Michael Broers is Professor  Oxford University. He is the author (ionary and Napoleonic Europe, *T 5–1814,* winner of the Grand Prix Napoleon in 2006, and of *Napoleon's Other War: Bandits, Rebels and Their Pursuers in the Age of Revolutions.*

Further praise for *Napoleon:*

'Judicious and magisterial . . . Broers' grasp of "violently changing times" is unimpeachable.' Roger Lewis, *Daily Mail*

'This is a masterly biography, both critical and empathetic.' Christopher Silvester, *Financial Times*

'Stimulating and genuinely innovative.' William Doyle, *TLS*

'[Broers] is steady and unsentimental, particularly when it comes to separating history from the myths created by Napoleon, his accomplices and posthumous admirers . . . I look forward to reading their exploits in the next volume of what surely will become the definitive life of Napoleon.' Lawrence James, *The Times*

'What [Broers] brings home brilliantly is the vitality, intelligence and phenomenal drive of this man, and the improbability of his achievements . . . The wait for volume two is going to be unbearable.' Simon Shaw, *Mail on Sunday*

NAPOLEON

VOLUME 1

Soldier of Destiny, 1769–1805

MICHAEL BROERS

FABER & FABER

First published in 2014
by Faber & Faber Ltd
Bloomsbury House, 74–77 Great Russell Street,
London WC1B 3DA

This paperback edition first published in 2015

Typeset by Donald Sommerville
Printed in England by CPI Group (UK) Ltd, Croydon, CR0 4YY

A CIP record for this book
is available from the British Library

ISBN 978–0–571–27345–4

2 4 6 8 10 9 7 5 3

For Jim McMillan

CONTENTS

MAPS

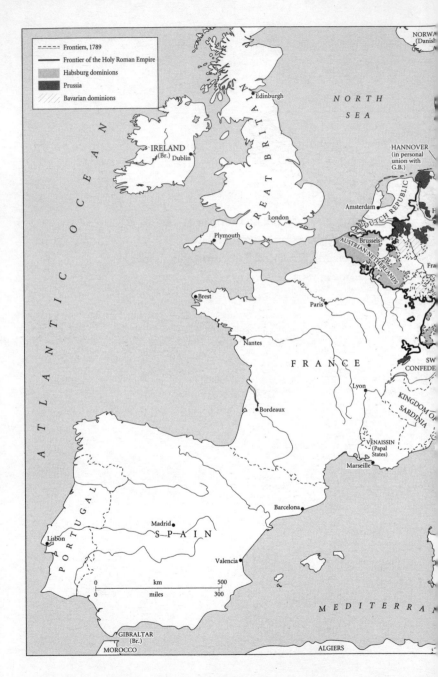

Map 1. Europe in 1789

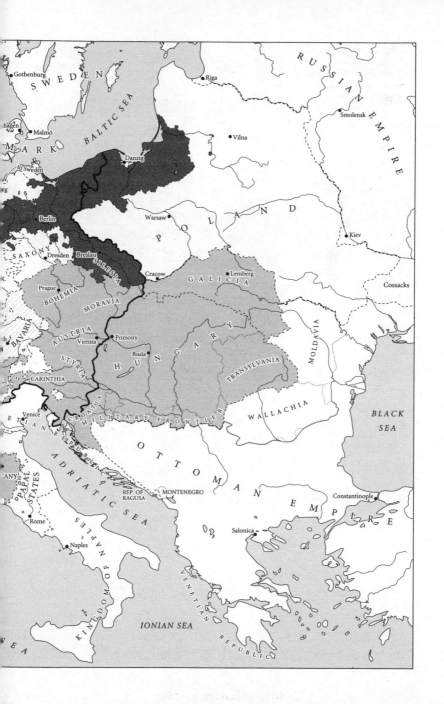

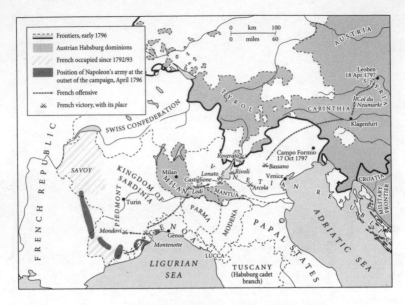

Map 2. Napoleon's First Italian Campaign, 1796–97

Legend:

- Frontiers, early 1796
- Austrian Habsburg dominions
- French occupied since 1792/93
- Position of Napoleon's army at the outset of the campaign, April 1796
- French offensive
- French victory, with its *place*

Labels on map:

AUSTRIA

TYROL

CARINTHIA

STYRIA

Leoben 18 Apr 1797

(Col du Neumarkt)

Klagenfurt

SWISS CONFEDERATION

FRENCH REPUBLIC

SAVOY

KINGDOM OF SARDINIA

PIEDMONT

Turin

Mondovi

MILAN

Milan

Lodi

Castiglione

Lonato

Roverato

Rivoli

Bassano

Campo Formio 17 Oct 1797

Arcola

Venice

VENETIAN REPUBLIC

CROATIA

MILITARY FRONTIER

PARMA

MODENA

MANTUA

Montenotte

Genoa

GENOA

LUCCA

PAPAL STATES

TUSCANY (Habsburg cadet branch)

LIGURIAN SEA

ADRIATIC SEA

km 100

miles 60

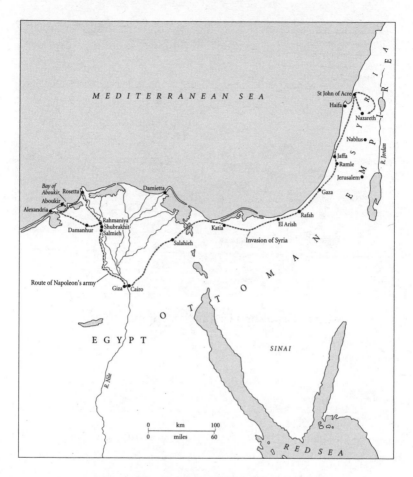

Map 3. The Egyptian Campaign, 1798–99

Map 4. Napoleon's Second Italian Campaign, 1800

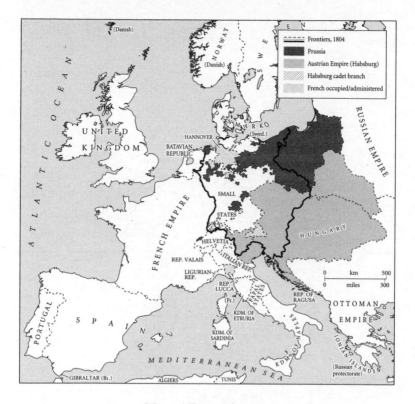

Map 5. Europe in 1804

PLATES

THE FORCE OF DESTINY

Liberty, Equality, Ambition

No, Monsieur the Count, you will not have her ... you shall not. Because you are a great lord, you think yourself a great genius! ... Nobility, fortune, rank, office, all this makes you so haughty! What have you done to have so much? You took the trouble to be born, nothing more. For all that, you are but an ordinary man; as much as me, sod it! Lost in an obscure crowd, I have had to use knowledge and every calculation just to survive ... and you want to fight![1]

... glad only that ... I could do my duty by him ... at my own risk. This I did all the time with an honesty and zeal, and a courage which deserved a better reward from him than in the end I obtained ... He was so incapable of self-control that even on a Saturday, the day on which almost all the couriers left, he could not wait for the work to be finished before going out, and continually urged me to hurry with the royal and ministerial dispatches, which he hastily signed before running off somewhere or other, leaving the majority of the letters without his signature ... it was necessary that someone should sign them, and I did so myself ... I endured his slights, his brutality, and his ill-treatment with patience ... But as soon as I saw he intended to deprive me of the honour I deserved for my good service, I resolved to resign.[2]

The first quotation above is the soliloquy of Figaro, the crafty, highly intelligent and ill-treated factotum of a brutal, dim, Spanish aristocrat, from the 1781 stage play, *The Marriage of Figaro*, by Alexandre de Beaumarchais. The next excerpt is Jean-Jacques Rousseau's account of his ill-treatment by another silly, arrogant nobleman, the French ambassador to Venice, while Rousseau was his secretary in 1743. It comes from his autobiography, *The Confessions*, written in 1765, but not published until 1781. *The Marriage of Figaro* and *The Confessions* were two of the greatest sensations of the 1780s, and among the very last great literary offerings of the old European order, before it was smashed into tiny pieces by the French Revolution of 1789. They were both quickly banned in France, but not before the damage was done.[3]

The eighteenth century had produced reams of serious literature on politics and society that strove to be subversive, propounding visions of new orders and lambasting the status quo, but none matched these two works in the chord they struck with the reading public, as the authorities were quick to spot, for they touched the nerves of many angry men, usually young ones. Louis XVI, the French king, had initially loved Beaumarchais' play for the fun it poked at an aristocracy whose obstinate refusal to surrender its independence frustrated him, but his advisers soon pointed out that Figaro made no subtle distinctions when it came to contempt for authority. Mozart's opera, based on the Beaumarchais play, met a similar fate in Vienna, where its performances were soon halted by Joseph II, who was the self-proclaimed most aggressive reforming monarch in Europe, but whose patience was tried beyond the limits by so candid an assault on the basic intelligence of a nobility he, more than Louis, found a nuisance. Beaumarchais knew that the joke was on them all, and that it was dangerous because it sneered back, rather than whined. Indeed, it was a classic example of going beyond a joke. There is swagger in Figaro's salvo, an arrogance based on hard fact, more dangerous than any cry of pain. Beaumarchais and Rousseau proposed something that was more dangerous than righteous indignation at the inequalities sustained by aristocratic privilege; they ventured a vision of society that was far more redolent of danger for those in power than a rage at social or economic injustice. This was not the righteous rage of the weak, but the defiance of those set on becoming the new masters. First Figaro, and then Rousseau, dared to say that their masters were not just cruel and callous, but that they were stupid. Next, they asserted that they, the 'doers', were more intelligent, and that it was simply stupid to obey the stupid.

Beaumarchais' Figaro and Rousseau knew they could do things better than their betters, as it were, and looked down on them. The goal was not to free the world, but to rise in it, to take it over, and then to exterminate those in power less because they were unjust, than because they were dimwits. It was talent that mattered, not the privilege of birth, yet those foolish enough not to see this – the mass of the people – were as hopeless as the masters. The world should belong to the best and the bravest. Steven Englund has described the atmosphere exuded from Napoleon's tomb in Les Invalides as 'the awe-evoking sense of human *possibility*, which is a different thing from hope'.[4] This was not about dreaming of justice; it was a question of seizing the day.

Awe was yet to come, but that sense of possibility – something less ethereal and altruistic than hope, liberty, equality or fraternity – burgeoned from the Figaro of Beaumarchais and the Rousseau of the Venice embassy. Men of this stamp were hardly ideologues, and so did not give the new political culture its new language of liberty, but they made it work, and they did so from self-interest based on confidence. Altruism came and went among them, but, as Robert Alexander has said of Napoleon, himself, 'will and talent are the bedrock of the reputation'.[5] They were the bedrock of the most potent element of the Revolution itself, and of the liberated generation it spawned. Ambition ruled Napoleon, and it was selfish. As Thibaudeau, one of his earliest supporters, put it, his genius was used only to serve his ego, his only passion was power, his mistress was France.[6]

Yet it is no less true that when he rose, all who wished to follow and had the talent to do so, rose with him. This was the Revolution – and the new Gospel – according to Napoleon. When 'liberty, equality and fraternity' had all frayed at the edges and been left behind by those who invented them, the Revolution's early promise of the 'career open to talent' remained. When Napoleon said – possibly – that he found the crown of France lying in the gutter, picked it up and put it on, he took revenge for Figaro and Rousseau. All Rousseau could do, as he said, was resign and rail at society with his pen. Indeed, he went on to invent a political utopia in *The Social Contract* and write two best-selling maudlin novels, *La Nouvelle Héloïse* and *Emile*, both of which concluded that subservience was 'the answer'. Figaro fared better, for this was fiction. He made a fool of his master and got his girl away from him through pure guile, but the happiness he cleverly contrived for himself and his beloved was purely personal: 'I was poor and despised. I showed some spirit, the hatred has run its course. A pretty girl and a fortune!' he can exult in the statutory happy ending.[7] It took a seismic upheaval to make the step from the stage to power attainable for the likes of Figaro. The French Revolution made victory in the public sphere possible for such men, and Napoleon epitomised them. For men of this stamp, the Revolution was less an ideal, than a vehicle; and if its creators did not know how to drive it, any more than those they overthrew knew how to control the old order, there were men who 'had to use knowledge and every calculation just to survive', who could master the new order. If there was a word Napoleon clung to all his life, it was 'destiny', and if there is a word that encapsulates him, it is 'ambition'. He gave both to the men of his generation, and their sons, who were prepared to follow him. The liberation brought about by the Revolution – whether deliberately, through its liberal legislation, or inadvertently, by the titanic war it unleashed – offered the ambitious their opening, but it was Napoleon's ambition that turned these individual ambitions into a collective sense of destiny. 'Destiny' was his own, personal, contribution to his generation.

Many biographers and historians have accentuated the cynical and manipulative in Napoleon's character, and they are not mistaken. He possessed these attributes in abundance, and it would be unrealistic to the point of absurdity to believe he could have survived his times without them, to say nothing of triumphing over them. Nevertheless, to put the accent on this side of his character, to the detriment of so much else, is to give both a false picture of the man and to render inexplicable his most lasting achievements. As Annie Jourdan has put it, 'Napoleon sought the positive in everything.'[8] When this is set beside his extraordinary energy, a more rounded and plausible person emerges, for Napoleon was a powerful creative force in the life of Europe, during his own time and long after. Only a positive, optimistic mind would have thought in terms of progressive reform to the degree Napoleon did all his public life. His optimism envisaged new, modern systems of justice, public administration and education; his energy made of them working realities in his own time, the strains of constant war notwithstanding. These systems and institutions are his living legacy, and have survived long after his military achievements were swept away in the last years of his rule.

The scope of this first volume encompasses the most energetic, creative period of his life, although he went on to achieve still more in the brief moment of near-complete peace in 1810–11, as well. His vision of a world after the Revolution, as well as beyond the *ancien régime*, sprang to life almost as soon as he came to power, first in Italy, and then in France. It did so with a speed and clarity that came from within him, as he absorbed and reformulated the many rich intellectual currents of his times. His ability to grasp so much, so quickly, was driven by an insatiable curiosity about the world around him. From his youth, Napoleon's notebooks teemed with facts and ideas drawn from a remarkably wide range of reading. It has become almost a truism among historians that the last generation of educated Westerners able to absorb all essential learning was that which just preceded Napoleon's. People such as Jefferson and Franklin in America, or Voltaire, or Catherine the Great of Russia were the last to be so fortunate. Napoleon was fighting a losing battle, but his efforts to emulate them in the face of rapidly expanding knowledge were as heroic as anything he displayed in war. He had much to learn, he knew it, and his energy and curiosity drove him on a quest of self-improvement to the very end of his life. This reached beyond the personal quest for knowledge. Napoleon transformed knowledge into reform, at blistering pace. This was not the work of a pure cynic; he cared about the future, in a wider sense than just his own reputation, although he certainly cared about that, too. If Napoleon's reactions have the quality of quicksilver, of frenetic energy, the concrete reforms they gave birth to proved durable and exportable. This was quite unprecedented.

Napoleon's life is a remarkable story, and its wonder of endless possibility – the awe Englund almost smells oozing from his tomb – emerges in the telling. No other man from such relatively humble beginnings had ever risen so high. However, more to the point, no such figure had become his own master, to say nothing of being the master of Europe. In this, Napoleon belonged to his generation, or to the most dynamic part of it, those who had seized the French Revolution by the throat and made it work for them. Where he went, he took his contemporaries with him. He began by sharing the restless ambition and the sneering, swaggering contempt for the old order with the like-minded, but by the time he marched on Austria in 1805, he had become their undisputed chief. The Revolution in France unwittingly opened the way for this, but no one had emerged with the personal capacity to seize the day, save Napoleon. The revolutionaries feared such a thing, and Napoleon often went to great pains, in these years, to disguise his ambitions, for they all had the example of the Roman Republic before them, hijacked from its patrician elite by Julius Caesar and, more effectively, by Octavian. Yet even the remote classical past could not quite provide an analogy for Napoleon. The Caesars were patricians among patricians; Napoleon was a Figaro among a generation of Figaros, who had seen off their old masters. His achievement looms all the larger because it came to pass in times of dangerous, unprecedented flux. It took more than energy, acute intelligence or ambition to triumph in this world.

Many who came to know Napoleon spoke of his self-control. Some, like Madame Junot, saw it as a virtue, others, Madame de Staël chief among them, felt it to be a dangerous, hypocritical mask which hid his egotism. Whatever its rationale, it was the product of iron self-discipline, for Napoleon was a man of powerful, often violent emotions, which makes it all the more impressive that his 'extraordinary reserve' was so remarked upon when he first entered the limelight of Parisian high politics on a daily basis, in the months before and after his seizure of power in 1799.[9] Those in subservient – and therefore exposed – positions often know how to wear masks, as did Figaro and Rousseau, in front of their masters. Part of Napoleon's ability to emerge as the head of this fraught political world stemmed directly from his capacity to hide the sneer and the swagger that the old regime had bred in him. Napoleon displayed all this in his rise to power, but his show of reserve to the world had deeper roots in his background. He came by it honestly. Caution was a central part of his character, and his particular Mediterranean origins gave him this schooling that more than once saved his life, as well as fuelled his success. The hero of Joseph Conrad's masterpiece, *Nostromo*, was – like Napoleon – of Ligurian origin, drawn from a people known for their taciturn probity in equal measure to their expansive spirits and deep emotions. Ambition and passion had to be tempered with self-control. Conrad's view of his central character – 'that man could command himself even when thrown off his balance'[10] – fitted Napoleon as well as the charismatic Gian Battista Fidanza of the novel. They were cut from the same cloth.

No one hated Napoleon more than Germaine de Staël, perhaps the most brilliant woman of her times, if also a dilettante born to *ancien régime* privilege. She was among the first to label him as power-hungry, although her repeated assertion that Napoleon was intrinsically tyrannical can hardly stand without a powerful effort of refutation. Nevertheless, Staël's view of his seething impatience and energy, lurking under the cool, authoritative exterior, are as accurate and cutting as Napoleon's own famous gaze. For Staël, Napoleon feigned intellectual curiosity to lull the intelligentsia into a false sense of security; he spoke of reconciliation and unity, while carefully constructing his support around factions he could play off against each other. Staël's judgements must form a shrill counterpoint to Napoleon's career. Many pages are needed to assess Staël's verdict, but her grasp of a central element of his character is beyond dispute. Whether Napoleon 'spoke with forked tongue' or not is one matter; that he spoke calmly, amidst

a sea of daggers, is undoubted. The precarious joust between passion
and prudence was intrinsic to Napoleon's character.

Passion – passionate loathing – always won out in Napoleon's
dealings with Staël, but while much ink has been spilled accounting
for the bile she stirred in him, Napoleon's detestation of Staël deserves
more thought than it is given. This was more than a political or ideological contest, as important as this was for two such sharp minds,
and it was certainly not a product of the groundless claim that
Napoleon disliked 'intellectual women', a jibe repeated even by so
powerful a mind as that of Pieter Geyl.[11] His close relationship with
his step-daughter, Hortense, his singular efforts in the realm of girls'
education, and the power he gave two of his sisters – Elisa, in Tuscany,
and Caroline, in Naples – readily belie this. Napoleon viewed Staël
in no small part with the eye of Figaro: she was a spoiled product
of *ancien régime* privilege, the daughter of a powerful minister and
financier, the wife of an aged aristocrat she played for a fool; she was
just a ponce, however clever. To Napoleon, she was patronising the
parvenu. As with Figaro, confrontation with such a creature could
cloud the mind, but this was the exception to the rule.

Napoleon's character was less complex than multifaceted. He
was energetic, imaginative, optimistic and cynical as circumstances
demanded; his personal ambition was boundless, yet so were his
aspirations for the society he belonged to. There is much of Homer's
'sharp-eyed Odysseus' in Napoleon. Both were quick-witted, observant,
persuasive, and utterly ruthless; they were made so because success
was all, and they came from cultures where failure meant obliteration.
Theirs was a world with little room for manoeuvre, be it in the cave of
the Cyclops or the political arena of revolutionary Paris. To make such
a comparison across millennia is not facetious. Anthropologically,
Odysseus and Napoleon were products of insular, Mediterranean
elites: their respective worlds, although divided by centuries, were
still set against and moulded by a geography that produced poverty,
and fuelled ambitions that could only be fed by emigration, usually
facilitated by war. Napoleon knew the classical past from literature,

and the Greco-Roman world was the common cultural currency of all educated Europeans of his times, a currency whose value had increased markedly during the eighteenth century, as secularism displaced the other, hitherto dominant cultural trope of Europe, Christianity. Yet the classical past was very much alive for Napoleon, the Corsican bourgeois, as a guide to life – for its heroes and the forces that drove them were still relevant to his own circumstances; men like Odysseus were recognisable types in Napoleon's Ajaccio. Ambition dominated this narrow, competitive world, and the lessons of antiquity were learned anew by every generation of the poor but vibrant islands that dotted Homer's 'wine-dark sea'. Napoleon came by ambition honestly: it was his inheritance. He was the scion of generations of tenacious men, whose common, defining element was the determination to rise in the world. Their world was a narrow one, but every generation of his family, on both sides, never ceased or shirked from the 'project' of social and economic advancement, collective and individual. This was Napoleon's birthright: ambition coursed through his veins. However thwarted, constrained or crushed, ambition never abated in these families. It was an all-consuming passion, but one which had to be tempered with careful calculation and cunning.

The earth-shattering events of the French Revolution gave atavistic ambition a different context of wider horizons, but also of volatile circumstances where calculation often had to be over-ridden by opportunism, where caution had to give way to daring. Napoleon readily adapted to this world, displaying an innate ability all his own to seize every chance that came his way in the midst of the most dangerous, uncertain times the western world had ever known up to that time. His mental and physical energy, his unique talents – the sum of which can rightly be called genius – set him apart from ordinary people, yet the ambition which drove him put Napoleon at one with a whole generation of Frenchmen who wanted something for themselves from the Revolution that the old order could not permit: to rise as high as their talents allowed, and to revel in their success. No one should dare identify with a genius, but many can relate to shared aspirations. Awe is something that unfolds before one, just as Europe did for Napoleon. The years immediately after his seizure of power in 1799 were still dangerous, but they were also those of the swagger and the sneer. This was far from all, however.

The Revolution produced many remarkable politicians and soldiers; that Napoleon came to overshadow them all, and then lead an entire generation across a hostile continent to unparalleled hegemony is, indeed, staggering, and so best told in stages, perhaps. 'Journey' is a word much cheapened in contemporary parlance when applied to the course of a life, but the years covered in this volume constitute an extraordinary journey, where the physical movements of a man are, precisely, the measure of Napoleon's progress in life. Napoleon was born, in 1769, in Ajaccio, a bastion of Italian civilisation that clung to the narrow ground between the sea and the barbarism of the mountains of Corsica; it pauses in 1805, as he begins the march to Austerlitz. No one propelled Napoleon on this course but himself. His journey amounted to the conquest of Europe. This was no easy matter, but it was, at that point in history, a unique achievement. In 1793, he had fled his native Corsica penniless, with little more than the shirt on his back and his head barely attached to his shoulders. By 1805, he was the head of state and had created an army ready to overcome all his enemies. No one of common birth had ever made such a 'journey'. It cannot be said too often or too loudly: there had never been anyone like Napoleon before.

Many *literati* say a good biography should flow like a novel, and Napoleon is often said, perhaps apocryphally, to have seen his life as one. Authentic or not, his 'journey' certainly provides the narrative structure of the novel. To attempt a life of Napoleon that is not a narrative would be to cheat the reader as much as the subject, for it was, indeed, as unheralded a tale as it was spectacular. One wonders, if presented to a publisher from another galaxy, how so incredible a story might be received, which parts of it might have to be rewritten in the interests of reader-credibility.

This volume stops at a point when Napoleon wondered if his journey might have run its course, if he had over-played his hand. He now faced a larger war, with stronger enemies than ever before. Both his army and he himself were untried at war on this scale. He had scraped his realm bare of men and money to fight. His gamble worked. Thus there was more to come, and therefore motive would reassert itself over narrative as the driving force of the plot. That motive was power. If Napoleon's life was, indeed, more like a novel than a documentary, then power is the red thread of its plotline. His life was about how he got power, but also about what he did with it. Napoleon's military and diplomatic exploits, and his political machinations, were a springboard to power, as well as an assertion of it; his great reforms were what he did with power, once he had taken it. More than this, he had to defend the power he held, and this aspect of the story is too often overlooked. The constant need to protect his gains was why his caution so seldom left him, at least in the years covered in this book, and why he placed such value on self-control. Napoleon's career is not just a story of a meteoric rise, it is a cautionary lesson in the fact that what is seized has to be held. Flux is all in the Napoleonic adventure; his search for political and personal stability becomes all the more poignant when this is remembered.

Napoleon lived in violently changing times, and it was part of his personal genius to recognise that the world would never cease changing, ever again: he put his finger on modernity when he said that his son would have to rule differently from himself. It is, therefore, equally legitimate to ask if a man so aware of change around him changed, himself. If anything marked Napoleon's life, it was the acquisition of power from a position of exposed danger and subservience. In a penetrating review of an exemplary exercise in biography, David Runciman asked the question of the fourth volume of Robert Caro's life of President Lyndon Johnson: Does the acquisition and exercise of real power reveal or occlude a personality?[12] The question looms even larger in the case of Napoleon than in that of Johnson, for power came quickly to him, whereas Johnson had waited years to reach the presidency; when achieved by Napoleon, it was very close to absolute, not that of a democratic leader. By 1805, it was clear to the whole world that Napoleon was no longer Figaro or Rousseau-in-Venice: he had built a whole new political order to ensure this for himself. He was now set to prove his superiority over his old masters, be they the aristocrats of the old order, his contemporary European rivals, or the revolutionary politicians who had sought to use him. Did success bring out latent aspects of his character, or did it engender new ones? The clues are in this narrative but, if there can be any definitive answer – and it is most unlikely – only the later correspondence, on which volume two will be based, can offer any hope of enlightenment. Runciman's question is worth trying to answer, but its value rests in the exercise, not in the result.

There is much to draw on when trying to understand Napoleon, but the human dilemma will always remain that a person is, ultimately, unknowable to others. In their foreword to Conrad's *Nostromo*, Jacques Berthoud and Mara Kalnins draw attention to Conrad's genius for recognising this:

Conrad was keenly aware of how partial and limited any interpretation of an event or assessment of another individual is. Juxtaposing different perspectives not only reveals that limitation but underlines the fullness and complexity of any given moment so that the artist can 'bring to life the truth, manifold and one, underlying its every aspect'.[13]

If this is a difficult task for a novelist, it is all the more so for the historian, for even a writer as committed to realism as Conrad still creates his own world, while historians have to cope with the fragments left to them by the hazards of the past. Napoleon's written legacy is, perhaps, the first to pose the biographer with a very modern problem. His nephew, Napoleon III, set out to preserve his uncle's image for posterity by compiling a copious edition of Napoleon I's correspondence. There is no shortage of first-hand material in the thirty-two volumes published under the auspices of the Second Empire, between 1858 and 1869, but their contents are, as everyone has always known, carefully tailored to say the least. The official correspondence serves only to deepen the problem which so troubled Conrad, and that is why many of Napoleon's finest biographers have turned to the memoirs of others to resolve it. It was always a choice between the lesser of two subjective evils, and a trawl through the footnotes of his foremost chroniclers reveals their heavy dependence on perceptions and assessments of Napoleon made by his contemporaries, surely a towering irony for a man who was a prodigious correspondent in life.

This monumental anomaly is being rectified after a century and a half by the new, still emerging *Napoléon Bonaparte, Correspondance générale* being compiled by the Fondation Napoléon in Paris, under the direction of Thierry Lentz, which has now reached the year 1809. Through the concerted effort of a team of researchers, archives and private collections all over the world have been combed to yield a correspondence that will be two and a half times larger than the existing edition, and it is already almost double the size of Napoleon III's version.[14] What has emerged is a more reliable, complex and essential body of evidence to reveal 'Napoleon-in-action', as well as in his own words. The history of the man and the epoch has been changed for ever, as a result. Obviously, Napoleon was too ambitious, too aware of 'destiny', and too cautious a man to let his guard down consciously, and so most of what he wrote was self-serving, but the flow of his daily correspondence, unexpurgated by subjective considerations in the new edition, cannot hide reality.

The many memoirs about Napoleon can now be balanced beside his own words, as he confronted events in moments of almost constant stress and crisis, when there was no time for myth-making. The Spanish historian Jesús Pabón asserted, with enviable acumen, that Napoleon's many and often contradictory pronouncements could only be of use to historians when they were matched by his actions.[15] Before the publication of the new correspondence, this was, indeed, the only sane way to approach the subject. Now, however, words and deeds can be brought together as never before, making a new biography imperative, if only as the first salvo in a reassessment of Napoleon, the end of which cannot, and should not, be predicted. Indeed, that end will never come, happily. If history has taught us anything about the man, it is that any assessment of Napoleon can only be provisional, just as the entirety of another human being can never be known to others. Those who belong to the ages see their legacy shift with the tides of time.

1

LIFE ON THE EDGE

The Corsican Cradle, 1769–1779

Napoleone Buonaparte was born on 15 August 1769, the Feast of the Assumption of Our Lady the Virgin Mary, in Ajaccio, Corsica, to Carlo and Letizia (née Ramolino) Buonaparte; he was their second surviving child, his brother Giuseppe having been born the previous year. Letizia returned from Mass at the cathedral and gave birth to him at home, with the help of her servant, Camilla Ilari, who became Napoleon's nurse. Myth was spun around the birth – that Letizia had brought him into the world alone; that she had done so on the floor of the front room; that the new-born had first been laid down on a carpet woven with scenes from Homer's *Iliad* (this according to his ardent admirer Stendhal) – all of which Letizia, in her own lifetime, dismissed as so much nonsense.[1] No one had carpets in Ajaccio in 1769, certainly not the Buonaparte, and they were not for summer use in any case. Camilla could always be counted on, so Letizia was not alone.

There was a strange occurrence that day which was real enough, for a comet appeared in the skies over Ajaccio. People naturally saw it as a portent of something, but opinions varied about the momentous event it foreshadowed. Only a few days before Napoleon died on St Helena, in 1821, a comet appeared in the skies over that little island as well. For those who set store by such things, there was no doubt about what that one meant. The lesson is not that superstition has weight, but that there is never any need to mythologise the life of Napoleon Bonaparte. The truth is more than enough to cope with.

AJACCIO: A COLONIAL WORLD

The single most important circumstance of Napoleon's birth, in trying to understand him, is not that he was born in Corsica, but that he was born in Ajaccio. It is not enough to say he was simply a 'Corsican', for there were two very distinct Corsicas in 1769, which did not mix with each other much, and neither respected nor trusted the other. Like everyone else, Napoleon belonged quite firmly to one of these Corsicas. Napoleon's final nemesis, the Duke of Wellington – that self-appointed epitome of the English grandee – is reputed to have rebuffed a man who called him 'Irish', with the withering reply: 'Just because a man was born in a stable, it does not make him a horse.' Napoleon's ancestors, to a man and woman, would have given the same rebuke to anyone who called them merely 'Corsicans'. When a French historian of the mid-nineteenth century said of Napoleon that 'Italian blood ran from vein to vein' in him,[2] he should not be dismissed, but 'Italy' was, and is, many things.

Corsica was, in most ways, part of 'Italy'. This meant that, like most of Italy, its cultures divided sharply between the highland periphery and the lowland, coastal world of urban culture. The Genoese imported this division to Corsica when they acquired it in 1453, and compounded it by creating the new settlements of Bastia and Ajaccio. In this act, they simply took for granted that the indigenous people of the highland interior – the 'insulars' as they always called them – were alien. The Italian rulers of the island excluded the people of the interior from the outset; this division between urban and rural, highland and lowland, was brought from the mainland, and did not change as long as Genoa ruled Corsica. Napoleon belonged somewhere in this complicated heritage, but as with most parts of Europe, simple geographic labels serve little purpose.

The Buonaparte and all their friends and relations belonged to the small cities of the coasts and, when they looked up to the high, jagged peaks that led to the isolated interior, they felt the same mixture of contempt and dread known all across the Mediterranean by the dwellers of the towns and plains for the barbarians of the uplands, of the isolated, violent, unlettered world the Jesuits called 'Our Indies' – our American frontier – a feeling shared by English-speaking, Protestant 'north Britons' like David Hume, when he looked out from his study in Glasgow at the 'Highland Line', or by Wellington, when he contemplated his 'fellow Irishmen' beyond the English Pale of settlement. This was a common feeling, and in Corsica it expressed a very clear division. Genoese rule made of both Corsicas an immobile place, where individuals might – and did – seek advancement by leaving Corsica, prepared to go anywhere in the world. However, Corsicans remained bound to their roots, whether in the interior or the coastal towns, a fundamental division that did not change over three centuries. These roots were immutable, however varied the experiences of the Corsicans beyond the island. In Corsica, as in so many other peripheral parts of Europe, the past counted.

The mountains of the Corsican interior did, indeed, merit being called 'our Indies' by the Jesuit and Franciscan fathers who were the only outsiders who took a real interest in these upland regions. Ajaccio was founded in 1492 by the Genoese, in the same year that Genoa's most famous citizen crashed into the New World. The first Genoese settlers of Ajaccio may not have been in 'first contact' with the people they called 'the insulars', but they ventured less far, less fast into the interior of their new home than did those Genoese and Spaniards who followed Columbus across the Atlantic. The founders of Ajaccio clung to the coast, always. That was their job. They were part of a deliberate plan by the Genoese for Corsica, which they had acquired in 1453 for purely strategic reasons. The Republic of St George, with its capital in Genoa and its small hinterland spread out along the coast of Liguria – the modern Italian Riviera – was a commercial and banking power, with a considerable merchant fleet, and its only real interest in Corsica was to use it to secure the sea lanes. To this end, the Genoese destroyed most of the native aristocracy in ruthless wars in the late fifteenth and early sixteenth centuries, leaving only three families with noble status and any estates of note in the south of the island, the Bozzi, Ornano and Colonna-Istria houses.

The other prong of Genoese colonialism was the creation of new towns on the coasts, to serve as bases to protect shipping and to contain the 'insulars' of the interior. Ajaccio was one such foundation; the major town and capital was Bastia, in the north of the island, founded in 1476. Neither Ajaccio, on its large harbour, in the south-centre, nor Bastia, had any economic or commercial purpose: they were simply military colonies. There were other settlements that came to little, such as that attempted at Porto Vecchio, and the two older towns of the coasts – Bonifacio in the south-west and Calvi to the north-west – dated from before the Genoese, but they had been created purely as defensive positions, and contracted as Ajaccio and Bastia grew. Henceforth, Genoa ignored the interior as long as it got its taxes, and it dealt ruthlessly with the 'insulars' when it did not, or when they tried to ally with dangerous outsiders – usually the Turks, French or Milanese – against the Republic. Its manner of government in the mountains was one of manipulation, not control. The early destruction of the great nobles had left the natives leaderless at all but local level. In this way, highland Corsica became a world of petty clan chieftains, whom Genoa could use to collect taxes and then ignore.

Genoese indifference is brought home by a simple fact: they neither knew nor cared about the geography of the interior in any detail. They were indifferent to anything but the most rudimentary idea of where its settlements were or their size. Genoa did not care what went on there, only what came out of it, in taxes. When they had to deal with serious unrest on the relatively accessible lands of the southern nobles in the early seventeenth century, it emerged that no one in authority really knew the size of the local population; when a serious revolt broke out in the highlands in 1735, it emerged there was no map of the interior in the offices of the island's governor in Bastia, although a Tuscan, Pinelli, had made one in 1729. Official distances to the interior were calculated on how long the trip took to and from the coast.[3] This attitude changed little between 1453 and 1768. As a result, the highland interior did not change, either. It remained the world of an uneducated, ill-disciplined clergy who were, first and foremost, part of their clans' elites; of a vendetta culture that soaked many areas in blood for generations; of ancient superstitions; of 'honour' and little formal learning; of shepherds who lived in almost complete solitude for most of the year. It was the Corsica of the bandits, who lurked in the passes that led from the coast to the hills. Only the very poorest of the Catholic religious orders, the humble Franciscans, remained among these people long enough to win their trust, for only they could share their hard lives on such barren land. The Jesuits came, looked, investigated, and went back to the coastal towns to found colleges for the education of the Ligurian settlers. This was the Corsica of legend, and of stereotype. It had nothing at all to do with the Buonaparte.

Napoleon's world was that of small urban settlements, clinging to the seaboard, proud but wary behind their walls, whose more ambitious denizens looked out to sea for advancement and gain, not inland, while all of them allied and vied with each other to hold the narrow ground they called home, competing and co-operating, as needs be, for the small rewards that came from the equally small metropole of Genoa, and what could be extracted from the inhospitable island itself. It was a society whose horizons were at once the very narrowest and most petty, and the most adventurous and restless. The same Ajaccian might offer his services – military, professional, artisanal – to the Italian states, France, Spain, and even the Turks, while he was engaged in bitter litigation over a few square metres of ground within the walls of his town. The Buonaparte were no exception. They did not like the 'insulars' anywhere near them. Soon after its foundation, the mountain people flocked to Ajaccio, but in one of the few major concessions the settlers ever wrung from the Republic, by an 'ethnic treaty' of 1579, the two thousand or so settlers forced the 'insulars' to live outside the walls, in *il Borgu*, near an insalubrious marsh, and soon denied them the right to own property or carry arms within the walls.[4] Ajaccio and all the other coastal towns were officially called *presidii*, military posts, the same word used by the Spanish in the New

World for the same reason. One such *presidio* grew to be Los Angeles and another, San Francisco. It did not work out this way for either Bastia or Ajaccio.

As with their compatriots who followed in the wake of Columbus to the Americas, the Ligurians who took up the challenge of Ajaccio and Bastia came from all social classes and groups. What they had in common was their origins in Liguria, a poor, small stretch of ground, which could never hope to support its population. Such areas produced conquistadors in these years and, just as most of the Spaniards who overthrew the great civilisations of the Americas came from poor backwaters like Estremadura in Spain, so the Genoese government found its readiest volunteers for Corsica not from the great city, but from its impoverished hinterland, the Riviera. The Riviera is today a playground of the very rich and one of the most fashionable coastlines in the world, but it was nothing of the kind when Genoa needed colonists for Corsica. Indeed, as the imperial 'department of the Apennines', which it became between 1805 and 1814, it was one of the direst backwaters of Napoleon's own empire, as incapable of attracting good administrators from the outside as it was of supplying its own. It was the kind of place that produced men ready to risk all on the longest of chances. In this case, they traded one backwater for another, but at the turn of the fifteenth and sixteenth centuries it must have seemed worth the gamble. Napoleon sprang from a long line of gamblers.

In the period after Genoa transferred control of the island to France by a treaty of 1768, Napoleon's father, Carlo, and his uncle, Luciano, desperately – often pathetically – tried to create grand Tuscan origins for the family, less from snobbery than from the very sane need to stake their claim to nobility with their new French masters, whose standards in such matters could seem too high and exacting to the Ligurians of Corsica. They were determined to be seen as settlers from the mainland, never – even after three centuries – wishing to be identified with the 'insulars'. It was much the same in Napoleon's mother's family, the Ramolino, who had more immediate links with the Genoese elites, but also claimed, spuriously, to be of Venetian and Florentine origin.

The sophisticated standards of record-keeping in the Republic of St George stretch back well into the Middle Ages, and the real story of the Buonaparte is easy enough to chart. They came to Corsica as the Old World's equivalent of the conquistadors, just like most other Ligurians. The first Buonaparte to take service in Ajaccio was Francesco, who came from Sarzana, the largest town of the eastern Riviera. He went to Corsica in 1514 as a mounted crossbowman. Although he stayed in close contact with his brother, a priest, in Sarzana, Francesco never left Ajaccio again, save on active service.

Thereafter, the fortunes of the Buonaparte were bound entirely to the city and its immediate hinterland. Francesco's son, Gabriele, was also a soldier of the garrison, but in the 1560s he became one of the *anziani* of Ajaccio, the annually renewed city council, on which the family would be represented henceforth. Like his father and the other Ligurian soldiers, he was a *stipendiato*, a citizen of the town within the walls, not an 'insular', and so did not have to ask permission to live, own or buy property within it. He returned to Sarzana to find a bride. When the 'insulars' rose in the late 1550s, he fought them, as he was paid to do.

It was Gabriele's son, Geronimo, who took the most important step in the history of the Buonaparte under Genoese rule, when he became a member of the local legal classes. Through Geronimo, the Buonaparte took a step away from the world of the 'gamblers', of the soldier-adventurers who created Ajaccio, into a different culture. Henceforth, they learned the cautious ways of the lawyers, and adopted the careful calculations of the provincial Mediterranean bourgeoisie of which they were a part. Valour in arms had made this advancement possible, but the opportunity it presented was seized with both hands. From that time onwards, no Buonaparte ever performed paid manual labour. Probably as a reward for the family's loyalty to the Republic against the 'insulars', Geronimo became a clerk of the local registry – the *cancelleria* – and the family maintained its place in the literate, educated legal classes from then onwards. This allowed them to enter the most well-entrenched, durable section of the urban elite, for the lawyers were the literate manipulators of urban society. 'They not only monopolised municipal government, they monopolised the knowledge of how it worked', as Michel Vergé-Franceschi has put it.[5]

It was as a lawyer and a minor government prosecutor that Napoleon's father, Carlo, rebuilt the family's fortunes from their lowest point, during Napoleon's infancy. The family had its ups and downs over the centuries, but it never quite lost its place among the middling levels of settler society in Ajaccio, simultaneously intermarrying and disputing within its ranks. Marriages with the Bacciochi were common, the last being that of Napoleon's sister, Elisa, to Félix, who served Napoleon well as a general. There were alliances and litigations with the Pozzo di Borgo, a somewhat wealthier and more fortunate family: Charles-André, Napoleon's contemporary, became his arch-enemy and would-be nemesis in the service of Napoleon's most potent foe, Tsar Alexander I. Their fathers had been alternately rivals and allies in local politics, and in the law courts, over property.

Ajaccio was typical of the urban, provincial world of the western Mediterranean in most of these ways, with its local elite as competitive as it was tightly knit. The law, the army and the Church were sought-after professions; property within the walls was the mark of status, while the ownership of lands and mills in the surrounding countryside funded a style of urban life as ostentatious as possible, which in Ajaccio was not great but all the more coveted for that. It was a secular world, by the standards of the times, where benefactors preferred civic improvements to building churches. In its way, this was a sign of growing, if still unconscious, independence from the metropole. The Republic had welcomed the Jesuit order, with its insistence on adherence to Roman orthodoxy and its mission to imbue every aspect of life with the Catholic faith, from its foundation. It was the Jesuits who, with the support of Genoa, founded the only source of secondary education in Ajaccio for the notables. Their college served the sons of the settler elite well for three centuries, until the Jesuit Order was abolished in France in 1773, but the Jesuits, for all their guile, did not instil the notables of Ajaccio with a spirituality that outweighed their hard-nosed secular view of life, nor did their influence curb the appetite of this ambitious milieu for the learning – first Humanist and then Enlightened – that came from the mainland.

The legal classes used the Church more than it used them; places in the great Italian universities, with their Humanist learning, were sought when they could be afforded. The Jesuit monopoly of secondary education under the Republic of St George did not prevent the spread, first, of the Humanist teaching of the Italian legal schools, so necessary for worldly success at home, nor, later, the writings of the *philosophes*, nor that ultimate expression of heresy, Freemasonry, a society to which Napoleon's father and many of his uncles belonged. The Corsican diaspora ensured that, however isolated and inbred Ajaccio's bourgeoisie might seem, its members were never as marginal as they might appear. Above all, marriage to a 'passing' Genoese official – an officer of the garrison or an administrator sent out on a short period of service – was highly prized, both for the patronage it could bring and as a way of reasserting the 'apartness' of the urban community from the hinterland.

The law was what mattered in the little world of Ajaccio, for if military prowess was the ticket out, legal skill was the defence mechanism to 'hold the fort'. There is a much more profound point buried in the endless litigations and revealed by the very centrality of the legal classes to this society. The law was how they fought each other, for the vendetta culture of the interior was anathema to this world. Its bitterness did not translate into violence for, in so tight-knit but ambitious a milieu, alliances often had to be made among families who had been at law with each other a generation before, in utter contrast to the clan system of the interior.

No one could afford a vindictiveness that allowed no point of return. Carlo Buonaparte, Napoleon's father, was the busiest lawyer in Ajaccio:

in 1770 alone, he pleaded in 98 of the 184 cases that came before its
court, and he defended people that he himself had gone to law against
on other occasions.[6] After the peasant revolts of the early seventeenth
century, the three surviving insular noble families were drawn into
this world, too, as their lands became fragmented, and they sought –
almost cap in hand – admission to Ajaccio and the protection of its
laws. By the late eighteenth century, the Bozzi, especially, had married
into the Buonaparte, but also fell into a bitter property dispute with
them over a house in the town, a sign, over the long term, of how their
power had declined. Carlo fought them hard in court in the mid-1770s,
backed by his uncle, Luciano, a very uncharitable priest whose grip
on the family finances gave him great power over his nephew. For all
the bitterness of the legal battle, the 1780s saw Buonaparte – Carlo
and Luciano among them – standing as godparents to new children
of their former rivals in court, an emphatic sign of reconciliation after
the case was concluded. As Michel Vergé-Franceschi has put it, trouble
between bourgeois families lasted three years, not three generations,
and did not involve violence. Carlo was the orchestrator of this
particular instance of reconciliation, just as he had, as the family's
lawyer, prosecuted the family's case until it was resolved.

Carlo passed on to his son the received wisdom of his culture, that
men were there to be reconciled, not alienated.[7] It was the way these
bickering, litigious families conducted their business, through the law.
It was the same within the family, for, although often disunited, its
members rarely became enemies. Whether at home or within the walls
of the *presidio*, cohesion was all.[8] It was the mark of the civilised world
of the Greek *polis*, from which the Corsican *presidio* was consciously
derived. Aristotle's classical trope of the civilised urban *polis* and the
alien 'barbarian' world beyond its walls was a living reality for the
Buonaparte and their ilk. In the shadow of the mountains, they wore
the law as a badge of civilisation, as a symbol of their 'otherness', rather
than as 'vendetta by other means'.[9] The Bozzi, certainly, had been
'civilised' by the time they went to law with Carlo, and he treated them

accordingly. Even many of Napoleon's bitterest enemies noted his lack of vindictiveness, despite the power he wielded and the temptation before him to exert vendetta on an unparalleled scale. He came by this restraint honestly, for it was a cultural and social attribute, as well as a trait of his character. It arose from the culture of the elites of the Ligurian *presidii*.

The Buonaparte had but one marriage with the insular elite in three hundred years. Geronimo's son, Francesco, followed his father into the *cancelleria*, and also exercised the very important functions of a notary. His skills led to his employment by one of the three insular noble families, the Istria, and to marriage to a niece of its *signore*. Francesco rose to be the *luogotenante* – the chief steward – of the Istria domains, but after a violent revolt by their peasants in 1615 broke their real power, Francesco largely turned his back on this rural world. He never gave up his role as a notary in Ajaccio, and by the 1630s his considerable energies were devoted to urban renewal. The family had little to do with the rest of the island until the generation of Napoleon's parents, and, in this, they followed the growing power of the state. The infighting among the three insular noble families deepened the divide between the *presidio* of Ajaccio and the surrounding countryside, for the humbling of the Bozzi, Ornano and Istria marked not just a victory for the remote Republic of the metropole, but for the bourgeoisie of the *presidio*. The dominant class on the south of the island was now the settler, urban elite.[10]

The early and mid-eighteenth centuries saw a decline in the family fortunes, but good marriages within the local elite and with the Genoese colonial administrators continued, as signs that their standing was not measured in wealth, alone, however 'middling' even by local standards.

As Michel Vergé-Franceschi, one of the finest historians of Corsica, has said, it is not enough to look only at the Buonaparte, for 'a family does not come down to one line. A family is never a name, it is a milieu.'[11] Napoleon was Letizia's son, as well as Carlo's, and, in his own mind, he was more hers than his father's, for he always said that his mother had given him his *fierté*, a mixture of pride, arrogance and determination. *Fierté* means indomitability, what another European island, Ireland, terms 'fierce'. If this was indeed so, she defined him.

Letizia was so widely acclaimed the prettiest girl in Ajaccio when she married Carlo in 1764, at barely fifteen, that it is probably true, but her physical charms played no part in the union. Carlo openly confessed in his memoirs that he was in love with another girl, so much so that even Letizia's beauty could not make him forget her.

For the Buonaparte, however, this was the best family alliance they could hope for. Letizia's family, both the Ramolino and, still more, her mother's family, the Pietrasanta, were on a higher rung than the Buonaparte. Letizia was firmly part of the colonial 'establishment'. Her father's family, the Ramolino, arrived in the 1560s, and the first known Ramolino, Gabriele, was, like the first Buonaparte, a cavalryman, but of higher social standing than Francesco, for he fought in the company raised by the great Genoese patrician Andrea Doria, was wounded, and then, as a reward for bravery, was given command of a frigate which guarded the harbour of Ajaccio. The Buonaparte had left the profession of arms long behind them, but the Ramolino, especially, and the Pietrasanta, still held prestigious military commands until the end of Genoese rule in the 1760s, as well as being notaries. Her father, Giovan Geronimo, who died when Letizia was only five, had been a captain of the garrison of Ajaccio and a government inspector of roads and bridges, as well as the magistrate of the village of Bocognao, where the family acquired lands, while his father – who outlived him and spent much time with Napoleon as a child – had also been a soldier and the mayor of Ajaccio. Like the Buonaparte, the Ramolino had nearly all been *anziani* in their time but, unlike them, they had held firmly to the military tradition that had originally brought them to Corsica. Like the Buonaparte, too, they were desperate to create a Florentine ancestry for themselves. This in no way diminished their intense loyalty to the Republic, and a major moment in their family lore was the participation of Morgante Ramolino – 'a cavalryman of Ajaccio' – in the killing in 1567 of Sampiero Corso, the legendary leader of a great revolt of the 'insulars'. In one strand of many Napoleonic legends, Letizia is depicted as the female embodiment of an atavistic, 'pure' Corsica, as a classical matriarch stuck in a later age, a child of the wild mountains who instilled in her son a vendetta-like passion for revenge and political independence. Nothing could have been further from the truth.

The marriage of Letizia's father into the Pietrasanta family only deepened the Ramolino's firm roots in the 'Establishment'. The horizons of the Pietrasanta reached beyond Ajaccio, to the island's capital, Bastia, for they had risen as high in the service of the Republic as a Corsican born in the *presidii* could hope; in the early seventeenth century, a Pietrasanta had held the highest office open to an islander, as Commissioner General of Genoa in Corsica. Nevertheless, the family remained pure Ajaccians, and had married into the Bacciochi and the Pozzo di Borgo in the eighteenth century. Unlike the Ramolino or the Buonaparte, the Pietrasanta never felt the need to create a noble lineage for themselves, even under the French. The Pietrasanta had produced one of the few Corsican-born captains of the citadel of Ajaccio, a sign of the great confidence placed in them by the Republic,[12] but they seamlessly transferred their loyalties to their new masters when Genoa passed control of Corsica to France in 1768, as a true Establishment would. They retained considerable influence with the new rulers, as they had with the old.

When the politics of the island became convulsed in the mid-eighteenth century, and when the change of masters made it essential to create new networks of patronage and protection, it was the Ramolino–Pietrasanta axis that saved the future of the young Napoleon, for these families possessed a standing, won long in the past, that the Buonaparte did not. Letizia's grandfather passed easily into French service, becoming a member of their Conseil Supérieur in Bastia in 1768. The good relationship Giuseppe Maria Pietrasanta quickly established with his new French masters would save the Buonaparte from near oblivion in the first years of the new order.[13]

When Carlo Buonaparte married Letizia Ramolino in 1764, she brought him the biggest dowry in Ajaccio, the fruits of generations of local notability and the recognition of the metropolitan sovereign.

Letizia's family had never stepped out of line until her aunt, Angela Maria, like her niece a great beauty, but widowed at an early age, took the extraordinary step not only of remarrying, but of marrying a Swiss Protestant mercenary naval officer of the garrison. François Fesch half-heartedly converted to Catholicism, and their son, Giuseppe – Joseph – although Napoleon's uncle, was close to him in age, and grew up with the Buonaparte children. Joseph Fesch entered the Church along with another Joseph, Napoleon's older brother, and was later elevated by his nephew to become Cardinal Archbishop of Lyon, the primate of all France. Raised by his Protestant father, Fesch was a man of moderate religious views, which counted for as much with his nephew as did the ties of kinship. François Fesch, and the Istria, a few generations before, were the only people from outside the walls of Ajaccio to enter the realm of Napoleon's family, on either side, in almost three centuries. Napoleon was born in a fortress, in every sense.

This was the cloth from which Napoleon was cut, but this world, so long in place, would soon be rocked by the wider currents of European history to which so many of its ambitious sons had set out so determinedly to belong. When the age of revolutions came to Corsica, however, it was not from within the society of the *presidii*, but from the bowels of the mountains. It shook the faith of many in the world as it was, Carlo and his second son included.

CORSICA IN THE AGE OF ENLIGHTENMENT AND REVOLUTION

The Republic of St George was a weak state, and it ruled by exploiting the weakness that came naturally to most Mediterranean societies, the almost eternal antipathy between the mountain and the plain. Its 'colonial policy' transformed an anthropological trope into a political system, that of two Corsicas. In the course of the eighteenth century, however, the wider world began to impinge on the island, and this seemingly permanent division almost – but not quite – threatened to change. The Buonaparte were caught up in this rather more than many other families.

The 'insulars' had always retained their own tradition of resentment and rebellion. The first real assertions of Genoese authority had crushed the great native *signori*, the Leca and the Rocca, but the middle decades of the sixteenth century had seen the rebellion led by Sampiero Corso, a remarkable leader sprung from the mountain people, who won recognition from the French and the Turks before he was crushed. At the end of the century, the remnants of the insular aristocracy rose again in the 'wars of the Cinarchesi' that definitively broke the independence of the three southern *signori*. In a static world, these memories remained vivid on both sides of the walls of the *presidii*. Resentment came naturally to the 'insulars', as did revolt when circumstances seemed propitious.

It was more complex within the city walls. For some, Letizia's family chief among them, the bonds to the Republic had seemed insoluble, and yet new ties to their new French masters had been relatively easy to forge when the island changed hands in 1768. Nevertheless, for all the privileges and financial advantages the Republic accorded the descendants of the men it sent to found its colonies, Genoese rule had always had a 'glass ceiling', which was less important to the alien world of the highlands but could be felt acutely by a minority of the settler elites in the *presidii*. As colonists, the 'Ligurians' of the coastal towns could not hope either to attain standing in the Genoese metropole, or to command the highest offices in the island, for the Governor in Bastia and his immediate staff, as well as the military commandants of the *presidii*, were always Genoese patricians. True power and influence beyond the parish pump could be found only in the service of foreigners. The elites of the Corsican *presidii* were not alone in this, nor in their growing feelings of impotence as the demands of the metropole grew and their own voices diminished in the early eighteenth century. The settlers of the Americas, British and Spanish alike, began to feel restive, as did the Anglo-Irish, closer to home, but such elements in Corsica, if vocal and intense in their resentment, never gained a real following within their own walled communities.

The highlands and lowlands shared the limited expectations imposed on them by the Republic, but their respective diasporas met, mingled and explored their common frustrations only abroad, not on the island. In Rome, Florence and Naples men from otherwise different, alien worlds began to find a shared identity impossible on the island they all called home. Limited prospects and the increasing realisation that they had a common enemy in the Genoese Republic brought some of them together by the early eighteenth century, but only in the context of the diaspora. Those who remained at home in the *presidii* were, in the main, either too cautious, like most of the Buonaparte – epitomised by Carlo's uncle, Luciano – or too intrinsically loyal to the Republic, like the Pietrasanta, to think in terms of sedition. It was easier for the expatriate 'insulars'.

The series of rebellions which broke out in Corsica from 1729 onwards were part of a wider phenomenon, yet they were also rooted in the past. The core of resistance to Genoa was centred where it had always been since 1453, in the highlands. The elites of the *presidii* were in two minds about supporting rebels drawn from a culture they feared and despised, or, at worst, prepared to fulfil their original role as a colonial garrison of Genoa. This was the world in which Carlo and Letizia married in 1764, and into which Napoleon was born five years later.

The first uprising against Genoa, in 1729, began as these always had, in the mountains, and it had two different sources, as had been the case since 1453: peasant grievances over taxation erupted into a series of violent local revolts, and leadership was found, first, among the local clan chieftains, but came also from Spain and Venice, which both saw an opportunity to oust Genoa from the island. This time, however, a single local leader emerged from the insular elites; this was Giacinto Paoli, a judge and minor official from the small village of Morosaglia, in the mountainous north-east of the island. Giacinto was a remarkable product of the peasant elite, educated at the Collegio De Bene in Genoa thanks to a relative in the clergy. A brilliant classicist, he returned to his area, surrounded by a family of illiterate farmers and shepherds, deeply immersed in the traditional culture of vendetta and clan loyalty. For Giacinto the classics of the Greco-Roman past were something of a guide to life in his remote rural world, and he imbued the revolt with more direction and purpose than was normal, and thought in terms of a central government and an independent Corsica. Nevertheless, the revolt itself was still anchored in the mountain communities, and the *presidii* stood firmly against them: Paoli's men sacked Bastia when it offered resistance and 'Ajaccio welcomed them with cannon fire'.[14] By 1736, the Genoese had crushed the revolt, and Paoli fled into exile. Unrest rumbled on, however, aided and abetted by the insular diaspora. As a result, Giacinto's son, Pasquale, was raised mainly in exile, educated in Naples and Rome, and served in the Neapolitan army, at one point seeking service with the French.

The upheavals of the wars of the 1740s and 1750s – the War of the Austrian Succession and the Seven Years War – in which Genoa found itself unwillingly involved, allowed Pasquale his chance to reassert his father's hopes for Corsican independence, and he returned to the island in 1755, well educated, articulate and, at first, somewhat detached from the hard realities of insular clan politics. Nevertheless, facing a much weakened Genoa, Pasquale Paoli forged a rebel state in the mountains, with its 'shadow government' in Corte, the pre-Genoese medieval capital of the island, and the only town of consequence in the interior. Paoli held his ground here for thirteen years.

Little had really changed at the heart of the revolt: Paoli's support, like his father's before him, came from the clans of the mountains; the gates of the *presidii* remained closed, and its elites, epitomised by families like the Pietrasanta and Ramolino, were set firmly against him. However, Paoli's long experience of the wider world – he was the product of Enlightened Europe more than of the society he sought to lead – gave him aspirations to forge a government based on representative institutions; Paoli asked Rousseau to draw up a constitution for Corsica, a task he accepted with alacrity and completed in 1765.

Rousseau's enthusiasm for the Corsican cause was emblematic of a change in the wider context of Paoli's revolt. Paoli presented his rebellion and his rebel state in exactly the light that progressive European opinion had been waiting for in these decades, and Paoli knew how to manipulate educated opinion in the salons of metropolitan Europe. Paoli played on the aura around him, but he did so in the sincere belief that he could create a genuinely Enlightened state, in his rebel stronghold, between 1755 and 1768. To the intelligentsia of urban Europe, Paoli incarnated the pure virtues of Roman antiquity, among a people untouched by modern corruption. He became their ideal of the disinterested freedom fighter, the father of a free people, leading them to modern democracy – itself an unknown but much discussed quantity in the eighteenth century – but determined to preserve the innate values of community and sense of natural justice they thought they saw incarnated in the Corsican highlanders. When foreign intellectuals came to Corte, they did not see the barren countryside or the jumble of impoverished houses that formed the small town bereft of amenities, the Corsica Paoli himself was determined to change for the better. Instead, the cultivated *bien pensants* were mesmerised by what they took for the remnants of a lost classical Arcadia. The Romantic haze had descended on educated Europe, and so, somewhat ironically, Enlightened opinion was 'ready' for Paoli and his mountain republic in the 1750s, to an extent it had not been for his father or for less sophisticated, obscurantist peasant rebels. He was visited by the Scottish intellectual James Boswell, like Paoli an enthusiastic Freemason, and many others. This time, the wider world knew about Corsica, even if it did little, in practice, to help. Nor was Paoli himself free from a romantic, idealised vision of his people and his country. His idealism was born in a diaspora he had known since early childhood, for his real life had been spent largely abroad, where he nourished hopes and visions almost as abstract as those of his admirers. He did not abandon these hopes, to his credit, in the face of harsh realities, even if he learned to navigate the world of vendetta and clan loyalty. This was really the idealism of a displaced person, raised in exile, rather than of a recent emigrant.

Paoli's state continued to exist in its mountain bastions largely because the Republic was now too weakened by debts and the costs of war to exert itself, beyond defending the *presidii*, which were now in effect isolated outposts more than at any time since their foundation. In reality, for all his genuine aspirations for a modern, prosperous Corsican nation, Paoli's power base was rooted in the world of the highlands. The 'insulars' were just as inclined to emigrate as the settlers, and probably more so, in search of betterment. Many members of the broken and reduced indigenous elite, and the families of the local clan chieftains who now dominated the highlands pointedly took service with the Venetians, Genoa's bitter rival; others found their way through Spanish service as far as Latin America. A few, usually through family members in the lower clergy, were able to gain educations in Genoa, alongside the sons of the settlers, in the Collegio De Bene, where a handful of places were reserved for deserving Corsican boys. The world they returned to was very different from that of the *presidii*, however. The highland elites were drawn from the peasantry. Local judges, parish priests and clan leaders were part of a violent world; no one was far removed from the culture of vendetta or the practice of banditry, even if they were not actively engaged in either, and part of their role in village society was to mediate the threat of violence and the consequences of theft. This was a world people like the Buonaparte or Ramolino visited as rarely as possible, if at all, and then only on official or commercial business.

The intellectual world of the *presidii* was far from frozen in these decades, however. This was where some small cracks began to appear in their walls, less literally – for the vast majority of the townspeople did not see in Paoli a bearer of modernity, but the harbinger of their worst nightmare – than intellectually. Among the very few who looked to Paoli's vision of an independent Corsica was Napoleon's father,

Carlo, much to the discomfort of his in-laws and most of his own family. Like Paoli, Carlo was a Freemason, a progressive thinker who had spent time abroad, mainly in Rome, and acquired a similarly negative view of Genoese rule to Paoli's. In Carlo's case, this was based not so much on the traditional sense of oppression felt by 'insulars' of all levels of education, than on a dislike of the backward, conservative ethos of the Republic and a growing sense of the very limited opportunities it offered its 'Corsican garrison'. Carlo had had a 'shady' young manhood, it seems, although it is unlikely that the more sordid accusations levelled at him by anonymous denunciations in Ajaccio were true, some of which involved seducing a virgin. However, his reaction to his unwanted marriage to Letizia was to leave for Rome, officially to study law, which he failed to do. Instead, he ran up considerable debts, as did his wife in retaliation, pressing Ajaccio's capacity for high fashion to admirable and resourceful limits.

Whatever he got up to in Rome, when Carlo returned home he had changed. Indeed, he came back a man, but one now highly influenced by the insular Corsican émigré community he had come to know in Rome, and offered his services to Paoli. It is impossible to know with certainty the relative degrees of careerist calculation and idealism that went into Carlo's decision, but it was, in terms of the society of the *presidii* to which he belonged, an unpopular gamble. That said, they all knew that Paoli had been 'up there' for a decade in 1765, when Carlo returned from his travels and moved to Corte, initially without Letizia, whose spending sprees continued unabated. Several of the younger Buonaparte went with him, notably his brother, Napoleone, and his sister-in-law, Geltrude, who was estranged from her husband. By contrast, and more representative of the Ajaccio elite, Carlo's uncle Don Luciano, the cautious, calculating priest, weighed up Paoli's chances of survival, remembered his real sources of support and so rejected the idea of moving to Corte, which he called 'a foreign country'.[15] Paoli's assurances that 'loyalty would be well rewarded' were too vague to reverse centuries of enmity between the interior and the *presidii*, save among the young and restless. Carlo was able to rescue his own position when Paoli fell, in no small part thanks to his in-laws, but his decision to go to Corte would have fundamental implications for Napoleon, for Paoli became a pivotal figure in Napoleon's early life, if not in the manner his father would have wished.

One of Paoli's inducements to the ambitious, educated youth of the *presidii* was the new university he created in Corte. Although small and with limited resources, its courses were a model of the new, progressive learning and were free from the control of the Church, present in most European states. Carlo took his studies more seriously in Corte than he had in Rome. More importantly, he rose high and fast in Paoli's service, becoming something like a private secretary to *Babbù*, 'the Father'. Carlo probably did not wield as much power in Corte as he claimed in his memoir, or as his sons continued to believe, but he undoubtedly had a considerable degree of influence on day-to-day affairs. Geltrude proved a great favourite at Paoli's semi-official 'court', a role subsequent myth assigned to Letizia, who arrived later in Corte. Letizia cut a dash, and her lavish spending now found its justification, but her sister actually seems to have been closer to Paoli.[16]

Letizia's first son Joseph was born in Ajaccio, in January 1768, but was removed to Corte, where Napoleon was probably conceived in the first week of November the same year. Something crucial changed in that year, however. Napoleon may or may not have told Paoli, in June 1789, that 'I was born as the nation died', for the authenticity of the letter is highly questionable,[17] but the observation, whether real or not, is correct.

On 15 May 1768, the Republic of St George 'entrusted' Corsica to French protection. As Michel Vergé-Franceschi has made clear, the Republic did not actually sell or otherwise cede the island to France. Rather, in what he terms aptly 'a game of dupes', the Treaty of Versailles authorised the French to govern and pacify Corsica, in the interests of both states, and then return it to Genoa.[18] The Genoese knew full well that they could never hope to regulate their finances sufficiently to meet the conditions for its return, and the French had no intention of giving it back. Nevertheless, Corsica remained as strategically important in the western Mediterranean as it was under-developed economically, and both states feared, following the emphatic defeat of France by Britain in the Seven Years War, that Paoli's popularity among the London intelligentsia was evolving into links with the British establishment, and that his 'mountain republic' – the modern early Rome – might actually become a puppet state of the modern Carthage and its powerful fleet. This prospect intimidated both parties to the treaty, and, on 19 May, two battalions – the first of nearly 15,000 French troops – landed in Ajaccio to a warm welcome. Paoli was now facing, not an inert, minor Italian city-state, but – for all its recent defeats in major wars – the greatest land power in western Europe, able and determined to protect the island, and the *presidii* above all, from the British at sea, and the rebellious 'fifth column' in the mountains.

However progressive Paoli's experiment in statehood had been in Corte, the conflict now returned to its traditional contours very quickly, although this time the 'occupier' was one to be reckoned with. Paoli decided to strike at the large, mainly 'settler' *signori* of the north, but the city of Bastia, where the new Governor of Corsica, the comte de Marbeuf, had been installed in the name of Louis XV, quickly rallied to the French.[19] Paoli won a few engagements, but the French juggernaut proved too much for what was, in the end, a peasant militia. Foreign observers had waxed lyrical for decades about Corsican valour and their ferocity in arms, plaudits that were not embroidered fantasies, but at Ponte Nuovo, on 8 May 1768, a large, newly arrived French contingent under the comte de Vaux caught the main Paolist force at a narrow crossing and, in a terrible slaughter, Paoli's resistance was effectively broken. Paoli himself had already been put to flight a few days before and was away in the hills. His absence has cast suspicion on him ever since, and has never been explained, nor has the fact that some troops – German volunteers with Paoli – turned on the retreating rebels and opened fire on them. Nor does Carlo seem to have been at Ponte Nuovo, later mythology notwithstanding, as he was more likely to have been with Paoli's staff. Later legend had Napoleon's uncle and namesake dying heroically on the bridge, but his earlier death from natural causes is easily proved. What is incontrovertible is that Carlo and Letizia's world now crumbled under the sledgehammer of French arms.

Paoli and what was left of his army fell back to Corte, but, knowing it could not be held, he and several thousand others made for the coast, where the Royal Navy collected them. A generation of exile would follow. To his credit, Carlo did not desert Paoli, and freely admitted in his memoirs, written for his sons, that he would have followed his leader into exile without Letizia, now carrying Napoleon, had Paoli himself not reminded him of his duty as a father and husband.

Accordingly, Carlo led his young family home the hard way. Order had broken down in the mountains after Ponte Nuovo, and it was probably as much to protect his vulnerable wife and infant son, Joseph, from the depredations of bandits, as from the French, that he took them over high, small passes in dreadful, freak snowstorms, to the safety of Ajaccio. This journey became the stuff of legend, a brave, stalwart Letizia rallying the rebel womenfolk and urging Carlo to make a last stand high in the mountain caves. It was nothing of the kind, for the family moved almost alone, leaving the diehards behind.[20] Nevertheless, their ordeal was proof enough that there was more to this couple than the other reality of a vain, spendthrift wife and an ambitious, preening husband. Their reasons were more personal and prosaic than the stuff of the legend, but Letizia made the hard journey all the same, heavily pregnant, in awful conditions. It was proof enough of the *fierté* she imparted to her son. Such people could face hardship when they had to. If there is any truth in that current of medical opinion that says children are already learning actively while in the womb, Napoleon's first subconscious lessons in life were those of privation, danger and rugged persistence. Whatever the truth of this, Napoleon certainly showed very early in his military career a taste for physical hardship worthy of a Spartan, and forced marches in blizzards, over forbidding mountains, became the forte of his armies.

The battered Buonaparte family arrived home, in every sense. Carlo's days as an idealistic Corsican patriot, and as part of a national government, were over. He settled down to the hard work of making something of himself and securing a future for his children. He became a busy lawyer, took an interest in his properties and, above all, set about working with Letizia to give their sons a happy, secure upbringing after the deluge was over. Napoleon treasured his parents' efforts for him, and the happy childhood they gave him. The Buonaparte returned to the family home, but under the tight grip of Don Luciano, who continued to control most of their finances. That home continued to expand, despite property disputes and lack of funds. A terrace was built at the rear, as both a gesture to fashion and to give the two boys a safer place to play than the street. The legal dispute with the Bozzi, across the road, rumbled on in the first half of the 1770s, while in the mountains Paoli's supporters planned a new revolt, which broke out in 1774 and was quickly and ruthlessly suppressed by the French. Carlo kept his distance from it, thus confirming he had broken definitively with his former politics. It is generally agreed that Carlo was not regarded as a traitor to Paoli by Corsican society, for he had stood by him for as long as he remained on the island, and his new collaboration with the French was regarded in Ajaccio as simply conforming to the general attitude of the urban elite, a return to the fold and to sanity, after a noble, but misguided aberration.

Napoleon's early years were spent in comparative peace, playing with his family and friends, surrounded by a secure, loving home to which he always paid tribute. There were dark moments, for Carlo and Letizia were never entirely at ease with each other, and Napoleon recalled with distaste his mother's orders to go and spy on Carlo in the *caffè*, 'to see if he was gambling', and admitted freely that he was not a truthful child, incurring her strap for it. He was boisterous, a trait perhaps over-egged in the myths surrounding his childhood, but his exuberance probably stood out less for its intensity, than in contrast to the affable, tranquil nature of his older brother. His love of playing soldiers, so stressed in the legend, is not unusual in little boys, but it appears true enough that he befriended the French garrison, and appalled Letizia by preferring their coarse rations of black bread to the family's meals. He was sexually normal. He had a little girlfriend whose hand he held and whom he played with happily.[21] His life at home was punctuated by trips to the family's country properties that gave glimpses of the Corsican uplands – for these excursions were not protracted – that came to grip his memories after he left home. For his first ten years his was the normal life of a child of the notables of Ajaccio.

There were very adult manoeuvrings kept well away from the two older boys, and of the siblings who followed them in quick succession – Luciano (1775, known as Lucien in France later), Maria-Anna (1777, nicknamed Elisa at school in France), Luigi (or Louis, 1778), Pauletta (Pauline, 1780), Maria-Annunziata (1782, later called Caroline) and Gerolamo (Jérôme, 1784). Through the Pietrasanta, with their presence in Bastia, Carlo used his social and intellectual skills to ingratiate himself with Marbeuf, and gained access, however limited, to a whole new dimension of patronage and possibilities. Carlo proved the ideal spy for the newly arrived Marbeuf, an able informer on the inner world of Ajaccio and of the remains of 'Paolism'. In return, Marbeuf allowed Carlo entry into the Byzantine world of the patron–client networks of *ancien régime* France, which Carlo knew all too well dwarfed anything a Corsican notable could have aspired to under either Paoli or the Republic. Carlo and Don Luciano were very much the poor relations to their in-laws under the new regime, but Letizia was not, and Marbeuf, a widower, was undoubtedly captivated by her. From 1771 onwards, he came frequently to Ajaccio and paid court to her, and invited her, definitely, and Carlo, possibly, to his official residence in Bastia.

At the time speculation was rife, and has been since, as to whether this obvious infatuation escalated into an affair. It is impossible to prove, yet perhaps a few things can reasonably be asserted about the many rumours this liaison generated. It has been speculated that Marbeuf, not Carlo, was Napoleon's real father, but Dorothy

Carrington has shown how impossible this would have been: when Napoleon was conceived in Corte in early November 1768, Marbeuf was in his winter quarters elsewhere on the island, and Corte was under siege by the French. Indeed, Napoleon was, with Joseph, the only Buonaparte sibling who could *not* have been fathered by Marbeuf.[22] Marbeuf agreed to become Napoleon's godfather, but could not be in Ajaccio in time, and appointed a deputy, Giubega, a powerful notable from Calvi who was high in French service; he did, however, stand godfather to the Buonaparte who followed, a clear sign that the French rulers of Corsica had found themselves integrated into the roles of their predecessors under the Republic. All this would count for much, in the unforeseeable, dangerous times ahead. Behind the flamboyant face they presented to the world, Carlo and Letizia showed caution, taking out the best insurance they could for their children under what seemed a new, unshakeable hegemony, and it worked until it all came crashing down in 1789.

Napoleon owed his rapid rise to power to the Revolution, and supported it from the outset, but it proved a catastrophe for the family. Well integrated into the French system of patronage through their friendship with Marbeuf, Carlo and Letizia secured better educations and career prospects for their children than Genoese rule had afforded them, aspirations destroyed by the Revolution. The difference between the educations and early years of their four eldest children is in marked contrast to the struggle that Joseph and Napoleon had to provide for the futures of Louis, Pauline, Caroline and Jérôme in the 1790s. The transfer of Corsica to the control of the Bourbon monarchy had been a short, but real, golden age for the Buonaparte, relatively speaking. The young Napoleon soon came to sense the 'glass ceiling' that stifled the minor nobility under the Bourbons, rather than the opportunity his father saw flowing from entry into the service of a larger state. Napoleon became wholly 'French' when he came to see limitations where a Corsican notable saw only possibilities of advancement. In this sense, Napoleon and the Revolution were made for each other, but that time had yet to come.

It is only too true that Carlo would not have gained some of Marbeuf's favours had it not been for Letizia.[23] Although the relationship between Marbeuf and Letizia is, ultimately, unfathomable one way or the other, if the question is posed differently – to ask if Carlo and Luciano were capable of encouraging a real affair between them to advance the family's collective interests – the answer might reasonably be 'yes'. Carlo gained his position in the local court, and help with his pretensions to the Tuscan ancestry he felt he needed to qualify as a noble under French custom and law. The French commandant in Ajaccio was the comte de Narbonne, who had done much more fighting against Paoli than Marbeuf, and he suspected Carlo; Marbeuf's higher status kept him at bay. In 1771, when Carlo stood for election to the noble house – the second estate – of the newly created Estates of Corsica and failed to win, Marbeuf had the result quashed and pushed Carlo's candidacy through. This made him a 'noble', from which much else flowed. Above all, noble status gained his two sons proper French educations. Together with the young Joseph Fesch, Napoleon and Joseph were enrolled in their respective academies – Joseph and Fesch in the seminary of Aix-en-Provence, and Napoleon in the military academy at Brienne – thanks to Marbeuf's patronage. Lucien would follow Joseph to the seminary at Aix-en-Provence in 1786, although he left under a cloud in 1789, to throw himself into Corsican politics, while the eldest sister, Maria-Anna, obtained a bursary to the prestigious girls' college, the Maison Royale at St-Cyr, where she became known as Elisa, and excelled academically. The Buonaparte children were far from the only young Corsican notables Marbeuf helped in this way, for this was an integral part of his policy of binding the more reliable elements of the Corsican elites to their new country, but his liking for Letizia and his reliance on the Pietrasanta in a more official sense made the way much smoother for a man who had been so prominent a member of Paoli's close entourage.

Carlo had made more than a choice in local politics when he turned from Paoli to the French, and he did more than simply set his sons on the path to better careers when he sent them off to school in France.

Henceforth, the Buonaparte belonged to another culture, to another world, and the transition would prove anything but pleasurable or easy. Carlo had but pointed his children on the road; the journey through a new, alien land was left to them, and to Napoleon in particular. Even had Napoleon's later life not become the stuff of legend, Carlo's decision to tear them from their homeland decided the destiny of his son. The father cast the die; the son lived with the consequences.

2

FRANCE: A DANGEROUS PLACE

From Stranger to Saviour, 1779–1797

In December 1778, Napoleon and the other young Buonapartes set out for France. They went together with Carlo, first, to the Jesuit school at Autun, a cathedral town in Burgundy, where the two Josephs were to remain for some time, arriving on New Year's Day 1779. Napoleon stayed only a few weeks, in an attempt to give him what is now termed an 'immersion course' in French, which had only limited success. He moved on to Brienne, to the beginning of the military life that, more than any single agency beyond his own will, would mark him the most. Napoleon's severance from his childhood was abrupt, and he felt it acutely, yet he now entered on a career path to which he was immediately suited, and the contrast between his progress as a cadet – together with his natural affinity for institutional life – and the rude shock of being plunged, aged nine, into a new landscape, language and society obviously shook him. 'Culture shock' has become a debased term through trivial over-use, but it is not inappropriate to apply it to Napoleon's state of mind over the next fifteen years, for he came to feel as at sea when he returned to Corsica as he did in France. These years spent in French military academies and quiet provincial garrisons were punctuated by increasingly traumatic brief returns 'home', interrupted in 1785 by the premature death of his father, probably from a hereditary form of stomach cancer that would kill Napoleon at a similar age.

It is not enough to dismiss Napoleon's reactions to the experiences of his adolescence and early manhood by seeing them as normal in a society which sent many of its sons away to school, be that milieu the conformist French nobility or the ambitious notables of the Corsican *presidii*. Napoleon's childhood in Ajaccio was markedly different from that of many of his fellow students in Brienne. He had been surrounded by an exuberant household of Mediterranean women and a warm extended family, rather than the austere, more remote traditions of the French nobility. More prosaically, he did not speak the French language well, a powerful barrier to integration, for even when he did begin to cope his peculiar accent marked him out, regional variations having long disappeared among the French upper classes, wherever their provenance. On one level, Napoleon found himself very quickly in his studies, where he mastered mathematics and the little science he was offered. Emotionally, however, Napoleon reacted to his fate by spending a great deal of time and effort trying to be things he was not. He stood defiantly apart among the French, even as all the force of a French school regime bent on making him the target of its cultural imperialism crashed down on him. He created a Corsica of the mind, much as had the young Pasquale Paoli in a similar situation. The regime at Brienne forbade returns home, save for exceptional reasons, and severely limited parental visits, circumstances which allowed the mind to shape its own vision of home, divorced from reality. Napoleon sought to become the very kind of Corsican he was not – 'insular', brave and tenacious in revolt, indignant and unyielding in his quest for freedom and justice.

All educated young men of the times devoured Plutarch's heroic *Lives of the Noble Greeks and Romans*, readily available in a French edition that was derived from North's sixteenth-century English translation. This was extracurricular reading, unmediated by scholarly interpretations, stories and examples the young could take to their own hearts as they wished, untarnished by the boredom induced by formal teaching. Napoleon, like the Paolis – father and son – before him, transposed the lives of the heroes of Republican Rome into the recent history of the Corsica he was now inventing for himself, one quite alien to his real heritage as a product of the culture of the *presidii*. He asked for histories of Corsica from his father, in particular the one written by Boswell, Paoli's British admirer and propagandist. In the process, Napoleon came to idolise Paoli. He had a living hero, as well as dead icons, to pin his hopes on, or so he imagined. It was doomed to fail if put to the test of reality. This Corsica had nothing to do with Napoleon, but he would not find this out for many years to come.

In reality he was becoming his true self, a professional soldier, not an irregular bandit partisan, and his vocation seeped into him, almost at times in spite of himself. Napoleon learned much from this, but they were lessons about himself he was loath to admit. He had become a Frenchman, almost instinctively, but against his conscious will. He was not quite a Romantic, however much he sought solace in Romantic ideals in his cultural and emotional limbo. Romantic heroism was eventually put to the service of self-advancement, of *gloire*, not self-sacrifice in the name of abstract duty or a lost cause. He devoured Romantic melancholy at an age when most of his fellows did the same. The resonances of Rousseau and Goethe were powerful for a displaced adolescent, and Napoleon was surely that, yet they did not dislodge his natural energy and drive, nor turn him for long from his curiosity about the world and its ways.

Put another way, he outgrew Romanticism, although he could never own up to that. At the end of all things, on St Helena, he found a practical use for it, in constructing his memoirs in the tone that was perfect for its intended readership, a new generation imbued with Romanticism, and his own cohort, who were assured by Napoleon that no one could ever hope to understand them, not their fathers, not their sons, because of their wholly unique experience of the Revolution and his own exploits. Only the classical past – the Plutarch they had all read by candlelight under the bedcovers – could offer them any empathy. Even before St Helena, as a leader of men Napoleon was able to transform the heroism of the ancient world into a very tangible source of inspiration. His ability to transmit this to his armies 'made everyone feel they could be classical heroes', as Luigi Mascilli Migliorini has put it.[1] Napoleon was the rationalisation of Romanticism. He got his generation and the next right, and used the ripened fruit of his early self-delusion to feed them their dreams of glory.

These early years were full of the mistakes and delusions that evoke, eventually, the true character of a man. No institutional programme or intellectual current can hope to dominate so powerful an intellect or strong a will as that possessed by Napoleon, but youth is a vulnerable time, and Napoleon's youth was more vulnerable than many. His individual character can be seen less in the way he followed the herd into Romantic melancholy and classical heroism, and more in the way he absorbed them in later life by bending them to his own will.

Brienne proved a formidable proposition, even for so singular a spirit. In its daily life and curriculum, the nine-year-old Napoleon confronted the well-honed system of assimilation to the most advanced culture in Europe, and it imposed itself on him, more than any other influence he ever encountered. Napoleon was always grateful for his education, and he admitted it had made of him a Frenchman. He fought it, however. When Napoleon confessed his intrinsic 'Frenchness', he openly admitted defeat. He was probably sent to Brienne because, among the twelve royal military academies, it happened to have a vacancy at the time. The environs of this small town in the northern region of Champagne could not have been more different from Corsica; it was surrounded by an expanse of open fields covered by vines and wheat, where in winter the harsh east wind whips across the North European Plain from the Baltic. Though he went there more by chance than design, the French monarchy could not have chosen a more alien environment for its new subject.

Napoleon arrived in April 1779, the first time he had ever been separated from his brother Joseph. The school was part of an experiment that was soon to end. Perplexed by their continued military failures in the course of the eighteenth century, the French monarchy heeded a particular line of Enlightened thought that argued environment was the key to forming character, and created scholarships for the children of the minor nobility to attend military academies where the atmosphere was designed to shape future officers. The schools also attracted the sons of greater noble families, as they offered the surest path to military careers. The monarchy would soon despair of this, when defeat in war continued, and it turned to the recommendations of the marquis de Ségur, whose committee of inquiry proposed a shift from the 'institutional approach' to one predicated on family upbringing, assuming that only noble families with very long military traditions could produce officer material. His findings were accepted with modifications, and would have excluded Napoleon, but they were presented to the King's Council only in 1789, months before the old order collapsed.[2]

As with all the educational institutions under the French monarchy, Brienne was run by a religious order, the Minor Franciscans, although much of the teaching was done by laymen, again very much the norm by the late eighteenth century. It was a small establishment of about 110 boys, of whom 45 were recipients of state scholarships; that is, they were from poor noble families, and Napoleon was of their number.[3] It was a mixture of the monastic and the military, in that the boys slept in their individual, very spartan cells, rather than in large dormitories, and corporal punishment was rare, but the common denominator of the life of the cloister and that of the barracks was austerity. Life may not have been harsh, but it was very hard, and Napoleon seems to have had no qualms about it.

Brienne inculcated in him his frugality, his aversion to ease and his iron self-discipline. The habits he acquired there followed him across the battlefields of Europe, and were so ingrained that the luxuries his later triumphs offered him were politely declined. Napoleon might seize the best palace in Cairo or Vienna for his headquarters, but he usually slept in his camp bed. When Napoleon first read Rousseau's diatribes against the modern world and its corruption of morals, and his railings against the degenerative power of wealth, it all came quite naturally to a young man who thrived on the austere egalitarianism of Brienne. When he encountered the relative luxury of the military school in Paris after he left Brienne, with its servants, its expensive surroundings and elaborate meals, he complained that this not only distracted the cadets from their studies, but weakened them for future service:

Since they are all ... destined for military service, is that not the sole and
real education they should receive? Subjected to a sober life, to take care of
their appearance, they will become more robust, able to brave the rigours
of the seasons, to bear the strains of war with courage, and above all, to
inspire respect and blind devotion from the soldiers who will be under their
orders.[4]

Brienne left its mark on Napoleon. If Corsica had become an unreal
dream, Plutarch's ancient, and Rousseau's modern, theoretical Sparta
– made real in Brienne – were his daily routine. He had been practising
what he preached for some time, it seems. On her only visit to him at
Brienne, in 1782, Letizia was shocked to find her son so thin and gaunt.
He probably saw himself as 'lean and keen'.

The available records suggest that Napoleon worked hard. The
inspector of the military academies, the chevalier de Keralio, obviously
saw promise in him and marked him down as a model pupil in his
report of 1781. When, towards the end of his time at Brienne, in
1784, Napoleon asked to apply for the navy, de Keralio supported his
request. This was something of an accolade, for the navy had become
a highly sought-after branch of the service among the brightest, but
least well-connected, students at the academies. Its standing had risen
enormously after its successes against the British during the American
Revolution, and it had been the object of great financial investment
by the state. Above all, the navy required considerable intelligence
and technical expertise from its officers. De Keralio obviously felt
Napoleon had all these attributes, but he had not had the requisite
six years at the school, and so de Keralio's recommendations were set
aside. Napoleon opted for the obvious alternative, the artillery, then
the most technologically sophisticated branch of the service, and in the
midst of major reforms and advances.[5] Naval warfare would emerge as
one of Napoleon's worst blind spots as a strategist during his abortive
attempt to invade England, revealing a profound ignorance of every
aspect of the sea. History can be made by bureaucratic rigidity as much
as by the abstract forces of climate and geography, or the will of the
'Great Man'. Napoleon did not go to the great naval base of Toulon yet

– when he did, it was to make his name as an artillery expert against the British fleet in 1793 – but to the military school in Paris, which he attended for not quite a year, from October 1784 until September 1785, when he passed out forty-second of fifty-eight, a creditable record given his brief stay, if hardly outstanding.

Napoleon's schooldays are shrouded in myth, much of it improbable. Even how he got there was subjected to fantasy, by his father Carlo, who claimed in his memoir that he took the boys via Florence, where they had an audience with the model enlightened monarch of the age, Peter-Leopold, the Habsburg Grand Duke. Napoleon and Joseph lied like troopers to the end of their lives that this was true, in the face of its obvious impossibility. Philip Dwyer has astutely pointed to the incongruity of de Keralio's report on Napoleon as a model, well-behaved student and the carefully cultivated myth – begun by himself as soon as he was in a position to write his own story – of a rebellious, sullen outsider.[6] There are various 'epic moments' of the myth that actually sit awkwardly with other aspects of it. Napoleon was supposed to have displayed his early prowess as a commander when he organised a particularly heroic snowball fight in the schoolyard, yet it is highly unlikely that such an unpopular boy would ever have been able to lead his peers in this way.

Nevertheless, the realities of Brienne and much of Napoleon's behaviour in the army after he left it, and especially his youthful attempts at literature, reveal deeper currents of loathing and rebelliousness – the rage of the displaced person – than anything concocted later. Napoleon did, indeed, endure the snobbery of the sons of the higher nobility that the ethos of Brienne was meant to stamp out, in order to amalgamate the boys into a homogeneous corps, and he was taunted for his accent by all and sundry. He may or may not have taken it out on them at the time, as he wanted the world to believe, but he certainly did so when he put pen to paper, while on garrison duty after leaving Paris in 1785.

His rage manifested itself in a Corsican patriotism that exploded into nothing short of hatred of the French. As Andy Martin, who has delved into Napoleon's literary output, has said: 'Existence was struggle and writing was resistance – a series of guerrilla raids on the canon and the big guns of French history. Words were actions.'[7] He stabbed with his pen, with all the ferocity and venom of the dispossessed victim he felt he had become. He seems to have been planning to write a vitriolic, anti-French history of Corsica from about the age of sixteen, but the closest he got was the unpublished – and unpublishable – *Novella Corsa*, probably written in 1791. Many of his other writings, such as 'On Suicide', where he describes his own death, were 'fashionable' in a generation in thrall to the tragic hero of Goethe's *roman-à-clef*, *The Sorrows of Young Werther*, and Napoleon was no exception to this. He retained his admiration for the book and its author all his life, but his writings in this vein are signs of his assimilation less to France, than to what might fairly be called the 'youth culture' of late eighteenth-century Europe. The *Novella Corsa* was something quite different, however. It juxtaposes an unspoilt, innocent Corsica to the corrupt, morally degenerate French invaders, the last in a long succession of brutal outsiders who arrive to 'rape' the island. Its central figure is an Englishman, shipwrecked on Corsica, through whose intelligent but alien eyes the story is told. The choice of an English protagonist was far from innocent; it was a political statement, for, at the time, Paoli was in exile in London, a much admired figure in its salons and working hard to win British support for a new rebellion. Even Napoleon's supposedly deeply personal 'On Suicide' turns into a political statement, for a major cause of his imagined mental collapse is not existential, but highly topical and public: 'Frenchmen! Not content with having carried off all that we cherish, you have also corrupted our morals!'[8] He could never quite leave the real world around him for the aesthetic realm of true invention, and this failure revealed more of his true nature than he probably ever realised. Napoleon was a 'political animal', however hard he tried to be something more 'profound'.

Napoleon the 'novelist' and essayist of the late 1780s and early 1790s emerges as not just a fervent Corsican nationalist, but as an anti-colonialist. While still at Brienne, he had devoured one of the most widely read and controversial books of the age, the Abbé Raynal's *History of the Two Indies*, first published in 1770 and widely translated – most of it was actually ghost-written by Diderot – a work which has rightly been seen as the founding text of anti-imperialist discourse. Napoleon absorbed its message of the cynical, avaricious European exploitation of the rest of the world – the East and West Indies of the title – and applied the process to Corsica. It was a perceptive intellectual breakthrough on his part, and a theory that remains as potent as it is contentious, that the ruthless process of colonialism began and continued to be applied, not just to the 'other' of the extra-European world, but to Europeans by 'fellow' Europeans. Raynal's book had been subjected to harsh censorship by the more relaxed standards of the late eighteenth century, when many disciples of Voltaire within the French establishment infiltrated the Church-controlled censorship apparatus, and exercised a lighter touch than the norms stipulated.[9] Not when it came to Raynal. In 1780, when Raynal allowed a new edition to appear under his own name, a warrant for his arrest was issued, his book was burned publicly by the royal executioner and he fled abroad, returning only in 1785, and settling in Marseille.[10]

Seen in this context, the young Napoleon's views were more subversive still, and he was quick to make contact with his idol, second only in his personal pantheon to Paoli among the living. In 1786, now an officer in Valence, relatively close to Marseille, Napoleon wrote Raynal what amounted to a fan letter, and set out his views on the colonial condition of Corsica. Raynal encouraged his hopes to write a thorough-going anti-imperialist history of the island, and soon invited him to join his salon. Napoleon became a frequent participant and vocal contributor to Raynal's salon in Marseille, even after he had moved further north, to Auxonne.

His adherence to the ways of the French intelligentsia was just as evident when he entered that most Enlightened of events, the essay competition. This format of open competition for a cash prize put up by a salon had catapulted Rousseau to fame and, when Raynal offered a large sum for an essay 'On Happiness', in 1791, Napoleon cut

himself off from the world in order to write. He failed to secure the
prize, but his determination to win acceptance is all too evident from
the copious notebooks he compiled in the attempt. Napoleon is often
derided as a parvenu, a desperate, insecure arriviste, and his obsession
with this competition reveals that, in these years at least, this was part
of him, even as he clung to his Corsican patriotism.[11] If he was being
patronised by the French liberal elite, he did not notice, or did not
mind, and his ideas on colonialism – for he put his own interpretation
on 'Happiness' – imposed on Europeans by Europeans truly did push
the limits of the acceptable, and still do.

Napoleon's own career as the greatest of European imperialists laces
all this with irony, for no imperial hegemony ever sought to impose
itself so rigidly, or displayed such contempt for non-French European
cultures, as his own. Yet the colossal ironies of the future should not
obscure the incongruities that surrounded Napoleon's adhesion to
Raynal and his salon at the time it happened. Napoleon, the aspiring
scourge of French colonialism – economic, political, cultural – craved
admission to the very society he so sincerely hated. By seeking out
the salon, and trying to integrate himself into it, Napoleon revealed
how assimilated into French culture he had become; he looked to the
oppressor for approval, less by turning to Raynal, who was sincere in
his loathing of the conduct of his fellow Europeans, than by throwing
himself into the cultural medium itself, for the salon remained the
symbol of French civilisation, and Napoleon's own imperial servants
always saw it, and its social rituals, as the benchmark of true civilisation.
Napoleon at seventeen did not see the incongruity, so much a part of
French society had he now become. His eagerness to enter this milieu
reveals him unconsciously being himself – pushing his way into the
heart of the world he had been partially absorbed in at Brienne – while
the views he expounded sat ill with this same integration.

On paper, Napoleon was desperate less to assert his real, suppressed
sense of self than to escape both his acquired French identity and, even
more, his family background. The 'subaltern', oppressed Corsica from
which Paoli had sprung was not his, for he was one of the oppressors;

he was a scion of the Ajaccio 'garrison', wholly and completely. How aware Napoleon actually was of this, after a youth spent divorced from the realities of the island, is far from evident. His vision of himself as at one with the Corsicans of the interior was probably genuine, sharpened by the snubs he endured at school and the frustrations of his career. Nevertheless, he knew his family had begun as outsiders – whether as the Ligurian colonists of fact, or the Tuscan nobles of fiction – and his *Novella Corsa* and the papers he gave to Raynal's gatherings were, at a semi-conscious level, exercises in 'post-colonial guilt'. They show Napoleon's most impassioned efforts to be something he was not, whereas the manner and setting of their exposition reveal him as the French bourgeois he had become.

The death of Carlo in 1785 transformed Napoleon. He still clung to his youthful passions, personal and political, but he emerged as the leader of a family deep in debt and in need of a champion in the courts and among the authorities. Many stories, some true, some false, some embroidered, float about Napoleon's early years, seeking to detect the early master and commander, but the real proof of these innate qualities exists in his determination to shoulder responsibility for his mother and siblings. Don Luciano was now old and ill with gout; Joseph soon revealed himself unfit for the task of arguing and harrying, if not for quiet negotiation. While still in his teens, Napoleon showed himself someone ready to face up to difficulties. It was Napoleon, while still a schoolboy, who took it upon himself to collect his father's papers and go to Paris, to try to arrange his outstanding affairs and ensure the family got his pension; it was he who wrote to the head of the seminary in Aix-en-Provence to apologise for Lucien's misconduct, while he himself was supposed to be serving with his first regiment.[12] Napoleon rose to this challenge, having no qualms about writing directly to the Intendant of Corsica, or to the Controllor-General of Finances in Paris – the King's first minister – to press cases concerning the family. Carlo had begun a public-spirited project to drain marsh-land close to Ajaccio, and, when the promised government aid did not arrive, it was the seventeen-year-old Napoleon who reminded the Intendant of his promise of financial aid, while also asking him to pay for Lucien's education at Aix, for the family had suffered the double blow of the death of Marbeuf, its patron, in 1786, which really did leave Napoleon alone as its head.[13] A year later, he badgered both the Intendant and Loménie de Brienne, the Controller-General, about the marshland, and Carlo's ambition to see it planted with mulberry trees to provide the basis for a silk industry in Ajaccio.[14] The problems he encountered were clear lessons to Napoleon that Corsica was a distant, unheeded outpost of France, but the process also taught him that the monarchy was an unjust and inefficient regime. More than this, almost subconsciously, he reacted to these difficulties as a typical notable of the *presidio*: litigious, persistent, determined to defend his family's patrimony and to realise his father's hopes. Certainly, this stiffened his dislike of the French, and reinforced his sense of injustice, but it also shows how deeply he respected Carlo's legacy.

Just as much has been fabricated about Letizia as the embodiment of 'the true, pure, Corsica' as about Napoleon's relationship with Carlo, after his departure for Brienne, which has usually been portrayed as that of a son resentful of his father's treasonous collaboration with the French. Relations between father and son have been depicted as angry, as Napoleon branded him a collaborator, a traitor to Paoli and to his people. There is very little to support this, and Paoli certainly never felt this way about Carlo, for when Paoli returned to Corsica in 1790 the young Buonaparte were initially welcomed by him, evoking Carlo's loyalty to 'the cause' and to Paoli personally. Whatever rancour there may have been between father and son, it did not last long, and Napoleon – from the outset – showed loyalty to Carlo's hopes, whether for urban renewal or the advancement of his siblings in the French system, and real affection for him. Napoleon's venomous anti-French feelings did not include Carlo, at least not when it mattered, when he had to take his place as the head of the family.

Nor did his hatred of the French extend to women. It was on one of the visits to Paris on family business, probably in 1787, that he lost his virginity to a young prostitute he met around the cheap restaurants of the Palais Royal, one of the more rakish if down-at-heel parts of the city. He said he was moved by her tale of woe, and spent his first night ever with a woman. It may or not be so but it is a tale pedestrian enough to be true.

Napoleon's absences from his postings, after leaving military academy, were protracted to say the least, between 1786 and 1793, but he had good reason for them. If ambition played a part in his long trips to Corsica and then Paris, he was not just – or even primarily – trying to advance himself, but to protect his family from ruin, as the Revolution brought new tensions to Corsica. If he often neglected his routine duties as an officer, he never shirked the more demanding problems of leading his now fatherless and patronless family. He was a leader born, and there is no need to mythologise the fact.

Garrison life was not that dull or fruitless for Napoleon when he was there, but it drove home to him, as it did to many others of his generation, the disappointments of professional service under the Bourbon monarchy and the sheer boredom of peacetime. He had some fine senior officers at Valence and then at Auxonne, between 1785 and 1789. Once assigned to artillery regiments, he escaped the worst of army snobbery, the scions of the great houses preferring the cavalry or older infantry regiments. He was among other bright technocrats, from whom he learned much, both from their own ideas and experience, and from the modern reading on tactics and scientific advances to which they introduced him. Uturbie, in Valence, and then Du Teil and Gassendi, in Auxonne, were leaders in the field of modern thinking about gunnery and wider issues, such as the quality and production of gunpowder, range-finding and the manufacture of cannon, all of which they drew from scientific knowledge. This led Napoleon to interest himself in scientific theory, to an intensive study of chemistry and calculus, and to an abiding passion for astronomy, derived from the study of lenses, that stayed with him all his life, and which he imposed on secondary schooling in France almost as soon as he had the power. His commanding officers opened his mind to science, and also to the concept of a more mobile approach to warfare. It was a seed time, for all the ennui of garrison life. It also pulled him in the opposite direction from Romanticism, but he did not really grasp the struggle within him. The quiet world of provincial, sedentary soldiering had thus been punctuated often enough by the demands of family, but in 1789 it came crashing down.

THE FRENCH REVOLUTION:
THE END OF ALL THINGS, 1789–1793

The French Revolution changed the whole world, for ever. It marks a watershed in human experience, but no one saw their world more changed than the Buonaparte, and few places saw more change than Corsica, when the pillars of the old monarchy cracked, definitively, in the spring and summer of 1789. From the outset, the French revolutionary governments posed a series of stark choices to the society they ruled. It was impossible to avoid taking sides, however reluctantly, and it was even more impossible to avoid the results of those choices. They had to be lived with. The people of Corsica – the most remote in the new French nation – were no exception to this, Napoleon included. Even so powerful a will as his had choices imposed on him and had to face their consequences.

The origins of the French Revolution remain one of the most tortuous subjects in history, but by the late 1780s it was clear to all that France was in crisis and that the institutions of the absolute monarchy had reached an impasse about how to reform a state all felt to be in desperate need of change. On the one hand, the monarchy believed it needed more powers to raise revenue, and a more powerful, centralised administration to do so, thus challenging the traditional privileges not just of the Church and nobility, but of the French provinces and many private individuals who had acquired exemptions from some taxes and duties. This view was opposed with increasing frequency, and in ever more vehement language, by the *Parlements*, courts of appeal led by a magistracy which had noble status, one of whose tasks was to pronounce on the legality of royal legislation. Long-present tensions became urgent when France proved powerless to intervene to its advantage in a civil war that erupted in the Dutch Republic, and the Controller-General, Calonne, pronounced the state bankrupt. The monarchy and the *Parlements* called each other's bluff and chose to break the institutional impasse by summoning a body representing the entire realm, the Estates General, to meet in Versailles in May 1789 to discuss Calonne's reform project. The Estates General had not met since 1614, and there were explosive arguments about its powers and composition when it finally met. Divided as it was into three orders – the clergy, nobility and the commons (the first, second and third estates) – and elected, within each order, on a remarkably inclusive, quasi-democratic franchise, the meeting of the Estates General marked an unheralded watershed in French history. For the first time, ever, an elected assembly existed for the whole realm, as opposed to similar bodies which had a permanent existence only in specific provinces like Brittany, Languedoc or, indeed, Corsica. New men, hundreds of them, were now brought unwittingly into the corridors of power, and a new generation of leaders, unique in human history, was created at a stroke. The calling of the Estates General in the spring of 1789 began the voyage of this generation of men whose experience Napoleon would incarnate. They would change the world, and Napoleon, once their overlord, would change them. They marked themselves out as special from the very beginning, by seizing their chance with both hands while they could.

The deputies of the Third Estate quickly found common intellectual and ideological ground and seized the initiative, declaring themselves the true sovereign body of the nation, the only institution with legitimate authority to rule, and set about drawing up a constitution for France which promised a permanent, elected legislature as the new centre of power and authority. In so doing, they reduced the king, Louis XVI, to a constitutional monarch, still possessed of important powers, particularly in the realm of diplomacy and war, but hardly the absolute ruler he had been before he had summoned the Estates General, which soon rechristened itself the National Assembly. Louis had lost the initiative, but many of the reforms driven through during 1789–90 were not distasteful to him, should he be able to rid himself of their creators. On the night of 4 August 1789, the Assembly abolished all forms of privilege, swept away the old provinces of France and soon replaced them with a rational, uniform system of departments – of which Corsica was one – administered by elected committees. Freedom of religion was decreed and soon all Church properties would be 'nationalised', the regular orders abolished and, by the Civil Constitution of the Clergy of 1790, the only arm of the Church remaining, the bishops and parish priests, became part of the civil service. The Assembly soon began demanding allegiance from its officials, the clergy included, by public oaths, which caused much unease. The debates over the new Constitution, essentially over how inclusive the franchise was to be, would tear the revolutionaries apart in the years to come, while Louis bided his time and planned to reassert his power.

Unprecedented upheaval at the apex of the state led to disorder elsewhere. The vast unrest which swept France presented the Assembly with a dangerous choice: it could ask Louis to unleash the army to restore order, but then risk him turning it on them, or it could 'ride the tiger' of popular tumult and keep Louis paralysed. The deputies chose the latter course, and retained power at the centre, however tattered their new regime may have looked beyond Paris. It was the their best course. However, there was soon more popular violence in Paris, where the Assembly had transferred itself and soon dragged Louis along with it, first to protect the Assembly from the threat of a coup by the king. The riots were also designed to coerce the deputies into agreeing to concessions for the city. Tax strikes and attacks on noble properties, the burning of government tax rolls in the towns and the sacking of many chateaux in the countryside marked this first phase of the Revolution, while the new generation of politicians manoeuvred for power in the uncertain but energising new political culture – and the gaping power vacuum – they had created for themselves.

The new legislators revelled in rhetoric and forged many lofty phrases: 'liberty, equality, fraternity' – although not actually coined until much later – still serves as the best known and all-encompassing of them. What really drove them was the desire that dared not speak its name in the atmosphere of self-declared selflessness and national unity in which politicians of all factions swathed themselves: ambition. This ambition was often as selfless as selfish, for the new leaders couched their concepts of citizenship in the terms and images of the early Roman Republic they had absorbed from Plutarch, part of their common culture. The pervading belief among both those who were out for themselves and those who were genuinely committed to self-sacrifice for the Revolution was that they could run the nation better than the traditional ruling class, and this kept them together for some time.

Napoleon shared their feelings. In a letter to Don Luciano in late March 1789, he set out his views on the last ministers of the old order: Necker, a Swiss Protestant and an outsider, had saved the finances in the 1770s, while a noble, Taboureau – 'who was only a phantom' – held the official post. Returned to power at the height of the 1789 crisis, Necker was now proving inept at handling the Estates General, lost in the new world of open politics. Calonne, Necker's aristocratic rival and a product of the *ancien régime* establishment, 'ran the state's finances as he did his own. He ruined himself, and he ruined the kingdom', while having Necker forced into exile. Brienne, who overthrew Calonne, was intelligent and enlightened; he carried out useful reforms at the apex of the state, '[b]ut the deficit had to be cut and current expenditure had to be paid', and all Brienne could do was borrow; the *Parlements* simply blocked him.[15] None of them had the answer, in Napoleon's eyes. They were a spent force, taken together. His judgement was not infallibe, for Calonne became something of an *éminence grise* to his own regime; many of his staff went on to play powerful roles in Napoleon's councils; above all, Napoleon turned to many of the ideas that Calonne fought, unsuccessfully, to implement on the eve of the Revolution, when the revolutionary reforms later began to flounder.

Nevertheless, Napoleon's attitude to his present masters was very much of the times. A few weeks later, the 'glass ceiling' of *ancien régime* privilege seemed gone; elections opened the way for new men to reach for a national, as well as a local, platform for advancement. The new regime declared the one maxim to which all its successors would cling, 'the career open to talent'. Like the Rousseau of the Venice embassy or Figaro, many had now had their revenge, and were poised to rise in the world. This was the spirit in which frustrated men like the Buonaparte brothers – Joseph, Napoleon and even the young Lucien – threw themselves into the Revolution. When Napoleon lambasted Buttafoco, the leader of the Corsican nobility in the Estates General, for his opposition to the Revolution and its reforms, he called him a man 'who hides under an intelligent exterior, the greed of a valet'.[16] It was a long tirade, defending Paoli from Buttafoco's accusations of treason, but Napoleon put a very telling sting in its tail. Buttafoco may have been the closest thing to a noble Corsica could summon, but to Napoleon, he was nothing but the lackey of a dead world. The contempt for the past is palpable.

Napoleon's only conscious objective was that Corsica gain from the Revolution, but by adopting this vision of the future he turned his back on the cause of independence. It was a gigantic step. He had thrown in his fate with that of France, yet, as with so many defining acts, it did not come from meditation, but from something almost instinctive. Napoleon had become a Frenchman by second nature, a second nature born of the Revolution. The opportunities Carlo had sought for him had not been there, under the old order. They were now. Even so, the seismic events of the first years of the French Revolution did not immediately change Napoleon's view of the past. He continued to feel passionately about Corsica's abuse at the hands of the colonial masters of the Bourbon monarchy, as in his *Letters on Corsica* to Raynal, written in 1790. The Revolution, however, had galvanised Napoleon's view of his adopted country and the possibilities it offered his island, and to men like himself. In June 1789, he wrote to his godfather, Giubega, at the moment when the fate of the new Constituent Assembly in Paris hung in the balance and the king seemed ready to crush it, of his hopes that 'centuries of feudal barbarism' would soon be over, and that representative government would end the rule of a regime whose 'insolent hand we have to kiss as it oppresses us . . . a degree of ignominy that shames me'. There was hope, however, for France would soon have a written constitution and a monarch who was no longer absolute; its administration and system of justice were being rationalised under his eyes.[17]

In 1789–91, his preoccupation remained the position of Corsica in this new political order, and he had to hope Paoli saw it in the same terms. For this reason Napoleon was soon at real odds with Matteo Buttafoco, not just dealing out ritual insults. Buttafoco became a rallying point for those opposed both to the Revolutionary reforms and to the return of Paoli. Napoleon had to hope that Paoli wanted to make common cause with those, like himself and his brothers, who now saw France rather than independence as the future. It all makes the words he supposedly wrote to Paoli – '30,000 French [troops] have been vomited up on our coasts' – all the less likely to be true. There is no doubt that Napoleon was a 'revolutionary of the first hour', and he risked his position in Corsica because of this. Buttafoco and many who had transferred their loyalties easily from the Genoese to the French – personified by his mother's family – were now set against the sons of Carlo Buonaparte.

Meanwhile, Joseph and Lucien, having left their seminary in Aix-en-Provence, became determined spokesmen for the new order in the political clubs of Toulon and Marseille. They, not Napoleon, were the Buonapartes at the forefront of the new order. Lucien made his name as a radical firebrand in Toulon and Joseph returned to Corsica to seek election to the new departmental administration. Paoli, their father's patron and leader, returned to the island in 1790. Should Paoli embrace the Revolution, they could assume their father's mantle in his entourage. If not, they would be on narrow ground. It came to depend on the course of the Revolution itself, something no one in Corsica could control.

Napoleon's movements from the outbreak of the Revolution in the spring of 1789, until 1793, were tortuous, as he bounced back and forth between his official postings in the Rhône Valley and Ajaccio no fewer than five times, with a stay in Paris between May and September 1792, one of the most turbulent periods of the whole Revolution.

As Napoleon dashed between France and Corsica in these months, something fundamental was going on in his mind. His thoughts on how to to master the Revolutionary crisis were clarifying. Napoleon watched his world with a careful eye, certainly when in France, and drew lasting lessons from it all. More than many others, he was at the mercy of events, but he increasingly realised the nature of the threat as well as the promise. Initially, while his brothers did the talking, Napoleon watched events in France unfold from the vantage point of his provincial garrison. It proved a useful position, and drew from him thoughts that proved of lasting importance for the development of his ideas and for the character of his regime once he achieved power.

Napoleon and Joseph showed their commitment to the Revolution in the way many bourgeois families did, when they bought some of the very first nationalised Church property to come up for sale in Ajaccio, overcoming the initial scruples of their young uncle, Joseph Fesch, the only family member still in holy orders.[18] This was more than just a way of profiting from the fall of the old order, although it was certainly that, for to buy former Church property put the purchaser firmly on the side of the Revolution. Royal displeasure at these reforms ensured that those who did so were effectively 'blacklisted', a threat that did not remain idle as resistance to the Revolution grew. When Napoleon, early in his tenure of office, was unequivocal in his support for all who had bought these 'national lands' – the *biens nationaux* – against the court-in-exile, he stood among his own. Nevertheless, from his observations on the growing anarchy around him in eastern France, Napoleon emerges as anything but a blind optimist, however strong his revolutionary convictions. His words to Joseph, in the aftermath of the momentous reforms of the night of 4 August 1789, are more of a window on his character than all his literary excursions, his memoirs included:

All that is brilliant, but it still only exists on paper. I forgot to tell you that all the provinces have renounced their particular rights. That is a great step for the best. They are very busy with the Constitution, but they are going very slowly. They babble too much.[19]

These laconic words, in their very terseness, give the true mark of the man. Napoleon saw the new unity of the nation, made possible by the abolition of provincial privileges, as a vital step forward, and no single man of the era would do more to forge a highly centralised state while in power. His impatience – budding contempt – for the new parliamentarians and their convoluted debates on the new constitution presages his later disregard for elected assemblies, just as it shows an acute early awareness of the dangers ahead for the Revolution, for this was the issue that tore the early consensus to shreds. Yet, when in search of Napoleon's character as opposed to his views, the words 'but it only exists on paper' say the most. The early ruthlessness of the revolutionaries may have put an end to those institutions Napoleon – following his acute grasp of Rousseau – had said 'set man at odds with himself',[20] but he did not then assume the new order would fall naturally into place. He had seen action putting down a riot in the small Burgundian town of Seurre, in the summer of 1789, which left him in no doubt about the hard road ahead, even before the Estates General had met.[21] There was caution and a degree of intelligent pessimism in his character, which was essential to the hard task of turning reforms into reality. When the mantle of leadership came to Napoleon after 1799, this cast of mind, present here long before the Revolution turned sour and vicious, was what, finally, made real the reforms he chose to pursue.

This cautious pessimism was an attitude Napoleon shared with Paoli, when 'the father' returned to Corsica from exile in London in 1790 and embraced the sons of Carlo. Joseph was able to settle permanently in Ajaccio and was by far the more prominent of the two brothers in local politics, but, as the Revolution began to change course, both Joseph and Lucien – yet not Napoleon – began to fall foul of Paoli. Paoli quickly ensconced himself in Corte, his old stronghold and that of his core supporters, rather than in Bastia, the official capital of the new department formed by the island. Paoli was dismissive of the material improvements the French had made in their attempt to win over the Corsicans, such as roads that 'led nowhere' as there was no commerce to pass over them, just as he disparaged the attempts of Carlo Buonaparte and his associates to foster mulberry groves and silk production, because there was little good soil, and it was goats that mattered for the poor, not cash crops for the rich. This was a clear marker thrown down that, for the 65-year-old *Babbù*, his stronghold was still the mountains, and that his people were the 'insulars'.[22] This was not necessarily a bad omen for the elites of the *presidii*, but as events in France created ever hardening divisions, circumstances in Corsica led to new fissures developing along the atavistic fault lines between the mountains and the coast, between the 'insulars' and the settlers. It was not inevitable, but that was what happened.

Initially, all Corsicans, royalists, radical revolutionaries or neither, shared the common fear that France would rid itself of the island. To these exposed communities the assertion of the National Assembly in 1789 that it was indissolubly part of the nation was empty rhetoric. In November 1790, there had been talk in the Assembly of handing Corsica over to the Papacy as compensation for the seizure of Avignon, a papal enclave in France; more ominously, Corsica had been excluded from the new internal free-trade area created by the abolition of all provincial privileges – tolls included – after 4 August.[23] Paoli, like Napoleon, saw great advantages for Corsica within a reformed France, if it could count on remaining part of it.

As the Revolution changed course, however, tensions rose within the complex political world of the island. The Civil Constitution of the Clergy produced very little trouble among the Corsican secular clergy; only a tiny minority refused to take the oath of loyalty to the new regime, but the abolition of the regular orders led to disturbances in both the mountains and in Bastia and Ajaccio. The Masonic lodge of Bastia was destroyed by an angry mob, and Paoli – one of the most prominent Masons in Europe – began to distance himself from his brothers, to maintain his popular standing. When order was restored, however, it was by his militias raised in the mountains, which unnerved the city more than the initial riots.[24] In 1791, when Louis XVI tried to flee Paris and was captured at Varennes, a significant wedge was driven between the Corsican elites who had integrated themselves with the French since 1769, and Paoli, who remained unmoved by this and supported the anti-monarchist government that began to emerge. His stand kept his links to revolutionaries like the Buonaparte brothers intact, while Buttafoco and others followed the lead of many French nobles and emigrated. More worrying than emigration for many in the *presidii* was the vengeance taken on the émigrés by Paoli's militia, who sacked their properties and harassed their remaining families in a manner more akin to traditional insular vendetta than revolutionary justice.[25] The advent of war with Austria and Prussia posed a new threat to Corsica, for it was a vulnerable outpost, made worse still when Britain – and its Mediterranean fleet – entered the war against France early in 1793.

Napoleon had spent more of the period 1790–2 in France than in Corsica, but the build-up to war led to the creation of a new citizen army with elected officers, and he saw his chance to claim a place in local politics at last. When he returned to Ajaccio in April 1791, he was elected lieutenant-colonel of the second battalion of the Ajaccio National Guard. Amidst fears that the French regular troops in Ajaccio would turn against the Revolution, an affray broke out on 8 April between Napoleon's men and the regulars, but this was followed by something far more serious. The next day, the town was seized by a general fear that insular National Guards were advancing on Ajaccio to support the regular troops. Napoleon and his superior, Quenza, armed both their men and the general population against a force of mountain shepherds who were wintering with their flocks nearby, and who were loyal to Paoli, and who were ordered to attack Ajaccio by the authorities in Corte, also nominally under Paoli. Martial law was declared in Ajaccio, and it seems clear that Napoleon ignored calls for a ceasefire; his battalion opened up on the shepherds, driving them off. This made him a hero to the town and even more to its Jacobin club, the hub of pro-Revolutionary loyalty, of which Joseph was a leading light. It was a striking instance of traditional, atavistic enmities being rekindled by the new pressures of the Revolution. In the face of a nightmare that had haunted the *presidio* since 1492, all the new political rivalries and older family conflicts within the walls were suspended. Charles-André Pozzo di Borgo, who became Napoleon's most determined enemy, made common cause with the Buonaparte brothers at the prospect of the 'insulars' storming the walls; they were, in that moment, 'as thick as thieves', in the words of the historian of these events.[26]

The crisis really began in response to the overthrow of the monarchy in August 1792 and the declaration of the Republic. Paoli's loyalty was deeply questioned by many Revolutionaries on the island over the winter of 1792–3, and in Paris. Napoleon went to Paris at this time in an effort to clear Paoli's name with the new Revolutionary assembly, the National Convention, and witnessed the violence of 10 August, when the armed people of Paris stormed Louis' palace, the Tuileries – later Napoleon's own residence – and butchered his Swiss Guards. The bloodbath did not shock Napoleon as much as the anarchy he felt attended it. In his eyes, the mob had taken hold of the politicians, and he recalled in his memoirs the fear and loathing he felt when stopped in the street by drunken men 'with hideous faces' who seemed, in those days, to be running the world. Napoleon had no real qualms about what they did, for the old monarchy was rotten to the core and Louis unfit to lead a great nation. Yet this was not the victory of the able and the clever but of the dregs of society. He had seen the peasantry 'off the leash' in Seurre, and the provincial populace on the rampage in Auxonne. Now the capital itself was in the grip of the mob. To a generation steeped in the history of the late Roman Republic, where similar scenes were drawn so luridly by Plutarch and Sallust, it seemed that all was on the point of being lost. Fearing for his sister's safety, Napoleon withdrew Elisa from St-Cyr, leaving Paris on 15 September. His calculations were precise, for the city saw a bloodbath directed against suspected 'fifth columnists' – mainly the clergy, prisoners and royalist sympathisers – on 21–2 September, which did not spare convent girls. He brought her back to what he hoped would be the safety of Corsica.

Things turned out very differently. The unity of the Paolisti in Corte was beginning to fragment, as some of them, uneasy at the radical turn the Revolution had taken – the deposition of Louis, the destruction of the 1791 Constitution and the declaration of the Republic – returned to hopes of independence. Paoli remained unmoved by this, although many around him were trying to change his mind and, as the new government in Paris became aware of this, its suspicions grew once more. The revolution of 10 August 1792, which led to the creation of the National Convention and the declaration of the Republic, necessitated fresh elections in Corsica for deputies to Paris. Angered that he had failed to win a seat, Joseph provoked a breach with Paoli when the latter refused to help him overturn the results. Napoleon strove to restore Joseph to Paoli's favour, but to no avail.[27] Only Napoleon now stood between the family and the loss of its powerful patron. Paoli and Napoleon still shared much in common, a loyalty to France and the Revolution, but Napoleon had a growing unease at its course, for the events of 10 August had left a deep impression on him of mob violence and the seeming willingness of the radicals to be led by it. For his part, Paoli was becoming angry at the growing accusations of treason against him in Paris by a regime he felt was acting irrationally.

Early in 1793, shortly after the entry of Britain into the war, the government ordered French forces in Corsica to invade Sardinia, in an effort to dislodge the British from their friendly bases there. It seemed a perfect opportunity for Paoli to prove his patriotism and for Napoleon to distinguish himself. In fact, it proved the undoing of both of them.

The revolutionaries had regarded Sardinia as a threat for some time, before Britain entered the war, as it was ruled by the House of Savoy, which was rabidly opposed to the new French Republic. A

French fleet was sent to Ajaccio to ready for the invasion, but there was soon serious trouble between the sailors and the National Guard, in which Napoleon himself was almost killed by French volunteers from Marseille who were to be part of the invasion force. Paoli refused to release all but a handful of Corsican volunteers for the expedition, and those French forces which were delegated to the expedition proved of very poor quality. The whole force numbered barely 3,500 against 11,000 Sardinians. The French were commanded by Admiral Truguet, the only friendly figure among them as far as Napoleon and his men were concerned, for they spent more time fighting their compatriots than readying for a complex landing in combat conditions. Truguet was entertained and courted by the Buonaparte and other prominent families, as passing military commanders, Genoese or French, had always been in Ajaccio; he seems to have taken a shine to the sixteen-year-old Elisa, but she did not take the bait.[28] Given what then happened, it was as well.

Truguet decided to use the Corsicans, with Colonna-Cesari, a former deputy, as second in command, to attack the small island of La Maddalena, as a separate unit from the main force. Napoleon commanded a small battery of three cannon. After several mishaps, they arrived off La Maddalena on 22 February, but only Colonna-Cesari and Napoleon with a handful of men actually landed; the rest refused to follow, afraid of the Sardinian galleys, of which, in fact, there were but two. Napoleon did indeed distinguish himself. In freezing rain, his small unit bombarded the main town of the island, San Stefano, for two days, 24–5 February, and reduced its batteries to silence. He drove the Sardinians back to a narrow corner of the island, but then the French ship supporting him withdrew. Fearing they would be abandoned, the main body of the Corsicans fell back to the beaches in panic. No one told Napoleon and his battery; he did not hear until late in the evening. After a vain attempt to save his guns and get them to the beaches, he spiked them and scrambled with his men into the very last boats. The recriminations that followed changed the fate of the Buonaparte family for ever.

The fiasco of Sardinia was used in Paris to brand Paoli a traitor, definitively. He was accused by Salicetti – a Corsican deputy close to the Buonaparte at home and to the most radical elements of the Revolution in Paris – of corruption in the preparations for the expedition. Salicetti was anxious not to be associated with Paoli in the face of a hostile government, and he took his protégés, Joseph and Lucien, along with him in this. Paoli, for his part, began to reconsider his position. Napoleon may now have been disabused of Paoli as an effective leader,[29] but he rose to his defence when he was openly denounced in France.

Even before the expedition had set sail, on 5 February, the Convention had ordered Salicetti and three other commissioners to Corsica to investigate the situation on the island. They reached Toulon in early March, where they got their first news of the Sardinian fiasco, which only increased their suspicions that Paoli was a traitor.

In these same days, Napoleon experienced the first of many assassination attempts on his life, after a stormy meeting with Paoli. The attack was probably not Paoli's work, but it was almost certainly that of his partisans in Corte. Napoleon had complained to Paoli that he had been left out of the new reorganisation of the island's National Guard ordered by Paris in his absence. This was a sign of how exposed he now was, but worse was to come.

While Salicetti was in Toulon, he met with Lucien, who had become disaffected from Paoli and, away from Corsica, was inclined to believe what he heard from his fellow Jacobins. Lucien always denied it, but it seems certain he spoke out in the Toulon Jacobin club and denounced Paoli as a traitor to the Revolution. It was certainly in line with the order from Paris, of 2 April, to sack Paoli and dismantle the whole administration he had put in place; Pozzo di Borgo was tarred with the same brush as Paoli. This was the news Salicetti carried with him when he reached Bastia. After meeting Paoli in Corte, Salicetti hesitated, but on 18 April he made the orders from Paris public.

Every municipality in Corsica, from the remote interior to the *presidii*, rose as one to defend Paoli. It was an historic show of unity among all but a few Corsicans. Napoleon drew up the protest of the Ajaccio Jacobins himself, and risked his position with the government by joining Paoli in Corte, in defiance of direct orders to return to his regiment. However, at this very moment, the news broke that Lucien had been the instigator of the denunciation of Paoli in Toulon. Napoleon was, according to insular tradition, also a traitor to Paoli, and he fled Corte for Ajaccio on 30 April. The die had been cast for all time. The Buonaparte, a settler family within the walls of the *presidio*, now found itself the target of traditional highland vendetta. Napoleon reached Bocoagano on 5 May, where his family were the major land-owners. He claimed he barely escaped from forty Paolisti bandits bent on killing him, but this seems unlikely. The village was loyal to the family and any such incursion would have been risky.[30] A cousin guided him to Ajaccio by the back roads, and he found safe passage on a boat to Bastia, where he had no choice but to join with Salicetti and the other commissioners of the Convention. Once there, certainly by 9 May, his only thought was for the safety of his mother and the younger children still with her, and he was not wrong to emphasise the danger to them.

On 31 May, Paoli's new assembly in Corte, the Consultà, now in open opposition to the government, proscribed the Buonaparte family as 'born in the mud of despotism, nourished and raised high under the eye, and at the expense of a luxuriant Pasha, the late Marbeuf, to their perpetual infamy'.[31] This was in the old insular tradition, meaning death on sight, if the family did not abandon all it owned and flee the island for at least seven generations. Not only the old ways, but the old enmities, revived as a result of revolutionary politics. However, traditional loyalties within the *presidio* held firm as well. Letizia fled Ajaccio on the night of 31 May, accompanied by a small group of friends, who got her the eight miles to her small property at Campitello. More tellingly, although the Buonaparte house had been sacked by National Guards from outside the town on 25 May, no one in Ajaccio tried to arrest her; she was the victim of mountain, insular barbarism, something alien to the *presidio*. When Letizia did return to Ajaccio, once things were safe again after the French expelled the British in 1796, she found her house, battered but still hers, and friends to help. For the moment, it was simply a matter of staying alive. At Campitello, Letizia was warned by a local bandit, Costa, that Paoli's thugs were still after her; she shifted to another cottage, only to be warned to move on and get to the coast, where Napoleon had organised a French ship to transport his family to him in Calvi. Elisa took Pauline and Caroline by the hand, Letizia carried Jérôme in her arms, and they fled to the beaches, where they waited in the open until the rescue ship arrived on 2 June and took them to Napoleon, in Calvi. Nine days later, the Buonaparte sailed for Toulon. Corsica was over for them. Napoleon remembered Costa in his will.

The flight from Corsica amounted to a bitter rejection for Napoleon, as well as a trauma, and it has often been regarded as the point at which he became wholly 'French', as a reaction to being, literally, chased from his homeland under threat of death. Had it not been for Lucien's rashness in Toulon, it is hard to know what Napoleon would have done when Salicetti and his colleagues from Paris attempted to force the hand of all Corsicans, but it is clear that Napoleon's reaction to the vendetta placed upon his whole family destroyed in him his romantic, quite irrational faith in 'Corsica' as he had come to believe in it: a fusion of his own world of the *presidii* and that of the mountains, into one people. There were two cultures, after all, and he had been victimised by the traditional 'other' his forebears had shunned, despised and yet feared for centuries. It did not require a complete embracing of France to see this, and his assimilation into French culture was far from complete in the summer of 1793.

Napoleon had embraced the radical wing of the Revolution; he had absorbed the military values and daily life of the army of the old monarchy; he continued to crave entry into its more intellectual salons. The next three years would show how alien Napoleon still found some elements of French society, however, and how much he had to learn about the France of normal, bourgeois life that he found

in Marseille among the Clary family. He could not wholly embrace
what he did not yet know. He could, and did, reject what he had
come to see as alien and barbaric. By turning away from the world
of Paoli and the mountains, Napoleon partly reverted to his natural
type, that of the settler elite of the *presidio*; he cast his lot with the
French and 'civilisation'. There would soon be more to this. Before
long, Napoleon detected the vices of the Corsican interior in the
back country of southern France in his new postings and, as his own
rule spread across the western Mediterranean in the years to come,
this drove his views of the whole region: civilisation was a thing of
the towns, the plains and the coasts; barbarism still pervaded the
mountains and their peoples. The hard, time-worn lessons of the
Ajaccio elite became the given of a new imperialism.

For now, 'civilisation', in the form of the French Revolution, was
running for its life from Corsica. Salicetti followed the Buonaparte in
flight, along with the other commissioners, on 21 June. For his part,
Paoli was now isolated too, in his own way. He had broken with the
Corsican counter-revolutionaries, who were loyal to the Bourbons,
and with the *presidio* elites, but he was now also an outlaw, condemned
as a counter-revolutionary by the National Convention. He was
thrown back on his core support, the 'insulars', and soon turned to
the British, who took over the island in the following months. Bastia,
Ajaccio and Calvi held out for a time into the autumn of 1793, as
much against Paoli and the 'insulars' as against the British, but they
fell, inevitably, cut off from all support. Unable to control the unrest
of the highlands, and abandoned by Pozzo di Borgo and the urban
collaborators who had rallied to him for a time, Paoli came to be seen
by the British as a liability, and he departed into a self-imposed, final,
exile in London in October 1795, a bitter man.[32] For all that, it was a
far more comfortable banishment than the one he had imposed on
the Buonaparte.

THE REFUGEES

On 13 June 1793, the Buonaparte were washed up on the shores of
the Riviera their ancestors had left three centuries before. They
returned, penniless and homeless, to the mainland those two mounted
crossbowmen Francesco Buonaparte and Gabriele Ramolino had set
out from on their great gamble. They had been the victims of the
collective nightmare of the people of the *presidii*, namely the vendetta
of the 'insulars'. It had happened at last, and it had happened to them.
Generations of careful accumulation, begun by the bold risks taken by
the first men-at-arms on the frontier, had collapsed in the fury of the
spring of 1793, all because of Lucien's carelessness. Six years later, his
brother's capacity to speak first and think later would set Napoleon on
the path to supreme power, but for now he had, almost single-handed,
undone three hundred years' work. Lucien had gambled by entering
the bear pit of revolutionary politics and lost, dragging the family
with him. Elisa's school had been closed in the midst of the September
massacres, and her prospects – the brightest possible for a girl of modest
means at that time – had vanished. Now, their properties sacked and
lost, all the large family had to live on was Napoleon's meagre pay.
They were a colonial garrison no more, poorer immigrants than their
forebears, at the mercy of a country in the throes of a bloodbath.

The France they had landed in was the least safe place in the
western world in the summer of 1793, and about to get worse. The fall
of the monarchy on 10 August 1792 had ushered in a period of tension
between the factions in the newly elected National Convention,
created to replace the government set up in 1791. Although all united
in support of a republican regime and were opposed to any return
to the old order, the new deputies soon clashed over the conduct of
the war, what to do with Louis – who was eventually executed early
in 1794 – and the details of the new constitution the Convention was
drawing up. Above all, they vied for the support of the armed local
government committees of Paris, the Sections, which led to yet more
bitter infighting. This tangled web was reflected in the towns and

cities of the provinces, as local clubs and municipalities split along the lines drawn in Paris, grafting their own, parochial quarrels on to those of the capital. In the spring of 1793, the pressures erupted into open violence almost independently in the large southern cities of Bordeaux, Lyon, Toulon and Marseille, and in Paris. The more radical factions of the Convention coalesced around a group centred on Maximilien Robespierre to overthrow the leading ministers in the government, led by Brissot, and their more prominent supporters in the Convention, known as either 'Brissotins' for their leader, or 'Girondins' because some of them sat for the Bordeaux area, the Gironde department. Among the deputies executed or driven out by the Robespierrist faction – known as the 'Mountain' because they sat on the highest benches in the assembly chamber – were those from Marseille and Toulon, which crystallised the political divisions in these cities and produced violent confrontations in the late spring and early summer of 1793. This was the world the Buonaparte now found themselves in.

This was far from the whole of it, however. Now firmly in control of the Convention, the Mountain seized control of the machinery of government, such as it was, and galvanised it, first to arrest the tide of the war, which was running against France, and then to quash both the new civil war in the south, and the growing counter-revolutionary opposition in the countryside, as peasant communities rose in revolt against the Convention's new policy of mass conscription. The policy the Mountain evolved to confront this crisis was called, without nuance or a shade of irony, 'the Terror', for, as one its spokesmen, Saint-Just, declared – drawing directly on Rousseau – the French were to be forced to be free.

There was much Napoleon found to admire in all this. The sheer energy and determination of the Terrorist government, its ability to organise and mobilise even the most recalcitrant sectors of society in a national war effort, all enthused him. The Mountain waged a ruthless, pitiless war on that other 'mountain' Napoleon had come to see in Corsica as the enemy of civilisation, as well as on its own rivals within the Revolution, and the vestiges of the old order. However, the Terror also meant a stifling, dangerous political correctness, the emergence of a police state of denunciation and counter-denunciation, a disregard for the rule of law and, ironically, an inclination to mob rule when the support of the Parisian Sections or their local equivalents in the provinces was needed. The Terror built a society of fear and potential anarchy, yet it was manifestly saving the new France from destruction. Napoleon learned many things from this particular period of the Revolution, and he lived in tension with its contradictory messages for the rest of his life: the need for authoritarianism to confront crises or even to enact great reforms; the dangers of pandering to public opinion; the importance of the rule of law, juxtaposed to the possibilities of real power. For the foreseeable future, however, the Buonaparte had to weather this storm as best they could.

The Buonaparte found shelter and support from three very different sources. Joseph and Lucien had made friends and contacts in the Jacobin clubs of the Provençal cities of Toulon and Marseille, and they used them. The war and the internal civil war now raging soon offered Napoleon chances for more rapid advancement than even he had dared dream of only a year earlier, and he took them. Quite separately, and seemingly a world away from the turmoil the boys were exploiting, the Buonaparte girls found their way into the friendship of the wealthy Clary family, who became central to their lives. Every member of the family had a part to play in helping to set this bedraggled immigrant household on its way in a new world, but every one of these connections led them into yet more danger.

The Buonaparte were now in the hands of the very men – and the very revolutionary faction – whose precipitate actions had broken their links to Paoli and led to the violent loss of all they possessed. Salicetti, still influential in the Jacobin clubs of Toulon and Marseille, and now bound to Lucien since the latter's rash denunciation of Paoli in the cause of the Jacobins and the Convention, did what he could for Letizia and the younger children. They soon moved to Marseille, where Joseph, through his own Jacobin connections, had found a post. Napoleon was promoted and posted to Nice, while Salicetti's lobbying in Paris had acquired a fund for the relief of Corsican exiles, from which Letizia received some help.

However, the family had only escaped from the frying pan of Corsica into the fire of the French Midi, which was about to become the arena for the next phase of revolutionary civil war. Both Toulon and Marseille erupted into violence as pro- and anti-Convention factions tore the cities apart over Robespierre's ruthless purge of those of their deputies whom he suspected of wanting to broker a peace with the Allies, among many other things. The anti-Robespierre factions won control of both cities, and the family – now inextricably bound to the Jacobins through Salicetti and Lucien, whatever Napoleon thought of the events of 10 August 1792 that brought them to power – found itself almost as endangered by their associations with the Jacobins as they had been in Corsica. One set of difficulties had been traded for another, but in this case the Convention was in a position to counter-attack, and did so.

Early in July 1793, Napoleon was ordered from Nice to Avignon to pick up gunpowder and other supplies for his unit. He arrived to find the city falling into the hands of the advancing anti-Convention forces of Marseille, now dubbed 'the Federalists' by the government in Paris because they were accused of trying to destroy the unity of the Republic. Napoleon claimed at the time and afterwards that they tried to arrest him, although there is no proof of this. What is certain is that his own side, the forces of the Convention sent to take retake Avignon under Carteaux, did arrest him on suspicion of being a noble, something his father would have been proud of even had it cost Napoleon his life. He was vouched for by Salicetti and allowed back to Nice.

Napoleon responded to this, not with anger – he was probably too shaken – but by writing a pamphlet based on a meeting he had had in the nearby town of Beaucaire with several merchants, hence its title, 'Supper at Beaucaire'. Its pro-Convention tone was obviously part of a pragmatic effort to clear himself after the fright of his arrest, but the essay should not be lightly dismissed as simply opportunist. Napoleon sees strong, central direction as all that can hold the French state together and preserve the gains of the Revolution, and castigates the 'Federalists', less for their politics than their refusal to see the risks they are running. Unity in the face of the threat of a triumphant counter-revolution of savage peasants led by vicious nobles and clergy was the only way. This became the cornerstone of much of his own policies in the years ahead: however brutal first the Convention, and then Napoleon himself might have to be, the alternative was unthinkable, even for people who thought they were royalists.

In 'Supper at Beaucaire', Napoleon has two characters, men from Marseille, argue foolishly that it might be better to bring in the British – as Paoli had done – until the Convention was made to see sense. The pamphlet made no impact at the time, but his two fools turned out to be prophets, for that is what the Toulon 'Federalists' actually did, a few weeks later, offering up the city to Admiral Lord Hood's fleet on 27 August, so enabling him then to bring in about 17,000 Allied troops to secure it.

Marseille proved an easier task for the forces of the Convention, however, and Napoleon was probably with Carteaux when the Convention's forces retook it, two days before the defection of Toulon. Although Marseille fell without serious resistance, and the Convention did little to persecute more than a handful of the 'Federalist' leaders, Carteaux's ill-disciplined volunteers – composed of Marseille Jacobins and Parisian militants – wreaked havoc in the first weeks of September. This provided Napoleon and the other professional officers there with yet another sickening example of popular excess, to add to a growing catalogue.

The Buonaparte were to have their own experience of mob violence in the near future. The city, unleashed, was as cruel and savage as the Corsican Mountain. When the obligatory, 'politically correct' venge-fulness of 'Supper at Beaucaire' is stripped away, the events of 1793 can be seen to have ingrained in Napoleon's mind, for ever, the conviction that the society he lived in could only advance under a strong, centralised state.

Real war, its challenges and opportunities, soon presented itself to Napoleon with the need to retake Toulon. For the first of many occasions, the prospect of active service in proper military conditions must have seemed a relief from the madness of populism and politics. Napoleon had returned to Nice after the fall of Marseille, but the incompetence of the Convention's commanders before Toulon, with no experience in siege warfare or grasp of gunnery, soon exposed the operation to disaster in the face of the well-honed expertise of the Royal Navy. Salicetti remembered Napoleon and, with help from his colleague Augustin Robespierre, younger brother of Maximilien, Napoleon took command of what passed for the French artillery at Toulon. He may have been a political appointment – there was no other sort at this time – but he now put all his training and the combat experience acquired in Sardinia to full use, impressing all around him, some to the point of jealousy. Even historians often disparaging of Napoleon admit he displayed exceptional ability as an artillery commander in the field during the siege, and that he shone even more as an organiser.

THE SIEGE OF TOULON

Toulon was the chief French naval base on the Mediterranean coast, and was one of the best-defended ports in Europe. With its harbour now held by the British fleet, and its inland batteries manned by its well-trained crews, retaking it was a daunting task. The troops sent to do so by the Convention could not have been more ill-suited to the task: most were local volunteers, with little or no military training, and their commander, Carteaux, was, in Philip Dwyer's perfect pen-portrait, 'a good choice when it came to brutal reprisals against local populations in revolt ... but ... incompetent in matters of siege warfare'.[33] The deputies of the Convention present at Toulon, Salicetti and Augustin Robespierre among them, could not tolerate him, particularly when he began to frustrate the initiatives Napoleon was trying to undertake, after his arrival there in mid-September. They gave Napoleon independent command of the artillery and promoted him to major, and he galvanised the pitiful force he found. The deputies of the Convention who bestowed this independence on Napoleon did him one of the greatest services of his life: by recognising his talent and giving him his head to use it, they reminded him what the Revolution was supposed to be about, the promotion of merit. It was a principle with which Napoleon imbued his own regime, at the level of policy, but it was also enshrined in how he treated his subordinates, the men and some women (like two of his sisters and his second wife). They were all potentially people who could be delegated to, trusted, and brought on, on the basis of their abilities.

Once he was left to himself, Napoleon proved as energetic as he was resourceful, scouring the surrounding area for more ordnance, harrying the local authorities for supplies of gunpowder, setting up a foundry manned by skilled workers he requisitioned from Marseille, and putting his military education to use by organising an artillery park along the lines of the professional royal army. He used naked threats of terror against many local authorities to get what he wanted: Valence, recently implicated in the Federalist revolt, was reminded of this in thinly veiled terms, for example.[34] Napoleon soon conceived a dislike and distrust of Provence that he never lost. It was a nest of reaction, of counter-revolution, not unlike the Corsican interior.

Starting with a couple of mortars, four cannon and a few light field guns manned by untrained volunteers, Napoleon forged a force to be reckoned with.[35] Somehow, he collected more and more large guns – 24-pounders – and long-range mortars fit for siege warfare; he searched out retired army artillery officers in the area and set them to work. He filled the ranks by retraining regular infantry intensively, under his direct supervision. This was not without its frustrations: wrong size shells arrived from Marseille; mortar tubes were made but until he intervened no one had thought about their ammunition. Nevertheless, by early November, he had a hundred cannon and siege mortars, regular supplies of ammunition, and good gunners. They were well placed and sited, all thanks to Napoleon, in positions to cause the city and the British fleet maximum damage, given the positions the French held. Napoleon also showed flashes of the charisma he later made his own. One battery was in an especially dangerous, exposed position, where casualties were higher than average: he put up a placard there, naming it 'the battery of the fearless'. It became a much-sought-after posting from then on.[36] On 30 November, he proved himself a frontline commander when he led the successful repulse of an Allied assault on the French positions. He claimed he had captured the commander of the Allied ground forces himself, although this seems unlikely. He had no need to gild the lily, however, for Dugommier, his new commander, praised him highly in his dispatches, even if he could not spell his name.[37] He pounded Toulon and its harbour for twenty hours a day, day in, day out. It was superhuman effort, if on a small scale. He was still only twenty-four.

Toulon was too major a position to be reduced by artillery alone, and the deputies, vociferously prompted by Napoleon, persuaded Paris to replace Carteaux with a professional soldier, Dugommier. The besiegers were soon reinforced by a brigade of experienced troops, under André Masséna, older than and senior to Napoleon, who would become one of his finest commanders. The deputies at Toulon also included Paul Barras, another who would soon exercise a profound professional and personal influence on Napoleon's life. At Toulon, Barras, Augustin Robespierre and Salicetti proved more than useful to Napoleon, for they knew talent when they saw it, admitted they knew nothing of military affairs and left him alone to do his work, as they now also did with Dugommier and Masséna, while ensuring they got what they needed from Paris.

The key to Toulon was Fort Eguilette, because it controlled the entrance to the harbour. If it could be taken by the French, the British fleet would have to withdraw or become trapped in the harbour, the city would be cut off from its only source of supplies – the sea – and would soon fall. It looked easy on paper, and this plan had long been discussed, but only through Napoleon's efforts with the artillery and

Dugommier's ability as the overall commander could it have any chance of success. Napoleon sent the plan, reworked considerably by himself, to Paris and passed it off as all his own work, a ploy both self-serving and politically astute, as he had become the commander-on-the-ground most trusted by the government.[38] When the big French assault came, it was a combined effort. The attack began on 17 December, three days after Masséna's arrival. Six thousand troops under Murion stormed Fort Mulgrave, supported by an intense artillery bombardment directed by Napoleon; it was taken, for the heavy loss of a thousand men; a few hours later, Masséna's fresh troops took Fort d'Artigues. The key, if less well-defended Fort Eguillette was left to Napoleon, who proved himself again an able and very brave field commander, not just a skilled gunner. He had a horse shot from under him and received a bayonet wound in the leg, but carried on to seize the position, get his own guns in place, and soon had ten cannon trained on the inner harbour. When he opened a murderous fire on the British ships in harbour, Admiral Lord Hood, the commander-in-chief at Toulon, ordered a general evacuation. It was over. Dugommier was rightly praised at the time as the hero of Toulon, but no one minimised Napoleon's contribution. It had been vital, and a tribute to his professionalism, leadership and initiative.

What followed the fall of Toulon was anything but heroic, and disgusted both Napoleon and most of the other professional officers present. As at Marseille, the political commissioners sought and took savage revenge on the 'infamous city', not only unleashing the ill-disciplined volunteers on its population, but opening the prisons for the same vengeful purpose. There were appalling scenes on the *quais*, as civilians scrambled in vain to get on to the departing British ships – which still managed to evacuate over 7,000 people – as Napoleon's battery at Eguilette rained down an indiscriminate fire that sank four ships containing fleeing women and children.[39] It is doubtful that he targeted the helpless deliberately, for they were embarked on well-gunned warships, but the terror unleashed on Toulon by the deputies was only too well calculated. Sidney Smith, one of the British commanders at Toulon, tried to inculpate Napoleon in these atrocities, but his accusations are dubious, to say the least.[40] It is indisputable that, along with other officers, Napoleon attempted to mitigate the worst of the slaughter.

It can never be known with certainty, for the times did not allow people's real thoughts to be committed to paper or confided to friends, but it seems a reasonable assumption that Napoleon had become as disgusted by the politicians he served as he was by the urban mobs they led. This was a loathing outweighed only by his hatred of the reactionary, anti-revolutionary 'mountain', which was as real in southern France as it was in Corsica – an atavism now assimilated into contemporary politics. In a very *ancien régime* way, his family had now come to depend on the patronage of the Jacobins, through Salicetti. At least the leaders of the mob had a use for him, but Napoleon was reduced to choosing the least of many evils. For the moment, however, his fortunes improved. By 19 December, Toulon was back in French hands; Napoleon was moved to other duties and the dirty work of repression left to the politicians. He was soon promoted to brigadier general, and given the unglamorous post of inspecting the batteries along the coast of Provence. The new regime, however unsavoury, rewarded talent and effort.

The siege of Toulon was Napoleon's first major action, but it is not really true that it launched his career, as is sometimes claimed. The times were still too convulsed for any success to provide security; notoriety under one revolutionary faction could prove fatal when power changed hands. The hard truth is that his prominence in a great triumph of Jacobin arms nearly got him executed. It took him over two years to rebuild his career, but Toulon did reveal Napoleon at his best as a leader.

Many of the qualities that would become his hallmark in the field emerged in these months, as the precision and decisiveness of his orders reveal. The qualities found in his exercise of command seem to have been unique to his nature. Napoleon was forced to be menacing and authoritarian by circumstances, but the real point is, he came to it quite naturally, for all his qualms about the Jacobins. 'Send me someone intelligent,' he barked to the civil administration of Beausset, as he set about fortifying the area around their town.[41] 'I will not hide from you, that if Citizen Constantin makes the slightest delay in executing the present order, the representatives of the people and the General will act very severely against him,' was a threat to a subordinate.[42] 'There are two kinds of alarmists in the Republic, those who cry famine and those who are always afraid to be without [gun]powder,' he advised a colleague, in a clipped tone worthy of Robespierre himself.[43] Clarity went with his threats, however, for no one was left in doubt about what they had to do, and this clarity reached far into the particular. In a letter to a quartermaster, his views on how supply trains should be run are set out succinctly, devoid of ambivalence: 'There are two very distinct ways of harnessing [teams of draft horses] in the army: that for supplies, and that for artillery ... [they] have nothing in common with each other, and can never form the basis for a serious discussion.'[44] Here, the eye for detail engenders precision, not confusion.

There were more profound characteristics emerging, too. In a letter to Gassendi, another brigadier, Napoleon showed that he was prepared to speak up for his colleagues, and knew well, even at twenty-four, that they needed to be reassured, especially in times when professional shortcomings could be treated as high treason. Gassendi had been hauled before the dreaded political commissaries – Salicetti, Barras and Augustin Robespierre – for slackness, which could easily be inflated into a charge of sabotage. Napoleon spoke with an honesty that carried potential danger for him:

I learned with displeasure of the scene that met you in Marseille [his interrogation] ... [I]t was all easily put right ... I have spoken to the representatives; they are not at all displeased with you, they only thought they were making political concessions. This business is over, and we will speak no more of it.[45]

This was leadership of a subtler kind, knowing beyond its years.

Many of the signs of the future commander can be seen at Toulon, particularly in the way he instilled trust, and it is no coincidence that he forged two close friendships here, with his two immediate subordinates, Junot and Marmont.

Not all the omens were good, however:

I have told you of this brilliant success ... it is enough for me to tell you that the English have not captured one of our guns ... The enemy has been thrown into the most unheralded retreat ... They did not even have time to set fire to their ships ... They have not burned our stores of wood or rope. I have visited the naval arsenal, and I can assure you that even the worst they have done to us is reparable.[46]

The young officer had not the slightest hesitation in lying *in extremis* even to the Ministry of War. The British had sunk twelve French warships in Toulon, and made off with another twelve; they had burned all the timber stocks needed for repairs and construction, carefully accumulated under the monarchy. Philip Dwyer has placed these losses to the French navy in their full perspective by recalling that they were greater than those Nelson would inflict at the Battle of the Nile.[47] Letizia had always chastised Napoleon's habit of lying, to no avail, and as his wars progressed a waggish expression took root in France, 'to lie like an army bulletin'. The above may well be the first such example. The full flush of success that spawned it did not last long. For the moment, however, he was one of the heroes of Toulon.

ANOTHER FRANCE: THE CLARY FAMILY

Napoleon was able to rejoin his family in the last days of 1793, and to spend more time with them during the first half of 1794, in his new posting as inspector of the local coastal artillery. There are times in a life when the most uneventful occurrences – and these months were probably the most mundane, even normal, days of Napoleon's life – yield understated moments that leave deep traces, often all the deeper for their quiet nature.

Napoleon never neglected his family, but he was away during their first hard months in exile. Once in Marseille, the Buonaparte found their way, initially, through the Jacobin contacts Joseph and Lucien had established and the help that came through Salicetti. It is not clear how they came to know the Clary family. Their first contact may have been at the most menial level, beginning with Letizia and Elisa doing domestic chores, and then Elisa advancing to tutoring the Clary daughters, Julie and Désirée, on the basis of her very good Parisian education and her even better intellect. More certain is that when the city was subjected to the political witch-hunt that followed the end of the 'Federalist' revolt, Joseph saved one of the Clary sons, Étienne, when he fell foul of the Revolutionary Tribunal – a thinly veiled kangaroo court to weed out rebels – in September 1793. Joseph had considerable influence in Marseille, following his brother's efforts to restore it to Jacobin rule. It is not clear why he helped Étienne; it may have been because of links already established with the Clarys through Letizia and Elisa, or because Étienne, Salicetti and himself were all Freemasons.[48] The family became grateful to him, most certainly, and from that point the Buonaparte were welcome in the Clary home as more than domestic servants. Joseph could not protect them completely, for they were obviously detested by the Marseille Jacobins, and another son, Justinien, disappeared in the winter of 1793–4, his body later being found in a derelict house in the city, where it had been left to rot after his murder.[49] Nevertheless, in dangerous times, Joseph obviously did a great deal to prevent things getting worse for them, his diplomatic skills emerging in the murky world of Marseille politics in the same months as Napoleon proved himself in the field.

Napoleon probably did not meet the Clarys until early in 1794, and they did not seem very impressed by him, the aura he had acquired at Toulon probably counting for little in a family harassed by the government in whose service he had shone. Like the Buonaparte, however, the Clarys were so afraid of the revolutionary turmoil they could ill afford to rebuff anyone with a semblance of influence. Their

tepid reception of the unkempt, often gauche artillery officer – hardly
the most glamorous arm of the service in society – is almost irrelevant,
given how Napoleon seemed to regard them. In *Brideshead Revisited*
(1945) Evelyn Waugh makes his narrator fall in love with a family, with
what it embodied, more than with any one of its members. Napoleon
perhaps followed this path with the Clarys, whatever they may have
made of him.

The Clarys were in trouble in Jacobin Marseille because they were,
frankly, nice people at a moment when honestly won wealth and ease
were suspect. They were a genre of French people to whom Napoleon
came late, and his time among them was as eye-opening as it was
influential. Their treatment in the name of 'equality' appalled him.
When Napoleon met them, the Clarys had no aristocratic pretensions
and took no interest in their ancestry. They were well-established
Marseille entrepreneurs. The father of the family, François, who died
early in 1794, and probably knew Napoleon hardly at all, had risen
high in the merchant community, by his own efforts, as an importer–
exporter of many commodities, from silk and soap to arms, between
France, Italy and the eastern Mediterranean. The Clarys were outward-
looking, secular and imbued with a sense of risk and adventure in
business, but careful and cautious in how they used the money they
made, and they made it by a combination of hard graft and acumen.
Their house in Marseille was gracious and well appointed, but not
opulent; they loved their large but simple country house, *la Casa*.
Their mixture of risk, openness to the wider world, good sense and
closeness of family were all things Napoleon responded to with
approval. Gabriel Girod de l'Ain caught their world perfectly in her
classic, elegant study of the family:

... refined by the progressive ease of many generations, they had acquired
a taste for luxury, for lovely lodgings, for French gardens. By going to
concerts, to the theatre, by holding literary salons or philosophic circles,
they knew how to fill their leisure time, a sign of distinction ... *Coquetterie*
and *gourmandise*, those pleasant sins of civilised souls ...[50]

It was a way of life Napoleon took to heart, just how much would only unfold as his own life progressed. Those who knew him well, especially Junot's wife, remarked on his affinity for this open, clever, lively and warm milieu.[51]

Napoleon may only have been able to watch this from the edge, but it did not detract from his admiration for what he saw. This was a new France for him, one altogether more likeable and tangible than anything he had found since he arrived at Autun on New Year's Day 1779. It was a universe apart from the institutionalised world of Brienne and the barracks. It was the counterpoint to the savagery of the urban mob and the mountain peasantry, just as it was more open and human than the salon. The world of the Clarys was everything that Ajaccio wanted, in vain, to be. It was the *presidio* blessed by geography. Joseph – urbane, calm, polished by the seminary – found it easy to integrate into this world, and married Julie, the elder of the two Clary daughters, in August 1794. By contrast, Napoleon had his chance but could not bring himself to take it. The world of the Clarys came to be the France he adored and championed in all his work in power, but he could not quite bring himself to join it. The world of these solid, cultivated people was dear to Napoleon, but he was not meant for it.

Nevertheless, his sojourn among them was an influential stage in his life. It revolved around the second daughter, Désirée. Napoleon met the Clarys at their lowest ebb, but at their personal best. Harried and harassed by the Marseille Jacobins, their wealth branding them as of suspect patriotism, the men were either still in gaol or in hiding in early 1794, and those alive were only so because of Joseph. The women – Julie, Désirée and their mother, who did not like having Napoleon in the house – proved themselves resourceful and cheerful in their independence. Their optimism in adversity was a much-needed lesson for Napoleon. He felt he was there to help. It was, however, the wrong moment. Napoleon was a young man who had just had his self-confidence confirmed in the heat of battle; he had shouldered immense responsibility and emerged from it well. When he met

Désirée, barely seventeen, he was prepared to impress and she – open, exuberant, intelligent but not well educated – seemed interested in what he had to say. Her sharp mind and his need for companionship might have made it a meeting of equals, but his burgeoning self-confidence, and her youth, tipped the balance towards him in an unfortunate way. Their romance was ungainly, but their friendship endured many vicissitudes over the years to come. She took to him, for all his gauche demeanour that oscillated between the garrulous pedant and the taciturn man too used to the bivouac, and he to her. Désirée appreciated his only half-joking suggestions on how to improve her education, the reading lists he sent her, his offer to buy her a piano and find her a good teacher. Yet, underneath this rough exterior, Napoleon was the one who was not a little in awe of the Clary world, however battered by the revolutionary storm, and of his older brother, who had entered it with such ease. In truth, the gap in their ages was not important in the normal sense, for there was much about the relationship that showed how immature Napoleon remained in this sphere of life. It did not long survive their separation when he was sent to Paris in the autumn of 1794.

When Julie married Joseph, an official bond was created between the two families, but he was often callous towards her, and it was Napoleon's enduring liking for them, and for Désirée in particular, that led to their own rise under his rule. His generosity turned the next generation of Clarys into grasping people, now bent on fabricating a noble lineage for themselves. In 1793–4, Désirée became love-struck on Napoleon, but soon got over it.

There were other aspects of their liaison that were odd, however. He took to calling her by one of her other middle names, Eugénie, which was not how she was known to her family, and he would do the same with Joséphine, whom he met not long after his time with Désirée. This trait has given rise to much speculation about what it might say about Napoleon's psychology, all of which is impossible to know. He did not persist in 'redubbing' his women after this phase of his life, for neither his second wife, Marie-Louise of Austria, nor Maria Walewska, his most serious mistress – and arguably his happiest relationship – were 'revamped' in this way.

Napoleon wrote an utterly silly novel about the affair, with himself as a classical hero, 'Clisson', who triumphed in war but failed to find happiness when it was offered to him by 'Eugénie', from whom he was torn by the call of duty. Napoleon expressed these feelings in terms all the more juvenile for being pretentious, but beneath the posturing, a quite profound truth about his state of mind may lurk: 'Clisson' longed for a normal life, but could not achieve it, just as Napoleon adored the world of the Clarys, but after his experience of Toulon, which allowed him to live as he now knew he was intended to, that happy, sane, settled world – the world of the French provincial notables he would do so much to make the foundation of his state – could not really hold him. There may be more to this flimsy novel than meets the eye.

AN IDYLL SHATTERED: THE POLITICS OF SURVIVAL, 1794–1795

Another aspect of *Clisson* that should strike the reader as significant is its very timing. The book is about an idyll shattered by the greater tides of history, and between his time with the Clarys and its composition, Napoleon had seen the precarious world of the Buonaparte come close to collapse. In the months after Toulon, Napoleon spent his time on routine duties, courted Désirée and, on his increased pay, was able with Joseph and Lucien to rent a large house for his mother and the younger children in Antibes, the confiscated property of an émigré noble, now in the gift of Salicetti. Antibes is now a playground of the rich, as is Sarzana, along the same coast, from where the family originated; then, it was a quiet fishing village, where the air was better for the children, and less fraught than the great port of Marseille. Letizia soon opened it to friends and patrons, actual and potential, as she and Carlo had done in Ajaccio.

Napoleon was now given a more demanding posting to the front, where he faced Piedmontese troops between March and mid-May

1794, as an artillery commander. He participated in several successful, if minor, engagements, but his main role in these manoeuvres was as a strategist. His plans proved effective, but it was Masséna, commander of the largest forces, who carried them out. Napoleon's ideas and Masséna's ability to execute them led to the fall of the port of Oneglia and the pass of the Tende to the French.

He was now a general, and to Letizia her sons' very different careers seemed to have advanced by leaps and bounds in the course of a few months, and life as it was lived from the winter of 1793 to the summer of 1794 must have seemed like a dream – a return to a semblance of normality for her. And so it was, a dream. Events in Paris came within a hair's-breadth of shattering the family yet again.

Napoleon was once more the target of men intent on his death, for his greatest source of patronage – the Jacobin government of the Mountain – drowned in yet another bloodbath in August 1794. In June, he had been on a fact-finding mission to Genoa, to assess its political climate, and the feasibility of a French invasion of the coast. When he returned he was arrested, in reality because of his links to Augustin Robespierre, whose older brother had been overthrown and executed in one of the most sudden, unheralded coups of the Revolution; the actual charges against Napoleon were that his mission to Genoa had been a cover for treasonable dealings with the Allies. He was seized in Nice, where he was due to be posted, on 8 August, almost immediately on his return from Genoa, and less than two weeks after the execution of the Robespierre brothers in Paris, on 27 July. He may have been put in the prison of Fort-Carré, but, as Philip Dwyer has pointed out, there is no evidence for this, and it is more likely he remained under house arrest.[52] It does not matter, in truth, for in the climate of the times his survival was anything but assured, and the even deeper, if less obvious, links of his brothers to the now defunct Terrorist regime made their chances of survival far from certain.

Napoleon was lucky in that a good friend, Laurenti, soon emerged to vouch for him. The order for his execution by guillotine had already been authorised, but it was not carried out. Two weeks later, Napoleon was free, thanks, it seems, to the same man who had denounced him in the first place, Salicetti. His patron had turned on him in a blatant, desperate attempt to save his own skin, and momentarily dragged Napoleon down with him, as he distanced himself from the Robespierres, but perhaps also fuelled by jealousy and a growing fear of Napoleon, after his success at Toulon.[53] Salicetti quickly saw that if Napoleon was tried, in however perfunctory a manner, he might in turn remind the world that Salicetti himself was far more involved in the horrors of the Terror than he had ever been. It was a near-run thing, yet again.

Although alive and at liberty, Napoleon and the fortunes of the family had been rocked. They did not escape the latest regime change unscathed, for Napoleon returned to his quarters to find he had been relieved of his command, and that his release was only provisional. Although he was soon asked to use his recently acquired knowledge of Liguria to prepare an invasion plan, which he did with great skill, this was a far cry from his independent command at Toulon. These plans went into his pocket, and he used many of his ideas, and all the information, in his own first major campaign there, in 1796, but all this was hardly to be imagined in the last months of 1794.

Napoleon was one of many officers with clear links to Robespierre's faction who were arrested after his fall on 9 Thermidor, but this was no comfort to any of them. Coming just a year after he was hounded out of Ajaccio, it is less of a wonder that iron can be seen in his soul by the summer of 1794 than that any semblance of loyalty survived in him. However, Napoleon's relations with Salicetti were restored quite quickly, as the initial trauma of Thermidor passed, even if it is likely that he never really trusted Salicetti again, however many important posts he charged him with once he was firmly in power. That he did not turn on Salicetti, or turn him away, was an early mark of Napoleon's capacity to forgive, although his latent caution was too well developed to allow him to forget. This quality is often neglected in him, as it sits almost incongruously with his pessimism about the Revolution, which was growing apace in the face of the vicissitudes of the Terror, but it was real enough. He never considered taking revenge. Nothing was further removed from the insular culture of vendetta, but nothing closer to the culture of the *presidio*.

The politics of Paris had brought all this about, as so often in the life of the family in the 1790s. Events at the heart of the Revolution in the spring and summer of 1794 created their new predicament. The triumph of the Mountain at the purge of the Girondins did not bring about a period of peace in Parisian politics any more than it did in the provinces. While the purge led to the 'Federalist' revolt in the cities of the south, by the spring of 1794 the success of the coalition that had overthrown Brissot shattered the unity among those who had dragged him to the guillotine. Tensions grew between the Mountain (which controlled the Convention, the Sections of Paris, the senior committee of government – Public Safety – and the Jacobin clubs) and the municipal administration of Paris, under Hébert, whose power in the Convention and the Committee of Public Safety was limited. The rivalry between them turned Paris into a cauldron. When Robespierre led a coup against Hébert in the spring of 1794, it was preceded by a spate of denunciations of collaboration with the British to sabotage the war effort, all of them patently ludicrous yet which were accepted as real; and finished in bloodshed comparable to that which had dispatched Brissot and his adherents. Following this, the Mountain turned in on itself, when Robespierre successfully denounced his long-standing ally Danton as a traitor because the latter had seemed to advocate a negotiated peace with the Allies at a point when the efforts of the Terrorist government were yielding military successes. Much of Robespierre's fear of Danton probably stemmed from a growing recognition, which Danton had haltingly articulated, that with victory in sight it was time to dismantle the machinery of the centralised Terrorist government. It was at this point that deeper fissures appeared, probably less between Robespierre and Danton themselves than between those in the Convention who saw the Terror as a means to an end – winning the war – and those who had come to regard it as an essential period of purging and regeneration for the emergence of a people worthy of republican liberty. Robespierre and his faction succeeded in sending Danton and his small following to their deaths, but this only increased a climate of fear in the Convention that amounted to paranoia.

By July, a shadowy coalition had emerged, convinced that Robespierre and his own following were bent on totalitarian rule, both ideological and factional. They seem to have been a very heterogeneous group, and their incongruous nature accounts for the confused political world that emerged when Robespierre, in his turn, was denounced in the Convention after he had made a series of threats against yet more deputies, as vague as they were brutal. On 27 July, he and his colleagues were hounded from the Convention, hunted down and executed.

Although this was a catastrophe for people like Salicetti and the Buonaparte brothers, who had risen in its service – and for many energetic officers like Napoleon, who had responded to the crisis of the regime – the end of the Terror was like no coup before it. The fall of the Mountain unleashed social repercussions, not just policy changes. Paris had been in the grip of a dark culture of mutual denunciation and suspicion, which the purge of Danton had revealed to have no ideological limits. It was a world where no one was safe. The fate of Napoleon is – almost – an important corrective to any vision of the post-Robespierre regime as a haven of tolerance or that a clean break with the darker side of the Revolution occurred with his demise. Nevertheless, those most directly affected by the politics of the Parisian Terror breathed a collective but cautious sigh of relief. This manifested itself not just in politics, but in that untranslatable French term *sociabilité*. 'Dressing down', frugality and a certain puritanism derived from middle-class assumptions about the life of the artisans had been an important element in the dissemination of Jacobin values and the propagation of republican virtue. Like so much else, it had its roots in a vision of Republican Rome. The victors – or, more aptly, the survivors – of the coup of Thermidor, as the fall of

Robespierre came to be known – took a social and cultural revenge on the defunct regime that went beyond disarming the Sections and drawing up a new constitution that removed all but the wealthiest from the franchise. Paris dressed up, as ladies' necklines plunged and men donned buckles and expensive riding coats for the first time in years. Champagne flowed, parties were thrown and affairs flaunted.

The Revolution, that of the new Parisian chattering classes at least, had acquired a *sociabilité* all its own, where *ancien régime* elegance might help but where money talked, and connections – political, social, financial, sexual – were all. Those connections had all been forged since the collapse of the monarchy, and were now liberated from the controls of the Terrorist government. It was a world in flux, operating in a new political system that reflected at once the opportunism and the unease of those who framed it: a government with a weak, rotating executive of five men, the Directory, to ensure that the dominance of a Robespierre would not repeat itself, and two assemblies, regularly destabilised by frequent elections, to prevent the emergence of solid factions within them. Its politics reflected the social world of ever-changing but ever more daring fashion, just as it mirrored the fluid alliances – sexual and entrepreneurial – of the world the new constitution was meant to represent. This was the newly liberated and libertine France of the post-Terror Revolution. Between 1794 and Napoleon's seizure of power in 1799, the country was a bonfire of the vanities whose champagne-fuelled gaiety was impinged on by the continuing threat of defeat in foreign war – which would bring a royalist restoration and potential purges worse than those of the Terror – and by the recent memory of so many close escapes from death, to say nothing of impoverishment and imprisonment, at the hands of leftist extremists. The past had been dangerous; so might be the future: so the present was for living. Napoleon set off for the dizzy world of Paris in May 1795 to be disquieted by its atmosphere and under the shadow of fresh trauma.

Napoleon had seen himself rehabilitated in the course of 1794–5 and was able to resume life at Antibes and court Désirée once more, but he was no longer accorded an active part in the war. The closest he appeared to come to reviving the career that had seemed to open before him at Toulon was when a projected reconquest of Corsica was mooted in the spring of 1794, in which he expected to play a prominent role. He was entrusted with drawing up invasion plans but the project came to nothing. Greater things awaited Napoleon than reprising the role of his early ancestors, the mounted crossbowmen. The news that reached him in early April 1795 threatened to point him in quite a different direction. He was reassigned to the infantry, to serve against peasant and royalist rebels in the Vendée, the bastion of counter-revolutionary resistance. Napoleon was shaken by this. Later, he always liked it to be thought that he baulked at these orders because he recoiled from the prospect of fighting 'fellow Frenchmen'. This is unlikely, in the climate of the times, when the success of counter-revolution was dreaded by everyone with a stake in the new regime. If it was indeed his view, it was a poor miscalculation on Napoleon's part.

In the event the campaign against the Vendean rebels in 1794–5 proved very successful and even more popular. It created a new hero of the Revolution, a man well suited to the more colourful, glamorous times that followed Thermidor. Lazare Hoche, blond, tall and dashing, became the darling of Parisian society, precisely because he crushed a revolt the metropolitan elite regarded as being composed of semi-savage, superstitious bumpkins. Napoleon could not have predicted Hoche's success, for the Vendée was a nasty guerrilla war and the graveyard of the reputation of some good professionals. It was, for all that, a posting in which success could bring popularity with the politicians.

Napoleon's dislike of his appointment was more likely because he dreaded being removed from the artillery to the infantry. He would have seen this as a waste of his hard-won expertise, both in the field and at the drawing board. The artillery arm had evolved a well-honed inverted snobbery towards the infantry and even the cavalry, seeing itself as the intelligentsia of the army, and Napoleon epitomised this. For whatever reason, he felt frightened enough by the prospect to set

off for Paris in the first week of May, after having become engaged –
albeit rather informally – to Désirée on 21 April. He took with him
Junot and Marmont, the loyal staff group he had assembled around
him at Toulon, whose fortunes were now bound up with his, along
with his younger brother, Louis, whom he kept with him as much as
possible, hoping to groom him as the next leader of the family. Désirée
tearfully saw Napoleon off in Marseille on 8 May, and the friends
reached Paris by a leisurely route, on 25 May. What he found there was
quite beyond him.

1795–1796: THE LOWEST DEPRESSION
ON THE MAP OF LIFE

Napoleon arrived in Paris in a state of desperation, and for most of the
next five months he stayed that way. He soon became more fully and
consciously dependent on the patronage of one man, Paul Barras, than
at any time in his life, because he could not fathom the fast and furious
world in which he was now obliged to operate. Sheer survival had kept
Napoleon alert and driven since his flight from Corte, barely two years
before. Now he had to confront a new problem, the frustration of
trying to avoid obscurity in a milieu in which he had nothing obvious
to offer. He was shown up even more than in the Clary home as a
gauche, inarticulate hanger-on, possessed of considerable technical
expertise that might best be used in an army office but not a leader
of men, here in the glittering world of Hoche and Masséna, both of
whom were socially in demand and knew how to use the connections
they made at table and in bed. Napoleon contrasted feebly with them,
what a later age would term a 'geek' in the midst of knights errant.
The depths of his frustration emerged, in the professional sphere,
by his willingness – always denied later – to accept his fate with the
foot soldiers in the Vendée, for he made arrangements for his horses
and personal baggage, and those of Junot and Marmont, to go ahead
of them to the headquarters of the Army of the West. The spirits of
Francesco Buonaparte and Gabriele Ramolino must have stirred

in him when he put his name forward for a military mission to the Ottomans, which he openly hoped might lead to permanent service with the Turks. In August, he was assigned to the Topographical Bureau, a most emphatically obscure office job, and in mid-September he was taken off the list of generals on active service. Effectively, he had been broken back to major, put behind a desk and forgotten. The exhilaration and responsibility of Toulon had evaporated.

His initial refusal of his posting to the Vendée landed him on half-pay in a very expensive city and on the charity of others. For the only time in his life, he was generally reported to be scruffy and dirty, which could be put down to long hours of work, but also to personal neglect. If such descriptions are correct, Napoleon was showing every sign of depression. The letters from Désirée seemed too infrequent, even as his dependence on her began to slip away, and it was in the summer of 1795 that he wrote *Clisson*. If that period yields an insight into Napoleon's character, it is that boredom and inactivity led him into depression and could affect his judgement. He moped, and when he knocked on the doors of the influential he did not know how to impress them; if, that is, he found the courage to knock on their doors at all. It is arguable that this depression led to the greatest mistake of his personal life, his marriage to Joséphine, but in the forlorn summer of 1795 that society goddess was as unknown to him as she was unattainable.

Thermidor seemed to have destroyed the network of patronage that had saved Napoleon from Paoli's henchmen and raised him from the ranks, and these months soon taught him as much. Augustin Robespierre had volunteered to go to the guillotine with his brother; Salicetti was concerned with his own survival and hardly to be trusted even if he could be of any use. The one Jacobin deputy who had been at Toulon and who had thrived after the fall of Robespierre, and for whom the post-Terror whirl was tailor-made, was Paul Barras. Barras was unsavoury, corrupt, clever, and now a rising star in Directorial Paris. He remembered Napoleon when the champagne bubbles seemed likely to burst on them all. He emerged as a most unlikely saviour.

Paul, formerly vicomte de Barras, was just the sort of man Napoleon was disposed to loathe and despise from the age of nine, when he entered Brienne, and, for all the twists and turns of Barras' future career, at every step of the way each manoeuvre made him all the more abhorrent to Napoleon. It is the clearest sign of his desperation that, by the autumn of 1795, and for some time thereafter, Napoleon had to throw himself upon Barras' patronage. As will be seen, he rid himself of the man, in generous and fair fashion, at the first opportunity. In 1795, that was some way off, however. Barras was the scion of a very old noble family from Provence; one of his ancestors had been a Crusader knight. None of this heritage seems to have survived by 1755, when Paul Barras was born. At sixteen, he became the kind of privileged, unprofessional army officer Napoleon hated, made a cadet-gentleman of the Languedoc Regiment, and was then sent to the Pondichéry, his family's regiment. He had an adventurous early life, serving in French India and all around the Indian Ocean.

At the outbreak of the Revolution, Barras adjusted with consummate skill to the new political culture, being elected first to local government in Provence, and then, when the Revolution entered its most radical phase, as a deputy to the National Convention, following the fall of the monarchy. He proved himself among the most bloodthirsty of the Terrorists, and was sent back to Provence to galvanise conscription. He obviously used this mission to forge, or – given his family's long-standing position of prominence there – to re-establish, client networks. One to benefit from this was Joseph Buonaparte, whom Barras appointed to the Jacobin administration in Toulon, just before the city turned against the Convention. Barras was the man with local intelligence among the deputies sent to the region by the Convention, invaluable to outsiders like Salicetti and Augustin Robespierre. He led the vicious reprisals after the falls of Marseille and Toulon which so disgusted Napoleon; it was from Barras' henchmen in Marseille that Joseph had to rescue the Clary brothers, and it was probably the same thugs who murdered Justinien Clary. Barras proved too cruel for Robespierre and too lawless; he was recalled to Paris and received a stern reprimand, as did other 'overzealous' Terrorists, such as Collot d'Herbois, who retook Lyon and tried to blow it up afterwards, or Carrier, who drowned hundreds, possibly thousands, of Vendean prisoners on rafts in the Loire.

From that moment, Barras and others in his position made a cautious, secretive devil's alliance with more moderate deputies that resulted in the coup of Thermidor and the destruction of Robespierre. He led the armed force the Convention had gathered against the Mountain, and emerged as a leading politician in the rump Convention and the Directorial regime created by the new constitution of 1795. He profited financially from his new position, as he had from the powers he had wielded under the Terror in Provence. Now, his tentacles reached to the apex of the state, and across France, but he concentrated his efforts on Paris. In the hard winter of 1794–5, Barras scoured northern France for food to supply the city, guillotined those who resisted him and made a fortune in the course of it all. He was now very powerful and popular in working-class Paris for his efforts, the fact that he had crushed two revolts led by ex-Jacobins notwithstanding. Unlike their previous champion, the austere Robespierre, Barras 'knew how to live'. He made the rounds of the salons and the beds of the great hostesses – Tallien, Récamier and de Beauharnais, the future Joséphine – while keeping a mouse of a wife in Provence and a number of official mistresses, often leading actresses. He was easy-going in his use of power. Barras epitomised the fusion of shady finance, glittering *sociabilité* and parliamentary horse-trading that was very much of the moment. He combined the military office of brigadier general commanding the army in Paris and that of deputy in the rump Convention by the summer of 1795, and was easily elected to the legislature when the new constitution came into force. He was, in sum, the antithesis of Napoleon.

In October 1795, the regime was challenged from a new source. The right-wing western quarters of Paris, well-heeled and still often royalist at heart, rose in revolt and attempted to overthrow the post-Thermidor Convention by armed force, before the new constitution could come into being. Their anger was triggered by the infamous 'decree of two-thirds', by which the rump of the Convention perpetuated itself in power, restricting elections for the new legislature of only one-third of all the seats. It was a blatant way of keeping themselves in office and, to the right-wing Sections of western and central Paris, it was a way of keeping Jacobins – however repentant for the moment – in power. Other Sections supported them in an incongruous alliance of left and right, but it was the bourgeois west that did the fighting. They were well-armed and disciplined; this was not the mob. Barras was the commander of the army in Paris, and although he had military experience his forte was organisation, not combat.

At this point, he turned to Napoleon. Barras knew quality when he saw it, be it in a woman, a business deal or a soldier. He had been deeply impressed by Napoleon at Toulon, once Salicetti brought him to his attention, and he had kept an eye on him ever since, but Napoleon only swam back into Barras' ken because, when Barras called upon soldiers to come forward to defend the Convention, Napoleon – by now bored to tears in the Topographical Bureau – did so, along with several others. He was not unemployed, and he admitted in his memoirs to reservations about getting involved so directly in a political conflict, but it was worth it to escape office drudgery. It was another deputy who had been at Toulon, Fréron, who pointed out Napoleon to Barras when the officers assembled in the Tuileries, and he was given charge of the artillery. Napoleon was no friend of the right, and so close to the Terrorist regime that he was thoroughly reliable in these circumstances. Above all, he was almost penniless, he was ambitious and he could be controlled. At the time, Barras read Napoleon well.

As with so much else, legend surrounds Napoleon's role in the last great Parisian rebellion of the Revolution, called Vendémiaire after the month in which it was fought. By 5 October, the rebels, well-armed, numbering between five and six thousand, held the area around the Convention, the Tuileries palace; they had made their headquarters in the church of St-Roche. Napoleon is supposed to have commanded an artillery barrage on them, the moment, he liked it to be thought, when he told Barras that 'a whiff of grapeshot' would see them off. It was not true, yet it should have been; the lie speaks for his attitude to civil unrest well enough. Napoleon was probably not present when the firing took place at the church, and it is highly unlikely that massed artillery would have been used in the closed, urban space around it.

The facts speak well enough for Napoleon. As he had at Toulon, but with record speed, he found out where his poorly armed force could find cannon and muskets. He had the good luck to have with him a young Gascon cavalry officer imbued with the same energy and resourcefulness as himself, Joachim Murat. He sent Murat racing to the artillery park at Les Sablons, six miles from the Tuileries, to bring the guns to him. It was the first of many 'dashes' Murat would make for his future brother-in-law – he married Caroline in 1800. When the guns arrived, Napoleon knew where to place them, and made the Tuileries impregnable. When the rebels did try to storm it, Napoleon did not hesitate to turn the guns on them, in the more open spaces close to the building, and there were hundreds of deaths. It was over, and however subordinate his initial role in the defence of the Convention, his had been in every sense the 'killer blow'. He was christened 'General Vendémiaire', with neither affection nor respect, by the Parisian society he had saved.

When it came to it, Barras was not actually ready to raise up Napoleon when he delivered his account of the revolt to the Convention, although he probably made full use of Napoleon's report when he addressed the deputies in the flush of victory. It was, again, Fréron who said Napoleon deserved some credit, and Barras quickly corrected himself, changed tack, and made him a hero. Fréron, it should be added, was quite taken with Caroline at the time.[54] If Barras had been wrong-footed, he still had a protégé he could manipulate, and both men knew it. When the new constitution came into force, Barras became one of the first members of the five-man Directory and managed to stay on it until the regime fell in 1799. This post was incompatible with the command of the Army of the Interior, and he handed it to Napoleon, exactly because, however able he seemed,

Barras felt he controlled him. It was the first of several instances when the leading men of the Directory under-estimated Napoleon, but at the time it was not a stupid miscalculation. Napoleon was a client of Barras, he had no political connections of his own of any consequence and even fewer social contacts.

The last months of 1795 were spent in a certain frustration, for all Napoleon's new status as a general of division. Outwardly, his fortunes had been rapidly transformed. He rented a fine house in central Paris, and used it as his headquarters; he now owned a coach of his own. Thanks to an advance from Barras, he bought a decent if modest and appropriate uniform, of a general of artillery. Later, even as the Emperor of the West, he usually wore the simple green uniform of an officer of the Chasseurs-à-Cheval of the Guard. He had good new boots and a good horse. The family saw more of his money than he did. A large sum was sent to Letizia; Jérôme was found a suitable school; Joseph Fesch and Lucien were given posts in the army administration – Lucien rewarded his brother by neglecting his job shamelessly – and Louis, who had followed Napoleon into the artillery and had often been with him, was made one of his aides.

Just as his months in the Topographical Bureau had not been wasted, despite his boredom – Napoleon continued to study the Italian front, as he had in Genoa and Nice – so in his new command he began a major reorganisation of the army behind the lines, a considerable force. He purged as many royalists from its ranks as he could, while also carrying out Barras' orders to close the Jacobin club of Paris. This was the first sign – among the first actions of his new-found authority – of the 'even-handed', carefully balanced repression of the political extremes Napoleon would make his own after he took power in 1799.

In these months he also used his post to begin his reforms of the Gendarmerie, then a ramshackle rural police force hastily assembled early in the Revolution, largely incapable of fulfilling its role of policing the highways, keeping order in the army, or patrolling a very violent countryside. Through the ministries of police and war, Napoleon began to gather information on the force, although he could do little at this stage to reform it. Once in power, the resuscitation of this corps became a priority, but already, in his brief tenure as commander of the Army of the Interior, Napoleon had grasped its potential.

His experience of Paris itself, since his visit there on behalf of Paoli in 1792, was also now cohering, and was completed at Vendémiaire: 10 August 1792 instilled in him a loathing of the Jacobin Sections and their mob-like savagery; Vendémiaire taught him a hatred and fear of the middle-class western neighbourhoods, a feeling that was mutual. The personal experience of social humiliation sowed in him a dislike of the metropolitan intelligentsia, laced with a certain contempt. He would make his peace with the Jacobin east, but he never trusted the city. For all he lavished funds on its rebuilding when in power, his projects aimed better to control it, even to empty it. Napoleon was not intrinsically anti-populist, for he had embraced the Revolution at its outset, nor was he by nature an anti-intellectual product of the parade ground, still less a philistine: he had craved the praise of Raynal and his salon. His loathing for the masses and the intelligentsia, like that for the peasantry of highland Corsica and all places akin to it, had been learned at first hand between 1792 and 1795, at almost the cost of his life and certainly of his pride.

When Marmont returned to Napoleon's staff from a posting in Germany, he found him much changed, more self-confident, with an air of aplomb, even of grandeur.[55] Napoleon had certainly risen to his new and vast responsibilities and quite obviously relished them. The events of Vendémiaire had seen him surpass the expectations of Toulon, his last real success by his own lights. However, Napoleon was regarded as a political appointee, and he knew it. Barras had placed him in his job, and kept a close eye on him. Napoleon had responsibility, he had status, but he lacked real independence, more so than on the batteries at Toulon. It made him appear stupid to many in Parisian politics, who did not see him at work, and this was in Napoleon's favour for several years to come, when so many in power under-estimated him. It was hard for the metropolitan sophisticates to take him seriously beyond the parade ground, the planning rooms or, later, the battlefield, and so he amassed his power unnoticed for a long time. Nevertheless, at this stage his subservient role galled him and kept him in the hunt for a field command where he could be left alone.

He was just as aware that, in a world where social life was the route to power, he was as ill prepared for action as the men he found at Toulon. He still needed a patron; he was still, by his own standards, lost in Paris. His emotional insecurity was there for all to see, once he left his duties behind. No one knew this, or thought he could use it to his advantage, better than Paul Barras. Napoleon was lonely and adrift, even in his success, for its manner was demeaning. He had one haven, the home of a fellow Corsican, Madame Permon, a wealthy widow in her forties. She often fed and comforted Napoleon, and he actually proposed to her, hardly a rational act and one devoid of emotional intelligence. She let him down gently, but it is revealing of his state of mind. Her young daughter, Laure, who would marry Junot and become one of his most devoted followers, was most unimpressed by Napoleon, nicknaming him 'Puss-in-Boots' because his legs were too thin for his army-issue boots. The image lingered even when he bought some better ones after he had been promoted.[56]

This was still his state of mind when he met Joséphine, born Marie-Josèphe-Rose de Tascher de la Pagerie on Martinique in 1762, to a family of the old nobility, long in service to the Crown. Martinique was merely a posting, but one they had held for decades. She was married at sixteen to the vicomte Alexandre de Beauharnais, two years her senior, of an old noble house, and one of the vilest men of his era. She bore him two children, a son, Eugène, and a daughter, Hortense, and he proceeded to abandon them, although his many creditors did not lose her trail as easily as Alexandre's. He seems to have returned only to abuse his young wife, who was able to obtain a legal separation from him, which put Alexandre under an order not to come within several miles of her residence. None of this prevented Alexandre from embracing the cause of humanity in the shape of the French Revolution, however. He was a rising star in the politics of the National Assembly, and then in the army, where, by 1793, he had risen to command the Army of the Rhine. Joséphine first fled home to Martinique to avoid her husband's creditors in the last months of the old order, only to flee back to France in 1790 to escape a slave revolt ignited by the Revolution's abolition of slavery, which cost most of her family their lives. Returned to France, she found her husband's fortunes much changed. Alexandre was an aristocrat, and he thus became a suspect under the Terror. He was arrested early in July 1794, on the grounds that he was a counter-revolutionary; Joséphine was arrested for complicity, their long-standing estrangement notwithstanding, and her two children were gaoled with her, in Paris. Husband and wife, such as they were, were condemned to death, and Alexandre was guillotined just before the fall of Robespierre, on 23 July; Joséphine was released on 6 August. It may have been as well for Alexandre that he died before Napoleon came to power, for his presence on earth may well have been Napoleon's one enticement to embrace the vendetta culture of the Corsican mountains.

Myth began to surround Joséphine, too. It was said a prison officer, in thrall to her beauty, ate her order of execution to save her. She did bestow a large sum on him later in life, but the connection can never be known. It is the sort of thing that *should* have happened.

Release from prison let her back into a world where, with two young children and no source of income, she had only her charm to serve her, and she used it. Even in prison, under the shadow of the gallows, Joséphine had no difficulty in making Hoche, facing the same fate, fall in love with her. When they emerged, the affair continued, despite his absences in the Vendée once the post-Thermidor government had reinstated him, and the pleas of his pregnant wife to rejoin her. He spent his leaves with Joséphine.

This liaison did not prevent Joséphine from enjoying the social whirl that followed the end of the Terror. She was not long in making Barras' acquaintance, which Hoche interpreted in only one way and ended their affair. It is more than probable that Barras had already usurped him, to a degree. Barras was powerful, and he was there; he did not hold commissions, he handed them out. Joséphine – Marie-Rose as she still was – often acted as his official hostess, and there were highly believable rumours of erotic dinners where Joséphine, Récamier and Tallien acted as his private harem. Barras tried his best to blacken Joséphine's name after Napoleon excluded him from office in 1799, branding her a high-class prostitute prepared to indulge in a list of perversions that probably revealed more about Barras than it did about Joséphine. Nevertheless, she knew how to combine survival with pleasure, and was at the centre of society, polished, affable, beautiful.

Joséphine shared one character trait with Napoleon, but it did nothing to help the relationship they formed: she, like Napoleon, had lived through hell. She had been driven from her home by violence, then cast into uncertainty, and had faced execution. Beneath the 'good-time girl' was a cautious survivor; indeed, the very purpose of the party was survival. Joséphine found it dangerous to commit to one man in so volatile a world. She was not wrong: Hoche was dead by autumn 1797, from tuberculosis contracted after almost drowning in an attempted invasion of Ireland at the end of 1796. Barras soon lost control of his own fate, once Napoleon learned the ropes of politics for himself. When they met, Napoleon was hardly in Joséphine's league, and she probably thought she could relax, just like Barras and the rest of the smart set.

There is, predictably, a wonderful lie regarding how they met. It began when Napoleon, as commandant of Paris, was carrying out the disarmament of the city with his usual thoroughness, and had Alexandre's sword, that of a general of the Republic, collected from the Beauharnais home in the process. Eugène took his courage in his hands, went to Napoleon and demanded it back as his heritage. Napoleon was so impressed by this that he did so, and asked to meet the boy's mother. In another version, Eugène went home with the sword, and his mother, in her turn, was so impressed she asked to meet Napoleon. As so often, there is a deeper, different, but important truth behind the myth. It was fabricated by Eugène and Hortense, after Napoleon's fall. It was how they wanted things to be, and it is a testimony not only to their wish – which Napoleon shared – to bury the lurid tales surrounding Joséphine, but to the love they came to feel for Napoleon. In truth, they did not like him when he first came into their lives. They feared he would take their mother away from them and Hortense, especially, found him rude, recounting how he talked around her to Joséphine when she was placed between them at a dinner.[57] This may be a story, too, but it rings truer to form than most.

The story the children concocted reflected how first appearances deceived so much in these months. Napoleon raised them as his own, and they rewarded him with a love and loyalty neither their mother nor Napoleon's own family ever matched. The Beauharnais children became the twin pillars of his life, Eugène in the public sphere and Hortense in the private. He, and he alone, was entrusted with Napoleon's dearest political possession, 'his' Kingdom of Italy. People of exceptional intelligence, they mirrored the different sides of his own sharp mind: Eugène, that of the careful, meticulous planner and competent administrator; Hortense, the quick-witted, insatiably curious polymath, although she could expound her learning without being a bore. She married his favourite brother, Louis, as unworthy of her as he proved of Napoleon, but through that marriage the dynasty lived to fight again. They became indispensable to him, but he had raised them to be so and they loved him for it.

The truth of when Napoleon and Joséphine met is uncertain, but it was probably soon after Vendémiaire.[58] 'How' seems clearer. Barras had begun to drag his 'hero' around the salons and their hostesses in the early autumn of 1795, and it was at one such gathering that Napoleon was dazzled and Joséphine polite and mildly amused. Napoleon's memoirs show both honesty and some self-deprecation on the first encounter. Amidst his description of her beauty and her grace, he added:

... my character rendered me timid before them [women]. Madame de Beauharnais is the first to have reassured me. She said flattering things about

my military talents, one day when I found myself placed next to her ...
[after this] I followed her everywhere. I was passionately in love with her.[59]

That never changed, for the rest of her life. In late 1795, the lonely
Napoleon, even more isolated and self-conscious in society now that
he had been thrust into it, fell in love with the first beautiful woman
who was civil to him. He had never been so vulnerable than in these
months; the fame he had won at Vendémiaire had done him no good,
in society or even in politics.

   Joséphine enchanted him, but what made her take an interest in
him is harder to know. She saw all his limitations, with her cautious
eye, however charming she had been to him almost as a matter of
course at dinner, although in so doing she also showed that she had a
kind nature, however patronising, so unlike many of her friends. The
catalogue of hard truths about the Napoleon of 1795, often recounted
by contemporary critics and hostile historians, swam around in
Joséphine's mind long before they hit on them. Who was he? Who
had this soldier actually beaten? What had he actually commanded?
Why all the fuss from Barras and no one else? What did he say? Where
did he get that accent? How much of this is self-promotion? Can
he actually establish himself and stand alone or will he always be in
Barras' pocket? Does he ever shut up in that awful accent? Conversely,
does he ever speak? The record did not augur a bright future, and she
weighed this up. The British press and secret service may have picked
up the phrase 'Corsican upstart' from the gossip of Joséphine and her
circle in these months, with no need to invent it, save that Napoleon
was of even less interest to them than to the glitterati. This caution
was reflected in her very modern, hard-headed marriage contract:
Napoleon was to have no control over her finances – something she
should have come to regret, given her incompetence with money –
and she had full custody of her children. Her misgivings were utterly
unfounded in this regard, too, but she could not have known how good
a man Napoleon was in this respect. It was a predictable, reasonable
response to her own experiences, and Napoleon accepted it, a sign not

just of his passion for her, but of genuine understanding, of empathy with another orphan of the storm.

For all that, he did have prospects. Hoche was a better bargain, but he had at last ended their affair, not long after Napoleon began to pursue her, and it was increasingly clear that Barras was phasing her out as a mistress. She was now well into her thirties. They slept together for the first time in December 1795, and he wrote to her, impassioned, the next day; she took it in her stride. Napoleon was hardly her ideal, but it was clear he was sincere and, since breaking with Désirée, unattached. She did not have to worry about divided loyalties, wives, or competition of any kind: Napoleon was too open and honest to have to chase. There was something else for Napoleon. Letizia and Joseph suspected Joséphine; they did not like the relationship, nor did many of his close, loyal friends, and this made Napoleon all the more determined. He rose to criticism of her, and he always would, for the opposition or plain dislike of her among the family actually made their bond stronger in the years ahead. Only Barras, among those he confided in, thought his proposal of marriage, in January 1796, a good idea, which in rational terms was equivalent to the kiss of death. Napoleon had steeled himself for a long courtship, but like so many of his great victories – and to him this was always the most important – it came quickly, seemingly out of nowhere, and carried a heavier price than he anticipated. The banns appeared on 20 February 1796. Napoleon was now legally 'Bonaparte', among other things. The heart can only be known to he who carries it in his frame, and this is really how the love between Joséphine and Napoleon will always remain, and rightly so. There was no real logic to it. Nor was the manner in which he rapidly renamed her 'Joséphine' – just as Désirée had become Eugénie – but, like their love, it stuck for ever.

If Joséphine had a sixth sense about Napoleon's prospects, it was soon vindicated. He had bombarded the new minister of war, the intelligent, hard-nosed ex-Terrorist Lazare Carnot, about the present dilapidation of, but potential for, the Italian front. Napoleon had been gathering information about the region for years, and had now come to see himself not just as an expert on it, but as the man to put his own theories into practice. Carnot paid more attention than many to Napoleon, but it was the inaction and indifference of the general commanding the Army of Italy, Schérer, that made him listen harder. His impatience with Schérer grew when Salicetti returned from a visit to the front and confirmed Schérer's seeming passivity in the face of Napoleon's ideas about carrying the fight over the Alps, not to the main Austrian army, but to the Piedmontese, who were closer to the French lines. The capture of enemy territory envisaged by Napoleon as the first stage would, both the Corsicans argued, help rectify the army's lack of supplies, for Napoleon agreed fully with Schérer's complaints about this, but he seemed to have a positive solution that would cost the French little, whereas Schérer had reasons only for staying put.

It was in the end not the patronage of Barras, but the sober opinion of Carnot – no fool, who knew Salicetti's links to Napoleon – that won Napoleon the command of the Army of Italy on 2 March 1796. Napoleon's hard work, his mastery of the sector, had impressed a hard man, all the more so because Napoleon was soon arguing with him, tooth and nail, for complete freedom of action: the plan was his; only he could carry it out. Carnot, piece by piece, gave way. He also knew the storm this would cause, for it raised all the angry questions Joséphine had pondered, from her own, different point of view. Napoleon was an unknown; he could barely speak French; there were far more experienced men available. It was all true, but Carnot, who would serve Napoleon in his turn, was known already as 'the architect of victory' and he followed his instincts. He was more right than anyone could yet know. Barras' main role in the appointment came after it had been made, as he reassured all and sundry that Napoleon had no interest in politics and even less capacity for it.

Until he assumed the independent command of the Army of Italy in March 1796, at the age of twenty-seven, there had been many profound influences on Napoleon. There was the atavistic heritage of Ajaccio, quite distinct from that of Corsica, that of the calculating if ambitious provincial, urban notable, divorced from the violence of the rural world; more obvious was his institutionalised military upbringing – not a mere education – that marked his character at every level, marked it all his life. His affected but sincere Romanticism, crystallised by his reading, had now transferred itself from his adoration of Paoli and his hopeless dream of finding a pure society in the Corsican mountains, to Joséphine, where it found an abiding, if hardly tranquil, home. Few men, even in an age which so prized the polymath – and this was the last era when the western world could produce them – were as widely read as Napoleon, save perhaps Thomas Jefferson, who would one day thwart Napoleon's American dreams because he was his intellectual match. Napoleon's curiosity made him a bore in elegant company, but it informed his every thought, and, indeed, made those thoughts informed. All of these attributes counted for much, and would never leave him. They had left indelible marks on him, yet none of them had defined him. This is the hallmark not just of the exceptional human being – for this he had yet to prove himself to be, although Josephine seemed to sense his innate greatness better than anyone else – but also of the complete individual he was and would remain. Napoleon was less a disciple of Rousseau than a kindred spirit. He cut a romantic figure but he was not a Romantic. In the months ahead, Italy would define him. Independent command, conquest followed by power, followed by the knowledge of how to wield power – the ability first to create, and then to rule – would define Napoleon. Only then, in quite exceptional circumstances, would Napoleon 'Bonaparte' be defined as a man.

For the moment, there was much of the mundane and comic left to get through before he left Paris for the Italian front on 11 March. Napoleon and Joséphine married on 9 March 1795, in a civil ceremony in a town hall in north-central Paris, in the rue d'Antin, which now squeezes between the elegant department stores Au Printemps and the Galleries Lafayette. Nothing of this future elegance was presaged by the ceremony, however. The room was spartan, to say the least. Napoleon arrived two hours late (because he had been going over his brief with Carnot), which caused the registrar to go home, leaving the ceremony in the hands of his deputy, who may or may not have been qualified to carry it out. Joséphine made him pay for this faux pas by excluding him from their bed that night in favour of her yappy little dog. Neither had dared tell their families about the wedding, so the only witnesses were Barras and the long-suffering Madame Tallien. The sole sign of grace present was Joséphine herself in a white muslin gown. Even this was marred by a vulgarity, and one that was not invented by legend. Across her gown she wore a sash in the tricolour of the Republic. On it was a medal Napoleon had given her. It read, simply, 'Destiny'.

3

THE CONQUEST OF ITALY

A Star is Born, 1796–1797

The Directory sent Napoleon to take over the dishevelled Army of Italy with a vague but ambitious strategic plan to cross the western Alps, defeat the Piedmontese and the Austrians, march across the top of the peninsula, then cross the eastern Alps into Austria, defeat more Austrians, and link up with other French armies advancing from the Rhine to the Danube and take Vienna. Napoleon did not quite manage that, but he found a strategy of his own, and it dwarfed anything any of his superiors or his opponents, or perhaps even he himself, had foreseen.

When Napoleon crossed the Alps for the first time in April 1796, many people saw many things in him. To some Italians he was a liberator; to others he was a rabid revolutionary fanatic; to others still he was merely the next in a long line of barbarian pillagers from the savage north. To some in France he was a nuisance, sent out to lead an underfunded sideshow and get himself lost; for others – mainly his own men – he was their last hope of victory and better conditions. He soon proved to be all these things. He had no choice. This is obvious in the two proclamations he issued on the eve of his descent on the lands below him. In one, he told his men he was leading them into the richest fields and cities in the world:

Soldiers, you are naked, ill fed; the government owes you much; it gives you nothing. Your patience, the courage you have shown in the midst of these wastes, is admirable, but it can bring you no glory, no renown will reflect on you. I want to lead you into the most fertile plains in the world. Rich provinces and great cities will be in your power; you will find honour, glory and riches. Soldiers, are you lacking in courage or constancy?

In the other, he proclaimed to the Italians that he had come to free them from centuries of servitude, not only political and diplomatic, but spiritual and cultural.

It is doubtful that many people actually read either document at the time, but they reveal a great deal about the future of Napoleonic Europe, for all his regimes, right up until his fall in 1815, balanced precariously between the desire to reform and enlighten and the equally powerful impulse to plunder and extort. More than Napoleon could possibly have realised, he had set his own agenda, from this cold, clear Alpine vantage point. What he saw in his own mind's eye was an unparalleled opportunity to make something of himself, and he took it with both hands.

First, he had to fight for it, and his entire life so far had made him more than ready to do so. In a matter of weeks and months, his military, diplomatic and political judgement would display something far more than marked ability. Verve and genius would emerge as he descended the passes to the valley of the Po. The descent of the passes was, in every sense, his rite of passage from being a talented survivor to becoming the master of his own destiny, and that of countless others.

Napoleon arrived in Nice, in modern parlance the GHQ of his new command, the Army of Italy, on 27 March 1796. He had never commanded a field army before, and this should always be remembered when the First Italian Campaign is assessed. Sensibly enough, the Directory had awarded a novice a sideshow, and the army he inherited had been treated in exactly that fashion – it was under-fed, virtually unpaid, under-armed and had been idling for over four years, most recently under the command of the ageing Schérer, an *ancien régime* officer for whom Napoleon had considerable respect and sympathy. Schérer had harassed Paris for supplies and reinforcements, and, having been denied them, had had to watch his army deteriorate in morale and material effectiveness. Although Schérer has often been maligned by posterity, Napoleon spoke well of him, as 'an honest and clever man ... worn out by the war, which has affected his health', 'a talented man ... for whom something ought to be done'.[1] Napoleon suggested a diplomatic post for Schérer, possibly because he gave the young commander a warmer, more civil welcome than the rest of his senior officers.

Schérer had a potentially brilliant staff: Augereau and Masséna, especially, would shine under Napoleon, but their first sight of him left these hardened veterans, both a good ten years older than Napoleon, feeling unimpressed rather than threatened. They shared the view of the 58-year-old Sérurier that this could only be a 'political appointment' courtesy of Barras' corrupt indifference to the military. They soon changed their minds, however, and the transformation of their opinion is all the more striking because they had not yet seen Napoleon in action. Masséna recalled that when 'he put on his general's hat [he] seemed to have grown two feet'.[2] He did this by asking the right questions of them, questions that were both intelligent and imbued with a positive, aggressive approach to the projected offensive. Napoleon wanted to know how to get the army ready to fight on the attack, and he was in a position to be both precise and realistic. He knew what he was talking about, because the previous year, from his desk at the Topographical Bureau in Paris, he had made a careful study of the western Alps – the terrain, the state of the roads and ports, the weather – for a projected offensive that never took place. He knew, at least in theory, what he needed to assess and what was required. More than this, he impressed by his presence – by his very glance – not simply by his attitude. Although almost intangible, the impact of his person is very clear. There was something about the man, not just his approach to command.

There was also something about the small group of staff officers he brought with him. His new chief of staff, Alexandre Berthier, was among them, at forty-three a military engineer who soon became Napoleon's right arm and was dubbed 'the Emperor's wife' by a later generation of French officers. He had served in the region before, and had a phenomenal capacity for sustained concentration on paperwork. His complete antithesis, Joachim Murat, was at his side, a hot-tempered, none-too-bright Gascon cavalryman who had had the supreme nerve to suggest his own appointment – and got away with it. Murat had boundless energy and courage, reacted bravely in a crisis, and so compensated in the field for his other shortcomings. Then there were Napoleon's close friends and contemporaries: Marmont, twenty-two, his fellow artilleryman, and Junot, twenty-four, Napoleon's 'flatmate' in Paris who had been with him since they first met at the siege of Toulon.

In human terms it was an almost prophetic coming together: henceforth, the fates of all these men were bound to Napoleon's. Murat would marry Napoleon's sister, the redoubtable, menacing Caroline, become the king of Naples, betray him and then die ludicrously, repenting of his treason. Marmont, too, rose high, only to turn on Napoleon in the darkest days of 1814 and be calmly damned for his ingratitude to his face by Napoleon. Masséna proved the most distinguished commander among them, and the most corrupt, avaricious individual of an exceptionally greedy milieu; Napoleon's appeal to the material cravings of the army, on the eve of its descent into Italy, might have been penned with Masséna in mind. In the light of their future careers, David Chandler's observation that 'rarely had such a galaxy of military talent served together at one time and place' is redolent of understatement.

What drew Napoleon to both Masséna and Augereau was their pure military ability, for he never established a good rapport with either man, although he rewarded them well, both when they got into the rich Italian plains in the spring of 1796 and for the rest of his career. They did not much care for Napoleon either, once he took off his transforming general's hat. Napoleon's attitude has been attributed to his preference for surrounding himself with men who would not become potential rivals, in response to finding himself surrounded by proven commanders who were jealous of his rapid promotion over them. This is unfair, for although he was initially wary of his colleagues – no doubt because he was still untried as a commander – it does not reflect his future conduct towards them. Napoleon soon learned to respect talent and promote it, whatever the risk to himself.[3]

A very interesting trend of the last, desperate days of the empire, in 1814, was that Napoleon's finest commanders – the ones he should have been jealous of and have alienated according to the 'envy theory', as it were – were exactly those who stood by him: Davout – often an outspoken critic on campaign – and Soult, arguably his equals, fought for him to the end, and joined him during the Hundred Days the next year. It was the other, lesser lights – Marmont among them – who turned on him at the death.

Napoleon showed very early that, with the exception of Berthier, whose role demanded it, he did not like 'yes men'. One of his greatest personal attributes – and one that he built his whole policy around – was to get men to work with and under him who could not normally bear the sight of each other, but who were also men of considerable talent in their respective fields.

Together with Augereau and Masséna, who had come to respect him, Napoleon's new staff headquarters immediately came to resemble the mixture of *ancien régime* professionalism, first-hand revolutionary experience and youthful verve he would seek to foster and maintain in both the army and the personnel of the civil state for the next decade. This was the blending of the old order, the revolutionaries of the 1790s and of newer men, like Junot, Marmont and himself, which has been labelled *amalgame* – amalgamation – twinned with *ralliement*, rallying around Napoleon personally.

He soon applied this approach to political factionalism among the Italians during 1796–7, but honed it to perfection, to the great profit of his country, when in power after 1799, bringing men like the aristocratic Talleyrand (his foreign minister), the revolutionary radical Fouché (his minister of police) and the technical experts Carnot, Cambacérès and Lebrun together into his Council of State. These were men of enormous ability but diverse, indeed opposing, backgrounds. If Napoleon had a prejudice, it was a marked preference for men of his own age and experience; he found it hard to trust older men, and his memoirs on St Helena targeted directly those of his own age and the younger generation – those he called *les enfants du siècle*, the children of the new century – whose historical experience he considered unique. Something of this was already evident at GHQ, Nice, in 1796, and he would try to 'move on' from dependence on the older generation as soon as he could.

Before anything could happen to any of them, they first had to get over the mountains and beat the Allies, and their glittering future was by no means clear in the spring of 1796, however piercing Napoleon's eyes or bracing his approach to the onset of war.

THE WAR OF THE FIRST COALITION IN ITALY

Napoleon arrived with a determination to overcome the mass of problems and shortcomings he found on the Italian front. His dynamic approach to the situation made it impossible to be anything but angry about the apathy and inertia he found all around him.

The anger is obvious, but always balanced by the determination to turn adverse circumstances around. What Napoleon saw, more often than not, were self-inflicted wounds, not intrinsic flaws. His men had been let down by a corrupt army administration and indifferent, often actually hostile, local authorities in their rear. He pointed directly to this the day after he reached Nice:

The four departments which the army occupies[4] have paid [the army] neither the forced-loan, nor their grain quotas, nor the payment in forage required by the law of 7 Vendémiaire, nor have they begun the levy of ... horses. These administrations have reacted very slowly. I have written to them, I have met with them, and I have some hope of some action ...

The administrative situation of the army is shameful, but not hopeless. I have been obliged to threaten its personnel, who have stolen a great deal and are in credit, and I have won over many of them by flattery. The army will eat good bread and it will have meat ...[5]

Old animosities and future ruthlessness lurk in these words, along-side Napoleon's current pressing concerns. His experience at Toulon had taught him about the latent counter-revolution and blatant recalcitrance of the south-eastern departments, and what he now found came as no surprise to him; once in power, after 1800, Napoleon would be quick to unleash a ferocious campaign of repression in Provence. The corruption in the military administration was a timely reminder of how debilitating this had become since the end of the Terror; again, one of Napoleon's first acts as Consul was to carry out a purge of the army administration. In both cases, although he neither dared nor wished to say so, Napoleon was reminded that his first patron, Robespierre, had been right about the corruption of the War Ministry – it had marked his denunciations of his rivals for power (it was one of the few of his accusations that was true) – and in his determination to crush not only provincial rebellion, but the indifference of local government. Napoleon went on to attack these problems with brutal verve. For the moment, he occupied himself with, literally, securing his rear as well as provisioning his troops.

The other most obvious self-inflicted wound was the heavy-handed attempt by the Directory to threaten, cow and intimidate the neutral Republic of Genoa into letting the French occupy its territory and allow the Army of Italy safe passage over the passes into Piedmont. The large-scale troop movements this entailed in early April attracted Austrian concern, and led them to concentrate more forces along these passes than they had hitherto. Most notably, it all but deprived Napoleon of the only obvious advantage he held at this stage, the element of surprise. He had to set about correcting this as best he could. Napoleon's first brush with international diplomacy was therefore to oppose the bellicosity of Paris, and avoid the overt coercion of the Genoese. On his second day in Nice, he wrote to the French ambassador in Genoa that 'in my view, we must win them over quietly, and continue to live in peace and friendship with this Republic, whose animosity ... would upset our military calculations'.[6] In his thoughtful biography of Napoleon, the Italian scholar Luigi Mascilli Migliorini made the acute observation of the profound resemblance of Napoleon's memoirs to Caesar's *Gallic Wars*.[7] One of the recurrent themes of Caesar's own self-publicity was the skill of his diplomacy with the Gauls; the battles and campaigns were glorious, but it was his ability to avoid confrontation that really raised Caesar above his contemporaries. At the outset of his public life, Napoleon successfully reversed the blunt, counter-productive policy of his superiors, and so was able to move his army close to the front without provoking the Austrians further. Thus, he made the passes passable, just in time.

As his troops moved into position, he cautioned Masséna: 'Citizen general, you should now reoccupy the positions you held ... Your soldiers should rest up; take care not to stir the enemy, and do nothing that might make him think we have hostile intentions.'[8] The success of this is borne out by the fact that the Austrian troop build-up was halted, which meant that the main body of their army was still concentrated away from the passes, allowing Napoleon to cross over against forces he could contend with. It was his caution, as much as his daring, that allowed him to boast after the event that if Hannibal had crossed the Alps, he had outflanked them.

While his men rested, Napoleon also had to rebuild the army. He applied the 'carrot and the stick' to his new command, but with the confidence and assurance of a far more experienced leader, and with an insight into his men's minds which seems beyond his years. His first trial of leadership came hard on the heels of his arrival. The incident itself may appear insignificant in light of his future career, but for a young man in his first command it was a test of resolve. The 3rd Battalion of the 209th Demi-brigade at Nice had just mutinied, refusing to join the advance and assume active duties because it had not been paid. Napoleon responded ruthlessly, decisively and immediately. The unit was dissolved and its men distributed among others; his wrath fell on its officers, for 'not having shown enough nerve',[9] and its NCOs, who, 'not having set the example by setting out but having remained in the ranks without speaking, are all guilty', were dismissed the service immediately and sent home. The grenadiers who incited the mutiny were all court-martialled.[10] There was no over-reaction – no one was executed – but there was firmness, clarity and authority in his very first act as commander. This was how he would carry on, when far greater challenges reared their heads.

In March 1796, the Army of Italy nominally numbered 67,000 men, but its real fighting strength amounted to about 37,000, which Napoleon had brought up to 41,000 by the start of the campaign in mid-April, although there was as yet no prospect of replacements. Supplies were low and had to be raised from Provence; there were only sixty field guns in the army. In every sense, the army and its leader were on their own, in the wilds of the mountains. The troops were originally scattered over the Alpine front, but Napoleon brought them together, along the Apennine passes on the Ligurian coast, and consolidated them into the new divisional system, sanctioned recently by Carnot, the Director most immediately responsible for the war effort. The divisions broke down the *ancien régime* regiments; they were subdivided into brigades and, below them, *demi* (half) brigades; each division contained units from all three arms – infantry, cavalry and artillery – all of which foreshadowed the corps system Napoleon would make the organisational core of his armies.

It was not easy to provision large concentrations of troops in poor, mountainous regions, or to keep them supplied where the roads were so difficult and poor. For this reason alone, Napoleon knew he had to move quickly and fight his way into the more fertile Piedmontese lowlands over the hill. It was that crude. These constraints also largely explain the configuration of the Allied armies facing Napoleon, as well as the need to defend a front with several usable passes over a long stretch of mountains. Half of Colli's 50,000 Piedmontese were spread out in this way, over thirty miles of front, backed by 10,000 Austrians in a second line of garrisons. Those Allied troops who were concentrated and able to move amounted to 9,500, who had advanced to Voltri in response to the Directory's aggression, and another 11,500 around the town of Acqui. For all the shortcomings in numbers and supply, Napoleon had his force ready to advance; his 41,000 men were all mobile and none of them tied to defensive positions.

Napoleon's strategy was speed in attack and a less concentrated advance than originally planned. The loss of complete surprise now required considerable co-ordination in command by Napoleon and Berthier, for there were now more enemy troops in the passes than before the Directory had blundered in. The first effect of this was that Napoleon had to begin the campaign four days early, on 11 April, but the Austrian advance had also had the unintended result of disclosing to him where their larger troop concentrations were. The perceived need to advance on Genoa had also disrupted the enemy: Beaulieu and Colli, the Austrian and Piedmontese commanders respectively, had only the vaguest of general orders – to drive the French back as far as they could – but no clear objectives, and their response to Napoleon's concentrated advance was fragmented, if determined. Napoleon, too, had no specific directives, but he saw this as an opportunity and decided to drive a wedge between the Piedmontese and Austrian forces, directed in such a way as to take the bulk of his army into the fertile lowlands of the Po Valley. He went after a concentration of 6,000 Austrian troops near the Ligurian town of Montenotte on 12 April. This began with a frontal assault by La Harpe, but victory was clinched by a highly risky night march by Masséna's division over very treacherous terrain, which surrounded the Austrians under Argenteau and scattered most of them. They were forced to retreat, leaving more than a thousand muskets to the French, which were promptly issued to Augereau's division, which had had to advance almost unarmed, behind La Harpe.

Napoleon was now slowed down and almost undone by a combination of stubborn resistance from isolated Austrian garrisons and the desperate condition of his own troops. While the former element threatened to fragment his own advance, the latter resulted in Masséna's men, who were holding the important town of Dego, dispersing to pillage the locality; this allowed the Austrians briefly to retake the town and forced Napoleon to divert troops and time to secure his lines. He did this swiftly, but it was a warning of how fragile his hold on the army could be, in such straitened circumstances.

Once regrouped, he returned to his course: divide and conquer. Napoleon ignored the largest Allied force under Beaulieu to the east, at Acqui, and swung north-west to attack Colli's Piedmontese at Mondovì; these had fallen back on the town – which is on a formidable crag – in haste. Again, the key was swift pursuit, for Colli was not given time to prepare a good defensive position. Augereau's newly armed division was thrown in, fresh, alongside Sérurier, who led the attack with a verve and ruthlessness that defied less his advanced years than the surly pessimism that had been almost his hallmark until now in the Army of Italy. Colli withdrew, still almost intact, but Napoleon followed.

At this point, it can be seen that his strategy was at least as much diplomatic as military. He did not swing east to attack the main Austrian army at Acqui, but on 23 April drove down the valley of the Tanaro, towards the relatively undefended Piedmontese capital of Turin. This opened the plains of the Po to his men's empty stomachs – the capture of the arsenal at Mondovì had given them arms but little food – and the king, Victor-Amadeus III, to negotiation. Napoleon halted at Cherasco, where the rivers Tanaro and Stura meet, and the road to Turin opens on to the lowlands; only now did he send La Harpe towards Beaulieu at Acqui, who began, in turn, to fall back to the Austrian strongholds in Lombardy. In diplomatic as well as military terms, Victor-Amadeus was now alone and he sued for peace.

Napoleon could not, as a field commander, make a permanent treaty, but the Armistice of Cherasco, concluded on 28 April, gave the Army of Italy exactly what it wanted. Victor-Amadeus' state was left almost intact, thus relieving the French of the need to rule and occupy the country, something they could not do and hope to pursue the Austrians at the same time. Instead, they were allowed to occupy key points across Piedmont south of the River Stura, and given free passage across the south of the country, with the right to provision themselves there. This amounted to power without responsibility: the local Piedmontese administration was to work for the French, who received supplies, had a secure rear and, above all, an easy passage towards the Austrian fortresses in Lombardy. It was ideal, and its achievement had taken Napoleon only two weeks.

The results of the first phase of the campaign in April 1796 were far from flawless but all the more remarkable for a beginner, and the conquest of Piedmont displayed many of the hallmarks of Napoleon's future military operations. It was swift, decisive, relied on the offensive and, as Jonathon Riley has shrewdly observed, it showed that 'envelopment was already Napoleon's favourite tactical gambit'.[11] The Directory's blunders had forced him to become a 'scrambler' from the very outset of his career as a commander and he turned this to his advantage, but only just. Even more, he had been landed in a considerable mess by poor, aggressive diplomacy. Within two weeks, at the Armistice of Cherasco, he had extricated himself and his army from this mess not only by intelligent, improvised generalship but, like Caesar among the Gauls, by shrewd diplomacy that mixed magnanimity and menace in the right measure. In two weeks, his limited forces had won impressive victories, secured his rear, created a whole new range of possibilities for his advance and acquired the supplies his men desperately needed; and he had divided his enemies by diplomacy, thus knocking a formidable power of the second rank, Piedmont, out of the war. It was a pattern that repeated itself over and over again. This was a startling beginning for a young man new to command, but it was only a beginning. The true confrontation was yet to come.

The Armistice of Cherasco allowed Napoleon to advance eastwards along the unprotected southern bank of the Po. This, rather than the crossing of the Apennines, was the outflanking that really mattered. Moving along the south bank, he did not yet have to ford the line of difficult rivers that flow down from the Alps and join the Po on its northern bank. Napoleon could move quickly and deeply into Italy this way, and that is just what he did. On 3 May, he created a diversionary movement near Valenza, where Beaulieu had regrouped, while driving an elite advance guard further east, to Piacenza, where the French actually crossed the Po – again outflanking and almost enveloping Beaulieu – on 7 May. The advance guard was entrusted to Jean Lannes, a sharp-witted Gascon who had caught Napoleon's eye at Dego. Lannes, showing skill and ability, established a bridgehead at Piacenza in a careful, potentially fraught operation. Beaulieu reacted promptly, and Lannes defended the bridgehead with his small force well, forcing Beaulieu to pull back. His quick work allowed Augereau's and La Harpe's divisions to cross within hours. A sharp engagement followed, in which La Harpe was killed by friendly fire. Beaulieu got away, but the Po had been crossed and he had been outflanked. Lannes now began a rise that made him Napoleon's most versatile commander and ended with his death at the Battle of Aspern-Essling in 1809.

When Beaulieu withdrew north-eastwards over the Po and back into the Austrian province of Lombardy, it was into the traditional 'comfort zone' of those defending Italy from western invasion. This was the area known in military terms as the Quadrilateral, because its four corners were guarded by the strong fortresses of Mantua and Peschiera on the River Mincio, and those of Verona and Legnago on the Adige. Of these, only Mantua was actually in Austrian territory, the other three belonging to the Republic of Venice, but any Austrian retreat further east would bring them into defensive service. The Quadrilateral was a traditional deterrent to any threat to the Lombard plain and the rich city of Milan. The Armistice of Cherasco had given Napoleon a very useful strategic opportunity, which enabled him to advance as far as Piacenza on the easier terrain on the south bank of the Po; but that was all it was, an opportunity, not a decisive advantage, for sooner or later he would have to confront the Austrians on the northern bank, with its multiplicity of rivers to ford, the Alpine passes to the north, to which the Austrians could fall back and through which they could bring in reinforcements from their imperial heartland. They also held the redoubt of Mantua, from which they could harass French lines of communication. When Lannes secured the bridgehead at Piacenza and the rest of the army followed him, this was what they were faced with.

Between the rivers, and before the mountains, lay the great valley of the River Po. Its lowlands had once been true 'war country', on a par with the fields of Flanders – vast, flat, easily manoeuvred plains that were also, like Flanders, a corridor between the rival great powers of Bourbon France and the Habsburg Monarchy, a place where conventional armies could collide head-on. No more, by the 1790s. The agricultural revolution of the late seventeenth and eighteenth centuries had brought rice and maize to the region, depopulating much of it and replacing its people with rice paddies which, if neglected or abandoned, rapidly degenerated into muddy, malarial swamps. The Army of Italy pushed into these 'killing fields' in spring, when they were at their most sodden and mosquito-ridden. Having enough to eat, at long last, had its price, even when the food was plundered, as it was. That price was a war with 'General Mud', who can harass an army on the march better than any band of partisans. The reality of the French advance was usually a muddy slog; the image Napoleon crafted around it – the one which endures – is of bridges heroically crossed. All kinds of obstacles had to be surmounted – boggy paddy fields, narrow bridges over swift-flowing rivers, hard mountains yet again – and they were. The reality was more heroic than the myth, as is so often the case, and Napoleon knew it. He heaped praise and plunder on the sodden army, but he exported something more glamorous home.

The Austrians decided to avoid all this and withdrew gradually and carefully to the passes, making Napoleon follow them over the difficult, soggy flatlands. They established rearguards on the major river crossings, and put a strong garrison in Mantua, but virtually abandoned Milan, the regional capital. The fighting between the Po and the Adda, the first of the Po's northern tributaries Napoleon had to cross, displayed the ability of his troops – in this case, infantry, Lannes' grenadiers – to pursue the enemy at real pace across marshy ground. Relentless, unexpectedly quick pursuit of retreating enemies became a hallmark of later campaigns, and this early example at Lodi forced the Austrians back in haste beyond the Adda.

Napoleon chose to use a later, similar but less serious, engagement at Arcola in November – the bridge crossing on the River Alpone near Mantua – to glamorise himself, but Lodi was his real triumph as a leader from the front. Austrian artillery covered the advance to the bridge and the causeway leading to it from high ground across the Adda, and the crossing was taken by sheer courage. Napoleon, Masséna, Augereau and even – indeed, especially – the paper-shuffling Berthier led the infantry columns personally, both across the bridge and wading through the river, assailed by fire. This was all done after hours of hard marching over sodden ground. It was a collective effort, as the subsequent propaganda made clear. The later self-glorification of Arcola, immortalised by Gros' famous painting of Napoleon leading the charge alone, was for civilian consumption. Napoleon had no need of this with his own men after Lodi, and he could paint himself as he liked for mere civilians. Now the ranks knew he could fight, sword in hand, alongside them. His officers had long had confidence in him; henceforth, he was a legend to the men. Lodi was the birth of 'his army', of the bond with his men. More pertinently, Beaulieu fell back and, most importantly, the road to Milan lay open.

It was after Lodi, Napoleon later said, that he first felt the hand of greatness upon him – 'that I believed myself to be a superior man'. This was tested immediately. Before the army even reached Milan, orders came from Paris that the command of the Italian front was to be divided. Napoleon was to turn a much reduced force south to coerce the petty states and token armies of Tuscany and the Papacy, while the main body of the Army of Italy was to amalgamate with the Army of the Alps, which had been brought up behind Napoleon, under the experienced Kellermann, who would assume the main task of attacking the Austrians in the passes. Napoleon vigorously and successfully opposed this, and showed both his own convictions as a strategist and a new-found ability to play politics in the process. He argued that it was dangerous to divide a command at the best of times, but particularly in the present circumstances, when the enemy's intentions remained unclear and the Austrians still had several offensive options open to them. Knowing Carnot understood strategy, he wrote to him from Lodi, '... it would be better to have one bad general than two good ones. War is like government, it is about tact ... Yet I wholeheartedly do not want to lose in eight days [the gains] of two months of exhaustion, difficulties, and dangers, and do not want to see myself ensnared.'[12] To the Directory collectively he stressed that Beaulieu was far from beaten, that Mantua remained a threat, that to divide the army now was dangerous, and that Beaulieu had been reinforced with 10,000 fresh troops because the French delay in reopening an offensive on the Rhine had released Austrian troops for Italy.[13] Two days later, from Milan, and with almost composed, sarcastic understatement, he informed the Directors: 'I am sending you a letter of exchange for 650,000 *livres*. Perhaps you will find a use for it.'[14] He balanced reason with an appeal to avarice, not for the first time, and not for the last. He kept his command, and received Kellermann's troops as reinforcements into the bargain – the first Paris had ever accorded the Army of Italy.

Napoleon was now also the master of Milan, the city and the capital of the province that would become his first personal power base. The French entry into Milan was a strange affair, but it spoke volumes for the state of things present and yet to come in northern Italy. The wealthy, prosperous Milanese beheld a ragtag army, unprepossessing men led by an equally scruffy youth, but they beheld victors, nonetheless. Milan was the largest, richest city the Army of Italy had yet to encounter. Its population was something between 111,000 and 120,000 – larger than most French provincial cities by some way – and dominated by a commercial bourgeoisie made wealthy by the agricultural richness of the well-cultivated Lombard plain and by its position as a route centre. It was wealth that dated from time immemorial, even if Milan was primarily a regional centre. It was still a medieval town, for the most part, its elites still content with the splendours they had inherited, a cityscape where vast open spaces were rare, but with a rich architectural heritage.[15] The city was dominated then, as now, by its magnificent cathedral of St Mary the Virgin, a

Gothic mass of intricate statuary and lace-like masonry on the outside
– all surmounted by a gleaming gold Madonna – and a stark, austere
interior, the work of its great sixteenth-century reforming Archbishop,
St Carlo Borromeo. Milan may have lacked modern industries – its
artisan classes still relying on small-scale, high-quality production –
and its commercial classes might have tended to provincialism, but the
eighteenth century had seen the city emerge as the unofficial capital
of the Italian Enlightenment. The more cultivated among the French
were captivated by it. Henri Beyle, better known under his pen name,
Stendhal, served there under Napoleon, and fell in love with a city he
felt rivalled 'all that the imagination . . . could dream of', in the beauty
of its architecture and above all, its great opera, La Scala, 'the premier
theatre of the world'.[16] His was not the view of the rank and file. What
the French troops saw was a soft, defenceless society they soon came
to regard as degenerate and, for all its material wealth, inferior to that
which produced men who could fight with half-empty stomachs and
march forever in rotting boots, if they had them, or on calloused feet,
if they did not. Their contempt for the city, and for religion, can still
be seen in the graffiti some of them carved with their bayonets into
the beautiful statues at the west door of the cathedral. Napoleon, for
his part, saw his chance to be more than a soldier. It was in Milan that
Napoleon transformed himself overnight from an inspired 'operator'
into a visionary. He saw in Milan his very own capital city.

There was still fighting to do, however. Napoleon had not lied to
Paris about the danger Beaulieu still posed, and he wasted no time in
laying siege to Mantua and pushing north-east after the main Austrian
army. This time, Napoleon risked being in the same position in which
he had found Beaulieu and Colli in Piedmont – sitting in the lowlands,
with an enemy in the passes ready to swoop. For the first time, he was
on the defensive. It was his opponents who had more options: not
only could they attack from several or all the Alpine passes and retreat
easily to safety, but any successful advance might see the 12,000-strong
garrison at Mantua sally forth to disrupt the French rear. Worse still,
Beaulieu could count on a stream of reinforcements and supplies

directly from Austria, which Napoleon could not match. This, at least, was how Napoleon had to calculate his odds.

Napoleon's first siege of Mantua, in July, was abandoned with the loss of 179 cannon, which had to be left behind when he needed to divert these troops rapidly to counter an Austrian thrust from the Alps. The siege proved very costly to the army, a practical loss of materiel. The looted art treasures and huge indemnities extorted from Tuscany and the Papal States by Augereau – in what was little more than a barbarian raiding expedition south, in June – made a big impression on the Directory, but it only deprived the real front of much-needed resources. Napoleon had learned the hard way that he could not besiege Mantua and stem the assault of the main enemy forces at the same time. An Alsatian cavalryman, Wurmser, had replaced Beaulieu, and brought another 25,000 fresh troops with him, building the army in the Tyrolean Alps and around Trento up to about 50,000 men, although those battered by Napoleon were demoralised and in need of reorganisation. The new general now sent three columns to relieve Mantua: one went down each shore of Lake Garda, and the third down the valley of the River Brenta, to the east. The French were driven out of Verona and now Wurmser threatened to undo everything.

What followed was desperate, but it vindicated Napoleon's emphatic belief in a centralised command. His only hope was to co-ordinate his defensive line against Wurmser's relatively ill-timed assaults, and this he did. Masséna bore the brunt of the first attacks by Quasdanovitch's column, and he was turned back; Napoleon carefully positioned Augereau to protect his flank, and when Wurmser attempted to envelop Masséna and link with Quasdanovitch – who was no longer in the field – Augereau checked him at Castiglione, on 3 August, which is generally regarded as the prototype of how Napoleon preferred to fight. A hallmark of Napoleonic tactics became securing his flanks from being overrun by placing one of his best commanders wide on a potentially exposed wing. Wurmser did not know the whereabouts of Quasdanovitch, but Napoleon knew where all his own forces were. He was able to bring his three divisions – totalling 30,000 men – to bear on the now isolated Wurmser's 25,000. Numerical inferiority had been turned, through centralised co-ordination, into unsuspected parity. Masséna and Augereau took the brunt of the fighting, forced marches bringing their troops together, while Sérurier closed off Wurmser's left, leaving him no alternative but to withdraw back up the valley; even had he fought his way through Masséna, he risked being cut off still further from his support. The French retook Verona on 7 August. Napoleon had lost about 6,000 killed and wounded, the Austrians 16,700 and 4,000 prisoners.[17] Quick, clear thinking at the top was matched by hard marching and the ferocious fighting ability of the troops. The army had come a long way, in every sense, and shown it could respond not only to pressure exerted by an enemy with all the advantages, but to complex orders in difficult circumstances. David Chandler rightly concluded: 'The Napoleonic method of campaign was rapidly evolving.'[18] So, from top to bottom, were the men who did the campaigning.

The Austrians were far from finished, however, and d'Alvintzi actually broke through to Mantua in late September. Again, carefully co-ordinated hard marching simply cut him off and left him trapped there. In early November, the Austrians under Quasdanovitch and d'Alvintzi tried again to raise the siege with a twin-pronged attack down the Adige and the Trento, which almost worked. The French were initially thrown back, with heavy losses, while d'Alvintzi was receiving reinforcements and now had 23,000 men in the field. Napoleon's response was already his trademark manoeuvre – 'the advance on the rear'. He moved up the Adige, behind d'Alvintzi, and cut his lines of communication, forcing him to halt his advance and to face the French on ground of their own choosing, a narrow marsh between the rivers Adige and Alpone. The result was the fierce three-day Battle of Arcola, 16–18 November. Despite the heroic imagery of the battle, it ended with the Austrians retreating intact, if badly mauled. Napoleon had indeed charged the bridge, colours in hand, on the first day – a desperate as much as an heroic reaction to stiff resistance – but had actually been held back by his staff officers, so great was the danger.

At the end of it, d'Alvintzi was still there, at the top of the passes, still with a choice of three routes to Mantua, which was still holding out; he was reinforced and now had 45,000 men – numerical parity with the Army of Italy – but Napoleon had to detach 10,000 troops to besiege Mantua. Paris had grand designs, set on seeing him advance on Vienna, yet in truth Napoleon could do little but dig in and await the next assault as best he could. It came in January 1797, when d'Alvintzi advanced down the Adige with 28,000 men and was met by the French at Rivoli, a good defensive position that d'Alvintzi could only approach by narrow roads. In the main battle, the Austrians succeeded initially in cutting off Napoleon's main force, but his break-out – which saw the use of shock tactics by both cavalry and infantry – split the Austrians and isolated them from another column heading directly for Mantua. Napoleon had to turn to deal with this, allowing the Austrians one last stand at Rivoli, the command of which Napoleon had turned over to Joubert. His confidence proved justified: the Austrians were trapped in the narrow gorges, more than 11,000 prisoners were taken, while another 3,000 had been killed or wounded. Retreat was all that was left. This was a victory for the infantry, above all; in close, prolonged fighting, the Army of Italy had reduced 48,000 fresh Austrian troops to a hounded, scattered rabble of 13,000. For the first time, there was no orderly, tactical retreat. At last, the imperial army had been properly routed. Finally, on 2 February, Mantua and its 30,000 men capitulated.

Northern Italy was now in Napoleon's hands, and the first thing he did was raid the Papal States – his instinctive response to the recent 'peace dividend' – to extort thirty million francs from the Pope for the French war effort – and to remind Paris it had all been worth it. The Directory actually agreed. Italy was now seen as the main theatre of operations, because it was Napoleon, now ensconced in the Venetian Alps on the edge of the Tyrol, who was within striking distance of Vienna, not his rivals on the Rhine, Hoche and Moreau. The Army of Italy was brought up to 80,000 men, and advanced over the Alps, on the offensive again, and headed 'down the hill' as in Piedmont a year before. The Austrians had a new commander, Archduke

Charles, the son of Emperor Francis, and he would become one of Napoleon's most formidable opponents. On their first meeting, he forced Napoleon to take an enormous risk, to advance, almost cut off, from his base at Trieste. Napoleon reached Leoben, only seventy-five miles from Vienna and, knowing how exposed he was, turned to diplomacy. He sued successfully for an armistice and gambled that the French offensive on the Rhine would place such pressure on Vienna that a permanent peace would follow. On the last day of the truce, with Hoche and Moreau poised to break through across the Rhine, Emperor Francis agreed to a permanent cessation of hostilities. The peace was not formally concluded until the Treaty of Campo Formio on 17 October 1797, but the fighting was over. Fittingly, the great gamble had ended with an act of supreme brinkmanship.

Behind the Alpine lines, much had been going on, all of it of tremendous import both for Napoleon and for the future history of Europe. As so often the case in Napoleon's career, the sound of battle had proved an effective cover for other, deeper happenings.

THE 'HOME FRONT': ITALIAN REVOLTS

Another, utterly inglorious but indelible, pattern of behaviour accompanied the lightning advance into Italy. The advancing French army brought havoc, resentment and civilian resistance in its wake, and saw it stir anew in its rear. Peasant communities suffered pillage, rape and random murder; they responded – where the terrain allowed – with guerrilla war, ambushes, and behaviour that bordered on banditry. In May 1796, as the army advanced into the 'richest plains in the world', even in exposed, heavily occupied urban centres like Verona, Pavia, Rimini and Lugo, resistance was attempted, even though the result – brutal French repression – was all but inevitable. This was a legacy of the Revolution Napoleon was never able to shake, but something he would later devote considerable time and energy trying to reverse and appease. The spring and summer of 1797 saw the valleys of the Piedmontese Alps and Apennines rise in a spate of atomised but genuinely savage revolts, after a year of vexatious requisitions, heavy-handed military occupation and the supposed complicity in all this of local royal officials and pro-French 'Jacobins'. The *barbetti* – semi-bandit local militias of the Alpine passes – reconstituted themselves, only now they fought eastward from the mountain passes; the bandit-smugglers of the Ligurian border – so long a thorn in the side of Victor-Amadeus – now became his champions. Urban centres rose as well, despite being so exposed to their occupiers. Verona, the great city of the Po Valley, was the most brutal in its reaction to the French occupation. In April, its people exploded in rage, killing over 400 French troops. A by now predictable sacking followed, but the revolt of Verona would have wider consequences. It was in Venetian territory, and the rising helped serve as a pretext for Napoleon's abolition of the whole republic at the Armistice of Leoben, only days later. This was an early sign that Napoleon could not keep order in the areas he occupied, save by brute force.

The leitmotif of his attitude to civilian resistance, with the war his priority, is summed up in what became his most famous quote on the subject, 'Burn a village.' Nor was it an idle utterance. The unfortunate victim of the word made deed was Binasco, in Lombardy, where on 25 May 1797 the French responded to local resistance the previous day by massacring the 600 or so peasants who confronted them and levelling the village to the ground. It was hardly the first village obliterated by the Revolutionary juggernaut, nor would it be the last, but Napoleon made it famous as the manifestation of his will. Binasco was a window on his mind that spring, and, as such, a policy statement. His own, crisp report to Berthier says it best:

A vast conspiracy was hatched against us: Milan, Pavia, Como, all rose against us at the same moment . . . While returning [to Milan] on the side road to Pavia, we were met by 1,000 peasants from Binasco, we beat them. After having killed one thousand [of them] we burned the village, a dread example and a useful one; in an hour, we will march on to Pavia where they are said still to be resisting us.[19]

Pavia did indeed resist, its local militia bravely defying Napoleon's veterans. On 26 May, Napoleon stormed the city, and every armed man was immediately killed: 'I take it that you have shot those who were taken in arms,' he calmly wrote to his subordinate, Despinoy.[20] It is what followed that really was chilling. He turned the city over to the troops for a twenty-four-hour spree of rape, looting and murder. If he could not obliterate the great city, as he could Binasco, he took out its heart.

There was more to this than the shocked, fearful vengefulness of a tired, exposed army in alien territory. Napoleon's orders to his troops mouthed platitudes about respecting the religion and mores of their 'Italian hosts' whom they had, after all, come to liberate, but in truth he did little to curb the desecration of churches, monasteries or even convents – and the Army of Italy had a particular penchant for terrorising nuns – as they advanced into the heart of the Catholic world. As Tim Blanning has said, 'anger often overruled prudence'.[21]

Many of his most hardened, long-serving soldiers were, in fact, the remnants of the Parisian *sans-culottes*, the stormtroopers of radical Jacobinism whose anti-clericalism was deeply ingrained and whose brutality towards Catholic, rural populations had been honed in sweeps around the outskirts of Paris in search of grain during the Terror, and in the bloody recapture of rebellious cities like Lyon and Toulon while suppressing the Federalist revolts. Napoleon did nothing to change their opinions or their conduct, for he shared them.

Contempt for Italian culture was always evident, and sometimes it had firm foundations. In February 1797, Napoleon swung south again to raid the Papal States, partly with the intention of annexing the Pope's Adriatic port of Ancona to the new state he would proclaim in April, the Cispadane Republic, which he was carving out of the Duchy of Modena and papal territory around Bologna. In July, he would unite the Cispadane to the Cisalpine Republic, which he had carved out of Austrian Lombardy. On 10 February, in a letter to the Directory, he called the Papal States 'the most ridiculous of governments'.[22] There was a concrete reason for this, not just a general, anti-clerical prejudice. The previous day, possibly for the first time, Napoleon had encountered an organised Jewish community, for Ancona had one of the largest in western Europe. As Jews did throughout the Papal States, they lived in a ghetto, under evening curfew, and were forced to wear yellow stars. As corroborated in a contemporary Jewish chronicle, Napoleon's spontaneous reaction was to send a detachment composed of Jewish soldiers to tear down the walls and rip off the yellow stars. He emancipated them from all papal restrictions, and the community hailed him for it. Later, he invited a Jewish delegation from Ancona to see him in Milan, where he welcomed them warmly.[23] In the meantime, he appointed three Jews to the municipal council and told Paris, 'My plan is to gather together as many Jews there as possible' to make Ancona into the Cisalpine's entrepôt for lucrative commerce with the Middle East.[24] His trip to Ancona reinforced Napoleon's contempt for Italian Catholicism, however much he might later try to appease the Church.

It has often been assumed that Napoleon's Corsican background created a natural affinity between the Italians and himself, but the complete reverse seems to have been true. Napoleon understood the Catholic, Mediterranean world, but he had turned his back on it and come to despise it. However, the bonds he had severed helped forge a useful one with his men. They all felt an intrinsic contempt for, as well as a new-found fear of, the world around them. This is all the truer, because he had plans for Lombardy. He was going to educate its people, rich and poor, peasant and bourgeois and noble, to be French, just as he had his own family. It was the first instance in his public life of his assimilation with the 'civilising mission' Revolutionary France felt towards the rest of Europe. Town and country burned in his passing and in his wake, but his resolve to conquer and to build a new France in Italy remained unshaken. Only a few miles from the rotting corpses and smouldering embers of Binasco, in the splendour of his new headquarters at Mombello, Napoleon would issue constitutions for new states, see visions of a new Italy, of a new society – and of a new Napoleon.

MOMBELLO: THE MEETINGS OF THE PUBLIC AND
PRIVATE SPHERES

The agenda of the Armistice of Leoben shows how far both Napoleon
and his country had come by the spring of 1797, although its very
existence was also an admission of partial weakness: Napoleon and the
Austrians had fought themselves to a standstill, with the odds slightly
in favour of the latter, until Hoche and Moreau appeared on the point
of tipping the balance in favour of France through their victories
over the main Austro-Russian armies on the Rhine and in Switzerland. Nevertheless, Napoleon and his masters now at least had gained
enough time to pause for thought and consolidate their gains.

Napoleon – as quite distinct from the Directory – now held
northern Italy; if Emperor Francis wanted it back, he would have
to fight for it without the pivot of Mantua; he had effectively lost
the Austrian Netherlands, the left bank of the Rhine and military
control of Switzerland. This is not to say Francis could not regain
them – he would do so, fleetingly, two years hence – and Napoleon
knew this better than he did. Two factors made Napoleon divert
from the diplomatic course his masters in Paris wanted to impose on
him between Leoben and its formal sanction at Campo Formio, in
November. The weakness of the army was the more obvious of the two.
His army had done all it could and needed rest and reinforcements
after prolonged Alpine fighting, therefore Napoleon knew better
than Paris that this was no time to drive hard bargains or antagonise
Vienna unduly. The Directory's policy was always in flux: if they were
winning, they wanted to drive hard bargains, but Paris was not aware
of the price of the fighting – it did not want to know that the army
needed to rest. As Steven Englund has put it, 'he was aware that the
final and most important battle of this conflict was to be won over a
green felt table, not in an Alpine valley'.[25] What made that last battle
– of what had begun as a secondary front a few months earlier and
remained so for Paris – so important for him, however? This was the
second factor that gave Napoleon a lesson in negotiated settlement.

Despite his successes, the Directory never regarded the Italian front as more than a sideshow, whereas it was everything to Napoleon. He, not the Directory, was the one with something to lose in Italy. Paris wanted dead Austrians and Italian plunder; Napoleon now had a country – a fiefdom, a power base – all of his own in northern Italy, and he wanted to keep it. Cobenzl, the chief Austrian negotiator at Campo Formio and a veteran diplomat, asked Napoleon at one point, 'Why do you have more interest in taking care of those little republics than you do in dealing with us?'[26] The answer would become clear, but it is interesting that it was not yet obvious, even to some of the brightest minds in European politics. Napoleon somehow concealed his new vested interest, and he learned how to negotiate to protect his gains without appearing to be self-interested. To keep the core of his new power base, Napoleon acceded to the Austrian annexation of the Republic of Venice, perhaps the oldest state in Europe.

The bartering of Venice was greeted with shock and horror by the Italian 'Jacobins', and Napoleon has been almost universally reviled for it by historians ever since. Only one Director opposed the bargain, however, and there was nothing unprecedented either in the nature of the horse-trading or in Napoleon's own behaviour. He had dealt gently with Genoa and Piedmont, when necessary, and harshly with Tuscany and the Papacy, when Paris wanted plunder. Now he adapted to the circumstances yet again. Napoleon seems to have coveted Venice – all his dealings with the Papacy and Victor-Amadeus reveal how hungry he was to expand the Cispadane and then the Cisalpine republics at every opportunity – but he had to bargain with something at Campo Formio, something he, not Paris, had in gift, to hold on to what he could.

What Napoleon was discarding in his treatment of Venice was less his Jacobinism than the foreign policy of their hated rivals, the Girondins, whom Robespierre had ruthlessly disposed of in the spring of 1793. The French Republic had long abandoned the near-insane idealism of 1791–2, with its lunatic, provocative promise to bring 'peace to the cottage and war on the castle' and to liberate Europe from the old order. Robespierre, then almost a lone voice, had told the Girondin ministry in 1792, when they declared war on the rest of the world, that no one likes armed missionaries. Napoleon had learned this at first hand, the hard way, at Verona, at Pavia, at Binasco. The real wonder is that he persisted with his constructive plans for the Cisalpine at all. Even to dream of such reforms, he had to hold on to Lombardy.

The crux of Campo Formio, from Napoleon's personal perspective, was the conjoining of his military weakness with his new-found self-interest in northern Italy. This was also true behind the lines. The French were hated with a venom by the Italian masses, and Verona had been one of the most violent expressions of this resentment. There was a very real possibility – which Napoleon could not admit to, even to himself – that to attempt to create too large a state in these circumstances would have weakened his grip critically. He had something considerable to lose and lacked the means to defend all of it. In terms of his personal evolution, the talks that took place at Leoben and Campo Formio, however cynical historians have judged their results to be, showed that Napoleon was capable of compromise. He has been loathed, particularly by Italian nationalists, for ceding Venice back to Austria in these negotiations, but, had he reverted to his earliest lessons in diplomacy in 1813–14, history would have been made differently. The emphatic nature of his huge victories between 1805 and 1809 led him to lose this ability. Clear eyes may be cynical, but they are at least realistic, and see the world as it is rather than as it should be. The supreme irony of Campo Formio is that it resembles the approach to diplomacy and international reordering that dismantled Napoleon's hegemony at Vienna in 1814.

Soon after his return from the Alpine front, an exhausted Napoleon established his headquarters in the sumptuous surroundings of the palace of Mombello, an elegant eighteenth-century villa near Lake Como, just north of Milan, which had been used as a political rendezvous, akin to a modern conference centre, under the Habsburgs. There, he did something as unheralded and singular as any of his military or diplomatic exploits since he crossed the Alps a year earlier: he set up a proto-royal court. His extended family joined him there, and Mombello became a magnet for every ambitious person within the confines of his creation, the Cisalpine Republic, who sought favour and advancement. Out of the blue, in the words of Philip Dwyer, 'Bonaparte received homage as if he had been born to it',[27] but, then, he had done many things since March 1796 as if he had been born to them, and receiving homage was the least demanding. A rigid etiquette, isolating Napoleon from all around him and regulating access to him, was quickly put in place.

How he knew the ways of a court are a mystery. On one level, Philip Dwyer has probably made the best assessment in speculating that he gleaned it from Joséphine's knowledge of *ancien régime* etiquette. Dwyer's other observations, however, that no other revolutionary general in occupied territory, with a potential power base at his feet, ever behaved in such a way, and that the most obvious impact of the new formality was to 'place a distance between the prince, or in this case the general, and those in his entourage, so that they were obliged to look up to him', as at Versailles,[28] suggest psychological motives driven by supreme egotism. Napoleon's self-belief was obvious, but the nature of his success was unique in western history up to that time. Men of obscure origins had won great victories and conquered extensive territories in the generations before him, but none had been free to rule or shape them as they wished. This was the direct result of the opportunities created by the French Revolution, with its mixture of democracy, chaos and now, at last, military success. Napoleon, a commoner, had usurped the prerogative of monarchs less by conquering northern Italy, than by making it his own.

There were no modern or recent historical precedents for the circumstances Napoleon, or his generation of Frenchmen, found themselves in. What marked Napoleon's generation was their sense of uniqueness. Luigi Mascilli Migliorini catches this well when he observes that the only period of human experience they felt they could identify with was the classical past.[29] Suddenly, the classical formation of Napoleon and his fellows became acutely relevant. There was one book they had all read that had something for everyone in it, the eighteenth-century French translation of the sixteenth-century English translation by North, of Plutarch's *Lives of the Noble Greeks and Romans*, short biographies in the vernacular – not the original Greek – of colourful characters. This was what they read in their own time, alongside the formal set texts of Caesar, Livy, Cicero and the poets.

For radical republicans in the 1790s, the history of democratic Athens, assailed by Persian despotism, or the struggles of the young Roman Republic against Carthage on the one hand and its home-grown, patrician enemies on the other, were the obvious analogies: the lives of the Gracchi, Cincinnatus, Cato the Elder and Aristides were exemplars for them. Rousseauist visionaries could turn to Romulus, Solon and Lycurgus. Even angry, dispossessed royalists had Coriolanus and Sulla to emulate.

Napoleon's propaganda drew on the image of Scipio Africanus, the stern Roman republican who finally defeated Hannibal, but the influence of Caesar's *Gallic Wars* was powerful on him throughout his life, as was Plutarch's life of Caesar. Plutarch's *Lives* were paired, however, and Caesar's life was matched with that of Alexander the Great, which was arguably at least as influential on Napoleon, and there was more to empathise with in Alexander's career. Napoleon, like Alexander – but unlike Caesar – had acquired new realms suddenly and as a very young man. Alexander had had to turn abruptly from being a leader of men to ruling a great but defeated and degenerate culture; he did so through *grandeur,* driven by the need to isolate his former comrades from decisions and politics that rough soldiers could not grasp. In comparing Caesar and Alexander, Plutarch heaped more praise on the latter as a state-builder, in terms that Napoleon would have found more inspiring for him and, he hoped, more apt:

Alexander was driven only by virtue to begin a great war worthy of a king, seeing its goal not as putting the throat of the world under the foot of the Greeks, but of organising the whole world under a peaceful and contented government.[30]

Every schoolboy had read Plutarch, but only Napoleon found himself in a position to live out the lives of Caesar and Alexander. He would often turn to Caesar, but in Italy in 1797 there was more to be learned from Alexander. He had to learn quickly how to rule a foreign people. For Alexander, the solution was to adopt the trappings of Persian despotism; for Napoleon, the answer was to be found at Mombello.

This was an atmosphere – indeed, a way of life – he was quick to recreate as First Consul in 1800, and Jacques-Olivier Boudon has seen in this behaviour an almost immediate manifestation of deliberately monarchical intentions. If so, the path to the imperial coronation was not set out in Paris, in 1800, but arguably at Mombello as early as 1797.[31] It is tempting to see the proto-court of Mombello as something almost instinctive – along with high military command or high diplomacy – in Napoleon, so swiftly did he turn to it, establishing it at the very first opportunity.

For contemporaries, as for historians, the most salient break with previous practice was extending court etiquette to his officers. The officers' mess was still a common table open to all his staff, where discussion took place and efforts were made to impress the commander, but one where he presided in a very formal fashion. It was a controlled gathering. If Alexander had a fatal flaw, according to Plutarch, it was that he spent too much time with his captains at table in far from formal carousing.

Behind this formality lay a deeper practice that Napoleon continued throughout his public life, but which he could not make explicit as he dined publicly, but often alone at the head of a formal table. He was no longer only a military commander, but the head of a civilian regime – the Cisalpine Republic – and he was conducting diplomatic relations with a major power. The army had to be kept out of this milieu, and the court etiquette of Mombello enabled this separation of the military and political spheres. At Mombello and for the rest of his career, Napoleon lavished honours and wealth on his soldiers, but he never let them near the running of civil administration or diplomacy. If the Cisalpine Republic, or the French Republic, or the First Empire were run for their benefit, they were not run by soldiers. Mombello may have betrayed the ethos of the Revolution and fostered an autocracy, but it prevented a military dictatorship. Napoleon – and no one else – ran Mombello, and diplomacy and the process of state-building that went on within its walls. His signature, and his alone, is on the Treaty of Campo Formio, and the most significant absentees are those of his comrades, not French diplomats.

Would that Napoleon had been able to compartmentalise his own family as well as he had his generals.

There was his new wife. It had been difficult getting Joséphine to come to Italy at all. She showed none of the desire of a newly-wed to join her spouse after so abrupt a separation, and probably only did so at the prompting of Barras, who grasped the likely consequences of gossip better than she, especially as it was all well-founded. She came, in the end, for her own good. Napoleon's letters to her are marked by passion, but a passion tinged by insecurity and desperation. The opening of a reply to one of her rare missives, which he found time to write as he strove desperately to prevent the main Austrian army relieving Mantua, encapsulates their unequal relationship: 'I am obliged for the trouble you have taken to send me your news. Your health should be better today, I am sure you are getting better. I strongly advise you to go riding, it cannot but make you feel better.'[32]

He had every reason to be insecure. Joséphine's attitude is marked not just by her behaviour, but by what she did not do – her letters to him were virtually nonexistent, if his to her are to be believed. Given her affair with a young officer, Hippolyte Charles, nine years her junior – with whom she actually travelled to Italy when she did at last come – there was probably not much with which she could have filled a letter. Joséphine had her own reasons for behaving as she did – she had had a life that was traumatic by any standards – but her conduct hardly offered the support and compassion someone in Napoleon's position needed, nor, arguably, what he deserved from her. Once in Italy, however, Joséphine responded to him affectionately – a case of loving the one you are with, as would be proved during his next absence in Egypt – but it was possibly also at Mombello, confronted with the most obvious manifestation of his achievements, that Joséphine realised there was indeed something very special about Napoleon. She played her public role to perfection, entertaining foreign diplomats and guests with the easy grace and charm that made her much loved, and with which the Bonapartes were as yet still unfamiliar. Lubricating the wheels of the 'court' of Mombello with the right blend of formality and warmth, she became central to its life.

His mother, Letizia, his three sisters, his brothers Joseph and Louis, and – at last – his wife and his stepson Eugène, also joined him at Mombello. Involving relatives in, and financing family from, the benefits of public success was not merely normal in this era, it was expected and Napoleon would have been a true monster had he frozen out his own blood; to do so would have been abnormal, almost sociopathic behaviour. Even Robespierre, the austere, fanatical 'sea-green incorruptible' of the Terror – who was never accused of financial corruption or favouritism even by his executioners – brought his Augustin along with him, the brother to whom he entrusted the dangerous posting of Toulon. In Napoleon's case, it was the company he had to contend with, more than what society expected of him as a sibling, that posed problems. The first Bonaparte to benefit directly was Louis, who accompanied Napoleon to Italy on his military staff; Joseph was next, becoming French ambassador to Rome. It was the attention he lavished on their private needs that really occupied Napoleon at Mombello, however. He dug into his own pockets to find dowries for his two sisters, Pauline and Elisa, who were engaged to be married at this time. Elisa married Félix Bacciochi, a fellow Corsican and a middle-ranking officer; it proved a good match, and they were notable among the family for their loyalty to Napoleon; Bacciochio never sought to exploit his connections. Pauline, still only sixteen, was pressured by Napoleon and their mother into marriage with General Victoire-Emmanuel Leclerc, a comrade from Toulon, as a means of curbing her penchant for unsuitable affairs. Pauline emerged at Mombello as a beauty to rival Joséphine, and a great deal of pettiness ensued as a result. As Philip Dwyer has observed, it was the first time the Bonapartes and Beauharnais had met, and in the hothouse of Mombello their animosities and suspicions festered, points were scored and, on the Bonaparte side, ammunition was gathered for later attacks on Joséphine.[33] Their attitude to her was more than justified, certainly at the time, but the future would prove how little they themselves had to offer the author of their good fortune. The milieu was held together by Napoleon's blind love for Joséphine, which no one dared challenge. As a result, he knew nothing of her affair with Charles throughout his time with her at Mombello, perhaps a revealing insight into the mixture of youthful vulnerability and the new-found autocratic isolation of the powerful, as Napoleon had suddenly become. Alexander the Great was indeed the most apt analogy.

There are two views about Napoleon's private life. One holds that he would have been a better human being had he been better loved; the other, that he would have accomplished more had he had the sense not to marry at all, or at least to rid himself of an ungrateful wife and restrain a grasping family. The latter seems the more sensible, and may not have been easier said than done, given that he had the example of his hero, Frederick the Great, before him, who lived the life of the bachelor Oxbridge don when he was not at war. Joséphine was a bad idea; in Louis, he pinned his hopes on the wrong brother; Joseph proved nothing short of a traitor. It was not until 1810 that, in Marie-Louise of Austria, he found a consort, friend and viceroy who was worthy of him. Nevertheless, his relationship with Joséphine brought him Eugène and Hortense – intelligent, loyal to the last, and indispensable in their different ways. This was all impossible to know at Mombello, however, though the evidence he had to hand should have made him turn away from Joséphine. The ruthless clarity of the public man – all the lessons in life he had learned in the saddle and at his desk – deserted him at home. Such behaviour makes him human, if to err is to be human. However juvenile or even obsessive, Napoleon's personal life at Mombello dispels all meaningful personal comparisons with true monsters like Hitler or Stalin, but it does make for a paradox which is best explained, perhaps, by recalling the dangerous, lonely paths he had been forced to tread since he fled Corsica, and the fact that he was still well under thirty. It is in his private life where Napoleon is seen actually acting his age – a twenty-something with a difficult background – whereas in the public arena he had shown, out of the blue, insight and expertise well beyond his years. It is the maturity of the public life that is to be wondered at, not the bewildered, confused passion of his intimate dealings.

Napoleon's ability to secure his advance into Italy and his new-found capacity to exploit his victories in such diverse ways stood in marked contrast to his inability to secure his emotional rear.

In the cold Alpine air a great many cobwebs had been blown away from Napoleon's vision of things. His capacity for clear-eyed ruthlessness was now evident in his approach to campaigning, to diplomacy, to self-publicity, to violent opposition, and, as will become apparent, to state-building. There was no small amount of cynicism in most of his actions. This is undeniable. He had emerged from the intellectual madness of the 1790s with his eyes open to political realities and, behind the grandiosity of Mombello and the carefully crafted, glamorous haze he cast around himself for the French public, he was a man who lived in the realm of the possible. He saw the world for what it was. There were unprecedented possibilities. The world was there for the taking, but it had to be won in battle of one sort or another. Nothing was secure. These insights were gained the hard way, from the straitened circumstances of his own past and the desperate beginnings of the bedraggled army he had found in the Alpine wastes. He could not apply any of this hard common sense to his personal life, however, neither to his feckless wife nor his grasping family. The gap between the personal and the public grew ever wider. Later in its life Mombello became a mental hospital.

4

THE CISALPINE REPUBLIC

An Apprenticeship in Power and a Warning Unheeded

Steven Englund, that shrewd biographer of Napoleon, has concluded: 'The eighteen months from May 1796 to November 1797 constitute perhaps the most complex period in all of Napoleonic history.'[1] Englund is right in his assessment.

Napoleon's military victories in the First Italian Campaign were nothing if not spectacular, but his real genius was in using that spectacle to conceal his real achievements. What the people and the rulers of France saw – and what fascinated them – were the brilliant defeats of the Austrian armies, the collapse of Italian resistance, the looted art treasures and, above all, the vast sums of money extorted by Napoleon and sent home. The Directory's coffers were much fuller than before; Paris could gawp and gloat as the bronze horses from St Mark's Square in Venice, and wagonloads of Renaissance masterpieces flooded into France. Some idea of this can be grasped from the contents of just one of the torrent of letters Napoleon dispatched to the French Directory, written on 14 May 1797 – at the very point when his work on the constitution and institutions of the new Cisalpine Republic were at their most intense:

The [one] million [lire] for [the naval works at] Toulon that I told you of will be sent tomorrow; another one million – half of which is in gold and silver – will go to Paris the day after tomorrow; it can help refit the fleet at Brest ... The Army of Italy has raised 7,000,000 millions [*sic*] since the new campaign. Twenty-five thousand hundredweights of grain and 100,000 francs [worth] of hemp, along with the steel, have left from Trieste for Toulon. The Pope has given us eight million [lire worth] in diamonds

... which should be worth no less than 4,500,000 francs. The costs of the
Army [of Italy] are assured for the months of Prairial, Messidor, Thermidor
and Fructidor ... The objets [d'art] from Rome have been assembled at
Livorno ... The Minister of the Navy must, as a matter of urgency, send
three or four frigates [to collect them].[2]

The constitution of the Cisalpine Republic was promulgated in July
and its committees were hard at work when Napoleon began to
bombard Paris with what it most needed – not just news of victories,
but the fat, juicy fruits of those victories.

The unease Bonaparte now began to cause among the politicians
arose from his independence in matters of foreign policy – the
cavalier way in which, on his own authority, he dealt with Vienna and
the rulers of Italy; at one point, General Clarke had been sent with
instructions to curb his initiatives, but without success. Even these
nascent fears were dulled by his ringing success on the battlefield and
his new-found capacity to make his theatre of operations not just
self-financing but profit-making. It is often said of Napoleon that he
had a remarkable, if thoroughly reprehensible, ability to play on the
weaknesses of others, and his manipulation of French opinion about
his Italian exploits is probably the first significant instance of just this.
Napoleon certainly orchestrated his military successes in the press,
which, as Philip Dwyer astutely notes, he had an uncanny and utterly
unheralded ability to use for his own glorification.[3] He fed publicity
to the French reading public and to the millions who were illiterate,
seizing upon the medium of the popular engraving with an innate
acumen for arresting images. He made sure France knew him as a
warrior and a hero, and all at one remove, for Napoleon was never
seen to be blowing his own trumpet – he paid the piper to do that for
him, as it were. What he intended to do was create a smokescreen to
mask his true intentions, and he succeeded.

This was an art that concealed art, be it the glorification of the art
of war as practised by Napoleon, or, literally, the art he sent home as
the trophies of victory. By portraying himself to the French people
and their rulers as a soldier and a diplomat, Napoleon ensured they

did not dwell on what he considered to be his real triumph – the creation of his own country and, even more so, his remarkable gift for shaping its institutions and making it all run the way he wanted it to. France saw only the spoils of war that Napoleon had accumulated by the autumn of 1796, the icing on the cake. The real prize was the rich territory of Lombardy and the Italian midlands. Napoleon's first, relatively harmless exercise in state-building was the 'Cispadane Republic', so-called because it was south of the *pianura padana*, the plains of the River Po, but this territory comprised the Legations – now the Emilia-Romagna – around the rich city of Bologna, far and away the most desirable province of the Papal States. The Cispadane was only a loose confederation of local patriot governments, however. The vital step was its amalgamation with Austrian Lombardy into the 'Cisalpine Republic' a few months later. Lombardy was the wealthiest province of the Habsburg Empire; it was its traditional milch cow, with a vast commercial agriculture based on rice, a hugely lucrative silk industry and the magnet of the great city of Milan, one of the most prosperous and populous in Europe. The new state was the largest of the 'sister republics' created by French arms; with 3,500,000 inhabitants, it dwarfed the Helvetic Republic (Switzerland), and was more populous than the Batavian Republic (the former Dutch Republic) of the Low Countries. The richness of its pastureland meant that, in a very real sense, Napoleon had seized the most valuable parts of the power vacuum to France's east. He was the virtual master of some of the most valuable territory in Europe.

Napoleon had contributed in no small part to his own good fortune, but even he could not have brought this about all by himself. Perhaps the most important reason for Napoleon's dominant position in his Italian conquests was the revolt of all the French commanders of all the armies over the conduct of the *commissaires de guerre*, the civilian agents sent to the armies by the Directory, who were meant to control the captured resources and civilian populations of the conquered territories. With the generals united against them and their very presence, the Directory's hand was forced and the agents were recalled from all fronts in December 1796. That left the soldiery as the sole French presence in these places. As Philip Dwyer has observed, 'For the first time since the sixteenth century, a French army in the field did not have a civilian representative at the commander-in-chief's side.'[4]

Paris' retreat gave unprecedented scope for all the generals to exploit their conquests, but of them all only Napoleon knew what to do with his, and this is the crucial point. In the hands of another man, it might have amounted to nothing. There are precedents for this assertion. Hoche had tried, without success, to weld his conquests in the Rhineland into a 'Cisrhenan Republic'; even earlier, Pichegru had attempted the same in Belgium. Napoleon succeeded, in the first instance, because he fed the government and the public what it craved; thus buying time, he was able to convert the Cisalpine Republic into a state on which he discreetly applied his own stamp. For the Cisalpine Republic was his work, a country moulded in his own image and by his own thoughts. It was, in short, the first tangible manifestation of his political vision. This was an apprenticeship sprung from a well-mediated, fully mature view of what a state should be; it was marked by few uncertainties and there was no groping around for ideas. That Napoleon knew his own mind and was already able to get what he wanted is the astonishing part of his Italian adventure.

His capacity for state-building once he reached Lombardy in May 1796 is all the more startling when viewed alongside his attitude in the immediately preceding months towards the Republic of Genoa, and then the Savoyard Monarchy. He took great pains to secure his rear through cautious conciliation of the conservative Genoese elite, writing to the Directory at the end of March that attempts to destabilise Genoa were misguided, and that it had to be handled with care if the entire campaign were not to collapse:

Our position with Genoa is very dangerous. It has been badly handled: we have done either too much or not enough; thankfully, however, nothing has come of any of it. The Genoese government has more pull and more power than might be thought. There are only two ways to deal with it: either seize

Genoa by a quick blow – although this is contrary to your intentions and to the people's rights – or live on good terms with them, and not try to extort money from them, which is the only thing they value.[5]

Three days later, he issued a proclamation to the pro-French Piedmontese 'patriots' along the almost standard lines of Directorial policy, inciting the radical elements in the kingdom to rally and rebel for the advancing armies of liberation, which were coming in response to local appeals to him.[6] Although Napoleon consistently protected the Piedmontese 'Jacobins' once in possession of the country, he emphatically dashed their hopes for a sister republic when he concluded the Armistice of Cherasco with Victor-Amadeus III.

Neither of these policies towards the first Italian states he encountered gave the least hint of what he would do in Lombardy only a few months later. Indeed, where he deviated from Directorial policy before he took Milan was in his caution and his apparent support for the old order. Compared to Pichegru and Hoche, Napoleon was – ostensibly – the least ambitious of front commanders. Nothing in Napoleon's previous conduct gave a hint of what he would do with the Cisalpine.

Napoleon did not leave his new realm as he found it. The Cisalpine was divided into twenty departments, once the amalgamation with the Cispadane was completed, and it was given a constitution modelled almost directly on that of Directorial France. Its legislature had upper and lower houses on the French model; the lower house, the Giuniori, numbered about a hundred elected deputies and approved the laws proposed by the upper house, the sixty Seniori, while above them was a five-man Directory, an executive on the French model, who appointed the six ministers of Finance, Interior, Justice, Police, War and Foreign Affairs. Seen in strictly institutional terms, there seemed no cause for concern – Napoleon was not an innovator; he merely cloned French institutions in northern Italy, as any other general would have done, bereft of political ingenuity or imagination. However, appearances were deceptive, as they were intended to be. Behind the institutional façade of the Cisalpine, in turn masked by the smokescreen of military romanticism, this was no Directorial clone. Napoleon was the effective – if half-concealed – chief and sole executive of the Cisalpine, and this practical concentration of power in one pair of hands was to be his trademark.

Napoleon governed the Cisalpine in his own way. He revealed practical approaches to administration and popular politics that were both original and unprecedented, when measured by the many experiments undertaken during the revolutionary decade in France. A plebiscite was used to approve the constitution of the short-lived Cispadane Republic in March 1797; the red, green and white tricolour flag was adopted by the legislature of the Cispadane, and passed on to the Cisalpine, by similar vote.

The process of creating a state typically began with a sleight of hand that could be, and was, interpreted one way, but which actually meant something quite different. Napoleon held a *concours* – in this case an essay competition very typical in eighteenth-century literary circles – for the best projection of a new constitution. The winner was a moderate republican, Melchiore Gioia. His choice pleased radicals because he favoured a united Italy, but Napoleon selected his essay because he believed in tight centralisation – and the Cispadane, with its fractious political life still rooted in localism, was about to be swallowed by the new, very different, Cisalpine. It was all very populist, but such things were superficial sideshows, certainly for Napoleon.

The Cisalpine was a larger, far more durable entity than the Cispadane. Napoleon took the new state seriously, an attitude that expressed itself through authoritarianism, rather than the game-playing that had sapped French strength under the Directory. The two committees that drew up its constitution were composed entirely of his own appointees, and he controlled their work tightly. The lessons he taught himself in how to manage committees would serve him well in the future, specifically in the drafting of the Civil Code in France, between 1800 and 1804, and, more generally, in his masterly ability to direct his greatest administrative creation, the Council of State. That lay ahead; the task in hand was the new republic. The document the two committees produced made the Cisalpine, on paper, the most democratic of the sister republics but, as ever, appearances were deliberately deceptive. The constitutions of the Batavian and Helvetic Republics were more overtly elitist than Napoleon's in Italy, but the former was the work of the Dutch themselves, and the latter reflected the wishes of the Swiss for a federal system. Both tended to preserve local elites in power, but they were not the fiats of foreign occupiers.

Modelled so closely on the French Directory, the constitution of the Cisalpine provided for the appointment of legislators by local electoral assemblies, but, as Carlo Zaghi has pointed out, the documents themselves reveal the extent of Napoleon's personal intervention in their work: he simply wrote over the lists sent to him by the appointing assemblies, putting his own men in. The most famous example of this was his literal crossing out of the famous physicist Carlo Caprare, who had been elected to the upper house, replacing him with a loyal republican, Antonio Aldini, whom Napoleon had known in Paris. Aldini went on to serve Napoleon to the end.[7] Napoleon appointed the five Directors himself, and kept in close correspondence with them at all times until he left Italy, late in 1797. This fundamentally altered the nature of the Republic, making it anything but a French clone, for the Cisalpine had a one-man executive over and above its Directory. No more crucial difference with the regime in France could be imagined. The constitution Paris gave to the Roman Republic, in 1798, had a smaller, more powerful executive than the Cisalpine; called the Consulate and composed of only three members, it foreshadowed the form with which exasperated French politicians would replace the Directory in 1799. The reality, as opposed to the outward appearance of the Cisalpine, showed what Napoleon had in mind for France, but no one in power paid any attention to that.

The few who understood the reality were not best placed to be heard. The only people who seemed to understand what Napoleon was up to – and what he was really like – were disgruntled Italian radicals like Buonarroti (a disciple of Robespierre) or the cynical French royalists of the 'Clichy' circle (named for the area of Paris where they met) – precisely those commentators no one in the political mainstream trusted or listened to, and that was fortunate for Napoleon. The first to feel the lash of Napoleonic censorship were the radical democrats of northern Italy. They took against him very quickly, as he tightened his grip on the spontaneous, anarchic explosion of publications that followed the collapse of the old states. For men like Ugo Foscolo, an Italian writer who was an early supporter of Napoleon, this was the beginning of a long, embittered relationship with a figure on whom they had pinned so much hope, but his sort were relegated to the margins by Napoleon exactly because they carried so little weight; a power base needed men with influence for it to become truly powerful. Likewise, within France in these later months of 1797 the only political commentators to target Napoleon as particularly dangerous and ambitious were the royalists, the 'Clichy Club' and its newspaper in particular. Even the French royalists and the Italian 'Giacobini' did not get it quite right, however. The Clichyans still saw Napoleon as a crazed disciple of Robespierre, a fanatic driven by Rousseauist abstractions[8] – the exact opposite, in fact, of the view formed by Foscolo and his fellow radicals in Italy. Even in his relations with the Italian radicals, Napoleon was not, however, all he seemed to them in their state of stunned disillusion. If he repressed their opinions and excesses, he never abandoned them, for Napoleon was as quick to release them from prison and give them jobs as he was to arrest them. Foscolo himself was given a post in the army administration, from the safety of which he poured out his loathing of Napoleon.

Napoleon had learned the complexities of post-1789 politics with incredible rapidity in Italy. This is probably what really should have caused most alarm. Italian radicals and French royalists made him into a stereotype, but from their own narrow perspectives. There was truth in the radicals' views, but not the *essential* truth; the royalists saw what Napoleon wanted them to see – the mask may have dropped in the Cisalpine, but in France it was still in place. He outlined much of what he had learned to the Directory, and with striking clarity, when he was trying to untangle the political muddle of the Cispadane in its early days. What Napoleon reported to the Directory is frequently quoted, but its importance is profound, displaying as it does his swift, ruthless mastery of complex circumstances. He identified three major factions, from a French vantage point at least:

1. There are the friends of the former governments; 2. The supporters of an independent, if rather aristocratic constitution; 3. The supporters of a French constitution, or of pure democracy. I repress the first, support the second, and restrain the third. I support the second and restrain the third, because the party of the second is that of the rich landowners and the priests who, in the final analysis, will win over the mass of the population, and it is essential to rally it around the French cause. The last party is composed of young men, writers, and men who, as in France and in every country, want to change the government and who love liberty just to have a revolution.[9]

This reveals more than simply an intruder who was quick to understand his new, convoluted surroundings. The addle-headed romantic of only a few years earlier had come a long way, for this is the analysis of a man far older than his years.

Nor did his development stop here. Napoleon would soon cease persecuting the conservatives, provided they co-operated, just as he did with the radicals. His true politics were emerging now, and they reveal what became the two key policies of his first regimes in France: *ralliement* and *amalgame*. *Ralliement* meant rallying to the new regime largely in terms of passive acceptance, of not opposing it, the most that might be hoped of from its reactionary opponents with their vested interests in the old order. This was about negative acceptance, convincing opponents that the game was up, that there was no alternative but to fall in behind the winners. The second, *amalgame*, 'amalgamation', was actually the harder to pull off – at least among civilian politicians – in that it entailed getting former adversaries to work together in the new political framework. It was a very intricate, as well as ambitious, construct, for such policies could never have sparked without a real genius for getting rivals to 'amalgamate'. 'Genius' is a word frequently applied to Napoleon, but it is wholly merited in this respect, and it is often forgotten – as he intended it to be at this stage. *Amalgame* was rooted in a mixture of pragmatism and genuine hope that the bloody fractiousness of the recent past could be ended in the name of efficient government. It could also reveal Napoleon's dark side.

The first president of the Cisalpine's Directory was Giovanni Galeazzo Serbelloni, a Milanese noble who had long supported enlightened reform. Napoleon commented to Paris that there were other, less cerebral reasons that made him reliable:

Citizen Serbelloni, by the good reputation he enjoys in this country, and the primacy his great wealth affords him, is fit to fulfil effectively a place on the Executive Directory; he is, moreover, so thoroughly compromised in the eyes of the Austrians that he is one of the people of whose opinions we can be most assured . . .[10]

Earlier still, in June 1796, Napoleon displayed the same clarity vis-à-vis Serbelloni and 'his comrades': 'they were at the head of the revolution here, and they know well that the House of Austria will never pardon them'.[11] This is not to say that Napoleon disliked or despised Serbelloni; quite the reverse – 'this is a very good man who wants his country to be free and happy', he told Carnot, a sceptical French Director.[12] Nevertheless, there are more sinister ties that bind, and few things bound more Italians to Napoleon than the ruthless repression that followed the brief restoration of the old rulers in 1799, who were often as blind as they were bloody in their targeting of 'collaborators'. It was a logic he would apply to France, and right across Europe, when he got the chance.

When the experience of *amalgame* is set in the context of actually trying to run the mess that was the Cisalpine, it can be seen that Napoleon also learned a hard, practical lesson. Henceforth, he not only knew what he needed to do, he knew who he needed in order to realise his vision, and he carried that lesson forward into his first years in supreme power in France. Circumstances would change, and a new, very different vision would take shape in his thoughts, but more immediately Napoleon had realised that radical republicans made the best secret policemen and the most efficient local administrators, especially in volatile areas. His choice for the Cisalpine's minister of police was Gaetano Porro, an ardent republican,[13] an appointment that foreshadowed that of Joseph Fouché – a man with a very bloody Terrorist past – to the same post in France in 1799. Conversely, the most technical aspects of administration – justice and finance particularly – were where moderate, enlightened reformers of the old order alone could arrest the disorders of the revolutionary years: Justice went to Giuseppe Luosi, a man of moderate reforming credentials,[14] just as judicial affairs would be led by the moderate royalist Cambacérès, when Napoleon came to power in France. He confided the disastrous finances of the Cisalpine to Lodovico Ricci, a cold rationalist of the eighteenth-century Enlightenment, whose reforming elitism had been formed serving the Duke of Modena, and who combined a loathing of noble fiscal privilege with a fear of democracy,[15] a background not unlike that of Napoleon's later choice to run French finances, Charles-François Lebrun. *Amalgame* was not just an ideal, it was a necessity. In time, a role would be found – and a niche created – even for aristocratic reactionaries, in the foreign service and the army. In the Italy of the *triennio*, as the period of French domination, 1796–9, was known, that time was yet to come, however.

For all the eloquent rage of the more intransigent radicals, Napoleon placed considerable trust and authority in those among them who would 'tone it down' and serve the Cisalpine. It was less their numbers at the top of the new state that mattered than the positions they held, and their relative durability in office. The only 'constant' among the Directors was the sole non-noble, radical patriot among Napoleon's first appointments, Marco Alessandri. A committed republican and a convinced believer in a moderate democratic franchise, he alone served throughout the life of the Cisalpine.[16] A very poignant example of *amalgame* in action was Napoleon's ability to persuade the radical Bolognese lawyer Antonio Aldini and the Lombard aristocrat Melzi d'Eril – a supporter of the enlightened, if authoritarian reforms of Emperor Joseph II in the 1780s – to come anywhere near each other. Once together, they represented probably the first example of the harnessing of opposites Napoleon most relied on: Aldini, like Serbelloni, had little choice but to support the French, yet he might easily have gone the way of Foscolo, discontented and full of hatred. Napoleon ensured he did not, and his voice was often heard defending the regime in the upper house. Melzi spoke out, too, particularly after Napoleon's departure, supporting and cajoling Ricci. Melzi's adherence to the Cisalpine was cautious, suspicious and uneasy. He loathed Aldini, favoured press censorship, and suspected Alessandri's competence; his vision was of a dictatorship of property owners. He entered public life, nonetheless.

They all rallied quickly to Napoleon in 1800, on his return: Alessandri became a senator of the Republic/Kingdom of Italy, the successor state to the Cisalpine, while Melzi became its Vice-President. Aldini remained a thorn in Melzi's side after 1800, but went on to hold very senior ministries under the republic and came to real prominence after 1806, when Melzi – with some irony – resigned, finding Napoleon too authoritarian. With equal irony, Aldini did not. Their joint story is a microcosm of *amalgame*, a tale repeated all over the empire in the years to come.

The bleating of radicals like Foscolo and the sullen withdrawal of reactionaries notwithstanding, only avowed extremists were ejected from Napoleon's republic. He found institutional means to include as many points of view as he could, and soon learned how to manipulate those institutions the better to control them. His upper house was largely composed of more moderate republicans and those supporters of the old order not quite disgruntled enough to ignore the new politics, whereas the lower, larger chamber was full of more radical reformers. They were all there, and they clashed. When they did so, Napoleon and the Executive Directory held the ring, arbitrated and got their way, but only after everyone, from a wide political spectrum, had had their say. It was a classic case of divide and rule that depended on a strong, one-man executive. After Napoleon was recalled in November 1797, it all fell apart, for the five-man Executive Directory could not control the two houses, and soon found itself at odds with them. Napoleon's system was inclusive, but its façade disguised one-man control with the illusion of the balance of power. The real lesson was that true inclusion had to be bought at the price of the concentration of power in Napoleon's hands. It is not possible to know precisely how Napoleon did this in daily practice, although the memoirs of certain individuals of the time speak clearly of his powerful magnetism and his ability to inspire confidence in those around him, in him as well as in themselves.

Napoleon's framework for the Cisalpine Republic stood on uncertain ground, for when the terms of the constitution were announced they ran the risk of pleasing no one. The constitution was too radical for moderates, too conservative for radicals, yet men of both tendencies came forward to serve it, and worked together. However, when Napoleon left Italy, *amalgame*, and not just the Cisalpine itself, fell apart. Ricci resigned, disgusted by the humiliating, exploitative 'treaty of alliance' Paris foisted on the republic in February 1798. Napoleon had a hand in the treaty, and its terms showed he could exploit as easily as he could create. His aims were purely military, as the treaty garrisoned 25,000 French troops on the Cisalpine at its expense, while demanding it raise its own army of about the same size. This was the first of many times Napoleon would make alliances on such terms. Conversely, with Napoleon distracted, the new French representative, Trouvé, abolished Porro's potentially powerful police ministry and purged the Cisalpine government twice in the space of a few months, imposing a new constitution on it.

Napoleon left a mess behind him, aspects of which he would probably not have been able to control, and so his absence from the helm of the Cisalpine by 1798 was fortuitous: its finances collapsed, its politics imploded and popular discontent seethed, even before the successful Allied counter-offensive of 1799. That being so, the impression he left among the 'amalgamated' was of someone less cynical and brutal than Trouvé, and who had at least created the skeleton of a reformed order and left hope in his wake. None doubted that what had been done, for good or ill, was Napoleon's own work.

Some of the successes of *amalgame*, and of the Cisalpine itself, are neither mysterious nor subjective. The Cisalpine was a product of Napoleon's personal will, but it was not a state built on the personality of a charismatic leader. The core reforms Napoleon drove through quickly had wide support from all Italian reformers, from Melzi to Foscolo, because they embodied the essence of the Revolution of 1789, which itself brought to fruition many of the projects of eighteenth-century absolutists like Joseph II. Most of these measures remained frozen on the statute books in 1796–7, but they returned, and were realised, under Napoleon, in 1800.

The composite nature of the new state made its administrative life more than difficult, but the principle involved – the smashing of long sacrosanct borders – set an exhilarating precedent for the future. Napoleonic legislation introduced open, public trials under laws that embraced the whole territory of the republic and paid no regard to the previous privileges of cities, nobles or clergy; internal customs tolls were abolished and thus one of the most hoped-for reforms of enlightened thinkers was realised – domestic free trade. Freedom of conscience and religion were embodied in the constitution. The state was now secular, and uniform across the whole national territory, regardless of the laws of the former Italian states. Taken together, these reforms reveal much about Napoleon's future priorities. A new political culture had entered Italy. Napoleon's commitment to legal reform – to the abolition of all privilege, feudal, regional, personal – was adamant in 1796, and would remain so. His unquestioning maxim was administrative centralisation and modern fiscal administration. Moreover, he was prepared to see these measures established and working, in the most adverse of circumstances. A wide spectrum of progressive opinion could rally to this determination; fewer – but enough – could amalgamate just enough to implement it. Napoleon took much from Italy, but these lessons were the most precious in the long run, and by far the most important for the future history of Europe.

Ruling the Cisalpine revealed for the first time Napoleon's determination to impose centralised, modern administration on whatever polity he might control; for Italian reformers, the Cisalpine became a beacon of what might be, with its flag, independent, sovereign institutions and its embryonic army. Napoleon did not get far, but after this apprenticeship he at least knew the odds stacked against his vision. His Italian domain was nothing if not a composite state, a proto-empire. At its height, the Cisalpine Republic comprised territories from six previously independent states. Its core was Austrian Lombardy, with 1,550,000 people; the Papal Legations, centred on Bologna, held 950,000; the Duchy of Modena over 380,000; former Piedmontese provinces 346,000; and there were also small parts of Switzerland and, briefly, Venice. These states had utterly different public spheres, yet Napoleon won fundamental support across a wide spectrum of the Italian elites in his determination to impose a French regime across this complex territory. There was little he could do in the few months circumstances allowed him in 1796–7, but his determination and the precise nature of that determination were very clear. 'Each department must not exceed 180,000 inhabitants,' he told the Cisalpine Directory in October 1797, a month before he left his power base.[17] It was a vain hope, for the local administration of the republic was a shambles, yet it revealed how seriously Napoleon took the minutiae of government at so early a stage. It was not the kind of thing that got back to Paris, and that was how Napoleon wanted it. More important than his failure to make such policies an instant reality in the Cisalpine was the very fact that no one in France knew he was running a state of his own, and so, they would continue to under-estimate him. Fate allowed him another, prolonged, opportunity to transform his Italian domain after 1800. It was one he would not waste.

Nevertheless, the contemporary reality was harsh. Napoleon could demand of his government 'the overview of the expenses of each ministry' and a 'general plan of the finances for the Republic',[18] but his own extortions rendered this a mockery. It revealed how hands-on he was determined to be, and showed how serious a very young general was, as a head of state, but the financial position of the Cisalpine degenerated relentlessly, and it was all his fault. Napoleon's apprenticeship in state-building took place in a climate of hatred and hostility among the Italian masses. The peasantry shared none of the aspirations of the reformers, and hated the depredations of the Army of Italy. Revolt preceded and followed the French. Napoleon confronted this with a ruthless logic. The peasant revolts, and the initial urban resistance he had found in places like Pavia and Verona, taught him the limits of inclusiveness; they instilled in him the sure sense that his regime could never be anything but elitist. Binasco proved to him not that the countryside had to be conciliated, but that there would always be villages to burn. So there would be, all the way from Lithuania to Portugal.

His departure in late 1797 allowed him to avoid confronting – or taking responsibility for – the massive revolts of 1799 that accompanied the renewed Allied offensive, but the rumblings left him in no doubt that his vision was not that of the masses. That knowledge did not deter him. His determination to reform civil society along the lines he first undertook in the Cisalpine is all the more striking in this context.

Napoleon had learned many things in Italy: how to lead large armies to victory; how to conduct diplomacy in both the old way and the new; how to manipulate committees and institutions; even how to create states and mould new nations. He had come to know the kind of men upon whom he could rely to run his state, and the kind of men he had to appease to let him do so – who he had to amalgamate, and who he had to rally – just as he now knew the soldiers who would serve him so well in the future. Above all, Napoleon now applied to the public world of politics and diplomacy the hard lesson of his inner life. He chose to use his Italian victories to make Italians into Frenchmen, to give them the public and the intellectual culture of the French Revolution, rather than to let them go their own way with their liberation. He intended to do to them what he had done to himself. He had learned, from the short-lived ferocity of the peasant revolts against his reforms, how elitist and narrow his vision of the future actually was, and so he learned not to concern himself with what the masses thought. He was no longer the angry, lost youth, so akin to the Brutus described by Cicero as someone who 'does not know what he wants, but who wants it very badly'. Napoleon had now, publicly at least, become the man Goethe would meet a decade later and call the spirit of his age. All this he had taken from a few months spent south of the Alps. Inwardly, Napoleon had already decided that a Corsican was something he had once been. He had become a Frenchman. Now Italy knew it, too, and soon France would know it. His was the grandest of all eighteenth-century grand tours. In November 1797, however, with all the self-publicity and redrawing of maps as a shield, this vision was still his secret. As he headed north again, that was exactly how Napoleon wanted it to be. He would now also have to confront what had been going on in Paris – and in the rest of Europe – while he had been south of the Alps.

5

WIDER LESSONS

Delusions of Grandeur, 1797–1800

The lands of Napoleon's new power base in the Po Valley are renowned for the fogs that envelop them in autumn, but they were as nothing to the political murk of the France he returned to in late 1797. Napoleon may or may not have told Miot de Mélito, as he set off north that November, 'I have tasted authority and I will not give it up',[1] but in the unpredictable world of the French Directory, and for most of the next four years, save for sixteen months in Egypt, he would have to keep his newly acquired craving a well-guarded secret. That he usually managed to do so speaks volumes both for his mastery of self and, perhaps even more, for his remarkable ability to be feared and suspected for the wrong reasons. His own self-promotion among the literate, urban French public had successfully depicted him as the bestower of victory, then of peace, and always of rich booty. Napoleon had not been idle in high Parisian politics during his time in Italy, however, and his interventions – carefully contrived and always at one remove – had made him friends and foes in equal measure, but none of them suspected his capacity for wielding power, even if some began increasingly to worry that he might indeed crave it. To understand how Napoleon was regarded in French politics, and why everyone missed the real point, it is best to examine the months before his return to France in November 1797.

The high-handed, arrogantly independent manner in which Napoleon arranged the Peace of Campo Formio may have disconcerted the Directory, but the rapturous reception it received from a considerable swathe of public opinion revealed a widespread desire for peace in France. This became clear in the elections of the summer of 1797, in which the moderate royalists – the clearest advocates of peace – won a majority in the lower chamber of the legislature. More importantly, they found support among two of the five Executive Directors, Barthélemy and the former Terrorist and leading Jacobin Lazare Carnot.

The first move against the royalist threat came from the republican deputies in the chambers, who turned to Napoleon's friend and rival, Hoche. Hoche impetuously took up their cause, and moved his army from the Channel coast against Paris, only to lose his nerve when sternly reminded by the government that he had no right to lead troops so close to the capital. He tamely returned to barracks, and died of tuberculosis that September.

This deprived the republicans of their first choice of saviour, Napoleon of his most glamorous military rival and Joséphine of a former boyfriend, but it also taught Napoleon several crucial political lessons. He was still widely perceived as a 'Jacobin general' in France, and the royalist press in Paris, centred on the 'Clichy Club', had long castigated him as a left-wing fanatic. Thus, from the outset, he knew he had much to fear from the new majority. Equally, the failure of Hoche's coup showed him that he could not rely on the republican deputies in the legislature.

However, when the call for action came again it was from within the Directory itself. The three anti-royalist Directors led by Napoleon's patron, Barras, turned to him to do what Hoche had singularly failed to deliver. Napoleon, still in Italy, dispatched his most markedly Jacobin lieutenant, Augereau, to carry out their orders. Augereau entered Paris with his own hussars – who were officially on leave and so not breaking the law – but only after securing the backing of Hoche's troops, upon whose republican sympathies Napoleon could count. The result was the successful Coup of 18 Fructidor, Year 5 (4 September 1797), which removed Carnot, Barthélemy and General Pichegru – who was unfairly tainted with royalism – from office, as well as purging the newly elected royalist deputies. The Republic had now been secured from the threat from the right, at least in electoral terms. The war would continue, which suited the generals and politicians, if no one else. The French ruling elite – and Napoleon, in particular – had confirmed their collective determination to hold on to the foreign gains made since 1795, at the cost of continued hostilities.

The coup announced the presence of the army in high politics, but it did not really lead contemporaries to associate Napoleon or the other generals with aspirations to power for themselves. Napoleon had acted at the bidding of his political patron, Barras, or so it seemed. Indeed, when the generals began plotting against the new regime installed after Fructidor, they did so as a team. This was crucial, for previously it had been their failure to agree that left their machinations moribund. Both Moreau, a general of the left, and Desaix, an ex-noble with ties to the right, approached Napoleon in the course of late 1797/ early 1798 with a scheme for a coup, but now the idea was always to act in concert, and to replace one defined group of politicians with another. Directors, individually, and political factions, collectively, were living precariously when the army refused to leave politics alone after Fructidor. When royalist generals were involved, the survival of the Republic might have been compromised had they succeeded, but civilian rule of one form or another was not really questioned by the commanders. None of the great commanders – of whom Napoleon was but one – had succeeded in creating a 'sister republic' of his own, save Bonaparte, and it was this singular achievement that should have marked him out as a real threat to whoever deployed him in their interest, yet it did not. Hoche, now dead, had been at least as successful a field commander, even if his victories had been less spectacular than those of Napoleon. Moreau was the true saviour of the nation in 1797, and would be so again in 1800; on both occasions, he led larger armies than those of Napoleon to victory on the main front in southern Germany and Switzerland. Neither, however, had learned to turn military victory into political power, a difference from Napoleon all the more striking in Hoche's case, when he had tried to carve out a 'Cisrhenan Republic'. His lack of initiative had seen his power base dwindle to four French departments before his death. In this respect, more than any other, Napoleon stood apart from all his peers. Fortunately for him, neither friend nor foe seemed to notice.

What the political classes did see in late 1797 was a military commander who had, it seemed, hitched his destiny to that of the Republic; who had remained loyal to his patron Barras and, possibly, to his Jacobin roots. Above all, they saw a conquering hero who could bring a modicum of peace, his hands untied by conniving politicians. Napoleon soon played on this image, dressing in civilian clothes when in Paris and appearing to shun attention while, in fact, drawing it to him.[2] He was right to do this, because the new Directory – however grateful to him it appeared – did, indeed, suspect him, as is evident in how they sought to deploy him after his return from Italy. Napoleon could not go to the theatre without being cheered, which is hardly surprising when many of the plays being produced in these months actually celebrated his achievements on the battlefield and, significantly, at the conference table. He had not just triumphed in war, he had seemingly delivered the peace that royalists could offer only through surrender. His presence was unsettling to those in power who now began to grasp how much they did indeed owe to him, and so began several months of wandering, as a new, safer role was sought for so awkward a hero.

Napoleon was first dispatched to the Congress of Rastatt, a diplomatic gathering between the states of the Holy Roman Empire and France convened to discuss the territorial problems created by the war. His stay there lasted a mere week, a sign that the government, however purged, still feared his capacity to win diplomatic concessions on his own terms. Napoleon's approach to diplomacy has been roundly castigated by his chroniclers, all of whom emphasise his bullying and his overtly 'military' sense of gaining advantage through fierce confrontation. Nevertheless, in 1797 his political masters saw that he had achieved more at the conference table than they had, and quickly had second thoughts about allowing him to do so again. Nor, indeed, was the new French Republic noted for its own skills in international relations. Rastatt was a particularly gross example of its attitude to negotiations with powers it still regarded as ideologically hostile. Directorial policy excluded all ex-nobles from diplomatic service in negotiations or as ambassadors, much to the frustration of their own foreign minister, Talleyrand. Instead, the French delegation at Rastatt was chosen by lot from the deputies, and it contained no men with diplomatic experience and, it seems, few of real intelligence.

Napoleon arrived among them like a whirlwind, in a Berliner coach drawn by expensive horses, but departed quietly, slipping into Paris as a private citizen. This lapse of self-effacing self-control had cost him his place at the centre of major negotiations, but he would not let it happen again, at least in France, until well entrenched in power. Nevertheless, his short stay at Rastatt proved of great lasting importance, if this was far from obvious at the time.

While there, he made the acquaintance of Debry, not the most tactful member of the French delegation, but the most alert, and put him in direct contact with Joseph, with whom he maintained a constant, perceptive correspondence throughout the duration of the Congress.[3] It was also at this time that Napoleon came to the favourable attention of Talleyrand. Their correspondence reveals how useful Napoleon was to the foreign minister in Italian affairs, as in January 1798 when he supplied classified military information – in some detail – to Talleyrand on the distribution and strength of the Army of Italy, of which he was no longer actually in command.[4] Talleyrand showed prudent good sense in cultivating Napoleon, the only successful diplomat the Republic then possessed. Napoleon was, after all, no more rough-hewn than the provincial clerks and former local Terrorists who became his colleagues at Rastatt simply by chance. For Napoleon, the knowledge acquired at one remove via Joseph and Talleyrand gave him an education in German affairs he would draw on immediately in 1800, when circumstances allowed him to take control of foreign policy.

A similar education followed, when the Directory appointed Napoleon commander of the Army of England, at that time strung out along the Channel coast, vainly preparing for an invasion of Britain. Napoleon no more wasted his brief posting here than he had at Rastatt, travelling about the ports, noting their strengths and weaknesses as launch pads, ripping apart the existing plans for embarkation, most particularly the quality of the barges the government proposed to use as landing craft. In a long report to Paris in February 1798, Napoleon outlined in detail the problems – but also the potential – of the invasion plans. He pointed particularly to the unsuitability of Boulogne as a military base, but his copious research was put to immediate use after 1802, in the construction of its military harbour.

As in Rastatt, and as on his mission to Genoa in 1794, lessons for a future yet uncharted were being learned, from the sphere of pan-European diplomacy to the micro-geography of the southern Alps and the Channel coast. Some insights acquired in these months were not retained, however, most notably the stark sentence with which his report began: 'Whatever efforts we may make, we will not acquire superiority on the seas for many years.'[5]

There has been much speculation about how projects for an invasion of the Middle East were becoming an obsession for Napoleon in these months, and he certainly took great interest in this policy, which originated with Talleyrand. His own correspondence reveals quite another preoccupation in the autumn and winter of 1797–8, however, and, again, it went unnoticed by those who should have recognised his real talents and powers. Napoleon was still the real master of the Cisalpine, even in his absence, and remained the real manipulator of Italian affairs, at least until he departed for Egypt in April 1798.

It is not until March 1798 that Napoleon's correspondence becomes dominated by the Egyptian expedition, and although the switching of emphasis from Italian affairs is dramatic, his first missives to Paris were to inform the government in precise terms of troop dispositions throughout Italy that were available for the new expedition.[6] In January, he was virtually directing the diplomatic mission of General Brune to Naples, ordered by the Directory, taking it upon himself to issue threats to the king in order to protect the French puppet government in Rome. The next month, he was administrating the Army of Italy – via its nominal commander, Berthier – in very detailed fashion, over the protection of the Italian Swiss communes which were loyal to France, to the point of reorganising the international border between these cantons and the Cisalpine Republic.[7] Again, while the Directors feared his popularity and his penchant for auto-diplomacy, and while the right feared him as a Jacobin, no one seemed to notice that he had not only built his own state, but was still running it from Paris. The Egyptian expedition would soon cut him off from his power base, and the military catastrophes France suffered during his sixteen-month absence temporarily robbed him of it altogether; but the decision to send him across the Mediterranean would give him yet another opportunity to learn the art of state-building, far from French eyes, even as it would also bring him to the brink of destruction.

In March 1798, however, the decision by the Directory to launch an attack on Egypt via Malta redirected Napoleon's energies, fixing his ambitions on a new horizon. His first steps on the road east led him back to Toulon, where he relearned his loathing of Provence, first acquired during the siege of 1793, and reinforced during the preparations for the First Italian Campaign. He found the postal service in the region disorganised,[8] and the local administrations all too ready to harbour deserters from his expeditionary force.[9] However, it was the flourishing culture of vendetta and local atrocities on both sides that lacerated him far more. He lambasted, in no uncertain terms, the cruelty of the forces of order in Provence for their indiscriminate judicial repression, writing to the Military Commission (Tribunal) of the region:

Citizens, I have learned with greatest sadness that old men of 70 and 80, and miserable women – pregnant or surrounded by young children – have been shot, accused of trying to emigrate. Have the soldiers of liberty become butchers? Is the pity they have shown throughout a thousand battles now dead in their hearts? ... I exhort you, citizens, that whenever the law sets before your tribunal men over 60, or women, to declare that, in the midst of the fighting, you have shown respect for the old and the women of your enemies. The soldier who signs a death sentence against anyone incapable of bearing arms is a coward.[10]

In the immediate local context of south-eastern France, Napoleon's stay in Toulon, and the practical problems he encountered in Provence in the course of organising the Egyptian expedition, brought home to him how dangerous a region it remained, and how little – in his eyes, at least – the Directory had achieved in trying to master it. It was no coincidence that, once in power and at peace after 1800, Napoleon turned very quickly to its pacification.

There is a terrible irony in his castigation of the draconian measures taken by the revolutionary authorities against Provençal communities, however. Napoleon's invocation of the chivalry of the French armies was hypocritical, but it did at least reflect the empty rhetoric of official orders. His own conduct in Egypt a few months later would fly brutally in the face of these sentiments and the norms they claimed – however cynically – to represent. No better contrast can be found between Napoleon's efforts to temporise within France during the uncertainties of the late Directory, when he himself was still a pawn in a dangerous game, and his unchained conduct on the other side of the Mediterranean. Philip Dwyer has speculated that the experience of Egypt changed Napoleon, that it hardened him into something close to a callous sociopath:

His contempt for humanity, already present before he left France, had been strengthened by his experiences in Egypt and Syria. He now seemed to be possessed of a cynicism that would grow over the coming years as his own warped philosophy of life continued to develop.[11]

While there is much to acknowledge and to contest in this judgement, there is more still to Napoleon which is simply unfathomable, but when his attitude to heavy-handed repression in Provence is set beside his subsequent behaviour in Egypt, the deranging impact of what was to come seems all too evident. While he was at Toulon, it was the power of restraint and concentrated energy that dominated Napoleon's conduct. The months between Mombello and Toulon had been fraught and uncertain, and Napoleon had risen to them in the manner of Plutarch's Caesar – with outward calm, studied calculation and the assurance of someone who had the measure, if not the mastery, of his circumstances.

The self-restraint and measured conduct which marked not just Napoleon's public image, but his judgements and actions, is all the more remarkable given the now farcical state of his marriage. It would not be unfair to regard Joséphine's treatment of her husband as appalling in these years. Her affair with Hippolyte Charles during the First Italian Campaign may or may not have persisted into 1798 – she was still fond of him and in close contact – but she took her time returning from Italy to Paris. The victor of Campo Formio and the delegate to Rastatt returned to an empty house in Paris, and it is possible that Joséphine's disgruntled maid, Louise Compoint, may have told him of the affair with Charles after Joséphine dismissed her. True or not, Napoleon had no domestic comfort to turn to in these months. Humiliation hunted him, for exposure as a cuckold would have damaged him immensely at this point, and his infatuated loyalty to Joséphine can be interpreted, almost according to taste, either as pathetic or as a sign of deeper humanity. It never seems to have affected his judgement in public life, for all that, at least not until he reached Egypt. Coincidence or no, Joséphine showed him no kindness when he left the splendour and relative security of Mombello for the uncertainties of Directorial high politics. That she sensed his career was too perilous to commit herself to him would be consonant with her character and her previous behaviour. Nor did she follow him to either Toulon or Egypt, but two letters from his flagship at sea, tinged with sadness to the point of pathos, reveal that Napoleon hoped she would join him. One was to Joseph, telling him Joséphine would stay in Toulon and await news that the main fleet was safely beyond Sicily, before setting out herself.[12] The other was to his mother, whom he had been unable to see when the fleet put into Ajaccio, telling her: 'It is possible that my wife will come to see you while she is on her way from Toulon to join me.'[13] A successful invasion of England, or of the moon, was more likely.

The task in hand, over the next year and a half, was as exhilarating as any that could be imagined. Napoleon had long been fascinated by the Middle East. Like all Frenchmen of his generation – indeed, far more so than was normal – he was steeped in the exploits of Alexander the Great and had devoured the works of the eighteenth-century Orientalist Volney. More pointedly, in 1795 he had volunteered for a French military mission to advise the Ottomans on army reform, but was summoned to deal with the Vendémiaire rising instead.[14] Napoleon's immediate interest in the Ottoman Empire, as distinct from Egypt, arose from his conquest of the north-eastern part of the Adriatic coast, which brought him into direct contact with Balkan affairs. These were things that remained at the back of his mind, until Talleyrand, the new foreign minister, convinced the Directory to turn eastwards. Talleyrand had returned from exile as an émigré in America almost directly to high office, and while abroad he had made a close study of Egypt and, above all, of British dependence on its trade in Indian cotton. If France seized Egypt and its cotton Talleyrand thought that Britain would be cut off from India and France – not Britain – would come to dominate the textile industry. As he saw it, to deprive Britain of the proceeds of Indian cotton would gravely undermine its whole economy.

One week after assuming office, in July 1797, Talleyrand bombarded the Directory with three memoranda to this end. Napoleon, who had yet to meet the foreign minister, supported Talleyrand's aim, though more for military than economic reasons. He was convinced that the seizure by France of the Ionian Islands in the Adriatic marked a point of no return for the collapse of Ottoman rule in the Balkans; the next logical step was to seize Egypt. The motive, as expressed to his superiors, was defensive more than aggressive: 'The vast Ottoman empire, which is crumbling every day, obliges us to begin thinking very soon about how to preserve our commercial interests in the Levant,'[15] he wrote from Milan. It was Talleyrand who made the expedition a reality, however, as Napoleon was first preoccupied with Italian affairs and then shunted from one posting to another. It took some time, but, greatly aided by the conclusion of a series of precarious peace treaties with the Habsburgs, the Directory adopted Talleyrand's project in March 1798. Napoleon, given his previous enthusiasm for the idea, his military prestige and, probably, the very awkwardness of his presence in Paris, was the obvious choice to lead the expedition.

Over the next two months, Napoleon gathered around him a heterogeneous group of soldiers and scholars, to take part in an expedition still, officially at least, shrouded in secrecy. His ability to draw men of diverse political views to him, and even more to hold them together when their expedition's destination and purpose were uncertain and the funds for it were scarce, displayed the skills in *amalgame* he had first shown in Italy, and which would mark the rest of his career. The hardened republican generals of his Army of Italy were now serving beside former nobles like Desaix and Menou, professionals of the royal army; indeed, his new army – a formidable force of around 36,000 – was itself a potentially awkward fusion of his own, deeply radical Army of Italy, and less overtly Jacobin troops from the Rhine front. What they all had in common was a shortage of supplies and arrears in pay. There were minor if persistent mutinies over pay, but these were quelled. The tensions among the troops and their officers were over-ridden by the prospects Napoleon laid before them.

There was also the unique, seemingly incongruous, presence of his team of intellectuals, academics and artists, assembled at Napoleon's own behest, with the dual purpose of studying Egypt, ancient and contemporary, and of disseminating French civilisation there. Napoleon rallied the troops with promises of untold plunder – just as he had on the frozen Alpine heights in 1796 – and the civilians with hopes of a regenerated Egyptian colony, recast in the mould of revolutionary France.

One of the most striking aspects of Napoleon's character to emerge both in the formation of the expedition and during the voyage was his intellectual depth and breadth, but, even more, his ability to listen. Intellectuals of all specialisms found in him an open mind and a sympathetic ear, not just to the well-established, such as the soldier-scholar Caffarelli, but particularly to the graduates of the new École Polytéchnique, the bright young engineers and archaeologists who went on to spearhead the Egyptian expedition, and subsequently so much of the intellectual life of France. During the organisation of the expedition, Napoleon displayed one of his greatest gifts, that of finding, nurturing and promoting young talent, of bringing forth new men and trusting them to carry on. Once he had them together, he could get them to work together. He had held Lombard and Bolognese 'patriots' together before; now it was the turn of the French themselves.

The sight of the fleet must have held them in hope and awe. There were thirteen ships of the line, led by L'Orient, Napoleon's flagship, and the largest warship in the world in 1798, together with other technologically advanced vessels, a heritage of the excellent fleet built in the last years of the monarchy. They were surrounded by forty-two smaller warships of various kinds, and more than 300 troop transports. The efforts made to assemble the expedition were frenetic. The whole enterprise, and the massive fleet in particular, is a reminder, as Philip Dwyer has pointed out, that for all its flaws the Directory could still summon considerable military force.[16] This is true, but events in 1799 would prove that French defences in Italy and Germany had been stripped dangerously bare to equip the expedition; the whole enterprise had been conceived and organised in months of relative peace which were shattered in April 1798, on the eve of its departure. A relatively minor incident in Vienna, centred on Bernadotte, the French ambassador, created a series of ruptures that led to a renewal of war between France and a new coalition – the Second – of Britain, Russia and the Habsburgs, soon to be joined by the Ottomans. Nevertheless, on 19 May, the fleet set forth from Toulon. The Egyptian expedition has been portrayed as a means by which the Directory sought to rid itself of Napoleon. His presence in France was certainly regarded as unwelcome by many, but it was a massive concentration of effort and expense just to get rid of one man. Were fear of him its true motive, then perhaps Napoleon might be forgiven his massive ego.

Throughout the creation of the expeditionary force, all that the upper echelons of Napoleon's entourage and the wider, educated French public knew about its purpose was that another way had been found of attacking Britain. Napoleon's pronouncements were steeped in references to the Carthaginian wars, and to himself as Scipio the Younger, the annihilator of Carthage. He was at one with a well-entrenched revolutionary paradigm when he adopted the mantle of Scipio, and identified his new expedition – wherever it was going – with the Punic Wars between 'virtuous', 'landlubbing' Rome and licentious, maritime Carthage. Revolutionary leaders of all hues, from the rabid Jacobin Saint-Just to the moderates of the current Directory, had cast the struggle with Britain in the terms of the classical models with which they were imbued from youth. Napoleon found the right nerve with little effort. As time progressed, however, his own mind was increasingly prey to the image of Plutarch's Alexander. At Toulon there was still enough of the calculating Octavian in him to keep well hidden any thoughts he may have harboured about advancing to India – any such noises had so far come from his civilian superiors – or of erecting Egypt into his own fief, something he had so well disguised in Italy. Yet his first landfall brought out the old Jacobin in him and, even more, the master manipulator who had first emerged in Italy.

Malta is at the crossroads of the western Mediterranean; it is a small place that has to be held by whoever seeks to control the seas between southern Europe and the Middle East. Napoleon well knew this. Fortunately for the French expedition, no one really did hold Malta in 1798. The island was ruled by the Order of St John, in theory the last of the great military monastic orders of the Crusades, but in practice a self-serving – if undemanding – corporation of nobles, the bulk of whom were of French descent, although their Grand Master,

Hompesch, was German. In military terms, Malta was there for the taking, and Napoleon seized it with alacrity. The expedition invaded Malta and its adjacent islands on 10 June, and Hompesch accepted an armistice as a prelude to negotiations. What followed was a swift, brutal re-enactment of Directorial policy towards any 'liberated' polity, but much more ruthless. How the process should have worked was outlined in Napoleon's orders to Berthier, who was to take effective charge of the island, on the eve of the invasion:

General Reynier will make an extremely simple proclamation ... to the effect that the French do not intend to change the customs or the religion [of the island] in any manner whatsoever, that the most severe discipline will be maintained [among the troops], and that the priests will be especially protected ... He will make it a particular point to respect the priests and monks, and will put under seal all the funds of the Knights of Malta; he will transport all arms to a single place. If some villages show themselves badly disposed [to us], he will take hostages and bring them on board his frigate.[17]

As had invariably been the case on the mainland – and would soon transpire in Egypt – respect and toleration for indigenous mores did not last long, while rapaciousness and the suppression of discontent soon became the dominant notes of French occupation. Within days, Napoleon had confiscated the wealth of the Order, using much of it to reprovision and refit his fleet and refill the coffers of the expedition, while also sending considerable sums to Paris, along with the flags of the Order, as trophies of a battle that never was. The island was put under direct French rule, and the entire French legal and administrative system was introduced; the new regime was staffed by a mixture of French soldiers and a handful of local collaborators. It all soon degenerated into revolt and repression after Napoleon sailed away, on 18 June.

Even before he left, the looting of churches was under way, the monasteries had been abolished and the scene was set for the collapse of French rule, even before the British arrived to prise them out. Significantly, most of the pro-French Maltese 'patriots' chose to be evacuated with the invaders rather than risk the later wrath of their own people. In every respect, events in Malta conformed to those in other territories before 1798 and what would happen the following year, when the French armies were thrown back from Italy and Germany. In one cardinal, if often neglected, respect the treatment of Malta differed from previous French conduct. On 14 June, Napoleon brutally declared to the French administration on Corfu that not only did the French flag now fly over Malta, but that 'the Order of St John of Jerusalem is destroyed'.[18] He went further; its ruling class was deported. Hompesch was put on a ship for Trieste, and directed back to the territory of the Holy Roman Empire, while all the knights of French descent were declared French citizens and shipped 'home', to be stigmatised as aristocrats in the increasingly tense atmosphere of late Directorial France. Perhaps even more irregular, all the knights of military age were carted off by Napoleon to serve in Egypt. It was an astonishing exercise in obliteration, and in some respects foreshadowed the rough treatment the Knights of the Holy Roman Empire received a few years later. They, like the Knights of Malta, were the most obvious surviving relics of the old European order, and they, too, would face virtual extinction, even if many German knights did ultimately hold on to their lands after long battles in the courts. Napoleon showed his Revolutionary credentials to the full on Malta; here was a world marked down for destruction, and he was its most thorough executioner.

Napoleon appreciated well Malta's strategic potential. He dispatched missives across the Mediterranean during his short stay, announcing the consolidation of the French conquest to the Republic's ambassador to Naples – he was now a matter of a few miles from the Sicilian coast – urging him to remind the Neapolitans that their claim to Malta would be judged in the light of their refusal to recognise the new 'sister republic' in Rome.[19] Likewise, he addressed the French consuls in North Africa, exhorting them to remind the beys of his presence, to release the slaves they had taken from Malta and 'to make them know that, henceforth, they must respect the Maltese'.[20]

The very day Napoleon announced a new *pax gallica* from Malta, Admiral Horatio Nelson, the commander of the British fleet in the western Mediterranean, convinced himself that the French were heading east, probably to Egypt, rather than west, into the Atlantic, and set off in that direction. The British had been suspicious of the large concentration of ships at Toulon since April, and had renewed their presence in the region accordingly, after having withdrawn from the western Mediterranean in 1796 to concentrate on the defence of the Channel. It was only now, however, in mid-June, that Nelson worked out in which general direction Napoleon was heading and this was confirmed when he reached Sicily on 20 June. The French fleet may have been numerically impressive, but it was a convoy, not a battle fleet capable of repelling the Royal Navy. Aware of this, Napoleon set off as quickly as the winds permitted. On 18 June, the French fleet weighed anchor for Egypt, reaching the coast off Alexandria on 1 July. The two fleets passed each other in fog on the night of 22/23 June, so near-run a matter was it, and Nelson, with more manoeuvrable craft than Napoleon, over-ran the French. He arrived at Alexandria on 28 June and, after trying to intimidate the locals into subservience, pushed on north, up the coast to Cyprus before turning back to Sicily to refit. The French landed in Egypt through a very narrow window of opportunity, for Nelson would soon be back, better informed and bent on destruction. For now, however, Napoleon and his forces had reached their goal.

The French had spoken a great deal about their objective during the voyage; they had read about it exhaustively before and during the preparation of the expedition, but nothing prepared them for what awaited them. The landscape and climate they literally waded into on 1 July 1798 was so alien and so forbidding to them that they took a little time even to begin appreciating the cultural gulf between the Egyptians and themselves. The main force, under Napoleon, landed near Alexandria, now a town of barely 6,000 people but once the greatest city of the Mediterranean; another force landed at Rosetta, to the east on the important Bay of Aboukir, where Napoleon would

direct the main fleet to find harbour, and another force, further east
still, at Damietta, on the main branch of the Nile. Alexandria fell
easily, but only after the French had had their first battle – with the
scorching heat, a lack of water and burning sands. It left them in foul
mood, and the city suffered from it in the same brutal manner the
soldiers of liberty and equality had dealt with most of western Europe
by then. These were the circumstances in which Napoleon issued his
famous proclamation to the Egyptians. In both French and Arabic –
the latter almost semi-literate if the Egyptian chronicler al-Jabarti is
to be believed[21] – he declared that he had come to liberate them, to
restore the fairness and equity of true Islamic law, and also to imbue
them with the liberty of his own revolution. Such incongruities would
henceforth mark his entire approach to ruling the country.

In the devastating heat of summer, however, the real concern was
survival. The three separate columns made rendezvous further up the
Delta, and headed for Cairo, the capital. They met scant resistance
in these initial phases. Their real enemy was a land with which they
had no experience, and the march to Cairo was, by all accounts –
Napoleon's included – sheer hell. Men dropped dead from heatstroke
and some even took their own lives, maddened by the heat and lack
of water. French armies normally lived off the land, but this was the
desert, not the rich, fat plains of the Po or the Rhine. The initial phase
of the march up the Nile to Cairo took the army through very different
parts of the Delta, and its progress was not helped by French ignorance
of the region. Each of the three columns – under Dugua, Desaix and
Reynier – following its allotted route, fared very differently. French
troops had lived off the land from the onset of the Revolutionary wars
in 1792, but they had never confronted anything like what they met
in Egypt.

Dugua's men found that their maps had not allowed for the
changing course of the Nile's branches, and discovered that some of
these had widened into lakes on the first part of their march, but once
across them, they found the countryside around the town of Rosetta
plentiful in fruit and bread, as well as abundant water, something the

army had lacked since it landed. According to Colonel Laugier, Dugua's division passed through 'cultivated fields criss-crossed by irrigation ditches filled with water', and met friendly peasants who allowed the troops to collect watermelons.[22] The fate of Desaix's division could not have been more different. Their route took them across barren desert; their woollen uniforms became personalised infernos; water was simply absent from the landscape and Napoleon nor any of his staff had even thought to equip them with water wagons. In contrast to the welcome Dugua's men received around Rosetta, Desaix's men found deserted villages and wells filled with stones. Many began to see mirages, but the Bedouin who harassed stragglers were real enough.[23] The third column, under Reynier, fared worse still, lack of water leading to its disintegration into small groups, but the march was not helped by the tradition of indiscipline this division was known for, or Reynier's inability to keep order.[24] Even the relatively fortunate men of Dugua's division paid the price for plenty in a land they did not understand. Their diet of Mediterranean fruit, to which they were unaccustomed, led to widespread diarrhoea among them.[25] The policy of 'living off the land' had always made the soldiers' diet the luck of the draw, but the experience of Egypt proved novel in all the worst ways. Still worse, large numbers of men went down with an eye infection widespread among the local populace and for which the army medics had no answer.[26]

Yet, even as the land frustrated him, human calculation – or lack of it – soon dealt Napoleon the military hand he most wanted, the kind of major, decisive engagement he always saw as the key to conquest. The rule and defence of Egypt was in the hands of the Mamelukes, with whose political legacy Napoleon would soon have to grapple. In mid-July, it was their military power he had to confront and exterminate. The three columns assembled on the western bank of the Nile, with Cairo across the river, to the east, on 20 July, with the Mameluke army drawn up on the sandy plain to the south of them, and with the great Pyramids behind them as a dramatic backdrop. The Mameluke army had an audience with it, a huge crowd of observers from Cairo, often playing musical instruments to encourage the army, come to see the slaughter of the alien invaders. The French had more mundane concerns. For the first time in weeks, they could gorge on goats' meat, food they understood.

When dawn broke, 'the French soldiers were greeted by a spectacular sight, the like of which not even the hardiest of well-travelled veterans had seen before', in the words of the historian Paul Strathern.[27] To their south, there were indeed the Pyramids of Giza, but to their east, across the river, was the far more alluring sight of Cairo. Cairo was a city of over a quarter of a million people – larger than almost all European cities – dominated by the minarets of its more than 300 mosques. After all their privations, this was the prize. All they had to do was fight for it. On 21 July, after issuing another proclamation that few, if any, heeded at the time, invoking the antiquity of the Pyramids to inspire the soldiers, Napoleon engaged the Mamelukes about twenty miles north of the Pyramids of Giza.

The Mamelukes were some of the finest light cavalry in history, but even on their own ground they proved no match for the French, even a French army bedraggled, half-deranged by thirst and heat and exhausted after a long march through the unknown. The battle lasted about two hours. The main French force formed into huge squares, which the Mameluke cavalry circled hopelessly, while modern musket and artillery fire raked them from all sides as they rode between the squares. Two other French columns, advancing up the eastern bank of the Nile, then caught the Mamelukes from behind, whereupon their cavalry left the field, as was their tradition. Although many were butchered or subsequently drowned in the Nile, the main body of their army survived and fled up the Nile, to more inaccessible country in the south. The disparity in armaments and tactics between the two armies notwithstanding, the 'Battle of the Pyramids' was a resounding tribute to the resilience and fighting spirit of French soldiery, given the state in which the troops had reached Giza.

However incomplete the French victory, Cairo – above all its plunder and supplies – now stood helpless before them. On 24 July, what was left of the civil government of Cairo sued for peace, and Napoleon and his men entered in triumph. The prize of Cairo was a double-edged sword for the French. The city was long past its heyday of the fourteenth century, when it was the jewel of the Islamic world and its great university and mosque were built, but it was still a thriving commercial centre, an important entrepôt in the eastern Mediterranean. Its markets were a welcome sight to the army, which at last could count on regular supplies. Although many of its great buildings dated from its past, the 1780s had seen Elfi Bey construct a beautiful palace, renowned for its gardens and galleries, on the northern-western side of the city, which Napoleon soon commandeered as his residence; before the large terrace which was the entrance to the palace, with its granite floor and marble pillars, spread the impressive Ezbekiyah Square, which became a lake when the Nile flooded.[28]

There was another Cairo, however. Close to 60,000 of its people were an under-employed proletariat, often dependent on the charity of the mosques, and under the influence of fundamentalist clergy. Well before the arrival of the French, this 'dangerous class' had been prone to revolts, and was well able to disappear into the maze of crowded, chaotic streets of the sprawling popular districts.[29] The French soon came to know and dread this side of Cairo, and it assailed their eyes and nostrils, first of all, for the populace relied on dried dung for fuel, whose fumes produced a horrid brown, pungent smog that hung over the city at mealtimes.[30]

Nonetheless, the taking of Cairo was nothing short of a triumph after the privations of the campaign.

It was short-lived. Nelson had not forgotten about Napoleon. Whereas Napoleon had assumed that Nelson would have to get all the way back to Gibraltar to refit and supply before coming after him, in fact he had been helped by the Neapolitan Bourbons who, in flagrant – if sensible – violation of the agreements the French had bullied them into, allowed Nelson to re-equip at Siracusa, in eastern Sicily. This cut his supposed voyage in half and, on 1 August, the British fleet arrived at Aboukir. The French fought bravely, but Nelson made short work

of them, a task made all the easier by Napoleon's prior orders to strip
the fleet of supplies, thus making it impossible for it to put to sea and
avoid an attack, while also ordering it to stay close to shore in case he
needed to return to France. This played into Nelson's hands.

French losses were horrific. Two ships of the line, including *L'Orient*,
were lost, along with two frigates, while nine ships were captured
by Nelson. Only two ships of the-line and two frigates escaped. The
French commander, Brueys, was killed in action along with 7,000
sailors, while another 1,500 were wounded.[31]

Perhaps an even more grievous loss was the treasure looted from
Malta that went down with *L'Orient* – treasure with which to bribe the
Egyptian elite to change sides, to mint a new coinage for the country
and, above all, to pay the troops.[32] A crucial element of Napoleon's
political strategy, together with his best hope of restraining his troops
from pillage, was now at the bottom of the sea.

At the outset of his infamous conquest of Mexico centuries
earlier, the Spanish conquistador Hernán Cortés had ordered his
fleet destroyed to quash any thoughts of turning back. Nelson took
the liberty of doing Napoleon the same service, and it changed the
character of the expedition, and its leader, as a result. Henry Laurens
put it perfectly: 'Prisoner of his own conquest, he [now] had to
succeed, and his dreams of Oriental conquest returned to raise his
spirits.'[33] The grandiose visions of Alexander were all that were left to
Napoleon, and they would take their toll on all around him, but on no
one more than himself.

Talleyrand's diplomatic pretext for the expedition had been to overthrow the Mamelukes and to restore direct Ottoman rule in Egypt,
through French arms, with the dual purpose of protecting French
commerce from their illegal, exorbitant demands, and of freeing the
Egyptians from their allegedly capricious tyranny. Even this thin fiction
was stripped away after Aboukir. Napoleon and his collaborators had
to confront, rule and try to comprehend a very alien culture, one they
would find as intractable, and themselves as unprepared for, as the
desert that had already almost overwhelmed them.

THE RULER OF EGYPT

Talleyrand's diplomatic hypocrisy came at the end of a long tale. Egypt had known almost a quarter of a century of upheaval by the time Napoleon floundered ashore in 1798, and the problems incurred by French businessmen there were but the tip of an iceberg of economic disruption, social disorder and political violence. Plague swept the battered country in 1791, and it returned during the French expedition. These were circumstances Napoleon reasonably hoped to exploit to his advantage, but to do so required a grasp of Islamic civilisation and Egyptian affairs that he and all his compatriots singularly lacked, and in which his unpaid, ill-fed troops had no interest.

The Mamelukes were a unique product of Ottoman culture, a caste of soldiers drawn from the Circassian peoples of the Caucasus, ethnically different from the Egyptians and, technically, slaves of the Sultan. They had ruled Egypt for centuries, but by the late eighteenth century they had become effectively independent of the Sultan. The political turmoil of the decades immediately before Napoleon's arrival had two fundamental sources: the increasing disintegration of the Mamelukes into rival factions vying for power, and the unsuccessful attempts by the Ottomans to reimpose their own rule on Egypt. Eventually, these fissures ran from top to bottom of Egyptian society, and the ensuing disorder disrupted commerce. This led to increasing incursions by the Bedouin Arabs, predatory raiders who terrorised Egypt in the absence of secure rule, but who also found allies among the settled communities in parts of the country, as Mameluke or Ottoman rule evaporated. By 1787, the country was roughly partitioned between the Mamelukes and the Ottomans. The two Mameluke factions under their respective leaders, Mourad Bey and Ibrahim Bey, had withdrawn together to Upper Egypt, and waged a guerrilla war with their light cavalry against the Ottomans in Lower Egypt. The stalemate was broken by the plague of 1791, which affected mainly Lower Egypt, and made a Mameluke reconquest possible. However, they were now confronted with continuing popular resentment at their rule, and their rapacious taxation especially, a resentment fomented by the religious leaders, the *ulama*. With the Muslim clergy turned against them, the Mamelukes became increasingly dependent on minorities such as the Greek and Coptic Christians for support. Throughout the 1790s, commerce failed to revive, law and order were not restored, and a popular alliance of clergy and people against the Mamelukes hardened.

What the French knew but could not understand was that an Islamic concept of legitimate revolt against authority underpinned the popular discontent against the Mamelukes. The Ottomans and the Mamelukes had also appealed to it on occasion throughout the 'time of troubles', as this period was known. Legitimate revolt was sanctioned by the violation of Islamic law that occurred when political authority threatened the community of believers in ways that transgressed religious rules regarding the protection of persons and property. Thus, it was the *ulama*, and they alone, who could pronounce resistance legitimate or otherwise. Napoleon's own proclamations were therefore at the very best presumptuous, and not based on any knowledge of the very Islamic laws Napoleon claimed the Mamelukes had violated. This meant the struggles the French sought to exploit were not of a kind they understood. These were not class conflicts, in the eyes of their protagonists, nor were they centred on the opposition of the privileged to the unprivileged, as in France. They turned on concepts that were anathema to the French revolutionaries, in so far as they were able to assimilate them to their own political culture: anti-Mameluke revolt concerned the defence of traditional, sacred rights – in their practical, as distinct from secular, context – by a religious community. There was no secular aspect to this struggle, nor was there any demand for radical change but, rather, a demand for the restoration of a sacred norm.

Napoleon never really grasped any of this, although he perceived its political results quickly enough. He drove ahead with his own reform of Egypt not so much in blissful ignorance, nor even in a haze of seeing what he wished to see, but in the yet more perilous condition of wary half-understanding. This was an alien culture, and he knew it, but too often he seized on what appeared familiar, not realising that it was in fact the most alien element of all. Napoleon the foreigner had had time to grope his way into France as a youth. In 1798, as a de facto potentate, he had no such breathing space in a very different place.

Western loathing of the contemporary Middle East in the eighteenth century hinged on its vision of Ottoman rule as despotic, capricious and unfettered, a political culture that fostered cruelty, unbridled lasciviousness in personal conduct and servility in the public sphere. Official French rhetoric sought to end this, and to regenerate Egypt through the values and institutions of the Revolution, mixed – it was never clear how – with an appeal to the Islamic sense of justice that legitimised revolt. Ironically, the conquest of Lower Egypt effected at the Battle of the Pyramids, coupled with both the inability of the Ottomans to strike at him and his complete isolation from France after Aboukir, turned Napoleon into exactly the type of ruler he was supposed to unhorse: an oriental despot. If his position was unpopular and precarious, this gave him all the more in common with the usual circumstances of such rulers. He marched into Cairo at the reluctant behest of its worthies because there was no one else to take over. These facts did not long escape him.

If Napoleon was now a despot, he sought to be an enlightened one, at least by the western standards he understood. Nevertheless, he did not choose to live modestly as a mere 'first servant of the people', as had his modern hero, Frederick the Great of Prussia. Napoleon established a new Mombello in the finest palace in Cairo the moment he entered the city, and he issued proclamations couched in terms he would never have dared pen, even from Mombello. He immediately placed Cairo under military rule, ordered its disarmament and instituted physical punishments for those who did not comply – including beheading – while prefixing all his decrees 'in the name of the Prophet'.[34] More worrying was his remark comparing himself to Alexander the Great:

When Alexander arrived in Egypt, they ran to him, greeting this great man as a liberator. When he . . . was declared the son of Jupiter by the priestess, he demonstrated that he understood these people: he played on their deepest inclination, which was for their religion.[35]

Unlike his hero, Napoleon did not find a way to manipulate Egyptian religious sensibilities. Instead, from his magnificent capital, there flowed reforms that, in their natural European soil, ranked with the most enlightened and advanced of any attempted by eighteenth-century reformers.

On 25 July, Napoleon decreed a new administrative regime for the city of Cairo, a council – the *diwan* – of nine men. He chose them from among the religious and academic elite, the *ulama* being the former and the *shaykh* the latter. This was hardly revolutionary government; rather, it corresponded to the most enlightened aspects of the enlightened absolutism of the old order. Napoleon hand-picked from the elite a council for consultation, in the manner the last reforming ministers of Louis XVI – Calonne, Necker and Brienne – had outlined just before the Revolution of 1789 made their plans redundant. Napoleon's political vision for Egypt amounted to what the conservative regimes that succeeded him in Europe after 1814 would call a 'consultative monarchy', but in the circumstances of an absolute master, freshly arrived in an alien world, consultation soon descended into a dialogue of the deaf.

In turning to cultural leaders and placing them at the summit of his regime, Napoleon showed that he knew who formed and led Egyptian popular and educated opinion, but events would soon reveal that he did not know what drove Egyptian culture, or what could mobilise it. Initially, too, Napoleon sought to exclude the Mamelukes from the higher administration, replacing them with Ottoman bureaucrats, a policy about which the *diwan* had its doubts. Undeterred, Napoleon extended this system from the environs of Cairo to the whole of Egypt: each province was to have its own *diwan*, although, outside Cairo, many Mameluke officials were retained. All of this was couched in terms of Napoleon's attempts to assimilate his policies into the Islamic tradition of justifiable revolt and renewal, but Egyptian opinion interpreted French ideology in terms of classic heresy, whatever the *ulama* of the metropolis might argue. Nor did anyone take seriously Napoleon's more secular claims – faithful to Talleryand's platitudes – that he was there as an ally and instrument of the Ottomans, to liberate Egypt from the capricious despotism of the Mamelukes.

Instead, almost unnoticed by the French, their measures handed moral authority to the local *ulama*, who saw them as simply foreign invaders and unclean infidels. The *ulama* were close to the people, and so knew at first hand the harsh realities of military occupation and the shocking conduct of French men, and even more, of French women, in the midst of an Islamic society. Unwittingly, Napoleon had cut the ties between the traditional leaders of opinion and the masses, and left the popular classes – whom their betters had come to regard as dangerous, superstitious and unpredictable – in thrall to the most traditionalist elements of the clergy.

Practical French reforms soon aggravated popular opinion, and played further into the hands of local leaders.[36] French attempts to prevent plague, which entailed disrupting traditional burial practices, left the people of Cairo disoriented and seething – a pattern seen in rural France and repeated in Italy and Spain – when burials in urban centres were banned in favour of cemeteries beyond the city walls. Napoleon swiftly created an 'Egyptian Institute', a local version of the French Institut, staffed entirely by the civilian experts of the expedition, to introduce western medicine and French high culture to the country. When the Institute confronted the *diwan* about legal reform, it was met with a mixture of bewilderment, unease and contempt.[37] Even potential collaborators were finding it hard to work with the French. The *diwan* was increasingly bound to the occupiers less by conviction than by a shared fear of popular disorder.

Although Napoleon was oblivious to what drove these shifts in opinion, he was, in practical terms, all too alert to the precarious security of Cairo and of his new Egyptian conquest. He fortified the citadel of Cairo against popular insurrection, but did so in ways that actually provoked the very unrest it was meant to intimidate, by blocking much used rights of way, turning large parts of the central area into forbidden zones under French control and, above all, failing to control the rough, often thieving conduct of his troops.

He was much more successful in wider, strategic terms, however. Napoleon moved quickly and sensibly to secure his southern borders, reaching agreements with the Mamelukes who had entrenched themselves there. He would later send expeditions south, as far as Aswan, but in the summer of 1798 he knew that securing the Delta, to his north, was far more important, for if the British returned or the Ottomans moved against him, they would approach through the Delta. Napoleon defeated the isolated remnants of Mameluke resistance there, and began fortifying the coast.

He also turned his attention to the Bedouin, and in trying to extirpate this endemic source of insecurity he probably played his strongest card with Egyptian opinion. The desert nomads had taken full advantage of Mameluke misrule, the most spectacular example of which had been their plundering of the refugees fleeing the French seizure of Cairo in July. However, this was but one example of their depredations at the moment of the French conquest. When Napoleon set about 'pacifying' the desert frontiers of Egypt, he initiated a policy that would become a hallmark of his regime, first in France after 1800 and then across Europe, but it was born on the banks of the Nile, and there it nearly worked. Napoleon reached the conclusion that the best way to win the support of the propertied classes was to restore law and order, to portray himself as the only political force capable of protecting their most basic interests, life and property, in the face of anarchy. Cut off after Aboukir, Napoleon's concerted attempts to intimidate, crush and harry the Bedouin reveal his determination to establish solid foundations on the only base he had left, security.

This policy was negated, however, first by the rapacious demands he, too, had to make on Egypt in order to supply his troops – something he tried to moderate by establishing a regular system of taxation – and by their ill-disciplined conduct. Worse, Napoleon was increasingly constrained to consign the enforcement of order to Ottoman troops under Greek Christian commanders, and the collection of taxes to the Copts, the detested native Christians. His inability to grasp the essence of Islamic social organisation militated even against his most potentially fruitful initiatives. This reliance on the marginal minorities, and an inherent disposition to offend the vast majority, would become another hallmark of Napoleonic rule in the years ahead. Regimes under his sway never lost the Revolution's commitment to legal and civil equality, almost inexorably finding support among those most detested by the mainstream. This was exactly the opposite of what Napoleon sought in Egypt, but the essence of French reforms, when they antagonised the majority, opened the door to rule by the minorities who benefited from them. Napoleon might speak of conversion to Islam, or adopt the local costume, but this mattered little in a system that offered political and administrative power to non-Muslims. He had slipped into the same abyss as the Mamelukes.

All this unrest took place set against one of strangest, most emotionally fraught moments of Napoleon's personal life. The cause – the only one possible – was Joséphine. Scarcely had Napoleon entered Cairo than the rumours of Joséphine's infidelity reached him, from the mouths of his own officers. He poured out his feelings to Joseph in a letter which fell into the hands of the Royal Navy, and hence into those of the British gutter press and the satirical cartoonist Gillray. Napoleon now became an international laughing stock, a cuckold held up to the gaze of the world in print and image. It was a small mercy that, stranded in Egypt, he did not actually see Gillray's images and only heard about them, but the master of the cult of celebrity now felt the machinery of celebrity pitilessly turned on him. Philip Dwyer has seen in this a defining moment, both personal and political, in Napoleon's life, as the point when he shed all idealism for naked ambition, and he changed definitively.[38] If this was so, if he did not really stop loving Joséphine, he at least did his best. That is, he began to act like everyone else around him. He openly took a mistress. Yet this conformity came in the disorienting – in every sense – atmosphere of Egypt, and the impact this had obviously had on the personal conduct of all around him.

Although French soldiers of all ranks were forever requesting permission to go home, they also found ways to make the most of Egypt. The lack of women travelling with the expedition had led the common soldiery to turn to local women. Many of the French officers also adopted Egyptian lovers with exuberance. Menou actually made a serious marriage with the daughter of the owner of the Turkish baths in Cairo, converted to Islam and was even circumcised. This was, however, the exception, not the rule. Many officers acquired whole harems, 'confiscating' those left behind by the Mamelukes *en bloc*. The normally reserved Eugène bought white slave girls in some quantity, while also expending his social energies with two black girls.[39]

In the midst of all this Napoleon first took an Egyptian slave (she was later killed for her association with him), but soon bored of her and turned instead to Pauline Fourès, the wife of one of his officers. By all accounts pretty and intelligent, Pauline became his public companion, after Napoleon sent her husband home on a thin pretext. She lived near him in his palace in Cairo, and was known as 'Cleopatra' to the troops. Napoleon wrote to her faithfully when on campaign in Syria, but his luck in love was thwarted by the Royal Navy when it captured her husband's ship. Fully aware of the whole business, the British sent him back to Egypt, where he confronted Napoleon and Pauline and obtained a divorce. Pauline seems to have hoped for something permanent from Napoleon, but he was reconciled with Joséphine on his return to Paris. Napoleon always looked after Pauline, however, and she lived on a generous pension during the Consulate and Empire.[40] If these experiences had, indeed, changed Napoleon, they had turned him into 'just another soldier' and his treatment of Pauline was anything but that of a monster.

There is perhaps another context in which Napoleon's infidelity should be set: he was a man among men in the most demanding of situations, men at this stage of his career who were often older and, until recently, more senior than himself. To remain faithful to a faithful wife was not the habit of many of them, but a man who did might still be respected. If his position as their leader was to be retained, remaining faithful to a woman who had so publicly cuckolded him demanded a different response. Whether or not this was how Napoleon thought cannot be known, but it was certainly the way of the soldier. By his own standards, however, this behaviour represented a serious loss of self-restraint.

For all the problems he confronted in the summer of 1798, these months were the lull before the storm. On 21 October, Cairo rose in mass revolt. Two months later, it was clear the Ottomans would move against him, and Napoleon took the offensive hastily, advancing into Palestine and Syria. In January 1799, the plague returned to Alexandria.

Disturbances broke out in Cairo on 21 October, originally over the issue of French taxation, particularly concerning the extension of taxes normally imposed on non-Muslims to the rest of the people. In the mosques of the popular districts the *ulama* had been agitating for several weeks at Friday prayers, and even in the calls to prayer, none of which the French could understand. They were spreading the official propaganda passed to them by the Ottomans, which imbued every French reform with menace, portraying it all as a plot to destroy Islam and enslave Egypt under their yoke. Both the Ottomans and the *ulama* were touching an already raw nerve, however. When the crowds killed a French general they mistook for Napoleon, the rioting spread and soon assumed the character of a real revolt, one already decreed and blessed as holy by the Sultan in Constantinople. French, Copts and Greeks alike were all targeted and blood flowed copiously in Cairo all that day and night as the French tried to barricade themselves in the citadel. The uprising had taken them completely by surprise and was a clear sign that the men Napoleon had regarded as the leaders of opinion, the major *ulama* of the central mosques and the university elite, had lost all real influence.

Napoleon was outside Cairo on 21 October, engaged in operations against the Bedouin, itself quite an irony. He chose to quell the revolt by his preferred means, doing what he did best. His artillery pounded the areas where the rioting was worst, as well as its main targets, the ancient university quarter and the Great Mosque. He followed up the bombardments with infantry incursions into the streets, with predictable results: houses and shops were looted, the university and its library were ransacked and vandalised. The Great Mosque was actually pillaged by the French after order had been restored on 23 October; the French general charged with its seizure entered it on horseback. Islam was now on a par with Catholicism, it seemed. Napoleon proclaimed a general amnesty, save for the instigators of the revolt, a category which the French interpreted with considerable latitude. He entrusted the hunting down of the ringleaders to a Greek soldier with a reputation for brutality, Bathélemy. The six leaders of the revolt were quietly beheaded and their bodies dumped in the Nile, and the French duly tightened their grip on the provinces to the north, in the Delta. The citadel area in Cairo was simply cleared of its inhabitants, and became a French military compound. This was now a naked military occupation.

Then, as if it had been summoned, the British fleet appeared off Alexandria at Aboukir on 24 October. Their bombardments caused little real damage, but they left no doubt that the French were now becoming the besieged. Ottoman ships took part in the raid, making it impossible henceforth to maintain any fiction that the French were there as allies of the Sultan or that the Sultan was not at war with them.

Nevertheless, even after the gore of Cairo, Napoleon remained sufficiently wedded to his concept of a 'consultative monarchy' to re-establish the *diwan* in late December 1798, even as he began his initial preparations to march into Syria. At this point, as Henry Laurens has noted, many of his proclamations began to take on a messianic tone.[41] Events in Egypt, both personal and public, may or may not have changed Napoleon permanently, but by the end of 1798 there were public as well as personal signs that he was not himself. In December, just before his departure for Syria, one of his proclamations demanded, rhetorically, 'Is there a man so blind as not to see that destiny itself guides all my operations? Is there anyone so faithless as to doubt that everything in this vast universe is bound to the empire of destiny?'[42] If this was how Napoleon's mind really did work, he usually kept it well to himself, but not this time. Cut off from any hope of escape, and now acutely aware of the mounting dangers around him, Napoleon drew on his own self-confidence which would, quite soon, lead to disaster.

Whether unbalanced by a mixture of events and environment or not, it was always Napoleon's instinct to act when threatened, to take the offensive and seek out conclusive engagement. In January 1799, with relatively little, and very hasty, preparation, he lashed out at the mounting threat from the north, and advanced into Palestine and Syria to confront the Ottoman forces assembling there.

THE SYRIAN CAMPAIGN

The invasion of Syria and Palestine brought out the worst in Napoleon and the whole army, but its leader set the tone. Napoleon's greatest accomplishment in the Syrian campaign was in extricating the army from a disaster of his own making in a state sufficient to fight another day. Egypt is a natural fortress, as Napoleon soon found when he had to fall back there, but in January 1799 he chose to quit it for the hard march across northern Sinai, over unyielding desert terrain with ill-prepared logistical support. The Syrian campaign was fought virtually without lines of communication or supply, and carried the Revolutionary 'strategy' of living off the land to its most extreme, but in some of the most barren, inhospitable terrain in the Mediterranean.

Napoleon's first major engagement taught him a very hard lesson about the Ottoman army, when his weakened forces confronted them at El Arish, to the west of Gaza, on 7 February. Although much inferior to western armies in pitched battle, Ottoman troops had mastered siege warfare and it took Napoleon two weeks to reduce the small garrison and seize its much-needed stores. This was the first of a series of sieges that would go badly for Napoleon. The army then pushed on north, up the coast towards Jaffa.

Napoleon's actual objectives are still cause for debate, itself an indication of how ill-conceived and badly prepared the campaign was. There seems little evidence that this was the beginning of a march on India, but his growing penchant for identifying himself with Alexander the Great cannot rule it out. More apparent was the idea of rallying the non-Turkish peoples of the region into a mass rising against the Ottomans, and advancing as far north as he could in order to intimidate the Ottomans, if not to march on Constantinople.

The Christian populations around Galilee were the only converts to his new cause of 'Arabism versus the Turks', which replaced his earlier appeal to Islam. Local militias and Bedouin alike harassed the army. Napoleon replied with ruthless raids on Palestinian settlements in search of supplies and, increasingly, in order to exact reprisals. He had hoped to capitalise on the ruthless rule of the Turkish governor of Jaffa, Al-Jazzar. Instead, he created a guerrilla army for the Ottomans.

On 3 March, the French cut off Jaffa from the landward side and the siege began. The city fell in four days, but it is what followed that still resonates two centuries later. Jaffa was sacked, in the midst of a pitiless massacre that Napoleon never explained with anything other than weasel words about his inability to cope with a mass surrender. Some 3,000 dead – women and children among them – is the generally accepted estimate.

Almost as chilling was the tone of Napoleon's proclamation to the people of the region, two days later:

It is as well you should know that all human efforts against me are useless, for all I undertake must succeed. Those who declare themselves my allies prosper; those who oppose me, perish ... [I]f I am terrible to my enemies, I am good to my friends, and above all, [I am] clement and merciful to the poor.[43]

The messianic tone is spine-chilling, and it raises the question of whether the evocation of a merciful conqueror was simply cynical –

for Napoleon was aping the style of his idea of an eastern despot – or if it really was self-delusion. One thing is very clear, however. The commander who castigated the vendetta-driven local authorities of Provence only a few months earlier, and had been a victim himself in Corsica, was now so distant an influence as to be on the other side of the moon. The strangeness and isolation of his circumstances were contorting and perverting Napoleon. So, too, perhaps, was the absolute power he wielded in this isolation, a degree of autonomy he would not really have again even as Emperor, but an absolute power under constant threat from everything around him, human, climatic and strategic. This may also have been the spirit in which he braved the plague hospital, touching the afflicted troops in an effort to calm them: western medical opinion believed that irrational fear played a major part in worsening plague, and that self-confidence and optimism were rational palliatives for it. Napoleon was well versed in all this, but his state of mind may have led him to behave in a less rational spirit.

His troops' behaviour mirrored their commander's throughout the campaign. The army pushed north to the major citadel of St John of Acre, centred on its forbidding Crusader castle. If Napoleon needed the jolt of modern reality more than a little at this point, it came in the form of the British fleet. Not only could the British keep Acre supplied by sea, they had captured the small French squadron sent from Egypt with all Napoleon's siege guns. He now had to assault the strongest fortress on the coast without them, and he failed, but not before sustaining huge losses which pushed the army almost to mutiny. The French depended for supplies on foraging raids into Galilee, where Murat's cavalry began to learn Bedouin tactics, to their great advantage. The siege itself descended into stalemate, but a small French flotilla from Egypt did break through the British blockade in early April, with the much-needed siege guns, and Napoleon took the offensive, but to no avail. By May, it was clear that a large Ottoman force was being mobilised to relieve Jaffa by sea, and Napoleon was helpless to stop it. On 17 May, he raised the siege of Acre and began the retreat to Egypt.

The march back was dreadful for the French. Their ranks were as decimated by plague as by the vain siege. Hounded by Bedouin, their plight actually worsened the closer they got to Egypt, for recrossing the Sinai desert proved to be the most ghastly part of the retreat. The only defence left to Napoleon was to run. His rearguard, under Kléber, was given the task of devastating Palestine, and it did just that. This was the only unqualified success of the whole campaign, and it made a lasting impact on the region. Lowland areas, only recently recolonised and newly cultivated in the 1780s, after Al-Jazzar had albeit brutally restored a semblance of order, were again abandoned until the late nineteenth century. The French policy of scorched earth allowed the Bedouin to rampage over these areas in their turn. The apostle of law and order, in both African Egypt and western Europe, brought devastation to the Holy Land as his legacy.

As the army staggered back, Napoleon's bulletins lied to the last. Although no one was fooled by these, Egypt had in fact been kept in good order during the campaign. The French administration carried out important financial and administrative reforms, and the scientific expedition continued its important archaeological and anthropological research.

When an Anglo-Ottoman fleet attacked Alexandria in mid-July, and managed to land a large force near Aboukir, Napoleon was still strong enough to crush them. The Ottomans were well dug in, but they were broken by Murat's cavalry, which also displayed for the first time what became one of the greatest of Napoleonic battle tactics: Murat pursued the broken ranks of the enemy with discipline and speed, hindering any major attempts to regroup and effect an orderly retreat. Indeed, many of the Ottoman casualties at Aboukir were caused by retreating troops panicking and drowning in the rivers of the Delta as Murat bore down on them.

Aboukir bought the French several months of respite, and put paid to domestic unrest, based on hopes of an Ottoman relief force. A French army held out there long after Napoleon's departure. Although badly depleted and increasingly reliant on locally raised troops of poor quality, the French were still able to quash a revolt in Cairo and to hold off fresh Anglo-Ottoman armies. It is unlikely they could have survived indefinitely, but British demands in the 1801 negotiations that led to the Peace of Amiens forced Napoleon's hand, in any case.

By late summer 1799, the Directory's military position in Europe was in far worse tatters than Napoleon's in Egypt and, on 10 September 1799, he was ordered home. Napoleon, however, had taken the initiative on this occasion, as on so many others: he had decided it was time to withdraw and slipped away surreptitiously on 22 August, with a handful of companions. He did not even hold a formal consultation with Kléber, his personally designated successor, nor did he leave from Alexandria, but from a small inlet on its outskirts that necessitated clambering into a rowing boat to be taken to his ship. However ignominious, even cowardly, Napoleon's sordid departure from Egypt, it at least served as a coming down to earth.

The Egyptian expedition proved the most spectacular moment in the whole incredible adventure of Napoleon's life. It led him into the unknown; it challenged all his natural abilities and found him more wanting than at any other point in his career as a soldier, as a state-builder, as a human being. It all but ended his bid for eternity. The sound and fury, coupled with the sheer exoticism of the whole episode, blinded contemporaries to its catastrophic failure, even some who were there, and hindsight has all but set it aside as an aberration in Napoleon's career, save for the mental scars it may have left on his character.

There were useful specifics that emerged from the campaign: Murat learned much from Mameluke cavalry tactics; Menou and many other officers who policed Egypt, such as Damas and Reynier, went on to form the core of the men who tamed the lands of the First Empire. In their different ways, Savary and Davout emerged as the best servants Napoleon would ever possess, the former as security expert and troubleshooter, the latter as a field commander.

The most important consequence of the Egyptian expedition actually developed before it took place, for its conception was the combined work of Talleyrand and Napoleon. Their common aim of redirecting the energies of the Republic towards the Orient was the first major step in forging a partnership – never cordial, always calculating and wary – which would aid Napoleon significantly in his bid for power in 1799, and would prove to be of spectacular, inestimable value to both men and their country over the next ten years.

As Henry Laurens has said, the essential legacy of the Egyptian expedition itself was scientific and ideological; the scientific committee's *Description de l'Égypte* and the academic research launched by the discovery and eventual decipherment of the Rosetta Stone surpassed any of Napoleon's endeavours.[44]

Its ideological heritage for later Napoleonic expansion was Janus-faced, to say the least. The most powerful impact of the attempt to rule Egypt along French revolutionary lines was wholly negative for all concerned among the French. They emerged from it physically and intellectually battered, disabused of any notion that Islam or its adherents were capable of assimilating to their political culture, to modernity as Napoleon and his collaborators understood it. Whatever personal animosities Egypt engendered, a collective French mentality, hostile and wary of exporting the Revolution, had taken shape. Yet, alongside this mixture of loathing and dread of what they saw as the alien and barbarous, there was also an unshaken, indeed strengthened, belief in their own culture's superiority to the Orient's which had not been there before. The determined popular resistance they met had left all those involved convinced that, however difficult or even impossible the exporting of their Revolution might be, it was still the only real hope for humanity. Even as he slipped away from them, this was a cultural bond between Napoleon and his men that would become even stronger as his empire grew.

The lessons for Napoleon personally were more tangible and useful. Some were learned to perfection, others not. He had been able to rule Egypt directly, unfettered, even more than had been the case in Italy, and from his experience of absolutism there he derived four features of his future regime. From the outset, he based his appeal for support on the re-establishment of law and order, which was to be the prelude to, and foundation of, a further reordering of civil government, based on regular, predictable taxation and professional administration. Finally, the freedom of Egypt had allowed Napoleon to try to build his regime upon those he chose, more than during the Cisalpine Republic. He reached out to the local, provincial elites, to the propertied classes who were beleaguered by misrule and violent disorder. His attempts to do so in Egypt may have been built on sand, but he returned to all these maxims as soon as he came to office in France, and here they turned into what he himself termed 'the masses of granite', the provincial notables who would benefit and appreciate his policies, even if Egyptians had not. The experiment did not work on the banks of the Nile; it would on those of the Seine, the Po and the Rhine. Italy had revealed his political skills. Egypt had sharpened his political vision, even if it had clouded his judgement in so many other ways. His failure as a state-building, enlightened despot left him undeterred, and his determination was justified. It did not prove so positive for him as a soldier. Egypt should have taught him that he was not ready to operate successfully outside wealthy, settled countryside, in topography and climates that were not western European. If he did learn this at the time, he had forgotten it by 1807 when he invaded modern Poland and Lithuania in winter.

Something more significant still is buried under all this. Until now, however adept at state-building or diplomacy or war Napoleon had proved himself, he had been at the beck and call of his government. He had been shunted from pillar to post since his schooldays, as an officer, even as a young, illustrious general; assigned his front, shifted from one command to another at the will of others. He had enthused about Egypt, but it was a plan concocted by Talleyrand, which he, not Napoleon, had sold to the Directory. Perhaps this sense of subordination, of being at the will of others, had exploded in the isolated, other-worldly freedom of Egypt. At few other points in his life had Plutarch's Alexander prevailed over Caesar more than in Egypt.

That he later wrote of the Egyptian campaign in terms more directly modelled on Caesar's *Gallic Wars* than any other reminiscence perhaps betrays his own sense of having betrayed his true mentor, Caesar, for the hero whose example proved his nemesis in Egypt, Alexander:

He was absent from Europe for sixteen months and twenty days. In that time, he took Malta, conquered lower and upper Egypt, destroyed two Turkish armies, captured their general and their equipment, their campaign artillery, ravaged Palestine and Galilee, and created the foundations, henceforth solid, of a most magnificent colony. He had brought the sciences and arts back to their cradle.[45]

In truth, he had lost his way, not just in the sands with his troops, but within himself. Egypt was to be the last such time he did this for quite a while. He recovered. As soon as Napoleon returned to France, 'Octavian' took over from 'Alexander'; self-control mastered impulsive egomania. After his first self-imposed fiasco, Napoleon became his own man, if not yet the master of his own destiny.

6

IN A SINISTER FOG

Seizing Office: The Coup of Brumaire, Autumn 1799

FROM OUTCAST TO OVERLORD: THE ROAD TO OFFICE

Napoleon received a hero's welcome when he returned to France on 9 October 1799. It lasted all the way from Fréjus, where he landed, to Paris. The towns and cities of the Rhône Valley cheered him all the way along the route; church bells rang out, crowds mobbed him, but it was all based on a gigantic lie and Napoleon knew it. Not until the catastrophe of Russia in 1812 would he need his propaganda machine as badly as he now did. Philip Dwyer is right to believe that the propaganda machine virtually saved him.[1] He was no fool: he knew the truth about Egypt even if the French public did not. Inwardly, Napoleon slunk back into France. He had sallied forth from Toulon with one of the largest fleets ever seen in those waters, at the head of the finest army the new Republic had yet to assemble. The warships were now almost all captured by the British or at the bottom of Aboukir Bay; the army had been decimated in Syria, Palestine and Sinai, its remnants left stranded over a thousand miles away. The only tangible trophies he had acquired in Egypt were archaeological finds – and many of those were now also in British hands. He did bring back a new vogue in fashion, furniture and frippery, and there was a giraffe as well, but it died on the way to Paris.

All this was in stark contrast to his return from Italy two years earlier, but Napoleon quickly fixed the attention of the public on the intellectual and scientific accomplishments of the expedition, while Joséphine soon made the Egyptian vogue her hallmark style. He had

benefited from the pure luck of irregular postal communications, as
Patrice Gueniffey has pointed out. When news of the British victory
of Aboukir Bay reached France it was quickly overshadowed by the
publication of his own glowing account of the land campaign, which
arrived in Paris two days later. The news of later disasters, contained in
Kléber's dispatches, did not arrive until after the coup of 18 Brumaire,
by which time Napoleon had taken power.[2] The truth dogged
Napoleon's false triumphal progress to Paris, and so it would be
unwise to conclude, as many have, that he believed his own publicity,
or that these were among the happiest days of his life.[3] He set off for
Paris, not to bask in fragile public adulation, but to search for much-
needed allies. Napoleon was now more alone and exposed than at any
time since he had faced the guillotine in a Toulon gaol cell, four years
earlier. Napoleon was all too aware that he was living a lie; had he
succumbed inwardly to the public adulation all around him, he would
not have survived.

Or so it seemed to him until he got the measure of France in the
last months of 1799. In truth, both his political masters and his fellow
generals in the field had fared much worse than he, and his own
spectacular failures had been successfully hidden from the public to a
degree impossible for those which now allowed the enemy to threaten
the borders of France itself. Napoleon profited more from the failure
of his colleagues to hold Italy than he did by any of his own actions.
'Would Bonaparte have lost Italy?' asked *Le Surveillant*, by no means a
lone voice. Napoleon was bolstered by the memory of his achievement
of peace at Campo Formio, as much as by his supposed victories,
because, in 1799, France now seemed too weak to win at the conference
table.[4] The fragile peace had collapsed even as Napoleon set sail for
Egypt, and the Allies had assembled a coalition against the Directory
which had had great military success in the spring of 1799, to the extent
that, for the first time since 1793, the territory of the Republic and the
life of the Republic itself were both in peril. Napoleon's successors
in Italy had lost all his conquests. Save for a tiny sliver of territory
around Genoa, all Italy, Switzerland and much of the Rhineland were

again in Allied hands. Fingers pointed at the corruption, inefficiency and incompetence of the Directory, and not just from both political extremes, but from within its own ranks.

The violent undercurrents Napoleon had perceived in Provence now seemed to herald a sinister 'fifth column' within, ready to explode should the Allies cross the Alps. Perhaps the most significant incident to occur along Napoleon's triumphal return to Paris was that brigands pillaged his baggage outside Aix-en-Provence. This, more than the cheering crowds, was the true indicator of the limits of his support, of the state of the country, and of the task awaiting whoever wound up in charge of it. A large, if ultimately disorganised and leaderless, peasant revolt had broken out in south-western France that summer, sparked by the new, more systematic laws enforcing conscription. In late 1798, the newly annexed Belgian departments had been rocked by a far more serious insurrection that had genuinely anti-French, pro-Austrian political motives. The Vendeans and Chouans of the west were still a real threat. The Republic had been alone and embattled before, but never had it been so unsure of how to react. In the midst of all this, Napoleon did not strike quite the figure of abject failure he might have had the truth of Egypt been more widely known. His military failures took place far away, and, whatever the losses of men and materiel, they had not opened the way to the invasion of France itself. The extent of his failures could be covered up, at least partially, for Egypt was still in French hands, while Italy – so highly prized and so well won by him – had been lost by others.

Napoleon had recovered his sense of proportion completely by the time he landed in the small, inconspicuous port of Fréjus. His choice of landfall is a clear sign of the discretion and caution he would continue to display, not just in the last months of Directorial rule, but in the years immediately after he attained high office. He remained exposed and endangered for some time. The isolated fugitive from Egypt became the target of assassination; the seeming pawn of the Directory became a leader embattled first by foreign armies and then by internal chaos. The abandoned husband assumed the headship of a difficult, untrustworthy family. Within months of landing at Fréjus, Napoleon took power not by force of arms, but through shrewd calculation; he secured his position more by making peace than by conquest. He steered himself from looming ignominy to real power and he did so with the clear eye that had first scanned Italy from the Alps. Strangely, perhaps, it was an English periodical of liberal leanings that caught the essence of the man in these dangerous years. 'Above all things,' the *Monthly Magazine* said of Napoleon in 1797, '[he] attempted, and in great measure obtained, the mastery over his passions.'[5] If he had lost his capacity for self-mastery in Egypt, this quality in him would now enter its crucial test.

The weeks between his arrival at Fréjus and the coup of Brumaire were among the most unreal of Napoleon's life. The urban public cheered him as he made his way to Paris. Amidst the routed generals of the European theatre, he seemed a shining success, a beacon of hope, at least to that part of France that wanted the Republic to win the war, and that may have been far from the majority. Napoleon knew the truth, however, and it went beyond his military failure. He no longer had a loyal army behind him. He returned to an empty house in Paris, Joséphine hedging her bets, for she knew the truth too, as did most in the higher political circles in the capital. Napoleon was aware of this and he also knew that the popular enthusiasm he still commanded – the only clear support he seemed to be able to count on – was as much a potential danger as the real news from the east.

In the eyes of an embattled, cornered political class there was only one thing worse than isolation and failure and that was mass adulation. With that in mind, Napoleon laid low in Paris, cultivating the relatively harmless world of the intellectual salons and their official organ, the Academy, picking up where he had left off before the Egyptian expedition. He had much to show for the scientific work carried out in Egypt, and the intelligentsia was suitably impressed, but this was of little relevance to the dangers of high politics. In Napoleon's early days in Paris, the regime sought to honour him officially with a banquet, but the guest himself and his entourage ate only the fruit and cheese they had brought with them, fearing assassination by poisoning. This event summed up the climate of the times. The long, unrelenting test of nerves of the autumn of 1799 was his masterclass in sangfroid.

The contrast with Bernadotte, his main rival for power in these months, says much about Napoleon's character under this kind of pressure. Patrice Gueniffey, a historian with a gift for sensing the measure of a man at the distance of centuries, describes Bernadotte thus:

His charm, his way with words, his cordial, open manner . . . even his cheek, gave him the appearance of a leader of men . . . Rare were those who did not succumb to his charm. Yet, this man who so seemed to . . . possess the ability to slake the thirst for the power he so craved, was also the most irresolute of men, hiding this defect behind a lot of bluff and diversion.[6]

His new wife of less than a year, Napoleon's former fiancée Désirée Clary, certainly had an eclectic taste in men.

Bernadotte had until recently been a field commander on the Rhine, as well as a calamitous ambassador to Vienna. He was an insider who tried to keep doors open to the two political extremes. A man with past links to royalism, by 1799 he was associating himself with the neo-Jacobins, as the misfortunes of war seemed to be proving them right. In so doing, he made himself the prisoner of both and the master of neither. Duplicity marked his later career, on the throne of Sweden that Napoleon procured for him, but in 1799 it lost him the initiative. Power slipped to Napoleon exactly because he was none of these things. Taciturn, but astute, keeping his own counsel and using his apparent weakness to his advantage, he became no one's hostage, was linked to no faction and set himself to create his own. In 1798, Bernadotte had hesitated to lead a coup, and his chance would not come again, because, when Napoleon was offered the role, he did not hesitate.

Napoleon's isolation and unease reflected the outlook of all those loyal to the Republic in the 'black year' of 1799. The only thing that had produced unity among the political leadership was its refusal

to acknowledge the victory of the neo-Jacobins in the elections of
1799. These had been quashed, in keeping with every other election
held since 1797. There was to be no return to the Terror. Beyond that,
even the ultimate loyalty to the Republic of a former member of
the Committee of Public Safety no longer seemed certain: Carnot, a
Director with just such a past, was now toying with moderate royalism
as a way out of the crisis. Generals like Bernadotte, a republican
volunteer in 1792, who owed his whole career to the Revolution,
seemed inclined the same way and he was actually the Minister of War
in 1799.

As the danger of invasion became very real, not only the soldiers
and the Jacobins, but politicians within the system as well, saw
that the day of the corrupt manipulator was over. Men like Paul
Barras could no longer be afforded, and as they were pushed to
the margins of politics the greasy but once effective networks they
held together dissolved. Corruption and profiteering had provided
much of the political glue of the Directory. Today, the Directory is
seen as a significant political laboratory for the future of republican
France, but then it was a fragile political world sustained not just by
corruption or the suppression of political extremes, but by shifting
alliances within the centre. The weak executive, with its procession
of Directors, actually led to real power devolving on men who were
often not in high office. The Directory withstood internal subversion,
endemic profiteering and inadequate political institutions, but it
could do so only if it was winning the war. Now, as defeat piled on
defeat, corruption and compromise were seen as dangers to survival.
Barras personified the weaknesses in this world, and his fading star
was a symptom of the times. He had come to embody the spirit of
the years of the Directory, nowhere better described than by Patrice
Gueniffey: 'There is a trait that strikes anyone who explores the
history of "the climate of opinion" [in these years]: its remarkable
stability. The prevailing spirit mixed [a sense of] being haunted
by the past, and distaste for the present, and a fear of the future.'[7]
Barras embodied this so well that, by the end, he was simply the past.

Napoleon soon saw that, in order to succeed, as opposed to survive, he had to dispel the fear of the future.

Conversely, Sieyès and Talleyrand were Napoleon's present and the future, respectively. At some point not long after his return from Egypt, Talleyrand brought Napoleon and Sieyès together to plan not just the demise of the Directory, but to devise a new, stronger regime to take its place, with themselves at its helm. Their plot became the coup of 18 Brumaire, their new regime the Consulate. Sieyès had had his great moment early in the Revolution, as an eloquent and courageous leader of the Third Estate when Louis seemed prepared to dissolve it at bayonet point, but ever since he had been shoved to the margins of politics. His proposed constitution had been pushed aside in 1795, and he had carped about the regime ever since, criticising its institutions as much as its measures, and devising new regimes on paper. Napoleon began to sense that the more absurd and complex Sieyès' constitution was – and it made that of 1795 appear streamlined – the easier it would be to subvert it. Sieyès' visions and systems were as flimsy and as thin as Joséphine's evening dresses, but at least Sieyès was assumed to have something to sell, and the determination to sell it to those who would be most needed to create a successful coup from inside the government. Events would soon show the contempt Napoleon had for both Sieyès and the men he carried with him into the conspiracy, but for now they were the key to office, if not yet to power. Without the support of so many politicians and intellectuals, the plot would have descended into what has so often been caricatured as a crude military coup. No such thing could have worked in 1799, as Napoleon, Talleyrand and especially Sieyès knew all too well. Napoleon saw parliamentary politicians as silly people playing silly games. If Sieyès was the silliest of them all, so much the better. Hence his wide appeal; hence his inability to grasp Napoleon's real nature. Sieyès saw only a dangerously popular soldier; he had paid no attention to Napoleon's exercises in state-building in Italy or Egypt, regarding them as crude imitations of his own ideas. When he called Napoleon 'the most civilian of the generals', he did not know what he was saying. Sieyès was perfect, the first useful idiot of the Napoleonic regime.

Sieyès was more than useful, however. In the planning stages of the coup, he was essential, and with reason. In two crucial ways his plan for a new constitution touched the right nerves among many at the apex of the Directory. His aim was now to adjust a creation he had tried, but failed, to influence at conception. Sieyès had objected to the weakness of the new executive from the outset. Now he set out to correct it, but not to destroy it. This was an attempt to protect the centre, to preserve moderate politics from the extremes by methods that, if ultimately reliant on force, were not intended to be extremist. The coup was not meant to be a purge, as such; no one was supposed to get hurt, and no one was. Above all, Sieyès' plan for reform revolved around the shared concern of the centrist politicians at the heart of the regime. Their over-riding worry, certainly since the coup of Fructidor in 1797 and probably ever since they had overthrown Robespierre and the 'tyranny' of the Committee of Public Safety in 1794, had been less the electorate or the legislature than the executive and how to make it work. There was a growing consensus that the Constitution of 1795 had made the Directory too weak, and Sieyès' plan to reshape it addressed exactly this issue within the parameters of the moderate republic created in 1795. Pierre Serna has traced four major themes in the moderate, 'establishment' press in the last years of the Directory: an emerging vision of the character of a centrist citizen; the question of a stronger executive; an emerging philosophy of moderation; and the justification of opportunistic measures led by a party around which republican institutions could rally.[8] Sieyès seemed to have the answers to the crisis many political insiders wanted to hear. He did not notice, however, that Napoleon had learned more about strong executives in Italy and Egypt – because he had first fashioned one for himself and then acted as its head – than all his peers, military or political.

The perceived need for a stronger executive reached beyond the 'establishment' of the centre, however. It explains partly the growing appeal of constitutional royalism, even among republicans with radical pasts such as Bernadotte and Carnot; the neo-Jacobins fought and won the elections of 1799 demanding a return to strong government. The wider appeal of strong government was something the men of the Directory, Sieyès included, failed to grasp. Their whole conception of politics was of an embattled centre, retracting into a safe laager. This was wholly understandable and a thoroughly sensible response in the climate of 1799. Napoleon drew a different lesson from it, however. His goal – well hidden in these tense weeks – was not to gather support for whatever new regime emerged from the plot, but to expand it to embrace all those elements whose major concern was a stronger, more effective and stable executive. In the meantime, he had to let Talleyrand do most of his 'fixing' for him, and was constrained to let Sieyès take the lead in the planning. It could not have been otherwise. As Serna has observed, 'Everything did not spring from the martial head of a general disembarked from Egypt. The members of civil society had already prepared the ground for enlightened opinion to accept a republic with an executive more powerful than any constitutional norm would tolerate.'[9] An important element of that preparation was the current Directors' own incompetence, which had strengthened the opposition, but royalism and Jacobinism had no power at the centre, and that was where Napoleon had to work. Sieyès had done a great deal of spadework here and in late 1799 the plot appeared to be under his control.

Ironically, in these months the Directory showed itself quite capable of confronting the crisis in practical terms. Late 1798 saw the beginning of the first systematic mass conscription in France, through the 'Jourdan Law', named after the general who drafted it. In June 1799, in the 'coup of generals', the army forced the Directory to enact neo-Terrorist measures, mainly the seizure of dangerous royalists as hostages and a 'forced loan' from suspected counter-revolutionaries to replenish the war coffers, now seriously damaged by the loss of Italy. True to their record since 1789, however, the Revolutionary elite remained brilliant administrators but inept politicians.

As they had been for some time, the generals were divided over the shape political change should take. If a lead was to come from the military, it could only come from an individual commander with the tacit backing of the rest. Bernadotte probably gravitated towards the royalists less from ideological conviction than because some form of restoration might take Britain out of the war, and so knock away the financial underpinnings of the Allied Coalition. Moreau, a man of the left and a force behind the measures of June, knew his views had no real support in the corridors of power. Masséna's army in Switzerland and Brune's in the Low Countries were actually doing most to turn the tide of defeat, making Russia reconsider the wisdom of fighting on. Masséna was the most apolitical of the generals, and the most corrupt, predictable only through his avarice. Without a command or a loyal army, Napoleon hardly came into the picture. The other generals knew what Napoleon's return from Egypt had really implied: he had abandoned his troops. He thus seemed the most harmless of all of them. The army was a powerful, if disjointed and rudderless, presence in high politics, unable to speak with one voice, still less to give a lead. So powerful in 1798, its moment had passed with the crushing defeats of 1799, and only when it could unite around one candidate could it hope to exert real influence again.

In circumstances in which nobody was to be trusted – when the highest decoration offered by the regime seemed to be the order of the double-cross – it was a minor miracle that sufficient men came together long enough to overthrow it. The politician with the clearest, most consistent desire for change was Sieyès; the man who really knew the game was up for the Directory was Talleyrand. Both were veterans of Revolutionary politics. Each had taken different things from his experiences. Talleyrand was a hardened operator; Sieyès liked to think he was too, and, in 1799, a few others seemed to believe this. What Sieyès had to offer in these months was a plan for constitutional change, something with which to steer through the fog, and he was prepared to risk a coup to bring it about.

Sieyès' ideas were complex, but those around him seized on only one. The Republic needed less powerful legislative assemblies and a smaller, stronger, longer-serving executive of three men, not five.

He felt, too, that he could 'people' his new system from among the existing leadership – which made his plans unthreatening, save in one respect: Sieyès had come to feel the government 'needed a sword', as he put it in his overblown manner. In other words, a general should be brought into the executive body, to ensure the proper co-ordination of the war effort. This was also an indirect acknowledgement that the neo-Jacobins had been right to demand a stronger government in the crisis, even if it did not spell a return to the Terror. Sieyès turned first to Moreau, a man of known Jacobin sympathies, whose integrity he deeply respected. Moreau gave crucial support for the plot, but refused to lead it. 'There's your man,' he is reputed to have told Sieyès, pointing to Napoleon. If he did so, it was a gesture both men would soon regret.

Talleyrand saw his chance here. He had been close to Sieyès for some time, and had secured him the embassy at Berlin, from which Sieyès returned to become a Director in the summer of 1799 after a successful, if controversial, mission. Napoleon and Talleyrand had been in contact since the First Italian Campaign, and had worked closely together during Napoleon's brief period at the Congress of Rastatt. The long-term importance of this short diplomatic mission now emerged. Either directly, or through his brother Joseph – very much a member of the Directorial diplomatic corps even without Napoleon's help – Talleyrand and Napoleon had come to know and respect each other. Trust was not a word in the lexicon of either man, but they had seen steel in each other and a mutual determination to seek safety in power. There was little to bind Sieyès and Napoleon, however. They despised each other, and when he spoke of Sieyès the veil of the cultivated intellectual fell away from Napoleon. He considered Sieyès a pompous man who inhabited a world of political theory, who believed that constitutional niceties, if properly calibrated, could secure the new regime. Talleyrand agreed with Napoleon but, ever the consummate diplomat, his behaviour concealed this. He brought them together and, once the three were in something like harness, those who looked to each of them individually were won over in their turn.

Lucien had also had his part to play. Elected a deputy for Corsica even though under age, he had not rested on his brother's laurels, but had carved out his own network of friends in the Council of the 500, the lower house, and had been noticed by Sieyès. He had to use all his powers of persuasion to help Talleyrand that October and proved himself, in the words of Isser Woloch, 'a dogged facilitator'. If the plotters won any support among neo-Jacobin deputies, it was the work of Lucien.[10] Indeed, the months immediately after the coup would show just how well-connected Lucien was, and how wide his network had become. It was through him that Napoleon recruited the first prefects and many other officials in key ministries. Once his brother was in power, Lucien became once again his intemperate, conniving self, but for the moment he worked with Talleyrand to hold Napoleon and Sieyès together.

In the labyrinthine weeks of private dinners, tense coffee mornings – that very bourgeois 'enlightenment' contribution to *sociabilité* – and altogether darker gatherings, those who were marginalised are as revealing as those who were drawn in. Paul Barras was now a man of the past; his networks had collapsed, and he could bring no one of real use into the conspiracy, a sign of changed times, even if his weakening position might have made him, personally, more trustworthy than usual. As Napoleon drew closer to Talleyrand, he left Barras, once his patron, in the dark about the plans.

Perhaps the clearest guide to the shifting tides is Joséphine. Once Barras' mistress and never really committed to Napoleon, she now put herself firmly among the plotters, using her connections with the financial world, and the Récamier family in particular, to help the new, murky cause. Her husband's venture was dangerous, but his stock was high enough to merit support, especially as she saw men of ability and influence turning towards him. Since his return from Egypt, their marriage had been marred by bitter rows, which threatened to become public as emotions became harder to control. He seethed bitterly over her infidelities, those that were certainly in the past and those that he supposed were going on in the present; she resented him, probably for being alive, and loathed his family's 'policing' of her. So often disloyal and ungrateful to him in other ways, the Bonapartes at least saw through Joséphine and tried to protect Napoleon from the worst of her. The state of the marriage in these months put Napoleon under pressure, given the climate of his public life, which would have broken any normal person. He coped with it all, however close to the edge his private life drove him. Perhaps Joséphine drew something from this, too, sensing the power of his self-possession and sheer will in the face of so much danger. Moreover, Joséphine was the most adept survivor of them all, and remained so to the end of her life, when she died of a cold caught from entertaining the victorious Tsar Alexander, in a flimsy dress, in 1814, and now she seemed to sense Napoleon's moment better than anyone else. Her connections were important to the plot, and her active participation in it would prove invaluable.

The people and means that each of the major conspirators – Sieyès, Talleyrand and Napoleon – brought with them to the common purpose was indicative of their own relative positions of strength, and of the political climate of the Directory in its last days. Napoleon knew his current illustrious reputation was built upon sand – and in the most literal sense. Sieyès had become a hate figure for the left in the assemblies. He had returned from his post as ambassador to Prussia, now a neutral in the war, with a reputation for 'appeasement', for talking in terms of a negotiated peace, a label that almost inevitably carried half-spoken accusations of royalism. He carried this baggage into the executive, when he became a Director.

The 10th of August 1799 was a tense day, the anniversary of the overthrow of the monarchy only seven years before, and Sieyès and the neo-Jacobin deputies in the lower house, the Council of the 500, took the chance to denounce each other for destabilising the Republic. The deputies of the left pronounced the dread words 'the country is in danger' – la patrie en danger – a phrase of deadly import. This had been the official decree of the Revolutionary government in 1792–3, the last time France had been invaded, which sanctioned the Terror. Now, the neo-Jacobins demanded it again. Sieyès closed their meeting hall, in spite of opposition from two other Directors, Gohier and Moulin. The left then mounted a press campaign vilifying him as a closet royalist. This culminated on 15 September, when Jourdan, the Jacobin general and deputy, again denounced him, along with Barras. With a menacing crowd outside cheering his every word, Jourdan rallied a large minority in the lower house to declare *la patrie en danger*, losing the vote by 245 to 171. It is easy to discount this incident with hindsight, but to those on all sides at the time the power of the left in the 500 was all too clear, and a return to the Terror was averted only by the refusal of the upper house, the Council of Ancients, to ratify a motion aimed directly at Sieyès, condemning to death anyone who tried to negotiate for peace on terms that rejected the natural frontiers.[11]

Sieyès was not fooled by the outward expressions of unity and of personal congratulations that followed on 23 September, the anniversary of the founding of the Republic in 1792. Instead, he took careful stock of who mattered, who did not, who was friend and who was foe. He concentrated on the power of the left in the 500 and the weakness and divided character of the executive, how to correct this and who to turn to. It was the approach of a political scientist as much as of a politician, but it was not inappropriate to the circumstances. Those who were not foes, and who also mattered, were shortlisted for the plot that now took clear shape in his mind. In the weeks in which Napoleon laid low and took refuge in Sieyès' preferred milieu, the Institut, Sieyès got to work in his own way. The torrid weeks of late summer had flushed out many potential opponents of regime change; the situation was now more perilous. Gohier and Moulin were dangers to the stability of the centre, ironically because they had stuck to the law in the face of a resurgence of Jacobin populism and street violence. It is significant that Sieyès did not turn for support to the other target of the left, Barras. Like Napoleon, he sensed that association with the most overtly corrupt Director was a liability in times of military crisis and Jacobin resurgence. A last-minute attempt by Barras to align himself with the coup was rebuffed by both Napoleon and

Sieyès. Instead, Sieyès set about creating a new network, a new form of political alliance, based on the new imperative: that it was time to survive, not to prosper.

In October, Sieyès did something remarkable. He not only pieced together the key elements of the projected coup, but he brought together most of the men Napoleon forged into the team that would rebuild and reinvigorate France in the years to come. Both Napoleon and Sieyès had an almost unerring eye for talent, even if they often looked for different things in the same person. Roger Ducos had proved himself the only reliable Director during the September crisis, and he now knew that most of his support in the legislature came from the upper house. The voting on the neo-Jacobin proposals had shown him clearly who was dangerous and on whom he could rely, which was crucial to his calculations on the day of the coup. Ducos manoeuvred Lucien into the post of President of the 500 in October, and his loyal colleague Lemercier into the equivalent post in the Ancients.

When Sieyès reached beyond the government, however, he brought together the core of the new regime. He had little work to do in rallying the intellectuals of the Institut to the plot, for Napoleon had already been elected to their number; one of the most prominent among them, Volney, had been with him in Egypt. Another was Pierre-Louis Roederer, whom Sieyès appreciated for his competence and clarity. Ironically, under Napoleon it would be Roederer, not Sieyès, who became the regime's 'constitution maker', as his chief role became that of creating French institutions in the German and Italian kingdoms assigned to various members of the Bonaparte family.

Sieyès' greatest contribution to the future of the regime was in rallying ministers around the plotters. The most important among them, Jean-Jacques-Régis Cambacérès, the justice minister, would be the key figure in formulating the new Civil Code, and shared Sieyès' aim to recast the failed institutional framework of the Directory. Cambacérès was one of the few colleagues Sieyès respected intellectually. Buried among the deputies in the 500, but raised to prominent roles for the coup, were Boulay de la Meurthe and Claude Régnier, the former a future framer of the Civil Code, the latter a future Minister of Justice. Someone who would speak first from the floor of the 500 against the Jacobins was Charles-François Lebrun, who was valued by Sieyès for his links to moderate royalism; under Napoleon, he created the Bank of France and finally halted the financial chaos with which the Directory had become synonymous.

To these must be added one of the most valuable, if relatively unsung, technocrats of the Napoleonic period, Martin-Michel-Charles Gaudin, whose efforts were to the disastrous finances of the period what Carnot's were to the war effort; in his sphere, Gaudin became 'the organiser of victory'. The son of an unsuccessful Parisian lawyer, he acquired a sound reputation in the late *ancien régime* working for the Farmers-General and had served with great ability in the financial committees of the early Revolutionary assemblies. He survived in office during the Terror, when his work in provisioning the armies and cities was facilitated by his knowledge of the complex workings of the commercial markets in Europe. Gaudin avoided public office under the Directory, however, accepting only a subordinate job in the postal service in 1798. It was here that he came to Sieyès' attention, and it was Sieyès, aware of his background, who persuaded him to become Minister of Finance on 19 Brumaire, a post he held until 1814, and again in the Hundred Days.

There were, of course, plotters who were very much their own men. Sieyès played a very astute game with Joseph Fouché, former Terrorist, butcher of the revolt in Lyon, and now Minister of Police. Fouché had often been brought in by the Directory when it felt threatened by the royalists, but recent experience had convinced him that his old comrades on the left were now the immediate problem, and that the constitution was inadequate to contain them. He expressed a willingness to help, and did so 'on the day', but Sieyès kept him in the dark about the workings and timing of events.

If Sieyès assembled this group with a specific task in mind, Napoleon kept them on afterwards and welded them into the greatest ministerial team France had known since the reign of Louis XIV. Not since Louis brought together Colbert, Louvois and Vauban would France know such a concentration of ability and energy at its head. The coup was a team effort; that team – minus Sieyès – would go on to reforge not just France but much of Europe.

Talleyrand was the only one of the three key conspirators who had actually felt the full force of the resurgence of the left in the summer of 1799. Napoleon, on the other hand, still held his general's commission, even as he watched his back and sniffed his food for poison, and Sieyès was technically one of the most powerful men in France, if also the most exposed. By contrast, there had been nothing veiled about Talleyrand's experience of the 'red summer' of 1799. He had been forced out of the Foreign Ministry in July, following the 'generals' coup' of June, blamed for the defeats and branded a royalist. He had taken to the shadows, where he proved more lethal to the regime that threatened him so brazenly than he would ever have been in office. Talleyrand continued to hold Napoleon and Sieyès together – just. Like Joséphine, he used his influence among financiers like Récamier, convincing them that this was the way out of the morass, for no one was more concerned about the prevailing instability than the money marketeers of the time. Above all, Napoleon trusted Talleyrand's judgement. His hand is hard to find, but it was everywhere.

Napoleon himself brought relatively little to the plotters' table, and what he had to offer came more from family contacts than the army. Jourdan still thought he could be attached to the neo-Jacobin efforts to preserve the constitution; Augereau, another general of the left, actually stated openly in the political clubs that Napoleon had deserted his army and should be disciplined. Bernadotte was not won over by Napoleon – a weekend spent in each other's company had nearly ended in disaster – and he may well have revealed Napoleon's true political opinions to the neo-Jacobin deputies. He was 'neutralised' by family ties: Bernadotte had married Désirée Clary, and so Joseph was his wife's brother-in-law. The loyalty of Leclerc, an important commander in the Paris region at the time, was ensured because he was married to Pauline. Moreau had been won over by deeply held principles and a respect for Sieyès. The only military support Napoleon could really guarantee was his own close circle. At the eleventh hour – the morning of 18 Brumaire (9 November) – he had still not been able to secure the loyalty of the key soldier in Paris, General Lefebvre, its commandant. Indeed, a few days earlier, Lefebvre had declared himself the protector of the constitution. On that morning, in a bold gesture, Napoleon met him, offered him the sword he had worn in Egypt and reduced the old warhorse almost to tears. It was about all he could do.

Two days before Napoleon had been summoned by the Directors and it had been made clear to him that Gohier and Moulin – and probably Barras – wanted him out of Paris. He feigned illness, when it was clear that he could not browbeat them, and so avoided a confrontation he could not hope to win, even with the support of Ducos and Sieyès. Then Sieyès, helped by Lemercier and Lucien, carefully arranged an extraordinary session of the two houses of the legislature. Napoleon was the spearhead of the plot; he and his men would run the real risks as dawn broke on 18 Brumaire.

The previous night had been one for Sieyès and the politicians, and they used it well. The conspiratorial Directors invoked legislation that allowed the chambers to be transferred out of Paris, for security reasons. This was the first step. The two presidents of the legislature, Lucien of the lower house and Lemercier of the upper chamber, spent the small hours issuing invitations to those deputies considered reliable to go to the Tuileries for an extraordinary session where they would vote to transfer the assembly to St-Cloud, the pre-designated temporary seat of both chambers, while those considered unreliable were simply not informed. As the day would prove, even this precaution was barely enough for the success of the plot. The military element of the plan was to escort the deputies to St-Cloud and secure the new meeting place from any attempt to thwart the legislature from convening, and this was kept secret even from Sieyès, as well as from Fouché, who commanded the Parisian police. The politicians knew there would be a military presence, but not of what it consisted. Nor did the military themselves. The commanders of the units known

to be loyal to Napoleon, as well as those who might be a danger –
Lefebvre chief among them – were all asked individually to come to
Napoleon's house in north-central Paris, at six o'clock. None knew
about the others. Even as they all took their places to go to St-Cloud
via the Tuileries, or prepared to hold down Paris if necessary, none of
the plotters – not even Napoleon – really knew the details of the entire
operation, a very poignant insight into the political climate they were
all united in seeking to destroy.

If the night of 17/18 Brumaire belonged to the most senior
politicians among the plotters, the rest of the day was the preserve
of the soldiers loyal to Napoleon and deputies loyal to the coup.
Another comparatively small but very significant part of the plot
took place on the morning of 18 Brumaire, however, which said
much about Napoleon's life at the time. Joséphine invited Gohier to
morning coffee at eight. He was one of the two Directors known to
be openly opposed to constitutional change in general, and to Sieyès
and Napoleon in particular. First, she kept him out of the way while
the troops assembled, and in the process ensured that he seemed to be
close to Napoleon, and therefore implicated. She persuaded Gohier,
even as events were unfolding, that the only aim of the plot was to
purge Barras. It also helped that he was trying to get her into bed.
Her actions bound her inextricably to the plot and to Napoleon, and
she knew it. There was no way back now. Her dealings with Barras
earlier that month had done more harm than good to the conspiracy,
for she had tried to steer Napoleon away from Sieyès towards her old
lover and their old patron, in what may or may not have been the kind
of game of double-bluff the hardened survivalist plays. Two nights
earlier, Barras had met Napoleon and seen that it was he himself
who was isolated. Joséphine then made her choice. When she invited
Gohier to take coffee with her, her fate was sealed, her options closed.
This was as much a watershed in Napoleon's emotional world as it was
in the history of the world itself.

The small hours of 18 Brumaire saw many significant comings
and goings, all of which marked turning points but none of which at

the time guaranteed the success of the coup or heralded real change. Indeed, all were looking warily over their shoulders with their eyes on the recent bloody past. Talleyrand had spent the night calming Barras down, even offering to pray with him, as if either man could remember how. Barras was persuaded to stay out of things, a crucial move crafted by Talleyrand, for without him Gohier and Moulin could not achieve a majority of Directors and successfully oppose a change to the constitution. As Barras slipped out of Paris for his country house, clutching the suitcase full of the money with which the plotters had bought him off, so he and the political era he epitomised slipped from history. At the time, however, he was really using his tried and tested survival tactic, that of being out of the way on the day of the revolution. When Sieyès, that other arch-survivor, swung into action in the early hours, he, too, took a case full of money with him to St-Cloud, lest he needed to beat a quick retreat from a failed coup.

As the selected deputies stumbled out of bed to the Tuileries, Napoleon gathered his troops around him, and Berthier summoned the commanders of the National Guard to meet on Place de la Concorde. Once assembled, Lebrun and Régnier, following the lead of the officers of the chambers, denounced a Jacobin plot to overthrow the constitution, and moved to leave for St-Cloud. There was no argument and they prepared to move. As Philip Dwyer has rightly said, all this fooled no one, for by 1799 such ruses 'had been fabricated . . . to justify the illegal machinations of a radical minority of deputies'.[12]

By now, Napoleon and the troops were outside; he briefly entered the Council of Ancients and made a short speech saying he had come to defend them. Crucially for his credibility, he had Lefebvre at his side, and the crowds that had gathered outside seemed more jovial and curious than hostile. However, even within so 'select' a gathering, several deputies remarked that Napoleon had said nothing about protecting the constitution. They were quickly silenced while Napoleon rallied the troops with a promise to purge a corrupt regime that had cheated them of their just rewards. It was probably the only honest thing anyone said all day, and the only promise kept. The civilian and

military wings of the plot now finally came together, as Napoleon's
7,000 troops took Sieyès' 'chosen' to St-Cloud. It was only now that the
politicians realised how strong a force Napoleon, through Berthier,
actually had at his command. Once the deputies were at St-Cloud, the
meeting of both houses was postponed until the next day.

Only at this stage – the night of 18/19 Brumaire – did the plotters
have the chance to concert a plan for confronting the deputies. That
night, it was Sieyès who was ready to abandon the façade of legality,
advocating the arrest of forty Jacobin deputies. Napoleon stopped this,
believing it could mark a return to the bloody purges of the Terror; nor
did he want to alienate irrevocably any group of republican politicians.
The only agreement they had was to overturn the constitution and
replace the Directory with a new executive.

The next day proved as disorganised as the previous one had run
like clockwork. The morning of 19 Brumaire was characterised by
dithering among the plotters and an increasing awareness among
the deputies of both chambers that, save for those who were part of the
plot, they were pawns in some sort of game. Only at this point did the
surest hope of success come to rest with the troops around Napoleon,
and this only because the politicians could not develop a strategy
to manipulate the chambers. The whole business was watched by a
curious, generally well-heeled crowd of picnicking spectators who had
come to see a coup in the country, which went some way to justifying
the plotters' decision to get out of Paris, for this was an altogether
different audience from the pro-Jacobin mob Sieyès, Napoleon and
the others knew and feared.

The rapid deployment to St-Cloud had created a potential
problem, however. Indeed, the chaos surrounding the last meeting of
the Directorial assemblies epitomised both the shambolic politics of
the doomed regime, and the riskiness of the coup bent on its demise.
The château of St-Cloud no longer exists; it was destroyed by Prussian
artillery in the Franco-Prussian War in 1870, and so the actual scene
of the coup of Brumaire cannot really be reconstructed, but the hasty
transfer of the assemblies there from Paris meant that their chambers

were thrown together at short notice. The Ancients were assigned a long gallery in the château, itself, the Gallery of Apollo, which was more or less ready; it had a quickly assembled podium for the president of the chamber and the speakers, and the room was wide enough for benches to be arranged in the semi-circular fashion that the French revolutionaries had adopted immediately in 1789, to avoid the 'oppositional' character of the British Parliament. The chamber assigned to the 500, the Orangerie of the château, was still being set up that morning, leaving the deputies of the lower house time to wander about, confer and, eventually, to gather themselves for action, if threatened. It all served to slow the impetus of the conspiracy. The whole setting of the Orangerie militated against an orderly meeting, or an orderly disruption of it; its entry was so narrow that only two deputies – or soldiers – could pass through it at one time so that both escape and 'invasion' were awkward. Orangeries were long, narrow annexes to châteaux, such as that near the Louvre in Paris. They were built as hothouses, and so that of St-Cloud proved to be, even on a cold autumn day. This Orangerie had a partition in the middle, which had only been partially dismantled, and, although the hastily summoned carpenters had managed to set up a raised podium for Lucien, its president, and the speakers to stand on, the deputies had to crowd themselves on steps along the walls, below the long, narrow windows, or mill about standing in the centre of the hall. There were also members of the public present, who could not be prevented from attending sessions; most of them were sitting on the window ledges above the deputies. This would not be an easy physical setting to control, when the moment came, and so it proved.

Sieyès, Ducos and Napoleon spent these hours nervously in a room above the Council of Ancients, waiting for their allies in the chambers to take control of the sessions, persuade the deputies to vote a state of emergency, dissolve the constitution and hand them power. When the 500 convened, chaired by Lucien, the deputies proved true to themselves. Lucien tried to assert the plotters' agenda, and the Jacobins, with considerable moderate support, turned on him, denounced

Napoleon as a traitor and howled Lucien down. They had seized the initiative, as they had learned to do in the course of the Revolution. Then, in an instant, they threw their victory away. An oath of loyalty to the constitution was demanded and approved, but this entailed every deputy swearing the oath individually, one by one. Time dragged on as they did so.

Now, finally, time had swung back in favour of the plotters, through the folly of the deputies, but Napoleon no more knew how to use this advantage than the deputies had theirs. Impatient, fed up and increasingly clouded in his judgement, Napoleon strode into the Ancients, the self-control and calculated self-mastery of the previous weeks evaporating with every step. The exchanges that followed between Napoleon and the deputies reveal a keen mind and a clear view of reality on his part, but absolutely no sense of what the circumstances required of him. His frustration tipped into petulance, telling them first that he was sick of being labelled a Caesar or a Cromwell, then warning the Ancients that they were 'sitting on a volcano'; but he did not elaborate on who he thought the volcano was, demonstrating the same fatal combination of vagueness and violence that had undone Robespierre just before Thermidor, when he had threatened the Convention with a 'hit list' he then failed to produce on the day. Then someone challenged Napoleon – just as someone had challenged Robespierre over Danton's death – with: 'And what of the constitution?' Napoleon's reply came from the gut: 'The constitution,' he sneered, 'you yourselves have annihilated that. On 18 Fructidor, you violated it; on 22 Floréal, you violated it, and you violated it again on 30 Prairial. It has no further respect from anyone.'[13] This judgement was devastatingly true, and spoke for a whole gamut of opinion, from right to left. He had put his finger on the flow of recent history, but the timing and tone could not have been more inept. It went from bad to worse. When pressed to name 'the traitors', he muttered 'Moulin and Barras', the first a blatant lie, the second a betrayal. As he swept out, he ranted, 'I walk with the god of victory and the god of war!', words for the soldiery, perhaps, but not for a parliament.

By the time Napoleon had reached the 500, his opponents – probably a considerable number by now – were ready for him. Lucien had lost all control of them, and Napoleon was greeted with jeers, calls for him to be outlawed and outright physical violence. Two-by-two, Napoleon and his men entered the Orangerie, pushing their way through the deputies who were standing, and running a gauntlet of abuse from those on the steps along the sides of the long, narrow hall. When some of them physically challenged Napoleon, he was on very narrow ground in every sense, trapped in a badly exposed position he would never have been caught in, in battle. He was saved by his bodyguards, for he had crossed the line of legality by entering the 500 with troops, something he had not done in the Ancients. With Napoleon and Lucien driven from the chamber, a motion to outlaw Napoleon was proposed, which could have led to his immediate death. This was the dread moment the plotters had all feared, and it had come to pass.

The plot was now, literally, on the outside of the political establishment. It would have to become, however briefly, an armed coup if it were to succeed. Three things saved the coup of Brumaire in those short moments: the inability of the 500 to unite under a spokesman; Lucien's ability to rally the troops not loyal to Napoleon to the coup; and the loyalty Napoleon commanded from his own men. Within the 500, no one emerged to direct the challenge to the plot, to drive through the motion against Napoleon or to quell the unease spreading through false rumours that four of the five Directors had resigned, effectively dissolving the constitution.

Outside, Lucien emerged as the coup's saviour. In Steven Englund's words, he 'uncorked an impromptu speech for the history books'.[14] His 'target audience' is another crucial reminder that the army seldom spoke with one voice under the Directory. He aimed his words at those troops who were not actually under Napoleon's command, but were the official guard of the chambers or part of the Parisian National Guard, soldiers whose duty was to turn on Napoleon if they believed he had come to overthrow the constitution or crush the legislature. His actual words also show that the old slurs remained the best ones, at least for republican troops. Lucien told them that a minority of deputies were in the pay of the English, were armed, had tried to kill his brother and were now virtually holding the majority of deputies hostage, at knifepoint. He drew a sword and swore that he would kill his own brother if he were to betray the Republic. The words were straight out of Marat's newspapers at the height of the Terror, the gesture redolent of the stern, if volatile, patriotism of Plutarch's Roman Republic; and it worked. It was just as well, since Napoleon himself had manifestly failed to inspire them just moments before. It may not have helped that his horse had nearly thrown him as he rode before the guards, trying to rally them. After his brother was met with their stony silence, it was Lucien – who had failed so badly in the 500 – who saved the day. These guards were the men who cleared the chambers and effectively ended the Directorial regime.

The other group of soldiers present were Napoleon's own men, under the loyal Sébastiani, veterans of Italy and Egypt, who had remained calm and resolute. This was very important, as in the course of the early afternoon Augereau and Jourdan had arrived and urged Napoleon to abandon the coup, while pro-Jacobin crowds had followed them from Paris and were milling about the gates. Neither general actually challenged Napoleon, however, for, even with the support of the republican troops before Lucien won them over, they would have had to fight Sébastiani.

Accounts vary as to the manner in which the halls were cleared. The official version and many military memoirs depict deputies diving ignominiously from windows and fleeing into the park, while those loyal to the plot clustered around Napoleon and the troops. However, Philip Dwyer has unearthed an account that speaks of a quiet, orderly withdrawal by most of the 500.[15] Whatever the truth, with the entry of the troops led by a composed Napoleon, everyone knew the coup had succeeded even if few really knew what it was supposed to be about. The Constitution of 1795 was over and a provisional government of three 'Consuls' – Napoleon, Sieyès and Ducos – took over. The day's work done, everyone went home to Paris. It seems that Napoleon said not a word on the journey back. Perhaps – it is impossible to know – he realised that he may already have said too much.

It was less a wonder that Napoleon lost his nerve when faced with the fury of the deputies than that Lucien, Lemercier, Régnier and the others kept theirs. This was a Jacobin chamber, red in tooth, claw and politics. These were the same men who, only a few weeks before, had demanded a return to the Terror, who had reimposed the Law of Hostages and sought the death penalty for anyone who as much as mentioned making peace. The lowest common factor among the plotters was to prevent a return to the Terror, and the only reason the neo-Jacobins clung to the Directorial constitution was that it provided them with the scope to do so, whereas their opponents had to resort to a coup. Less than five years earlier, men who had dared oppose Jacobin-led assemblies had been summarily executed. There was every chance this fate could have befallen Napoleon at Brumaire. The meeting had been removed from Paris to minimise this risk, and, had it not been so arranged, the balance would not have been in the plotters' favour. This much was obvious on the floor of the 500. No one could sleep quietly, with this knowledge of the past, amidst the uncertainties of the future. Nevertheless, thanks to Napoleon – not Sieyès, the supposed darling of moderation – it had remained a bloodless, if not quite a legal, coup. The centre had held against the Jacobins, whose response to the plot had shown they were still – albeit *in extremis* – prepared to return to the Terror, and they had been stopped, but only because Lucien had been able to 'out-Marat' them to their own guards. One vital, immediate lesson Napoleon had learned from the day was to keep the army out of Paris in future, as it had been kept out between 1790 and 1794. Henceforth, only troops under his own command, first the Consular and then the Imperial Guard, were garrisoned in the city.

Napoleon's resort to force at Brumaire is usually regarded as a manifestation of his innate militarism, as well as his innate authoritarianism, but the real proof of both is not to be found in the brute force he applied to the politicians. Violence, or its threat, had been the norm in the frequent regime changes of the 1790s in France; the

Directory had been no stranger to such tactics. Napoleon's bayonets were used with far more circumspection than in any previous purge, and with no loss of life. Rather, the future was clearer in Napoleon's inability to deal with an elected chamber. He was a fish out of water among the deputies, lost for a way of dealing with them face to face. Assemblies baffled him as much as they disgusted him. Napoleon's behaviour in the chambers at Brumaire, not the orders he issued, reveals his real authoritarian instincts. This aversion to parliamentary 'hubbub' stands in deep contrast to his genuine enthusiasm for serious discussion and debate in committee, behind closed doors. At Mombello, on board *L'Orient*, in Cairo, Napoleon showed himself to be open and desirous of criticism, thirsty for information and opinions from a wider political spectrum than any of the Revolutionary regimes were capable of tolerating, to say nothing of accepting it and putting it to use. The uproarious furore of parliaments was something quite different, however, and, at Brumaire, Napoleon found this out for himself. A pattern of government was set, provided, that is, he survived long enough to get his way.

7

THE PERILS OF OFFICE

The Shadow of the Assassin, 1800–1802

The first steps taken by the provisional government reflected the need to diffuse the threat of a renewed Terror, and show how it had been mounting in the last months of the Directory, even as the war emergency was easing. All power had been temporarily vested in the three Consuls, Napoleon, Sieyès and Ducos, who formed its executive; for the moment, until elections could be held, the Consuls were the only functioning arm of the new regime, but they used their power sparingly, wary of how narrow their victory had been. The great ministries were confided to those who had made themselves indispensable to the plotters, one way or another: the loyal Cambacérès received Justice, and Talleyrand returned to Foreign Affairs; Berthier became Minister of War. Fouché, whose greatest service to them had been to stand aside, retained Police. These were all clear, almost inevitable choices, but they reflected a desire for moderation. Sieyès got his way over Interior, which went to Laplace, as an acknowledgement of the support given to the plotters by the Institut; significantly, he did not last long, being replaced by Lucien Bonaparte a few months later.

It was in their initial legislation that the new regime did most to reassure the political world that they would not follow victory with revenge. The Law of Hostages and the forced loan were both repealed within days of the coup; a new set of 'extraordinary commissioners' was sent out to the provinces to placate the departmental administrators, as much as to enforce the will of the new regime, and the men assigned these roles were known more for their moderation than their loyalty to the new Consuls. This policy of 'pacifying rather than proscribing', as Jean-Denis Bredin has put it,[1] served to assure important figures who had either wavered or even opposed the coup. Barère, a former member of the Committee of Public Safety, wrote a public letter of support which had widespread influence in Parisian political circles, and Jourdan re-established good relations with Napoleon. Bridgeheads were quickly built with the Jacobins, at least in Paris: the thirty-four Jacobin deputies who were to have been banished immediately after the coup were actually left alone; the nineteen others who had been interned were theatrically released by Napoleon a few days later.

The real sign of confidence in the new regime came two weeks after the coup, when Napoleon was able to obtain an immediate advance loan of twelve million francs from the major Parisian bankers, which was the first step in stabilising the Republic's precarious finances. It was also a clear gesture on their part of the tacit support many of them had offered to the plotters. In February 1800, Napoleon created a national bank, the Bank of France, with Lebrun as its guiding intelligence, which was the first step in ending the financial and monetary chaos that had beset France since well before 1789.

Sieyès had seen almost immediately that real power now lay with Napoleon, but he attributed this to his military standing and to his general popularity, which might wane in the process of the complex political horse-trading that would surround the framing of the new constitution. He was wrong. Napoleon had learned to play this game in Italy, and he set about it once more. The weeks ahead revealed Napoleon's real power as stemming from his ability to chair committees with skill, to get diverse people of talent to work together, but under his chairmanship – to lead a talented government team. After Italy and Egypt, and even in assembling the Egyptian task-force, he was now better practised at this than the supposed masters of the revolutionary political game. Theirs had been a world of deals, betrayals and purges; his had been one of compromises, coalitions and real, if often cloaked, leadership.

There was a more specific game to play, however. The morning after the coup, Boulay de la Meurthe, one of the loyalest plotters, asked

Sieyès what sort of constitution he would now put forward. Sieyès replied that he had nothing in mind, a remark which left Boulay stupefied.[2] In the light of what he went on to dictate to Boulay in the following days, it would seem Sieyès had thought rather too much about it, so labyrinthine was the proposal, even if he had been careful not to put it down on paper in its entirety. In fact, Sieyès' construct was so precise as to play into Napoleon's hands, enabling him to use the details and the broad framework of Sieyès' institutions as empty shells for his own concepts.

The most dangerous part of Sieyès' project for the survival of a parliamentary republic was less his over-complicated network of assemblies or his convoluted voting system than his plans for the new executive. Immediately after Brumaire, all were agreed that one of the three Consuls would have to act as chair. This was offered to Napoleon on grounds of precedence, but he cautiously advocated a rotating chair, accepting it so long as it was taken in alphabetical order. It was Sieyès who introduced the idea of setting one of the Consuls above the others, but in a very singular manner. His project foresaw a new head of state, the 'Great Elector', technically set above the two other Consuls, chosen for life by one of the assemblies but holding no effective power. The two Consuls would be the real executive, one for internal, the other for external, affairs. Napoleon attacked this on two fronts, and in two different ways. He was quick to denigrate the idea of a powerless head of state, mocking Sieyès within the government. Roederer had tried to achieve a compromise between them by proposing that some additional powers be given to the 'Great Elector'. Talleyrand quickly brought them all back together, to enable the work for the constitution to go on, and Napoleon agreed, now in a position to be amenable because an important principle had been accepted: one Consul would indeed sit above the others. Sieyès had created the difference, now Napoleon played on it. Once at the head of the constitutional commission, Napoleon showed all his skills as a chair. He made Daunou, a long-standing critic of Sieyès, the secretary, and he drove the work quickly. The committee met in the evening and often worked all night. Daunou always started proceedings by presenting the texts that had been drawn up, then Napoleon gave his own, brief, overview, and opened the wider discussion. The work was done in twelve sessions. Sieyès could not, it seems, keep up with the pace and, although many of his ideas were outwardly maintained, their substance was hollowed out to create something very new. Napoleon won his first great campaign, post-Brumaire, in a committee room.

The first battle was to alter the role of 'Great Elector' beyond recognition, precisely through retaining the idea that one Consul – now the 'First Consul' – should be senior to the others, in order to create the strong executive the Directory had so badly lacked. The First Consul, like the other two, was no longer elected for life by the Senate, the senior assembly, but now only for ten years, although all Consuls could stand for re-election. The First Consul now initiated all legislation and appointed and dismissed ministers and all local officials and magistrates; he also conducted foreign policy. Sieyès had advanced a complex theory he called the 'absorption' of power into the executive from below; Napoleon twisted it craftily to produce something Sieyès soon saw for what it was. He simply lost interest.[3] From Sieyès' virtual resignation all else flowed. The committee retained something that resembled Sieyès' construction of a group of assemblies, each with its own attributes, but with so powerful an executive above them that, in practice, their characters changed greatly.

Sieyès envisaged three chambers: the Corps Législatif, which voted on laws, the Tribunate, which debated all the proposals that came to the government on legislation and, above them both, the College of Conservators, whose role it was to initiate legislation, and which was elected by local councils composed of the most 'notable' citizens of their departments.[4] It was this last body that disappeared, its role as initiator of legislation usurped by the First Consul, its role as the senior assembly replaced by the Senate. This new body's attributes show well how Napoleon reworked Sieyès' plan with care, rather than riding roughshod over it. The Senate was now appointed by the First Consul, its eighty members tenured for life. However, it was still the guardian of the constitution, as conceived by Sieyès, and it deliberated in private, not in public like the other bodies. It was consulted about all legislation, but that legislation now came from on high, from the First Consul. The differences were crucial in the creation of an authoritarian regime Sieyès had never imagined. The present was about manoeuvring himself into power and reshaping the executive, and Napoleon was successful at both. The Corps Législatif and the Tribunate kept their functions, but in the very different context of a First Consul who enjoyed all legislative initiative. Sieyès and Ducos were appointed 'senior senators', charged with appointing thirty-one others. Sieyès was relieved, telling Napoleon, 'I don't wish to be your aide-de-camp.'[5] Cambacérès and Lebrun took their places as the other Consuls. It was a set of tricks first learned in Italy but nobody had noticed.

Where Napoleon trumped Sieyès more overtly was in the changes the committee made to the electoral system. Sieyès had here come very close to breaking with many revolutionary, republican principles, but Napoleon saved their outward appearance. Sieyès had spoken of a 'pyramid', Napoleon of power flowing from the people, through mandate, to the executive. The new constitution itself was presented to the people for approval by plebiscite – a wholly new mechanism – and the voting system, while still elitist, offered a wider participation than Sieyès' proposal. Where their minds had come together was over the creation of a wholly new body within the government, the Council of State. Sieyès set it out as a council drawn from wherever and whomever the government – in his project the College of Conservators – felt was needed to draft and discuss legislation before it went before the legislative bodies. It was an official symposium of the best expertise available, given official sanction to conduct its research and to present its findings on anything of public interest. Napoleon had created similar bodies in Italy and Egypt, but Sieyès had spelled it out. Over this single but cardinal point, their minds met and it found its way into the new regime, under the chairmanship of the First Consul. By the mid-nineteenth century, every state that had ever been under

Napoleon's influence, however briefly, had adopted it. It balanced authority with technocracy; it provided a forum for opinions and ideas, as censorship began to bite, with the suppression, in January 1800, of sixty of the seventy-three political journals published in Paris and as elections waned in importance. Between January and March Napoleon ended the right of local authorities to elect their justices of the peace and local councillors.

On 17 February, a new local government official was created who would epitomise the regime, the prefect. Prefects were appointed by the First Consul on the advice of the Minister of the Interior and given complete authority and control over all sections of local government. Their initial selection was largely the work of Lucien. All these reforms will be examined later, in the wider context of the reshaping of France that took place between 1800 and 1804, but what is truly striking about them is the speed and clarity with which they emerged from Napoleon's mind and the team around him, in only a few weeks after he had, by the skin of his teeth, taken office. Napoleon's experience in political manipulation and state-building, which he had learned in Italy and Egypt, was now there for all too see. He applied his ideas, fully formed, with a swiftness that left Sieyès behind. Napoleon knew better than his peers how to forge a country's government, as well as how to steer a committee. Above all, in the midst of growing repression, the Council of State and the new ministerial team would be seen to work. So often ridiculed for his false affectations of modesty in these months, Napoleon's real achievement, as so often before, was in concealing his real talents.

On 7 February 1800, the new constitution was accepted by a vast, rigged majority in the plebiscite. The new First Consul may have traded on public confidence in his reputation as a victorious republican soldier when he presented his work, but he had drawn on his other, managerial and political, skills to create an instrument of government of his own authoritarian, technocratic stamp.

Napoleon got his way over everything of importance. If he could survive, he now had the tools with which to forge his own state, as he had in Italy. There was great danger ahead, it is true, but it was also less than twenty-one years since he had arrived at Brienne, an unwilling, uncomprehending French subject. It was less than seven since the Buonaparte had fled Corsica, penniless and friendless, for Toulon. When all this is weighed and assessed, Napoleon's rise can be seen as genuinely meteoric. Yet only a crisis of the highest magnitude could have spawned so phenomenal a career, and Napoleon and those around him had come to power because they said they could overcome that crisis. Counter-revolution still loomed in the provinces and, more importantly, the war continued. Success, personal and political, all depended on military victory. Without it, Brumaire would have been nothing but a parlour game, and the recently gallicised 'Bonapartes' might have become refugees again.

BACK IN THE SADDLE:
THE SECOND ITALIAN CAMPAIGN

The magnitude of the crisis presented such a clear and present danger that Napoleon threw his support behind the moves for peace being made by Talleyrand's emissaries to Britain and Austria. This was a stance that hardened many Jacobins still further against the new regime, but it was a policy which reflected the desperate plight of the armies, exhausted by the price of their recent victories, as much as by their defeats, their effectiveness constantly undermined by Directorial corruption. The negotiations were futile, but they bought precious time for rebuilding military strength. The Austrians had won back too much, particularly in Italy, to have good reason to sue for peace, and the British did not trust what appeared to be just another makeshift, plot-ridden French government of unknowns, one that was unlikely to last.

The first two months of the Consulate saw frenetic diplomacy and military refurbishment, as well as determined state-building. An energy born of desperation and fear, it was nonetheless clear-sighted. The main reason Sieyès and those around him sought 'a sword' in the first place was to give the military a direct presence on the executive, to foster a properly co-ordinated war effort. In this, if in this alone, Napoleon did not disappoint them. The armies' effective strength in January 1800 was only about 285,000 men, badly distributed across five army groups.[6] Napoleon acted with a ruthlessness worthy of Robespierre in doing what he could to repair the problems of arms and supplies, and the troops were paid for the first time in many months. The men at the front now knew there had been real change, that if they remained victims of civilian bloodsucking there was now a government determined to end it. At this early stage, Napoleon had to strengthen his forces through judicious organisation and redistribution, as mass conscription had still not taken full effect and it was still difficult to supply and arm vast numbers of troops. The next round of fighting had to be done with the remnants of the Revolutionary armies.

The armies of the Rhine and Danube were amalgamated, bringing their combined strength up to about 120,000, and the Army of Italy – in reality, because it had retreated so far, the Army of Genoa – was raised to 40,000, the reinforcements largely drawn from the disbandment of the supposed 'Army of England' along the Channel coast. A truce negotiated with the counter-revolutionaries in the western departments (the background to which is discussed below) enabled Napoleon to create a wholly new entity for the Revolutionary armies, an Army of the Reserve, of about 30,000 men concentrated in Dijon, in eastern France, later almost doubled in number by new conscripts and reservists. Thus positioned, it could be used on either the German or Italian fronts, as required. A central reserve became a hallmark of Napoleonic battlefield tactics and theatre strategy for the next fifteen years, but in 1800 it was so fresh a concept that Habsburg intelligence, although aware of its existence, had no idea of its purpose.[7] Berthier took over its command, which allowed Carnot to return from exile in Germany, where he had fled from Jacobin threats in the summer of 1799, as Minister of War. The Russians had left the war, but the Austrians under Kray, in Switzerland and southern Germany, numbered over 100,000, while Melas had just short of that number in northern Italy. The recent victories of Masséna and Moreau had given a degree of initiative back to the French, but from his position at the apex of the state, as well as from his role of supreme military commander, Napoleon knew only too well that real hopes of French success rested on quick victories. Therein lay the reason for the crisis. He left the main front, in Germany, to Moreau. Although Napoleon had undisputed control of running the war, the new constitution actually forbade the First Consul from commanding an army in the field. Masséna, almost trapped in Genoa, retained the leadership of the Army of Italy; Berthier, Napoleon's almost eternal chief of staff, had the new Army of the Reserve. Moreau was the real spearhead for the new campaign.

Nevertheless, this was still the convoluted world of the late Directory in all but name, and nothing was free from politics and paranoia. In his new position as *generalissimo*, Napoleon, now working closely with Carnot for the first time, set out an over-arching strategy for renewed hostilities which, although offering an interesting insight into his military thought, was soon undermined and over-ridden by the politics of having to deal with Moreau, still the most experienced, successful general of the Republic, still a leftist republican and still a potential threat to the new regime. If he lacked the ambition to replace Napoleon, he was nevertheless in a position to depose him.

The key to Napoleon's plans came from the advantage that the recapture of Switzerland by Masséna had given the French. If that advantage was used to the full, Switzerland could become the pivotal link between well-co-ordinated offences in southern Germany and northern Italy, thus splintering the Austrians in both sectors, and, sooner rather than later, opening two roads to Vienna and the prospect of swift capitulation. To this end, he wanted Moreau to concentrate his forces for a drive over the upper Rhine, while Berthier was to cross into Italy, not along the coast to relieve Masséna, who was now in Genoa, but to come down over the Swiss passes, behind the Austrians. Moreau interpreted this as a ploy to reduce the importance of his front while increasing that of Berthier's, and he still carried enough influence to force Napoleon to allow him to launch his own attack, in his own way. Moreau opted for caution, attacking on a wider front, better to ensure his supply lines and allow his troops more room to operate; it also kept him in country he knew well. Here Moreau showed not only caution, but a seeming unawareness of the wider circumstances of the war, for he failed to make the chance of a quick victory his priority, whereas Napoleon's whole strategy hinged on exactly this. The younger, less successful general had a far better grasp of the deeper weaknesses of the Republic, and of the imperative of a short war, than his senior, perhaps the real measure of what separated the two men.

Moreau moved forward as he saw fit and he did so brilliantly, delivering a series of hammer blows to the Austrians. The real key to the war, and to reigniting Napoleon's reputation as a commander, was his own creation, the Army of the Reserve. Neither the Austrians, nor perhaps Moreau, really grasped its potential. Positioned in eastern France and then moved into western Switzerland, around Geneva, it could turn either north or south, as needed. Napoleon, predictably, chose to turn it south: Moreau could not prevent this part of his plan, although he did partially thwart it by not providing the levels of support for the invasion of Italy which Napoleon requested of him, once his own sector had been secured. Most importantly, Napoleon had to readjust his plans, making the Swiss/Italian sector the more active theatre of operations. With Moreau determined to move slowly, Napoleon had to switch the offensive to Italy, but he had to do so with fewer resources than Moreau's. From the outset, as in 1796, the French would be heavily outnumbered when they crossed the Alps. Berthier had proved a hesitant commander, and the clear indications were that he would not cope well in the field once hostilities began. In the first week of May, Napoleon arrived in Geneva and effectively took charge, although Berthier retained formal command of the Army of the Reserve. When Napoleon seized its command and took to the field, he was in technical breach of the law barring the First Consul from leading an army.

In the light of the fraught months behind him, a return to the front, no matter how difficult the circumstances, must have come as something of a relief. Napoleon threw himself into the meticulous planning for the Alpine crossing. He determined to use all the northern passes, the Simplon, St Gotthard and the Great and Little St Bernards, to get his 50,000 troops and, more problematically, their artillery and horses, into northern Piedmont. Indeed, the Austrians were the least of his worries in May, for their main army was still preoccupied with besieging Masséna in Genoa. To keep things this way, Napoleon begged Masséna to hold out until early June, which he did, in the most dreadful circumstances. In great contrast to 1796, Napoleon was now in a position to supply and equip his men properly for the arduous crossing, and each soldier carried nine days' rations and forty cartridges; they crossed in five long columns, spread out between the base of the passes and Geneva, to avoid congestion, with supplies to follow. This formation would be used again and again in his later campaigns. The artillery proved a problem, requiring several impromptu, often ingenious methods of getting the guns over the narrower paths, such as using hollowed-out tree trunks as 'stretchers' for the barrels; sledges were also used. For the most part, however, the infantry carried the guns in large teams. It took longer than Napoleon had hoped – the first units arrived to face the Austrian garrisons in the area without artillery cover – but within three weeks, by 24 May, Napoleon and almost 40,000 men were in the valleys just north of Turin, having arrived in the rear of the main Austrian army under Melas, which was still concentrated in the south of the country, around the fortress of Alessandria, to the north of Genoa.[8]

Instead of marching south to confront the Austrians head-on, take Turin and then move south to relieve Genoa, Napoleon swung south-east and seized Milan, well to the rear of Melas and lightly defended. This was a cruel disappointment for Masséna, but it was undoubtedly the right thing to do, when the goal was a quick victory. Napoleon had now badly disrupted Melas' supply lines – he was all but cut off in Piedmont – and he had little choice but to turn and offer Napoleon the big, decisive battle he sought.

Napoleon had wanted to fight Melas from a good defensive position he had chosen at Stradella, a village at a point where the gap between the Alps, to the north, and the Apennines, to the south, was narrowest – that is, at the very point where Melas' supply and support lines were most fragile. Circumstances changed drastically, however, when Masséna – his men exhausted and on starvation rations and trapped between Melas and the Genoese, who had tried to revolt – capitulated on 4 June, having no idea Napoleon was so close. His hair had turned grey during the siege, but he had held out for exactly as long as Napoleon had asked.

Napoleon was welcomed like a hero in Milan, but he now had to rush to a front where it was in Melas' hands to choose the ground for battle. Two things still worked in Napoleon's favour, however: Masséna had delayed his surrender just long enough to keep an Austrian corps at Genoa, thus leaving Melas slightly under-strength. This much was by design. By luck, many of Melas' dispatches had fallen into French hands. Even without this intelligence, it was clear to Napoleon that Melas could now try, with superior numbers, to recross the Po and menace his own lines. He had to leave the safety of Stradella and march on Alessandria. Although the crossing of the Po was well organised, once the French were on the march there were serious breakdowns in communications; orders were lost, contradicted or issued in rapid confusion. Napoleon had left too much of the field command to Berthier, and the net result was a badly scattered army. None of this was helped by Napoleon's stubbornly held misconception that Melas was set on avoiding a major battle, when the exact opposite was the case.

Napoleon was still working on the assumption that Melas was trying to out-manoeuvre him and fall back on Genoa when, on Sunday 14 June, Melas launched a massive dawn attack on the French, at the village of Marengo, near Alessandria. As David Chandler has put it, the whole army, from Napoleon to the drummer boys who had to beat recall, were all caught off guard by Melas' quick-witted aggression.[9] The Austrians ran into a small French advance guard, and it was only after an hour that Napoleon really understood he was faced with the main enemy army, and rallied the troops in the immediate area on a plain near the River Tanaro, surrounded by vineyards. On this open ground, Napoleon tried to stem the Austrian advance. The fighting was furious and driven by desperation, to the point that it seems to have exposed the limitations of the French army musket. If one memoir is to be believed, the firing was continuous and the guns, if not those who wielded them, over-heated: 'Our musket-barrels were so hot that it became impossible to load them for fear of igniting the cartridges. There was nothing for it but to piss into the barrels to cool them.'[10] This ribald vignette rings true enough in its evocation of the intensity of the action, and the shortcomings of the standard-issue musket, but the troops were so occupied that they probably had had too little to drink to carry out the 'cooling exercise'. Thirst in the line-of-fire was but one more hazard of war. It is estimated that, by late afternoon, Napoleon had barely 6,000 men still fit to fight on.[11] In these circumstances, when he rallied them the prosaic optimism was tinged more than a little with desperation: 'Courage, soldiers! The reserves are coming.'[12] By chance, he was right.

Napoleon had dispatched Desaix away from the area just before the attack, and only problems at a river crossing as they moved away kept Desaix's troops within easy reach of the new battle zone, enabling him to return by mid-afternoon. His supposed comment to Napoleon summed up the engagement – the battle had been lost by mid-morning, but there was still time that afternoon to win a different battle. So it proved. Still obviously shaken, however, Napoleon threw his reserve troops into the action quickly, to try to turn the Austrian right. It was Desaix's intervention that stemmed the Austrian tide, his troops acting as the de facto reserve of fresh men who entered the battle when Napoleon's troops already in the field had been beaten. Desaix's mere appearance did much to revive the morale of Napoleon's exhausted units. It is a mark of how unnerved Napoleon had become that he broke his own cardinal rule and committed his reserve corps too early, but Desaix filled this gap. He paid for it with his life, however, shot by a sniper or perhaps a stray bullet, a loss which left Napoleon genuinely moved and saddened. 'I am plunged into the deepest grief for a man whom I loved and esteemed the most,' he wrote to Paris,[13] and his words were sincere. More moving still, for it was uncalled for, were those to Moreau: 'His family and the Republic have had a great loss; but ours is greater, still.'[14] Napoleon always acknowledged his debt to Desaix at Marengo.

The day was actually won in the most spectacular fashion imaginable. Desaix had done much before he was cut down, but even his counter-attack began to falter, and the Austrian infantry launched a ferocious, if ill-disciplined, attack on his lines. Into this mess, Kellermann suddenly appeared at the head of 400 dragoons, the very last of the reserves. His advance had been shielded by the high vines the region is noted for, then in full flower, which allowed him to charge at short range into the Austrians. The big horses ridden by big men, wielding sabres at close quarters, wreaked carnage on the fragmented Austrian infantry. Those who could, fled or capitulated.[15] In one burst, Kellermann's cavalry had delivered victory. Blood and dust mingled on the fields beyond the vines. When the dust had settled, and the blood dried in the hot sun, Napoleon was secure, not just on the field, but as master of France. Defeat would have spelled the end of the Consulate.

The Battle of Marengo was among the most important of Napoleon's career, but more in a political than a military sense, although it did not look like that on the field of battle on the night of 14 June 1800. Napoleon later said that the night before Marengo was when he sensed his great destiny, but even though the Austrians had lost 14,000 killed or wounded from a total force of about 40,000, Napoleon's Army of the Reserve, numbering just under 30,000 effectives, had lost about a quarter of its strength as well and was too exhausted to pursue Melas, who fell back towards the fortress of Mantua. Marengo had battered Napoleon, by the loss of his close friend, the awareness that by his own lights he had blundered in the field and by the clear, honest realisation that he had under-estimated Melas' spirit and ability, and over-estimated the power of his own aura to intimidate the Austrian.

However, the next twenty-four hours saw all Napoleon's assumptions about Melas realised, if after the event. With a large force still intact, and the garrisons of the major fortresses of north-central Italy still unscathed, Melas sued for an armistice. Napoleon seized the offer with both hands, and the Austrians withdrew from Italy, west of the Venetian provinces, leaving the territories of the former Cisalpine Republic to their former master. They also undertook not to fight until the results of Napoleon's offer of negotiations with Vienna were known. On 17 June, Napoleon rushed back to Paris, while Masséna and the Army of Italy recrossed into Liguria. The Armies of Italy and the Reserve were merged, with Masséna now in charge of the southern sector.

The dangers, internal and external, were far from over. Napoleon was still a relative outsider in Parisian high politics, the war was not yet finished – and was only concluded by Moreau's emphatic victory at Hohenlinden in December – but Napoleon had gone to Italy to win quickly and he had done so. This return to Paris was different from Napoleon's arrival barely nine months earlier. Marengo had been a very narrow victory, but a victory it had been. Within months, France was again the master of Italy, and held Switzerland and western Germany in a firm grip. The military success craved by the Jacobins had been delivered; a position of real strength had been achieved from which to negotiate the peace craved in turn by the moderate royalists. Nothing was certain, save that Napoleon had done what he had claimed he would.

APPEASING EUROPE

The victory at Marengo had secured the French reconquest of Italy with unforeseen speed. Melas agreed to terms that left all but the Venetian territories in the north-east at the mercy of the Army of Italy, and Napoleon was able to leave the subjugation of Tuscany, the Papal States and Naples to his subordinates, as he rushed back to Paris. Moreau's successes across the Alps notwithstanding, Napoleon's own position, and that of the Consulate as a whole, was by no means certain or secure. Technically the war was still on, and hostilities did indeed resume in a few weeks in the German sector, when peace had been promised. As long as this was the case, unrest at home would also fester. In the coming months, the truce with the Vendean rebels broke down and one of their leaders, Georges Cadoudal, would try to kill Napoleon, as would several other people. The triumphalism that followed the victory of Marengo was for the public. Napoleon knew all too well that he and his regime were in no position to drop their guard.

Napoleon was so conscious of the need for peace that he began looking for it immediately. He dashed off a letter directly to Emperor Francis from the very battlefield, on 16 June, 'to find a way to put an end to the grief of a continent'. It was a mixture of humanitarian pleading to end senseless slaughter, and threats based on a military power he knew France did not really have. He warned Francis that he could have taken the whole of Melas' army prisoner, but had chosen to let it march home when, in truth, the Army of the Reserve was a battered, exhausted force in need of reinforcements. The real thrust of the letter was that the terms of Campo Formio had been acceptable to Francis before the war, and, therefore, there was no reason why they should not be again. The problem, Napoleon argued adroitly, was Britain:

The equilibrium of Europe? The past campaign has shown well enough that the equilibrium of Europe is not threatened by France, and the last few days have proved that it is the power of the English [that is the real threat], which has seized the commerce of the whole world and the empire of the seas for itself, and which, today, is strong enough to resist the combined fleets of Russians, Danes, Swedes, French, Spanish and Batavians.[16]

Here he was alluding to a second front that had opened against the British and was hitting them where it hurt most, in damaging their commerce. Having left the Austrians to their own devices in the war, Tsar Paul soon turned on the British through economic warfare. Russia, Denmark and Sweden were all aggrieved by the British policy of stopping and searching neutral shipping, and when they united

under the Tsar, in the League of Armed Neutrality, vital Baltic supplies
for the Royal Navy – timber, pitch, hemp and tar – were threatened, as
well as food supplies. Napoleon sought to show Francis how alone he
now was. From Lyon, Napoleon wasted no time in assuring the King
of Denmark that he had the full support of the French Republic,[17]
while also reinforcing the army in the Low Countries and ordering
it closer to the border with the Holy Roman Empire; simultaneously,
Napoleon was busily forging a new Army of the Reserve, again based
in Dijon. All of this, he urged Carnot from Milan, must be kept secret,
particularly the military build-up on the German border, as it had to
be accomplished by withdrawing troops from the Vendée.[18]

France was close to exhaustion, as Napoleon knew only too well. As
he confessed to Brune, when he ordered him to take command of the
Army of Italy:

This is the principal army of the Republic, militarily, and especially from
a political point of view ... [T]here are a great number of extremely
weakened demi-brigades ... You will find the Army of Italy in a fairly good
state; but corruption is at its height, and those closest to Masséna are those
most often accused [of it].[19]

Reinforcements were accorded Brune, from the Army of the Reserve,
to bolster a front weakened at Marengo and further undermined by
Masséna's continued predilection for Directorial-style profiteering.
There were still more concerns on the main front. Napoleon told
Carnot that Augereau's northern army had been severely weakened by
the need to deploy so many troops in western Germany, in readiness
for war. Augereau had had to use his men to occupy fortresses that
Moreau, in his turn, had been forced to abandon, to reinforce his front
line; Napoleon wanted Moreau to send five battalions back to Augereau,
for there were no available new troops.[20] It is not surprising that, now
back in Paris and better appraised of the situation, Napoleon's next
letter to Francis – written in the course of an inspection of the Vendée
and the Channel coast – contained no threats, but, rather, an assurance
that 'France desires to make peace with England, as well.'[21] The wider

lesson for Napoleon was clear enough: if hostilities resumed, a quick victory in Germany was essential; to achieve it, internal security had to be compromised, so depleted were the Republic's forces. Italy would be exposed as a sideshow, without a decisive outcome north of the Alps.

This was a time of high tension, as the French awaited Francis' reply, and their best hope now appeared to be the pressure being put on Britain by the League of Armed Neutrality. Over the summer and early autumn of 1800, Napoleon's desire for peace was genuine enough. He urged Talleyrand to enlist Prussia, not as a military ally against the coalition, but as a conduit to Francis, to gain an armistice that embraced the German front, as well as Italy, thus opening the way for official peace talks.[22] As late as the last week of September, ten days after he had all but given up on a favourable response from Francis and ordered Moreau onto a war footing,[23] Napoleon was sending out similar requests for mediation to two 'friendly contacts' he had made among the German princes at Rastatt in 1797, the landgraves of Hesse-Kassel and Hesse-Darmstadt, telling them both that France wanted peace.[24] The only part of Europe where Napoleon actively provoked hostilities in these months was in Iberia, where his hard work to rebuild an alliance with Spain was driven by the need to push the British out of Portugal, and subject that country to Franco-Spanish control. Scarcely a month after he told Moreau to be ready to attack in Germany, he urged Joseph, to whom he had confided the conduct of the stuttering peace talks at Lunéville, to insist that Britain be kept out of the negotiations, and that the first steps should be to get the Habsburgs to agree to the terms of Campo Formio, and those he had proposed more recently, in Paris.[25] Napoleon's attitude hardened in the course of November, increasingly convinced that Francis, bolstered by British money, now wanted to fight again, and was stalling only to 'gain the winter' to rebuild, as he had told Carnot.[26] Before Brumaire, the deadly game of nerves had centred on Parisian high politics; now, it was transferred to the realm of international relations. Napoleon still walked a tightrope, and his resolve and composure were being tested, yet again, for still higher stakes. The 14th of July – now virtually the national high day of the Republic – saw the Austrian cannon and standards taken at Marengo paraded before the Parisian crowds, but those at the centre of affairs felt anything but triumphal.

There was need for caution very close to home, and, at times, Napoleon seemed to be the only one of his inner circle who grasped this. In November 1800 Lucien issued a pamphlet entitled *A Parallel among Caesar, Cromwell, Monck and Bonaparte*, which he made every effort to distribute as widely as possible. As Minister of the Interior he was well placed to do so. The pamphlet stressed that Napoleon was not comparable to any of the others, that he was not a general bent on making himself a king, unlike Caesar or Cromwell, nor was he, like Monck, the vanguard of a royalist restoration. Nevertheless, the pamphlet – probably written by Lucien and others, but ostensibly anonymous – also emphasised the importance of Napoleon as an individual and raised the sensitive, potentially explosive, issue of what might happen if Napoleon 'were to be missing'. The issue of the succession was suddenly made central to public debate, and the introduction of Caesar into the debate, however it was handled, ignited fears that Napoleon, like Caesar, might make himself Consul for Life or, like Cromwell, resort to nepotism if allowed to choose a successor. Everyone knew what was implied, but no one was more unnerved by this than Napoleon himself.

When Fouché confronted him with the need to suppress the pamphlet, he found Napoleon more than prepared to do so, and to confront his own brother – and right-hand man at this stage – over the issue. When Lucien launched into Fouché in front of his brother, he found himself alone. Stripped of his powerful ministry, Lucien was dispatched to Madrid, as ambassador to Spain, and effectively cast out of the circle of power for ever. 'My only natural heirs are the French people, they are my child' was Napoleon's public response to the affair, the only one he could give and hope to survive one more day. Nevertheless, Napoleon's reaction was not just ruthless, it bordered on the paranoid, if not without reason. He sacrificed his own brother, who had proved something close to invaluable both at Brumaire and in creating the first prefects. This may have stirred memories of Lucien's intemperate attack on Paoli in Toulon, which put the family under vendetta and drove them all from Corsica, but there was also no more emphatic sign of how insecure and vulnerable Napoleon still felt in the Parisian political world exactly one year after his seizure of office. He did not believe power was yet his.

Napoleon's reaction to the pamphlet also revealed the great extent to which the classical past was his guide during these months, rather than the examples of more recent history. If there was a true historical parallel with the political climate of the early Consulate, in terms of a paradigm that could guide its leader through the murky dangers that had not simply evaporated at Brumaire, it was the early Roman Principate. Julius Caesar may have served as a model for Napoleon in the First Italian Campaign, just as Alexander the Great had become a dangerous, unsettling exemplar in Egypt, but Napoleon had already learned, as the hidden hand behind the Cisalpine Republic, that the most useful mentor in times of trouble was neither of these dynamic supermen, but Octavian. Like Octavian, Napoleon was a young, relative outsider, a novice, among an older generation of skilled, devious and duplicitous political operators. He had to depend on generals still loyal to an older republican order; he was only there – according to the plans of others – as something close to a figurehead. Napoleon knew the classical authors, and he knew how dangerous it was to invoke the history of the Roman Republic among educated Frenchmen of the time. All would remember, when the pamphlet insisted on Napoleon's irreplaceable role in the Republic, how badly Caesar had come out of Plutarch's direct comparison of him with Alexander the Great:

[Alexander's] war did not bring tears to the Greeks: Caesar filled his country with fire and tears ... Caesar ruined some of his friends, and was abandoned by the others, he filled Rome with his military insolence, and sowed the seeds of infinite unrest which followed from his own blood ... Caesar's intemperance ... and his insatiable ambition is far, far more dangerous an excess than the rage or the blows from the fists of Alexander

... Caesar, having scarcely arrived at the summit of a shameful glory by an oblique route, and who had acquired the hatred of the leading men of the Republic, was soon brought down by those who loved good laws and the good of the state; this led to the civil wars.[27]

As every schoolboy knew, Napoleon included.

Luigi Mascilli Migliorini has said, with acute sensitivity to the intellectual culture with which men of that era were so imbued, that Napoleon was haunted by the ghosts of the classical heroes of his youth 'who spoke of the liberties of Rome, strangled by a military genius'.[28] He was not alone. Tronchet, a very loyal supporter who had organised the purge of the Tribunate for Napoleon, is reported to have told Thibaudeau that Napoleon 'was still a young man, but he has begun like Caesar, and he will end like him'.[29] Octavian was both the more apposite and the safer role model for Napoleon in these months. Like Octavian, Napoleon, too, saw that the way out of these dangers was not a straight one, however much decisiveness might be required to navigate it. Valérie Huet, with the coolness of the historian, notes slyly that, like Octavian, Bonaparte knew it was better to appropriate the Republic than to restore the monarchy.[30]

Caution was all, even when it came to censorship. There can be no doubt that, as the regime felt more secure, its goal was to foster its own legitimacy and avoid political confrontation, either between rival factions, or pamphleteers and the state, rather than to develop public opinion in a modern sense. Nevertheless, in the wake of the 1790s this could not be imposed abruptly. This was the climate in which public order was reassessed by the new government, and, surrounded by such pointed aggression, it is little wonder the Brumairians tended to agree about controlling the press and kept a watchful, ever more authoritarian eye on literary life, particularly in the capital. Even so, 'history' was complicated in all their minds. All had fresh memories of the unbridled fury of Marat, Hébert and Brissot, and their ability to rouse the rabble, but beside this stood both their attachment to their early victory over royal censorship in 1789 and the revival of an arbitrary and archaic, but vicious and politicised, censorship during the Terror, when the Montagnards had followed each purge with the suppression of each defeated faction's newspaper.

The last years of the Directory had seen a return to this, if one devoid of bloodshed. Each coup – or, to be more precise, the unacceptable election result that preceded them – saw the suppression first of royalist newspapers in 1797 and then of the Jacobin press between 1798 and 1799. The uneasy times produced a consensus among the new leaders based on the potential dangers of an unfettered press. The new regime easily coerced newspapers it deemed dangerous into closure or forced their merger with more reliable publications, because the Directory had left no legislation to prevent this, and none among the Brumairians wanted to arrest this process. If there was a difference with the previous regime, it was that the Brumairians had to be provoked over a sustained period.

The Consulate saw a vigorous rivalry between the *Journal de Paris*, edited by Roederer, and the crypto-royalist *Journal des Débats*, owned and run by Louis-François Bertin and his brother who had the same name, the bestselling journal in Paris up to its 'change of format' in 1805. It propounded an anti-*philosophe* doctrine, expounding traditional values of a distinctly Catholic character. In 1802, it said that civil law was an inadequate instrument to restrain human passions; in 1805, it called for the burning of the works of Voltaire, Rousseau and D'Alembert. Soon after the promulgation of the Civil Code in 1804, it launched a series of attacks on the law's intrusion into family life to the detriment of parental authority.[31] Above all, it appeared increasingly to extol the Bourbon monarchy, at a time when the Brumairians feared an attempted restoration.[32] It took until 1805 for Napoleon to lose patience completely and yield to his repressive instincts. He lambasted Bertin as a man in the pocket of the émigrés, and finally took full cognisance of Roederer's 'interested' insistence that the *Journal des Débats* was the harbinger of a restoration – 'one could cite a thousand ... articles ... written with evil intent,' he told Fiévée, the chief of the censorship office who had tried to defend it.[33] Napoleon ordered its name changed to the anodyne *Journal de l'Empire*, but two years later he was still complaining of its glorification of the Bourbons. The *Journal des Débats* was slowly pressured into passivity. It was not until Chateaubriand compared Napoleon to Nero, in 1807, that he confiscated and closed the journal of a man who had turned into a rabid opponent of the regime in 1804.[34]

Censorship would tighten over the years, accelerating under the late Empire when a comprehensive regulation was finally imposed in 1810, but during the Consulate the muzzling of opposition in print reflected the insecurities of the Brumairians, Napoleon included. Fearful as they were of the press either goading a Jacobin mob, or fanning the fires of restoration among a large middle-class readership – Napoleon noted to Fouché in 1805 that the press still commanded 12,000 francs in sales – the regime drew back from resorting to overt force in this sphere. Even as late as 1805, in the same letter to Fouché expressing fear at the wide circulation of the *Journal des Débats*, Napoleon still insisted on the limits of censorship, while foaming at the mouth as he imposed it, ad hoc:

... henceforth, the *Journal des Débats* ought not to appear until it has been sent to the censor, the day before [publication] ... These are the only conditions under which I will allow this journal to continue to appear. Censorship must not ever extend to serialised novels nor to literary articles, but only to politics and to literature that might have a political content.[35]

The year 1805 saw Napoleon more secure in power than at any previous time; crowned Emperor in December 1804, with peace on the Continent, he still preferred a 'case-by-case' approach to censorship, and reminded Fouché of its limits. A year later, the rechristened *Journal de l'Empire* was 'still at it', however. Napoleon felt constrained to tell Fouché to tell the censor to tell the *Journal de l'Empire* to 'stop talking incessantly about Henri IV and the Bourbons ... I don't want to see public opinion being steered in a fallacious direction'.[36]

The war against the free press was one of attrition. It is true that by the time a definitive, and punitive, censorship law was passed in 1810, the Parisian press had shrunk to a mere four journals, all mundane and under tight control, but this was the work of erosion, and the law, when it came, was driven through the Council of State by younger men, who were alien to both the clerical censorship of the old monarchy, and the ideological hysteria of the 1790s. However, as 1800 passed to 1801, the hesitancy over censorship was a sign of fear rather than toleration.

'OPEN SEASON'

Napoleon was a hunted animal in the first years of the Consulate. From the perspective of the man and those close to him, the restoration of order began at home, as shots were fired and bombs were planted under the new leader as he went about his daily business. These attempts on his life are often passed over too lightly, for from the perspective of the target they were paramount, and central to Napoleon's thoughts. These feelings of being the 'hunted' never left Napoleon, any more than did his self-discipline. The two were bound inextricably together. At one of the highest points of his career, only months after the military triumph of Austerlitz, the humbling of Austria and the consolidation of his hegemony in Germany – on the last day of May 1806, barely days after he had forced Francis II to dissolve the Holy Roman Empire, over which his family had ruled for centuries – Napoleon could still write to his brother Joseph, whom he had made King of Naples a few months before:

My brother, do not organise your guards in the way you have, by naming only one commander. Nothing is more dangerous. Sooner or later, you will have to change him, and it will be better from the start, not to go down a false road ... I have to tell you this, in what concerns your bodyguards and your kitchen: otherwise, you run the risk of being poisoned or assassinated. I specifically want you to keep your French chefs, that you are served at table by your own butlers, and that your quarters are always organised in such a way that you are always with your French guards. You have followed my own private life enough to know how, even in France, I am always under the guard of my loyalest and oldest soldiers.[37]

Napoleon's closest bodyguards were not his own men, but the Mamelukes he brought back from Egypt. It was a Mameluke, Roustam, who slept outside Napoleon's door and stood by his side at all times, entering 'the legend'. He was but one of a contingent of about 300 Mamelukes who served the French in Egypt as elite light cavalry, and were evacuated with them to escape certain death as traitors at the hands of their compatriots. Men with nowhere else to go were those who could be trusted most. The same was true later of the Polish lancers. There was a point at his bedroom door where even most members of the Imperial Guard, his elite corps, did not pass.

After Brumaire, and for many years afterwards, his own life now resembled that of Octavian in the dangerous months after the assassination of Caesar, more than that of Alexander, the conquering hero. The fate of Julius Caesar haunted Napoleon in the early months in power, to the point that he drove out his own brother, Lucien.

A year afterwards, in 1801, one of his most loyal supporters, Roederer, suggested he take the title of Emperor. Roederer's proposal may have been prophetic, but at the time it was made Napoleon knew this was the last thing he should do. He did not so much resist temptation as tremble at the thought of being murdered in the Senate.

Something of his character in these years emerges in the recollections of Lebrun, the Third Consul and a man who worked more closely with Napoleon than almost anyone else at the time: 'Bonaparte was always pleasant: there was nothing of that impetuosity I had believed formed the principal trait of his character.'[38] There were people and institutions – Germaine de Staël, the Vatican, the British – able to make Napoleon all but froth at the mouth, but these were the exceptions, not the rule. If restraint was an act, it was a good one, sustained even among his intimates. Surrounded by political sharks and real assassins, the hallmark of Napoleon in these years was an iron self-discipline.

In the wake of Brumaire, Napoleon was not alone in drawing parallels between the early Consulate and the late Roman Republic, or between his position and that of Julius Caesar at his weakest, for his steps were tracked by many a would-be Brutus throughout his years as Consul. Isser Woloch, a historian sympathetic to the Jacobins rather than Napoleon, has nonetheless noted that Napoleon had reason to be haunted by such fears from the outset at Brumaire, when 'Even if such deputies had not unsheathed their knives against Bonaparte ... their cries of *hors de la loi* [he's outside the law] against him could be deemed a knife blow.'[39] There were plenty of intemperate, if largely vain, threats from left-wing quarters in Paris and beyond it in the first months of the Consulate, such as a Jacobin of Langres who said of Brumaire: 'If I had found myself in Paris, I would have disembowelled Bonaparte like a pig.'[40]

Not all such talk was idle. On 24 October 1800, only a few months after his return from the Italian front, and but four days after he had issued an amnesty to émigré royalists, there was an attempt on his life outside the Paris Opéra. The assailants were never found, although at the time and ever afterwards Fouché claimed they were Jacobin extremists. Whether he was right or not, lying or telling the truth, the plot has gone down in history as 'the conspiracy of the daggers', the weapons used to kill Julius Caesar. Others followed, but the most serious came on Christmas Eve 1800, when a bomb exploded in the rue St-Nicaise, killing twenty-six people, although it missed the carriages carrying Napoleon and Joséphine, who continued their evening engagement at the Opéra. Fouché's intelligence showed fairly clearly that this was the work of royalists, probably in British pay and linked to the Chouan leader Georges Cadoudal, but Napoleon chose to blame the left and exiled 130 innocent Jacobins to 'the dry guillotine' of Guiana. Nine were executed.

The bomb shook Napoleon. In the days after the conspiracy of the daggers, only two months earlier, his official correspondence continued without interruption, with orders being dispatched to the armies and to the diplomats in Lunéville. In stark contrast, after the 'infernal machine' of the rue St-Nicaise, the orders ceased for five days. When he recovered himself, he set about using his newly acquired ability to invoke emergency powers to crack down on the Jacobins throughout the country in a harsh, if very short-lived, series of arrests and the closures of clubs and newspapers.

This did not mean that he had forgotten the royalists, however. Napoleon may have chosen to use the Christmas Eve atrocity to dispose of a clutch of potential Brutuses, but two days before he authorised their exile, in his first official letter to Fouché since the attack, he had collected himself and divined his real enemies:

Citizen Minister, there are three classes of individuals in Paris who merit special surveillance:
    1. The Italian refugees.
    2. The *colons*.
    3. Those from the West who have been amnestied.
I would ask you to let me know how many of each of these classes of people there are in Paris, and to provide me with steps to get them out of the capital . . .[41]

The methodology Napoleon used in designating and defining the political geography of opposition had a remarkable precursor in his outline of the sources of unrest in the Cisalpine Republic a few years earlier. His Italian apprenticeship had imbued him with a certain clear-eyed approach to analysing where the threats to him originated, and the specific forms in which they emerged.

Of 'the three classes of individuals' Napoleon cited, the first were largely pro-republicans enraged with Napoleon over his perceived betrayal of Venice; the second were French settlers from the Caribbean, angered over his failure to deal with massive slave revolts in modern Haiti; and the third were Cadoudal's men, Chouans, the very men to whom he had recently offered amnesties. Even before he cynically turned on the left, his eye was trained on the real danger, from the right, but it had taken him a little longer than usual to compose himself. This only served to illustrate to all and sundry how fragile the new regime still was.

Napoleon was now wholly dependent on someone or something else for the quick victory he needed. It came as autumn turned to winter.

THE PEACE OF AMIENS: THE TURNING POINT

Events outside Napoleon's new-found hegemony gave him the opportunity he needed to turn the gains of Lunéville and Campo Formio – which had confirmed the French annexation of Belgium and the left bank of the Rhine, and their gains in Italy against the Habsburgs – into a wider European settlement. In the first flush of victory after Marengo in 1800, he might reassure the Danes of his support all he wanted, but he could do nothing when the British turned their guns on them and wrecked the League of Armed Neutrality. Britain ruled the seas at the opening of the nineteenth century, something that would not change for over a century to come, and that rule was heavy-handed at the most tranquil of times. At the height of renewed war with France, and after the collapse of their Austrian ally, it was little short of despotic. British claims to the 'right of stop and search' enraged every neutral maritime power in Europe and, by 1800, the Danes were operating an effective convoy system against the Royal Navy, the success of which encouraged the creation of the League of Armed Neutrality in December 1800. In April, Nelson committed one of the most blatant acts of international terrorism of the period, rivalling Napoleon's own seizure of Egypt. He destroyed the neutral Danish fleet in harbour, in Copenhagen, thereby bullying the Russians and Swedes to quit the League. This may have ended the League and its ability to close off the Baltic to the British and block the naval supplies their fleets depended upon, but it served only to intensify the resentment that led to its creation. The Spanish, too, detested the British policy of 'stop and search', and had even deeper fears about their designs on the Spanish colonies in the Americas.

All were fearful of the British – and their timidity often infuriated Napoleon – but a collective will emerged to rally around French diplomacy to curb British aggression at sea, particularly at a point when Napoleon had the upper hand in the conflict on land: Britain's impotence on the Continent had been revealed for all to see with Austria's defeat by Moreau at Hohenlinden. Prussia had long withdrawn into neutrality, having been the first major power to recognise de facto the French Republic in 1795, while Tsar Paul had proved an unstable, unreliable ally when he was part of the coalition, and had been part of the League from its formation until his assassination in March 1801. Isolated, Britain came to the conference table with great reluctance, and very much in two minds at the apex of its government. On 28 July 1801, Britain signed preliminary accords with the French Republic, to allow negotiations to proceed, but it took over six months for talks to begin, as the destruction of the League offered the British hope of avoiding making peace; then Napoleon's initial refusal to make any preliminary concessions to them caused further delay, as he felt his own hand strengthened by the pan-European bitterness that British conduct inspired and by his own military ascendancy over Austria.

When both sides reached the table, at the northern French city of Amiens, there was a noticeable absence of goodwill, but Napoleon's chief negotiator, his brother Joseph, supported by Talleyrand, showed a propensity for compromise. They both had to draw deeply on their clerical training to steer the talks along, as Napoleon fulminated from the safe distance of Paris, and the British Cabinet shifted within its internal divisions of hawks and doves under the new Prime Minister, Addington. William Pitt, an intransigent advocate of the war, had resigned over the refusal of the king to countenance Catholic emancipation in the wake of the 1798 revolt in Ireland. His reason was of only marginal relevance to the Franco-British conflict, for Catholic emancipation was a long-cherished goal of many in the English liberal elite, but it did the French Republic far more good than Hoche's abortive invasion of Ireland or the 1798 rising there, as it opened the door to a Cabinet prepared to enter into talks and, ultimately, to accept a treaty of peace with a state it had demonised.

The British soon realised how isolated they really were in Europe. The talks at Amiens gathered together not just Britain and France, but all the northern maritime powers as well as Spain, Portugal, the Batavian Republic– formerly the Dutch Republic – and the small German states. The British delegation soon saw that the French cock had arrived with a flock of vultures hard on its tail feathers. Ultimately, their presence meant that Amiens produced several separate treaties, which enabled the forlorn French occupation of Egypt to be ended and the country returned to the Ottomans, and for colonial matters between the Dutch, Spanish and British to be settled, as well as those between France and Britain.

On the central question of a war that was now only between France and Britain, Napoleon felt the conclusion of peace was inevitable, and continued to tell Joseph so, even as the concessions needed for it had to be wrung from him. It was an attitude he held from start to finish, his bellicosity much at variance with the caution he showed in his dealings with the Parisian political world. Before the talks had even begun, he thundered to Talleyrand,

... it must be made known to the English that we will never cede two of the American islands ... That if they insist on these points, they are not in good faith, and so it is contrary to the [French] government's intentions these rumours of peace continue any longer ... It is absolutely necessary that the preliminaries are signed by the first decade of Vendémiaire [about 1 October 1801], or the negotiations will be broken off.[42]

'If peace is not achieved right away, I have no fear of war,'[43] he declared three weeks before the treaty was signed on 27 March 1802. Napoleon's confidence, as much as mutual suspicion, made Amiens a vexed affair. This was not to say Napoleon was mistaken in his estimation of British reluctance to make concessions, nor to accuse him of failing to meet the preliminary terms for negotiations. He withdrew French troops from Tuscany and the Papal States in October 1801, as stipulated, an action made all the more significant in his eyes when the British refused to recognise the transformation of Tuscany into the 'Kingdom of Etruria', under a Spanish Bourbon, an agreement he had brokered with Madrid. He accepted from the outset that France would have to abandon Egypt. Napoleon also wanted to seek common ground with the British on certain points, but still found it impossible to temper his suspicions. In November 1801, he asked Talleyrand to

reassure the British about his expedition to retake Saint-Domingue –
modern Haiti – from Toussaint l'Ouverture, and restore French rule
– and slavery – there:

Make it known to the English Cabinet ... that in taking the line I have,
that of annihilating the Black government in Saint-Domingue, I have
been guided less by commercial and financial considerations than by the
necessity of stifling any kind of unrest or trouble anywhere in the world
... That one of the principal benefits of any peace for England would be
the conclusion of one before France recognised ... the power of the Blacks;
and that, if this happens, the sceptre of power in the New World would
fall into the hands of the Blacks; that the resultant upheaval for England is
incalculable, in that this upheaval in the empire of the Blacks ... would be
confused with that of the Revolution.[44]

Even in the teeth of his own defeat at the hands of Toussaint,
Napoleon exuded confidence in his dealings with the British, presenting himself, on the one hand, as the antithesis of the Revolution
– as the new 'global policeman' of the exploitative status quo – but,
equally, as someone potentially free from a racism he correctly
assumed was prevalent among the British, and as being more than
capable of showing himself the friend of the new Black state. It was a
good diplomatic card, but, in his prose, shorn of diplomacy.

In February 1802, he told Talleyrand to put a new proposal to the
British Cabinet for a joint effort to be made by the two countries,
together with Russia and Spain, against the Barbary pirates

... to end the brigandage of Algiers, Tunis and Tripoli, that is the shame
of Europe, and of the century we live in ... Certainly, the undersigned
[Napoleon] has a high enough opinion of the [British] minister and of the
English people to believe that they can work out the motives which involve a
question which must be that of the dignity of European men and of public
morality; for in the end, God has given strength to the [great] powers as
individuals for them to protect the weak. It would be good to see a war which
has produced so many calamities end with an act of hope and consolation.[45]

There was one international law for black slaves and another for white
ones, at least when it came to courting the British.

Diplomacy – or, rather, monitoring it from arm's length – brought out the most cynical elements in Napoleon, yet only in his dealings with the British. The 'Haitian card' came to nothing, Napoleon's attempts to retake Saint-Domingue ending in catastrophe. The second appeal for a 'crusade' against the North African pirates was also ignored. Ironically, the protracted British naval blockade of the western Mediterranean was mirrored by intense French patrolling of the coasts they held, all in the interests of mutual economic warfare, but this inadvertent joint effort kept the western Mediterranean relatively safe from the corsairs until 1814. This was a side effect of the conflict, however, not a means to cement a peace. In 1802, both his proposals seemed practicable; a year later, they were exposed as little short of delusional.

Nevertheless, Napoleon never lost sight of the most important issues on which he had to stand firm at Amiens.

One issue in particular brought out the confrontational instincts he was so careful to suppress in domestic politics. The issue of the Italian Republic was a tightrope for Napoleon at Amiens. Even as the negotiations took place, he had gathered the political elite of the new republic to him at Lyon, and was drawing up its constitution and reviving its public institutions under the noses of those who had still to recognise it. When he got himself elected its President in January 1802, he had engaged in an act of diplomatic brinkmanship that made a nonsense of Talleyrand's attempts to portray the new state as an autonomous entity. It also made the issue appear personal for Napoleon, as indeed it was. The recognition of the new Italian Republic by the other powers was essential to him, and it almost became a litmus test by which he judged the reliable and the treacherous.

In the final days of the negotiations at Amiens, the recognition of the Italian Republic also became a way of reminding the British of their isolation on this point. On 12 March, he ordered Joseph:

You must announce directly to Lord Cornwallis:
    That the King of Prussia has recognised the Italian Republic . . .
    That . . . a courier [from Vienna] has announced to me, personally, at 5 p.m. tonight that the [Holy Roman] Emperor regards with pleasure that

the Italian Republic has been saved from the horrors of anarchy and that he
was pleased to receive the Italian ambassador . . .

That all the Italian princes have recognised the Italian Republic.

That . . . Emperor Alexander is more disposed than ever to work together
with France for all the great issues in Europe.[46]

This was a concoction of what was and what was not true, imbued
with the bluster Napoleon reserved for the British, but it revealed his
deepest concerns for the treaty, namely that his Italian creation be
legitimised and consolidated in international law. Less than a month
earlier, he had complained bitterly to Talleyrand that, by the Emperor
in Vienna refusing to receive the ambassador of the Italian Republic,
the new state was being treated 'as if the treaty of Campo Formio had
never existed'. His distrust of the Austrians was heightened because
France had withdrawn from central Italy and, like Britain, Austria was
proving reluctant to keep its side of the bargain: 'So then is the peace
considered nothing more than a truce? This is a painful perspective,
discouraging for a man of goodwill, but which could most probably
produce incalculable results.'[47] Napoleon asked that these last
observations be communicated to the British Cabinet. The sense of
imperative priorities was, even here, mixed with undiplomatic anger,
and soon turned to triumphalism when acceptance arrived by special
courier. The new state was simply passed over in silence in the final
treaty, a sign that Britain would not recognise it, but that it was too
weak to object to it. The issue of the Italian Republic had become a test
of nerve between Napoleon and the other great powers. He got what
he wanted, but at the price of British consternation and of unnerving
the continental powers.

When it was a matter of perceiving what was crucial to French
interests, and where he could make concessions, Napoleon had very
clear, well-defined goals. However, his attitude to the British often put
the negotiations at risk, and his brother did well to keep him away
from the conference table. At home, however, Napoleon could feel the
swell of his own success and of anti-British feeling behind him, for the
French business community, especially, feared too many concessions

to Britain, in particular a trade treaty modelled on the unpopular agreement of 1786, which had done much to undermine the credibility of Louis XVI. Napoleon was only too pleased to reassure the French merchants over this, but it fed his confidence to dangerous levels. Joseph had to curb this, warning his younger brother that:

I do not doubt success; it will take a few more days of patience and firmness on our part; these people can be beaten only with their own weapons, through imperturbability and inertia. They have always triumphed over what they call French petulance in all the previous treaty negotiations. Now it is possible to force them to lose hope in this . . . Wait a bit, and we will win over an article, with each day.[48]

In the same letter, he cautioned Napoleon, as did Talleyrand, that 'Neither the government nor the English people must be attacked directly.' Joseph was right. As Emmanuel de Waresquiel has said in his meditation on the career of Talleyrand, 'A good peace almost always rests on a sense of equity between the signatories.' This did not exist between Britain and France at Amiens, he concludes.[49]

Napoleon was quick to destabilise the western Mediterranean by annexing the mainland states of the House of Savoy within months of signing the peace; he did this reluctantly, when he learned his plans to restore the Savoyards were rendered dangerous by their double-dealing with Vienna, but in the atmosphere between France and Britain this fact was ignored in London. The peace was shattered within eighteen months, when Britain refused to evacuate Malta and return it to the Knights. Interestingly, when the vote came in the Council of State regarding peace or renewed war, Joseph and Talleyrand held out for peace.[50]

Amiens brought Napoleon almost inestimable benefits in the short term and for the consolidation of his long-term goals. The Peace gave him the breathing space he needed to rebuild his army, but it also gave him the platform he needed to rebuild his state: to move quickly to consolidate and extend his own power, and the time to forge a comprehensive range of new institutions for France. It allowed him, too, to integrate properly the new territories France had been acquiring – and temporarily losing – since the invasion of Belgium in 1795. Nonetheless, the victory of Amiens was not really his to claim. His own attempts at meddling, and his brinkmanship over the only aspect of the negotiations he controlled in full, the Italian Republic, brought the negotiations close to failure. Amiens was a triumph for his older brother, Joseph, and for Talleyrand, not Napoleon.

Napoleon showed another side of himself altogether in his dealings with the German princes and the new Tsar, Alexander I, and this element of the wider peace settlement truly did result from his efforts. He was much more adroit with them than with the British. He had begun to build up diplomatic contacts and mutual understanding with the rulers of the larger states of western Germany at Rastatt, and they had been nurtured by Joseph and Talleyrand ever since. Amiens now allowed them to take full form, to the advantage of France and the princes, and to the lasting detriment of Austrian power and influence. Now began the Napoleonic reordering of Germany. This was the point when Napoleon reoriented his strategic vision away from the Atlantic – the source of Anglo-French rivalry in the eighteenth century – towards Central Europe.

By far the most important German state, after Prussia and Austria, was Bavaria. Its new Elector, since 1799, was Max Joseph, who had shown himself to be an enlightened reformer when ruler of the small Rhenish state of Deux-Ponts before 1799. Napoleon, and then Joseph, had marked him out as a potential ally at Rastatt, and he had been a reluctant member of the anti-French coalition. By the time the conferences of Amiens began he had moved firmly to the French camp, supported by his chief minister, Montgelas, who had served Joseph II in Vienna and was not an admirer of Emperor Francis. Napoleon knew how to play on Bavarian fears of Austrian aggrandisement at Max Joseph's expense, for the new Elector, when still the heir presumptive in 1799, had opposed the presence of a large Austrian army on Bavarian territory, seeing in it a threat to its very independence.

When, in the summer of 1801, Vienna sought to acquire Bavarian territory, Napoleon opposed this. However, he was able to do so effectively because he fostered a working alliance with Tsar Alexander, who was equally wary of Vienna. In October 1801, he wrote to Alexander that:

The Elector of Bavaria, having consulted me about the proposition made him by the House of Austria to alienate part of Bavaria, I have assumed that I have been working in agreement with Your Majesty in advising him not to exchange . . . his hereditary states for those of another.[51]

It worked, and Alexander helped Napoleon not only in the case of Bavaria, but over the fates of Baden, Nassau and Württemberg as well. Napoleon's posturing as the new 'global policeman', or as the potential harbinger of the Revolution in the New World, had failed to impress the British, but this new stance, as the seeming protector of the status quo in the Holy Roman Empire, worked with Alexander just long enough for him to achieve his ends, for by 1804 the new Tsar was turning again towards an offensive alliance with Austria and Britain.

Napoleon's relationship with the German princes was based on positive factors, as well as the negative fear of Austria. Whereas Austria had offered these princes only aggression, Napoleon held out the prospect of aggrandisement. The pretext actually stemmed from the original harm that France had done to them. They had all lost territories to France when the annexation of the west bank of the Rhine was ratified with Austria at Lunéville. Napoleon took up their cause for compensation within the Holy Roman Empire, promising them new territories which would be adjacent to the cores of their states, and would enlarge them considerably. In reality, this policy of 'mediatisation' ripped apart the fabric of the old Reich, with scant regard for tradition, but Napoleon presented it differently to Alexander: he claimed they had a shared duty to protect their friends. Early in 1802, Napoleon took up the cause of Baden with the Tsar:

Your Majesty has an alliance with the House of Baden, which has suffered greatly during the war. I wish to know the degree of assistance Your Majesty would like to give to this House: this might be the appropriate moment to acquire for it a reasonable enlargement, proportionate to the honour of a state allied to Your Majesty. If this could be arranged, it would enable France to repay its debt to a very estimable prince ... who has always conducted himself well.[52]

Even before Napoleon had broached the subject of Baden with Alexander, article three of his treaty with Bavaria, concluded in August 1801, affirmed that 'The French Republic will use all its influence' to secure Max Joseph compensation for his losses at Lunéville.[53] His treaty with Württemberg, signed two months after Amiens, in May 1802, was more specific still on what kind of compensation Napoleon would help its ruler acquire: '... the French Republic will use its good offices to obtain for His Excellency, territories situated in so far as possible, [in places] convenient and beneficial to His Excellency, as recompense'.[54] Over the next two years, Napoleon made good these promises.

The destruction of the petty German states this compensation entailed was couched in terms of honour; the 'French debt' was paid by the independent imperial cities, the prince-bishoprics and the fiefs of the Imperial Knights that found themselves coterminous with Bavaria, Baden, Württemberg and Nassau. Franco-Russian co-operation, for the first time but not the last, shunted the Habsburgs aside. Bavaria was more than compensated: it became a considerable power of the second order. It had lost 4,600 square miles of territory at Lunéville, together with 73,000 inhabitants and approximately 4 million gulden (a gold coin) in revenue; with Napoleon's pressure behind it, Bavaria gained 6,600 square miles, 840,000 people and 6.5 million gulden in revenues by 1803. More would come over the years of Napoleonic expansion. Proportionally, Baden grew even more spectacularly, from a minor state of 1,400 square miles to 5,800 square miles, and saw its population and revenues quadruple by 1809. Württemberg made its gains mainly at the expense of the Swabian Imperial Knights and the Church, receiving 700 square miles of territory and revenues of 750,000 florins in compensation for the minuscule fief of Montbéliard, gains out of all proportion to its losses. By 1803, Napoleon had proved himself a more than useful protector of these princes. He was repaid with unswerving loyalty until the eleventh hour in 1813, and his influence on the internal evolution of these states in the years ahead was powerful.

It was a quiet but concrete triumph, for Napoleon had done more than help his new allies: he had secured French hegemony in western Europe and he did so without firing a shot. France had been strengthened directly at Austria's expense, not only through the obvious loss of influence and credibility within the Holy Roman Empire, but in very tangible terms. The petty states of the Empire – the prince-bishoprics, the fiefs of the Imperial Knights, the free imperial cities – were fertile recruiting grounds for the Habsburg armies and for imperial service. Metternich was but one of many such men drawn from their small territories into imperial – and therefore Austrian – service without any clash of loyalties. The rulers of the newly enhanced *Mittelstaaten* ensured that this supply of talent and manpower was choked off in future. Soon, the human and material resources of western Germany – rich, populous, highly developed – would flow the way of Napoleon, not of Vienna. The 'settlement' of the German princes was Napoleon's greatest diplomatic achievement. These gains, subtle in comparison to overt conquest, also secured Napoleon in power. Hegemony in western Germany was all the more real for its peaceful achievement. In hard, military terms, there was now an effective buffer between the eastern powers and France, in Germany and in northern Italy. The borders were safe, and would remain so until 1813.

Luigi Mascilli Migliorini has drawn attention to Napoleon's almost melancholy reaction to the conclusion of the treaties at Amiens, quoting his remark that 'the years ahead will be without victories, without triumphs, without robust negotiations which will shape the destinies of states', while admitting that the years to come would see France happier, if less glorious.[55] He was right in the short term. Nevertheless, peace there was, and it worked well for the Republic when it came. The peace gave Napoleon greater popularity than ever, and he transformed it into tangible power. Amiens allowed him to end the appropriation of the Republic, and begin the creation of a state truly his own. That is, to increase his powers to levels that would have been unimaginable to anyone but him at the moment of Brumaire. The period of furtive manoeuvring was over. The Republic had been well and truly appropriated. It was now time to think in other terms. He moved fast.

8

TAKING POWER

Towards the End of Politics, 1802–1804

'OUT OF THE WOODS': FROM FEAR TO CONFIDENCE

Brumaire had been a coup by, and for, the political world of the Parisian 'bubble'. In this narrow context, the immediate threat to the plotters had come from the left, and a fair proportion of the coup's supporters had been, at some point, well disposed to constitutional royalism. Napoleon had learned how to out-manoeuvre the supposed masters of the world of high politics. The semi-foreign arriviste coped with a certain kind of Frenchman in masterly fashion. Now, with peace as well-secured as it could be given the international climate, and his personal power as absolute as he dared make it for the present, Napoleon would be tested as to how well he understood his adopted country. The bloodless victory of Amiens had at last allowed him to rise above mere political survival, with the real power to act for himself. There were times, in these years, when he appeared to know the French better than they knew themselves.

Napoleon learned many lessons in his first months in power. Revolutionary politics, he discovered, was at least as dangerous for him personally – and for hundreds of thousands of other Frenchmen – as any battlefield, and that for this reason alone the Revolution had to be ended. It was a matter of simple survival as much as anything else. He also now knew at first hand that Paris was an island within France, and one just as blood-soaked and dangerous as the Corsica he had fled. It was divided into vendetta-ridden factions, a royalist west – where he was reviled as the author of Vendémiaire – and a recalcitrant Jacobin east, which could still, in the minds of some politicians, be relied upon to unsettle the world of high politics. Napoleon never came to terms with the western side of the 'island'; throughout his rule, he always entered Paris from the east if he could, and avoided the neighbourhoods in which he had made his name as an 'enforcer' for the regime he subsequently dispatched. His rapport grew with the Jacobin east, however. He conferred artificially low conscription quotas on it and before he left for the Russian campaign in 1812 he ordered his private army, the Imperial Guard, to scour the surrounding countryside for food to ensure the Jacobin *faubourgs* were well provisioned in his absence. Neither Robespierre nor the *Parlement* of Paris could have looked after the *sans-culottes* any better.

Paris was all the more dangerous in Napoleon's mind because of its very appearance. The city of his times did not at all resemble that of today, save in the areas around the twin Renaissance palaces of the Tuileries and the Louvre, and the Champs Elysées, the wide, tree-lined avenue created under Louis XIV in the seventeenth century. In the place of the wide boulevards and vast squares that are the hallmark of modern Paris, its centre was still a web of narrow cobbled streets – which were easily dug up and used as missiles during riots – where medieval houses leaned towards each other, blocking the sunlight. The ramshackle popular architecture was often punctuated by the elegant seventeenth century *hôtels* of the nobility, with their tall, narrow windows and splendid entry gates. The real life of the city was in the closed courtyards behind the narrow street entries, however. This was where Parisians congregated for work and sociability, away from the gaze of outsiders and authority. This world has all but vanished, although some tiny remnants of it can be glimpsed in the fashionable Marais quarter, between the Hôtel de Ville and the Bastille, and in the Latin Quarter, with their half-timbered houses and alley-like streets. In Napoleon's mind, as the assassination attempts on him multiplied, this cityscape increasingly took on the shape of a living nightmare. His would-be killers sallied forth from these dark, hidden places to assail him, and slipped back into them just as easily. The old centre was his most potent enemy. The eastern suburbs, home to the pro-Jacobin *sans-culottes*, might be won over and the subversive, if well-heeled royalist west, with its well-lit streets and elegant apartments, intimidated, but the danger of the 'vipers' nest' at the heart of the city seemed intractable to him.

Once in power, Napoleon was not long in trying to avenge himself on Paris, but in a subtle way. It was beyond his power to bulldoze the old centre, or to rebuild it. Instead, he turned his attention to recreating the public spaces of the city, where he could. Napoleon put special emphasis on the parks, gardens and other public green spaces of the capital. The physical urban ambience surrounding these spaces was intended to seduce and impress Parisians and visitors alike, as attention was turned to the parks and gardens of the city for the first time since the 1780s. In the hands of the new regime, the park became a tool of enlightenment, to stand in contrast to the closed, dark 'Gothic' world of the streets. To Napoleon, private parks, the preserve of aristocratic plotters, were relics of a drab but dangerous old order. It was time to put an end to the era of closed gardens,[1] if not yet of cobbled streets. Napoleon opened the restored gardens of the Tuileries to the public, in direct contrast to the monarchy, yet he kept them in the neo-classical style of the seventeenth century, as he also did with the Luxembourg gardens. The public parks of Napoleonic Paris were physical plebiscites, and an opening of a culture previously the preserve of the privileged, to the nation. Nevertheless, Parisian space was also used to affirm emphatically the authoritarian character of the regime. It was a benign but authoritarian way of coaxing Parisians out of their lairs, and into healthy, green places, where they could be kept an eye on.

Many of the other great spaces recreated by Napoleon doubled as public parks and parade grounds. Paris was the permanent head-quarters of the Imperial Guard, the cream of the army, which was under Napoleon's exclusive command, and the open spaces of the capital were used to showcase it. Parisians were now the spectators at these events, no longer the dangerous players they had been during the violence of the Revolution which had so terrified Napoleon.

The public spaces of Paris, its parks especially, encapsulate the contradictions, just as much as the aspirations, of the new regime, of openness and progress, set beside the ever-present reminder of its iron, military fist. Napoleon's real revenge on the city centre had to await the rule of his nephew, Napoleon III – the second son of Louis and Hortense – who ordered his architect-in-chief, Haussmann, to lay waste to the city his uncle so feared, clearing away the 'Gothic menace' and turning Paris into the city it is today.

Napoleon had to survive on this dangerous island, however, and the only way to do so was to reach beyond it to the 'mainland' of *la France profonde*. These were the circumstances in which Napoleon's key twin policies of *ralliement* and *amalgame*, first developed in Italy, were put to their first test in France. *Ralliement*, the passive acceptance of the regime, allowed people to stand aside quietly, without being forced to take sides; *amalgame* entailed working for the regime alongside former enemies. *Ralliement* was conceived as a safety valve to avoid confrontation; a*malgame* was intended to mark a new beginning. Now, it remained to be seen if it could achieve these ends.[2] This approach was geared to embrace as many people as possible, in direct contrast to the attitude of the late Directory, and it applied even more to the provinces than to Paris. This became the linchpin of his domestic political vision.

Napoleon's first attempt to reach out beyond Paris, taken even before the dust of Brumaire had settled, was a gesture of reconciliation to political extremism – to another 'island' within France. It was, quite simply, to do with arresting the flow of violence. On 14 December 1799, the government offered an amnesty to the rebels in the Vendée, which was extended to all the rebels in the western departments two weeks later. Conciliation was not the only policy of the regime, however. Fouché, for his part, soon made it plain that provincial royalism was still the public face of counter-revolution. It quickly became very clear that the real, lingering danger to any republican regime, whether radical and Jacobin, or elitist like the Directory, came from counter-revolution in the provinces, whose power had grown with every military reverse. Pacification at home – be it the internal reconquest of much of the south and west, or the peaceful reassurance of the landowning classes – was essential to the survival of any republican government.

The need for this kind of support became all the more apparent as the intellectuals of left and right turned away in disappointment and disgust from the Consulate, as its authoritarian character became clearer, and, even more, as it grappled with hard realities. Napoleon had seen this coming, even if high and fine minds like Madame de Staël, a noted author, the centre of an intensely intellectual salon, and the daughter of Jacques Necker, the last first minister of Louis XVI (in the centre), René de Chateaubriand, a pugnacious proponent of royalism, a devout Catholic and the author of several bestsellers, notably *The Genius of Catholicism* (on the right), or Benjamin Constant, Staël's sometime lover and an emerging political commentator (on the left), had not. They all stood at the forefront of Parisian intellectual life in 1799. Staël, whose loathing for Napoleon surfaced soon, and with a vengeance, interpreted the politics built on *ralliement* and *amalgame* in the most cynical optic conceivable, but she got it perfectly right:

In all his political nominations, Bonaparte followed nearly the same rule, of taking ... now from the right, and now from the left, that is to say, choosing alternately his officers among the aristocrats, and among the Jacobins: the middle party, that of the friends of liberty, pleased him less than all the others, composed as it was of the small numbers of persons, who in France, had an opinion of their own. He liked much better to have to do with persons who were attached to royalist interests, or who had become stigmatized by popular excesses.[3]

Staël was right about Napoleon but, more importantly, he was right about people like her. Intellectuals make very unreliable political allies, and, whatever the nature of the regime he would go on to forge, he was wise to prepare for life after their disillusionment. Even an eye as sharp as Staël's failed to grasp the deeper cunning at work in

Napoleon's mind, however. On the one hand, he knew how to draw more of her 'middle party' to him than she dared imagine, nor could she face the hard reality that many such people, after the convulsed decade they had lived through, felt they had more in common with him than her. More than this, Staël failed to look hard enough at the details of so many of Napoleon's measures. It should have been clear to her when she dissected *amalgame* so shrewdly in the last years of his rule – between 1810 and 1813 – that he had carefully planned for a time when he could dispense with the men of the older generation in favour of a younger cohort of his own making. In 1800, this lay in the future, yet even at the first hour Napoleon was bringing forward quiet, competent men who had already put 'faction' behind them. Beside Talleyrand and Fouché came Cambacérès and Lebrun, the men who would lay the foundations of a new regime rather than refashion the debris of the Revolution. As support from the revolutionary extremes waned – Staël's' 'extreme centre' included – their day was coming.

THE LIMITS OF INCLUSION, 1802–1804: CRUSHING THE RIGHT

For all this, the Parisian bubble was still far from safe. Plots and rumours of plots continued to dog Napoleon for years to come, particularly from within the army. Bernadotte, from the right, and even Augereau, on the left, grumbled about the results of Brumaire and were dispatched far from Paris; an embryonic plot among some officers at Rennes in 1803 was scotched by Fouché, and may have involved Bernadotte. The real problem was the open disaffection of Moreau, however, and, even more, the determination of the British secret service to cut off the head of the new regime. Napoleon did not fear Moreau as an individual, as, for all his convinced republicanism, he had little political acumen. Steven Englund has summed up Napoleon's attitude to him perfectly, in that Moreau 'more exasperated Bonaparte than rivalled him'.[4] This was even apparent when Moreau finally did become entangled with truly dangerous people.

In the last days of January 1804, Fouché uncovered a British-run plot, centred on the Vendean leader Cadoudal and General Pichegru, who had defected to the enemy early in the Revolutionary wars. Moreau had been meeting with them for some time before he was arrested on 15 February. In their plans, he was meant to be little more than the 'battering ram' to overthrow Napoleon, and would be quickly replaced by a noble, acting as 'Lieutenant General of the Kingdom', until Louis XVIII could return.

The following month, Napoleon ordered the arrest of the duc d'Enghien, a young, fanatical but ineffectual aristocrat living over the border in Baden on a British secret service pension. Napoleon had decided he was the Lieutenant General designate, which was preposterous even by the often demented thinking of the court-in-exile. Napoleon took a direct, personal interest in hunting d'Enghien down. He himself gave the detailed orders for the kidnapping, which involved violating Baden's territory, and entrusted its direction to Berthier and the arrest itself to Caulaincourt and the Gendarmerie, the military police force he had recently resurrected into an elite unit.[5] Napoleon may have had very genuine fears about d'Enghien, given his links not only to the British, but to General Dumouriez, like Pichegru an early traitor to the Revolution.[6] D'Enghien was executed on 21 March, while Cadoudal was hanged and Pichegru died in prison, in murky circumstances. Moreau, by contrast, was only sent into exile, then went to America, only to emerge in 1812 as a military adviser to the Tsar. The most ardent republican among the generals of the Directory thus found himself the henchman of a self-defined autocrat. He would die at the Battle of Dresden in 1813.

It was d'Enghien's demise that has gone down in history, however. His death alienated true royalists definitively; it separated the moderates from the diehards very effectively. Chateaubriand abandoned his initial hopes of Napoleon as 'a powerful genius, the conqueror of anarchy, a chief who had emerged from the principle of popularity'.[7] The deed 'fell upon me like thunder' and sent him into self-imposed exile, and other, less notable aristocrats followed suit. Chateaubriand claimed that this one event turned the courts of Europe against Napoleon, which was hardly the whole truth, but his personal response to the deed marks a real turning point in Napoleon's always fragile relationship with the royalist right. Chateaubriand had remained an active supporter of the regime far longer than other members of the caste of which he made himself the champion after Napoleon's fall. Unlike many nobles, he did not shun the regime when the defects of the Concordat Napoleon concluded with the Papacy in June 1801 became clear, for example. He ignored the defiance of the bishops and the court-in-exile, and was not discouraged by the resumption of war with Britain in 1803. Indeed, if his memoirs are to be believed, Chateaubriand rallied to Napoleon exactly because he did not represent 'a king of continuity, of a usurped monarchy', but something new and genuine, a break with the past. Now this had been sullied for ever by the gratuitous murder of d'Enghien, marking the point when he began to rule by fear.[8] A host of other aristocrats had already withdrawn to their own closed world, as they had in the mid-1790s, for all Napoleon's entreaties. Napoleon had prepared for a world without them.

The rupture with Chateaubriand proved that all Napoleon had left to offer the old nobility was the prospect of suitable careers in public service, which events conspired to provide. The army and the diplomatic corps beckoned, as military victories swelled the army, and brought the courts of Europe to Napoleon's door. Even this, however, was only a prospect to tempt a new generation; sons might rally, but not their parents.

Chateaubriand was right about one thing. D'Enghien's execution was as cynical and calculated as the exile of the republicans after the bomb attack in the rue St-Nicaise, but it was far more brutal, for a pattern emerges in Napoleon's retaliations: republicans are exiled, royalists die. He was ready to exterminate those he had now learned, over the course of four years, to be his real, irreconcilable enemies, but he could not, nor did he wish to, drive an everlasting wedge between the republican past and himself. As he moved towards seizing the imperial title, however, he had to 'separate his destiny from that of the Bourbons in an irrevocable manner'.[9]

This break with extreme royalists was real, not merely ideological. The conspiracy of 1804 worried Napoleon far more than that of the 'infernal machine' which nearly killed him in the rue St-Nicaise, for he saw it in the context of his policy of 'rallying' and, in concrete terms, the very limited success of his early amnesties for the émigrés. Three days before d'Enghien's execution, he told Talleyrand:

Write to Frankfurt and Hamburg and [get the French secret service] to send us the lists of émigrés living in those cities, their age, their details, their first names and, if possible, the departments they come from, and that you want it in a fortnight. It might also be necessary to ask [the Bavarian government in] Munich to arrest the Bishop of Châlons.[10]

Napoleon had done a great deal to try to appease French Catholics in the first years of the Consulate, as we will see, but the wider ramifications of the d'Enghien conspiracy were fraying his nerves, witnessed in his wish to seize a senior cleric even if he was an émigré. His heightened fear and seeming hatred of the royalists was much clearer when he wrote to his brother-in-law and comrade Murat the next day. Murat was the military governor of Paris, and he had suspicions that a very senior member of the royal family, the duc de Berry – known for his intense hatred of the Revolution – was in Paris, along with other nobles of similar feelings. Napoleon lashed out:

If [they are in the city] ... I want them arrested tonight, and I want them shot, but I also want the foreign ambassadors arrested, and they will get the same treatment, and [international] law will afford these people no protection ... And arrest the man who gave you this information, the miserable creature ... Everyone knows the ambassadors' houses only serve as safe havens for crimes of state. Don't be fooled by the nonsense of those who say otherwise, and don't let anyone talk thus to you.[11]

Napoleon had himself succumbed to a rumour circulating in Paris that several royal princes were hiding there, in the homes of foreign ambassadors, awaiting the success of the assassination of the First

Consul. Fortunately for them, the Bourbon princes were not in Paris and only d'Enghien felt Napoleon's wrath.

Napoleon had been pushed to the edge by these events, yet not quite over it. D'Enghien's murder was brutal, but it served a purpose. He was less a scapegoat than a warning shot fired at other royalist conspirators. Napoleon's brush with paranoid bloodletting came in response to fears of a wider plot, in his own capital. As he moved towards taking the imperial title in the following months, much would be done to placate republican sentiment, and the assassination attempts themselves were often invoked as a reason to 'entrust the Republic to an hereditary emperor', but there was no similar courting of the royalists. In the wake of the plot of the 'infernal machine', Napoleon had told the Council of State that 'the Chouans and the émigrés are simply a skin disease, while the Terrorists are an internal infection'. Henceforth, he reversed his position with all his exact, geometric precision.

THE REALITY OF POLITICS: LIVING WITH THE CENTRE

In truth, d'Enghien's death is the exception that proves the rule. Stalked by assassins, the overt target of British policy, treading a line between the embittered factions bequeathed to him by the Revolution, Napoleon never lost sight of his own goal of real power, but nor did he tip into blind, rabid retaliation. Even his cruellest acts were calculated, with a clear political purpose. In deliberate and complete contrast to the previous generation of revolutionary politicians, there was no descent into paranoia or bloody, random purges.

His caution and ruthless self-possession, his ability to keep a sense of perspective, come out in his dealings with opposition from within the regime by those who had initially supported Brumaire. The uneasy, fundamentally incongruous coalition that disposed of the Directory started to fray when Napoleon put his authoritarian stamp first on specific legislation, and then on the new institutions of government. Many, most notably Sieyès, could simply be bought off with well-paid sinecures, but other uneasy Brumairians were not so easily neutered. Faced with a minority of influential opponents and a much wider body of politicians who felt unhappy with many of his actions, it is less surprising that Napoleon sought to thwart and stifle them, than that he did not actually turn on them. The years of the Consulate were filled with subtle manoeuvres, political pressure and shrewd bargaining, punctuated by occasional – and often reciprocal – tongue-lashings, but in genuine contrast to the Directory there were no mass purges. Above all, no member of the elected assemblies or any journalist ever came to harm. Violence was reserved for those on the political extremes – and this should not be forgotten, for the memories of the Terror were still very fresh in the minds of everyone, but most especially those who had supported the coup of Brumaire.

The proximity of the Terror did much to aid Napoleon in his dealings with those politicians of the centre who were becoming worried by his actions. Carnot and Napoleon, agreed on so many aspects of the war, soon fell out with the advent of peace. Forced out of the War Ministry, Carnot became a member of the Tribunate, the assembly charged with debating legislation sent to it by the Senate and the Council of State. Although he had been driven into exile in the late Directory for his links to royalism, Carnot now chose to refresh his Jacobin roots, opposing the creation of the Legion of Honour and, more importantly, casting the only vote against making Napoleon Consul for Life in 1802. Carnot's own views were widely shared, but his past as a member of the infamous Committee of Public Safety always undermined his standing with the republican centre, 'a troubling aura that now weakened his moral authority as a lonely defender of elective government'.[12] Napoleon never harmed him and retained him as a Tribune until the assembly was abolished in 1807. When Carnot left public life, between 1807 and 1814, Napoleon left him in peace. Indeed, he rallied to Napoleon during the Hundred Days, serving as Minister of the Interior, and was exiled by the restored monarchy as a result. For all Carnot's fulminations against him, Napoleon turned out to be his best friend in politics.

Carnot's lack of credibility made him an irritant, but Pierre Daunou presented a more influential voice of dissent within the regime. Daunou had opposed Brumaire, which was hardly surprising given the key role he had played in the creation of the constitution of 1795, which the coup had overthrown; appointed to the Tribunate, he harassed the new legislation at every opportunity. His election as President of the Tribunate in 1802 was probably the high point of legislative independence during the Consulate; it coincided with his fortieth birthday, which made him eligible for the Senate and the prospect of becoming a yet sharper thorn in Napoleon's side, and his election was avoided only by the exertion of considerable personal pressure on the Senate by Napoleon, foreshadowed in his exasperated warning to Lebrun and Cambacérès, his co-Consuls:

I will make it known to the Senate, myself, of the situation we are in. I don't know how it will be possible to carry on, when the constituted authorities are composed of our enemies: and the system has no greater [enemy] than Daunou . . .[13]

Napoleon proposed – and carried out – the removal of twenty 'dissident' Tribunes, replacing them with twenty *bien pensants*. Napoleon called them Senators, in his rage, perhaps a Freudian slip of the pen as his frustration welled over and he imagined the worst. He did this legally, and Daunou was among those removed. Yet Napoleon had always tried to work with Daunou; he respected him and used him as a counterweight to the hapless Sieyès on the committee which framed the 1799 constitution. He acknowledged the wide respect Daunou commanded by offering him a post on the Council of State – the true centre of power – after his election to the Presidency of the Tribunate. This olive branch was brusquely rejected at a dinner between the two that was meant to bring them together. The two egos traded snide remarks, but it ended only in Daunou being shuffled into, first, the directorship of the library of the Institut, and then to that of the National Archives, where he served brilliantly until the end of the regime. Napoleon appointed him to this post for life in 1804. When eyebrows were raised, he wrote darkly to the Minister of the Interior:

[M]y intention is that [this post] should be perpetual . . . and as M. Daunou, who holds this post, should enjoy all the rights and prerogatives which are attached to it, and that no one should dispute this. I wish you to take steps to ensure that all difficulties about this object should cease.[14]

The same day, Napoleon wrote to Daunou: 'I very much hope that the circumstances present themselves which now allow me to make use of your talents in a very eminent post for the good of the state, and my service.'[15] The removal of Daunou and his nineteen fellow 'irritants' from the Tribunate represents exactly the warped legality they most feared, but the level of influence he wielded in the first precarious years of Napoleon's rule could have led to a much worse fate. Napoleon's treatment of Daunou reveals more than a ruler bent simply on autocracy. His first instincts were to try to attract Daunou into the 'system', as he called it to his closest collaborators, perhaps opening a wider window on his political thought than he would have preferred. In the end, he held on to Daunou, and Daunou to Napoleon. Daunou stood on the very edge of *amalgame*, but not completely outside it, his distinct distaste for *ralliement* notwithstanding. That Napoleon did not lash out at this sort of opposition shows a sense of proportion utterly absent in his predecessors at the helm of the Republic.

The Tribunes who rallied around Carnot and Daunou were not the only sources of 'moderate' opposition to the new regime. A group of elitist republican intellectuals grouped around the journal *La Décade Philosophique*, some of whom were deputies in one or other of the Consular assemblies. Their specific points of collision, and even more of collusion, with Napoleon in the early years shed sharp light on the nature of the politics of the centre, and on why Napoleon could live with their criticism. Quite naturally, they proved sensitive to repression of the press, and spoke out, in line with Daunou, against the first two articles of the proposed Civil Code because they did not invoke directly the 1789 Declaration of the Rights of Man. Their

opposition was potent enough to force Napoleon to withdraw the
Code from public discussion, if not to divert him from his course. Led
by Ginguené and Say, the journal had always advocated making peace
with the other powers, as long as the Republic was not endangered,
a position which almost endeared Napoleon to the two men at the
outset of his rule, when he needed the press most.

His indulgence faded once war with Britain resumed in 1803. *La
Décade* was forthright in its opposition to Napoleon's attempt to
retake Saint-Domingue from Toussaint l'Ouverture's slave rebels in
1802, and vehement in its hatred of his chief colonial adviser, Moreau
de Saint-Méry, a protégé of Joséphine from the French West Indies,
who successfully advocated the restoration of slavery. It is interesting,
however, that *La Décade* argued primarily not against slavery, as
such, but for the independence of the colony under its local Creole
leadership.

This is perhaps the clearest sign of the innate elitism of the men
grouped around the journal, for they had supported the ejection of 'the
masses' from politics with marked enthusiasm at Brumaire. Indeed,
they railed most against Napoleon in these years when he sought to
mend fences with the Church, through the Concordat, seeing in it a
return to state sanction for superstition and obscurantism. In line with
this outlook, *La Décade* devoted several long articles to attacking the
leading apologist for Catholicism, Chateaubriand and in particular
his recent bestselling book, *Le Génie du Christianisme*. In any case, by
1804 the murder of d'Enghien had turned Chateaubriand into a fierce
enemy of Napoleon.

In the end, the men of *La Décade*, which was not shut down despite
its sharp words, were on the same side as Napoleon, and he knew
it, even if they did not. Most of their pages advocated agricultural
improvement, an end to corruption in public administration and a
political system centred on the responsible, propertied classes. What
exasperated Napoleon about them were their stands on particular
issues, not their adherence to an enlightened philosophy that looked to
the eventual 'improvement' of the lower classes. In practice, however,

they saw this as a distant future, and their intrinsic elitism bound them to a powerful protector, whether they liked it or not. Their programme was one of elitist, enlightened absolutism, which was exactly what Napoleon sought himself his whole public life. There was a deeper identity of interest between Napoleon and the elitist intelligentsia than some of their number perceived. This was why, ultimately, so deep-rooted a resentment towards the regime remained an 'unexploded conflict', as Yves Bénot has put it.[16] It was his ability to master this sort of opposition, rather than trample on it as Thibaudeau feared, that enabled Napoleon to advance from one Consul among three to Emperor. He amassed power in committee, by skilful use of the chair rather than from the saddle of a warhorse.

One of the greatest of the many books ever written about Napoleon was by a Dutch scholar of true genius, Pieter Geyl. In the immediate aftermath of the Second World War, with an eye to recent events, Geyl compiled a book from excerpts of quotes from Napoleon's contemporaries and later historians and thinkers, entitled abrasively *Napoleon: For and Against*. Its title polarises discussion about its subject, but if read carefully Geyl is playing a much subtler game than many of those who think they are taking their cue from him often realise. Geyl saw that many of those who came to oppose, indeed to hate, Napoleon the most intensely actually supported him fervently at the outset, led by Staël and Chateaubriand, and that they never lost their admiration for his personal abilities, nor ever disparaged his ferocious intellect.

Few contemporaries of comparable intelligence or originality ever doubted that Napoleon was something extraordinary, for good or ill. Conversely, many of those who actually backed him consistently in the first years of his rule were those who under-rated him or simply assumed he had no vision of his own. Men like Sieyès or Cabanais simply saw what they wanted to see; many were, frankly, mediocrities whose egos had become inflated by their seemingly unshakeable grip on power, and actually handed Napoleon the constitutional weapons he needed to undo them. They were never 'for', as they could not assess Napoleon, nor were they truly capable of turning against him, for lack of a viable alternative once he had wrong-footed their own plans. There were others still, epitomised by Carnot, who so wanted to be 'against', but whose common sense told them, in modern parlance, to put up and shut up. Talleyrand and Fouché were less emphatic than Carnot, but later events would show that they were less 'for' than realistic enough to know that, for the time being at least, to be 'against' was folly for themselves and their country. Lebrun and Cambacérès represent genuine collaborators, men who saw enlightened absolutism as a creative force and parliamentarianism as a proven danger. Napoleon placed and retained them at the apex of the state. To be 'for' or 'against' in Napoleonic France was a shifting, evolving process, and the closer his contemporaries were to him the more complex were the meanings of 'for' and 'against'.

One of the first and most bitterly opposed measures taken by the Consulate, which united all liberal voices against the regime, was the creation of the Special Tribunals, new courts composed partly of soldiers, partly of civilian judges, to deal more ruthlessly and consistently with provincial unrest than either the regular criminal courts or pure courts martial. That they also lacked juries angered Daunou – but not Carnot, interestingly – the contributors to *La Décade*, and Madame de Staël, in equal measure. These courts embodied the tyrannical instincts they suspected Napoleon harboured, but their opposition also reveals how out of touch they were with provincial realities, or the preoccupations of the propertied classes most exposed to disorder of all kinds. However noble its instincts, this was the voice of the Parisian 'bubble', and Napoleon saw he had to resist it if he was to extend his support to the propertied classes beyond Paris. The violence of the provinces swirled all around the Parisian politicians, even after peace was delivered on the frontiers, and Napoleon put the real domestic issues of these years first.

Napoleon knew that his priorities were those of the people he needed to win over. The flood of official petitions and unsolicited letters of support from the provinces which followed the plot of the 'infernal machine' gave him early proof that his policies were attracting the local elites – the 'masses of granite' – and the rank and file of the departmental administrations. As early as January 1801, Napoleon could see for himself that the work of his first year in power was creating a power base in *la France profonde*, whatever Parisian politicians or elitist intellectuals might think of him. There was nothing high-minded or nuanced about those policies. A state was forged in the midst of murky 'politics' and the dodging of assassins' bombs, and it was accomplished with astounding speed. The lessons of Italy were now applied to the *Grande Nation* itself.

THE CONSULATE FOR LIFE, THE CONSTITUTION OF THE YEAR 10: POWER SECURED

No one benefited more from the Peace of Amiens than Napoleon himself. The treaty was signed on 27 March 1802, and by the end of the first week of August he had become First Consul for Life, and a new constitution at last gave him the kind of political system he wanted. There was no doubt the regime revelled outwardly in the double triumph of Amiens and the official adoption of the Concordat, on 8 April (although actual agreement had been reached the previous July). On 18 April, Easter Sunday, the new First Consul for Life went to Notre-Dame from the Tuileries with the papal legate, Cardinal Caprara, to celebrate a Mass, trumpets sounding the entire way. Napoleon was escorted by the Consular Guard, rapidly swelling into his private army. They were in new uniforms, their weapons gleaming; the Horse Grenadiers 'seemed to make their horses march in step'.[17] Napoleon wore a new striking red uniform, that of his new office, and a new ceremonial sword, in whose hilt had been set the most precious stone of the old royal treasury, the huge Regent's diamond. He was still outshone – literally – by Joséphine, who dripped and blazed at once, with new diamond jewellery. This was the first appearance of the new liverymen of the First Consul, who drove his coach. Although this marked the revival of a royal office, they wore new colours, green and gold, 'colours of youth and power, which would soon be familiar throughout Europe'.[18]

The ceremony marked peace of two kinds, cultural and political. The central actors, Napoleon and Caprara, were covered by a traditional sign of thanksgiving for reconciliation, two crimson canopies surmounted by white feathers,[19] Napoleon had lost no time in decorating Notre-Dame with the battle flags of the army, which hung above the 'panoplies of peace' as a warning that peace came from might. Alongside the coach and its liverymen rode Napoleon's private guard of mounted Mamelukes, their uniforms 'fairly blazing with gold'.[20] Their presence was a reminder that Napoleon was still fearful, that he trusted only hunted refugees like himself, with his life.

One of Napoleon's most potent arguments for the Consulship for Life was the continuing threat to his own life but, in truth, although still very much a target after Amiens, his great accomplishment of a comprehensive, advantageous peace settlement made him invulnerable in political terms. It was now unthinkable for all but the furthest political extremes to overthrow a regime that had delivered an end to ten years of war. From the royalist right, Chateaubriand hailed him (if not for long) in his new bestselling novel *Atala*, and, from the left, even that perpetual nuisance the Tribunate proposed that Napoleon be offered some gift of thanks. The swift move to real regime change embodied by the new constitution was only the first sign that Napoleon did not see his new-found security as durable, still less the moment to stand still. That gift turned out to be the Consulship for Life, and the Constitution of the Year 10, which finally embodied Napoleon's own work, reflecting his own vision.

The proposal to reward Napoleon took its formal shape in the Senate, with the proposal to extend his term to ten years, but Napoleon soon used all his skills in committee to switch the debate to the Council of State. He did this in order to change the proposal to a grant of office for life, and then to argue that this change was so fundamental that only a plebiscite could give it legitimacy. Technically, the Council of State was exceeding its powers by amending the Senate's proposal: its official task was to draft new legislation for the chambers to vote on, and to assess the legality of its own proposals. The manoeuvres Napoleon initiated over the Consulship for Life skirted the bounds of legality, but were well crafted enough to work. It was, for Isser Woloch – whose account of these events is exceptionally incisive – 'a devious stratagem',[21] and it shows how intelligent a strategist Napoleon was in his favoured civilian milieu, that of the closed committee of experts.

This measure did not have an entirely easy passage even in the Council: several members spoke against it, but none *voted* against it. The five councillors who expressed reservations preferred, when it came to the vote, to abstain. The attitude of this, most loyal of the organs of state, served as a useful warning to Napoleon of the rougher passage his bid for true, sole power would receive in the Senate, to say nothing of the Tribunate, where Carnot spoke out powerfully against the proposal. What happened in the course of the debates in the Council of State shows Napoleon's genuine political acumen in these months, of his sense of what was possible within the confines of Parisian parliamentarianism even at the height of his popularity to date.

The real spur to the whole debate about the nature of the executive office, what had made the issue important to those beyond Napoleon's clients and family, was the issue of the succession. Overnight, between the appointment of a committee by the Council to draft a proposal for the Consulship for Life, and the debate on it the next morning, probably with the connivance of the committee's chairman, Cambacérès, Napoleon removed the proposal to allow him to appoint his own successor. All discussion of the very issue which had prompted the majority of Senators to broach the change in the constitution was removed. Napoleon had shown more sense here than those around him, not for the first time since Brumaire. He knew that the issue of the succession, however important to so many politicians concerned for the future of the new regime, was a trap; it raised the spectre of monarchy, of restoration – of the ghost of

Caesar. At this stage Napoleon knew the time was not ripe. This is all the more striking because many of those closest to him – those he still considered indispensable, such as Roederer and Talleyrand, and those he was shedding, like Lucien – shared the wish of many Senators to see a return to a form of monarchy under Napoleon. In contrast, the two men who were Napoleon's most invaluable collaborators – and the greatest architects of his future state – were reticent about the issue of the succession at this stage. Lebrun and Cambacérès had no doubts about the desirability of strengthening Napoleon's executive powers, but they, too, saw that the Republic, so hard won, was not yet ready to shed its identity.

The proposition that came back to the three chambers – the Corps Législatif, the Tribunate and the Senate – was that the issue of the Consulship for Life and the new constitution be put to the nation by plebiscite. In 1788, Louis XVI was driven to call the bluff of those resisting change in the representative institutions of the old order, the *Parlements* and the Assembly of Notables, by asking them to let him call the Estates General, the long-defunct body whose behaviour would be unknowable. The gamble failed. Fourteen years later, Napoleon turned once again to the nation, through the plebiscite, but from a position of infinitely greater strength. Typically, no one in Paris seemed to remember – or even to know – that Napoleon had already learned how to use a plebiscite to his advantage when he created the Cisalpine Republic in 1796. Yet again, his Italian apprenticeship served him brilliantly.

Napoleon achieved acceptance of his Consulship for Life partly by stealth, as we have seen, but he found the confidence to bring it into the light of day because Amiens had at last given him a position of real strength. The plebiscite was a more genuine vote than any held before because it was based on a single issue, unlike those previously held in 1793, 1795 and 1800, which approved entire constitutions.[22] Napoleon had the confidence to hold it, and to rig it. The plebiscite was also a clear sign that he was now ready to widen the political nation, reversing the assumption of the Directory that only one section of the Parisian elite could be trusted to run the Republic. This was, as Steven Englund says, 'a form of democratic authoritarianism'.[23] The plebiscite of 2 August 1802 was falsified, corrupted and sanctioned a more authoritarian order, but it was born of a confidence no regime had really felt since 1790. The 'yes' vote was emphatic, so the rigging turned out to be unnecessary.

The constitution was not put to the same test. Two days later, the project was drawn up in the Council of State, with Cambacérès at the helm, and enacted by the Senate by special decree, a *senatus-consultus*. This was the point when the question of the succession was quietly reinserted into the constitution, the *senatus-consultus* according Napoleon the right to nominate his successor. Now Napoleon finally revealed his hand. Even the manner in which the constitution was promulgated foreshadowed a new authoritarianism.

After Amiens, Napoleon set about transforming the state in his own image. Much of what he did bore the outward marks of a restoration of the old order, but to accept this at face value would be to underestimate his ambition and self-confidence. Napoleon was too assured to need to ape the past, just as he was too astute to emulate a political system that had collapsed in failure. There was much of the old order in the Constitution of the Year 10, but only those elements Napoleon felt had survived the Revolutionary storm and proved their worth through that survival. The image of a Bourbon king was not among them.

The true predecessor of the new constitution is found in the spirit of the Cisalpine Republic, not the checks and balances of Brumaire. The weak executive of the Cisalpine was modelled in theory on the French Directory. In fact, Napoleon appointed the Italian Directors and worked above them as a one-man executive. These Directors were purged by Napoleon until their composition suited him, just as he did later with the likes of Lebrun and Cambacérès. It was the working model that mattered. The experience of the Cisalpine allowed Napoleon to test this method of executive rule, which he adapted again in the framework he was handed by Sieyès in the wake of Brumaire, and now honed in the Constitution of the Year 10, which created a new body, the 'Private Council', composed of the two other Consuls, two Senators, two Councillors of State and two ministers. All but the two Consuls could be chosen by Napoleon, depending on the matter under discussion. Those matters were anything related to constitutional change; the possible suspension of the constitution; and the possible suspension of due judicial process, such as the suspension of juries in disturbed areas and the creation of special military courts where unrest merited such steps. This last provision soon acquired real importance during the campaign of internal 'pacification'. All this resembled the actual workings, if not the official framework, of the executive of the Cisalpine Republic.

In the Cisalpine Napoleon had kept for himself the right to appoint the members of the two legislative bodies, the Council of Elders and the Grand Council, after having examined the nominations sent to him by the local assemblies. Under the Constitution of the Year 10, the electoral colleges of the departments took on this role, and their members were appointed for life. The French Senate was greatly modified by the new constitution. Its membership, numbering eighty, was chosen directly by Napoleon from candidates proposed by the electoral colleges, from original lists drawn up by Napoleon, although many members of the existing Senate were co-opted into the new body.[24] It made a travesty of Sieyès' vision, and even of the system as it had evolved since Brumaire, but the blueprint had been there for all to see in Milan. No one chose to pay attention in 1796–7, and a mere five years later the price was being paid.

The creation of the Private Council changed somewhat the role of the Council of State, but it would be wrong to see it as having reduced it to a mere talking shop. Rather, its role came into sharper focus in the reorganisation of 1802. Henceforth, the Council of State was the preserve of technocrats, but it always got the full attention of Napoleon, and it was most often chaired by Cambacérès, particularly, or by Lebrun, when Napoleon was absent, especially after 1805, when war began anew. Napoleon set great store by the opinion of experts, and valued the free discussion that the secure environment of the Council of State afforded. With his preferred *modus operandi*, the committee, he created a system with two key councils for different purposes.

In many ways, the Council of State after 1802 came to fulfil the role Sieyès had envisaged for the Tribunate: 'the Tribunate, which proposes', placing before the Corps Législatif – 'which decides' – the projects for new laws, whether derived from its own ideas or from petitions from the public; Sieyès' Tribunes were to be 'talented, enlightened men', capable of generating, elaborating and articulating new ideas and projects.[25] Such qualities were now confined to a committee, not an assembly, the mark of the new order. Sieyès' logical emphasis on the need for oratorical abilities for this role was replaced in Napoleon's system by the need to assemble a good case on paper for open discussion. The atmosphere was unfettered and almost informal, often resembling the learned, intense but open discussions on board *L'Orient* on the voyage to Egypt, without the problem of seasickness.

As for the Tribunate itself, Napoleon showed his growing confidence by taking a quiet revenge on it. Already subdivided into three permanent sections, it now had its numbers reduced to fifty, renewable by a third every three years, its members serving for six-year terms, and saw itself further subdivided into five sections. Its nominations were controlled by the Senate and by electoral colleges appointed for life. In brief, it was now 'awarded' a parcel of weaknesses – impermanence of membership, instability in its ranks and subordination to other bodies. It could be dissolved at any time by the Senate, and in 1807 it duly was.[26]

In keeping with the ethos of the regime, Napoleon took his revenge bloodlessly; his method of exclusion usually included a sinecure and a good financial settlement, as with Sieyès or Daunou, rather than exile or death. Even at the apex of the state, nothing sinister happened to those who had opposed the changes of the Year 10. Most of them, men like Roederer, who had unnerved Napoleon by his lack of judgement more than his opinions, were moved to other duties, only to find new, important careers at a later time. Even a scholar as hostile as Isser Woloch draws attention to this trait of the regime and its leader: 'Very few of his chosen servitors lost Napoleon's confidence completely.' Those dismissed under a real cloud, for good, were very few, and the worst that happened to anyone on this short list was exile.[27] The worst punishment was in fact reserved for his brothers, for, contrary to myth, he was far more ruthless with his close family than with his collaborators, as Lucien's treatment showed. It was matched only by that of his generals. Any one of them deemed to be rather too interested in politics – of whatever colour – was, like Lucien, packed off to a foreign embassy for a while. This was the temporary fate of the pro-Jacobin Lannes and Augereau, and of the always suspect Bernadotte, who remained tainted by royalism. Napoleon's treatment of his generals was a clear indication that however authoritarian his rule was going to be – however dictatorial – it would never be a military dictatorship. The army and its leaders were kept well away from the Council of State and the Private Council. Only the Ministry of War was ever held by a soldier, and that only by Napoleon's most loyal, most compliant general, Berthier.

Real power passed to Napoleon himself. The Consul for Life retained all his existing powers, and gained still more, most significantly in the realm of foreign affairs. The extension of his scope for action in foreign affairs would be of cardinal importance in the war-torn years ahead. His treaties no longer needed any ratification. This meant all foreign policy was now in his hands. The monarchical power to pardon paled into insignificance in comparison.

The Senate was the only part of Sieyès' edifice that emerged from 1802 with any real gains, but its new-found status failed to mask its loss of power when set in the context of the reforms as a whole. Its members were elected for life and given generous financial conditions of service; they now took precedence over the members of the Council of State on official occasions. The Senate could dissolve the Tribunate and the Corps Législatif, but these were in any case now powerless bodies. If the government – that is, the Consul – requested it, the Senate could amend and interpret the constitution, but only if and when he did so. The few powers the Senate retained would prove fatal for Napoleon in 1814, but this had to await a set of circumstances when executive power had momentarily slipped from his hands.

Napoleon did not raise the status of the Senate without also elevating his own. Very quickly, the Consul set up a proper court for himself, as he had at Mombello, but this time in the Tuileries. He recruited Bourbon courtiers to reinstate formal court etiquette; Joséphine was now given official status as 'La Consulesse' – which jarred, rather, with other attempts to ape the *ancien régime*. His face now appeared on coins, something no one had dared do since the abolition of the monarchy, but, thanks to Gaudin's work at the Ministry of Finance, they were also the first French coins for a considerable time to be worth anything. Increasingly, he began to use only his Christian name. Nevertheless, Napoleon always shunned Versailles, letting it fall into ruin. Outside Paris, he preferred Fontainebleau and, later, Compiègne, to the east and north, respectively. His choice of the Tuileries was symbolic, for it was where the National Assembly had dragged the court of Louis XVI against its will, specifically to keep it under the eyes of the Nation and the people of Paris.[28] Napoleon paid more than a nod to his Revolutionary heritage, even when aping a monarch, and even when he was Emperor.

This was not a restoration of the old monarchy, it bears repeating: it was another emanation of Napoleon's confidence in the security of his rule. He knew it did not fool true royalists, and that it was more likely to offend than reassure them. It was a clear sign to the court-in-exile that he was no Monck, the Cromwellian general who had been the architect of the Stuart Restoration in 1660. They could return to France only as private individuals, to well-heeled obscurity or not at all. When, early in 1803, he offered Louis XVIII a generous – but not extravagant – pension were he to return to France, it came with the obligation to renounce the throne of the Bourbons in perpetuity. This was an insult and Napoleon knew it. There was no restoration of noble privilege; the new Legion of Honour, in March 1802, carried honours earned in state service, but no tax exemptions or anything that resembled the markings of *ancien régime* caste.

The nature of the Napoleonic regime will be explored in the following chapter but, even as he revived a court, Napoleon made it clear that this was a distinctively new regime. Taking on some of the trappings of royalty was, in the political climate of the times, perhaps the surest indication that there was no going back, neither to the radical phase of the Revolution or the monarchy.

Outward appearances meant nothing. They were there to deceive. At the most workaday level, Napoleon may have been busy refurbishing the former royal residences of St-Cloud and the Tuileries, to reflect his ever-increasing executive powers, but he grumbled about the extravagant cost of refurbishing his own home, the Malmaison, at Joséphine's behest. When he employed the same architects, Percier and Fontaine, for his official home, he kept a close eye on the budget; it was after all public money.[29] This was not the style of a Bourbon, least of all that of Louis XIV, the creator of Versailles.

There were more important examples of a turning away from *ancien régime* practice where it counted most. By 1802, at last, the real instruments of government were two committees and their chairman, the First Consul. The reversion to rule by committee was perhaps the real restoration in 1802. Napoleon's preference for this form of the exercise of power marked less a conscious return to *ancien régime* ways than an instinctive reversion to the natural methods of executive administration. The King's Council had been an integral part of Bourbon government since Louis XIV, and it had resurfaced during the Terror when the two great committees of Public Safety and General Security had emerged as the effective government of the Republic. Napoleon had honed and structured his system in very different, more rational ways than either previous regime could have imagined, but the vesting of policy formulation and decision-making in tight-knit committees of trusted experts was so deeply rooted in French political culture as to be almost atavistic. The emergence of the two committees represents a blend of the collective heritage of the French political class with Napoleon's personal preferences, but the future was outlined in what at first glance appears to be one of the more minor changes that followed Amiens.

A year after the promulgation of the new constitution, on 9 April 1803, Napoleon created sixteen 'auditeurs' of the Council of State, young men who were to be trained as the leaders of tomorrow. They were later taken directly from the new University set up in 1806 and the Grandes Écoles, first to serve as assistants in the Council of State, where they drew up the paperwork; they could not enter into the debates unless asked to explain a point. This training was followed, for the ablest, by a posting as a sub-prefect, or possibly as prefect, to departments chosen deliberately for their difficult political circumstances, their long distance from Paris and their generally inhospitable character. No one seemed to grasp the long-term import of this, nor were they probably meant to: Napoleon had taken the first step towards bypassing the whole revolutionary generation – friend and foe alike – as soon as he could, in favour of a younger generation schooled according to his own precepts. Napoleon was quietly giving up on the fathers, who either shunned him or could not be trusted to put the past behind them, so he turned to the sons.

Another constitution was issued by Napoleon's fiat in 1802, that of the Italian Republic, for whose existence he had risked so much during the Amiens negotiations. Napoleon simply summoned its loyalest leading lights to Lyon, early in 1802, and directed the terms of the new document. This manner of proceeding in itself crushed the hopes of many Italian revolutionaries who had been stalwarts of the original Cisalpine Republic between 1796 and 1799, but Napoleon was, even more emphatically than in France, their only defence against the restoration of the old order, and most of them knew it. He was very clear who he trusted, and who he wanted to 'run' the framing of the constitution: Melzi d'Eril, Antonio Aldini, Fernandino Marescalchi and Gio Galeazzo Serbelloni. All had emerged as loyalists during the Cisalpine and were now recalled to the colours. These four men almost incarnated the policy of *amalgame*. Melzi was a liberal aristocrat who had served Joseph II and backed his detested centralising policies; Aldini was a former radical republican, from the radical enclave of Bologna; Marescalchi was a friend of Melzi's with a similar social and political background; Serbelloni was a duke, a former chamberlain of the Habsburg Empress Maria-Theresa and one of the wealthiest men in the new state. As Napoleon brought the Republic increasingly under French control and reduced its autonomy, it was the Jacobin Aldini who proved his most loyal, most effective minister in Milan, ousting Melzi when the latter resigned at the creation of the Kingdom of Italy, in 1805, although the final straw for Melzi was actually his opposition to Napoleon's Concordat with the Papacy for the new kingdom, which he felt to be far too lenient to the Church. In Lyon, in the winter of 1802, however, all four did their work well. Theirs were the views he most wanted on the new constitution.[30]

The general lines of the Italian constitution followed those enacted for France later in 1802. It was proclaimed in January 1802, a full eight months before that of the *senatus-consultus*, but in one detail it was more restrained: Napoleon named himself its President, but for ten years only, with the possibility of re-election. Napoleon appointed Melzi as Vice-President, an increasingly unappealing post, as the art of delegation proved more than difficult for Napoleon as time went on. The Republic's two assemblies broadly corresponded to those of France: the lower house of seventy-five members, the Corpo Legislativo, chosen by electoral colleges from lists drawn up by the executive, and the upper house, the Consiglio, composed of fifteen members, all appointed by Napoleon. To this, Napoleon added the Consulta di Stato of eight men, which presaged his French Private Council.[31]

A revealing difference between the French and Italian constitutions was the greater latitude and influence Napoleon accorded the electoral colleges of the Italian Republic, in contrast to their French counterparts. The Italian colleges were not based on departments, but on the three major regions of the Italian Republic, with colleges in Milan,

Bologna and Brescia, each composed of 700 members and with extensive powers to debate important issues. Napoleon divided each college into three houses, one each for the major landowners, the merchant and business communities, and for the *dotti*, men of letters and intellectuals. It was all a clear sign he had considerably more faith in the urban elites of northern Italy than those of France, and of the place he would like to accord local elites, when he felt safe to do so.

Embedded in this organisation is a vision of society, a window on his mind, and a hand he never quite felt he could play in France, where even at the height of his power and popularity he had to build on the foundations of others. Napoleon recognised a truth evident to Calonne, Brienne and Necker, the last ministers of Louis XVI, that the local assemblies responsible for the administration of taxation, and charged with helping the new prefects since Napoleon's advent to power, had to comprise those who paid those taxes or the system would collapse. The years immediately preceding the Revolution had seen all these ministers, who virulently loathed each other, put forward reforms centred on local assemblies to administer taxation. This was true representation according to an authoritarian regime. Whereas Napoleon's vision for the Italian national assemblies was far more dismissive than anything he dared impose on France, restricting real debate to a small committee of the assembly, the role he accorded the provincial elites was central and relatively unfettered.

In Italy, business interests and what might be called the intelligentsia had to be accorded an important place in the flow of information that would inform executive decision-making, and, in Napoleon's vision, this merited corporate status. The 'masses of granite' were the most essential component of this; the larger representation of landed wealth in the three Italian colleges is an emphatic indication of the cardinal place Napoleon accorded this source of wealth and local influence, because he saw it as the most stable. Yet it was not enough, and the large number of ex-nobles embraced by this definition of wealth had to be balanced, but not outweighed, by other sections of elite society. This was Napoleon's method of regenerating a new elite, and he chose to give his real trust to a wider range of people than the landed element in society. Above all, in Italy, he set great store by the provincial intelligentsia; they were the men to heed.

Nothing like this really came to fruition in French local government. Napoleon's vision of three Italian electoral colleges was a completely original creation. His whole ordering of the Italian Republic offers powerful insights into his concept of government partly because he simply had a freer hand than in France, but also because he knew this part of the world and its elites far better than he knew France itself. Napoleon had ruled this region; he had had close contact with its political and economic leaders during the creation of, first, the Cispadane, and then the Cisalpine Republics. He had campaigned across its territory, had dealt with its officialdom at the most local level, initially as a military invader in search of provender for his troops and then as a civilian ruler. This is obvious in the speed and confidence with which he turned to Melzi, Aldini and the others at Lyon, for he knew his men and his team in Italy far better than he did his French collaborators, even those he came to trust wholeheartedly, like Lebrun and Cambacérès. This intimacy reaches deeper, however. Napoleon felt a familiarity and confidence in the provincial elites of northern Italy that he did not yet feel in France; the French 'masses of granite' remained something of an abstraction for Napoleon in 1802; the provincial worthies of the Italian Republic, by contrast, were familiar, trusted friends, and those he did not really trust, like the nobility, he at least could read.

The character and role of the Italian electoral colleges is perhaps the clearest, most emphatic institutional expression of Napoleon's belief in the primacy of a stable, predominantly landed but not over-wealthy elite as the bedrock of society. The creation of separate chambers, given equal freedom of expression, for the business community and the intelligentsia expressed a belief that intellectual life and creativity were not necessarily the preserve of the metropole, be it Paris or Milan, and that the new forces of commerce had their distinctive part to play in the state. Napoleon had sprung from such a milieu. This vision was hardly a triumph for the uncivilised, backward mountain hinterlands;, it was, rather, his assertion that the small to middle-sized cities and towns of this prosperous, advanced part of Europe were what truly mattered. This was the core of society, for Napoleon.

Georges Lefebvre was one of Napoleon's greatest biographers, his classical Marxism giving him penetrating insights into what lay behind Napoleon's actions, and he was one of the first historians of the period consistently to look behind his political reforms for deeper meanings. Lefebvre's vision may have been too restricted by his insistence on the all-pervading importance of socio-economic class for Napoleon, but he discerned brilliantly that there was more to the creation of weak assemblies and influential committees than appropriating personal power to himself. This was about embedding the new regime in society, but in those parts of society that were the most stable, an assessment that did not always equate with great wealth, which was often amassed through inherently unstable financial speculation. In the Italian electoral colleges, where Napoleon accorded an important place to Lefebvre's 'classic bourgeoisie' of merchants and manufacturers, he gave pride of place to localised commerce and industry, which operated in the relatively secure environment of assured micro-markets, not in the murkier, fluid world of international speculation.

When given a free hand, Napoleon thought in terms closer to caste than modern socio-economic class; his vision of social control by these elites over the popular masses stretched far beyond Lefebvre's Marxist stricture of the power of employers over their salaried workers. Society at the turn of the eighteenth century was more complex than this, and Napoleon showed how well he understood it in his ordering of the Italian Republic. Nonetheless, what Lefebvre's remarkable intelligence grasped was Napoleon's search for effective methods of social control that embraced society as a whole, and his belief that indirect influence was needed, as well as the power of a professional, centralised state. Lefebvre believed Brumaire had been the work of the higher bourgeoisie, and he was largely right, but

Napoleon quickly saw that he could not rule with them alone,[32] nor did he wish to, as his actions in Italy make clear. Lefebvre discerned that Napoleon had come to fear the atomisation of society created by the Revolution – the splitting of society into 'grains of sand' – and that 'masses of granite had to be thrown onto the soil of France' to hold them together. Italy was, for the moment, the repository of the purest form of the Napoleonic vision.

The French Constitution of the Year 10 was essentially Napoleon's blueprint for government and represents his preferred method of wielding power. It was little changed by the creation of the Empire. The trappings of authority came in December 1804, with the coronation, but the powerful motor of government – designed, made and driven by Napoleon – was in place in 1802, and it was based on a Italian prototype. It was now high time to get on with business, freed both from foreign war and meddlesome parliaments. The instruments of power could now be put to real use.

9

THE GREAT REFORMS

The Sinews of the New Regime, 1800–1804

Napoleon had served three very different apprenticeships in public life in a short space of time. He had learned to command at a high level in the field, although it would not be until 1805 that he actually commanded the main French army in the major theatre of operations; he had learned how to survive, manoeuvre and master high politics; most of all, in Italy, he had learned how to become a ruler. To all three, he brought clarity of thought, a ruthlessness that veered easily into cynicism, and a very good judgement of character, an ability to spot talent in less obvious candidates, and to delegate to them. He now brought all these lessons to bear on France. To date he had not quite succeeded as Alexander; but he had survived admirably as Octavian. Now he could begin, carefully, to be Augustus.

THE NEW STATE EMERGES

Napoleonic administrators at every level of responsibility referred often and reverently to the doctrine of 'the separation of powers' that defined the character of the machinery of state. However, by this they did not mean anything like the 'balance of powers' theorised by Montesquieu in the early eighteenth century, and still invoked by Anglo-Saxon constitutional experts. It had nothing to do with executives and legislatures providing checks and balances on each other. Far from it. Rather, it expressed the clear demarcation between the different branches of public administration, which all came together only in the executive – in Napoleon and the Council of State.

This meant that the civil bureaucracy, the two branches of the police – Fouché's administrative police and the Gendarmerie – the financial administration and the judiciary were all independent of each other, answerable only to their own ministries for routine orders, and that there was to be no plurality of office, and as little overlap in spheres of responsibility as possible. In one important respect, this system did provide an element of the more usual understanding of the separation of powers, in that it established an independent judiciary which, in marked contrast to the *Parlements* of the *ancien régime*, had no administrative powers. This did not prevent clashes between the different branches of the service – far from it – but the regime was determined from the outset to ensure that each ministry and its local agents ordered their own internal business without interference. This did not mean that the civil authorities could not call on the police – during the conscription levies, the Gendarmerie was under the direct orders of the prefects, for instance – but it did mean that old regime practices of individuals amassing too much power and influence by holding more than one post were now impossible. Indeed, anyone who held a government post and who was elected to the Corps Législatif had to resign his job.

What it produced, in effect, was a spider's web of different strands of local government that all came together at the apex of the state. In less sane, responsible hands than Napoleon's, the system could have degenerated, or been manipulated, into a cynical game of divide and rule by the head of state. He did not operate this way; he did not play pointless power games with his machine of government; in this, he remained a soldier by temperament, far more than many later military dictators who purported to emulate him. This did not preclude ruthlessness bordering on cruelty in individual cases, but for Napoleon the priority was getting his machine to work.

This was just as well, for France was (and remained) an under-administered country, and the number of civil servants – as opposed to magistrates and policemen – actually fell under Napoleon.[1] The system worked because of the quality of the men who ran it, at least

Young Napoleon: In his early career, Napoleon cultivated the image of the
Romantic hero, but carefully crafted it to adhere to Revolutionary austerity.
This portrait is typical, but it also catches his powerful gaze, which all who
knew him remarked upon.

Letizia: Napoleon's mother was reputed to be the most beautiful girl in Ajaccio, in her youth, and was a powerful influence on her son.

Carlo: Napoleon's father had a raffish reputation as a young man, even joining Paoli's revolt, but he later became a pillar of the Ajaccio establishment.

Joseph: Napoleon's older brother by one year, to whom Napoleon was probably closer than anyone. Joseph was a skilful diplomat and was indispensable in Napoleon's negotiations with the Pope and the British, in 1801–2.

Lucien: The third of the Bonaparte brothers, six years Napoleon's junior, by turns a hot-headed liability and the invaluable ally who saved the day at the coup of Brumaire. He was eventually expelled from Napoleon's inner circle.

LE JEUNE NAPOLÉON ET PAOLI.
Vas, mon fils, tu seras un homme de Plutarque, 1789.

Paoli and Napoleon: Napoleon was devoted to Paoli in his youth, and both men were steeped in Plutarch's lives of classical heroes. Paoli here gives Napoleon the greatest praise, but in reality, this scene is a Mafia 'kiss of death'.

The Flight: Although highly romanticised, this print captures the fear and desperation of the Bonapartes as they were forced to flee Corsica for their lives, now penniless, to escape Paoli's vendetta, in 1793.

The Battle of the Pyramids: A victory famous for its setting as much as its results. Napoleon told his men that 5,000 years of history looked down on them but it is doubtful anyone listened after the hellish march up the Nile.

The Battle of Marengo: The battle which won the Second Italian Campaign and Napoleon's first victory as First Consul; it secured him in power after a shaky start.

Napoleon and Josephine: An idealised portrait, almost a parody, of domestic bliss that hides their tempestuous, often fraught relationship, which was marked by Josephine's affairs in its early years.

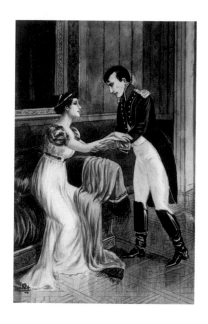

Barras: Paul Barras was the *éminence grise* of the Directory, Napoleon's controlling patron at his lowest ebb. Corrupt, suave and powerful, Barras was soon outwitted by Napoleon, and pushed out of power.

Hortense: Josephine's daughter by her first marriage, she disliked Napoleon at first, but soon found in him a father, as he did a daughter. She married Napoleon's brother Louis, and was the mother of Napoleon III.

Coup of Brumaire: Even this piece of Napoleonic propaganda does not seek to hide the resistance Napoleon faced from the deputies of the Directory, the regime he was about to depose. Napoleon is shown as he was, isolated and in danger, as his Guards push forward to save him.

First Consul: Despite the dangers of the coup, Napoleon succeeded in taking power at Brumaire. He appears here in his uniform as First Consul, the undisputed head of the French Republic, vested with near-autocratic authority within a few months of seizing power.

A coronation sketch by David. Aggressive and martial, this was how Napoleon originally wanted his coronation immortalised by his favourite painter.

After consideration of David's portrayal, cooler heads prevailed, and the far more formal, glacial painting by Ingres – done two years after the event – became the official image of *Le sacre*.

The Coronation by David: The moment of triumph. Most dictators 'airbrush' inconvenient people out of official images, but Napoleon ordered David to paint in his mother, Letizia – sat prominently in the centre of the balcony – although she had refused to attend.

in its middle and higher echelons, although the competence of many of its mayors and justices of the peace was often rightly questioned. Indeed, the historian Marie-Cécile Thoral has shown how much this very centralised bureaucracy had to rely on volunteers at local level, to maintain for example the infrastructure of roads and bridges of which Napoleon was so proud.[2] Mayors and justices of the peace were unpaid. When all this is set in the wider context of the difficult topography of France and the still low levels of technology of the early nineteenth century, the success of the new regime in imposing hated burdens like taxation and conscription is still very impressive.

Napoleon assigned very ambitious, modern tasks to his bureaucracies, but the technology at their disposal still had more in common with the late Middle Ages than the world of only a generation ahead. Ships still moved by sail or even oar, however good their navigational equipment; there were few paved roads and no tunnels through mountains, however accurate the maps drawn by Napoleon's Topographical Bureau; troops – and gendarmes – still rode or marched. Steam was in its infancy as a tool of transport. This was the world in which authoritarian government had to operate. Yet, for all these impediments, the Napoleonic state moved well beyond mere aspiration.

Napoleonic government relied on its personnel and the system its leader devised for its success, not technology. It was a triumph of human resources. The Consulate very quickly confirmed the basic structures of local government created by the Revolution, with a few adjustments to the internal organisation of the departments. The basic units of administration created in 1790 remained; there was to be no restoration of the old provinces, still less of the jumbled, overlapping institutions which 'governed' provincial France before the Revolution. The real change came, predictably, in the shift of power from elected bodies to centrally appointed officials. Elections still took place for the membership of departmental councils which carried out the work of the distribution of taxes and advised the government on local issues; there were also still elections for the justices of the peace, although mayors were actually appointed by the Minister of the Interior. These elections, based on a multi-tiered franchise that 'filtered out' the masses, were not binding on the government, however; Paris appropriated for itself the right to choose its local servants, but the elections provided important indicators of the climate of local public opinion, and their results were taken seriously by the regime.

Nonetheless, the appointment of officials marked the clearest, single most significant shift from the Directory to the Consulate. It was the most emphatic sign, at local level, that things had changed; the state was now the arbiter and commander, not the repository of the electoral will. Local officials had long ceased to call the people they governed their 'fellow citizens', referring to them instead as their *administrés*,[3] 'the administered ones'. Now it was official.

The hub of this system was the prefect, created by the law of 27 Ventôse, Year 8 (18 March 1800). The prefects were appointed by the head of state, on the advice of the Minister of the Interior; indeed, they still are, not just in France, but all over Western Europe. This official controlled the entire civil service within his department, and was directly responsible to the central government. Prefects were almost never local men, as was also the case with gendarmes and public prosecutors, and they relied for their local information on their immediate subordinates, the sub-prefects, who administered the tier of government below the department, the *arrondissement*; they took their orders from the prefects and had little power of initiative. Below them both were the mayors of the communes, the lowest unit. There was indeed a clear chain of command within the department. The role of the prefect, however, has been the subject of some debate among historians, although Napoleon never had any doubts that, ultimately, he was in charge and moved many of them around at will. They were seldom men who naturally took a lead of their own, unlike the royal *intendants*, who were more often than not left to their own devices.

The way they were chosen was another example of the genius of delegation. Lucien, in his short-lived tenure as Minister of the Interior, often consulted Talleyrand and Cambacérès. Napoleon knew very few of the first prefects personally, although there were notable exceptions. He appointed his old school friend from Autun, Hugues Nardon – a prominent Terrorist in his native Burgundy, under Robespierre – to the convulsed department of Maine-et-Loire, on the axis of the Vendée and the Chouan country of the Normandy–Brittany border. Most were men Lucien had come to know as a deputy during the Directory, and whose conduct at Brumaire he had monitored carefully. Most were of proven moderate politics, but, as in the case of Nardon, ex-Jacobins could have their uses. Of the 300 men who were prefects between 1800 and 1814, only 21 had been in the assemblies of the early Revolution, although most had been in local government before 1795; 240 of the first appointees had been deputies during the Directory – and were thus known to Lucien – and only 26 had had no previous experience of government at some level. The first generation of prefects were usually over forty, but the changes in the corps, if not massive numerically, still show how Napoleon's mind was working, and where he was moving. By 1814, 60 prefects were auditors of the Council of State, young men 'fast-tracked' by Napoleon to overtake the revolutionary generation;[4] in 1811, all sub-prefects of the *arrondissement* where the prefects had their residence, the *chefs lieux* – and thus their effective deputies – had to be auditors. There were obviously some poor appointments, but, to a remarkably high degree, Napoleonic prefects proved competent and devoted to their duty. Lucien had chosen well for his brother, for he had a good knowledge of the political class of the Directory period. This allowed him to produce a new administrative elite for Napoleon, the desk-bound equivalent of Moncey's gendarmes, and far better disciplined.

In March 1800, Lucien issued the following exhortation to the first prefects: 'The task you must fulfil is great; your attributes are multiple, they embrace everything connected to public finances, to national prosperity, and to the well-being of your *administrés*.'[5] He did not mention the need to enforce conscription, to help the Gendarmerie keep order, or the possibility of getting killed out there.

THE 'OTHER WAR': THE INTERNAL PACIFICATION OF
FRANCE AND THE STRATEGY OF REPRESSION

'Despite efforts to regularize the new regime, the escalating level of violence made it obvious that people did not like Bonaparte's republic any more than the Directory's.'[6] Howard Brown has put the state of France in the wake of Brumaire more starkly, and better, than most historians. The first two years of the Consulate were war-torn and, with the government's attention drawn to the need to survive militarily, local government often sat tight in the face of banditry and general lawlessness, as there seemed little chance that the men of Brumaire would last long in office. Disorder actually increased during the last phase of the war, 1799–1800, and the brutal repression set in motion by the Directory in 1797 either stalled or escalated into desperate outbursts of atrocity that proved counter-productive.

Napoleon's regime could not restore order in its own way until after the Peace of Amiens in 1801; the Consulate had to await the 'peace dividend' to unleash itself on the rampant brigandage of the south-east and the revivified counter-revolution of the west, but when it did so it was not only with a vengeance but with more direction and structure than any previous revolutionary government. Napoleon had seen the potential for this as soon as he took power. Between Brumaire and the resumption of fighting in the spring of 1800, he told his commander in the Vendean region to proceed with disarming the countryside:

Pursue it [disarmament] with the greatest energy, for this is what, and on what, we can most count, [for] the moment will soon come when I shall have to withdraw a considerable corps of troops from the Army of the West [for the war] ... it is essential to take advantage of the moment to consolidate [the present] calm.[7]

Napoleon 'targeted' the parts of France where he knew circumstances were the most desperate for the regime. He reserved the most ruthless means of repression for certain places, while he let the new, professional judicial institutions assume control over the rest of the country. The Rhône Valley, Provence, the western departments centred on the Vendée, the six new Piedmontese departments, and the Belgian departments – the scene of a massive anti-French revolt in 1798 – all felt the brunt of the new regime's wrath. This took the form of military commissions with wide powers of arrest and judicial competence.

Initially, Napoleon had to continue to use discredited local republican National Guards to enforce the will of the military commissions but peace allowed the regime to change the character of law enforcement. Napoleon now transformed the military commissions in the Midi and the west from essentially sedentary courts into mobile judicial units. He continued to use the 'flying columns' of troops devised under the Directory to strike out from provincial centres into troubled rural areas, but he attached a military commission to each. Justice was meted out on the spot, usually within twenty-four hours. However, in the new Piedmontese departments, Napoleon retained the Directorial method of keeping the military commissions in the major regional centres, Turin and Alessandria. These commissions executed more people in four months in 1801 than the Directory had managed in over two years, but the new regime refrained from branding their work – their victims – as overtly political. It was not a matter of helping local republicans settle scores with priests, nobles or other known royalists; their victims were labelled as pure criminals, and rough justice was carried out within specific, well-designated areas.

This was still something of an ad hoc, inherited approach, however. By 1801, the Consulate had come into its own. The Gendarmerie had been created early in the Revolution, but had remained a toothless force, riddled with slackness and corruption, a virtual dumping ground for the worst elements of the army. Napoleon transformed it into an elite corps in a remarkably short period, and his contribution to its creation was seminal. He found new men, and revitalised a moribund institution to carry out the same brutal work. In its Inspector-General, Moncey, a career soldier before the Revolution, he found the able, intelligent and ruthless leader he needed. Moncey had served in both Italian campaigns, as commander of the military Gendarmerie; he came from a legal family,[8] and this served him well in a position that straddled the military and civilian spheres of law enforcement. It was another important example of Napoleon's ability to choose excellent collaborators and delegate to them with confidence.

As with so much else, the Directory had launched a series of initiatives in its last months, aimed at reinvigorating the Gendarmerie, but the law of 17 April 1798 did little more than call upon the corps to act. The prototypes of a reformed Gendarmerie were shaped by generals Wirion and Radet, sent to organise policing and counter-insurgency in the new Belgian departments and the Rhône Valley, respectively, in 1798, while Napoleon was in Egypt. Wirion, in particular, developed a vision of the Gendarmerie as an elite unit, and stressed the need for its men to acquire precise knowledge of the people and places they policed. Napoleon appreciated their work, and sent Wirion first to reorganise the western departments in 1800, and, a year later, to establish the corps in the new Piedmontese departments, while Radet would go on to work in Corsica, and then throughout Italy after 1805. Nevertheless, the real initiative, one of genius, came from Napoleon himself.

In November 1800 Napoleon had outlined the command structures and territorial distribution he envisaged for the new force. As with so many of his genuine, fundamental insights, it is difficult to know how Napoleon arrived at this approach, but he had experienced guerrilla harassment during the crossing of the Alps in the First Italian Campaign and had observed the convulsed state of the Rhône Valley and Provence at first hand. The probable origins of his concept of counter-insurgency tactics are here, and it was certainly no coincidence that Moncey had borne the brunt of this harassment, as commandant of the military Gendarmerie, charged with protecting the Army of Italy's communications. Napoleon's vision of the role and the character of the Gendarmerie emerged clearly formed and ready, with only a few adjustments to be made. He insisted on its dissemination down to the level of the canton, the second-lowest tier of local government, above the commune but below the arrondissement and department, the seats of the justices of the peace.[9]

Napoleon always remained a passionate defender of his creation, and he also took a very detailed interest in its composition and conduct, particularly in its early years. In 1802, he told Berthier, then Minister of War, 'I want you to send me the exact circumstances of the Gendarmerie legions, to inform me of their distribution over the departments, the strength of their reserve forces, and what is still missing in their organisation.'[10] A month later, he sent General Gouvion to inspect the legions of the Norman and Breton departments, 'to observe their conduct, the morality of the officers and men, and the manner in which they perform their duties [and] if the brigades are well distributed'. What also emerges in his orders to Gouvion is the close interest Napoleon took in the actual repression of brigandage. On a recent tour of the Norman departments, he had noticed numerous well-fortified farmhouses, which could provide potential bases for bandits, and he ordered Gouvion to dismantle them.[11] His trust in the higher officers of the Gendarmerie was unerring, even when Moncey's robust defence of his independence from the civilian police under Fouché led to tensions.[12] When Napoleon began his initial preparations for the abortive invasion of Britain, he entrusted the secret mission to report on the reliability of the local administrations of the Channel departments to one of the Gendarmerie's senior inspectors, Lagrange.[13]

The corps was far from perfect, its men often falling short of the high standards set for them by the regime, just as it was often not as well paid, provisioned or armed as it should have been. Nevertheless, the progress made under Moncey was remarkable. From the outset, Napoleon saw the Gendarmerie as an elite corps: its men had to be non-commissioned officers of the regular army with a clean disciplinary record, literate, tall, and with at least three campaigns of active service behind them. In sum, they had to meet the same requirements as members of the Consular – later Imperial – Guard, the acknowledged cream of the army.

Gendarmes soon showed themselves a very different proposition from the ill-disciplined, revenge-crazed National Guards of the 1790s.

The flying columns remained, but their practice had changed from savage amateurism to hard-boiled, battle-hardened professionalism. Atrocities could still occur and brutality was routine, but ultimately the new corps was under military discipline and subject to a chain of command. It was dispersed systematically and comprehensively across the entire country in six-man brigades, most of foot soldiers, some of cavalry, and eventually housed in barracks away from the communities they served. They were paid by the government, not by the local authorities, and efforts were made to ensure they were not local men, although this was not widely successful.

The Gendarmerie gave a new set of sharp teeth – real fangs – to the regime. It now had an armed, experienced, professional police force under central control, disseminated all over the nation, loyal only to the state, ready to enforce the will of the Consulate. Only now, through this corps, did 'absolutism' start to become a reality in the daily life of hitherto isolated rural communities. The most important single ordinance was that of 12 Thermidor, Year 9/31 July 1801, which created the 2,500 six-man brigades, and set the total for the corps at 16,500 men.[14] By 1801, for the state's enemies, whether truly political opponents or common criminals, or any troublemaker in between, a weapon had been forged to ensure they would never be left alone again. The 'other war' of internal pacification now had its own army.

However, that army was far from ideologically or politically neutral. The first veterans to fill its ranks were largely soldiers of the Revolution, men who had fought the Republic's wars abroad and often also in the western departments of the Vendée; if they were not convinced republicans when they entered the ranks – suspicious of priests and peasants to the point of hatred – they were by the end of the three campaigns required to become gendarmes. However much the regime vaunted itself as 'above faction', its loyalest and most effective servants on the ground were often quite the reverse. It is very significant that Napoleon knew this very well, and that he adored the corps. *Ralliement* and *amalgame* were policies for the urban elites; when there was dirty work to be done, the enemy remained the same – the heterogeneous coalition of the counter-revolution, now misleadingly rebaptised as 'brigandage' – and the task of smashing it could only be entrusted to uniformed sons of the Revolution, men like Napoleon himself.

The Gendarmerie was Napoleon's creation; it was one of his most imitated innovations and fundamental to the future history of Europe, its importance reaching far beyond the immediate needs of the early Consulate. Through Napoleon's reform of the Gendarmerie in these early years, one of the most profound changes in the life of rural Europe began, and the importance of his work first in moulding and then in wielding the Gendarmerie cannot be overstated. Napoleon was obviously a supreme tactician in the arena of conventional warfare, but he deserves equal, perhaps even greater credit, for his approach to counter-insurgency as embodied in the territorial dissemination of the Gendarmerie. Dissemination was conceived as the permanent replacement for the rapid, mobile penetration of the flying columns. Flying columns spread terror and pushed back insurgents from urban centres and important lines of communication; the disseminated brigades, by contrast, allowed the Gendarmerie to acquire the local knowledge needed to smash local networks of resistance, and to provide regular surveillance.

Napoleon's correspondence with Moncey in the first years of the Consulate reveals close attention to the tactical deployment of the brigades, always with an eye to the complex needs of combining the protection of highways, urban centres and isolated communities with the need to penetrate the most inaccessible parts of the country-side where insurgency of any kind found a safe haven. It was on his initiative that the emphasis was shifted from a predominantly mounted corps, mainly concerned with patrolling the highways – as had been the role of the Maréchaussée, the military police of the old monarchy – to units of foot soldiers, better adapted to the difficult terrain on which 'brigands' operated.

It was an approach to law and order that worked, and its post-Napoleonic history offers clear proof that imitation is, indeed, the sincerest form of flattery. The Gendarmerie was introduced into all the non-French parts of the Empire and the satellite kingdoms; even more significantly, it found ready imitators among Napoleon's sworn enemies in Austria, Russia and Prussia, and, later, Spain. Above all, corps modelled or even derived directly from it were retained after 1814, in the successor states to the Empire, notably the Royal Dutch Gendarmerie, the Piedmontese Carabinieri Reali and the various state police forces of the south German states.[15] Napoleon created the working model that transformed the power of the European state.

The other institution Napoleon introduced, which set repression on a firm, regular footing, was the network of Special Criminal Tribunals, created by the law of 19 Pluviôse, Year 9/8 February 1801, the prospect of which had caused such consternation among the leaders of the moderate centre. The new courts represented a partial return to the military *prévôtal* courts of the old monarchy, in terms of their competence to deal with serious crimes, the presence of soldiers as judges, usually high-ranking officers of the Gendarmerie, and the abandonment of juries, a much-cherished innovation of the Revolutionary reforms. However, their procedures were essentially those of the normal, civilian courts, and the majority of their judges were also civilians. The law of 19 Pluviôse met with vociferous resistance in the Tribunate, but the fact that it was passed easily in the end is a clear indication that the Consulate's determination to deal with disorder in a systematic, coherent manner had won substantial support in the Parisian political world.

The Special Criminal Tribunals, like the military commissions with which they initially worked but would eventually outlive, were introduced only in those departments generally considered to be the most disturbed; in practice, this amounted to almost one-third of France by 1803. As the Empire grew apace after 1805, all the new Italian, Dutch and German departments also received them. Nevertheless, as Howard Brown has shown, this 'hybrid of provostial justice and revolutionary experience' marked a distinct improvement on the ad hoc, highly partisan and unprofessional instruments of exceptional justice deployed in the 1790s.[16] Together with the Gendarmerie, the

Special Criminal Tribunals represent the emergence of a policy of repression, regulated by law, and gave the state a permanent, potent presence in its most troubled hinterlands.

These new institutions came to life at a unique point in 'Napoleonic time', coming into their own in 1801, the height of the period of the 'peace dividend', and this allowed them a crucial breathing space, created by Amiens, for both a general and a particular reason. This was the only moment during his rule that Napoleon was able to demobilise troops: approximately 27 per cent of the army was released from service and conscription was momentarily reduced to very low levels. This gave what Howard Brown has called 'the Consular Terror' three key advantages in its infancy: the end of foreign war allowed more resources of men and money to be devoted to policing than ever before; the demobilised veterans – often men who had been in the ranks from the beginning of the war in 1792 – provided an ample pool of recruits for the expanded Gendarmerie; and, most importantly, the easing of conscription briefly removed the single most serious source of collective, public violence. In the early summer of 1801, on the eve of the conclusion of the general peace, it is estimated that there were on average two attacks per day on the Gendarmerie related to the enforcement of conscription.[17] These now ceased, for the moment.

With this burden lightened, the regime could turn the bulk of its new-found repressive power on general lawlessness such as highway robbery and other forms of banditry, and on the last bastions of deeply rooted counter-revolution in the west and the Midi. Every act of collective defiance was labelled as common crime – brigandage – and so divested of potentially reasonable, legitimate motives.[18] This fitted perfectly with the policy of the early Consulate, which was predicated on rising above faction, but it hardened into a credo which also served to deny the continued existence of a very real popular counter-revolution in southern and western France. In the same letter in which he exhorted his commander in the Vendée to act with as much impartiality as possible to prevent the further shedding of French blood, Napoleon referred to the need to 'destroy these men of ill repute, and the bandits who profit from the spirit of frenzy which has seized the masses to lure them into their criminal ways'.[19] The truth could only be spoken by Fouché's secret police; even Napoleon had to stick to the script, and even with his commanders. The 'peace dividend' of the early years at least allowed all forms of brigandage, political or not, to be beaten back without the added problem of resistance to conscription. This was a blessing for the regime in every way. It allowed it to restore internal order to a degree hitherto thought impossible.

Like the war, Napoleon inherited conscription from his Revolutionary predecessors. The sporadic mass levies imposed by the republican regimes had finally given way to a regular system of conscription with the 'Jourdan Law' of 1798. This set an annual quota of conscripts for every department, based on its population as assessed by the État Civil, but only the new machinery of the Consulate could make this a reality. The work was co-ordinated by the prefects, and enforced by the Gendarmerie; while the prefectoral bureaucracy drew up the lists of those eligible, the prefect toured his whole department with a company of regular troops, assisted by each Gendarmerie brigade, in turn, to coerce those who had been 'balloted' into the ranks. Where resistance was met, the gendarmes reacted accordingly. Moreover, these tours took place at least three times a year from 1804, and, in the last years of the Empire, usually four. Prefects came to know their departments better than any previous officials of any central government, taking note of the needs and grievances of rural communities, while forcibly crushing resistance and extracting the most active elements of their communities for long periods of military service.

Bloodshed was the norm, but so, eventually, was submission. The statistics alone of the Napoleonic wars speak for this – the army got its men by the hundreds of thousands; something between three and three and a half million Frenchmen alone – to say nothing of the occupied territories – were conscripted during the Revolutionary and Napoleonic wars. No French family could have remained untouched by conscription.[20] The machinery was far from perfect, but it worked well enough to furnish the armies with men, and its deficiencies were not so debilitating as to dissipate hatred of what became universally known as 'the blood tax'. The theoretical distribution of quotas lacked precision, causing real injustices in some areas,[21] but everywhere the fact of forcible enlistment alone was enough to evoke permanent loathing of the regime among the rural masses upon whom the burden fell. The system appeared all the more vicious because the annual levies normally took only a proportion of the men eligible, not all of them, so to escape the call-up in the year one became eligible did not ensure exemption: when needs be, and by the end of the Empire that meant permanently, men of 'later classes' could be conscripted. No one was ever safe, nor was Napoleonic France ever free of 'brigandage' as a result; for, having been so successful in curbing so many aspects of disorder, its own dependence on conscription from 1804 onwards ensured that other forms of unrest continued to the end.

Nevertheless, at the moment of its uncertain birth, the regime had delivered peace abroad and then drove home this advantage by not shirking the unsavoury task of restoring internal order. The new regime had created real, if never entirely placid, conditions in which further reforms were possible, and they were no less necessary, if less dramatic, than internal pacification.

STABILITY FOR THE 'MASSES OF GRANITE': REORDERING PUBLIC FINANCES

The Directory had inherited a colossal financial crisis from the early Revolutionary regimes which, in their turn, had taken over the original crisis that had erupted under the monarchy. The Revolutionaries had compounded the problems they found in three serious ways: they had issued paper money, the notorious *assignats*, based on the unrealised hopes of the sales of confiscated Church properties, which had destabilised every sector of economic life and ignited inflation; they had started a major European war without the means to finance it, and were unable to bring it to an end; finally, the general chaos in provincial France, unleashed by the Revolution, had led to the near complete collapse of tax collection until the Terror, 1793–4, and it was still far from regular under the Directory. These were the domestic circumstances which made the contributions of looted foreign assets by successful generals like Napoleon so crucial to the survival of the Republic.

To its great credit in the longer term, the Directory began to tackle the underlying problems of the state finances in a coherent fashion. However, this courage came at a severe political price in the circumstances of the late 1790s, and earned it deep hostility, especially among the popular classes. By 1795, the worthless *assignats* had created hyperinflation, and the Directory began the painful return to hard currency which, in turn, had created a deep economic recession in France by the time of Brumaire. The Napoleonic regime would claim sole credit for solving the crisis but, in truth, the Directory had taken the first steps and endured the unpopular immediate consequences. The Directory and its successor regime had come to realise that nothing they might try to do would much matter unless basic economic stability and a modicum of prosperity was restored in France. Together with the restoration of civil order, it was the bedrock of all else.

Nevertheless, just as in the realms of law and order, legal reform and education, whereas the Directory had only a series of initiatives the Consulate developed concrete, coherent policies based on fundamental institutional reforms. After 1802, these reforms were able to take root in a climate of peace; even the resumption of war with Britain in 1803 made little impact on the internal situation, military confrontations being limited to a naval war itself constrained by the strength of the British blockade. This single fact alone permitted the Ministry of Finance and the Treasury first to restore state finances to manageable levels of debt and then to produce reasonably balanced budgets until 1806–7, when the demands of renewed continental war began to be felt again.

The creation of the Bank of France, on 6 January 1800, and the reorganisation of the Ministry of Finance and tax collection, which began soon afterwards, were crucial moments in the reform. An attempt to create a central bank on the lines of the Bank of England had been undertaken in the 1720s by the Scottish financier John Law, and had ended in catastrophe, so the initiative of the Brumairians was regarded as equally risky. So bad a name had projects of this kind that, at the outset, the Bank of France was not actually a government institution, and it almost came undone when, ill advised by Ouvrard, a financier, it attempted to speculate on the Spanish-American piastre. This at last led to direct government intervention to supply sufficient capital to underpin its work, and to tighter regulation. At its foundation, however, the Bank was a private venture. It was really a vote of confidence by the Brumairians in their coup, a very tangible pledge of allegiance to the new regime. In essence, they were voting with their wallets. Its founding capital of thirty million francs was raised from the ranks of the leading plotters; among its chief investors in the shares set at 1,000 francs each were the men who had 'bankrolled' the coup, Récamier, Lecouteulx and Perregaux, and the Bonapartes themselves. In April 1803, the Bank was given the monopoly on the issue of paper notes; other banks doing the same were bought out. Its capital was increased by 50 per cent, and by 1805 its 200 leading shareholders included the foremost Parisian financial magnates.

The real architect of financial success was Gaudin, who had stood uneasily aside during the Directory but was persuaded by Sieyès to assume the challenges of the post of Minister of Finance almost immediately after the coup. This would prove by far Sieyès' greatest contribution to the new regime, indeed to the future of the nation; it made far more of a useful, lasting impact than any of his over-elaborate constitutions. Napoleon admitted his lack of expertise in this area, his mathematical prowess notwithstanding, and it is a tribute to his ability to delegate effectively, where he knew he was not competent, that he allowed Gaudin to get on with such crucial work unhindered. Gaudin developed a comprehensive policy for financial administration, which began with the separation of the Ministry of Finance, responsible for the collection and administration of revenues, from the new Ministry of the Treasury, the main expenditure office,[22] which was put under Barbé-Marbois, a young aristocrat originally highly prized by the regime as a living symbol of *amalgame*. In 1806, he was replaced by Mollien who, like Gaudin at Finance, held the post until 1814. Mollien had directed the Sinking Fund of the Bank of France since its creation, and he quickly introduced double-entry bookkeeping into both institutions. In the spring of 1800, his intelligent hard work, supported by Napoleon's insistence that the rest of the central government co-operate with Gaudin, produced an understated, rather boring, but genuinely historic achievement. That April, Napoleon asked Gaudin to draw up the information sent to him for the finances of the first six months of the Year 8 (from September to April) 'to establish once and for all the actual budget of the French Republic and to consolidate the national debt by establishing it in a regular manner'.[23] (The political unrest that undermined the old monarchy had become a crisis when Calonne, the Controller-General of Finances – the first minister – had to confess to a handpicked Assembly of Notables that the chaotic financial administration of the *ancien régime* did not allow him to present a proper budget. The ensuing unrest of the revolutionary decade did not improve matters, although progress was made under the Directory.) Mundane as this achievement seems, when set against Napoleon's military exploits or even his great administrative and legal reforms, it was fundamental to all the rest of the regime's work; and, furthermore, it was done quickly.

Tax collection is never a popular business, and Gaudin, like Napoleon, was a realist. They contented themselves with a degree of fairness and a drive for honesty and transparency. Initially, Gaudin did not add many new taxes to the existing ones; rather, he set about a thorough reorganisation of how they were collected. The main source of revenue, just as before 1799, remained the land tax, the brunt of which fell on the peasantry. However, the other direct tax brought in by the Revolution, on personal incomes and those from business, had fallen mainly on urban areas and proved very difficult to collect. It was increasingly replaced by direct taxes, many abolished during the Revolution, but now revived: these direct taxes on consumer goods fell largely on the towns. The *octrois*, and many of the most hated direct taxes of the old order were also restored, on alcohol, tobacco and salt between 1804 and 1806. Now, all these taxes were collected in a better way than before; the direct taxes were always resented but the central source of revenue, the land tax, was set on a clearer, fairer, basis than hitherto. The key to this was the creation of a new, comprehensive land register for France, the *cadastre*.

Napoleon had been deeply impressed by the national land register the Savoyards had compiled for Piedmont and Savoy in the eighteenth century, but to imitate this in a country as vast as France was a major undertaking. Gaudin, working with the army's topographical office, made major progress, however, and the work continued after 1814. Although the *cadastre* was not finally completed until 1827,[24] there was soon enough with which Gaudin could work. The cadastral map not only allowed the state to collect revenue more effectively, it gave the public confidence in the accuracy and, up to a point, in the fairness of the workings of the system. For the first time, every piece of property in France was registered and its value assigned, and these results were in the public domain for all to see. The revolutionaries of the 1790s had made much of the virtue of 'transparency' in public life, but it was Gaudin who actually brought this about, in the most important aspect of the state's activities for ordinary people.

Gaudin's most lasting legacy was the restoration of a sound metallic currency, nicknamed the 'Germinal Franc' after the Revolutionary month in which it was first issued, April 1803. It proved difficult to erase other hard currencies which had crept into France in the 1790s and retained the confidence of local markets, but the new franc, convertible into both gold and silver, emerged as a stable currency. It survived until 1928. From the outset, Napoleon realised his debt to Gaudin and did not hesitate to tell him so. A fine example of his 'man management' is the warm letter of thanks and encouragement sent to him in late March 1800:

It is because our needs are great, and our position delicate, that your talents, your honesty, your zeal for the public good are so needed. You have already done much. There are still great obstacles you must surmount, and some distasteful things to endure, but better days are coming![25]

Napoleon was right, and when the good days came Gaudin had played his part in bringing them about.

It took more than technical reforms to restore public confidence in the government's ability to handle its money, something Napoleon perhaps grasped faster than the technocrats around him. His skills as a politician have often been overlooked, which is understandable in the light of his aversion to public speaking and his growing contempt for parliamentarianism, but they were very real, and were less to do with self-publicity than the effective exercise of power in ways seen to be in the public interest. The extirpation of corruption within the civil service was one such instance. He took a direct interest not only in cases where corruption damaged the flow of revenue to the state, but also when public opinion was obviously aroused. In November 1800, he asked Gaudin to look into the conduct of the senior tax official of the major northern city of Valenciennes, against whom 'many complaints have been raised', and, a few months later, against his counterpart in the second city of France, Lyon, about whom 'many complaints have been put forward'.[26] In September 1801, he drew Gaudin's attention not only to the sloth and negligence of the tax collector of Voiron, but to the 'extreme harshness' of his colleague in Léman.[27] Napoleon's great faith in Gaudin notwithstanding, he was more than prepared to nag him when public opinion was ruffled. He told him in no uncertain terms in August 1801:

Paris is complaining that requests for tax reductions by several individuals ... remain unanswered for eight or nine months, which overburdens the people. I want a report from you about this business, and to know what steps can be taken to get [these things] settled within a month.[28]

Nor did Napoleon hesitate to strike at the apex of the administration. In September 1801, a judicial investigation found twenty-five minor Treasury officials guilty of fraud, but Napoleon pushed this further, and when their superiors were convicted of negligence, he ordered Gaudin to inform them that, in his eyes, their negligence 'had facilitated the crime', and that, although not guilty of a technical offence, they would 'no longer merit the confidence of the government' – the regime's preferred euphemism for dismissal.[29] Napoleon had always suspected the financial administration he inherited from the previous regime; as a soldier in the field, he had seen his men and his campaign plans suffer from official corruption. His assault on malpractice in the Treasury and Finance was coupled with a quiet purge of the personnel of the War Ministry. This was an admission – only made overt in his memoirs – that the leading light of the Terror, Robespierre, had been right in his own suspicions about the civil service, but whereas Robespierre's preferred method was the guillotine, Napoleon used prison if the courts supported him, dismissal when all he could prove was culpability, and pensioned redundancy when he could not. Nevertheless, the war against corruption was crucial in winning a degree of public confidence for the new regime; the dates of Napoleon's interventions in such matters show that it was one of his immediate concerns on his return to Paris, after the Second Italian Campaign.

His interest in ending corruption and scotching the circumstances that might give rise to it were not confined to his first years in power, nor was even an entity so powerful as Fouché's police exempt from his sharp eyes. In September 1804, he told Fouché:

The police commissioners make an immense amount of money from [legalised] gambling, and people are complaining loudly. I intend ... the profits from this gambling should go to the cities ... I shall put them to public use. I will use the 200,000 francs profits at Bordeaux to build a bridge or a canal for the town, and will do the same elsewhere. Each police commissioner, becoming so very rich, will become a power, with many agents under him, to use against the municipal authorities, which will only lead to the greatest discontent when such vast sums are diverted from their true purpose, the public good.[30]

This impartial, often ruthless approach gave people what they wanted and was far more impressive for many of them than more abstract political matters.

The financial reforms addressed the deep, permanent problems affecting the relationship between the French state and its taxpayers, not merely the regime's immediate need for revenue. In this important if prosaic respect, Napoleon, through the hard work and sharp intelligence of Gaudin and Lebrun, truly did return the Revolution to its original principles, as the first pronouncement of the Consulate had sworn to do. The Estates General had been called in 1789 to help solve the crisis of the French state by setting its finances on a permanently sound footing. This the Revolutionaries had spectacularly failed to do, as the collection of revenues all but ceased until the mid-1790s and the madness of the *assignats* nearly reduced one of the most advanced countries in the world to a barter economy for several years. Napoleon managed to fulfil the Revolution's promises by taking full advantage of the respite offered by the peaceful circumstances of these years. He would begin to squander it as the wars accelerated, but the institutions and administrative practices he fostered, together with the land register he initiated, survived his own excesses to become the basis for a modern system of management. These characteristics were the hallmarks of the best Napoleonic reforms: clarity of purpose; institutional solidity; and an ability to build for the future, as well as to cope with a current crisis. The work of reform itself was delegated to the best technical minds available, with as little concern for the politics of the past as possible, but these men were still closely monitored by the young, energetic and highly intelligent chief of state. This was invariably Napoleon's approach to reform, but, as his educational and ecclesiastical reforms reveal, it did not always turn out entirely as he intended.

THE POLITICS OF THE FUTURE:
THE RESHAPING OF PUBLIC EDUCATION

Every step Napoleon took in his public life was imbued with a sense of 'the political', which, in hard reality, meant extending his personal grip on power, in order to turn that power into the creative force for reforming first France, and then Europe, as he saw fit. When the new regime watched the law on secondary education of 1 May 1802 glide with ease through the assemblies – even the often obstreperous Tribunate saw it pass by eighty in favour and nine against – Napoleon had both eyes on the future, although this would only emerge gradually. Up to about 1802, he had had to work through and with the men of the Directory, not only the parliamentarians, but Fouché and Talleyrand, who occupied the key ministries. As the Peace of Amiens bore fruit, his own men began to emerge to prominence, less in public than in the real corridors of power that led to the Council of State, where Cambacérès and Lebrun now came to the fore and the fundamental task of restoring order fell to Moncey and that of creating financial solvency to Gaudin. When the Council of State transformed Directorial aspirations into concrete policy, Napoleon and his men did so with the future of the regime, as well as of France, firmly – if discreetly – in mind.

Educational policy was one of Napoleon's ambitious reforms that would slip beyond his grasp, but his initial efforts in 1802 offer a clear window on to his over-arching vision for the future of his country. The intense interest he took first in secondary and then in tertiary education reveals a political intellect that had come to realise that nothing stands still. If there is a key to Napoleon's thinking about the world and its ways, it rests on his acceptance that he lived in an era of incessant change, and that the best chance for his own political survival – and that of the society he ruled – was to work to control the process of change: to accept the inevitable, but to harness it. In the *laissez-faire* culture of Britain this translated into embracing the dynamic, fundamental material change of the Industrial Revolution. Napoleon, first the product and now the ruler of a markedly different cultural and political environment, thought more in terms of generational change, and in terms of moulding that change, rather than letting it evolve of its own accord. The law of 1 May 1802, widely, if erroneously, referred to by many historians as the 'law of the *lycées*', is a clear indication of this mind at work.[31]

The old monarchy had left education at all levels almost entirely to the Church, whose authority and ability to fund schooling simply evaporated at the Revolution when it lost not just its official monopoly of learning but its income. The Revolutionary regimes of the 1790s were awash with rhetoric and schemes, but bereft of results. Inevitably, this meant that Napoleon's efforts would fall far short of his master plan, but it also meant that, in the long run, his relative success meant that his was the indelible footprint left on the future of the French educational system. The law abolished the *Écoles Centrales*, the state secondary schools set up under the Directory, and replaced them with the *lycées*, with one for every five to six departments, coterminous with the circuits of the Appeal Tribunals; forty-five were created in all, four for Paris. Napoleon retained the Directory's concept of a state-run and controlled system of secondary education although his intention to extend this tight control to primary education faltered simply due to lack of adequate teachers and funds. In 1804, he noted that forty former convents in Paris had regrouped and that, in contravention of the law, the nuns had resumed their old communal life; but because they were also all providing free primary schools for girls he bowed to necessity, telling Cambacérès: 'This reveals the need for the provision for women's education. Talk to Portalis [the Minister of Religion] about what might reasonably be done in this matter.'[32] He had little choice at the primary level, any more than any previous regime had, but Napoleon was more concerned about female education than many Jacobins. Thoroughgoing reform of university education would not follow until 1806–8, but Napoleon left a stamp on the character of the *lycées* to reveal his intentions, and his outlook on society, not just on education.

Private education was not outlawed or abolished, but henceforth the state dominated education in France. Beside the *lycées* were the 'special schools', the progenitors of the *Grandes Écoles*, led by the *Polytéchniques* and the new military schools which have over-shadowed the French universities ever since. The goal of both institutions was to restore professionalism to the French elites, to produce – and soon – a new generation of technocrats with modern educations.

Napoleon's hand was very firm in the formulation of the new curriculum, devised in its details by A.-F. Fourcroy. It was not by chance that Napoleon turned to a distinguished scientist, rather than a classical scholar, to guide these plans, for the new *lycées* were a real, and for many aristocratic families brutal, break with educational tradition. Although the classics were retained, the emphasis was now on science and modern languages; the Humanist tradition of a literary schooling supported by Catholic theology was downgraded to the point of indifference in favour of modernity. Napoleon took a direct, intense interest in ousting traditional Humanism from its pride of place. He charged René Haüy, one of the most distinguished mineralogists of the times and the driving force behind the introduction of the metric system for weights and measures in the Revolution, to write a new textbook for mathematics in the *lycées*. 'I await the greatest results one could hope for from this: the propagation of enlightenment in so important a branch of human knowledge. I want you to give yourself entirely to this work.'[33]

The dislike of this approach by more traditionally minded parents was underscored by the military atmosphere of the *lycées* as opposed to the monastic character of most *ancien régime* colleges. Uniforms were soldierly in style; drum rolls signalled the start and finish of lessons and students marched from one class to another. The essential ethos of the *lycées* reveals an outlook deeply authoritarian but determinedly progressive, the hallmark of the excellent military mind. In common with all the best commanders of his times, Napoleon embraced technological progress; ignorance spelt disaster, and such men had no time for anachronism.

If any single facet of his reforms sets Napoleon apart from tradition, and refutes any accusations that he was a reactionary bent on a cultural restoration in France, it is the *lycées*. This emerges not just in their character, but in their reception. The generous 6,400 scholarships offered by the government were shunned by most noble families, and many bourgeois parents as well. Some 2,400 of the bursaries were reserved for the sons of state servants; the other 4,000 were intended to form the basis of a true meritocracy by examination, but it soon became clear that only those attached to the regime were interested in them. In this, at least, the ferociously innovative vision of the First Consul proved too much for the majority of the 'masses of granite'. Under the restored Bourbons, once shorn of their overt militarism and with a reassuringly Catholic ethos reintroduced, their modern curriculum reconciled with traditional Humanist subject matter, the state-controlled *lycées* entered the mainstream of French elite culture, and became (and remain to this day) its nursery.

Although shunned by those it was meant to serve at the time, Napoleon's vision is manifest in the *lycée*. The niceties of Ciceronian prose and the delicacy of Ovid's poetry gave way to the slide rule and the chemistry laboratory; the doctrines of the Church Fathers faded beside the need to learn German and English. A handful of girls' colleges, similar, if hardly equivalent, to the *lycées*, were founded in 1805. The new elite were to have wives who, if not their equals, would at least be spared traditional ignorance and be able to support them intelligently. The new generation was truly to be new, no longer the product of an education that Napoleon saw as little short of useless and antiquated. There was, simply, to be a changing of the guard; it was to be educated and turned out quickly. Men, as well as elite culture, were to move on as swiftly as the generational process allowed. The new auditors were to emerge from the *lycées* and take their place in the councils of power as soon as possible. In its first decree, the Consulate had declared that it had 'ended the Revolution'. By setting the educational process on a new footing so quickly, Napoleon showed he meant this, and in the most basic terms imaginable. If the *lycées* and the special schools did their job, and did it using the mould he had cast for them, all the men he had inherited from the past – royalist and revolutionary, friend or foe – would be gone. Very different people would take their place.

The creation of new national educational networks was the key element in a process that might be called the re-professionalisation of French working life. When the Revolutionaries had declared the 'career open to talent', they deliberately abolished the need for all formal qualifications to practise any trade or profession whatsoever, with only a handful of exceptions that did not embrace medicine, engineering or the law. Almost by chance, through nationalising the properties and other sources of the wealth of the Church, they precipitated the collapse of those institutions which offered professional training. The Revolutionaries' real targets were the guilds and corporations of tradesmen, whose restrictive practices had, indeed, hampered the prospects of many in the artisan classes. They brought everything else down with them, however. The Consulate soon set about changing this, but in a more authoritarian fashion than the old monarchy.

Georges Lefebvre has noted 'a progressive specialisation in the functions in the hands of bureaucrats'[34] and this trend extended to the whole of professional life. Napoleon famously distrusted both doctors and lawyers, something he had in common with the majority of his subjects, but he went far towards reviving their positions in French working life. The Consulate and then the Empire progressively increased the standard of formal qualifications needed for every level of both professions, but Napoleon always kept the educational process and entry to the professions firmly in the hands of the state, rather than allowing it to slip into the corporate independence of the *ancien régime*. Inevitably, there was favouritism and nepotism, especially within the law, and the numbers admitted into the legal profession were heavily reduced compared to the earlier free market of the Revolution, but qualifications in themselves were the preserve of the state. Those qualifications were uniform and accepted across the whole of France, and then the Empire, in contrast to the localism of the old order. In 1810, the École Normale was founded in Paris to provide a standard training for the professors of the *lycées*. The whole edifice was determinedly elitist, but it set standards of worth and did not entirely snuff out the possibility of rising by merit alone, save perhaps in the law. More than anything, the process of resurrecting the liberal professions under the tutelage of the state represented normalisation, a turning away from the abnormalities of the 1790s, which was not the same as restoration.

THE POLITICS OF THE PAST: THE CONCORDAT AND THE FAILED RECONCILIATION OF THE RIGHT

Napoleon often admitted that the achievement of the Concordat with the Roman Catholic Church in 1801 was the hardest thing he ever did. He was all too right, because few of his reforming initiatives failed so comprehensively or were seen to falter so quickly. The hard reality that before long his religious settlement with Pius VII not only foundered but began to backfire on him is seldom acknowledged even by his most vehement detractors. For those on the left then and now, the very existence of such a settlement provided a clear indication that the Revolution was being discarded in favour of a crypto-monarchist restoration. To the left, Napoleon was a would-be traditional absolutist; as such, he bowed to the inevitable and sought to restore the Church as a pillar of the monarchy. To a more right-wing political tradition, the same logic has a different appeal; it proved the power of counter-revolutionary resistance to Napoleon, and his need to compromise with it. None of these interpretations stands up to the reality of the situation. Not unlike his educational reforms, Napoleon's agreement with the Papacy unravelled in his own time, if in far more spectacular, calamitous ways.

Napoleon did undertake this difficult task with hopes of some success. He would not have sought terms from the Church had he not seen the need for its support in the wider task of pacifying France; his key policy of reconciliation with the royalist right would have been little short of a nonsense, had he not been prepared to engage with the Papacy to restore the Catholic faith to some official position in the state. Above all, he was opposed to a complete rejection of the French past, and he realised how central to French culture Catholicism remained. Napoleon did everything for a reason, and to seek rapprochement with the Church seemed entirely rational to him. There was a neo-Darwinism about Napoleon *avant la lettre*; he respected – even if he did not always admire – survivors of trauma; in the primordial jungle of the 1790s, he had seen the Church survive against the odds of Revolutionary persecution during the Terror, and less overt vexation under the Directory. Along with elements of the nobility and, above all, the 'masses of granite', the Church simply had to be reckoned with.

Napoleon needed to retain ultimate power over what had been the wealthiest, most powerful entity of the old order after the Crown itself. His power was rooted in the Revolution, and he knew it, while the Church proved the most intractable element in the France of *ralliement*. It soon degenerated into a choice between the retention of the state's monopoly on authority in all its forms and a genuine reconciliation with the Church. In practice, Napoleon could not bear this, nor could the post-revolutionary French state. Nowhere is his conscious rejection of a true restoration of the monarchy more emphatic than in his dealings with its greatest single surviving institution.

There was more to it than this, however. Napoleon's whole view of the world baulked at the prospect of the Church exercising real, independent influence over society. To permit this to happen was to abort the hopes he placed in the *lycées* for a more professional society based on utility and modernity; the spectre of a peasantry in the thrall of superstition appalled him for, however much Napoleon demanded obedience, he never wanted it to be blind. The First Consul carried a wide spectrum of the political classes with him in this, for the 'masses of granite' viewed the prospect of the confiscation of their *biens nationaux* – national lands appropriated from Church and aristocracy – with equal horror.

Relatively soon, he found himself thrown back on the support of
the republicans of the 1790s when relations with the Church soured;
the issue of religion came closer than any other to driving him back
into the republican laager of the Directory. From necessity and from
conviction, Napoleon recoiled from the prospect of the Church as
anything but an instrument of the new regime. He found a way of
keeping 'the altar' under control, but it soon ceased to be a positive
force for the regime. A true return to an *ancien régime* where the
intellectual life of the nation was controlled by theology revolted
both the enlightened intellectual and the absolutist ruler as nothing
else did.

No other confrontation provoked by the Revolutionaries had had
such an effect throughout France, territorially as well as ideologically,
as the reforms of the Church in 1790. The regular clergy – the
monks, nuns and friars – were abolished and their vast properties
were confiscated with far less acrimony than the trauma caused by
the insistence of the new assembly that all priests and bishops – who
now had be to be elected by constituencies which could include non-
Catholics – had to swear an oath of loyalty to the new constitution,
just like civil servants. When Pius VI forbade this, the French Church
split into those who took the oath – the 'Constitutionals' – and those
who refused, the 'non-jurors' or 'refractories'. Successive governments
nominally supported the former and outlawed the latter, treating
them as traitors and rebels. At various times the refractories had
the death sentence hanging over their heads, and they were always
hounded; but when the Directory made France a secular state, the
Constitutionals were effectively abandoned, if not actually harassed.
Thus, alongside the confiscation of so much Church property and
wealth, and the generally hostile attitude of the regimes of the 1790s,
the Catholic Church in France was now bitterly divided within its
own ranks, for there was no love lost between those who had accepted
the oath and those who held out against it. The former regarded the
latter as dangerous agitators, little better than the 'brigands' with
whom the Revolutionaries bracketed them, while the latter saw the

Constitutionals as heretics. In the last years of the Directory, after the coup of 18 Fructidor in 1798, official persecution of the Church, in the wider context of the regime's assault on the sources of counter-revolution, actually intensified, with non-jurors facing the guillotine again, and Constitutionals, too, came under increased suspicion, given the links many had with the moderate royalists who had won the aborted elections of 1798. These were the circumstances Napoleon inherited in 1799.

For all its woes, the Church had survived throughout most of France in one form or another, and the non-jurors, who had to be supported in secret, often by poor peasant communities, were probably the more vibrant of the rival factions. Napoleon saw that this was too strong a force to fight, if he could avoid it, and that any talk of reconciliation would look ridiculous unless he tried to deal with it. Even before the Second Italian Campaign and the negotiations with Rome began, Napoleon had started to reach out to both factions of the Church. In December 1799 – after only a few weeks in office – he allowed the clergy, by definition at this stage the Constitutionals, to reoccupy all derelict churches which had not yet been sold off as national properties; in a gesture to the illegal non-jurors, he offered them an amnesty and a return to their duties, for a simple promise not to disobey the new constitution. He also allowed religious observance on Sundays again; previously, the Revolutionary governments had permitted this only on the *décadi*, the last day of the ten-day Revolutionary week, which Napoleon maintained until 1806. These were his own initiatives, however. He knew nothing was possible without Rome, and when talks commenced in November 1800, the real work began.

Napoleon was partially helped by the death in 1799 of Pius VI, whom the French had been holding captive in Avignon, and the election in early 1800 of the Bishop of Imola, Chiaramonti, as Pius VII. Napoleon's knowledge of him in Italy, where he had urged his diocese not to oppose the French occupation, seemed to offer some hope of dialogue. It proved possible, but it was far from amicable. Negotiations began in November 1800, when papal representatives arrived from Rome, but even before they began Napoleon had laid down two points he considered beyond discussion: Church properties sold as *biens nationaux* during the 1790s were to remain untouchable, and the French episcopate had to be reappointed from scratch. Unless these two terms were agreed, Napoleon told the envoys when he met them in northern Italy – he still with the army, they on their way to Paris – there was no point in proceeding. Rome had to concede these points, but over the next three months the envoys proved as unyielding as the conqueror of Italy, as sets of proposals and counter-proposals were drawn up and rejected by both sides.

Napoleon then entered the negotiations in person, and set a time limit of five weeks for a definitive text to be agreed. He got his way. Pius VII approved the agreement in June 1801, and Napoleon ratified it the following September. Portalis, a member of Napoleon's inner circle, was entrusted with managing the passage of the Concordat through the assemblies, but his calculations nearly backfired. His failure to understand the depth of anticlerical feeling among the deputies is revealing, for Portalis did not assume the deputies were in favour of a society imbued with religious sentiment; he made his case in terms of pure utility, that organised religion was a necessary ingredient of social stability; it was a component of pacification and normalisation.

Even couched in such Voltairean terms – of not discussing atheism in front of the servants – the Concordat faced very substantial opposition in the assemblies. It was only passed in April 1802, and, despite the 'halo effect' of the Peace of Amiens, the government only succeeded in getting it through the Corps Législatif by amending the text to ensure that the Church would remain emphatically under state control. Even then, more than a third of the deputies either abstained or voted against any formal rapprochement with Rome.[35]

The message was clear: for many men of the moderate centre the Church was still peasant rebellion at prayer. There were even rumblings of discontent from within the Constitutional Church, the very group of men Napoleon was most determined to protect. The Abbé Grégoire, one of the leaders of the Constitutional Church from its inception, argued that the Consulate had already done enough to restore public worship, and had no need to deal with Rome.[36] If Fouché is to be believed in his predictably unreliable memoirs, he shared this view completely, claiming that although he saw the 'resurrection of the altars' as the basis of stability, involving Rome directly in French affairs would lead to trouble.[37] Napoleon had fought his first war on two fronts.

What the deputies failed to see was the hard battles Napoleon's negotiators were fighting with Rome and, as at Amiens, it was probably as well that Joseph did most of the real work, alongside the Abbé Bernier, a former Vendean chief and non-juring priest who had rallied to Napoleon soon after Brumaire. Talleyrand hovered in the background, and his skills proved invaluable. Napoleon's direct correspondence with Pius VII ceased altogether during the period of the negotiations, and his exhortations of Joseph and Portalis, even as they drew to a conclusion, reflected the impatience of a secular leader who grasped the huge political capital he could gain from bringing off a major, unexpected rapprochement but had no real idea who he was dealing with in order to achieve it. In July 1801, he told Joseph he wanted the papal bull authorising the agreement to be published as quickly as possible, to coincide with the new session of the assemblies.[38] In October, he ordered Portalis to hurry the Pope along in drawing up the bull, and to send it to him in time to publish it throughout France alongside the texts of the Concordat and the Peace of Amiens.[39]

Napoleon never learned how to deal with the Roman Catholic Church. As Nietzsche put it, 'the eagle of empire can never lie down with the lamb of God'. He had to get Joseph to confront Consalvi, the head of the papal delegation, over the status of the Constitutional bishops, insisting that the Pope could not order them to retract the oaths they had taken to the government in 1790. This would, Napoleon stormed, dishonour the Constitutionals, and also 'above all, the temporal authority which has sustained them since the [time of] the Constituent Assembly'.[40] Napoleon showed a fierce loyalty to his revolutionary roots here. His increasing exasperation with the Vatican, and the latent contempt he had for Catholicism, would certainly have wrecked the negotiations, and with them the whole political edifice being built on *ralliement* and *amalgame*, but it would also probably have reassured the core of the French political classes. Indeed, Napoleon's staunch defence of those bishops who had remained steadfastly loyal to the Revolution met with a fierce riposte from the thirty-seven *ancien régime* bishops who refused to resign, even on the Pope's orders, and thus rejected the Concordat. Thirty-five of them were in exile abroad,[41] which was fortunate for Napoleon, but they continued to exercise influence within their French dioceses. Above all, their furious reaction to the very idea of a reconciliation sanctioned by Rome points to the mountain the politics of *ralliement*, to say nothing of *amalgame*, had to climb in the sphere of religion.

People on both sides saw only the principle of engagement between two sworn foes. The most important thing about the Concordat of 1801, for both parties, was less what it granted the Church than what it did not. Its terms reveal why the Papacy had to be bullied into it. Napoleon's vision of the Church's role in society becomes clearest in what he did not restore, more than in what he allowed to return. Conversely, the Papacy and the French faithful were left with no illusions that Napoleon would grant them the full restoration they had hoped for. The regular orders were not restored, and the actual Church remained what the Revolutionaries had sought to make it in 1790: a working arm of the state, composed almost solely of bishops and priests with only a handful of teaching and nursing orders left from the powerful regular clergy of the old order. The festivals of the Church were cut to a handful of High Days, and their celebration was largely confined within the walls of the parish churches, as was almost all public worship unless it involved celebrating a French military victory or, later, a birth in the imperial family. At a stroke, the great public processions and carnivals that had punctuated the calendar of the French Church for centuries were done away with, again as the Revolutionaries had wished. The only High Days not relocated to

Sundays were Christmas and the Assumption. The lay confraternities, for centuries the fulcrum of social life in much of France, were reduced to one per parish, and lost their independence. The field chapels and roadside shrines, which were the centres of piety for the peasantry-at-work, were still banned, as were the missions often sent into the countryside in the eighteenth century to provide the Catholic Church's equivalent of Methodist revivalism.

Above all, after a determined intervention by Napoleon, the Vatican conceded a crucial point: Catholicism was not made the sole, official religion of the state. All the existing faiths – Lutheranism, the Calvinist reformed church and Judaism – were recognised as equal and under the direction and protection of the state; the Roman Catholic Church had to settle for being officially recognised as the 'religion of the great majority of Frenchmen'. Freedom of conscience was as non-negotiable as the *biens nationaux*. Any among the French faithful who had hoped for the restoration of traditional piety were soon disabused of such hopes, as were those royalists who saw in Napoleon a French Monck. This was the victory of the Revolution.

The method of appointment of the clergy, the territorial reorganisation of the Church, and its whole position vis-à-vis the state, was a victory of the old regime of Louis XIV and traditional Gallican liberty from Rome, however. Louis XIV, although very pious, had always defended the independence of the French – 'Gallican' – Church from undue interference from Rome, especially over the appointment of bishops, and Napoleon resurrected this attitude. The Concordat reprised the terms of the 1516 Concordat of Bologna, made between Francis I and Rome, which allowed the French head of state to nominate the French bishops, choices which Rome had to sanction. All the French bishoprics now had to be filled, however; effectively, everyone had to reapply for his see. Napoleon also forced the Papacy to agree to important diocesan boundary changes, which reduced the number of bishops considerably. A window on Napoleon's future conflicts with Pius VII opened when the French insisted on – and won – the right to extend all these reforms into the newly annexed

Piedmontese departments, which were only incorporated on the eve of the agreement.

Pius VII swallowed the Concordat because, however unpalatable, it represented an improvement on the vulnerable position in which the Church found itself within France before 1799, but to push these terms beyond the boundaries where Revolutionary persecution had prevailed for a decade was seen as a dangerous precedent. The Piedmontese Church had been untouched by such ravages, and there the Concordat was, in effect, damaging for the Church's position. Pius had little choice but to concede; it left a bitter taste in his mouth, but prepared him for further confrontations of this kind as Napoleon's realm expanded.

If Napoleon won anything for his own political purposes from the Concordat, it was the *carte blanche* it gave him to reshape the French clergy through a vast exercise in *amalgame*. Jacques-Olivier Boudon encapsulates Napoleon's vision succinctly: 'His principle was simple; he sought to amalgamate the two episcopates, and to appoint half the [new] bishops from new men.'[42] Rome would get the return of some non-jurors; the republicans would see many Constitutionals saved, but – or so he hoped – Napoleon would ensure that the majority of his new episcopate were neither, that they would be his own men. The proportions did not work out as he intended, however, as he extended the amnesty on émigrés to the refractory bishops: thirty-two of the new appointments were intransigent counter-revolutionaries, while only twelve were Constitutionals, and the other sixteen were men of the pre-1789 episcopate. Among the new appointments, he placed his uncle Joseph Fesch in the senior see of Lyon, making him the head of the Gallican Church, while the relatives of several of his generals also received bishoprics.[43] Napoleon placed considerable hopes and responsibility on the new bishops; they were to be his 'prefects in purple', charged with the appointment and supervision of the parish clergy, and charged with making three pastoral tours of their dioceses a year, just as the prefects toured their departments.

Napoleon was soon disappointed. His concessions to the refractory clergy won him nothing, and he was soon more reliant on Fouché's police, and his trusted Gendarmerie, to inform him of the priests' conduct. Before the ink was dry on the Concordat, his correspondence reveals how widespread clerical dissidence remained. Boudon puts it perfectly: 'The notion of "the policing of worship [*la police des cultes*]" found its full meaning, in so much as that, throughout the whole period, religious questions became one of the sources of opposition to the regime.'[44] It was not long before responsibility for this policing passed from the Ministry of Public Worship, under Portalis, to Fouché and his former Jacobins, at Police-Générale. Fouché and his men were actually panicked by the widespread enthusiasm for public worship that followed the Concordat, and they were not fools.

There is ample evidence that the signing of the Concordat did little to abate clerical opposition where it existed, save to allow the reinstalled refractory bishops to marginalise Constitutional priests and promote their own men. Napoleon was not exempt from clerical defiance. On a visit to Rouen in 1802 – an area Napoleon actually liked for its moderate politics and economic vitality – he reported to Cambacérès, 'Monsieur the Archbishop, who is greatly loved and esteemed here, very much wanted to give us a Mass, but he gave us neither holy water, nor a blessing, nor a sermon. We will get our own back tomorrow, which is All Saints Day.'[45] One ponders if Napoleon wrote to Fouché to spring a Jacobin version of 'trick-or-treat' on the cleric.

When Fesch took up his post in Lyon in November 1802, Napoleon stressed the need to help the Constitutional priests there, and not to let them be pushed aside; he had no illusions that 'there are a great number of priests who were sworn enemies of the state' in the second largest city in France. Fesch was ordered to employ a few of them and to keep Napoleon informed about their conduct, 'and I will dismiss them by my own will'.[46] Lyon remained a centre of clerical disaffection to the end. When Napoleon ordered Moncey to send his men on their provincial tours of inspection, their orders always stressed the need to keep a very close eye on the clergy. There was worse. In May 1804, Napoleon informed Régnier, his Minister of Justice, that 'a great number of priests in [department] Deux-Sèvres have come to my attention. They are rebels against both Church and State ... All these individuals will be arrested by the Gendarmerie, without any intervention by the civil authorities.'[47]

Régnier was being told in no uncertain terms that this was a matter for the heaviest hand of the law. The following month, it was the turn of fourteen priests in neighbouring Poitiers, whose arrests 'caused considerable "emotion" in the region'.[48] Such things went on until the end, and, as will be seen, got much worse when relations with Rome collapsed altogether by 1809.

Outside even this mass of untrustworthy priests there remained a rump of non-jurors who still refused to accept the Concordat, but who had managed to remain in France or re-enter it from exile in the period of toleration during the negotiations. They became known as the *Petite Église*, the 'little church', and remained an illegal but persistent presence until 1814. Predictably, the *Petite Église* found its strongest support in the Vendée, its position always bolstered by the fear Constitutional priests had of accepting posts there, the considerable financial inducement offered by the government notwithstanding. It also gained considerable support in Lyon, where it drew on older, Jansenist sources of resentment of both the state and Rome, but in the other scattered areas where it had a following the *Petite Église* was based on influential local bishops and clergy who lent it support. Its followers probably never reached much beyond about 100,000.[49] Never a real danger, it was nevertheless always an uncomfortable reminder of how Napoleon's gamble had failed. It drew its strongest support from exactly those regions of France, and those elements of French society, Napoleon had most hoped the Concordat would rally to him, the counter-revolutionary peasantry of the west and the old, local aristocracy.

In 1805, arrests were made in the Vendée of priests of the *Petite Église* who were under the protection of the aunt of one of the most prominent aristocratic leaders of the Vendean rebels, La Rochejaquelein.[50] This is hardly surprising, but it underlines the disappointment of the hopes

Napoleon placed in the Concordat, and the sincerity with which he had sought to prepare the ground for it in this troubled region. In May 1800, he told Bernadotte, then commander of the Army of the West, that the priests in the region seemed to be conducting themselves well and that 'it is essential to make them as happy as possible. Full freedom of religion.'[51] It failed. Napoleon is all too often credited with pacifying the Vendée through the Concordat, but in truth the reinforcements he sent there almost as soon as he took power, in January 1800, and the low conscription quotas he allowed these departments did more 'to prevent this effusion of French blood'[52] than the offer of a religious settlement so lacking in appeal for this very conservative people.

It was relatively easy to persuade the Vendeans to lay down their arms, as fresh troops released for internal service arrived to bolster local garrisons that Napoleon freely admitted were badly under-strength.[53] It was quite another to coax them into rallying to him. At the end of 1803, a rising of more than 400 men was reported in the region, among whom were seven émigrés newly landed from England. Napoleon referred to them in the new parlance as 'miserable creatures with neither hearth nor home, *mauvais sujets* created by the impunity during the licence of the civil wars', but he ordered 'fairly considerable forces' into the area and admitted they had been organised enough to disperse quickly and without trace.[54] Two days later, he complained to Régnier that the mayors of the region did not seem to merit the confidence the prefects said they had in them, otherwise the 'lesser chiefs, deserters and other sinister people' would have been dealt with. There was an ever-increasing need, he felt, to press the mayors for proper lists of 'these brigands and, above all, the foreigners, who have only been drawn to the area by the civil war'.[55] If the Concordat had been meant to end this sort of thing, it had failed to do so, certainly in the eyes of its architect.

Napoleon deserves much credit for this initiative, its failure notwithstanding. He was sincere about ending the bloodshed in the Vendée, and, unlike the regimes of the 1790s, he swallowed a well-honed contempt for the rebels' piety in order to achieve it. He had come to respect their leaders – the men he would later call 'the giants of the Vendée' – if not their principles. He was ready to compromise, as he was with the entire Church. Staël knew at least half her man when she said of Napoleon, 'his intelligence made him do what conscience would have dictated to others',[56] but as a cosseted child of the enlightened 'bubble' of the Paris salons, neither her own conscience nor that of most revolutionaries, whatever their factional allegiance, extended to trying to appease an enemy most of them regarded as simply bestial. Napoleon shared their prejudices, more than many later cared to admit, but in this failure, perhaps more than in some of his more durable successes, he showed himself a statesman, albeit one who soon abandoned the path of compromise when he saw it was futile. In 1795, after the fall of Robespierre, many of the rebel leaders in the west had taken hope from the change of regime, and some had even come to Paris in the hope of dialogue with the Directory. They were quickly disappointed, the election results in which the constitutional royalists had done so well were annulled, and they were soon back in arms. When the west shunned Napoleon, however, it was because it did not like his terms, not because he refused to try to compromise. The difference amounts to little, in terms of the course of repression, but it is indicative of a more sincere approach to reconciliation than had been tried hitherto. The failure of the Concordat needs to be viewed as part of a much longer struggle between elite and popular culture, of which the clash between the Church and the French Revolution was only a part.

The most poignant manifestations of this failure are not to be found in the social or territorial bastions of counter-revolution. The prefect of Loir-et-Cher, hardly a troubled region, still complained that 'what is angering here in Vendôme, is that religious dissidence . . . is favoured by the richest and best thought of families, the women, especially'.[57] Unlike Chateaubriand, they had not waited for the death of one of their peers to reject *ralliement*. Nor did Napoleon see it in the same, resigned terms as his prefect. In July 1804, he ordered the arrest by the Gendarmerie of the priest he felt to be the leader of 'dissidence' in Vendôme, 'the rebel named Thouagniers': 'I want a report on the mayor of Vendôme, who protects this priest, under the influence of his wife, and I want to know why this mayor let that priest bury a man who died recently, without turning to the parish priest.'[58]

Vendôme is a quiet place, then as now, not far from Paris. Its *ancien régime* bishop was an émigré who had refused to resign as part of the agreement, but there had been no violence there. This was neither the 'wild west' of the Vendée nor the malevolent Midi, but Napoleon still felt threatened by the clergy and considered sending in troops. A degree of recalcitrance in the see of a refractory bishop was to be expected, but it is Napoleon's over-reaction that matters. The regime itself did not trust its own agreement with Rome, even at this early stage.

The erosion of the compromise Napoleon desired from the Concordat was not all the fault of his ferociously traditionalist opponents, of course, and its failure reveals the limits of Napoleon's own tolerance of the religious culture of his times, and of popular piety above all. His utterly deaf ear to the spiritual sensibilities of the Vatican and the higher clergy was buffered by his selection of and faith in good diplomats, but his vision of the Church proved too 'progressive' and elitist in the eyes of the masses, not just royalists and clerics. This was not a personal opinion of Napoleon alone. He shared the intellectual outlook of almost all Frenchmen of his generation who accepted the tenets of the Enlightenment (and even some who did not) – that popular piety was too overlain with superstition, that its worst excesses had been aided, abetted and prolonged by the Jesuits, and that their pernicious influence had outlived the order itself, which had been banned in the 1760s. Most educated people – from Staël to Napoleon and back again – recoiled in horror from the world of local saints, their riotous festivals, powerful relics, and, even more, from the very orthodox, highly rigid forms of Catholicism inculcated in forgotten peasant communities since the seventeenth century, as was the case in the Vendée. The terms of the Concordat set in stone the fact that Napoleon could not go this far in reaching out to the Catholic masses, and he would have carried no one in the circles of power with him had he wished to do so. The Concordat enshrined in law a certain view of religion that was moderate, opposed to popular piety in many forms, and would inevitably alienate large swathes of the peasantry. It had many affinities with Jansenism, a current within the Catholic Church in the late seventeenth and eighteenth centuries which placed a strong emphasis on personal devotion and an austere approach to religion that stood in deliberate contrast to the ostentatious, atavistic elements of popular piety. Indeed, the Concordat was initially good enough even for Chateaubriand, who accepted his appointment as the French Republic's ambassador to Rome with alacrity, in hopes of fostering the new relationship. The French elites outside the minority wholly opposed to Christianity envisaged a Church imbued with the more intellectually rigorous spirituality of the Jansenist tradition, in its religious form, as opposed to that political strand of Jansenism which rejected state control. Its core values found expression in those aspects of the Concordat that suppressed traditional, popular piety. Napoleon was clear about this even to the most favoured among his family. His letter to his uncle, Cardinal Fesch, upon the latter taking up his new post as Archbishop of Lyon and, thus, head of the Gallican Church, cautioned: 'The bishops and archbishops of today are no longer the bishops and archbishops of [17]89; they are closer to the primitive Church ... Take good note of what I have said in this letter.'[59] In the same breath, he exhorted Fesch to rally both clerical factions around this vision. It did not work.

This was an elite consensus that included Napoleon, in which a neo-Jansenist Catholicism co-existed with secularism, and it served ultimately to embellish the elitist nature of the new regime. Put another way, if *ralliement* was meant to be inclusive. Napoleon's religious policies worked actively against winning over the largest section of the population. Napoleon's dilemmas in appeasing the right and the rural, Catholic masses – and his commitment to the Jansenist tradition prevalent among the educated elites – are encapsulated in a letter to Fouché of late 1804, not long before his coronation as Emperor of the French. Napoleon knew that, however much Fouché and his largely ex-Jacobin police suspected them and wanted them barred from the local assemblies, former émigrés who had been amnestied had to be left in peace, even if he wanted them carefully watched:

The art of government is to punish the miscreants, to reward honest people. You know that many of these émigrés have returned of their own free will; it is thus impossible to deny them the enjoyment of their political rights . . . The general idea is to keep a watch on everything, and to make exceptions for those who conduct themselves well . . .[60]

At the same time, however, he revealed the limits of appeasement of the right. Napoleon reacted with a ferocity bordering on hysteria to the rumours circulating after the Concordat that he might allow the Jesuits – the bugbear that united the educated classes, from royalist reformers to rabid Jacobins – back into France:

My principal aim has been to prevent the Jesuits re-establishing themselves in France. They take all sorts of forms. I want neither the Sacred Heart of Jesus, nor the confraternity of the Holy Sacrament[61] nor anything that resembles a religious militia; and under no pretext do I intend to take one step that will allow the existence of any other clergy than secular [parish] priests. My equal intention is not to allow [female] convents . . . it is not, however, inconvenient to allow former nuns to end their lives in their communities or to wear their habits, but they will not be allowed to take on novices or to recruit them . . . they must not be under the supervision of priests, or in communication with their bishops, for any group which diverges from this path must be dealt with pitilessly.[62]

One community of Parisian nuns had developed a devotion to the Sacred Heart, combining Napoleon's two worst nightmares: Fouché was told to look into it discreetly at first, and then to take action if needed. He was also to look into another community which was running one of the girls' primary schools Napoleon himself had recently approved. He was now having doubts – 'How do you tell a novice from a pupil?' The liberal elites had nothing to fear from the Concordat, but the Church was already being told where to stop. The same day he ordered Talleyrand to inform the Spanish government that he regarded their decision to re-admit the Jesuits 'with difficulty', and advised Madrid to think again, 'and that I shall never allow this to happen either in France, or the Italian Republic'.[63]

These official responses to perceived clerical reaction give credence to the story recounted by Madame Junot in her memoirs of Napoleon's ferocious reaction to 'the affair of St-Roche' at around this time. A much-loved Parisian dancer, Mlle Chameroi, died in childbirth, unwed, and her funeral cortège, followed by a large crowd, was refused entrance to his church by the priest of St-Roche. The police barely averted a riot, and diverted the funeral to another church, where the priest carried out the funeral. This evoked a rare violent outburst from Napoleon, according to Madame Junot, 'and excited him to let fall some of those expressions which never escaped him but when he was violently agitated'. Napoleon put successful pressure on the Archdiocese of Paris to admonish the priest of St-Roche publicly; he was suspended for three months and an account was published in the official state organ, *Le Moniteur*. Madame Junot remarked that the phraseology in *Le Moniteur* bore more than a passing resemblance to Napoleon's own peculiar prose style. Of the recalcitrant priest it said: 'recalled to a sense of duty by meditation, he may learn that all the superstitious practices preserved by some rituals, but which begotten in times of ignorance, or created by the over-heated imagination of zealots, degrade religion by their frivolity, were proscribed by the Concordat.'[64]

In August 1805, in the midst of all his preparations for 'the descent on England', and writing from his headquarters on the Channel coast, Napoleon could still find guns to turn on the Church when it tried to push the bounds of its authority into daily life, as had been its duty before the Revolution. When several prefects supported clerical demands to ban dancing outside churches, Napoleon asked his Minister of the Interior sarcastically, 'I don't know where this will end. Is dancing now an evil? Do we want to return to the time when villagers were not allowed to dance?' Then he exploded:

If everything the bishops say is to be believed, we would have to ban balls, entertainments, fashion, and turn the Empire into one big convent ... Make it clear to them ... that the civil authorities do not involve themselves in this kind of thing . . . and write directly to the prefects who have followed or set such an example.[65]

Hundreds of thousands of conscripts might be forced to drill, but all were free to amuse themselves in peace as they wished. His defence of secular society from a creeping theocracy was as ferocious as that of the French coastline from the 'new Carthage' of the British.

Madame Junot always remarked on Napoleon's powers of self-control; they were, for her and her husband – his old friend and comrade-in-arms – one of the hallmarks of his character. The only other time she reported such a complete loss of control was when the Peace of Amiens was broken by the British.[66] The Church and the English clearly had an effect on Napoleon few other things could rival.

The suspicions and resentments on both sides did indeed make the Concordat resemble Napoleon's uneasy peace with Britain, more than the healing of the wounds of the Revolution it is often portrayed as. Like the Peace of Amiens, the Concordat would collapse in mutual hostility; it just took longer, as the Pope had no divisions to deploy against Napoleon. In both cases, Napoleon was dealing with people and political cultures he neither liked nor properly understood. The labyrinthine ways of the Vatican eluded him; he could not understand that a papal bull was not to be hurried, nor the depths of soul-searching the Curia had to subject itself to in order to come to terms with the concessions it had to make. The rise and demise of parliamentary ministries at Westminster was equally mysterious to him. On each occasion, direct intervention in the process of negotiation would have ended in disaster, and on each occasion the end result proved irksome to both parties and hostilities were resumed, with Britain in 1803 and with the Vatican, after a long 'phoney war', in 1809. Ultimately, Napoleon lost both contests, but in the short term his imperfect victories bought him some precious time. That they were achieved at all stemmed from his remarkable ability to delegate the right problem to the right men, and to heed them, when he needed to hold himself in check. If Amiens and the

Concordat expose Napoleon's limitations – cultural and personal – they also underline his great strength, that of never surrounding himself with mediocre sycophants.

The work for the Concordat produced one of his most fascinating collaborators. Although this exercise represents a general failure of both *ralliement* and *amalgame*, it brought the Abbé Étienne Bernier into Napoleon's ken. Bernier had been a leader of the Vendean revolt from the very outset, and was a member of its non-military 'supreme council' created only weeks after the outbreak of the rising, in the spring of 1793. In 1796, following a string of disasters, he was very influential in persuading some of the military leaders to fight on, and was the author of a flood of proclamations to the peasantry to remain in the field, even as they abandoned him. Throughout the fighting, Bernier set himself up as a clear rallying point for a scrupulous adherence to clerical and royal authority. He remained in opposition after the collapse of the revolt, well into 1799, and tried to foster links with émigrés in England.[67] However, he approached Napoleon by letter almost immediately after Brumaire, and soon got in touch with the military commander of the west, General Hédouville, offering to act as an intermediary with the rebels, a chance Napoleon seized: here was *ralliement* where and when he needed it most.

Napoleon saw Bernier's first letter to him as 'that of an enlightened man, worthy of co-operating with for the well-being and glory of the fatherland. Tell him I will see him with pleasure.'[68] When Bernadotte took over, he assured the new commander that 'Bernier is a very able man who has greatly aided the [process of] pacification. Show confidence in him.'[69] Bernier did, indeed, succeed in halting the fighting and persuading most of the rebels to accept the amnesty. Napoleon discerned that his talents were not tied to his regional influence, but were highly transferable: he could be amalgamated.

Bernier proved a born negotiator, and Napoleon used him in the negotiations for the Concordat alongside some of the most senior men in his regime, where he proved his worth. Bernier was rewarded with the diocese of Orléans in 1802. He died in 1807, at the moment when his counsel was most needed, but his example was a small ray of hope for Napoleon in an ever darker sea of clerical black.

Napoleon had confronted theocracy before, in Egypt. His frequently quoted assertion that he would have converted to Islam to consolidate his grip on Egypt, and that he saw the Concordat in the same light, is something that is both true and untrue. The statement did, indeed, encapsulate his cynical indifference to the spiritual, in general, but it also shows how he over-estimated his tolerance of what he considered backward and obscurantist. Napoleon soon turned on the Egyptian clerics and their faithful when he discovered their religion did not match the vision he had acquired of it from Voltaire. When the Catholic clergy again reared its many heads after 1801, whether as traditionalist local priests in the cause of counter-revolution or as bishops intent on the restoration of their privileged position in society, Napoleon drew back, the better to ponder the advantages of lashing out. Unlike in Egypt, however, he could not simply turn his back and walk away from what repelled him. Within France, the Concordat was Napoleon's most ambitious application of the policies of *amalgame* and *ralliement* to the most serious rift of the 1790s, and it failed.

THE CIVIL CODE

In his presentation of the work of the Council of State for the new Civil Code, Jean-Étienne-Marie Portalis made one of many resounding points, on 21 January 1802: 'The law is made for men, not men for the law.'[70] This aphorism has lived on in European jurisprudence, among many others in his remarkable work. It was a maxim arrived at by a committee of the Council, which began its work days after Brumaire, if only formally constituted in August 1800, and saw its code promulgated on 21 March 1804. The men and the nation it was made for were highly politicised, and the men who made it were far from untouched by the politics of the 1790s, yet they managed to forge a document just as lasting, as concise and as clear as any of the age that gave the Western world the American Constitution and Bill of Rights.

Like its American counterparts, the Civil Code – renamed the Code Napoléon in 1807 – was, in essence, a product of the conservative strand of the Enlightenment, based on a pessimistic but grounded view of the human condition, determined to provide a template for interpretation, rather than an unalterable, detailed set of strictures. Like those documents, the Civil Code of 1804 was concise, precise yet flexible, and written in clear prose, accessible to any reasonably educated person. It was meant to free the civil law from opaque language and legal jargon, and it succeeded. The committee produced a model of clarity and comprehensiveness, which Stendhal, a Bonapartist admittedly, called 'the best family novel ever written'. The Napoleonic jurists drew on their previous work on codification during the Revolution, but it is undeniable that they succeeded in creating one of the most durable, influential documents in modern history.

The men of the committee succeeded in this, for the Code endures in France, and across Europe and the world, in the basic form they gave it. Napoleon always regarded it has his greatest and most useful achievement, more lasting and useful to society than any of his military victories. In the first instance, however, it had to navigate the turmoil of its own place and times, the aftermath of the French revolutionary upheavals. When it was written, the Civil Code was the product of politics, what Portalis called a transaction between the old and the new.

The Council of State, still in its infancy, had learned many lessons before it sat down to work, mostly at the expense of Cambacérès, who would chair 52 of its 107 sessions – Napoleon would lead the other 55 – and settle its finer points once the matters of principle were mastered in committee. Even when Napoleon presided, Cambacérès was present, and he often had to take control. The Second Consul had presented three projects for a civil code to the assemblies of the 1790s, the last and fullest in 1796 and, in the process, he and his colleagues had learned the limits of reform the men of the regime – the post-Terror political elite – were ready to support, and where their desire for a return to older certainties began. In this sense, the Code succeeded because it reflected the human experience of the 'masses of granite' and their representatives as of 1800. Napoleon did not so much lead them in this as reflect their prejudices to a remarkable degree. His views on those aspects of the law which mattered most to them matched their own, as did his sense of what was important to the mainstream of French society, and what could be left on trust to the legal experts; his personal interventions reflected the concerns of the stable and prosperous classes as no other leader had. This, rather than any inspired insights of jurisprudence, of which he knew little, is why the Code thoroughly deserves to carry his name, united with his ability to steer the committee to its goal as an astute chair.

Napoleon's sessions began at midday and could run until 7 p.m.; the discussions were more wide-ranging and less methodical than those chaired by Cambacérès, and the Second Consul would steer the discussion back on course when needed.[71] Indeed, although ready to assert his own opinions, Napoleon showed himself willing to bow to the experts, particularly on points of detail, as when Cambacérès forced him to reject his own proposal for an unworkable set of definitions of 'people and the law' for the first section of the Code. Napoleon thought not in terms of 'society', but of individuals who had three forms of relationships with others. Individuals had relations with the state, with their spouses, and with their other relatives. Cambacérès pushed these generalisations aside as unworkable, and the committee's division into nine categories stood.[72]

The 'transaction' Portalis described was of two kinds. The first was an emphatic reassertion, once and for all, of the gains of the Revolution which the men of the Directory had come to believe were the untouchable heritage of the great reforms of 1789. The Code also retained those elements of *ancien régime* law which even the Revolutionaries had come to see as less the product of royal rule than as universal truths. The second 'transaction' lay within the received wisdom of the old order, which even the Revolutionaries had found hard to ignore, the division of French legal culture between that of the written, Roman law tradition of the south, and that of customary law,

in the north. That so many within the French political elite now felt
able to think in terms of blending the old and the new, that the very
term 'transaction' was so easily accepted, was a clear sign that, in the
realm of law at least, the political climate was ready for compromise.
The Revolutionaries felt secure enough to incorporate the best of the
ancien régime, and more conservative elements had come to accept
that many Revolutionary reforms were here to stay.

There was also agreement around how all this should be carried
out: the real point was that a legal framework rooted in enlightened
thinking, not tradition, was so readily accepted. The preferred method
of enlightened thinking was a concise, abstract, but comprehensive
legal code. The basic concept of a single, uniform law code for the
entire country was seen as axiomatic. Portalis was open about how
hard the task of reconciling regional variation in legal practices was
when he spoke to the assemblies: 'How can we not be as attached
to customs as we were to privileges? And how can we not see them
as barriers against the shifting will of arbitrary power?' The answer
was equality before the law, which could only be achieved through
uniformity; too many concessions to particularism were a return
to the undesirable past. The Code had to find a way to assimilate
different practices, not to create 'special regions': 'We have made a ...
transaction between written and customary law ... [by] conciliating
their terms, or by modifying some by others, without breaking the
unity of the system, and without breaking the general spirit [of the
Code].' 'Uniformity is a form of perfection,' as Portalis put it in his
preliminary remarks in 1802.

With uniformity came much else. The Code enshrined the principle
of equality before the law for all, perhaps the achievement of the early
Revolution that had the widest support. This whole approach spelled
the death of *ancien régime* corporatism in all its forms. Meaningful
regional autonomy died forever, alongside noble privilege; the right of
association among workers was banned, alongside clerical immunity
from civil justice. The Code confirmed and defined a social order based
on the rights of the individual; the citizen's only legal accountability

was to the state; he was obliged not to infringe the rights of others, but had no special claims on anyone or anything. The consensus reached so readily over this should not be surprising, among the men who rallied to Napoleon, for it had been their goal since 1789.

The early Consulate provided the first moment in ten years when the protracted work of reforming French law could proceed, and it was taken. Napoleon had to cajole, to get the work done and to make the experts and assemblies jump the necessary hurdles, but there were few real arguments about the 'general spirit' or framework of reform. On one level, the Code proved how much consensus for the working reality of the new order there actually was. This was what enabled Napoleon to turn the seeming recalcitrance of the Tribunate to his own ends and purge it of elements he could portray as 'out of step' with the ethos of the greater 'project'.[73] As an exercise in politics, it was invaluable to the regime, but there was some irony in this. Napoleon himself, and many of the members of the commission, did not think in terms of the 'eternal' or 'immutable', in any sphere of life. One of Napoleon's most profound insights is his concept of life as being in perpetual flux, and his attitude to the law code that was given his name in 1807 was no different. The Code was a response to the circumstances of contemporary society, its needs and its politics. If its framework was indeed meant to last, its content was not. As a response to changing times, Napoleon anticipated that its particular dispositions would also change.

The harmony praised by Portalis was not easily won, nor was it seamless, for the Code that emerged was eclectic in content.[74] Yet it had a guiding ethos, what Portalis called 'its general spirit'. However, this 'general spirit' derived more from the immediate political consensus that drove its creation than the disparate legal principles poured into it in the search for compromise. 'Unity', not just uniformity, formed the 'general spirit' of the Code, together with its secular view of the world. Portalis, a convinced Catholic, was prepared to declare on behalf of his colleagues, at the tribune of the nation, that 'the laws are made for man'. This was a seismic shift in how the world was now viewed, even by sincere believers. It marks the culmination of a process of gradual, almost unconscious secularisation of educated society that had been going on in the course of the eighteenth century in urban France. As David Bell has put it, the triumph of the 'creeping secularisation' of civilisation was under way,[75] if only in certain urban, well-read quarters. A reaction to this realisation was also well under way. Louis de Bonald and René de Chateaubriand, to say nothing of the Church itself, were already ranging themselves against the 'godless' Code. However, theirs was a reaction to the consensus of those who now held real power.

The Tribunate rejected the first draft of the Code, an act which marked it down for destruction by Napoleon – a vengeance eventually extracted when he abolished it in 1807 – but its negative reaction was based largely on the technical failings and imprecision it found in the draft, not on differences over theory or substance. In fact, the consensus around the major elements of the Code in the assemblies was considerable. Many of the real battles came in committee. When Napoleon and Cambacérès needed to counteract the more conservative views of Tronchet or Portalis, they brought in members of the Council of State with more revolutionary views, such as Berlier, who had been a member of the Jacobin Convention, while they could also use and then exclude men of genuinely radical views, notably Merlin de Douai, exploiting their opinions and expertise while keeping them out of the decision-making. The Code was the product of excellent expertise and extensive discussion, but controlled by Napoleon's authoritarianism.

Above all, the Code was meant to reflect what the French elites wanted. In this, it represents a more successful attempt to attune the regime to public opinion than its rigged plebiscites or propaganda. What emerged was a three-way 'transaction', which the committee saw coming. This is encapsulated by Jean-Louis Halpérin as a revolutionary element, based, first, on the sacred nature of property as the foundation of society, and the right of the citizen as an individual to enjoy it in peace, and reflected directly in its articles on contracts and property, which were based on Cambacérès' 1796 project. The second element was reactionary, looking back to the norms of the monarchy, which had been shaken by the legislation of 1792–3, and re-established the hierarchical, paternalist family, which royalist deputies had demanded since 1796–7, but which had also gained much support among prominent liberals, Benjamin Constant in particular, who applauded tighter controls of fathers over sons, 'as a way to make children more obedient', an interesting comment on where liberty stopped for even its most outspoken proponents.[76] Nevertheless, calls for a return to the full-blooded application of Roman law, which placed sons under the domination of their fathers for life, were resisted, and an age of majority of twenty-one was established, although it was set at twenty-five for marriage and the consent of both parents was needed. Under the Code, a precise hierarchy was established within the family, with the father its indisputable head, the mother in second place and all the children equally under them. Fathers could reserve up to a quarter of the family property for one child, but primogeniture and discrimination in favour of male over female heirs were abolished. It is, indeed, arguable that the family member who lost most by the provisions of the Code was not the wife, but the eldest son.

The transaction included a pragmatic compromise over the marriage and inheritance laws, which blended both traditional and revolutionary legislation, and the legal traditions of north and south.[77] Consensus was reached relatively easily over these issues, but family law proved one of the most difficult and controversial aspects of the work of the committee and the Council of State as a whole.

Divorce in particular proved a thorny problem and, while the stance of the Code on this issue is viewed as reactionary by contemporary lights, in the context of their times the measures adopted represent a compromise between extreme positions, based on a consensus that saw marriage in secular terms, as a civil, legal contract, something that was more important to any of the French Revolutionaries than the rights of women. Most of the legislators of the Consulate had grave reservations about divorce, but few were prepared to abandon the institution altogether, as this would have been regarded as too great a concession to the old order, even among the most conservative members of the committee who cherished 'family values'. Where a consensus arose, behind all the arguments over the position of women in the family and divorce, it stemmed from a shared Romantic sensibility. There was a general sense that something was rotten in the state of contemporary marriage. The problem was what to do about it. Portalis, who was not an enthusiast of innovation in social matters, to say the least, still adhered to the general view that there was a deep malaise in the institution of marriage that had been inherited from the old order, and that the Revolutionaries had been right to try to address it. He made quite open reference to a world in which many unhappy unions had been contracted, for mercenary reasons and with scant regard for the feelings of those involved, but he balanced this by affirming the view of many that the legislation of the 1790s had gone too far: 'if ... the centuries of ignorance are the theatre of abuses, the centuries of philosophy and enlightenment have only too often been the theatre of excess'. Liberal divorce laws played havoc with property and inheritance; they were easily manipulated by the extended family; they undermined the social order. Above all, the committee argued, marriage, if seen as a civil contract, should not be entered into lightly, but neither should it be reneged on at will.

However imbued with traditional Catholicism the personal opinions of men like Portalis may have been, he knew he could not speak in such terms and couched his discourse in firmly secular terms. Indeed, had he done otherwise he would not have carried Napoleon with him. The most politically radical of the revolutionaries of the 1790s, Robespierre and, especially, Saint-Just, had very traditional ideas about the place of women in a republican society, to put it mildly, and it is doubtful the liberal legislation on divorce or the property rights of married women would have survived long had they not been overthrown in 1794. This aspect of the reforms of 1792 had been argued over during the Directory, and the liberal views expressed by Cambacérès were far from popular. What emerged in the Civil Code was, indeed, a 'transaction' far more conservative than the increasingly disliked reforms of 1792, but far less retrograde than some of even the radical legislators wanted. Napoleonic divorce laws were still by far the most liberal in Europe, simply by the very fact of their existence. Divorce was abolished altogether, for any reason, by the restored monarchy in 1816.

It was in his opinions on the balance of these 'transactions' that Napoleon emerges as a leader who reflected public opinion, rather than as one determined to shape it, and herein lay the foundations of his success. He emerged as a radical revolutionary over property rights, their exercise, and their moral origins; as a reactionary over social matters, though not from a Catholic perspective; and as a mediator between the legal traditions of north and south, even though he had a marked personal preference for the tradition of written, Roman law. Napoleon continued the political balancing act between left and right that characterised his politics in these years, but, given his willingness to enter the most sensitive issues without hiding his views, it is reasonable to think that his opinions were genuine. An *ancien régime* practice abolished in 1792 called *rentes perpetuelles*, which was not actually linked to noble privilege because it could be enjoyed by any property holder, but resembled feudalism as a source of income, had caused the committee to hesitate, for many favoured its reintroduction. Here, Napoleon showed himself an outspoken enemy of the old order, and quashed all talk of the restoration of these rents in a forceful intervention.[78] Napoleon showed himself at his most reactionary over the question of the rights of illegitimate children to inheritance from their fathers. 'Society has no interest in recognising bastards.' Gone was the more sensitive term 'natural children',[79] yet in this he expressed the opinion of many families, shocked at the prospect of legitimate children being pushed aside over inheritance. Paradoxically, few men ever loved, acknowledged or provided better for their own 'bastards' than Napoleon, but this aspect of Revolutionary legislation had never been popular, and Napoleon shared the preoccupations of the mainstream.

There is much in the Code's provisions for the rights of wives and the treatment of illegitimate children that jars with the sensibilities of a later age, but by the more hard-nosed standards of the times, and for several generations to come, they represented a return to normalcy, influenced by the new experiences of the Revolutionary decade. If the conservative reform of divorce was a victory for husbands – over their in-laws, as much as their wives – then the exclusion of 'natural children', as they were still called, Napoleon's direct language notwithstanding, from the family inheritance was a victory for wives, who no longer had to fear that their children's share of the family property would be diluted because of their husbands' infidelities.

If Napoleon's strictly personal experience can be seen in any of his opinions, it was probably in the argument over divorce. He supported that wing of the committee which wanted to retain it, but on much more difficult grounds than had been possible in the 1790s, which had been in large part the work of Cambacérès. Napoleon sided with men of the Directory like Thibaudeau on the Council of State who sought to retain divorce by mutual consent, subject to stringent proof, and did so with more conviction than the now repentant Cambacérès. It took Napoleon six unyielding interventions to get the committee to find a compromise on this, and was a rare example of a determined challenge to the mainstream, which had come to fear this innovation on practical, as well as moral, grounds.[80] Napoleon also fought for a wider applicability of the *ancien régime* practice of 'bodily separation'. This measure had been the preserve of the Church before the Revolution, and forced violent men to live apart from their wives, usually under a form of curfew and at a regulated distance, but did not entail divorce. Napoleon now fought for its revival under the supervision of the police and courts. Joséphine had been saved from the cruelties of her first husband by such a measure.

Because the Council of State listened to the French as a living society, not as an ideal polity or a community of religious believers, the regime found a more permanent foundation than its shifting constitutions, so much so that the Code outlived it. The First Consul had his part to play in this process, but he was not the leader. Napoleon emerged from the seemingly endless sessions as something close to an 'everyman' of the French provincial propertied classes. By instinct and preference, and of course by manipulation, Napoleon steered the Code in the direction that most of his subjects wanted. It was, as it finally emerged, the charter of the hopes and aspirations on which the 'masses of granite' came to rest. His intuitive sense of what such people wanted from the law in their daily dealings was the most emphatic proof imaginable of the journey he had made into the mind of *la France profonde*, which marked something of a return to his roots in the Ajaccio elite, and an emphatic rejection of the primitive, rebellious Corsica of Paoli. It is tempting to say that the Clary household had begun a process that culminated in one of the most important documents of the age. Napoleon had steered his new, usurper regime towards a firm legal foundation. It endures to this day, but to Napoleon it was only a springboard.

No one hated Napoleon more that Germaine de Staël, but she had the measure of Napoleon at times better than anyone else:

This man, at bottom so impatient, has the faculty of remaining immoveable when necessary; he derives from the Italians who know how to restrain themselves in order to obtain the object of their passion, as if they were perfectly cool in the choice of the object.[81]

This was a time for youth. If the new prefects were older, the men who appointed them were not. If the men who were doing the fighting were beginning to age by the time of Marengo, their commanders were younger than those of 1792. The giants of the Revolution had all butchered each other; the old men of the old order had emigrated in horror and loathing. The field was left to the young. All the achievements of these years bore the mark of youthful energy. This was a whirlwind of thrusting reforms – it was the work of a young, energetic man in his very early thirties – and the Revolution had allowed this to happen. Only in France could such a person have seized power – much of the unique ability of the French Republic to use the peace dividend in so dynamic a way springs directly from Napoleon's very youth, allied to genius. It all stems from his own person, and that person could only have emerged from the chaos of the Revolution. Staël was but three years his senior, Chateaubriand only a year older. They embraced and then spurned his cause with the passion of the young, just as Napoleon drove himself and those around him with equal verve. The impatience and ambition Staël so brilliantly exposed stemmed mainly from Napoleon's age. His patience and self-discipline, the magnitude of which even Staël could not quite comprehend, were indeed characteristics of Mediterranean culture, but they had been refined in the viper's nest of revolutionary politics.

By 1804, the time of waiting was almost over. The object of passion, real power, was now close at hand for Napoleon. Only those as astute as Napoleon himself, like Staël, could see how close he was to taking it.

10

INTO THE BRIGHT SUN

Confidence and Reverses, 1802–1804

The new regime was not yet enjoying anything like ease and serenity, despite its administrative triumphs. As late as 1804, Napoleon's fear of royalist exiles led to the murder of d'Enghien and relations with the Church deteriorated rather than improved after the conclusion of the Concordat. Nevertheless, the Peace of Amiens bought Napoleon time and popularity, and he used it well.

It was now increasingly clear to friend and foe alike, and to all those still biding their time, that Napoleon was the master of the Republic, and that the Republic was being recast in an authoritarian mould. The hesitant could still 'rally' to him, without strings; the more confident could 'amalgamate' and take part in shaping his new state. All profited from stability. For those opposed to him, the years between the Peace of Amiens and the resumption of the general European war, in the last months of 1805, were a time to turn away. Carnot and Chateaubriand could only shrug – one with his left shoulder, the other with his right – and slink off; they had no 'sword' with which to challenge Napoleon now. He dealt with the plots against him with a ruthlessness born of insecurity, but he dealt with waverers with the confidence of one doing them a favour. He took the resumption of war with Britain in May 1803 almost in his stride, as he was no longer the unsteady head of a weakened body politic. There were now firm institutional foundations beneath the flux of politics. The time was now right to secure power still further, and in a more public, emphatic manner than seemed possible at Brumaire. He had been the real architect of his own security. New problems came with mastery, however: the future was unresolved, as he had no heir. The Republic still needed to assert its hegemony over western Europe. The threatened renewal of war hastened the need to rebuild the army. However, Napoleon could now handle these issues in his own way, and on his own terms. It was time to move.

WESTERN EUROPE:
THE CONTOURS OF A NEW EMPIRE EMERGE

Steven Englund has cleverly charted Napoleon's shifting political vocabulary during his rise to power. He has noted the gradual abandonment of the use of 'Republic' – the politically correct term of the Revolutionaries – and the parallel emergence of 'nation' in its place, while Napoleon was always judicious in invoking 'France', with its proprietorial connotations of the old monarchy. Englund astutely comments that Napoleon did not actively wish to jettison the Republic but sensed that it was a divisive, politically charged term that would hinder his attempts to rally the country to him and amalgamate its best and brightest to his regime.[1] This change of emphasis signified more than the reconciliation of political factions. It was embedded in the practical, more prosaic reforms of the Consulate: the educational reforms set out national standards for the first time; the land register was conceived of on a national scale; the regime continued the Revolutionaries' drive to establish the metric system as the norm for the whole of France; the new army Napoleon began forging after 1803 mingled men from different regions in the same units; conscription was meant to turn peasants into Frenchmen, the army to become 'the school of the nation'; the Gendarmerie was becoming an effective national police force. The list of policies designed to impose uniformity is as long as the Loire. Indeed, they stretched into the Rhineland, to Belgium, and over the Alps to Piedmont. This desire for uniformity was far from new – the French elites had enjoyed a linguistic unity rare in Europe – but now uniformity was geared directly to the needs of the new state, and driven forward with unprecedented determination.

Moreover the new regime sought inclusiveness not just in political terms but in cultural, legal, administrative and religious matters, encompassing toleration for Protestants and Jews. The busts of Turenne and Condé, the great Huguenot commanders of Louis XIV – the former a convert to Catholicism, the latter who chose his conscience above his king and country – stood side by side in the Tuileries of the First Consul,[2] an emphatic signal that religious discrimination and the imposition of confessional conformity would not happen again. The Napoleonic regime had a vision that sought to match the nation to the state, rather than to create a state that suited the people of the nation, but its inclusiveness and its drive for unity marked every step Napoleon took; Napoleon forged a template for French society which it had to conform to.

Yet Napoleon was far from well travelled in the country he had so doggedly sought to master. His meteoric rise had taken him around much of northern and central Italy, and as far afield as Egypt and Syria, but his direct experience of France itself was confined to something of a 'rabbit run' between Paris and Provence, via the Rhône–Saône corridor, and he did not like most of what he saw. Paris was familiar, but it was full of dangers: to the east lay the latent mob, to the west the well-heeled suburbs where he had made his first bloody mark. Its better-heeled districts were a snakepit of snobbery. Provence and the Rhône were little more than extensions of the Corsica he had come to loathe, hotbeds of hotter heads, of superstition, counter-revolution and a vendetta culture that was a nightmare made real for him. The Saône was calmer, but a cultural wasteland of dull garrison towns, hardly the nursery of a great people.

Now, however, as First Consul, Napoleon actually began to explore the country he called his own. Lyon had long been merely Napoleon's main halt on the rabbit run, but he visited it for two weeks early in 1802. His main purpose was to re-found and consolidate the Italian Republic, but his stay gave him the opportunity to talk with its civic leaders and assess its complex economy. He had little success with its clergy, but, while he was there, he began the successful process of winning back the loyalty of the second city of France: 'I have some reason to be very satisfied by the proofs of loyalty the Lyonnais have shown me, and by the progress I can see in all the owners, and in all the workshops, to revive this, the major manufacturing centre of the Republic.'[3]

These brief words conceal a deeper story. Lyon had fallen very foul of the Jacobin Republic, despite its own staunch republican leanings; it had become the centre of the Federalist Revolt of 1793–4; it held out longer than Toulon. When it finally fell to the government, the Parisian commanders, Collot d'Herbois and Fouché, set about systematically levelling the city and ordering the mass killing of thousands of people. During the siege, the Lyonnais republicans had made common cause with local royalists, which stained them in the eyes of many prominent politicians under the Directory, long after the fall of Robespierre. It was during the Directory that the refractory clergy began to make real ground in the city.

Napoleon set about reversing this trend during his years in power. He achieved this at the expense of the Italian Republic. Lyon's wealth was largely based on textiles, a fragile industry subject to 'boom-and-bust' cycles that led many royal *intendants* actually to fear it, but Napoleon instituted a policy of economic colonialism in his Italian domains specifically for Lyon's benefit. In a return to mercantilism on an imperial scale, he ruthlessly ran down the silk manufacturing industry in northern Italy, and gave Lyon the monopoly on the manufacture of silk goods, while ensuring that the raw silk produced in Italy reached it at preferential prices. In the Hundred Days of 1815, Lyon was one of his bastions of support, and when his Italian kingdom disappeared after his fall – and with it, cheap silk – the city soon became a dangerous thorn in the side of the restored monarchy, the scene of several bloody revolts in the 1830s and 1840s.

Napoleon visited Normandy in the autumn of 1802, and his curiosity is palpable in his first impressions, as is his clear sense of himself as something of a tourist. 'The Normans do not seem to me at all as Citizen Lebrun told me [they were] ... I still do not know the Norman departments, and I have taken the greatest pleasure in travelling around this rich and fertile country.'[4] What Lebrun told Napoleon about his compatriots is not known, but despite the awkward reception he got from the clergy of Rouen and his wariness about the proximity of rebels on its western limits, Napoleon obviously liked this green, rich, advanced region. This was in utter contrast to his loathing for Provence and the southern Rhône. In the same letter, he remarked on the good state of Norman manufacturing 'These departments appear extremely agreeable,' he remarked to the Minister of the Treasury the next day.[5] These impressions remained. Napoleon was learning where his true constituency lay, in a northern, prosperous France of commercial agriculture, industry and intense local commerce, a France that was not a hotbed of Jacobinism, and whose royalist elements chose not to vaunt their opposition by taking to the *bocage*. He was beginning to see this with his own sharp eyes.

In the years ahead, as Gavin Daly has shown in his local study of Rouen, departments like Seine Inférieure became the kinds of places where things worked as they were meant to: where the prefect and the ordinary civil administration could, indeed, dominate local government without the constant need for military commissions to keep unrest at bay with their flying columns; where conscription was enforced without the risk of rebellion; and where, despite the later ravages of the economic blockade of the Channel coast, the propertied classes remained essentially loyal.[6] The regime had gained widespread support here, the economic privations of the last years notwithstanding.[7]

The characteristics he found so agreeable in Normandy were absent from the west and the Midi, including highland Corsica, but he soon detected them in western Germany, as he had already in parts of northern Italy, as well as in the Belgian departments. His dealings with the German princes and the Swiss cantons came much more easily to him, and achieved much more success than his relations with the people of much of France itself. The contours of the heartland of his state – as distinct from the French nation his policies were originally meant to weld together – were emerging.

If eastern Normandy epitomised Napoleon's preferred template for his own country, his enduring settlement of Switzerland (known as the Helvetic Republic after 1797) shows how *amalgame* of the elites was supposed to complement his wider, European goals. In the late 1790s, the Swiss cantons were anything but the havens of peace and prosperity with which they later became synonymous, for the Revolutionary wars between 1797 and 1800 had turned them into one of the most intensely fought-over parts of Europe. As a result, their economic life was disrupted, their resources ravaged by the demands of the armies, and, above all, political and social tensions long latent in their communities spilled over into open conflict, which crystallised around competing views of the reforms of the French Revolution and whether it was worth imitating them.

In Switzerland, these divisions concerned not just the adoption of French concepts of civil liberty but also whether the country should remain a loose confederation of largely independent cantons or adopt French centralism. Conservative elements, determined to preserve the traditional order of privileges – which were particular to each canton – coalesced around the retention of local autonomy. These were the Federalists, while social and economic reformers – the Unitarists – looked to the French model of 'one nation' and an all-powerful central government. French occupation led to the momentary triumph of the Unitarists in 1797, and the creation of a sister republic, Helvetica, with a constitution closely modelled on that of the Directory. Their control was always fragile, and all but collapsed during the Allied advances of 1799, but Masséna's victory at Zurich in September 1799 restored the Unitarists to a precarious authority. Napoleon withdrew his troops under the terms of Lunéville, but he gave the Swiss a constitution a few months later, at the request of both factions, in January 1802. Its attempt to balance federalism with the essence of the French reforms failed.

Without the presence of French troops, there were four coups within a year, and the republic was on the verge of civil war when Napoleon intervened for a second time, late in 1802. He called seventy delegates, drawn from both sides, to Paris. The result was the 1803 Act of Mediation, which gave the Helvetic Republic a period of complete peace until the fall of the Empire, and reveals Napoleon's thoughts on the politics of reconciliation. The failure of the first constitution – called the Malmaison Constitution, for the residence where it was drawn up – led Napoleon to reject the idea of trying to get opponents to work together directly. However, he did not then proceed to impose a neo-French solution on the country from above. Rather, experience and consultation had proved to Napoleon that the cantons were the natural unit of the Swiss polity; no settlement could survive save on that basis. Nevertheless, the implosion of *amalgame* did not necessarily spell the impossibility of *ralliement*, and Napoleon's astute – and quite cynical – insight in these circumstances was to separate the two. The Unitarists were neither strong enough to impose their will nor to maintain Napoleon's original compromise, so he turned to the Federalists, the traditional elites, in the sure knowledge that the Unitarists would have to acquiesce when their rivals rallied to him, as they had no other source of support than the French.[8] Napoleon could do this to an extent not possible elsewhere, because the Swiss conservatives were as isolated, diplomatically, as the pro-French reformers. The allies had shown no real interest in them, in sharp contrast to the Italian states, where the Habsburgs continued to hold out the prospect of restoration, or in the Batavian Republic, where the British were actively committed to the restoration of the House of Orange, or even in France itself, where the British continued to try to stir up the Vendée and the Bourbons could always claim that allied victory would culminate in their return.

These conditions allowed Napoleon to hand over control of the Helvetic Republic to the sort of conservative elements he distrusted collaboration with elsewhere, but felt confident of in Switzerland. The old elites regained office in most of the nineteen cantons, in return for agreeing to supply Napoleon with a considerable number of troops – which they found almost impossible to do – and funds. Internally, each canton went its own way; many saw the reinstatement of harsh *ancien régime* penal laws, and concerted attempts to thwart the abolition of feudal privileges which had been abolished after 1797. However, several cantons also chose to pursue reforms in their own way, blending their own ideas with French influences. Napoleon did insist on one thing, however: equality before the law was maintained, although he was less successful in persuading the Swiss to retain religious toleration.

From his own point of view, however, the Act of Mediation was a success for being a rare exercise in pragmatism. The cantons were weak and divided, just as their equivalent of the 'masses of granite' were bereft of foreign support; it was safe to cede local power to reactionary patricians, who, in their turn, had no choice but to give Napoleon what he needed from them. In these circumstances, he was able to secure this strategically important region without the need to rule it directly. 'Tell the Swiss often that they must forget all their hatreds, calm their passions,' he told Luis d'Affray, a patrician of Fribourg whom Napoleon appointed his deputy in the Confederation after the conclusion of the Mediation.[9] The Act of Mediation was a fine achievement, all the more so as its essence survived his fall in 1814, despite the best efforts of many Swiss patricians to put the clock back. Napoleon genuinely deserved the title he appropriated to himself, 'Mediator of the Swiss Confederation'.

Napoleon had developed a respect, and an affinity – hardly natural – with the stern Protestant urban patricians who moved swiftly to reimpose the Calvinist Sunday in many places.[10] His Minister of Justice, Régnier, was an Alsatian Lutheran, as was Roederer, one of his right-hand men from the outset; the Concordat had turned its back on exactly those aspects of Catholicism most despised by Protestants. Napoleon was drawn to cold rationality, and so to the ethos of self-discipline of these Calvinist communities and the highly literate culture fostered by their official religion. In northern Italy, Switzerland, among the princes of western and southern Germany, and in north-eastern France, Napoleon was finding his natural power base. Switzerland would always be a safer haven than the Vendée; Lyon would always be more 'his' city than Paris. The Italian constitution reflected his hopes more than any other. 'Citizens,' he told the councils of Berne in June 1803, 'I have seen with great pleasure that your new arrangement is working in calmness ... The durability of the well-being you now enjoy depends on your loyal adherence to the Laws, and to the spirit of concord which you have created, to forget the divisions of the past.'[11] In this instance his smugness was justified.

The letter to the leaders of Berne, written from Amiens, ten weeks after the peace forged there with Britain had broken down, is a poignant indication of where and with whom Napoleon could work, and where and with whom he manifestly could not. Those he found impossible emphatically included the British, but it stretched to a great many southern Europeans as well. Napoleon had developed an ever-widening dislike of his Mediterranean subjects that went far beyond his atavistic loathing of the 'Mountain'. It came most revealingly in outbursts over relatively small matters. His early-acquired distaste for the Lombard nobility exploded in a letter to Murat, the French commander-in-chief in Italy at the time. 'In the country you find yourself in, you must ... reunite all the patriots', the 'Italian Jacobins', who alone could really be trusted. Napoleon vented deeper loathings, however, for Italian elite sociability, in a revealing choice of words. When faced with a request to allow casinos to reopen – gambling houses preferred by the aristocracy – he exploded in the same letter to Murat, 'casinos are institutions which harm many people, and which are not at all the French way'. It was private balconies at the opera that most incensed him, however, heightened by Murat's toleration of such things:

It is not acceptable, either, that the balconies you use at performances carry any exterior decoration [a coat of arms]. The character of Italians is one of intrigue and lies: you have not taken your guard enough against this ... I have already been very discomfited in seeing you drawn into this petty, small town bickering ... You must not mix, not go to dinner, nor dancing, anywhere, except ... [officials] of the Republic who have a private house.[12]

This was the zeal of the convert. Gambling was not the French way, nor was the Italian obsession with outward show. As full of contradictions as Napoleon's prejudices might be, they were very real. He was more charitable to the Corsicans of the interior, a sign, perhaps, that he had mellowed about his own expulsion at their hands. He told his military commander there that 'The Corsican is difficult, but he is basically all right. Talk to them patiently and listen to what they say; but be a bit severe in carrying out your duties.'[13] Geographic lines, based on culture, were taking shape in the mind of an increasingly powerful leader. The Mediterranean world of petty vendettas, superstition and baroque intrigue was foul; the Atlantic world of commerce and parliamentary 'talking shops' was perfidious. Napoleon at least had an ever-tightening grip on the former, but the latter was a powerful threat.

THE BRITISH: A DIALOGUE OF THE DEAF

The Peace of Amiens was very effective in many ways. However, the accords at Amiens failed to settle what mattered most, the conflict between Britain and France. There was a practical reason for this, rooted in a realpolitik stretching back over a century, and the more immediate, highly subjective inability of the two governments to understand each other in 1801. Napoleon had no real comprehension of the twin pillars of Britain: its commercial economy, based on free trade and industry, was anathema to his innate mercantilism, already clear in his 'squaring' of Lyon by awarding it a monopoly of the silk industry, and he was exasperated by its parliamentary system of government, a point that need not be laboured. Nor could the British grasp the nature of the new Napoleonic regime. France was the old enemy for Britain, whether under the Bourbons or the Revolutionary Republic, but Napoleon's presence at its head added an unfamiliar uncertainty to the old enmity. Stuart Semmel has put it well, digging into the British press of the time to find how often Napoleon was regarded with puzzlement, that he had

... broken free from historical models; he defied classification ... From an early point, Napoleon was seen as 'an unclassifiable being', a slippery, enigmatic figure who did not fit ... The mixed signals he sent made it more difficult to treat France as a simple antithesis of Britain ... Napoleon became as 'shadowy, undefinable and terrific' as Milton's Satan.[14]

The British grasped the difference between Napoleon and the republican regimes on one level, in that they sensed his mixture of republican and authoritarian tendencies, but this only served to frighten them. Some visitors to Paris during the brief window of peace felt relief at a return to a semblance to pre-1789 normalcy, but those in power were grappling with what they correctly perceived as the unknown. No other European political culture reacted to the Consulate with such insight, but it was an awareness that poisoned, rather than appeased, relations.

The analogy with Milton's Satan is as apt as it is potent. Napoleon was, indeed, a self-made man in British eyes, but he had risen through the army and he did not behave like a parvenu, although he was one. He was Cromwell devoid of a Calvinist conscience or any lingering sense of awe for the institutions he had inherited. For the Habsburgs and Romanovs, as for Pius VII, he was nothing but another phase of the Revolution, and from their perspective they were right. Yet, in the complex world of British politics, Napoleon's increasing authoritarianism did not go unremarked, to the extent that it lost him the admiration of that part of the parliamentary establishment, the Foxite Whigs grouped around the Holland House circle, who turned on him as a betrayer of liberty, thus broadening the base of the 'war party' as never before. Napoleon would pay for this later, in 1808–9, when the Holland House clique played a vital role in mobilising British opinion for the anti-French resistance in Spain.[15] The British sensed the differences and complexities of the new leader, but could not fathom them.

The gutter press, led by Gillray's cartoons, had mocked 'the upstart' from the outset, but as of Amiens, the ludicrous little cuckold in the silly hat had had the last laugh. The general consensus in the British corridors of power was that the 'Corsican corporal' had bested them at the conference table. The British had at least expected to force the

French into a lopsided trade agreement, as they had at the end of the American Revolution, but found Napoleon prepared to put up tariff walls against British goods. For his part, Napoleon did not know what to do about a nation of revolving governments, changing leaders or a set of economic interests which seemed to depend on permanent expansion and insatiable expectations in every corner of the globe. Nor could he hope to challenge their naval might, any more than the British could fight him on land, without the aid of other powers.

All this was compounded by the long-standing rivalry between them in the wider world, which both Napoleon and the British government under Addington had inherited, and sought, in vain, not to reignite. Napoleon's was actually the first French regime for a century the British did not really have to fear in either India or the New World, certainly not in his first years in power. A long instruction to Admiral Decrès, his Minister for the Navy and the Colonies, early in 1803, shows how overwrought Napoleon's feelings were about the British, but how very realistic were his actual intentions in India. Napoleon ordered a senior officer to go to the remaining French enclaves in India, to prepare for the eventuality of war with Britain. However, he stressed that this operation was to be a tactical withdrawal, because, 'it is essential to work on the hypothesis that we will not be masters of the seas, and that we can count on very little support'. The policy was anything but aggressive, yet Napoleon still lashed out at the British, in the belief that they were hated by the Indian princes 'who tolerate impatiently the English yoke ... They are the tyrants of the Indies, they are restless and jealous ...'[16] The choice of words says much in little; they are rooted in Raynal's vision of imperial exploitation.

For Napoleon, jealousy and insatiable restlessness marked the British character and dictated their policy. They were odious, but, more important, they would never stay still. Just as many historians see in Napoleon the leader who had to feed on war and expansion, so Napoleon thought that British capitalism could also lead only to expansion and exploitation at someone else's expense. The 'Atlantic world' of commerce and colonies was the Devil's whirlpool to

Napoleon. His actual policies show him recoiling from it, as far as French business interests allowed him to.

THE GRAVEYARD OF THE NEW WORLD:
THE END OF AN EMPIRE

Some of those business interests, however – those of the great merchants of the Atlantic ports and the Parisian financiers who backed them – led Napoleon into the most disastrous military and political fiasco of his career before the Russian campaign of 1812. It was time to 'call in' the favour advanced by the financiers at Brumaire, but it proved a costly debt. As calamitous as his Egyptian expedition had been, he had at least been able to negotiate something like an orderly withdrawal of the remnants of his army in the course of the Amiens conferences. His attempts to reassert French control over the valuable Caribbean colony of Saint-Domingue ended in the most emphatic failure of the Consulate, something Napoleon himself admitted when he was finally exiled on St Helena. He confessed to Gourgaud, one of his aides:

The business of Saint-Domingue was a great stupidity on my part . . . It was probably the greatest error of judgement I ever committed in administration. I should have dealt with the black leaders as I would provincial authorities, appointed the black officers as commanders of their own regiments, left Toussaint l'Ouverture as viceroy, not sent out any troops, left the blacks in charge, with only a handful of white advisers, a treasury official, perhaps, and I should have encouraged them to marry black wives. That way, with the blacks not seeing any whites set over them, [they] would have come to trust my system. The colony would have proclaimed the slaves free.[17]

Perversely, Napoleon was perhaps somewhat hard on himself in this assessment. Hindsight is one thing, but Toussaint was playing a triple game of diplomacy with the British and Americans, as well as the French, and Napoleon had first to think of preserving by far the most valuable colony in the French Empire, the island most productive of sugar and coffee in the whole Caribbean.

The Consulate inherited anarchy on Saint-Domingue. It had been triggered by the sudden abolition of slavery in the French colonies by the Jacobin National Convention in 1794. This led to intense unrest on Saint-Domingue, and in the other, smaller French islands of Guadeloupe and Martinique, which fell to the British for a time. Saint-Domingue was evacuated sooner by the British, but it was plunged into a very complex series of civil wars which, although they had begun as slave revolts aimed at pressurising the plantation owners to enforce abolition, evolved into power struggles between factions in which race played a key role but was not the essential point.

By 1799, two warlords had emerged as the most powerful men in the colony. Toussaint l'Ouverture was a former slave of African origin, who commanded the north of the island, supported by a large, formidable army that was mainly black, although his elite troops, the mulattoes, were mixed race. By the time of Brumaire, Toussaint had acquired the grudging support of most of the white minority, both French and the Creoles (whites born in the Caribbean). His rival and erstwhile ally in the early days of the revolt was André Rigaud, whose power base was in the south, and whose mulatto officers had been quick to seize the plantations of fleeing whites and install themselves as slave owners; many of Toussaint's black commanders had done the same in the north.[18] As the most accomplished historian of the Haitian revolt, Laurent Dubois, has put it, 'While free-coloureds [mulattoes] made up a larger part of the ruling class in the south, their interests were not substantially different from those of the new ruling class of black property owners that had emerged in the north and west.'[19] That common interest was in getting the agricultural and commercial life of Saint-Domingue back to normal, which meant retaining the plantation system, with its labour force of black field workers. If no longer technically slaves, they were increasingly oppressed by Toussaint's series of ferocious decrees tying them to the land. Dubois has termed these decrees 'a status based on a past of enslavement ... rendered immutable and permanent' on the same plantations on which they had always toiled.[20] To the white population, Toussaint may have been the lesser of two evils, in that he offered them protection from both Rigaud and his own men, but their valuable estates and incomes were lost.

The Creoles had their supporters in Paris: Cambacérès, who had commercial interests in Haiti; and Talleyrand, who, having once favoured emancipation, now pressed for the wholesale restoration of slavery to appease the British and Americans. Joséphine, if hardly a direct influence on her husband, had deep-seated reasons to oppose any appeasement of the rebels, or to support anything short of the reimposition of slavery and, in this unique case, she could offer Napoleon local knowledge. Talleyrand, with the help of Joséphine, eventually foisted on Napoleon one of the worst advisers he ever employed, Médéric-Louis-Élie Moreau de Saint-Méry, a distant relative of Joséphine, whose family had lived on Martinique since the seventeenth century and who, as a deputy for his island to the Revolutionary assembly, had stridently opposed the abolition of slavery. (Moreau went on to become the French administrator charged with incorporating the Duchy of Parma-Piacenza into the Empire, where he failed to foresee or control a serious peasant revolt his policies had provoked. Napoleon had to turn to Lebrun – then in Genoa – Junot and Radet, old and able collaborators, to clean up his mess. Moreau then disappeared from public life, and died in relative poverty in 1819.)

At the outset, Napoleon resisted these pro-Creole counsels, and was coming to see the new class of black and mulatto plantation owners as something akin to tropical equivalents of the 'masses of granite'. In August 1800, he said in the intimacy of the Council of State:

It is not a question of knowing whether it is a good thing to abolish slavery ... I am convinced that the island would fall to the English, if the Negroes were not attached to us, in the interest of keeping their freedom. They will not make as much sugar [as under slavery], perhaps; but it will be ours, and they will be our soldiers, if there is need. If we have one sugar refinery less, we will have a fortress occupied by friendly soldiers ...[21]

At this stage, Napoleon's concern was to secure the island, and he saw Toussaint as the best person to do this. It was very pragmatic, and in the same session he advocated the exact opposite in the French colonies in the Indian Ocean. Here, where the abolition of slavery had never been enforced, he authorised its confirmation. It was the status quo that mattered to him in the colonies. Napoleon wrote encouragingly to Toussaint, and promoted him Captain-General and the Republic's commander-in-chief on Saint-Domingue. This was an act in accordance with the policy of *amalgame*, in that Toussaint had been playing off British and French interests very effectively up to this point, and had enticed American merchants back by his restoration of order. Toussaint was no different from any of Napoleon's less trustworthy generals at this stage, save only that he was being bought off in more lavish fashion.

Things did not stay this way for long, however. Three critical factors turned the relationship between Napoleon and Toussaint – who openly cited the First Consul as a mentor – into war. The first was Toussaint's suspicion that the French would, indeed, reimpose slavery on Saint-Domingue if they could: they had allowed the local commanders to do this when they reoccupied Martinique and Guadeloupe under the terms of Amiens, and Napoleon had couched his proposed approach to French rule on Saint-Domingue in terms of 'particular laws' adapted to local 'customs, climate and interests'. Napoleon was at pains to reassure Toussaint that this equated not to slavery but to his own policies. In Toussaint's eyes the risks were obvious.

The second circumstance was born largely of Toussaint's own ambition. In 1795, the French had acquired the eastern part of the island – now the Dominican Republic – from the Spanish. They had been unable to assert any real authority there, while the British controlled the seas and the war continued, and so had left the Spanish administration, and thus slavery, intact. Toussaint showed himself all too ready to march eastwards, partly because the region was providing a safe haven for his enemies. Rigaud had fled there in 1800, when he did not believe Toussaint's amnesty worth the paper it was written on. Toussaint, however, also had the thirst for expansion attributed to his French mentor. In December 1800, he crossed the border and soon controlled the whole island. He did not abolish slavery, however, and showed himself as much an apostle of 'gradualism' – outside his own power base – as Moreau de Saint-Méry. In orders that arrived too late, Napoleon had made it very clear that 'an army of Negroes' was not to cross the old border. Ironically, Napoleon's further orders, that the white landowners in the Spanish sector were to be left in peace, corresponded exactly with Toussaint's intentions.[22]

The next year, to consolidate his position and reassure the people of Saint-Domingue that he would not re-establish slavery, Toussaint called a 'constituent assembly' which drew up a French-style constitution and, anticipating Napoleon by a year, declared himself 'Governor for Life'. This tested the limits of Napoleon's exercise in pragmatism and his indulgence of Toussaint, who had, to his credit in Paris, restored coffee and sugar production through his ruthless militarisation of the plantations. The constitution was too much of a deviation from Napoleon's fundamental approach to ruling Saint-Domingue, however. The First Consul insisted that the key decisions were always taken by Paris, not locally; the concessions as to which local 'customs, practices and habits' were to be admitted were not for the locals to decide. Napoleon intended to hold the ring between the newly freed blacks and mulatto elites, and the white colonists. He was deaf to the demands the whites had been making since 1789 for devolution. If their position was to be restored, it was to be on his terms, not theirs. Toussaint could be his viceroy, but he could not be allowed to aspire to the status of Napoleon himself in, say, his Italian 'fief'. The invasion of the east of the island, followed by the promulgation of his own constitution, led Napoleon to see Toussaint as too independent; this was blatant disobedience. There was also an element of misinformation, in that Napoleon had received reports – exaggerated at best – that Toussaint was threatening the white landowners on the 'Spanish' side of the island.

The Peace of Amiens was now secured, and, after having won British agreement, Napoleon intervened on Saint-Domingue. Toussaint was cashiered from the army and stripped of his position. He was behaving as had Napoleon himself in Italy five years before, and the

First Consul was having none of it. Napoleon, not unlike Toussaint, had been playing a double game up to now. On the one hand, he had been trying to work through the man who held undeniable power on Saint-Domingue and had used it in French interests. In October 1801, after all, Toussaint had brutally repressed black popular risings in the north, to protect the white plantation owners on whom the economy still depended in the area, hardly a 'dangerous' action for Parisian interests.[23] Meanwhile, Napoleon was still also trying to appease the traditional colonial financial and commercial interests to whom he was beholden. Now, he swung sharply towards them.

A fleet of more than fifty vessels was amassed in the western ports and, an obvious benefit of the peace, a force of 20,000 experienced troops was put under Napoleon's brother-in-law, Victor Leclerc, who had married Pauline in 1797. It was to be the vanguard for a projected army of 80,000. Napoleon still hoped Toussaint would work with him, rather than oppose this force, but he was quickly disabused of this. Jacques Norvins de Montbreton was one of the regime's most devoted imperial civil servants, and the author of the first life of Napoleon, a work of unashamed hagiography. He served in Leclerc's expedition, and he made it very clear in his memoirs that Napoleon was wrong to send out Leclerc, for Toussaint had offered an amnesty to the white planters who had fled to France, where many were harassed by the Revolutionaries before Brumaire; that Toussaint was an able leader, who would have been a loyal viceroy; and that Napoleon had failed to 'examine the wider sense':

If someone still asked me today if the First Consul should have ordered the expedition . . . I would reply no, a thousand times, no . . . [I]nstead of a fleet of fifty-four vessels carrying 20,000 troops . . . one frigate carrying an aide-de-camp with a letter or a decree from the First Consul . . . would have been enough to assure the relationship between the metropole and that great colony . . . Recognising Toussaint in his powers, and confirming him as governor for life, would have saved France.[24]

Napoleon came to agree with him. 'I reproach myself . . . It was a mistake to have wanted to subjugate it by force; I should have contented myself by ruling through Toussaint as an intermediary.'[25] Even so, perhaps because he saw something of himself in Toussaint, Napoleon may have been wise to try to stop him.

Napoleon's political strategy was very clear in his orders to Leclerc: divide and rule. A strong French presence was to be the tool that would rally the various factions to France; Leclerc was to present himself as an ally and protector and so help create an alternative local leadership to Toussaint. He was to rally the mulattoes, especially Rigaud's former supporters in the south; he was to appeal to the fears about Toussaint on the Spanish side of the island; the black small farmers, who had been thwarted by Toussaint's support for the plantation system, were also to be approached. While all black officers loyal to Toussaint were to be arrested and deported to France, to cut off the head of the revolt, any who rallied to Leclerc and Napoleon were to be regarded as the core of the new government.[26] This was still very much at odds with the pro-slavery lobby now entrenched in the Colonial Ministry, but it did not stop Napoleon presenting the expedition to the British and Americans – and to Thomas Jefferson, especially – in utterly different terms, as a thinly disguised racist crusade to save the world from black anarchy. Jefferson had made public his fears that an independent black Saint-Domingue could become 'the Algiers of the Americas' given to 'predatory expeditions against us'.[27]

The window of peace provided by Amiens was all that allowed Leclerc's fleet to sail in the first place, but Napoleon would not have secured such ready British support had he not been able to convince them that Jefferson, the new American President, was already behind him, driven almost to hysteria at the prospect of an independent black state on his doorstep. As a Southern slave owner, more than as Vice-President, Jefferson had been obsessed by events in Saint-Domingue from the outset, telling a friend in 1797 that 'only a single spark is wanting' to see the rebellion spread to the mainland, in which case 'we shall be the murderers of our own children'.[28] His support for the reassertion of French control, as well as his fears of race war at home, were heightened by the discovery of a very serious conspiracy for a large-scale slave revolt in Virginia itself – the Gabriel Conspiracy – in 1800, which had links to Saint-Domingue.

When he took office as President, in January 1801, this was his cast of mind – to starve out Toussaint and see French rule re-established. As one historian has put it, 'The menace of contagious rebellion . . . never left his mind.'[29] Jefferson often struggled with his conscience over the issue of slavery, but he was quite brilliant at overcoming its promptings. Pro-slavery declarations, Jefferson's long-standing francophilia, and his stated policy of supporting the French in the Caribbean to foster a balance of power with the British, all led Napoleon to conclude he could count on Jefferson for practical assistance in supplying Leclerc as well as diplomatic support. It was bolstered by the $150,000 the President authorised to help equip Leclerc.[30]

Jefferson would soon change his mind when he saw the size of Leclerc's expedition. In April 1802, James Madison, the American Secretary of State, asked the French ambassador, to the latter's surprise, to explain why the fleet was so large.[31] Jefferson now began to worry that Napoleon had wider ambitions in the New World, and that he might actually turn out to be an emancipator; that he would appease the blacks if they switched sides and create a black army to use against America. His fears were well grounded on both counts, but by then Leclerc had sailed. Indeed, Jefferson was increasingly convinced the French could not win, and that it would backfire on them.[32] He was not alone. Even before it sailed, Leclerc's expedition aroused fear in the American South, as news spread of Napoleon's offer of high office to Toussaint, and of commissions for his black officers.[33]

Napoleon and Leclerc still hoped they would not have to fight Toussaint; he had expressed his loyalty to the Republic, even as he had defied it, and this lingering hope of an agreeable submission was reflected in Leclerc's tactics. He planned a series of small landings, thus forcing Toussaint to fight on several fronts at once, and allowing the French the hope of getting at least some troops ashore without serious opposition. Leclerc planned a landing of the main force, led by himself, at Cap-Français on the northern coast, on 29 January

1802. It proved a rude awakening: Toussaint had dispatched one of his ablest and most ruthless lieutenants, Christophe, to the region and he fought Leclerc off. The French had to land in a very difficult jungle area further west. Toussaint's intentions were now all too clear. Leclerc's multiple landings worked, however, and all the major coastal centres fell to the expedition in a matter of weeks. What followed was a much harder lesson for the French, however. Toussaint simply pulled back into the rugged, mountainous interior and the real war, a vicious guerrilla conflict, now began in earnest. On 17 February 1802, Leclerc finally declared Toussaint an outlaw, and he proceeded to live up to his new station in life. Ambushes accompanied by horrific torture and mutilations hounded the French; Toussaint initiated a scorched-earth policy, depriving the large French forces of much-needed supplies; the greatest enemy of any European intruder in the tropics – yellow fever – came to his aid in force, killing 2,000 men, one-tenth of the French army, by May. Nevertheless, Leclerc's troops prevailed through sheer force of numbers. Toussaint was forced to surrender on 6 May 1802. Napoleon offered him a comfortable retirement, but – in an almost eerie foretelling of his own behaviour in 1815 – Toussaint soon began to plot a new attempt on power and was arrested and deported to France, where he died in prison, cold and ill, the next year.

This was far from the end. The revolt was deeply rooted and powerfully motivated by a desire to escape slavery; it was bigger than one man. Toussaint's former lieutenants and allies continued the guerrilla war. Nor was there safety behind the lines for the French. Napoleon had not understood the way the black population had been changed by the events of the 1790s. They had experienced a short period of real freedom and, more importantly, many had grasped that, however brutal Toussaint's plantation regulations were, they were not as bad as slavery. Perhaps Napoleon's greatest error was to permit the re-establishment of slavery on neighbouring Martinique – Joséphine's homeland – and Guadeloupe. This had been the work of the French commanders, supported by the white elites; it was not ordered by Napoleon, but he accepted it, and the repercussions on Saint-

Domingue were catastrophic. He had failed to understand that the black majority there would assume their turn would come. Norvins recounted the culmination of all this, in the rising in the cities, by the supposedly pacified urban populations, of 13 September 1802:

[T]he general insurrection had been planned for a month . . . and had been definitively set for that day; all the blacks, men and women, all the street vendors who had been so welcoming . . . everyone, without exception of age or sex, all of them knew. However, thanks to the most extraordinary, fanatical loyalty, none of them, even the children, would ever have given away their bloody conspiracy, even under pain of death . . . It was all only a bloody truce, and I am a living witness to it.[34]

Norvins' account had earlier marvelled at Toussaint's ability to hold together the three ethnic groups on the island, for even some whites had seen him as a better protector than the French. Rigaud had returned to an uneasy alliance with him, the exact reverse of Napoleon's calculations. Now, after his demise, the fruits of Toussaint's own capacity for rallying people to him were realised.

Resistance was hardened by changes in the French command. Leclerc died of yellow fever in November, having weathered the September revolt, and his successor, Rochambeau, proved a brutal and blunt instrument. Rochambeau behaved with a cruelty at least equal to that of the rebels, using specially trained dogs to hunt them, and applying ghastly methods of torture to prisoners. By the spring of 1803, he held only a small part of the island, and had been abandoned by most of the whites. With the renewal of war with Britain, Rochambeau was cut off from all hope of reinforcement from France. He surrendered to the British in November.

Although the French still held the Spanish part of the island, there was nothing they could do to prevent the independence of their own colony, which became an 'empire' under one of Toussaint's commanders, Jean-Jacques Dessalines, a former slave born in Africa, now Emperor Jacques I. The warlords soon fell out, and a series of bloody internal revolts followed between 1803 and 1806, but Napoleon was no longer in a position to exploit them. When he went to war with Spain in 1808, the Spanish colonies in the Caribbean ceased to be safe havens for the remaining French troops in the region. Napoleon had to stand by helplessly as the British seized Martinique in 1809 and Guadeloupe in 1810, the year he divorced Joséphine.

Not even the admiring Norvins denied the scale of the blunder. More and more troops had been poured in to help Leclerc, until over 50,000 French men and women had perished in Saint-Domingue, 45,000 of them from disease. Norvins compared the ravages of the tropics to those of the Russian snows in 1812.[35] Among the dead were some of the best veterans of the wars of the 1790s, for most of Leclerc's troops had been drawn from the Army of the Sambre-et-Meuse, which had borne the brunt of Revolutionary wars under Hoche and Moreau. France's only truly valuable colony had been lost for ever.

What later became known as the Haitian Revolution also raises several important questions about Napoleon himself. The most obvious is that of racism. The key to his thinking is to make a clear distinction between racism and slavery. Napoleon showed a general indifference to slavery, per se: he made it his policy to leave it in place in the French colonies in the Indian Ocean, and allowed it to be re-established in Martinique and Guadeloupe, but he always drew back from doing so in Saint-Domingue, where it would have undermined his hopes of reconquest. He was surrounded by the pro-slavery lobby, led by Moreau de Saint-Méry, but he was no more dominated by them than by any of his other collaborators. They did have considerable presence in these discussions, mainly because the strongest supporters of abolition were Ideologues (like Volney, a loyal supporter of Brumaire who had earlier gone to Egypt with Napoleon), many of whom had been marginalised by 1801. Nevertheless, Napoleon did not turn against Toussaint until he felt he had been defied, and ordered Leclerc to work with whichever black leaders he could convince to change sides. The black rebels deported to France were eventually incorporated into the French army, and many served well; some, ironically, were deployed to repress banditry in southern Italy, where they fought with distinction. Napoleon applied much the same policy of reconciliation to Toussaint's troops who were captured or surrendered as he did to Vendeans who laid down their arms. (In 1803, he created a new unit, 'which must be composed of officers and men who have fought against us in the Vendean war', under a rebel commander he respected greatly, d'Autichamp, who had surrendered in 1800.[36]) The crucial difference for Napoleon was nothing to do with race: black officers who behaved like d'Autichamp and surrendered would keep their commissions; those who did not were allowed to serve as NCOs, and then promoted after an interval. The latter was mostly the case in Saint-Domingue, and it ignored race as an issue. Napoleon showed none of the bitter racism of Moreau de Saint-Méry or Prime Minister Addington, let alone Jefferson. He decided to crush Toussaint because he was a dangerous subordinate; he never used terms like Jefferson's description of the new black leaders as 'the cannibals of the terrible republic'.[37]

Where slavery is concerned, his attitude was one of cynical, callous pragmatism, although he showed a marked respect for Toussaint and the black troops under him. This hardly makes Napoleon admirable, even by the standards of the times, which saw the emergence of a powerful abolitionist movement in France, whose work he undid in many places, but his views were untainted by genuine racism. Toussaint and his men were a menace, but hardly his inferiors, and he knew it.

On St Helena, according to his secretary Las Cases, Napoleon said of his black enemy:

Toussaint was not a man without merit, even if he was not what he was portrayed as at the time. His character, it has to be said, did not inspire real trust: he was sharp, astute; we have much to blame ourselves for, [but] it would always have been necessary to stand up to him.[38]

Napoleon's self-discipline, so often an asset in similar circumstances, worked completely against him when he dealt with the new leaders of the New World. Napoleon played his cards too close to his chest; he did not make his position on slavery clear enough either to Toussaint or to his Parisian advisers. Toussaint did battle. Jefferson simply abandoned the French and, hiding behind neutrality, cut Leclerc off to starve while allowing American merchants to supply the black rebels with all they needed.[39]

One important effect of the failure of Leclerc's expedition, with far wider consequences for the future of France, was that it strengthened Napoleon's innate mercantilism. He had been led into the Caribbean quagmire by the commercial interests of the western ports and the Parisian financiers. These were the kind of people who made Britain both alien and anathema to him, and he came to dislike their French equivalents just as much. They had fed him bad advice, set him off on a disastrous errand, and his future economic policies did not favour them. Many colonial merchants were notoriously royalist aristocrats, in any case, or so he came to think: 'Even if it had succeeded,' he told Gourgaud in St Helena, 'it would only have ended by making the Noailles and the La Rochefoucauld rich.'[40] The blockade against Britain he initiated in 1806, and the very essence of the Continental System that evolved from it – with its concentration on market strategies aimed at continental Europe – militated against these interests. Napoleon was more indifferent to them than to slavery, telling Joseph openly at the advent of the blockade that the support of the colonial merchants and western ports simply had to be written off. They were not his natural constituency, and Saint-Domingue may have underlined this for him. He never looked their way again.

Napoleon had learned another important lesson. Never again, with the important exception of Spain, would he allow any subordinate the local power and authority he momentarily accorded Toussaint; his empire would be highly centralised, on the strict French model, and this was the end of all talk of 'special laws' for specific imperial provinces. Although the episode of Saint-Domingue was something of a sideshow in the great events of the Consulate, the experience convinced him of the need for authoritarian centralisation and a universalist interpretation of imperial governance, from which he would never deviate. If, at enforced leisure on St Helena, he lamented not showing more latitude to Toussaint and adopting a devolutionist approach to empire, it was never something he practised during his active public life.

No other campaign of the Napoleonic wars touched the Bonapartes so directly or intensely as the assault on Saint-Domingue. Pauline Bonaparte accompanied her husband, Leclerc, on the voyage and on campaign, and showed herself to be brave, resourceful and very lively in the face of hardship and danger. During the shock of the urban revolts of September 1802, Norvins marvelled at her leadership in calming and organising the embarkation of the women and children of the garrison at Le Cap, but even more at her own refusal to leave, and her determination to take command of the rearguard: 'You can die, you others,' he said she told the troops, 'but I am the sister of Bonaparte, and I fear nothing! They will take me dead, along with my son!' For Norvins she showed herself to be 'a Spartan woman'. There were no weaknesses in her farewells; she took on a dignity and courage that her natural beauty transformed into something almost supernatural. Norvins tried to haul her out by tying her to a sedan chair, but she would not leave her husband, even as the fighting reached the port.[41]

Norvins was an admirer of the family, but Pauline's remarkable bravery was beyond question in this very real crisis. It was quite a revelation. Napoleon had ordered Pauline to go with her husband, to keep her roving eye at bay, and she had tried every trick she knew to get out of it. She claimed to be pregnant: Napoleon had her examined by his own doctor with the predictable result; she said she could not cope with the coach drive from Paris to Brest: he sent her in a sedan chair. She retaliated by going on a ruinous spending spree in Paris, which she landed on Napoleon, before her departure.[42] Yet once on Saint-Domingue, she travelled everywhere with Leclerc, including to the fighting – her beauty and flirtatious behaviour raising morale – and she took particular interest in the victims of yellow fever. Her letters home were still frivolous. She told Napoleon she would not come home unless she was given 100,000 francs, to keep up with Joséphine.[43] Napoleon took this to heart because he knew the campaign had brought out the best in Pauline and he wrote to her with genuine love and warmth in March 1802, to 'ma bonne petite Paulette':

Remember that the hardships, the obstacles, are nothing when shared with your husband, and that it is for the good of the country ... make yourself loved by your kindness, your affability, and by conducting yourself seriously, and never lightly. We will put some trunks together for you of the new fashions, which the captain of *La Syrène* will take to you. I love you very much; make everyone happy with you, and I know you are worthy of your position.[44]

She did indeed make her brother proud of her in these dangerous months. The danger proved fatal for Leclerc, literally, and for Pauline, as a person. Revealing more about himself than he perhaps intended, Napoleon wrote to her in July:

I have learned with such pleasure of how bravely you have borne the hardships that go with the manoeuvres of war. Take care of your husband, who I have learned is rather ill. Don't do anything to make him jealous.[45] For a man under pressure, even the smallest thing can be intolerable. A wife needs to be accommodating at such times ... Your husband now really is worthy of being called *my brother* for the glory he has won ... Stay united in love and tender friendship. My wife will send you the latest fashions.[46]

He hoped this would be the making of his sister and he was being proved right. More revealing, however subjective the evidence, is his yearning for the kind of marriage the Leclercs appeared to be forging in the tropical swamps. Sharing the dangers of campaigning obviously moved Napoleon. It was more than Joséphine ever did for him; he had to wait until his second marriage, to Marie-Louise, and his penultimate campaign in 1814, to have a wife at his own side.

Napoleon's request that Pauline look after her husband in illness had a tragic prescience he could not have imagined. Leclerc died of fever on 2 November 1802, Pauline nursing him to the end. It was also the end of the 'Paulette' Napoleon had so come to admire, although he always loved her, and she alone of his family came to see him in his first exile on Elba and organised his living quarters. After her husband's death, Pauline returned to France with his body. She seldom left her cabin during the voyage, and arrived, broken and silent, in Toulon. She cut off all her long, beautiful hair as a sign of mourning, a Roman custom. This gesture drew a sarcastic response in the memoirs of her supposed friend, the acid-penned Madame Junot, who said she found it immoderate and ostentatious, and claimed that even Napoleon mocked it: 'she knows full well it will only grow the more luxuriantly for its cropping'. Such a remark, if it rings true in the usual tone in which he spoke about Pauline, does not fit with his behaviour to her in her darkest hours.[47] She still had an open wound from being stabbed during the retreat, which meant that she was quarantined on arrival and then only able to travel to Paris in stages; she could not attend Leclerc's funeral. Pauline was only twenty-two. She stayed with Joseph, and Napoleon saw her as often as he could.[48] When she recovered, she would emerge as a vain, callous socialite. Her shopping expeditions, always extravagant, now became pathologically ruinous. Napoleon soon rechristened the brave, cheerful 'Paulette' of the jungles 'our lady of the fripperies'. The renewed colonial empire was not the only one, and certainly not the dearest, of his hopes Napoleon saw destroyed by yellow fever on Saint-Domingue.

If he exploited any aspect of the greatest family tragedy suffered by the Bonapartes, it was in using Leclerc's death to revive the royal etiquette of court mourning. Miot de Mélito, a councillor of state, recalled in his memoirs, 'this return to former Court customs made a profound sensation, and was looked upon as a bolder venture than others of greater importance made by the First Consul'.[49]

Though Napoleon used Leclerc's death to assert his new public power, it was soon obvious that he wielded little within his own family. Napoleon, Joseph and Lucien had always had trouble keeping Pauline away from unsuitable men and, with the trusted Leclerc gone, they had little hope of success. In August 1803, against the firm advice of all her siblings, Pauline married a wealthy Roman, Camillo Borghese, of high family and low morals, but she matched him in all of the latter. They soon all but separated, and she had a succession of young officers paying court to her. When told that one of them had lost a leg in Spain, she icily replied that it was a shame as he was a good dancer. For all this, the change in her was probably wrought by loss. This was no longer the behaviour of a beautiful young woman enjoying life, however inappropriately for her station. It was a morbid decadence. Her beauty was immortalised by Canova's statue of her as Venus, leading Laurent Dubois to reflect, 'Pauline would . . . live on in stone, a mute witness to the debacle she had survived in Saint Domingue.'[50] Pauline was a victim of the wars, a war widow like millions of others; but, as Napoleon's sister, her story is well recorded and her fate was gilded, unlike that of so many.

Napoleon Bonaparte and Thomas Jefferson were the two most intellectually gifted leaders in the western world at the dawn of the nineteenth century, and their interaction, first over Saint-Domingue, but even more over the Louisiana Territory, ensured that they both left indelible marks on the futures of their respective continents. Their mutual dealings brought out the best and the worst in both men, a reflection of the mixed – if spectacular – blessings those same dealings left on their world.

They had fenced over Saint-Domingue, and Jefferson's volte-face in abandoning Leclerc to his fate had done much to ensure French defeat. However, to Jefferson certainly, Saint-Domingue – if the black revolt was contained on the island – was as nothing when set beside the issue of the territorial claims of the infant USA. His victory over Napoleon in Saint-Domingue was Pyrrhic. The result was his original nightmare, of an independent black state in the Americas, which his subsequent policy of economic embargo and diplomatic isolation threw into the arms of the British. He paid so repugnant a price to prevent Napoleon from advancing to the next stage of his American ambitions, the reacquisition of the vast Louisiana Territory from Spain, and its colonisation by France. Jefferson prevailed in this, too, but ultimately only because Napoleon reached his own conclusion that France, like America, was meant to be a continental power. When their tense confrontation was resolved on 30 April 1803, with the sale of the entire territory to the United States by France, the two titans of the new century turned their backs on each other, Jefferson to the physical colonisation and subjugation of the American west, Napoleon to the conquest of western and central Europe, and the enduring imposition of his political system on its peoples. One was meant to open new horizons for a new nation; the other to embed a new political culture among old states. The term was coined soon after both men had left power, but what emerged for both leaders and their peoples was truly 'Manifest Destiny'.

By the time Napoleon came to power in 1799, France had lost all her territory on the North American mainland. France had once held Canada, the lands between the Appalachian mountains and the Mississippi River, and a vast region called Louisiana, west of the Mississippi, which contained the port of New Orleans at the river's mouth on the Gulf coast. One of the few things all French governments since the Revolution had in common was the desire to get as much of this lost empire back as possible. Canada was now part of the British Empire, and the lands east of the Mississippi belonged to the new United States, but Louisiana had been ceded to Spain in 1795, and in 1800 Napoleon had succeeded in prising Spain away from the Coalition, into an alliance with France. Talleyrand, whose time in America had kindled his enthusiasm for regaining Louisiana, now saw a window of opportunity to get it back, which was realised within months: Louisiana became French again in October 1800, but it continued to be administered by a Spanish governor. The French did not actually take possession of Louisiana until the spring of 1803.

Napoleon took an active interest in Louisiana as part of a wider colonial vision for France in the New World. He hoped he could settle its interior with farming colonists and develop it to supply Saint-Domingue and the other Caribbean islands with their basic needs, so freeing them of dependence on the United States. New Orleans was to serve as the great entrepôt for this integrated, very mercantilist vision of empire, all provided that Leclerc could wrestle back Saint-

Domingue from Toussaint, which seemed realistic for much of 1802, when his expedition appeared to be successful. Napoleon equipped another expedition under General Victor with 3,000 experienced troops to occupy New Orleans and the Mississippi delta; he even made civilian administrative appointments to run the territory. The expedition is thought to have cost the considerable sum of two million francs to assemble.[51]

Napoleon had good reason to occupy Louisiana quickly. The United States had cast covetous eyes over the territory, and the delta especially, for some time. The unregulated frontiers of the region – a wilderness in the eyes of Europeans and Americans – allowed American settlers to pour into 'French' territory unchecked. In 1801, Thomas Jefferson became the third president of the new Republic, a man with an imperial vision to rival Napoleon's. Jefferson thirsted for continental expansion and American settlement beyond the Mississippi. He did nothing to discourage illegal settlement there, however close to the delta and New Orleans, which vexed the Spanish governor to the point that one of his last acts, in October 1802, was to forbid Americans the right to trade via New Orleans, which provoked hostilities with the settlers.

In the meantime, however, in late 1801, Jefferson began probing the French about buying Louisiana, through his agent in Paris, Robert Livingston. His first requests were limited: Livingston was told not to raise the question of New Orleans or the delta, but to try to acquire only the real wilderness, to the north and west.[52] Negotiations stalled in these months, and Jefferson did not make things easy for himself. In a style of negotiating more associated with Napoleon, he oscillated between aggression and conciliation. However, by the autumn of 1802, with Leclerc dead and his expedition in tatters, Napoleon began to think in terms of cutting his losses, and divesting France of Louisiana, which seemed useless to him without Saint-Domingue. He lost the initiative in any case by November 1802, when an early winter swept the Dutch coast, leaving Victor's fleet unable to sail. In the meantime, thousands of well-armed, warlike American settlers had gathered on

the borders of the delta, prepared to invade Louisiana and take New
Orleans to forestall Victor, unaware that he would not be coming.
Jefferson was now alert to the crisis on the Mississippi, and to scotch a
war, he sent his protégé, James Monroe, to Paris. Monroe was not only
a consummate diplomat, he was trusted by the frontiersmen.

Monroe's arrival coincided with Napoleon's own volte-face over his
entire colonial policy, and the sale was completed on 30 April 1803.
The territory was sold for eighty million French livres, less than the
opening price Napoleon set of a hundred million, but far more than he
had actually dared hope for. It was a great deal of money by American
standards, but Jefferson did not hesitate. The Americans were all
taken aback by the reversal of Napoleon's position, which made them
move all the faster for fear Napoleon would change course yet again.
Livingston had been in despair in early March, and convinced a show
of force would be needed.[53]

The latent aggression of both men lay beneath the surface of the
talks. Napoleon ordered Victor to form alliances with the Native
Americans, whom Napoleon was convinced were pro-French, a belief
probably derived from Raynal as much as anything else. To this end,
Victor's expedition was supplied with a vast amount of firearms, sabres,
gunpowder and munitions for them, and a consignment of new state-
of-the-art carbine rifles for the chiefs.[54] As Wilson Lyon remarked,
'The figures of the list are cold but an accurate commentary on what
would have been the fate of the western American settlements' had
Victor arrived. The Dutch ice had saved America from Napoleon in
the manner in which the Channel saved Britain from him in the same
months.[55] If Jefferson's nightmare was a slave revolt across the Old
South, his dream was of a republic of free, self-sufficient white yeomen
moving westwards; if his vision of hell was the black race liberated on
Saint-Domingue, his ideal was the white Anglo-Saxon freed from the
need for slavery by plentiful new lands in French Louisiana. He was
prepared to risk the emergence of the former for the chance to realise
the latter. Above all, he was ready, in the last resort, to fight for his
dream, just as he was ready to live with his nightmare to stop Napoleon

thwarting that dream. In the end, Napoleon and Jefferson pulled back from the brink. Jefferson got his territory, Napoleon his money. In this way, France and the USA were able to maintain reasonable relations.

There were deeper currents at work in the sale of the last French foothold in North America. In the autumn of 1802, Napoleon had lost 20,000 of his best troops in Saint-Domingue, the hardened veterans of the Rhine front bequeathed him by Hoche and Moreau. The timing was crucial, for by late 1802 the army of the 1790s was wearing out; the soldiers were older, retiring, and generally fewer in number by the time war loomed again; the quality of the men far outweighed even the large numbers of casualties, in relation to the new ranks of raw, unwilling conscripts who now formed the bulk of the army. He had seen his brother-in-law lose his life, and his sister lose her mind for a time, and her happiness forever. In January 1803, in the midst of a normal conversation, he suddenly screamed: 'Damn sugar, damn coffee, damn colonies.' Roederer stressed in his memoirs that these were Napoleon's exact words. He was obviously shocked by so intemperate an outburst, and he felt compelled to prove it as best he could.[56] If Jefferson represented the Trajan of the New World, whose dream was expansion, Napoleon – at this point in his reign – had become that Augustus who, after the loss of three legions in Germany, wandered his corridors at night, crying to his dead lieutenant, 'Varus, give me back my legions!', if Suetonius and Tacitus are to be believed. These legions had been lured into the forest primeval of Germany and ambushed by an army marshalled by Arminius, a German chief who had learned his trade in Roman service. It was a lesson from history both Napoleon and Jefferson had taken in with their mothers' milk. Napoleon was also, in 1803, still the Augustus who could withdraw to more defensible frontiers.

THE ANGLO-FRENCH ABYSS

Napoleon's ambitions were emerging as European and continental, but the British could not grasp that his interests in the western

Mediterranean, especially in northern Italy, were not directed against their control of the Mediterranean seaways. When war came, it was over their refusal to evacuate Malta in accordance with the terms of the treaty. For the British, the island was the hub of a Mediterranean corridor to India, which had to be secured, as was still the case in the Second World War, when the island endured a long, devastating siege for precisely these strategic reasons. One of the last British arguments for their failure to evacuate the island was their concern that, left to itself or the small garrison of 2,000 Neapolitan troops which was the only other military presence there, Malta's neutrality would become farcical.

Napoleon saw Malta in different terms. Indeed, he was frustrated that, although the British remained, they were doing nothing to police the seaways and deal with the Barbary pirates. This attitude changed in the years ahead, but in 1803 Napoleon complained to Talleyrand that, under the noses of the Royal Navy, raids were occurring as far north as the coast of the Papal States; Portuguese shipping in and out of Malta was being plundered at will. To this end, Napoleon had reversed traditional French policy, and was helping the Ligurian Republic to create its own fleet, but only because the British would not consent to an article in the treaty obliging the beys of North Africa to respect the Ligurian flag: 'it is the English who tolerate this absurd injustice'.[57] Napoleon's call for Britain to divert ships to fight the beys seemed to London only a ruse to scatter the Mediterranean fleet. Nor had Britain any wish to aid many of the states worst afflicted by the corsairs, like Portugal, which had joined the ruinous 1800–1 blockade. His actions in Liguria were merely another instalment in his aggressive expansionism in northern Italy. Napoleon's often warlike comportment worked against him. Understandably taken for a bully, his motives, as expressed to Talleyrand in January, would have been dismissed as humbug, had London known of them:

The Ligurian minister has made strong appeals to me to intervene with the powers of Barbary, to make them respect the Genoese flag. Please make it clear through our minister in Genoa, that this will only be possible when Ligurian has warships and maritime forces superior to those of the

Algerians, and when it will be able to display them publicly in Algiers ...
Until now, France has always opposed the creation of a Genoese navy, but
today, it is the first to support it, and I will press for it.[58]

Napoleon tried to use this issue to win Russian support for his
stance over Malta, playing on the Romanovs' traditional support
for the Knights of Malta, whom Napoleon himself had overthrown
enthusiastically in 1798 on the way to Egypt, and was now desperate to
restore, in order to undermine the British. He asked Alexander to help
him to drive the Barbary pirates from the seas 'and to force them to till
their own soil'. 'This is in the interest of the whole world, and above
all, of all the flags of civilised nations.' He went on to stress how he
had evacuated Italian ports, as ordered, but that the British remained
obstinate.[59] He made reference in the same letter to how well they had
worked together, in the reorganisation of the Holy Roman Empire,
which had seen the status of the southern states increase. Napoleon
appealed in similar terms to the King of Prussia the same day.[60]
Napoleon was probably sincere in his frustration, but too many of his
actions ensured that his plea fell on deaf ears. This did not mean that
his former partner in the blockade, Alexander, was pro-British at this
stage – far from it – although he was under pressure from powerful
and potentially dangerous court factions to turn on Napoleon. Nor
was Prussia ready to oppose Napoleon, but Berlin was in no mood
to abandon the neutrality it had assumed in 1795. Britain and France
were both alone in 1803.

Napoleon – unlike Talleyrand and Joseph – continued to believe
that the British wanted to construct a new coalition against him.
Throughout March and April 1803, he reinforced his armies all along
the Channel and into the Low Countries and Germany, and he set
about preparing the Normandy coast for a direct British invasion,
aided, he was increasingly convinced, by a new Vendean–Chouan
rising, led by returned rebels 'who the English vomit up on our coasts
from Jersey'.[61] This plot lurked in every corner of his mind, to the
point of paranoia. When the mayor of Orléans wrote to him early in
1803, to ask his support in erecting a statue of Joan of Arc in honour of

her first great victory over the English there in the Hundred Years War, the release of mounting hatred is palpable in his reply:

... this is very agreeable. The illustrious Joan of Arc proved that it was no miracle that French genius could prevail in circumstances when national independence was threatened. United, the French nation has never been defeated; but our neighbours – more calculating, more adroit – abusing the openness and loyalty of our character, constantly sowed dissensions in our midst, from which stemmed all the misfortunes of those times, and all the disasters in our history.[62]

He paid for the statue from his own pocket.

Ironically, the British spoke of the French in exactly the same terms in these years. Perfidy, sly calculation, the abuse of the inherent honesty and trusting nature of a good-hearted people by vicious foreigners, it could all have been Tom Paine railing against the Norman yoke in *The Rights of Man*. The French could play at this game, too, and had the historical tropes to do it.

When modern politicians invoke stereotypes of this sort, it is always with a strong dose of cynical ingenuousness. As a leader often credited with being the first to drape authoritarianism in democratic trappings, Napoleon was doubtless being calculatingly cynical in exactly this way. In personal terms, however, this outburst is another indication of Napoleon embracing a certain vision of France as his own: he extols the values of the classes all his policies promoted, and of that vision of the peasant smallholder – hard-working, self-sufficient – to whom the ethos of the Civil Code so appealed. His outburst invoked that most ethereal of the republican values, *fraternité*, with its roots in the inherent generosity of a free people, contrasted openly with the debased commercialism of the British.

Political hyperbole apart, Napoleon was right to be on his guard, but the British political landscape was an unfathomable wilderness to him. British circumstances were beyond him, as was Parliament's attempts to cope with them. Whereas Addington's relatively friendly cabinet collapsed after Amiens mainly for economic reasons – the crisis in manufacturing engendered by the return of peace – Napoleon saw in it only a desire to bring back the 'war party' under Pitt and Grenville with the sole aim of destroying him. This accentuated his propensity to resort to arms, less because he wanted to shatter the peace than to get his retaliation in first, as it were. There was as much irony in the wider clash of political cultures as in Napoleon's depiction of Joan of Arc as a Gallic 'John Bull'. Napoleon strove to mould a polity based on compromise and mutual toleration, but he did it through the exercise of authority over warring factions – the state as arbiter – which was the antithesis of British politics. Napoleon sought consensus and co-operation among the French elites as anxiously as the desperate Whig grandees trying to pick up the pieces of a shattered House of Commons in the decade after the loss of America, a confusion which eventually led to the emergence of William Pitt the Younger as the only hope of appeasing the factions. Yet the concept of a loyal opposition, of a system that actually demanded open defiance and public acrimony, was inconceivable to Napoleon, and anathema to many of those French politicians who had seen its results in the 1790s, when the attempt was made to import it to France. Napoleon worked harder and more earnestly to weld the French together; *ralliement* and, even more, *amalgame* were ambitious and sincere exercises in the politics of consensus, but to bring the French together through a parliamentary system was impossible for Napoleon to imagine. If the British could not classify Napoleon, neither could he classify them. Neither side understood the other, at any level.

Weakness heightened the tensions on both sides. Both parties had come to Amiens because they knew their own military frailties. Britain had been brought almost to her knees by the blockade, and her navy was severely over-stretched, denied essential supplies from the Baltic. Napoleon, too, knew his armies were exhausted, depleted and incapable of a long war. The response of both sides to peace was to rearm, regroup and stand ready. Within eighteen months, mutual paranoia ensured that their worst fears came true.

Contrary to what many historians have assumed, the resumption of hostilities was not the result of Napoleon's blind lust for war. On the eve of the actual declaration of war, he lashed out to Talleyrand as the last, desperate, efforts were made on both sides:

I don't want the conference to degenerate into chatter ... Appear cold, arrogant, even a bit fierce!!! If their note contains the word 'ultimatum' let them know this word means war, that that way of negotiating is one of a superior to an inferior ... If the note does not contain it, make it be there,[63] observing to them that they should know who they are dealing with, that we are fed up with this state of anxiety ... that they will not get from us what they did from the Bourbons;[64] that we are no longer the people who received a commissioner to Dunkirk;[65] that if 'ultimatum' is used again, it will all be broken off.[66]

The letter was written in his own hand, at 4.30 in the morning, as his spelling – always fragile – had disintegrated. He made one last, ill-tempered offer of compromise on 13 May, that he would accept a ten-year British occupation of Malta if the French could continue to keep their bases in the Kingdom of Naples,[67] but the issue was already decided in his mind. The pent-up fury Napoleon had felt in his dealings with the British could only be relieved in building a new army. In 1803, however, with both powers bereft of allies, they could do little real harm to each other, making them most surely the elephant and the whale.

The British acted first, as it happened, and war resumed on 16 May 1803. They seized all French ships in their ports, and Napoleon arrested and detained all British nationals in France; he also occupied Hannover, of which the British king was elector. War came as a release of tension to Napoleon. It was about all the whale and the elephant could do to each other at this stage. They did their best to find other ways to strike at each other, but to little avail.

11

TOWARDS EMPIRE

Unspoken Ambitions, 1802–1804

THE GOOD YEARS

The war meant little in its first two years. It did nothing to dent the growing confidence of the regime, nor the general sense of stability felt in France, which, ironically, went along with the frenzied creative force of the Consular reforms. There are times in a life that are not marked by momentous events, public or private, but which in hindsight seem the happiest moments. The years between the Peace of Amiens and the entry of Austria and Russia into coalition with Britain by the summer of 1805 were such a time for the Bonapartes. It was punctuated by the deeply felt tragedy of the death of Leclerc, which changed Pauline's character for ever, but even this brought them together as a family. The Bonapartes, Napoleon included, shared in some measure the normality their young head was trying to foster in France, but they were too turbulent to relax completely.

The fulcrum of family relations was, obviously, the marriage between Napoleon and Joséphine. None of the Bonapartes had ever liked or trusted her, but now, as Napoleon consolidated his hold on power and elevated them along with him, they felt they would at last be able to oust her, particularly as the problem of the succession was discussed more and more openly around them. They were quick to use whatever means they had against her. Lucien and Joseph were the best placed to do so during the Consulate, when Lucien sought to use his post as ambassador to Spain to broker a Spanish marriage for his brother, with the active help of Joseph, who had emerged from the Amiens negotiations with the reputation of a fine diplomat. They were wasting their time, however. Napoleon always loved Joséphine, often despite himself. It is almost as if all his suppressed irrationality, all his buried, tightly disciplined passion, was directed towards their relationship, and so away from the rest of his life. Napoleon said many things on St Helena, but when he told Bertrand, 'Joséphine was a liar; she said "no" first, to have time to think, she ran up debts I was obliged to pay . . . I would never have left her if she had had a child!', he probably spoke the truth. It is supported by a quite extraordinary remark he made publicly at the very moment of their official divorce: 'She has made fifteen years of my life beautiful.'[1] It was only when his new Empress Marie-Louise insisted, that he sent her away from court. Moreover, to the frustration of his brothers, the internal life of the marriage was probably at its strongest in these same years of the Consulate.

Joséphine had always sought security, to be close to power, not to wield it, but to be sheltered under it. Life with Napoleon had been anything but safe or secure in the years immediately after Brumaire. She herself had been shot at and almost blown up . With the political stability that came after Amiens – and before the problem of the succession arose with the creation of the Empire – came marital stability. They could at last enjoy each other in conditions of peace and wealth. Joséphine, 'la Consulesse', fostered the new court with all the skill of a woman bred to the sword nobility, the oldest aristocratic families descended from medieval knights, who counted Crusaders in her ancestry. She was in her element, just as Napoleon was when he was in the Channel ports forging a new army. They often toured the provinces together, and when apart – she taking cures at spas, he exploring his new realm – they seem to have borne the separations with more mutual trust or, at least, less paranoia, than in the past. Napoleon always wrote to her, as he did to everyone else. Although Joséphine was not a good correspondent with anyone, he now seems to have understood this and accepted it. That is not to say it always went smoothly. Joséphine's failure to put pen to paper drew a waspish but humorous swipe from Napoleon while he was preparing for war at Calais and she was taking the waters: 'I didn't know that the waters at Plombières had the same qualities as the river Lethe',[2] the river that symbolised forgetting for the ancient Greeks. The tone is more teasing than angry, more resigned amusement than the paranoid cajoling of a few years before. It was all a sign of a growing bond, even in their quarrels.

The marriage seemed strong to contemporary observers who were seldom charitable. Madame Junot recounts a scene of genuine 'banter' between Napoleon and Joséphine, perhaps all the more endearing because it revolved around the often fraught subject of her propensity to spend money that was not hers. Napoleon told her she had to look good in public, lavishly dressed, to which she replied smiling, 'Yes, and you find fault ... or you erase my warrants of payment from the margin of my bills.' 'She pouted,' Madame Junot recalled, 'like a little girl, but with the most perfect good humour.'[3] The vignette is imbued with a close, spontaneous familiarity. They presented a good-humoured solidarity to their friends, to match the formality of their union in public.

The change in their fortunes made it all the more necessary to keep this side of Joséphine's character on a tight leash. As Napoleon's secretary, Bourrienne, put it, she took pleasure less in the possessing than in the acquiring of luxuries. It was not simply about having things. She was all too ready to bestow gifts, and this was, in itself, a problem. As Consul and then Emperor, Napoleon insisted on being kept abreast of all Joséphine's engagements, simply because she was as unthinking in her support of others' petitions as she was of money. She was known far and wide as the softest of touches for old ladies who wanted jobs for their grandsons. Madame Junot, given her own place at court, saw this for herself:

[N]othing was forgotten [by Joséphine] in this long list, except the good sense which should have prevented such unbecoming interference ... The First Consul was aware that her favours were so unsparingly and indiscriminately distributed that she would sometimes make fifteen promises at a single breakfast, dinner or fête . . .[4]

This largesse was potentially more compromising for Napoleon than her extravagant shopping. Her attempts to make money, as opposed to ridding herself of it, were the most calamitous of all, for many of the schemes into which she was drawn were dubious. She had always mixed with corrupt army contractors – the worst sin imaginable for Napoleon – and she was involved in attempts to sell 'fake' thoroughbred horses; she tried to speculate on the foreign exchange when the Peace of Amiens was announced, and ruined the man she used as her agent as a result.[5] Her new-found success brought out the most worrying aspects of her character, though it also gave her natural grace and charm, and the inculcated poise of the aristocrat, their proper function in her role as the ruler's consort. Napoleon always paid debts promptly, and assumed those of the more wayward members of his family, while always remaining suspicious of business propositions. Although Napoleon set a fine example of personal rectitude in his own finances, she ruined hers; as he strove to foster meritocracy, she would dispense patronage – or make promises to – over a good lunch; but the marriage actually grew stronger in these years. They had come to know each other, and there was an underlying trust now that was needed in the face of a hostile family. Nevertheless, to that family, to his siblings and mother, it looked as bizarre as it was dangerous.

Of course it is difficult to try to grasp the inner life of any marriage, even one so public as that of Napoleon and Joséphine, yet in the climate of those years Napoleon's short notes to her from Calais, while with the army in 1804, have a ring of truth, simply because he made the time to write them:

Madame and dear wife, I have been at Calais since midnight. I am off to Dunkerque this evening. I am pleased by what I see, and am in pretty fair health . . . Eugène is off to Blois, Hortense is well . . . I want to see you so much: you are necessary for my happiness. All good things for you, and for your close ones and friends.[6]

That he loved her children so much, and showed it in these years so clearly – making of Eugène his right arm and marrying Hortense to his favourite brother, Louis – counted for more than anything to her.

Whatever her own real thoughts of her husband, Joséphine could not but 'rally' to a man who wrote thus to her daughter that same month:

My dear girl, I so want you to write to me with your news – for I have nothing from you for a month, and your health is important to me, and your pregnancy must make you weak . . . I do appreciate your feelings for me, and you know that nothing can ever change my paternal feelings for you, and that I have sought the best for you from your youngest time. Your happiness, your health, your well-being, as those of your brother, are part of my most tender feelings. Write to me sometimes . . . and don't forget to give Mons. Napoleon [her first son, with Louis] two kisses for me.[7]

Events proved that these words were sincerely meant. When Napoleon went to Milan in the spring of 1805 to oversee the transformation of the Republic into the Kingdom of Italy, Joséphine went with him willingly. When she did so, it was not only as Queen-Empress, but as the mother of Napoleon's Italian Viceroy, Eugène: he had taken care of her two children as if they were his own, and she acknowledged this. He never let the divorce come between Joséphine's children and himself, nor the rapid floundering of the marriage of Hortense and Louis, nor the loss of their first child.

The incessant plotting of Joseph and Lucien seems to have served only to draw husband and wife closer together. Napoleon would hardly be dictated to in any circumstances, but their scheming, doubtless exacerbated when they saw the ascending stars of Eugène and Hortense, may have given them a powerful incentive to manoeuvre Napoleon into a divorce. Lucien's behaviour in Madrid smacks of reckless desperation to stop the relentless rise of the Beauharnais. Seen from their vantage point, the Bonapartes had every reason to fear the ascendancy of Joséphine's children. Lucien had been banished from the most important ministry of the early Consulate to the embassy to a second-rank power, and while Jérôme was given the command of a middle-sized warship, the brothers had to watch as Eugène was entrusted with the viceroyalty of Italy, the jewel in Napoleon's crown, his original power base. It was their own fault. Napoleon had offered Joseph the crown of Italy, first on condition of renouncing his claim to the French throne if Napoleon died without heirs, and then a modified solution, that he could succeed Napoleon in France if he renounced Italy in favour of Louis. Joseph refused both solutions, and even the usually pliant Louis would not accept the Italian throne in place of Joseph.

Napoleon knew where to turn, and this was not taken well by Joseph. Hortense bore not one but two sons in these years, the obvious heirs for all to see, but there was more. As Pauline's behaviour became ever more self-destructive, Caroline displayed her naked avarice and Elisa retreated from the family, Hortense became not only Napoleon's favourite, for her intellect and ready wit, but the darling of the new elite. Madame Junot remembered her as very pretty, if not a beauty like Pauline or her mother, and as 'the life of the party; her gaiety, good-humour, and spirit of pleasing, imparted the same qualities to all around her'. She had her mother's amiable nature, but not her frivolity; a good heart allied to a hard head. There was something else in Madame Junot's portrait of her that made the Bonapartes tremble, however: 'The young people grouped around her, looked at her and loved her, as the crowd would now and for ever follow her.'[8] She was a rallying point for a youthful court, and she had the intelligence to turn this into more than a mere social coterie.

Lucien's plans to marry Napoleon to a Spanish princess showed an utter lack of judgement and, if the memoirs of Miot de Mélito, a young rising star in the Council of State, close to Joseph, are to be believed, the usually circumspect Joseph was distracted enough to fall in with them. Miot's memoirs are based on 'reconstructed' secret conversations with Joseph on the plots for divorce and remarriage, and so of tenuous veracity. Nevertheless, Miot was all too justified in seeing 'the Spanish project' as sheer political suicide: The prospect of linking the Bonapartes to a branch of the Bourbons was the most dangerous path Napoleon could have taken: 'there were strong objections to bringing the race of the Bourbons back to France' was understatement at its most damning.[9] Lucien's subsequent disgrace was often attributed to a latent republicanism.[10] Nothing could be further from the truth. In the late Directory, as an influential deputy, Lucien emerges as a cynical game-player. During the military reverses of 1799, when he was trying to get elected, he linked himself to the neo-Jacobins; once in power, he suddenly became a defender of the government. Barras adopted the role his brother tried to assume after Brumaire, of reining in Lucien's naked ambitions, and did so with more success than Napoleon. Lucien's first clash with Napoleon, which cost him the Ministry of the Interior, had come from an excessive zeal to 'personalise' the Consulate at a premature moment. Now he was obsessed with naked dynastic ambition. If there was a true 'mafioso' among the Bonapartes, someone who thought of France as a personal fiefdom to be seized by the family and run for the family, it was Lucien. That his ambition was directed against Joséphine doubtless made it easier for the rest of the Bonapartes, led by Madame Mère, Letizia, to rally to his side. Napoleon at this moment was isolated from them, with the exception of Louis.

The war within the Bonapartes was further embittered when Napoleon demanded of Lucien and Jérôme precisely what he would not do for them: that they abandon unsuitable marriages. He finally bullied Jérôme into submission, but he could not break Lucien's 'unsuitable' marriage to the daughter of a currency merchant, Alexandrine Jacob de Bleschamps. Lucien was supported by their mother, who left Paris to join her son in Rome when he was finally ordered off by Napoleon. Nevertheless, Lucien's almost pathological hatred of Joséphine may have been the real motive for their estrangement, and it drove Napoleon to risk the enmity of his mother and sisters.

Bourrienne recounts Joséphine confiding in him, in about 1802, that Lucien had threatened her that if she did not produce a child, or allow Napoleon to do so by another woman and accept it as her own, she would be set aside. It was the same selfless but callous ambition for the family that had driven Lucien to go too far after Brumaire. If Bourrienne's account is true, then Joséphine's reaction to Lucien – that the surrogate baby idea was mad, that such a scandal could not be kept quiet and would ruin Napoleon[11] – has a certain symmetry with his equally miscalculated plans for a Bourbon marriage.

However tenuous Bourrienne's evidence, Lucien's doings in Madrid were real enough. Joséphine was now an official person, and a real companion to Napoleon at this time, no longer an equivocal, reluctant participant in a dangerous enterprise. In 1797, only the need to prevent the scandal of Joséphine's adultery seemed to hold the pair together, her reluctance to be seen to wrong the nation's hero, his to be seen as a cuckold. Now, they rallied to each other when Lucien's callous finger pointed to what would, eventually, become inevitable necessity: the need to think about a successor. Napoleon must have known all about Lucien's conniving, and it probably drove him to feel he had to break with his overly loyal brother. Whatever the reason, when Lucien had been sent to Madrid it was under a cloud. When he left for Rome, he was henceforth excluded from political life. Bourrienne soon followed. He was close to Joséphine and the pair had been embroiled in a financial scheme run by the Coulon brothers, corrupt army suppliers, which ended in scandal and the suicide of one of the brothers. Napoleon had to cut his close ties with Bourrienne, although he continued to serve the regime abroad, mainly in Germany.

When the marital problems of Jérôme broke upon Napoleon, he used the example of Lucien to cow him:

Lucien preferred a dishonoured woman . . . to the honour of his own name and that of his family. I can but lament of so great a waste of a man to whom nature granted so much talent, and who was torn from so great a destiny by an egoism without parallel, and who has strayed so far from the paths of duty and honour.[12]

The threat to Jérôme's future arrived in the beautiful form of Elizabeth Patterson, an American heiress, the daughter of an Irish immigrant who was now the wealthiest man in Baltimore. Faced with another marital crisis, the official version of Lucien's disgrace was of obvious relevance for the family. Jérôme met Betsy, as she was known, while on naval duty, at a society ball in the city, and married her there on Christmas Eve, 1803. When they returned to Europe, in the spring of 1805, Napoleon moved heaven and earth to stop them landing. He tried to buy 'Miss Patterson' off with a pension of 60,000 francs a year for life if she would only go home and disappear,[13] but Napoleon was truly out of his league when it came to bribing rich Americans. This time at least he had most of the family behind him: Jérôme was intended for other things. Napoleon kept Madame Mère well abreast of all his efforts to get Jérôme to see him in Milan, and to send Miss Patterson home – 'this prodigal son ... whom I will deal with severely', as he called him.[14]

The marriage was perfectly legitimate, but Napoleon was driven to conjure any slender legal hope of voiding the match, telling his own legal expert, Cambacérès, that as the marriage had not been contracted in France, and did not appear in any French records, it was invalid.[15] This was a vain hope, to say the least, but Napoleon gave a hostage to fortune when he pleaded with Pius VII to do something in a letter full of blatant, pathetic lies – Miss Patterson was a Protestant; the Gallican Church did not recognise the form of the marriage. He asked the Pope to issue a bull annulling it – but to keep it all quiet.[16] This could not have come at a worse time for Napoleon where Rome was concerned. Pius was increasingly aggrieved and uneasy about France's annexation of more territory in Italy, and Napoleon's extension of the Concordat to the new territories of Genoa and Parma-Piacenza, as well as the new Concordat he had imposed on the Kingdom of Italy.

All this won Napoleon a stinging rebuke from Rome on 31 July 1804, two months after his pleading letter to Pius concerning Jérôme. Napoleon had to reply to this papal reprimand with crawling, if still unrelenting, notes of explanation for his actions, singular for their deference.[17] In the meantime, Pius took exquisite pleasure in telling Napoleon he could do nothing, taking some little revenge for so many recent humiliations, Napoleon's recent coronation among them. Napoleon had one possible card to play: Jérôme was under age, and at only nineteen needed his family's consent to marry. Letizia supported Napoleon, but, unfortunately for Napoleon, when one of Betsy's brothers arrived in France to inform the Bonapartes that the Pattersons had no objections to the match – they had initially been as averse as Napoleon, exiling Betsy to a plantation, but had now given in – the Bonaparte he met was Lucien, who was obviously in no mood to support his brother in such a matter.[18] Lucien agreed to the union, leaving Napoleon 'blockade' as his only weapon.

Jérôme relented and Miss Patterson went home, although not before she had borne him a son in London, where she was forced to land when Napoleon enforced his only successful closure of the continent's ports, against a lone woman. The event 'has been the subject of great stirrings among the English', Napoleon told Jérôme.[19] Jérôme was forgiven, but was not given any imperial trappings; Napoleon set him to work as a naval officer, in command of one ship. When Murat, their brother-in-law, proposed that Jérôme be given the ceremonial rank of Grand Admiral – which he would in fact later acquire – Napoleon came close to telling his old comrade not to be silly.[20] This was one member of his family, at least, Napoleon found he could control.

Although the French government decreed the marriage void in 1805, Betsy Patterson only got a divorce on grounds of desertion from the American authorities in 1811. Jérôme 'married' the daughter of the King of Württemberg in 1807, the first – but not the last – Bonaparte 'marriage' that was illegal in the eyes of the Church. Betsy retained her beauty and returned to Europe after the fall of the Bonapartes, becoming quite a celebrity in high society.[21] To their credit, Napoleon and Jérôme always kept in touch with Betsy, and offered to bring the boy, Jérôme Napoleon, to France; she received a generous pension from Napoleon until 1813, and they offered her a title and a considerable domain in Jérôme's kingdom of Westphalia, and the dignity of an imperial prince for the boy.[22]

The birth of Jérôme Napoleon saw Napoleon change from a caricature of interfering severity into something very different, but wholly in keeping with his behaviour throughout his life. Henceforth, instead of driving her away, he sought to bring Betsy and Jérôme Napoleon into the imperial family. This was but one more incident for Gillray to conjure with – but it does match the warmth and generosity he showed to his own two illegitimate children and his refusal to deny or ignore them.[23] He had brought up Eugène and Hortense as his own. This generosity deserves to be set beside the justifiable opprobrium heaped upon him for his initial handling of Jérôme's marriage. Napoleon won his battle with Jérôme, but at the cost of turning into the British caricature of himself, that of the ridiculous bully, whereas in his treatment of Lucien can be glimpsed a man who was determined to stand against his own family, to protect his wife from the bullies.

The response of the three Bonaparte brothers to the assaults on their marriages merits some reflection on several levels. Napoleon came to see Lucien as expendable, but not Jérôme, and there is as much a political as a personal element to this. Lucien was not a neo-Jacobin but he was a remnant of the 1790s, his relative youth notwithstanding. Jérôme, in contrast, was scarcely in his twenties; he was the future, representing, along with Louis and Eugène de Beauharnais, the next generation Napoleon was beginning to promote in his greater aim of bypassing the factions of the *ancien régime* and the Revolution. They were the imperial family's equivalent of the auditors of the Council of State or the new officers emerging from St-Cyr, and the pupils of the *lycées* and the *Grandes Écoles*. Lucien and Napoleon demanded of each other what they would not do themselves: set their own wives aside for *raison d'état*. Lucien saw Napoleon's marriage not just in terms of high politics, however, but as a breach of family loyalty: high politics was merely an instrument for advancing the clan, but in his own case, as in Napoleon's, the personal counted for more. Neither gave way over the matter of his own heart, and it is arguable that this was really why Napoleon dispensed with Lucien. Jérôme's conduct was easily represented as the intemperate behaviour of a very young man. Napoleon wrote to Pius VII in exactly these terms when he vainly sought his help. Perhaps it was so.

For all that, it is worth speculating if there is here a glimpse in all three brothers of the new cultural sensibility they all avidly absorbed in the literature they preferred. When it came to personal happiness, they put sentiment first or, in the case of Jérôme, tried to, as he and Betsy sailed from one barred port to another. The youngest and most vulnerable, Jérôme, gave way; the two older brothers faced each other down, defiant to the end. Lucien lost his grasp on the power for which he had worked with demonic energy; Napoleon eventually had to admit that Lucien was right after all. Lucien never left his wife; he never behaved as other than a man who genuinely cared for her. Napoleon said often enough on St Helena that he truly loved Joséphine; in this case, at least, he acted as if he meant it. No hard-boiled scion of the Houses of Habsburg, Hohenzollern or Romanov would have behaved like the three Bonapartes when faced with such emotional choices. Nor would their own Ajaccian forebears. Only the regent of a very bourgeois realm, the future George IV, in his defiant – but still clandestine – marriage to the Catholic Mrs Fitzherbert, remotely resembled the private lives of the Bonapartes.

Louis seemed the only one of his brothers Napoleon could rely on or control in these years. Although he would soon go on to disprove this, Louis, in his marriage to Hortense, could not very well surrender to the Bonapartes who were so hostile to his mother-in-law. The union of Louis and Hortense, in its first days, seemed typical of the optimism of the period between Amiens and the renewal of war in 1805. The many hopes that rested on them seemed to be coming true. Napoleon had raised Louis virtually as a son, while his respect and affection for Hortense made them a 'golden couple' in his eyes, she above all for her powerful intellect. All this is touchingly clear in his letter to her sent from the Channel camps in August 1805:

My dear little girl, I read your lovely letter with pleasure, as with everything that comes from you. You make me imagine that I have actually become a grandfather, but what you tell me of the intelligence of Napoleon [Napoleon-Louis, their second son, who died in 1831] makes me see the third generation on its way, because I remember your own husband from

when he was so little that I think of him as the second ... I am so pleased
you write to me, and that you are nice enough to come to see me with little
Napoleon for five or six days ... it will bring a little lightness to our life in
the camps ... A thousand kisses to Napoleon ... I will be so pleased to see
you. Never doubt my love or attachment to you.[24]

She never did have to doubt this, and was one of the very few people
close to him who never disappointed his hopes. Napoleon's happiness
and confidence in the future rested on Louis and Hortense. Louis was
an investment; Hortense a gift from the gods.

These years saw the weddings of Berthier, Ney and Davout, among
others, and many lavish christenings among the families of the
military elite – the new marshals, after 1804 – at which Napoleon and
Joséphine invariably stood as godparents. The memoirs abound in the
recounting of lively breakfast and luncheon parties, of family picnics
and male hunting expeditions. Madame Junot, as so often, caught the
moment well:

... all my young married comrades, if I may apply that term to the wives of
Junot's brothers-in-arms ... and all in the beauty and freshness of youth;
so that no spectacle could be prettier than that our table exhibited, when
surrounded [by] ... young and cheerful faces, of which not one could be
called ordinary.[25]

These were the good times.

ULTIMATE POWER

The fears of the early years did not just evaporate. Napoleon, harried
for so long by blades, bombs and assassins' bullets, lost the growing
sense of confidence he had felt since Amiens in these moments, but
those around him saw the situation better than he could in the spring
of 1804. Fouché, scarcely the most reliable of witnesses to history,
perhaps precisely because he was one of the best informed, is searingly
honest in his account of the feelings of the old republican radicals
closest to power in 1804, and the links they drew between the demise of

Moreau in April, and Napoleon's first announcement of his intention to take the imperial title in May. Much more than the execution of d'Enghien, who was an enemy common to them all, Fouché and those like him realised that the sheer impotence and absurdity of Moreau's conspiracy revealed that Napoleon was their only remaining hope:

> Was it not absurd for the men of the Revolution to compromise everything to defend principles, when we really had nothing left for us but to protect the reality? Bonaparte was by then the only man in a position to conserve us in our property, in our influence, in our jobs. He profited from all these advantages . . .[26]

This stark confession of powerlessness is all the more striking because it came from the person who was, arguably, about to become the most powerful man in France after Napoleon. Dismissed from the Police-Générale for his opposition to the Consulate for Life, he was now poised to return, as a vocal supporter of the hereditary empire. For men like Fouché, the move towards the creation of the Empire was not driven by fear that Napoleon would be murdered by the likes of Moreau, but that Moreau and others like him had no real hope of success. Opposition by the right could, at least, rely on the support of the British, however bungling. It was now clear the left was defenceless.

The only men of the left with any autonomy of movement were those generals – the men who would become marshals the day after Napoleon became Emperor – who still harboured republican sentiments. There were several of them, but they were far from united. They had been bought off in the most generous fashion – as generous as a republic would permit, and, more importantly, deep bonds of loyalty had been forged between Napoleon and most of his commanders. Masséna and Bernadotte were neutralised more by bribery than loyalty, whereas for men like Berthier and Lannes it was much the reverse. They were the most spectacular beneficiaries of Napoleon's rise to power. Napoleon revived the old monarchy's rank of marshal without hesitation: the honour of the baton came naturally to him, and to all his commanders. None of them, whatever their past politics, ever refused it. In 1804 the great victories that would further bind them all together were yet to come, but Napoleon had developed another method of neutralising the marshals in the Channel camps. In 1804 his deliberate policy of fostering rivalries between the corps – and, inevitably, between their commanders – proved of immense political value to him. His commanders were all ferociously loyal to him but usually at odds with, and always mistrustful of, each other. The extent to which this actually influenced their opinions on the creation of the Empire in 1804 is hard to know with any real precision, but it was clear enough to all that neither the republicans nor the crypto-royalists still among them were hardly effective figureheads for a coup. The middle ranks of the officer corps proved the most zealous in their support for Napoleon, organising petitions from the soldiers in favour of the creation of the Empire and flooding the assemblies with them. This was the one point where Napoleon risked identifying himself not with Octavian, but with the most corrupt and unstable Roman emperors – he was proclaimed by the legions and foisted upon the Senate – but it still proved that the political mood of the army was that of its commander.

The world of Parisian politics, always paranoid, was thrown into confusion in the period between Amiens and the declaration of the Empire. This was the moment when those who had long occupied the corridors of power now saw that they were no longer in control. Mathieu-Louis Molé, a young aristocrat held up by Napoleon as a living example of the success of *amalgame*, caught the climate of the time in his memoirs:

From that moment ... it became the norm that no one spoke according to his conscience and – in the last stage of the corruption of the spirit – the atheists preached a mendacious religion, the Christians took an interest in philosophy; the republicans talked of monarchy, the partisans of absolutism espoused liberal ideas, the victims of the Revolution professed impartiality, and the murderers of Louis XVI lauded the virtues of their victim ... This was exactly where Bonaparte wanted to lead us. He was not wrong in thinking us deceived.[27]

Between 1799 and 1804, Napoleon had out-manoeuvred the French political world completely. It was as remarkable a series of tactical victories, followed by strategic successes, as any he achieved in war. In the days before Brumaire, he had gone in fear of being poisoned by some of his supposed supporters, to say nothing of the assassination attempts on him by his avowed enemies. He had been chosen for his role because of his weakness and lack of a discernible power base. Now the tables had been turned on everyone. The clearest winners, together with Napoleon, were not the would-be power brokers of the 1790s – led by Fouché and Talleyrand, for Sieyès and Barras had been left behind from the outset – but men like himself, Lebrun and Cambacérès, who had early taken the measure of the Revolution and bided their time.

The atmosphere depicted by Molé had, it seems, wider echoes than the rarefied political world of Paris. The process of turning the Consulate into the Empire did not follow political logic. It should have begun with the plebiscite, whose results would then be proclaimed by the Senate and finally affirmed by the coronation. That would have been to risk rejection, however, so Napoleon reversed the process. Less than a month before his coronation as emperor in December 1804, and a full six months after the official proclamation of the Empire in May, Napoleon held the now mandatory plebiscite on the new constitution which would create the Empire, which was then rigged in the approved manner, to produce 3,572,000 'yes' votes and 2,579 opposed. The real point, however, is that 65 per cent of the electorate abstained.[28]

There is no doubt that many of those around him – Roederer and his brother Lucien, chief among them – had urged a monarchical solution on Napoleon from the beginning, and they had been very firmly rebuffed, the latter discreetly, the former brutally. It would be wrong to take Napoleon's actions at face value, of course, and Jacques-Olivier Boudon has argued that the restoration of a monarchy was in Napoleon's sights even before Brumaire.[29] It is equally clear, however, that opportunism was a very important element in such uncertain circumstances: the Consulate for Life only heightened the uncertainties of what, never mind who, would follow Napoleon. The twin threats of d'Enghien and Moreau were manipulated to this end. Fouché recalled with dread that Napoleon moved not when he was afraid, but when he knew he had become indispensable. Napoleon had emerged as the sole repository of real power, and now, however fearful he could be, he knew it.

Napoleon had triumphed and if there is a key to this it lies not just in his desire for power, but in his preparedness to accept responsibility when others did not. The men of the Directory thirsted for power, but clung too readily to the shadows; they hid behind cabals, they schemed rather than planned; they either lashed out with violent retaliation or sought compromise within their ever-narrowing ranks. It was Napoleon who took essential decisions, even if he left the details to trusted experts; halting initiatives became clear policies. It was Napoleon who sought to break out of the shrinking confines of Revolutionary politics, and reached out to the Curia and the Chouans. However shameless a self-publicist, Napoleon also took the responsibility for his policies and his actions. He drove the work for the Concordat and the reordering of public finances, and the confidence he showed in his able ministerial team made it very stable, the only major casualty being his own brother, itself a sign of real resolve. Most of the great reforms involved some degree of unpopularity, but Napoleon did not sacrifice his collaborators in the face of it. This meant men rallied to him, both because he was loyal to those around him, but also because no one was prepared to take up the burden of leadership against him when it was still feasible.

There was one piece of timing that was carefully premeditated, however, and reveals how Napoleon's plans for personal advancement benefited from his clear and determined approach to fundamental reform. The Civil Code was proclaimed on the same day as Napoleon was proclaimed Emperor, 28 Floréal, Year 8/18 May 1804. It was a masterstroke of reassurance, promising that the new monarchy would be bound by the law, and that the law would be the same concise but immutable code for all. Napoleon had created the first explicit example of what came to be called 'the administrative monarchy', an authoritarian state held in check by a well-defined legal code. Nothing was further removed from the concept of Divine Right, and it drove a theoretical wedge between the old and new monarchies.

There was another reason for this emphatic coupling of the Code and the imperial crown, however. Although the Senate had agreed promptly to the creation of an hereditary empire, a move had arisen within its ranks to formulate the new monarchy on the lines of British constitutionalism. Louis XVI had famously and ironically declared he would rather be dead than be a king in the English fashion, and Napoleon felt no differently. To be bound by the law was one thing, to be a prisoner of a parliament was wholly unacceptable, and the assertion of an empire bound by law, but superior to its legislature, was the best way to scotch talk of imitating the British model.

The Roman paradigm of a kingdom that became a republic that became an empire was too deeply rooted in the collective psyche of the elites to be so easily bypassed, however. Educated opinion was aware that the demise of the Roman Republic was often seen as the beginning of Rome's decline, and marking the end of freedom and civic virtue. Nor did Napoleon wish to discard the Republic, but the transition had to be handled with care. Carnot had invoked this history when he opposed the creation of the Empire in the Tribunate – the name of the assembly was redolent of the Roman populism that had ousted the Tarquin kings – and the classical nomenclature Napoleon himself had fostered during the Consulate could easily have rebounded on him, had he not prepared his ground so well. The well-known lesson of Montesquieu's *De la Grandeur et de la Décadence des Romains* – a canon of eighteenth-century political thought – was that the decline of Rome was ensured when the virtuous republic turned into an empire controlled by corrupt generals. This was a deep-seated source of unease for Frenchmen of Napoleon's generation. He had allowed Moreau to escape into exile; he commuted the death sentences of two aristocrats who had plotted to kill him, the Polignac brothers, to life in prison. He brought Fouché back into high office and did nothing to dishonour or diminish the positions of the seven members of the Council of State who opposed the creation of the Empire. In the end, only three senators voted against the Empire, Sieyès, Grégoire and Volney. They were now men of the past. Napoleon did not harm them either. The only major 'casualties' of this change of regime – apart from Cadoudal and twelve of his closest associates, who were shot – were Napoleon's own brothers, Lucien and Jérôme. Both were excluded from the new hereditary succession, though Jérôme was restored to it when he repented, divorced and made himself ready to remarry as his brother ordered. Lucien went his own way. Napoleon never indulged in true vendetta politics. As Steven Englund has said, 'Corsican vindictiveness and a taste for feuds were not his way.'[30]

The transition from Consulate to Empire was one of the most dangerous Napoleon ever took. Although events soon proved how powerful he had become, the reintroduction of hereditary rule to a country which had beheaded its king less than ten years previously and dissolved a thousand-year-old monarchy in an orgy of blood was anything but a foregone conclusion. This was not a question of power, for the constitution bequeathed near-monarchical powers on the First Consul for Life; it was ideological and emotional. The final step was deemed so perilous that Napoleon took no direct part in it at any stage. The process was not so much opaque, as oblique. Every opinion in favour of creating an hereditary empire came from others, and although many voices were raised in favour of the move, Napoleon's was never one of them. He feared public reaction to this step, particularly within the army, and he did not so much tread carefully, as not tread at all. There have been powerful arguments put forward that Napoleon had sought an hereditary, monarchical regime from at least the coup of Brumaire, but even the most convincing exponents of this base their convictions on his cumulative behaviour, not on his words.[31] If they are right, this was one occasion when Napoleon either confided in no one, or when those he chose to trust carried their oath of silence to the grave.

There were two psychological currents at work within the French political elite. One sought to cast the transition from Republic to

Empire in terms of Roman history, but the other was more deeply rooted. It held that France could only flourish under a strong monarchy, and that the events of the Revolution had proved this. Napoleon, as Consul, had brought stability, but it was precarious, because there was no guaranteed succession. The instinctive response was expressed, with apt spontaneity, in the reply of the Tribune Carrion-Nisas to Carnot: 'Past experience has decided the question. France can only be at rest, in definitive calm, under hereditary institutions of power.'[32] It found official form in the collective reply of the Senate to Napoleon on the issue: 'an hereditary government alone can defend public liberty [and] maintain liberty'.[33] Monarchy was the natural system of government in France, but it need not attach to any specific dynasty; it was the method of government that mattered, and, sooner or later, what was natural would prevail or there would be – as there had been – chaos.

Another historical precedent reared its head in these months, the heritage of Charlemagne. Napoleon had to take an imperial title, rather than a royal one, for the obvious reason that he was not, nor could ever claim to be, the 'real' king, so toxic had the term become to all Frenchmen, for different reasons. 'Emperor' was the only relatively untainted title left. So imbued were all educated people with the history and relevance of the late Roman Republic and the early Empire that to conjure another title for an hereditary ruler would have amounted to trying to hide the elephant in the room. Yet the place of Charlemagne in French history still had to be reckoned with. Napoleon chose a mix of traditions, and did not draw on one historical precedent. As early as 1803, he had invoked Charlemagne's memory by erecting a statue to him atop a column in the Place Vendôme, and in September he made a highly publicised visit to the Carolingian capital, Aachen, and was visibly moved. In the first years of the Empire, the aspect of the Carolingian heritage Napoleon preferred to emphasise was less its attempted restoration of the Roman Empire, but its foundation of a new dynasty. Charlemagne was promoted as the man who rejuvenated France by his own efforts. He expressed Napoleon's desire to reconnect France to its entire pre-revolutionary past. The predominance of the

Roman rather than the Carolingian paradigm was, however, embodied in the beautiful medals that were struck for the imperial coronation. On one side were the words 'Napoleon, Emperor', on the other 'the Senate and the People'. As time passed and his hegemony became truly imperial and European – with the creation of satellite kingdoms and the need to remind his siblings that they were his vassals – Napoleon would begin to draw more on the example of Charlemagne. By 1810, their realms were territorially quite similar.

The ground for the transition to empire had been well prepared, which is all too evident in how little the Constitution of the Year 8 (1800) had to be altered. There were few executive powers Napoleon did not already wield by 1804. His fellow consuls, Lebrun and Cambacérès, had feared for the inevitable disappearance of their posts, but they were retained and rewarded with grander titles – Archtreasurer and Archchancellor respectively – and officially listed as among the six 'grandest' dignitaries of the Empire. Their influence did not diminish. Napoleon had formed his team, watched it do great things and was not about to disband it. There was only one significant ministerial change, in which Chaptal was replaced by Champagny as Minister of the Interior. Although this change involved the replacement of a republican intellectual with an *ancien régime* technocrat, there was nothing 'political' about it. Napoleon felt Chaptal had handled a subsistence crisis in Paris badly in 1803, arousing fears of popular disorder in the capital. Napoleon always regarded calm and order in Paris as a priority, and Chaptal paid the price, but in a gentle way. Napoleon attributed his failure to ill health, which was true, and allowed him to resign with honour.[34] Otherwise, the central government simply carried on.

In fact, the institution of the hereditary principle created new problems for the regime, rather than resolving uncertainties; it threw into yet starker relief how precarious the succession actually was. Napoleon had no son; he had excluded two of his four brothers from the line; Joseph had proved a very able ambassador and an indispensable negotiator, but these posts kept him out of the public eye, and to point too clearly in his direction – as the eldest Bonaparte male – served only to underline how incongruous appeals to traditional forms of legitimacy were in the circumstances. As for Louis, his only claims to anything were that he was Napoleon's younger brother, and he had been educated under his wing; in time, he would discredit even this claim to succession. Louis' greatest asset to the regime was his wife, Hortense, whom Napoleon valued greatly for her considerable intellect, but even more because she had already produced two sons (and in 1808 would give birth to a third, Louis-Napoleon, the future Napoleon III). Yet they were infants in 1804 and the prospect of a long regency was unsettling. Napoleon decreed that the Senate in an emergency could nominate his successor, another recourse to Roman constitutionalism, but the spectre of the army tearing first itself and then France apart in a power vacuum was real enough in these years. Everyone knew Joséphine could no longer have children. The creation of the Empire had only worsened what it was meant to resolve.

In the short term he and the family, and the political elite, revelled in his triumph. The Bonaparte sisters and the new Empress rivalled each other in their embarrassing extravagance, from running up unpayable bills for haute couture to commissioning state-of-the-art carriages, which they raced against each other through central Paris. The most tangible signs of confidence began with the creation of the Consular court and the blatant pomp of public ceremonies, such as his reviews of the elite units of the army in Paris, or the great parades and public banquets that marked the Treaty of Amiens all over France. As with the constitution, the court needed very little fundamental change after the creation of the Empire in 1804, so regal had the public face of the regime already become. Titles were embellished, as were official costumes, which were far more ostentatious than those of the Bourbons. Napoleon, with the help of Talleyrand, had already put a strict, largely Bourbon-derived court etiquette in place by 1804. There were well-defined, rigidly adhered to hierarchies; Joséphine had her own household and ladies-in-waiting. Napoleon moved his private residence from their family home, Malmaison, to the old palace of

St-Cloud, to the west of Paris. In the most significant symbolic gesture, he moved his official residence from the Hôtel de Luxembourg to the Tuileries, and had it lavishly redecorated. As the negotiations for the Concordat began to assume a central place in his plans, Napoleon began attending Mass every day in the Tuileries. He adopted the 'royal waddle', a walk in which the monarch swayed from side to side, lifting his head and craning over the shoulders of the crowd, at official receptions, in imitation of the Bourbon kings. It was the only way the king – or Napoleon – could see who was there. Despite the grumblings of republicans and the cattiness of royalists, the court had its uses, as well as its sense of triumphant reward for Napoleon and his people, who embraced the pomp with a feeling of having earned it.

Napoleon was sending out a clear message to his own countrymen that the new regime was here to stay, that this was not another fleeting collation of Revolutionary politicians that could be undone tomorrow. Napoleon was in power for life; permanence was the price of stability. There were other aspects of the official face of the regime that underscored its novelty, and which rendered the notion of a Bourbon restoration null and void. This ranged from the most obvious to the smallest detail. Flunkies reappeared in full livery on state occasions, in the silk stockings and powdered wigs so despised and eschewed in the 1790s, but the colour of their liveries was not that of the old monarchy; they wore green and gold, the original colours of the Revolution, those of hope and youthful vigour.

Napoleon did not go back to Versailles; he chose the Tuileries, in the heart of Paris, and his choice resonated with both recent and older history. He did not want to associate himself with the symbol of a decadent monarchy, which Versailles had become; it was redolent of failure, and it was too far from Paris, from the centre of power, for a working monarch. Napoleon was associating himself with an older, more dynamic monarchy, and he affirmed this when he later renovated Fontainebleau, the favourite palace of Henri IV, one of the most popular kings in French history, who was widely regarded as having brought France out of the trauma of the Wars of Religion.

Recent history was at least as important in this symbolic strategy, however. The Tuileries was the palace to which Louis XVI had been dragged by the Paris mob, and where he had been held against his will by the Revolutionary government. It became a virtual prison for the royal family after the failed flight to Varennes. Above all, it was the scene of several violent confrontations between the people of Paris and Louis, which culminated in the most spectacular bloodbath of the Revolution, when the armed Parisian militia and the Swiss Guards had fought – literally to the last man – on the grand staircase on 10 August 1792. The Tuileries was the very spot where the old monarchy met its blood-soaked death: with the Swiss bodyguards annihilated, the royal family was hauled before the assembly and imprisoned in a real jail, the Temple, to await their trials and executions. Napoleon embraced this dark heritage when he moved house. It was the outward expression of the title Napoleon took when he became 'Emperor of the French', not of 'France', which recalled the patrimonial powers of a king by Divine Right. It was in the Tuileries that Louis had rejected, in his heart and then by his attempted escape, his new epithet, 'King of the French'. From that same palace, the Tuileries, Napoleon embraced the concept of the new monarchy envisaged in 1789 with pride and alacrity.

The matter of how Napoleon was to be proclaimed Emperor of the French still had to be decided. Nothing was simple in the transition from Consulate to Empire, however meticulously Napoleon prepared his plans. At this point, problems arose within the Council of State, hitherto his bastion of support. The arguments were over 'how' he should be affirmed as Emperor. The nature of the cavilling – the devil in the details – revealed the fissures, and fears of fissures, that still preoccupied those at the heart of power.

Napoleon knew what he wanted, and got his way, but not without a series of arguments. He wanted a religious ceremony in Notre-Dame, with the Pope in attendance, but not presiding, and he wanted control of the coronation firmly in the hands of his own people. Even those who knew him best failed to see that he intended to use this occasion to put the Church in its place – in a brightly gilded cage – not to abase either himself or the Republic before it. The very mention of religion could send the most moderate of former revolutionaries into apoplexy, and this affair was no different. Seen in the longer term, the arguments over the coronation were the first specific signs that the regime had set itself on the impossible quest for 'legitimacy'. Hitherto, as a republican head of state, election – of a sort – provided as much security as any regime enjoyed since the constitution of 1791 replaced the National Assembly, which began life as the very legitimate Estates General of the old monarchy. Napoleon was playing a different game now. In truth, most of the Councillors thought that the *senatus-consultus*, decreeing the creation of the Empire, followed by the plebiscite, was sufficient, but Napoleon argued that what the Senate could do it could also undo. (The events of 1814, when the Senate claimed that it had legally deposed him, proved he was more right than he had dared imagine in 1804.)

The Council of State through its spokesman, the loyalest of the Brumairians, Regnaud de Saint-Jean d'Angély, wanted a purely secular ceremony on Revolutionary lines; it was to be held in the open air, on the anniversary of the coup of Brumaire, on the Champs de Mars, where the Eiffel Tower now stands. This was where the constitution of 1791 – the Festival of Federation – had been celebrated in 1791, and where Louis XVI had sworn allegiance to the new regime. Napoleon had answers to this: it would associate the Empire with the greatest blunders of the Revolution and identify him with Louis far too closely. There was more, however: Napoleon argued that the 'public' would be solely the people of Paris, and that this would revive the illusion that the urban population incarnated 'the French people' which Robespierre and Marat had so disastrously imbued them with during the Terror, a sense of superiority that allowed them to think they could make and unmake governments at will. Napoleon added that 'The people was sovereign then, everything had to be done in its presence; we should be careful not to let them think it is still so. Today, the people are represented by legal institutions.'[35] Napoleon referred to 'the people' as a collective sovereign body when he spoke of the Revolution; now, however, 'the people' had become a group of individuals, not a whole. Napoleon revealed not only a crafty sense of recent history, but his genuine fear of the Parisians. The skill of the committee man, who could turn the problem back on its proposer, won this round for him, for he was not the only one on whom this return to a volatile past might backfire.

He did so again, when there was talk of moving the ceremony away from Paris, most probably to Aachen. Here, Napoleon relied on his only real ally, Portalis, who pointed out that, if the coronation was held elsewhere, Napoleon would still have to make a triumphal return to Paris. The significance was lost on no one, for this had been the practice of the French kings for centuries. When the new monarch left Paris for Reims for his coronation he was still always described as the Dauphin – the legal fiction being that the old king had not died until the new one had been anointed and crowned – and returned to his capital, miraculously transformed. At no point did anyone consider Reims, it should be noted, but the spectre of a 'royal' restoration would be evoked if the ceremony took place anywhere save Paris.

Finally, the Council proposed Les Invalides, where the Legion of Honour and the marshalate had recently been created, but Napoleon pointed out that it had yet to become a truly 'national' venue; it was still too closely associated with him personally. Notre-Dame had been at the centre of many things during the 1790s, for good and ill. It had been the 'Temple of Reason' under the radical city government of Paris during the Terror, and then of Robespierre's Cult of the Supreme Being, but since 1802 it had been returned to Catholic worship; Notre-Dame belonged to a shared French experience. Napoleon won the debate, not by force but by pointing out where other ideas might lead, and there is no doubt the discussion was open and the result in the balance. Napoleon could not override the Council on such a matter. The abandonment of an outdoor venue for a traditional building carried an anti-revolutionary significance, even if they were all united in wanting to avoid a ceremony that aped the *ancien régime* too directly. Napoleon ensured that the choice fell on a site that was a national icon, whose history belonged to everyone.

Napoleon did lose one battle, however. He wanted his official portrait in the imperial robes to represent him with his left hand firmly and visibly clutching the hilt of his sword, while holding the crown over his own head with the right. It was a very belligerent, aggressive pose. His favoured artist, David – a man of profound republican politics and the creator of very martial republican art – baulked at its provocative imagery, although he sketched it out in full, and the Council agreed. Napoleon, having been so skilful and measured throughout the process so far, had suddenly lost control and reverted to his idea of himself as the combat soldier at war with the world. He saw sense quickly enough, and the result was Ingres' famous embodiment of the remote, almost abstracted pseudo-Byzantine Emperor, sitting on his throne, impassive, his sceptres in his hands. The image perhaps reveals deeper currents within Napoleon. His insistence on public formality had been apparent since his time at Mombello, and had been given increasingly free rein since he became Consul for Life. Ingres' official portrait is redolent of the ruler's sense of himself, at once inscrutable and immoveable, anchored in routine and legality. It was not the only image of his civil role he would countenance – in 1812, he had himself represented by David as very much the human, balding, paunchy and overworked servant of the people – but this was how he chose to initiate the Empire, and himself as Emperor.

Then there was the question of the Pope. Napoleon put the question in at the end, as a bombshell: 'Would it do to ask the Pope?' Bernier had assured him it could be done. Joséphine quickly rediscovered intense religious devotion, and also set to work charming Cardinal Caprara, the rather worldly papal legate to Paris. They needed their respective skills, for the Papacy recoiled from the idea. Rome posed conditions that Napoleon was ready to meet: he was not to take his oath to the Concordat in the Pope's presence – he was to do so outside Notre-Dame, after the ceremony; there was to be no mention of the Concordat at all during the ceremony; if Pius was to leave Rome,

Napoleon would have to send him a handwritten invitation. Even so, Fesch warned Napoleon that Pius had really expected Napoleon to come to Rome to be crowned – in the manner of Charlemagne – and that the College of Cardinals would throw the whole matter out. It was the realpolitik of Talleyrand and Napoleon which convinced Rome in the end. Talleyrand intimated that, should Pius accept, Napoleon might be prepared to return some papal territory, namely the Legations around Bologna. Napoleon did nothing of the kind, but the hint worked. Pius could not be seen to refuse even the slightest chance of recovering part of his legitimate realm.[36]

On one point Napoleon and Pius were firmly agreed: Pius was there as the most honoured guest, not as a participant, still less as the celebrant. He did not want to touch the new, imperial crown, and Napoleon did not want papal hands on it. The Council of State did not like the idea of the Pope taking any part; Regnaud snapped that 'Peoples, not gods, give crowns',[37] but it was obvious that Pius was essentially coming on Napoleon's terms. The Pope's own reticence and his desire to keep a safe distance from the whole affair was, Napoleon argued, a sign of the Republic's success, not of its weakness.

One person did stay away, however: Letizia, the Emperor's mother. Napoleon was sufficiently embarrassed by this to take an exceptional step for a man of power. It is the usual practice of dictators to 'airbrush' awkward people out of official histories, but Napoleon ordered that his mother be given the most prominent position in David's official painting of the coronation, hovering in a balcony directly over Napoleon himself. Letizia was in Rome at the time, thus heightening the irony, and had been appalled by the entire idea, particularly by the vision of the loathed, philandering Joséphine becoming an empress, after the heartache she had caused her son and the disgrace she had brought on the family. However, she was even further upset when she believed she had simply been ignored in the official protocols. Fesch reported directly to Napoleon that she felt embarrassed by not being given an official title when all the other Bonapartes were now princes and princesses.[38] Letizia found more important family business in

Rome: Lucien's inappropriate wife had just given birth to a daughter they named after her. Madame Mère did not arrive in Paris until 19 December, a full seventeen days after 'the event'. Napoleon accepted all this quietly.

There were other family issues to settle as the coronation took shape. Pius, now in Paris, remarked to Napoleon that he and Joséphine were not properly married, and that 'whatever the many past differences between France and Rome, we should not be separated by a point of etiquette'.[39] It was an iron fist in a velvet glove. Pius had thrown the entire affair into potential disarray with a mere nod; the succession would be invalid should Joséphine have a son, and the entire ceremony rendered a mockery. Fesch did his string-pulling and paperwork in Rome, however, and Talleyrand summoned the parish priest of the nearest church to the Tuileries, St-Germain-l'Auxerrois, to marry the imperial couple the night before the coronation.

Many aspects of French royal history were invoked in the magnificent three-hour ceremony at Notre-Dame on 2 December 1804, but none could possibly have included anything like an emperor being snubbed by his own mother, for the most human reasons of family pride and resentment; nor would there have been a precedent for the very modern conundrum of the 'semi-married' couple caught out by convention in their bid for respectability. From time immemorial, future kings of France had spent the night before their coronations in deep prayer, after first being anointed with the holy oil given by Heaven to Clovis. The Bonapartes instead got married. This would be a very contemporary monarchy.

When the arguments were over, the Council of State swung to a man behind their leader: 'Regnaud did the organising; Cambacérès did the checking; Lebrun kept the books; Fouché kept watch; Berthier selected the [military] units to represent the army; Portalis and Champagny chose the civilian delegations; Maret kept Napoleon abreast of every-thing, as his master, to be sure, had an opinion about everything,' as Thierry Lentz has so wonderfully put it.[40] Napoleon was not the only one who did not bear grudges. They had all come to realise it was their day, too. Napoleon knew how to lead, to inspire, and this was one such moment. All his people had come a long way, and he let them feel it. Camaraderie and lack of animosity was markedly absent in the ranks of his siblings. They all choked with fury, in unison with their mother, at the prospect of Joséphine's elevation, and the sisters bridled at the prospect of carrying her train to the altar of Notre-Dame. It was not pure jealousy. Like their mother, they knew how much Joséphine had hurt the brother they loved over the years. They were not unjustified in these feelings. Yet they could not fathom the complex insecurities that dictated so much of Joséphine's behaviour. The Bonapartes saw only a gold-digger, and a fickle one at that, who had all but taunted their brother in his hours of danger and despair, and who only seemed to 'rally' to him once those dangers faded and his star was secure. To have been the mistress of powerful men in dark times was one thing, but it had been unforgivable of her to flaunt the insignificant Hippolyte Charles in so blatant a way that the affair reached the British gutter press. The Bonapartes were incapable of the self-restraint that had guided Napoleon to success, particularly when the occasion demanded it.

Napoleon himself knew that the occasion was not a success with the Parisian public. The whole idea repelled republicans and royalists alike. Although crowds thronged the area between the Tuileries and Notre-Dame, almost all contemporary observers agreed they were more curious than enthusiastic. It was all very predictable, and afterwards there was a spate of pamphlets from both extremes condemning it. As Thierry Lentz has observed, the popular reaction mirrored the results of the plebiscite of May 1804; it was far from a rejection, but it amounted to only a tepid acceptance, 'directed more to the personality of Bonaparte, than to the principle of a new monarchy'.[41] For those closely involved, for the truly 'amalgamated', and for the newly created Imperial Guard above all, it was a moment of triumph. They had seen their commander raised to the height of power. They were resplendent in new uniforms, their arms gleaming, as they lined the route between the Tuileries palace and Notre-Dame, while the most elite units, the Gendarmerie of the Guard and the Guard cavalry, on new mounts, rode as escort for the imperial couple to be. The day that was for the whole French people turned into a victory celebration for the insiders. This is not to say that all were not welcome. Every effort had been made to create a ceremony based neither on religion nor tradition, but *ralliement* and *amalgame*. Indeed, something of Napoleon's inveterate anti-clericalism permeated the affair. Certainly, he went back on many of his promises to Pius VII.

The papal cortège left the Tuileries well before Napoleon's, and Pius was kept waiting in a very cold Notre-Dame for almost two hours before the newly-weds – the Emperor and Empress – drove up in their carriage, drawn by no fewer than eight horses, made heavier by being over-crowded, as it also held Joseph and Louis. The doors of the cathedral had been opened well in advance, and all the invited dignitaries were in place. Napoleon arrived already dressed in his imperial robes. Most importantly, he wore a Roman-style laurel wreath on his head, to acknowledge that he was already, legally, Emperor. With him was Joséphine, uncrowned, but in her robes, her train constantly sabotaged by the three Bonaparte sisters; her only ally in this hostile crowd was her daughter, Hortense. The symbolism that greeted them was eclectic. The new emblem of the regime, the golden eagle, was everywhere – Napoleon had preferred a lion, and toyed with the idea of an elephant, but had been overruled in the Council of State – and the imperial robes were embroidered with the bees of the Merovingians. The costumes of the great officers of state, Murat's especially, as Governor of Paris, were modelled on those of Francis I, the great king of the French Renaissance. In its efforts to evoke all the acceptable epochs of French history, it risked becoming something of a costume ball, yet most contemporary observers were generally impressed. The Pope said a Mass; it had been agreed the imperial couple would not take communion but only be blessed by him. The imperial regalia were all new; there was no attempt to integrate any objects of the old monarchy, although some Carolingian relics, most of dubious provenance, were carried by several of the marshals during the ceremony. The new imperial crown had been placed on the high altar, and, at the appointed moment, Napoleon took it, turned to the congregation, raised it above his head and crowned himself. He then crowned Joséphine. Pius pronounced the blessing, and led the *Te Deum*, and withdrew to the sacristy. This was the point at which Napoleon went back on his word to Pius, who had had to accept the change, sprung on him at the last moment: Napoleon did not pronounce his oath to the constitution outside the Cathedral as he had promised but from the steps of the high altar, as Pius hid in a side room. The oath could not have been more republican:

I swear to maintain the territorial integrity of the Republic; to respect, and to make respected, the laws of the Concordat, and of freedom of religion; to respect, and to make respected, the equality of rights, [and] political and civil liberty, the irrevocability of the sale of *biens nationaux*; neither to levy nor to impose any tax, save in virtue of the law; to maintain the institution of the Legion of Honour; to govern only in the interests of the happiness and glory of the French people.

When Napoleon had finished there were orchestrated cries of '*Vive l'Empereur*'.

That day, what did not happen was as important as what did. Napoleon refused to revive most of the key elements of traditional coronations. At no point did he kneel in prayer or for any other reason; he entered already crowned, and in full robes, not dressed humbly in a thin shirt, as did the Bourbons; he did not take communion. No doves of peace were released, and Napoleon refused to give the royal touch for scrofula, a practice he abhorred as a superstitious affront to modern science. He did not invoke ancestors he did not have. Above all, although the ceremony contained a religious element – the Mass said by the Pope – it was far from a sacrament, as royal coronations were at their very heart. Only when it was all finished, after the Emperor and Empress had processed out of Notre-Dame, did Pius reappear and take his own leave. Although twelve days of public festivities followed, when the ceremony was all over – at three in the afternoon – everyone simply went home.

It was a very self-conscious, calculated affair which, in some ways, achieved what it set out to do. Whatever the coronation was, it was not, nor was it meant to be, a restoration. The combined work of Napoleon and the French Revolutionaries had driven a permanent wedge between the *ancien régime* and all things to come. In 1827, Charles X tried to revive medievalism in his coronation, transferring the ceremony to Reims, having himself anointed with the holy oil of Clovis the previous night, and insisting on traditional attire. It was a fiasco, which brought him only ridicule, and not only from partisans of the Revolution. Napoleon's coronation, by comparison, was a success, because it was born of success. Those who would mock dared do so only from the safety of exile, for however self-conscious, pretentious or vulgar, it marked a hard-won personal triumph for the man, his family, and for those who had stood with him through the perils of the early days in power. *Le sacre*, the official term for the coronation, was glorious, the triumph of ability, effort, intelligence, and no small amount of courage. It was, in the best sense, a celebration of merit. On entering Notre-Dame, the story goes that Napoleon turned to Joseph and said: 'If only our father could see us.' It is probably just that, a story. Most observers noted how pale and quiet Napoleon remained until he swore the oath. Yet it is a story that should be true.

What the ceremony was intended to generate – a new, legitimate dynasty – was another matter altogether. In this, Napoleon was no more successful than Charles X a generation later, and, in truth, he knew it. A rationale for the creation of a hereditary empire, put forward at the time and since, was that France needed to deal with the monarchies of Europe on an equal footing. If so, the coronation simply drew embarrassing attention to the lack of equality between the different regimes, for the only heads of state to attend were Pius and a collection of rulers from the smallest of the loyal German states; Baden was the largest of them. In all fairness, Max Joseph of Bavaria had intended to come, but chose instead to remain at the side of his heavily pregnant wife, a decision Napoleon applauded.[42]

Recognition, when it came, had to be won on the battlefield or at the conference table. The institution of the hereditary principle made internal, indeed domestic problems, even more acute. The search for an heir went on. When Joséphine knelt before Napoleon, in her seeming moment of glamorous triumph, it was as if a prelude to being beheaded. She had spent most of the last eighteenth months at one spa or another, seeking the epoch's equivalent of fertility treatment, to no avail, while Joseph and Lucien sought to undermine her with rumours of adultery and planned to engineer a marriage to a Spanish princess for their master, all behind his back. These were more important matters to France than Beethoven's famous striking out in anger of his dedication to Napoleon from the score of his third symphony.

There was something much deeper to be learned from this strange day of celebration. An 'ancien régime' cannot be conjured or commanded into being, as Napoleon wished, any more than it could have a second coming by necromancy, as Charles X imagined. The efforts of both Napoleon and Charles X were fruitless – in the case of the first Bonaparte poignant, in that of the last Bourbon bathetic – when compared to the last coronation of the *ancien regime*. Then Louis XVI had the nonchalance born of security to break with precedent and stage a ceremony with contemporary dress and music in Reims. Yet Napoleon had succeeded in other ways. *Le sacre* showed the world, if only semi-consciously, that there was no going back and, above all, it was the apogee of a very modern fairy tale for a political faction, for a family, for one man, and for all those members of a great nation who chose to join in. There had never been anything like it before, and there was more to come. Within a year, the glory of *le sacre* was surpassed by military triumphs as yet undreamed of.

12

WAR WITH BRITAIN

Birth of the Grande Armée and Death of the French Navy

Madame Junot recounted a story Napoleon told a group of young socialites sometime in 1803. One day, a rich Marseille merchant received a young man of good family, who bore him a letter of recommendation. The merchant read the letter and, seeing that the writing covered only one of four sides of expensive paper, tore off the three blank sheets and put them in a wallet full of scrap paper to be recycled. The young man was most unimpressed by this seeming parsimony, but accepted the merchant's invitation to dinner nonetheless. He was dumbfounded by the wealth and good taste that greeted him at the merchant's home, which contrasted with his grim counting house, just as his erudite, cultivated conversation little resembled his businesslike conduct at work. He admitted it was one of the loveliest occasions he had ever experienced, but could not hide his perplexity. The merchant explained thus: 'You are too young to understand how masses are formed, the true and only power; whether composed of money, water or men, it is all alike. A mass is an immense centre of motion, but it must be begun – it must be kept up. Young man, the little bits of paper which excited your derision this morning are one among the many means I employ for attaining it.' Madame Junot recalled her own reaction: 'I was much struck afterwards by this idea of masses as the foundation of power, so characteristic of Napoleon's policy.'[1]

She knew that of which she spoke. Even as he told this tale – perhaps an echo of what he had learned in the Clary household, where he first encountered such a culture – Napoleon had set about creating a new army of unheralded size, a mass of men. He 'began' his mass in the camps he set up along the Channel coast between June 1803 and the autumn of 1805. Napoleon had directed all his civil reforms of France to the *ralliement* of the 'masses of granite'; now, he would match them with a mass of bayonets, of which he was the undisputed master and creator. It was collated from little pieces, the conscription quotas of each department, to be forged into what a later age would rightly call a weapon of mass destruction. This 'mass' began – was set in motion – as the Army of the Ocean Coasts, intended to invade England, but it came to be known to itself and all who had to face it as 'the Great Army', *la Grande Armée*. When the Austrians and Russians joined Britain in the alliance against Napoleon, and reignited war on the continent, he was ready to set it in motion, a motion that did not stop until he reached the shores of the Baltic. The years of relative peace had been the good times. The years of war against the Third Coalition were those of greatness.

Just as in his cautionary tale to the young blades, Napoleon began creating his mass prosaically. The birth of his army – the first that was his own, a very personal creation – started with the grim reality of mass conscription, with its ruthless combination of terror and red tape, in the depths of *la France profonde*. It began with prefects and their clerks, with justifiably frightened justices of the peace and mayors in isolated towns and villages, poring over the lists of names of young men who would defy them, usually with violence, almost always with the support of their families and communities. It continued with the flying columns of gendarmes swooping down on these communities, to enforce the findings of the clerks. Even Madame Junot, a self-confessed idolater of Napoleon, called these scraps of paper 'the conscripts just snatched from their families'.[2] Few people out of uniform or the bureaucracy could speak with such authority. Her husband was one of those charged with welding these lost, defiant souls into soldiers; she saw them arrive at her husband's depot in Arras, and transformed into the Grenadier Division, one of the elite units of the Grande Armée. She wrote with glowing pride of the end result of her husband's labours, but she had no illusions about how it all began.

Napoleon risked much to create his army. He threw Gaudin's financial system into near chaos to pay for it, and the process of conscription, predictably, tested the process of pacification of the Midi and the western departments to the very limit; in some places – notably the rugged Massif Central and the Pyrenees – it almost made a mockery of the whole notion of 'pacification': '[T]he Gendarmerie's raids emerge as veritable acts of war more than simple policing operations,' for one historian of this process in the Cevennes mountains.[3] There were regional nuances to resistance, but these were due more to differences of topography – more or fewer places to hide, better or worse positions from which to ambush gendarmes – than to support for the 'blood tax', for which there was none.[4] In many areas, it is not an exaggeration to speak of an 'interior front', a war behind the lines, revived and expanded by the renewal of mass conscription in 1803, which endured to the end. Every sinew of the new state first conceived in 1789 was mobilised to create this mass of men, on a scale never possible in the past. The 'blood tax' of conscription was now levied with a bureaucratic precision and an armed force far more organised than ever before. There were teething troubles, most certainly; administrative errors existed: in 1804, the Ministry of War had forgotten to take into account naval conscription in the Bordeaux area – the department of the Gironde – when it assigned its quota for the army; the same error was made in Brittany.[5] Yet the 'mass' was made real, and swiftly.

When it came to enforcement, the new weapon of the Gendarmerie came into its own. Already burdened by containing the embers of counter-revolution, it dealt with its new orders remarkably well, given the magnitude of the task Napoleon imposed on its brigades from this point onwards. Simply amassing scraps of paper was a war, but long before Napoleon's troops ever fired a shot at the enemy, his 'other army' of gendarmes and civil servants had already won the first round of that 'other war', but lost many hearts and minds in the process. One of the clearest signs of this is that, by the time the new levies were assembling for the Channel camps, the problem of desertion – of escaping from army service – was more serious than that of refractory conscripts, those who simply could not be rounded up in the first place. Although there were spectacular instances of mass desertion – as in the department of the Eure, close to the Channel camps in Normandy, and along the Pyrenean border with Spain[6] – the fact that local forces had raised their quotas in the first place marked real progress. Napoleon saw the true problem as administrative, and the worst influence of resistance was on the morale of the troops already assembled. He felt the fines fixed for deserters were too low for the wealthy among them, but so heavy for the poor that they could never be paid, and so did not deter them. All of this could be corrected, however.[7]

One of the important coincidences of Napoleon's concentration of most of the new recruits in the Channel camps, coupled with his own frequent presence there, was that he saw the results of the mass conscriptions of 1803–5 for himself. When the first recruits started pouring in from the 60,000-man levy of 1804, he was quick to pounce on shortcomings. In August 1804, he told Berthier to write to the commanders of the local recruitment councils, warning them that too many disabled men were being allowed through, a waste to the public treasury, and speculating – with some menace – that 'the prefects are out-manoeuvring the soldiers'.[8] Visiting a particular unit in the Rhineland, he rounded on the slackness of the prefect of the Allier, in central France, whose conscripts were earmarked for the 58th Regiment at Cologne, 'of the 400 conscripts he has to furnish, 100 have not arrived, 100 have deserted, so that only 200 remain, and half of them are lame, deaf, and useless'.[9] Of the next levy, he warned General Lacuée, who headed the conscription bureau of the Council of State, that:

We cannot hide the fact that the existing conscription regulations have not attained our goal. Out of 82,000 conscripts, only 64,000 have arrived, of whom 14,000 are deserters. Thus, the conscription process has yielded only half of what was asked.[10]

The circumstances of these years enabled Napoleon to keep an unprecedentedly close eye on all this; that eye was sharp, if often unfair in its judgement, for the figures were soon rectified and the quotas met. Nonetheless, no one was left in any doubt what was expected of them. A handful of prefects, eight in all, were lambasted as 'the worst in the Empire' for their toleration of desertion in the course of recruiting the new army, most of them in the rugged Massif Central.[11] The reality was that Napoleon had little cause for complaint about the 'cutting edge' of conscription in these years, and his rebukes were few in relation to the scale of the task. Most of the local officials of the new regime, gendarmes and civil servants alike, heeded his exhortation to Lacuée to 'work at it, day and night'.[12] The very size of the Army of the Ocean Coasts was proof of this.

The financial perils of the operation put the regime's popularity and the basis of its support at some risk. The hatred stirred by the 'blood tax' among the peasantry was mirrored, if less dramatically, by the unease felt among the commercial community, from the modest shopkeeper to the great financier, not just at the costs of the 'descent on England', but at the drastic means Napoleon was prepared to employ to pay for it. Just as Napoleon jeopardised the restoration of order to create his army, he effectively destroyed the financial stability Lebrun and Gaudin had successfully fostered by 1803. The end of the Peace of Amiens made little real military impact, but it disrupted commerce extensively, and this was compounded by poor harvests. These were the general circumstances in which Napoleon insisted on undertaking the most expensive military preparations conceivable: he had to create large new harbours on the Channel coast, repair and build both a war fleet and a huge flotilla to transport his great army across the Channel, and pay, equip and replenish that army and navy.

To compound all this, Napoleon insisted that everything be paid for in cash, immediately. This was a reaction to the chicaneries of the Directory, and admirable in principle – it showed how traditional his views on public finance could be – but it required unprecedented amounts of liquidity in the public purse. This forced Lebrun, Gaudin and, above all, Barbé-Marbois, the regime's paymaster, down many unpalatable, damaging roads. As the budget deficits grew over the years 1803–5, it was increasingly obvious that ordinary revenues could not cope with the new demands of military expansion, and by 1804 the regime had begun an unending, incessant search for new sources of income. Old forms of indirect taxation were resurrected, of the kind abolished by the Revolution and, by definition, unpopular; a huge sum was imposed on the treasury of the Kingdom of Italy – the first of many – and contributions were extracted from France's allies, Spain, the Batavian Republic and the Swiss Confederation. In February 1804, the government devalued certain kinds of coinage, which many merchants and shopkeepers soon refused to accept. This was the measure that turned public opinion most decidedly against the regime. Hard currency became rare, especially in Paris. As a result, counterfeiting took off, and remained a bane of the regime until the end. Bankruptcies became increasingly frequent, often affecting some of the largest enterprises. Barbé-Marbois did not hesitate to warn Napoleon that foreign investment, which had found France so attractive since 1801, was now fleeing.[13]

France now faced a major war – intended for Britain, but then diverted to central Europe – in a state of financial crisis. The sound financial administrative methods and the underlying system of taxation established by Lebrun and Gaudin would endure for over a century, as would the powerful, effective policing apparatus forged by Moncey, Wirion and Radet in the same years. However, their hard work in restoring France to good order was now thrown into chaos until the fall of the regime. Public finances would not be set aright until the work of Villèle in the 1820s.

THE DESCENT ON ENGLAND

The cause of it all was Britain. The rage Napoleon manifested at the collapse of the peace – in no way buffered by his awareness of its inevitability – now found an outlet. His aggression was channelled, geographically as well as intellectually, into creating an army, a fleet and a strategy to invade England and deal directly and definitively with an opponent he found as baffling as it was dangerous. He moved with remarkable speed and decisiveness. Britain declared war on 16 May 1803; in early June, Napoleon went to Boulogne in person to begin work on refurbishing the harbours to accommodate the vessels needed for the invasion. Boulogne was the point on the coast whence Caesar had successfully invaded Britain, something lost on no one.

The task before Napoleon and his state was enormous. If his initial impulse, the invasion, would prove stillborn, its corollary, the creation of a new military establishment, was an unqualified triumph. On St Helena, Napoleon later said, with genuine foresight, that his greatest and most lasting achievement was the Civil Code. At the time, between 1816 and his death in 1821, the Code's longevity and wide diffusion were far from assured. It did endure, however, and spread itself from France across Europe and further afield. It outlived him, whereas the Grande Armée rose and fell with his own fortunes; its last stand was at Waterloo, but by then it was a shadow of the force that was being created along the Channel coast. In its own time, however, the French army was the arbiter of its age in Europe. If the Civil Code was indeed Napoleon's greatest achievement, the creation of the Grande Armée was the work in which he took greatest joy; it was what came naturally to him, however dazzling his range of competence in so many fields. It was a labour of love, and his time in the Channel camps, directing its evolution from his headquarters at Pont-de-Briques, was probably the happiest moment in an otherwise fraught time in his life, both public and private. Preparing for war was a relief after divorce, unruly parliaments, tedious committees, lost colonies and assassination attempts. His labour was, above all, driven by the hope of ridding himself of something he hated all the more because it befuddled him: Britain. What emerged was a masterpiece, and the source of an epic, however brutal, mundane and, at times, sordid were its origins in the mire of conscription.

There were two distinct aspects to the grand strategy of the invasion of England: the naval preparations, and the reorganisation of the army. Napoleon often showed himself uncomprehending to the point of incompetence when confronting with the former, and a master in directing the latter. He had to begin the entire operation virtually from scratch, and this was especially true of its maritime aspects, about which he knew little and learned virtually nothing in the process. If there were some causes for optimism, they were largely on paper. The French navy appeared strong in terms of numbers, and Napoleon worked on this principle alone. He had superiority in warships, but increasingly his crews were inexperienced conscripts, whom the British, through their successful blockade, had allowed little chance to gain experience at sea. It has been estimated that almost half of the French crews at Trafalgar were actually redesignated soldiers, and the Toulon fleet which led that action was itself the most experienced in the French navy, having spent considerably longer at sea – five months in all – than any of the others.[14] However, Napoleon could not really see beyond the raw statistics. This is all too clear in his unrealistic demands over the composition of crews. In May 1804, he ordered his Minister of the Navy:

I am convinced that the ship Le Lion will be ready in Rochefort. I want the frigate L'Armide ready, too, by the end of the month; and as it will be difficult to find a crew for this ship, I want you to send 200 men from the infantry garrison to the ... ships in harbour in Rochefort, and use 200 sailors for the crew of this frigate [Le Lion] ... In this way, we will have five ships of the line and four frigates [ready].[15]

Napoleon was not thinking of these soldiers-on-board as marines, infantry who were specially trained for combat at sea, although he certainly expected them to serve as gunners and to take the lead in boarding enemy ships. He thought they could serve as mariners, a skilled job of which they knew nothing. In the same letter, Napoleon showed a deeper ignorance of how ships' crews work, when he sought to apply a standard maxim around which he built his land army. Not only was it possible, in his mind, to swap soldiers and sailors about almost at will, but he tried to concentrate the best sailors in the best ships – 'My aim is to take the best sailors to form its crew,' he said of *Le Président*, thereby stripping other ships of much-needed experience. No vessel could operate without trained crew, all ships need technical capability; Napoleon was trying to concentrate the best personnel at sea, as he did on land, with the creation of elite units, notably the Imperial Guard and the Grenadier Division. It was all incongruous, to say the least.

This is not to say the British held the great advantages they would later enjoy. Napoleon had yet to hand them these. After Amiens, the British had deliberately run down their armed forces, the navy included, provoking Nelson's outburst in 1803 that 'ours [the navy] is clearly going down-hill ... we made use of the peace, not to recruit our navy, but to be the cause of its ruin'. There would be no margin to spare, should the French inflict heavy losses in the kind of large battle Napoleon always sought on land, and naturally looked for at sea.[16] The British blockade of Brest was hanging by a thread at the outbreak of the war. Once the Spanish entered the war on Napoleon's side, their combined fleets stood at 102 ships of the line, while Britain had only 83 in seagoing condition, but the figures were not the real story. Although the Franco-Spanish war fleets had more ships than the British, their European components were scattered over seven ports, and the largest squadron was at Toulon, on the wrong side of Europe. Bringing them together would have caused a major problem for the British, and Nelson, particularly, was not always sanguine about the prospect of major engagements with the French. The task of uniting the fleets was beyond Napoleon, though he should have seen the problems and not built so grandiose a strategy which hinged on it. The British may have been weaker, but they had a degree of control of the Channel that only the entire French war fleet could hope to challenge. Napoleon needed to control the Channel for between a week and ten days of good weather, to get his army across, and the British maintained a powerful presence at its eastern narrows between Boulogne and Dover. This sector was patrolled by 218 vessels, mainly smaller armed craft adapted for coastal defence.[17] It was here, less than at the level of ships of the line, where British superiority was overwhelming, and it was exactly what the prevention of an invasion required. Conversely the British raided the French coast with relative ease.

These were the problems his opponents posed Napoleon, but his own approach to the proposed invasion created many of his own making. At the level of major engagements, and in his plans to unite his fleets, Napoleon showed little faith in his admirals, merely using them as ciphers for his own ideas, all of which were, as Nick Rodger has shown with devastating precision, fatally flawed. After the debacle of Aboukir Bay, Napoleon may have had reason enough to distrust the naval high command. He damned Villeneuve, particularly, in unsparing language in the summer of 1805, as he began to realise that the British had gained an advantage he could no longer hope to challenge. 'It is impossible to have manoeuvred worse than Villeneuve has,' Napoleon raged on 15 August 1805, as he learned that the British had been able to concentrate their forces and blockade the French in several ports.[18] A week later, on 22 August, the day before he officially called off the invasion, his last outburst was directed at Villeneuve: 'I do not think Villeneuve has the necessary character to command a frigate. He is man without resolve, without moral courage.'[19] Napoleon was not entirely wrong about Villeneuve; even a sympathetic French expert has admitted his natural pessimism, which left him 'paralysed by the passivity ... in his character'.[20] Napoleon was naturally disinclined to take advice from such a man, but he needed it.

Napoleon had no grasp of the inherent problems of tide, wind and bad weather, believing he could move fleets about at will and to precise timetables; he assumed that the British would not react to these movements, and fail to read his intentions. Napoleon's correspondence with his admirals seldom asked about the prevailing conditions, and, when he did, assumed that they would remain unchanged throughout an operation. In July 1805, his exasperation revealed more by what was not mentioned rather than what was. 'I do not understand at all why Ganteaume [the commander in Brest] has not moved; how is it possible, as he knows my intentions, that he let the enemy appear without making any movement?'[21] It did not occur to ask about the weather or the relative strength of the enemy. A startling example of Napoleon's insistence on 'micro-management' without the slightest consideration of wind and weather was his order to the commander of the Rochefort squadron on 26 July 1805:

[I]mmediately after your receive this dispatch ... you will work to effect your linking with Admiral Villeneuve ... If Admiral Villeneuve has not appeared by 15 Thermidor off Ferrol, there is not doubt he will have reached Santiago [in the Cape Verde group] in twenty days, and will have gone on to Cadiz. If you do not meet him at Cape Verde, go on to Cadiz ... If you find four or fewer enemy vessels before Cadiz, you will attack them; if there are more than five ... our intention is that you do not attack. If you have to flee, head for Admiral Villeneuve, whose navigation you will be able to guess.[22]

The unworkable mixture of supposition, insistence on precision in the face of incalculable conditions, and then vagueness, was all too common.

Above all, Napoleon thought purely in terms of the numbers of ships opposing each other, and seldom distinguished between ships of the line and frigates in his calculations: if the French possessed superior numbers at a given time and place, why did they not attack? 'My intention', he told Decrès in August 1805, 'is that if there are at least 25 enemy vessels before him [Villeneuve], having eighteen French and at least ten Spanish vessels under his orders, he should attack the English.' In the same missive, he assumed that the British fleets were still scattered when, in fact, they were converging.[23] It was evidence of another, undermining characteristic of Napoleon's approach to naval warfare: he assumed knowledge and certainty he did not actually have. He relied on reports in the English press to tell him where the British were, and worked on the assumption that, by the time he had received the news and transmitted it to Decrès, and then on to the naval bases, it was still valid. Above all, Napoleon kept changing and cancelling operations, sending out squadrons only to recall them immediately. This mixture of presuming nature would obey his orders, and then changing those orders so quickly, threw his navy into confusion. Not only did he refuse naval advice, he became muddled in his own.[24] It did not help that the only senior naval commander he trusted, Latouche-Tréville, died in 1804, but he distracted Villeneuve, who commanded the major Toulon fleet, to the point that he asked to resign in January 1805, well before Napoleon began to insult him.

Napoleon was not entirely wrong to want to strike in these months, for there were things he did understand that his admirals did not. This was a moment of political turmoil in Britain, and there was no First Lord of the Admiralty for much of late 1804/early 1805; Nelson, Villeneuve's counterpart in the Mediterranean, had no direct orders from London for the first five months of 1805.[25] This is where Napoleon's mishandling of his naval command emerges most clearly: Nelson, in the Mediterranean, Keith, in the key sector of the Channel, and other senior commanders like Collingwood and Calder in the Atlantic, and even the harassed Cornwallis, guarding Brest and the western Channel against the odds, were at least not hampered by their political masters. In utter contrast, Villeneuve and his colleagues, particularly Decrès – who had the accursed role of being the navy's equivalent of Berthier – were driven to the edge of reason. Napoleon's mishandling of the situation allowed the British the time and latitude he hoped to deny them; while French squadrons set out from port, only to return at Napoleon's whim, Nelson, Calder and Collingwood remained committed to protecting the Channel as their priority. Napoleon had hoped to draw them off with Villeneuve to the West Indies, in an impossible plan to reinforce French defences in Martinique and Guadeloupe, and so clear the Channel and raise the blockades of the French Atlantic ports.[26] In fact, the British did not take the bait, while Napoleon saw those of his squadrons not contained in port scattered over the Atlantic. Nelson set out, with only ten ships, to harass and shadow Villeneuve; the main fleets remained in place. When Villeneuve managed to liaise with other units, he was forced back to port by bad weather, the fleet was scattered by storm and the British were well positioned to resume their blockades. All this was beyond Napoleon, and it was in these circumstances that he hoped to outfight the Channel Fleet, even assuming he got his forces to the area in one piece.

It was a counter-productive exercise in micro-management by a non-expert, as a later age would term it, and did Napoleon less credit than either of his major military defeats in Egypt or Russia, where he behaved rationally, if mistakenly. Napoleon is often compared with Cromwell as a military dictator who emerged from a civil war and whose intrinsic authoritarianism resulted in monarchy. Such parallels are fraught with qualifications, however interesting, but Napoleon's mishandling of a naval war does resemble Cromwell's attempts to apply his military knowledge to the Anglo-Dutch naval war of the 1650s, with comparably poor results. Neither regime really trusted its navy and for remarkably similar reasons: both the British navy of the mid-seventeenth and the French of the late eighteenth centuries were conservative in their politics; both had had large royalist elements in the officer corps, many of whom emigrated; those who remained were suspect, while vacant posts were filled by men who turned out to be more radical than the republican regimes to which they owed allegiance. The climate was one of deep suspicion for both leaders. What Nick Rodger has said of Cromwell's relationship to his navy – 'Soldiers disliked and distrusted the navy, but they could not do without it'[27] – was equally true for Napoleon. Thus, however important to their plans, neither Cromwell nor Napoleon could ever give the navy the latitude they accorded their trusted comrades on land.[28] This had serious implications, compounded by a common refusal to take advice when faced with a kind of warfare they did not understand, and which they refused to approach on any terms but their own.

Napoleon, like Cromwell, left his military commanders to get on with operations, but they both insisted on having a very precise idea of troop movements, positions and the strength of the formations under their subordinates' command before they felt able to delegate. This is exactly what it was impossible to expect in naval warfare. Cromwell would issue orders 'written in a military terminology which in the naval context is ambiguous',[29] as would Napoleon. The more precise orders both men gave sounded worryingly similar to the heavy cavalry manoeuvres both spent so much time developing, but ships are not cavalry. Rodger's damning verdict that Cromwell remained 'unaware how difficult it is to intercept anything in the vastness of the sea'[30] was equally true of Napoleon. Both launched catastrophic amphibious operations in the Caribbean. The similarities amount to a catalogue of blunders unthinkable when set beside their records as soldiers or rulers. Obviously, this was an aspect of Cromwell's career – which fascinated Napoleon – that the French leader had neglected to take on board.

The greatest contrast between them, in this respect, was that although Cromwell was prepared to delegate, it was to the wrong men, whereas Napoleon would not delegate at all. Napoleon stopped short of making his marshals admirals, unlike Cromwell, who sent the officers of the New Model Army to sea, officially titled – during an interregnum in the English tradition of irony – the 'generals-at-sea'. Instead, he attempted to tell them how to rule the seas. All these failings, personal and professional, emerged in Napoleon's dealings with his navy in the years 1803–5, while he still had one. It was fortunate for both men that their ability to carry out ruthless counter-insurgency campaigns – or, more correctly, to delegate them to colleagues with the right expertise – ensured that the threat of invasion receded in their first years in power. Their naval exploits did not.

Before Napoleon could even allow himself to fail at sea, he had enormous problems in creating a base for launching an attack on Britain. The invasion itself demanded complex and expensive engineering works on land, the construction of a huge flotilla of landing craft, and the co-ordination of all this with the war fleets and the weather. It was probably beyond the capacity of any military establishment of the era, and begs the question of whether the British – their unrivalled expertise notwithstanding – could have succeeded with an invasion-in-reverse. It also poses even more sharply the question of whether Napoleon was sensible ever to have thought in such terms. Boulogne, Étaples, Ambleteuse and several other, even smaller inlets had to be converted into major ports to carry the invasion, at a staggering cost. The result was failure. Boulogne was left with a serviceable harbour for peacetime civilian commerce, but the French could not make it anywhere ready enough to support the capacity for the invasion; the new basin they built could hold a thousand landing craft – far from sufficient for the invasion – and the main harbour could not be prevented from drying up, almost by half, at low tide. Rodger has shown that, after over a year's expensive effort, the maximum number of landing craft ever able to sail on a single tide was a mere 100,[31] not enough to carry one French infantry division. Less than half the craft necessary were ever assembled in Boulogne, in any case; it proved impossible to build that many in time. This was wasted effort on a very grand scale.

There was more, however. The landing craft themselves were little short of suicide machines. There was no prospect of transporting a large army in ships of the line, but the landing craft, *péniches,* proved helpless in any encounters they had with even the smallest British patrol vessels. Mounted with only one gun, low-lying and with a single sail, they were powered mainly by oar, and were sitting ducks in the water, and there was no hope of them evading contact with warships on the crossing. Moreover, these craft were very fragile, and vulnerable in bad weather. This should have been made clear on 20 July 1804, when Napoleon ordered a practice exercise during poor weather, against Decrès' direct advice. It resulted in the loss of over 200 men and twelve *péniches,* which shook the morale of the senior admirals but left Napoleon untroubled about his strategy, however concerned for his troops.[32] There was an even deeper problem, however. This incident should have made it obvious that the *péniches* could not cope with high winds, yet a good wind was exactly what they needed to cross the Channel, a wind which, on arrival, would create high surf on the beaches, driving them back at the last minute. Finally, even as the *péniches* needed a wind blowing from south to north to get near the British coast, the French war fleet – should it ever be combined and reach the Dover strait – would need a wind from west to east, in order to arrive in time to protect the crossing.[33] Napoleon never grasped this, nor did he heed those who did. As Rodger has said, 'His idea of the time and conditions necessary for the operation was completely divorced from reality.'[34]

Napoleon remained serious about the invasion project well into the summer of 1805, and confronted by growing threats on the continent it remained his priority. In July, even in the face of threatening Austrian troop movements on his Italian borders, he was very clear to Eugène that, the need to take precautions notwithstanding, 'I am working on the hope that there will not be war.'[35] At the same time, he was issuing Villeneuve with impossible but detailed plans for uniting the French fleets which, he felt sure, would give them control of the Calais narrows for four to five days – nowhere near long enough – telling him 'Europe is in suspense, awaiting the great event which beckons'.[36] He was busy concentrating the Dutch transport vessels at his disposal in Ostend, along with artillery units from the Rhineland, and insisting on speed.[37] On 20 July, he assured Berthier that 'at one moment or another, it is possible the right circumstances will arrive' and assumed Berthier was readying to set sail; that the artillery would be on board and at the ready; that Ney would lead the first wave, followed by Davout and then Soult; that they should all land at four different, but proximate points; that, above all, 'there is no time to lose'.[38]

However, the British had concluded an alliance with Russia in April; in July, the Russians and Austrians agreed a 'convention of war', and Alexander mobilised an army of almost 200,000 men to march into Germany while the Austrians began assembling their forces in early August. From that point onwards, whatever his preferred priorities, Napoleon had to think in terms of a major land war. In these circumstances, it is remarkable that he persisted in his invasion plans as long as he did. Continental war had to become his main concern when Austria joined the new coalition on 9 August; there was also the likelihood that Naples would follow, thus allowing the British important bases in southern Italy, and the possibility of Russian troops arriving there.

Even before the official Austrian declaration of war, Napoleon ordered Fouché to arrest all Austrian nationals in Paris.[39] Yet, even with the certainty of war on the Rhine, in the last week of July and the first days of August Napoleon had convinced himself, on thin evidence, that the British fleet had been drawn away from the Channel to support Nelson in the West Indies and issued a series of unfeasible orders to amalgamate scattered squadrons to enter the Channel from as far away as the eastern Spanish coast.[40] On the night of 2/3 August, he left Paris for Boulogne. A week later, he asserted that the British were afraid to fight, that the combined French and Spanish fleets had done the job – 'they [the British] sense that their end has not been accomplished', he told Fouché[41] – and that 'Villeneuve has fulfilled his goal: the junction [of the fleets]'.[42] He assured Decrès that the British squadron from Plymouth had been too badly mauled by Villeneuve to fight.[43]

In a flurry of letters to all and sundry, the moment of high expectation, of impossible, almost hysterical optimism, poured out of Napoleon, but the gleam soon faded from his eyes. He had not realised that the engagement of 22 July between the British and the combined fleets off Spain's Cape Finisterre had not been a crushing victory, even if it had not been a defeat, but finally, by 15 August, Napoleon knew that Villeneuve would not be able to enter the Channel. More important, he grasped that, even if he reached its entry, the British now had superior forces there that he could not hope to breach, and this was a sign that the balance had tipped irrevocably against him.[44] A week later, however, on 22 August, he was still hoping for a renewed concentration at Brest, but knew it was only possible if Villeneuve could return from Cadiz.[45] That same day, Tsar Alexander ordered his Imperial Guard to leave St Petersburg for central Europe.[46]

Had Napoleon persisted in his plans after this point, he would have been flying in the face of all reality. He did not. These were the dying embers of Napoleon's hope, for the next day, 23 August 1805, he told Berthier that the invasion 'is postponed', and the same day gave the more mundane, but far more definitive order to the Director of War Administration to have full rations ready for the entire army, when it was due to arrive in Strasbourg, on the Rhine, three weeks hence.[47] He told Berthier the change of plan was due to adverse winds; he told Decrès that Villeneuve was a disgrace.[48]

Napoleon had actually begun preparing the way for the great 'U-turn' from the invasion of England to the march on the Rhine after 15 August, when he asked Talleyrand to assess the loyalty of the German princes in the Rhineland and began discreetly to pull troops out of the Paris region and redirect them to the eastern frontier.[49] However, he could not quite let go of the invasion plan until he was convinced in his own mind, once and for all, that he was outgunned in the Channel, and that took a week. When his hopes flickered for the last time, in mid-August, the flurry of ill-considered orders, the selective interpretation of thin evidence and the oft-repeated optimism expressed to all his senior officials were the signs of a man grasping at the final straw, when he had just begun to turn away from a hopeless venture to the reality of the crisis he faced.

The final burst of enthusiasm for the invasion is all the more inconsistent, to the point of irrationality, because, on 13 August, he made his plans very clear to Talleyrand: 'My decision is made: I want to attack Austria and be in Vienna before next November, to be able to face the Russians, if they show up.'[50] He had admitted to himself by early August that it was the war with Russia and Austria that mattered, but he could not resist one last glimmer of hope that Britain might fall. Napoleon's behaviour was foolish on the strategic level, but it was not irrational in the greater scheme of things, for Britain was, indeed, the source of all his real woes.

Villeneuve and the Spanish sat in harbour in Cadiz for several weeks, until Napoleon gave them their last, impracticable order on 10 September, to return to Toulon, to counter a possible Russo-British operation in southern Italy. Nelson did not believe the French would make any such move, so effective was the blockade by now. It has been speculated widely that Napoleon wanted to see something dreadful inflicted on Villeneuve, and indeed his fleet initially refused to obey the order. Nonetheless, on 19 October, Villeneuve broke out, was caught by Nelson and Collingwood off Trafalgar two days later, and roundly defeated, if only after a very fierce battle in which Nelson was killed. Recent research has shown how very hard-fought the battle was,[51] but the outcome, if hardly predictable, was the virtual destruction of Napoleon's sea power for ever. British victory has been generally attributed to their superior gunnery,[52] a crushing irony for Napoleon, the master artilleryman, who had tried hard to improve the firepower and accuracy of the French squadrons he could visit along the Channel coast.

The consequences of Trafalgar were lost on many at the time, as the battle fell on the same day as Napoleon's first major victory of 1805 at Ulm, and was soon overshadowed by the great triumphs of the following months, but they were severe for the French nonetheless. Until then the British had not really recovered the naval superiority they had lost to Napoleon since Amiens and the Spanish alliance – Villeneuve actually outnumbered Nelson at Trafalgar by thirty-three ships to twenty-seven – but the serious losses sustained that day could never be made good. Casualties are difficult to assess accurately: the British losses of 449 men killed were probably only a tenth of the Franco-Spanish total.[53] A small French squadron which had not been at Trafalgar remained at sea for 161 days. In the course of fighting their way home, they captured three British warships and forty-three merchantmen, finally returning to port at Rochefort on Christmas Day, 1805.[54] Blinded by the sun of Austerlitz, Napoleon's most spectacular victory, no one noticed this heroic, forlorn feat of French arms.

Britain had long been the dominant maritime nation of Europe, but France and Spain had been considerable naval powers throughout the eighteenth century, nevertheless. Louis XVI had revived the French fleets at a ruinous cost, but at the start of the 1780s his efforts had seen the British navy overtaken by the French, enough to help the Americans to their final victory at Yorktown and deprive Britain of its greatest colony. All this had made the French navy the career choice of Napoleon, as an ambitious, talented cadet. Trafalgar was its swansong, the last stand of what had been the new, proud, great hope of a French Atlantic empire. The ferocious course of the battle itself reflected this. For all its problems of materiel, personnel and leadership, Villeneuve's fleet offered stiff, often inspired resistance to the British. The French and, to a lesser degree, the Spanish, may have been deficient in guns compared to the British, and the French were certainly poorly trained, but they fought tenaciously, and the British ships were often forced to withdraw from certain duels to search for weaker prey. Most French and Spanish ships that were taken had to be surrounded, not defeated in one-to-one combat. Over one-third of the fleet fought its way back to Cadiz[55] but was then blockaded there by superior British forces. Nelson was killed through the sheer tenacity of a small French warship, the aptly named *Redoutable* ('Formidable'), that clung to the *Victory*, his massive flagship, with the bloddy-mindedness of a Basset hound – that most French of breeds – on the scent of a truffle. It was the determination of a French marine, a dying breed by 1804, who climbed his rigging under heavy fire to pick off Nelson on his own deck, that won Villeneuve the most Pyrrhic victory of modern times. *Redoutable*'s captain, Lucas, had trained his crew very well,[56] and his small ship took two far larger British ships – one of them no less than the flagship *Victory* – out of the battle.[57] The fate of the *Redoutable* was typical of the day, and of the whole French naval war, for after valiant individual efforts it was finally surrounded, outgunned, and forced to lower its flag for lack of ammunition. Heroism was not enough.

Trafalgar had not annihilated the French at sea, but it gave the British an advantage in ships Napoleon could never redress. Above all, it had shown how superior in training, tactics and seamanship the British sailor was to his enemies, however matched in the raw courage of the French sailors, or the intelligence of their captains. Trafalgar decided the course of Napoleon's ambitions, once and for all. His natural inclinations were towards the European continent, rather than the Atlantic world; he was a mercantilist, drawn to protectionism rather than the wide open economic life of the oceans and world trade. He felt more at home with the landed elites and localised commercial networks of the alluvial arteries of *Mitteleuropa* than the life of the great ports. Trafalgar transformed his instincts into his destiny.

It was cold comfort. As Rodger has said, Trafalgar handed Britain unchallenged naval supremacy, materially and psychologically. Napoleon had thrown away the fleet he had spent so much time and effort creating, and this cost him dearly in the years ahead. He was now no longer able to control the coasts of his own empire; henceforth, British Royal Marines could raid almost at will across Europe, and Britain was now able to supply her major allies, as well as future insurgents in Spain and southern Italy, with ease. London would soon make a mockery of Napoleon's continental embargo against British goods; the sulphur deposits of Sicily, the richest in Europe and essential to the British war effort, were now safely behind the wooden walls of the Royal Navy, and would remain beyond the grasp of Napoleon's war machine. It is true that a substantial French fleet remained intact after Trafalgar – many squadrons had not been there[58] – but most of the better seamen had been killed or captured, and the best warships lost. Even Napoleon soon came to realise that it was not a matter of quantity but of quality. He began a furious rebuilding of his fleet, planning to construct 150 new warships after 1805, and set about revamping the harbours of Antwerp and Genoa as naval ports, but this was not the point. Trafalgar gave the British the strategic advantage: the French were blockaded, and the only way to break out was pitched battle, for which they were not ready in 1805, while the British forged ahead. After 1806, the British lost more ships to bad weather than to the French.[59] When Napoleon damned colonies, sugar and coffee to Roederer, he should have damned the sea and its ways as well. Having had the sense to abandon the French Atlantic, he should have renounced naval warfare on the open sea, and concentrated on coastal defence, as he later realised. In 1803–5, however, he was obsessed by the invasion of Britain beyond the point of reason.

Nelson was given the greatest state funeral in British history and became a legend almost on a par with Napoleon; Villeneuve committed suicide in a hotel in Rennes, in April 1806, six months after his fleet had been forced to do the same thing. Napoleon is often condemned for his conduct of the Egyptian campaign in 1798, not without reason, and his greatest disaster was the 1812 campaign in Russia. However, his handling of the naval war in 1804–5 is arguably the most incompetent, and disgraceful, act of his public life. Fortunately for him, it was outweighed by his concurrent work on dry land.

13

THE CREATION OF A MASTERPIECE

The Camp de Boulogne, 1803–1805

Had the invasion of Britain been attempted, it would have destroyed the finest army in the world.

The preparations for the invasion in the Channel camps were a unique opportunity to turn raw, unwilling conscripts into a professional army, but they made an equally important impact on the officers and veterans of the 1790s, who were the experienced core of the army. The chance was seized, and it worked. The soldiers of the French Republic had undergone many profound changes in the years between the outbreak of war in 1792 and its temporary end at Amiens, a decade later.

Those wars had been fought, first, by a mixture of those soldiers of the old royal army who had remained loyal to the new regime – over 60 per cent of its officer corps had deserted by 1791 – and the roughly 100,000 volunteers who had rallied to defend the Republic by the outbreak of war. The latter were the great exception to all the rules of the period; this was the only time in the history of the French new regime, be it under the Revolutionaries or Napoleon – that there was ever substantial, spontaneous, popular support for the war effort. The 'blues' – so called for the cheap blue coats they wore as distinct from the white of the royal army – were drawn mainly from urban, artisan and lower middle-class backgrounds; they were ideologically aware – if not universally politically motivated – and soon filled the gaps at every level of the army as the wars progressed. By the Peace of Amiens the army of the Republic was increasingly composed of what would, under Napoleon, become its mainstay: reluctant peasant conscripts. The core was very different from the mass.

These three elements had grown together by the time of the 'descent on England', but at the cost of losing the initial bearings of both traditional military culture and the new, ideologically fired zeal of the early Revolutionaries. The royal army had been a traditional force of the eighteenth century. Professional officers, almost exclusively of aristocratic birth, led a mixture of foreign mercenaries, conscripted criminals and volunteers who had signed on for lack of money and prospects or, for some, genuine motivation for a military life. The rump of this force brought into the new army of the 1790s much of its professional ethos of caste honour, but its touchstone – dynastic loyalty and a natural deference to nobility – was explicitly condemned by the new regime.

Few professional soldiers felt anything but contempt for the new ethos of 'virtue' – that of selfless service to the Revolution and the Nation propounded by the political commissaries, the representatives on mission, sent out to the army by the government. Napoleon shared this scepticism, however much he may have disdained many of his aristocratic brother officers. Men did not fight for abstract concepts, as he well understood. His famous address to the Army of Italy on the eve of the First Italian Campaign makes no reference to such things. However, it does make great play of the cynical and callous manner in which their own government had neglected the soldiers. Napoleon seized on the mood of the troops; he did not have to drum it into them. The armies of the Republic had been told they were citizen-soldiers, part of the Nation, and their duty was that of any and all able-bodied citizens, to protect it when needed. Under the Jacobin Terror of 1793–4, every effort had been made to support the troops in real terms, and in official rhetoric, for they were encouraged to believe France was behind them, and the Committee of Public Safety in its ruthless prosecution of the war certainly did prize their efforts, if not in ways traditional military culture respected. This was the apogee of the 'army of virtue', a chimera in reality, but an ideal that at least ensured the army could fight on.

The concept of virtue as a source of motivation – as a reason to fight – withered under the Directory, and the soldiers themselves – now mostly fighting outside France – lost a sense of themselves as citizens-in-arms. Military administration became thoroughly corrupt, but this was only the symptom of a deeper estrangement. The Terror had forced an uncaring nation to care about the armies; when the Terror collapsed, the public expected the war to pay for itself and the armies to look after themselves. The impact on morale meant the loss of a compass for the troops. The return of some elements of *ancien régime* professionalism filled part of the gap, and their loyalty to commanders like Hoche, Moreau and Napoleon, who tried to look after them – or allowed them to plunder – became paramount. It was the only sane response. The 'army of honour' made a partial return among the veterans; a fragment of the army of virtue remained in that so many of the officers owed their rapid promotions to the Republic – the chief of state among them – and knew all too well that their careers would have amounted to little otherwise. The commissions of most of the officer corps by the time of the camps in 1803 had become their equivalent of the national lands bought by the 'masses of granite' during the Revolution: their fortunes were bound up with defending the new order. It was a calculated political commitment to a regime they had profited from personally.

None of this mattered to the mass of the new Army of the Ocean Coasts, however. They had not felt the camaraderie built up in the previous decade, any more than they knew of the old army of honour or the new army of virtue. Something different was needed to drive them on. Napoleon achieved this, less by a thoroughgoing revival of the ways of the old regime, still less by appeals to civic patriotism. His insights were based less on recent experience than on an almost anthropological grasp of the culture of the new peasant conscripts. If he drew on some elements of traditional military culture – decorations, honours, pomp – he did so only when they touched deeper human, male needs. Many elements of the old army, social deference chief among them, remained consigned to the past. Napoleon chose to build on the hard experience of the career soldier, but moulded to what he perceived to be the atavistic instincts of those he – with the detachment of a 'Latin' – called 'the Gauls', thus expressing how deep were the roots of the national psyche he was harnessing to the task.

Of greatest importance was what it did for the bulk of the army, the mass of new, raw peasant conscripts. Their transformation was nothing short of astounding when the violence with which the conscripts were extracted from their homes is remembered. The process of discarding patriotism for honour was something that actually affected only a small part of the army: the officer corps as a whole, and that portion of the ranks who were veterans of the 1790s. This experience meant little to the men conscripted in 1800–1, under the Jourdan Law, and nothing at all to the peasant masses who were dragged to the camps after 1803. How Napoleon handled them showed real psychological insight, and what he imbued them with is very representative of his regime, just as his approach has been misconstrued by so many historians. The new sense of duty and the high morale he imparted to the raw levies in the Channel camps did, indeed, see off much of the revolutionary, highly politicised – and wholly unrealistic – policies of the Republic. They were meant to create citizen-soldiers infused with a sense of altruistic duty to the Nation. This had long been seen as risible by the veterans, Napoleon included, but with the army now filled with men whose natural inclination was to counter-revolution, it was essential to turn to something else.

Napoleon's self-confidence was not merited in naval matters, but on land, he knew what he was doing better than any other soldier of his era. That confidence was imparted to others. Whereas he distrusted his admirals, Napoleon showed immense faith not only in his senior commanders – the marshals – but in their subordinates, and in his elite troops, the Imperial Guard, the Grenadier Division and, increasingly, the specialist heavy cavalry and artillery arms. While hardly standing aside from detailed matters, he still gave them far greater latitude in how they carried out his orders. His many missives to his commanders in the Channel camps are largely free of the obsessive harping on the particular that characterised his dealings with the navy.

The hallmark of it all was trust, and it was epitomised by the central pillar of the military edifice, the corps system, which was brought to fruition in the Channel camps. The basic organisation of the Channel camps revolved around the ethos of self-contained independence of the army corps. Each camp was garrisoned by a corps, under its commander, usually a marshal, but in any case always an experienced, trusted general. There were six camps, and six corps: Utrecht, under Marmont, the furthest north, in Dutch territory; Davout in Bruges; Soult at St-Omer; Ney at Montreuil; Brest, the furthest west, under Augereau; and the hub of operations, Boulogne, which Napoleon directed himself, and where the Imperial Guard was based. In addition, Junot commanded the Grenadier Division at Arras, and Bessières commanded the cavalry of the Guard; Murat, the Military Governor of Paris, also took a major role in cavalry training. Bernadotte and Kellermann commanded the forces in northern Germany. Lannes and Masséna were seconded to Italy, to train the Army of the Kingdom of Italy and to command the French troops there, respectively. Berthier, the Minister of War, was, as always, Napoleon's chief of staff and co-ordinated the administration.

The whole concept of the corps was one of delegation and the formation of discrete fighting units, capable of sustaining independent manoeuvres and engaging enemy formations alone, initially, until reinforced. Corps varied greatly in size in the field, but in the camps they numbered roughly 25,000–30,000 each. It is a myth that a corps was a wholly self-contained unit, however: its main constituent was line infantry, with smaller proportions of light infantry units for skirmishing, and light cavalry for reconnaissance and cover, with units of medium and some heavy artillery.[1] In the old royal army, and during the 1790s, many infantry regiments had had two small cannon attached to them, but Napoleon abolished this, and concentrated his artillery in larger units, attached to the corps.[2] Corps were sub-divided into divisions, brigades, regiments, and battalions; there were about four stages of command between Napoleon and his basic unit, the battalion.[3] Heavy cavalry, heavy artillery and the grenadiers – usually tall men, skilled in throwing the dangerous hand grenades of the period – were concentrated in their specialist divisions, although some were distributed in the corps. It was the responsibility of the corps commanders to familiarise themselves with the different branches of the service under their command, and to train them to work together. This system of organisation was hardly novel: Moreau, Hoche and Napoleon himself had been developing it as they went along during the 1790s. It was not a new concept Napoleon plucked out of the air, and it was fully formed as a working model in his mind, and those of all his commanders, by 1803, but the exceptional circumstances of the Channel camps enabled it to become the familiar norm for the entire army.

Napoleon issued countless orders to the corps commanders, but these were usually about shifting units around, ensuring units were up to strength – not in any way a given assumption in the early days of conscription – and he often turned up to review their work, their men, and to oversee exercises. He was punctilious about this, and kept what almost amounts to a library of notebooks – the *carnets* – with him at all times; on campaign, they travelled with him. The *carnets* contained the staffing details of every unit in the army, and were updated both by himself, as he went along, and by his staff regularly every fortnight. Each regiment had its page on which were the names of its officers and the numbers of men who were effectives, sick, wounded or on leave at any given time, and the departments whence the men had been conscripted, and everywhere the regiment had been stationed.[4]

In his memoirs, the Baron Berthezène recounted how, in the days before the Battle of Austerlitz, Napoleon stopped to watch a cavalry regiment he knew well from the Egyptian campaign pass by. Puzzled, he drew out his *carnet*, checked it and snapped at its commander, General Morland, 'This regiment is listed as being 1,200-strong. I counted only 800. What happened to the rest of them?' Berthezène also admitted, however, that officers were so afraid of Napoleon's close interest in numbers that they would disguise the figures if they could.[5] This has led one historian, Jacques Garnier, to wonder how much Napoleon actually did know about the size of his armies, at least on campaign.[6]

Only in the artillery, and then most often in the specific matter of sea batteries, did he interfere directly in the training of their men. Nevertheless, a personal visit to a unit could result in direct action, as after his inspection of the 58th Line Regiment in the Rhineland:

The officers of the 58th are good, and this unit is in good spirits: but I am extremely unhappy with the major, he has not the least notion of manoeuvres; he will only be restored to the rank of major when I am assured he understands them perfectly, an assurance I will decide for myself, when I see him in Paris. If, within three months, he cannot prove he is very familiar with manoeuvres, you [Berthier] will delay his return to his unit by six months.[7]

Should Berthier himself slip in giving him the information he demanded, Napoleon was always quick to spot it. He remarked to his right arm – Berthier was the man the army called 'the Emperor's wife' – when looking at the composition of 4th Light Infantry Regiment, 'there is an error. You well know how important it is that the reports given to me should not contain errors of this kind.' It was a question of how many men were effectives, and how many in sick bay.[8]

Insisting on information did not mean, of itself, what a later age would term micro-management. On the whole, Napoleon left his trusted comrades to get on with it. Only once did he give direct, but gentle, advice to a camp commander, and that was to his fellow artilleryman Marmont, who, like Napoleon, had spent his early career in a specialist arm:

Get familiar with the details of large-scale infantry manoeuvres. The season will start soon when you begin exercising your troops; and you know how very important it is in war, above all, when those first moments are charged and decisive. You have to set the tone for the officers to keep them occupied.[9]

Keeping occupied was essential to Napoleon, and it was the key to the brilliant success he had in forging the army in these years, and the nature of the new army required it as never before. Just over half of the 180,000 men in the camps had seen active service, but most of these were the conscripts of the early Consulate, 1799–1801, and so had little combat experience; there were still a reasonable number of veterans of the earlier 1790s, but it is estimated that less than one in thirty of them had worn the white uniform of the professional royal army.[10] Napoleon was very conscious during the Second Italian Campaign of how badly trained were his replacements from the new conscript levies, and how much work he had to do with them in so short a time in 1801. After the Peace of Amiens, he set the pattern that would dominate the routine of the Channel camps: constant drill with full parades three days in every ten. The army as a whole was still a disparate, disjointed institution. What it possessed now, at its heart, was youth, from the senior commanders to the ranks, and the energy that went with it.[11] Napoleon harnessed all this. However, the ranks were thinning, and this led to new problems.

By 1803, when the Channel camps were created, the bulk comprised the unwilling conscripts of the post-1799 levies and so the task was yet more urgent. They had to be trained, obviously, but they also had to be won over, to be given something close to a new identity. Men had to learn how to fight, and at the same time to like their new life. The first step in this was to prevent them being bored. No one understood the debilitating boredom of barrack life better than Napoleon. As a young officer it had almost put him off soldiering, and he allowed nothing of the kind to happen in the Channel camps. If anything, he fired the men up too much. The intense *esprit de corps* he forged among them led to frequent, violent brawls between corps, regiments and, especially, rival arms of the service within the corps, the 'bourgeois' intellectuals of the artillery conceiving a special hatred for the 'posh rich boys' of the light cavalry, a prejudice deeply embedded in the commander-in-chief himself. The atmosphere of the camps was a recipe for potential disaster. Thousands upon thousands of young men, torn from home against their will, cramped together in makeshift conditions, waiting for orders to move for almost two years; underpaid, often poorly supplied despite their leader's best efforts; being ordered about by men who spoke in accents which may just as well have been Japanese to them at the outset. It should have descended into mayhem. Instead, from these dangerous circumstances the greatest army Europe had ever seen emerged to conquer all before it. The key was Napoleon's ability to steer his commanders to the task of blending training, instilling enthusiasm and, above all, avoiding boredom in the ranks – and then leaving them to get on with it in their own ways.

This devolved approach as exercised by Napoleon showed him at his best. It demonstrated his ability to win the confidence of his commanders by showing confidence in them; he fostered mutual trust at the highest levels through his letters, in much the same way as Nelson did, as Colin White has shown. Both men had proved themselves physically brave by the time they rose to high command, an elemental attribute for any officer. They both knew how to praise when it was deserved, and to cultivate friendship. All this glows from Napoleon's missives to his generals, as it does from Nelson's to his captains. Although Nelson was able to achieve this more easily as the commander of smaller units, and helped too by the close familiarity of life on board – as 'one who achieved results through a natural tendency for good fellowship and trust, rather than carefully calculated management strategies'[12] – Napoleon showed a remarkable eye for a 'job well done', even in the unprecedentedly large formations of the Channel camps. 'A good word to a French soldier from his general ... can often make him forget privations of all kinds and help him surmount the greatest obstacles,' he told Chaptal.[13] Napoleon practised what he preached. Writing to Davout after a review of his camp at Bruges in the summer of 1804, he noted:

Let General Sorbier [whom Napoleon had known as a young officer in Valence] and the garrison of the 48th Regiment know how pleased I am with them. During the various engagements [with British raiders], I saw, in as far as I could, the part played by the land artillery in [our] different successes.[14]

He took the trouble to remember an old friend, and his whole unit.

Napoleon's relationship with Davout himself epitomises his capacity to foster friendship from inauspicious beginnings, and to inspire loyalty by generosity of spirit more than awe. They had not got on well together in Egypt, where Davout's slovenly appearance irritated Napoleon – 'Davout, by the way, was at that time, the most dirty and ill-dressed man imaginable' in the unsparing words of Madame Junot, whose husband was a close friend of both men – and even more his grumbling, sardonic nature. The relationship could have soured for ever because Davout was among those left behind in Egypt, and many others like him understandably never reconciled themselves to Napoleon. Napoleon made a genuine effort with Davout, however, recognising a good man and a fine soldier. In the end, Davout married the sister of Leclerc, Pauline's husband, and he began to imitate Napoleon's neat, soldierly – but understated – dress sense and personal hygiene.[15] Professionally, very soon after his return to France Davout was entrusted with the training and command of the infantry of the Consular Guard, in the formative period of its organisation; there was no higher form of delegation or trust in the Napoleonic military. These are not trivial matters among young, strong-willed, confident men. When Davout won the Battle of Auerstadt virtually single-handed against the main Prussian army in 1806, Napoleon accorded him the honour of leading the triumphal parade through Berlin, a generous admission of his own strategic error for having misread the battles so badly as well as a recognition of Davout's prowess. The relationship had come a long way, because of Napoleon's character, and the friendship he inspired did not wane with defeat: Davout not only rallied to Napoleon in the Hundred Days, he stubbornly refused all the blandishments of the restored monarchy after 1815 and spent the rest of his life on his estates in his native Burgundy.

Like Nelson, Napoleon knew the perfect balance between delegation and control. Nelson, 'having given [his ship captains] a general sense of his overall aims ... was prepared to allow them to carry out his orders in the way that they thought best, and he made sure they understood this'.[16] Napoleon's corps system institutionalised this approach, and his trust in Davout secured one of his greatest victories at Jena-Auerstadt; he began building all this in the Channel camps. Nelson spoke of the 'band of brothers' he had drawn together around him by the time of the Battle of the Nile in 1798; Napoleon set about creating his own brotherhood in the Channel camps, elevating a dozen of them to marshals of France the moment he made himself Emperor of the French. This approach should never be confused with a collegial approach to command, however. Orders were set out clearly, the better to be obeyed; the latitude was allowed in the execution, not the formulation. As General Jonathon Riley, a distinguished field commander in his own right, has discerned, 'Napoleon seems to have recognized the dangers in group decision-making. He reserved this to himself alone, from the beginning of his military life – and he never departed from this.'[17] In the circumstances of the camps, it was devolution of day-to-day authority that mattered, and Napoleon handled it well.

Nevertheless, in practical terms it had mixed blessings. Soult, Marmont and Davout trained their men intensively; they gave detailed, precise instructions to all their officers, down to battalion level, and held major manoeuvres every fortnight, which allowed not only individual units to learn the basics, but gave the whole corps the chance to work together.[18] Soult, indeed, has been saluted by the best historian of this phase of the Grande Armée's history as its real father. In his timeless history of the imperial soldier, Jacques Morvan says of him, 'it is to Marshal Soult, particularly, that France is indebted for that nucleus of excellent officers who formed the camp of Boulogne, and who subsequently were diffused throughout all the other armies of the Empire'.[19] Augereau and Ney were different, however. They had very little training themselves, as was also true of Masséna in Italy.

They had enormous combat experience, as did the officers and non-commissioned officers under them, and the results were different from those of Soult, Davout and Marmont. After nine years of war, few trusted the manual. They went their own ways, and some devised their own drills; empirical experience was always the rule, and this did not produce uniformity.[20] For all that, the circumstances of the Channel camps gave Napoleon an important advantage for basic training. He always believed it took at least three months to train an infantryman in those basics; it was generally admitted it could take as much as three or four *years* to train the cavalry, horses and men alike. At Boulogne, Napoleon had almost two years. Stability itself was important, for the routine of drill, under the same officers and non-commissioned officers, had been frequently disrupted by changes of post in 1799–1802, and would be again, for most of the years before 1814. The camps offered a unique, priceless period of stability, when men and officers got to know each other and when the men came to know their drill, however varied it might be from one unit to another.

What that drill consisted of was twofold in the peculiar world of Boulogne. On the one hand was the normal, basic training Napoleon always set such store by; on the other were the unique demands of training for amphibious landings. The former was the bread and butter of contemporary warfare; the latter proved more useful and influential than might at first seem obvious. The most important, primary training was in learning how to fire a musket in formation, and all muskets of the period – especially those of French issue – were inaccurate and poorly made.[21] Most muskets were accurate up to only about a hundred yards.[22] Wisely, Napoleon stressed the need, well perceived by his commanders at every level, that men needed to learn to fire en masse, in volleys as regular as possible, rather than to attempt to create an army of sharpshooters with muskets inadequate for the task.

However, training for the battlefield went far beyond this. Formation was also crucial, and in this respect the time and stability provided by the camps were vital. To compensate for their poor muskets, formation and a high degree of co-ordination were essential for men to be able to survive and win. There were two aspects to this: the stationary firing line and the advancing formations of line and column. In the former, Napoleon imparted clear views to his officer corps. The normal formation was in three lines, but Napoleon became convinced that the third line was usually less effective or accurate than the first two; often, field commanders simply gave up on it and left the third rank to load muskets for the second rank. It took time to do away with this habit, and it was late in the wars before Napoleon successfully made the two-rank formation standard,[23] a clear example of his clarity of thought but also of his inability to control training at the lowest level. In the first phases of the Revolutionary wars of the 1790s, the new recruits – seasoned veterans by the time of Boulogne – were hastily trained and new combat tactics improvised by their officers. The complex formation of fighting in lines was set aside for the easier method of columns, in which men could simply follow the lead of those in front; they were used as shock troops, with the bayonet much in evidence. Columns were not abandoned in the camps, but all veterans, officers and men, knew that they were really only an expedient. With the time and experience available now, training in the more complex techniques of the line returned. The column was used to advance into a forward position; then the troops formed line for the real fighting, because this allowed for better mass musket fire. Columns would then form and advance to puncture enemy formations with bayonet charges.

The bayonet was the other standard weapon issued to the infantry and, like all good judges of soldiers even today, Napoleon saw its importance for fostering the fighting spirit, at least as much as an effective weapon for killing. The bayonet did little real damage in combat but when brandished it could inspire terror in opponents. One reason he liked his men was because of their preference for the bayonet, and he insisted on its standard issue: 'the bayonet ... has always been the arm of the brave and the principal instrument of victory; above all, it is that which most suits the French soldier'.[24] Napoleon soon saw that the mixture of column and line, bolstered by good bayonet work in attack, could be at its most lethal when he dispersed columns along his lines, to throw at enemy positions he perceived to be weak.[25] An enthusiasm for the bayonet is still the mark of a good soldier, even in an age that has long discarded it in combat. The bayonet was a weapon of contrasts in the hands of the soldier; it could bring out a grim determination to stand fast, but Napoleon saw that its offensive power – the blend of ruthlessness and élan it brought out in the French infantry – helped them give their best.

The hard work of the parade ground was not just about evincing a fighting spirit that depended on the blood rush. Combining line and column, firing in formation, demanded discipline under fire, and this need for attention to detail was also present in Napoleon's determination to curb bad habits among his men that had crept in during the 1790s. The French infantryman was issued with a sack containing fifty rounds of cartridges and his food, and Napoleon was adamant that he should not become separated from it or lose it; if he learned not to do so, it was also a good way of keeping him at his post, and not wandering from it in search of ammunition or food.[26]

The blend of old and new in attack, with the emphasis on the old, was very complex and required gruelling, concentrated drill, but it became the hallmark of the Napoleonic line infantry until the later stages of the wars, when the heritage of Boulogne at last faded under the weight of casualties and frequency of campaigns. By 1809, the column was in more frequent use, to the detriment of the line, but those days were yet to come. The key attribute for battalion and company commanders was flexibility in the use of line and column, and, in the ranks, close familiarity with both formations. Another important advantage of both the corps, as a mixed unit, and of the experience of the camps in allowing it to cohere, was the close support that well-drilled artillery could give to well-drilled infantry. Indeed, Rory Muir has seen this as the sign of how well the army as a whole was working.[27]

The cavalry was an even greater triumph for the hard graft of the camps. Each corps had two or three regiments of light cavalry, but the greatest achievement of the camps was to create a large cavalry reserve of light brigades, and divisions of heavy cavalry divided into dragoons, who could also fight as infantry, and the *cuirassiers*, so called for the armoured breastplates they wore. Light cavalry at the time consisted only of hussars and *chasseurs-à-cheval*, armed with swords and carbines, who were used for scouting, pursuit and patrol; Napoleon would not create lancer regiments until later, having been impressed by the Prussians in this respect. The heavy cavalry were very different. They were shock troops of the first order, big men in armour on heavy horses, but they were far from a relic of the Middle Ages. Like the infantry column, only far more deadly, the *cuirassiers* existed to be thrown into combat at a critical moment, to smash enemy formations in mass but very well-organised charges. The emphasis of their training was on their ability to re-form quickly after the initial charge, for their lack of discipline in this had led to heavy defeats during the 1790s, which the drill of the camps put right.[28]

Napoleon saw they needed more order and discipline than the other arms, and so they were given more officers in proportion to the ranks, as success depended on how quickly they reacted in the field. This could only be inculcated through hard drill, for 'science' was the key here, 'from man to horse', and Napoleon always believed that the heavy cavalry, held in reserve until the crucial moment, had been the decisive factor in his clearest victories.[29] They were an elite force second only to the Imperial Guard itself, and even more favoured than the grenadiers. These units always acquired the tallest and best-built recruits and the biggest horses, for their essence was not their armour but the size and power of the men and horses, 'their size, appearance and reputation enabling them to deliver a more fearsome psychological, as well as physical, blow than any other troops'.[30] They were expensive and both men and horses took a long time to train, for it was a matter of horse as well as man. There was still a serious shortage of good mounts in 1805, and the cavalry did not really enter its brief golden age until 1807, when the magnificent stud farms of Prussia fell into French hands, only for the vast majority of these horses to be lost in Russia in 1812. Until 1805 the French cavalry, under both the old monarchy and the

Revolution, had not been a formidable force on the battlefield; by the time Napoleon re-entered the land war, this had changed beyond recognition. The heavy cavalry, like the bayonet charge, can be seen as almost retrogressive in an era of increasing technological progress, a reversion to the primitive on the cusp of the Industrial Revolution; but this ignores the high degree of precision needed for both practices, in terms of discipline and training, to say nothing of the atavistic aggression they injected into both garrison life and the battlefield.

The camps also offered the chance to forge the light infantry into the best of their kind. The Revolutionary armies had begun by using skirmishers as an integral part of their tactics, spreading light infantry out as a fan to shield the advancing columns, and they were, for a time, among the least esteemed troops. However, throughout the 1790s experience showed them to be an integral part of the army, and by the time of the Channel camps they were very well trained, able to act closely with the line troops, and highly valued, to the point that they were among the first French innovations that opposing armies tried to copy. All of this took time, and for the only time in his career Napoleon had an abundance of the commodity. The artillery, although much improved by Marmont and himself, still suffered from poor guns, and while its officers now reached high standards, the ranks had not achieved the desired level of expertise by 1805.

The only branch of the army not to undergo the experience of the camps was the dragoons. The bulk of these versatile cavalrymen – twenty-four squadrons[31] – were sent for service in the 'pacification' of the Vendée and, although not lacking in combat experience as a result, Napoleon felt they did not perform well at Austerlitz or, later, in Prussia, and relegated most of them to secondary theatres such as Spain[32] or to duties similar to those of the Gendarmerie.

The other aspect of the intense training recruits underwent in the camps, and one common to every corps, was in embarkation and landing at sea. The entire army had to learn to swim during the summer of 1803, along with boating techniques, and the 'shock troops' designated for the first wave of landings – the 67,000 men of Davout's

Corps and Junot's Grenadier Division – could embark in seventeen minutes.[33] It has been argued that all this took up too much valuable time which should have been spent on conventional drill, and that it proved useless in the event of the invasion being abandoned.[34] This is to miss the wider picture. Swimming raised the army to levels of fitness hitherto unimaginable, and unmatched by any of its rivals; learning how to embark and disembark – although suicidal if it had been tried in an invasion of Britain so flimsy were their landing craft– inculcated intense teamwork and an ability to work as a unit. The cavalry and horse artillery learned how to cross rivers in good order, which stood them in good stead for the first time in crossing the Rhine; those units that did not undergo the maritime exercises were markedly less well trained than those that did. Above all, perhaps, this new form of training expelled boredom from the ranks. No stationary army had ever been kept so busy for so long.

When Napoleon brought the Guard to Boulogne, it was a galvanising moment for the rest of the Army of the Ocean Coasts, and one of his most incisive psychological actions in the process of turning the unprepossessing raw material of the camps into a magnificent force. The Guard had emerged as both the elite of the army and its spoilt child. The revival of the *ancien régime* concept of rank, if not caste, throughout the officer corps under Napoleon was important in changing the ethos of the army, but this shift was even more important among the ranks. The nature, and the very existence, of the Imperial Guard was central to this. The favouritism the Guard received in every conceivable respect – pay, uniforms, material support of all kinds, its proximity to the commander-in-chief – made it the lowest common factor of hatred and envy among all the other units of the army, whatever their mutual rivalries. Its officers were paid 35 per cent more than their colleagues in the line regiments; its ranks almost four times more than conscripts.[35] Conversely, it was the highest measure of ambition, and this is what really mattered. The Guard was a meritocracy: a good soldier with a clean record, who had risen through the ranks to non-commissioned officer with three campaigns' service, could aspire to join it. The same prerequisites were required for that other elite corps, the Gendarmerie. The Guard was, unlike the corps, a genuinely discrete unit. It possessed infantry – its bulk – but also artillery, cavalry of all branches, and, as of July 1804, its own Gendarmerie, mounted and foot, the elite of the elite. In practical terms, this meant that no branch of the service was denied the hope of joining it.

Detested as it was by the rest of the army, the Guard became both a model of what a soldier should be, but also an aspiration, something which the Revolutionary armies, with their creeds of equality and the duty of service of the citizen-soldier, had been sorely lacking. Napoleon understood men better than the politicians of the 1790s, certainly in this respect. Conscripts virtually kidnapped and thrust into a new, alien world now had a target for their hopes that might outweigh their resentments, a sense that grew as war thinned the ranks and opened up possibilities still unknown at Boulogne. 'A whole world separated the Guard from the Line,' as its historians have said.[36] The desire to enter the Guard gave a point to army life, and no small part of Napoleon's genius as a leader was to see just this.

Even so, he injected something of elitism into the life of the line. The light infantry were formed into specialist units, and accorded an elite status; it was a role specifically for the smaller men, who might easily be despised. Indeed, Napoleon had clear ideas about which regions bred which types of infantryman – 'the mountain country for the light infantry [voltigeurs], and the plains for the infantry of the line'[37] – in accord with the physical products of each. Just as the small men had their specialism, the grenadiers were for the tallest, and their relatively elite status came, like that of the light troops, from their role in battle. The skirmishers did a dangerous job ahead of the line, and the grenadier units allocated to the line stood right behind the voltigeurs, at the heads of the attack columns: 'the company must always find itself united, to take its place at the head of the column ... and, through its comportment, to give confidence to the troops ...'[38] Both sorts of men were needed in every battalion, 'which will create the best means for emulation possible between men', adding, in what was most certainly a cry from the heart, 'Big men despise small ones, and the small want to show, by their bravery and audacity, that they despise the big ones back. The *voltigeurs* are excellent. To set the small against the tall is a new idea all of my own.'[39] He was built like a *voltigeur* himself, and so, perhaps, he was the one to know such things.

The grenadiers and *voltigeurs* gave roles to special men, marked by their physique. Anyone could aspire to the Guard, however, and this made it a talisman for all. By 1804, the Guard numbered 11,500, of whom 6,800 were fighting troops at Boulogne, plus its support and the palace guards.[40] Its origins were primarily political, for when Napoleon became Consul he was acutely aware that he was a general with no army, and he created a small Consular Guard from veterans of the Army of Italy as a counter-balance to Moreau's forces, more than for his personal protection. During the Peace of Amiens, he used his new powers quietly to build it up into the force that he sent to Boulogne. Its main practical role was to form the reserve force of the army as a whole; it would always be held back in battle either to turn the tide at the vital moment or to deliver the decisive blow, once victory was assured. In this, Napoleon conceived the Guard as part of conventional military thinking of the time. However, he carried it to extremes that set a wholly new standard for the rest of the army, and for all its future victims. Throughout the period of peace, he assigned some of his best generals to oversee its creation: Davout to its grenadiers; Soult to the rest of the infantry; Bessières to its cavalry; Mortier to its specialist arms; Savary commanded its gendarmerie. To be entrusted with such duties was a mark of confidence unparalleled from Napoleon. No one other than himself ever held overall command of the Guard, however, and the Guard soon became the only military unit allowed into Paris. It became an assurance that Napoleon's regime would not be overthrown by a military coup and so, ironically if logically, this most militarist of institutions became a guarantor of the essentially civilian character of the regime.

These officers were there for a reason, and the drills and daily routine they set for the Guard in its Paris barracks during the Peace of Amiens created the pattern for the rest of the army in the Channel camps. When the camps were created, and its commanders distributed to their own corps, they took these values with them, and it was no coincidence that the work of Davout and Soult stood out so much from that of their colleagues. At Boulogne, Napoleon took direct command of the Guard himself. The Guard had formed the military presence at the imperial coronation in December 1804, and returned to Boulogne with splendid new uniforms and weapons that made a stunning impression on the rest of the army, but it was its expertise in drill that did most to set the standard for all around them. Furthermore, those non-commissioned officers recently promoted to lieutenants had received an award that summer. All had been given two extra pairs of shoes,[41] whereas even the Grenadier Division, their only near rivals among the infantry, were buying their own.[42] The point for the rest of the army was that all this had been earned. These well-paid, dressed, shod, housed and fed men who did not march to battle, but rode in horse-drawn carts, were hard-bitten veterans, unlike most of the men in the camps. Their elitism had been paid for in their own blood, and their status was open to all.

The Guard and its influence on the rest of the army was indicative of a deeper current in Napoleon's thinking, in harmony with his creation of the Legion of Honour and the imperial nobility soon after. However qualified its impact on civilian French society, this insight into human nature was as accurate as his own expertise as an artillery officer in the world of the barracks. There was more work to be done in the camps, however, that even the example of the Guard could not quite achieve.

The Grande Armée was itself an exercise in the Napoleonic policy of *amalgame*. Although the presence of soldiers from the army of the old monarchy had greatly diminished, the Revolutionary years had created new divisions and rivalries, as had Napoleon's own recent reforms. The young officers fresh from the new military academy at Fontainebleau received a predictably hard time from the veterans, officers and men alike, whose instincts were to despise them, but the veterans were themselves still young and the mutual energy of the two strands galvanised the new army, if in different ways. Camp life at least allowed them to learn each other's strengths, as well as weaknesses. As their historian has put it:

[The veterans] had confidence in themselves, [the cadets] had confidence in the future, and their many and different efforts created the way in which the Grande Armée – driven and trained by these young men – [became] the formidable 'always ahead' when it came to catching the enemy, and a 'living rock' when it came to resisting him.[43]

The raw cadets raised the general level of education in the army, and helped the veterans to adapt to the new manoeuvres and tactics that Napoleon was introducing in the camps; the veterans had the confidence of the new recruits, simply by their experience. Napoleon also did something else that helped ease the life of the new conscripts considerably, although here he was systematising what the Directory had already been forced to allow. He ended once and for all the idealistic hopes of the Revolutionaries of using the army to forge a new French identity, which they had done by separating men from the same region and placing them into deliberately 'pan-French' units composed of recruits from different regions – 'a scheme devised in the hope that they could emphasize their national character and dilute any vestiges of provincialism', as Alan Forrest has put it.[44]

This is not to say Napoleon no longer sought to rip them from their roots and give them a new identity, for he certainly did. He just had a more sensible way of doing it. The basic unit of the army was the *ordinaire*, composed of about fifteen men, roughly the same as a modern section. Napoleon made sure that the *ordinaires* were composed of men from the same locality, a direct break with Revolutionary ideology. Forrest's careful study of the surviving letters home of French soldiers has shown how important, particularly in the early months of service, was the presence of men from the same area, often kinsmen and friends, in helping the new recruits to adjust to their strange new world. Napoleon, a well-educated, highly intelligent man better equipped than most to keep his mind active, still understood depression and homesickness, and this approach to organising his lower units did a great deal to lessen these problems. The conscripts' own words – or those they dictated – bear this out. The recruits had to adapt to the more or less standard French of their veteran officers and sergeants, but at least they could speak their own local dialects – *patois* – among themselves, off duty. Napoleon understood that armies live and fight as units – this was how they survived – and he applied this common sense not just to drills and manoeuvres, but to their inner life, at the most human level, something the Revolutionaries had failed to grasp. Through the constant drilling and hard work, bolstered by close companionship, genuine bonds were forged where they mattered, among the men.[45]

The *ordinaire* was the unit on which Napoleon sought to focus his men's deepest loyalty; this was the unit that ate together and slept in the same barracks. This was where their initial sense of homesickness – *la maladie du pays*, which the army took seriously as real illness – and the more general isolation they could feel from society were cured. It became their home, but also their cause, for if most of the raw conscripts had any feelings for the Republic they were ones of loathing, and they knew nothing of the older values of the royal army. The *ordinaire*, particularly if it contained other men from home, became the new bedrock of their lives. This communal life often broke down on campaign, as foraging, pillaging and the need to live in makeshift bivouacs imposed itself, but it never entirely dissolved.[46] This was where the experience of the Channel camps mattered so much, however. During this prolonged period of training and regular routine, the new recruits were able for forge deep bonds among themselves. Their collective loyalty survived the irregular life on campaign. When this was extended 'up the ladder', to loyalty to larger units as far as the corps, it became the bedrock of the new *esprit de corps* of an army divorced from the mainstream of civilian life, as it moved beyond France and stayed outside it, in the years of campaigning ahead.

There were inter-revolutionary fences to mend as well. The Channel camps brought together the men of Moreau's and Napoleon's old armies, at the very moment Moreau was charged with trying to murder Napoleon, yet the mixture of the two did not produce political problems on any appreciable scale. The real tensions came because Moreau's officers emerged as generally more disciplined and more austere than Napoleon's protégés from the Army of Italy, and better able to keep discipline in the ranks, at least on the parade ground. The different armies of the Revolution, operating in isolation from each other, had evolved their own customs of honour and daily routine. Napoleon did not attempt to undermine or harmonise these, any more than he seriously attempted to curb the ferocious rivalries between the different branches of the service, which spread beyond brawls among soldiers to duels between officers. Punishments for these things remained largely on paper, looking severe, but seldom applied.[47]

Napoleon balanced this sense of the collective with that of personal ambition. This is where the influence of the traditions of the old army was most obviously revived. The Republic had despised awarding medals and the creation of consciously elite units like the Guard; this ran directly against the ethos of equality. Many generals in the field, Napoleon foremost among them, had turned their backs on such attitudes well before the creation of the Channel camps, when the armies were still mainly composed of Revolutionary volunteers and ex-royal professionals. 'Swords of honour' were bestowed on men for courage in the field in the Italian campaigns, for example. Now, Napoleon made this his policy: courage, especially, was rewarded with pomp, and this recognition was sought by the men, because a wider environment had been created around them, where this recognition was valued by all. Personal recognition reflected on the *ordinaire*, as a whole. Napoleon did not abandon the values of self-sacrifice, but he defined them for his men in terms of virtue given for their comrades, and for their commander. The veterans had learned that wider society did not care about them, but that their leader and their comrades did. Promotion came most often in ways the ranks understood and appreciated: as often as not, it was for bravery in action, not for competence behind a desk.[48] Men ripped from the plough into the world of war understood this, and it bound them to the values of the army, and the leader who created this world. Self-interest was a spur, but it meant nothing without a collective ethos. Now that ethos was tangible, real, the *ordinaire* replacing the tight-knit rural hamlet, but with the crucial innovation of personal reward within the community, a blend of the old and the new societies that Napoleon brought about within the army. The return of honours, promotion and elitism was still an open system; it was predicated on the Revolutionary belief in the career open to talent.

There was something else, however, all too often overlooked by posterity but very real to contemporaries, and something Napoleon rightly trumpeted before his enemies. Unwilling conscripts the mass of his new army may originally have been; they may have been hauled to their depots by brutal, cruel force, but they were not slaves. The French soldier was now an imperial subject, but he was not a Prussian or Russian serf. He was not flogged excessively at the whim of some aristocratic officer who saw him as chattel, for that officer, however brutal, was not his social superior. Flogging was abolished, for 'to discourage people is not the way to bring them in', Napoleon told Savary, who commanded the Gendarmerie of the Guard, the elite of the elite, adding how much better this made his army than the British, where discipline was as savage as in the feudal east.[49] The raw levies were unwilling peasants, but they were not the dregs of society, criminals who had been scoured from the prisons to fill the ranks, 'a bad practice ... That was what the Neapolitan [Bourbons] did, as do countries without armies,' he warned Eugène.[50] 'The armies of the Republic did great things because they were made up of the sons of tenant farmers and good smallholders, not of rabble, because these men took the place of the officers of the old order,' Thibaudeau recalled Napoleon saying in his memoirs; they were decent people who would respond to the incentive of personal honour.[51] 'Napoleon's men' were anything but aristocrats, but honour, in a new guise, was their preserve as much as that of any noble. Respect and obedience were restored, with the return of some traditional military values, but obedience was owed to the uniform, not to any social status acquired beyond the army. Soldiers were listened to by their superiors; individual initiative was encouraged in training and combat, and rewarded.

Petitions by units were permitted, received, read, and often acted upon. No one was afraid to speak out, if it was done properly, and with due respect for rank. This trust, running from the top down, as well as in the opposite direction, was often expressed in ways that were no less profound for being mundane in their origins, for garrison life is, of its essence, just that, mundane. By August 1804, while in the camps himself, Napoleon had become aware of a growing wish among the troops for changes in their uniform: to abandon hats, to adopt trousers instead of breeches, to have hooded coats for winter, to switch from shoes to boots. He noted that the French army had done such things before, and usually gone back to the uniforms previously in use. Nevertheless, he listened carefully, because 'it is entirely possible that these changes may have their roots in the bad organisation the army has gone through at various times'. He ordered the corps commanders to call together committees of the regimental colonels, who were, in turn, to canvas the men for their views and then draw up reports for Napoleon to consider, in order to reconcile the needs of the soldiers with the costs involved, concluding, 'get them all to me in Paris ... by the first week of next month'.[52] Napoleon had faith in his troops, assuming their complaints were reasonable and should be heard fairly. It was a practical example of how the whole army was becoming familiar within its ranks, and that its members trusted each other. This was not the world of the old army.

Nor was Napoleon's army a mercenary force, in the way of so many armies of the old order, that of France included. He did not hire foreign mercenaries, as had the Bourbons: such regiments had been used by the crown against the people of Paris in 1789. Among the honours a soldier could earn for courage in battle, money was never included, for Napoleon would not countenance any return to the mercenary culture of the old order. 'Bravery is not paid for in cash,' he declared in 1804, as the new army was emerging in the camps, 'it dishonours the soldier.' '[The army] must serve without the hope of extra pay, which could tarnish the noble duty of the soldier with venality', he told Berthier.[53] A code of honour was at work, unthinkable to the early Revolutionaries, but it was of a very different kind from that of the aristocratic cadets Napoleon had learned to loathe at a tender age. Trust permeated the army, from the high command to the ranks. There are many romantic myths about the Grande Armée, most of them fostered by its own veterans, but the relative openness within it was not one of them.

It was a very pragmatic ethos, one to which the peasant conscript could relate, but it was not without its dangers, if not to the army then to the civilian world at large. The army was now a world unto itself and it acted like one. This was symptomatic of a wider phenomenon, a reminder of how volatile and dangerous an army of this period could be. Napoleon always walked a tightrope with the men. He may have despised ill discipline in any form, which is only to be expected from a man who lived his life under tight self-control, which, if it occasionally disintegrated, had kept him alive and given him victory. The fundamental place of discipline was second nature to him, but that is the point, it *was* second nature; it did not come naturally to him any more than to his men. Napoleon looked deeply into the minds and character of his men, and this had taught him basic truths about the French soldier. In his memoirs, he put it clearly:

There is nothing that cannot be got from the French with the lure of danger, it is the Gallic heritage. Love of glory and *valliance* is an instinct among the French, a sort of sixth sense. How many times, in the heat of battle, have I not seen our young conscripts throw themselves into the fray: honour and courage seeped through their pores.[54]

If he thought in stereotypes, he came by them honestly. The deeper point, for the shaping of the army, is the tension this caused between the needs of fighting spirit and orderly conduct. Napoleon let them have their 'safety valves'.

The discipline and routine Napoleon and his officer corps shaped did not extend far beyond the barracks or, indeed, beyond the parade ground. Duelling officers set a tone for the ranks, in their dealings with each other but also with the civilian communities around them. The habit – now a virtual tradition, claimed as right – of pillage was endemic in all the French Revolutionary armies, and Napoleon did little about it, for he knew these 'dark arts' of foraging – a euphemism for theft, usually with violence – would be needed on campaign. It was yet another 'survival skill' the new levies had to learn from the veterans, and they began by practising on the people of Flanders. Napoleon's best efforts to reform the army administration had gone far, but not far enough for the task of supplying so large an army, and it would break down badly when campaigning actually began. None of the barbaric habits acquired in Italy under Napoleon, or north of the Alps, under Hoche and Moreau, were lost. Napoleon seldom sought to curb this, for he understood the two essential things about these men: they were as brave in battle as they were savage in garrison, and this brutality was a clear sign of their devotion to duty as they understood it.[55] When the time came, they led from the front.

Transgressions on the parade ground or manoeuvres were dealt with by brutal measures but this severity often melted away when it was a matter of aggression directed towards civilians or other units. The Revolutionary governments of the 1790s, particularly under the Jacobin Terror of 1793–4, had tried to impose strict discipline on the army as part of its ideological programme of creating citizen-soldiers out of their recruits with a wider sense of responsibility to the Nation. In practice, this often led to the execution of soldiers by the civilian 'army commissioners' and the representatives on mission from the central government to the fronts. This was largely a confession of impotence in the face of an uncontrollable tide of ill-disciplined brutality, but when they got the chance these civilian officials lashed out.[56] This was curbed under Napoleon. Gross acts of ruthless, mass brutality against civilians could provoke death sentences, but, on the whole, the Napoleonic councils of war reserved their worst punishments for desertion, cowardice in battle and disobedience. At Boulogne, and thereafter, soldiers were almost always dealt with by soldiers: courts martial tried these offences, not civilian politicians or magistrates. The army sorted out its own business.

All this helped to draw the army together and to set it apart from the rest of society. Forced into poor, often murderous, relations with the communities around them, soldiers looked inwards. Thus, circumstance as much as design cut the army off from society, the Guard by its privileges, the rest by the need to forage and get rough with civilians. Looking away from the rest of society, it drew in on itself, another, more oblique way to forge *esprit de corps*. These conditions had existed from the outset of the Revolutionary wars but whereas the revolutionaries had sought to reconcile the soldier and the citizen in the common cause of the Nation, Napoleon drew on them to change the relationship between the army and civilian society fundamentally. David Bell has seen this process beginning under the Terror, as the Jacobins began to prefer professional competence to ideological purity, but this is to confuse pure professionalism – always under the gaze of politicians – with a sense of caste. It was only under Napoleon, and only after the experience of the Channel camps, that recruits 'left "civilian" society to join "military" society', as Bell has put it.[57]

There were other ways to reinforce its sense of difference. Napoleon continued the practice of the Revolutionaries – revived under the Third Republic in the First World War – of refusing to allow chaplains in the army; only Polish troops and the Swiss, much later, were allowed this privilege.[58] It was a decision taken on principle: men were offered the companionship of others from their own areas, but not the essence of peasant sociability or the spiritual and cultural traditions they had been raised in. Soldiers could go to Mass only with their officers' permission. During the First World War, Catholic clergy circumvented this by enlisting as stretcher-bearers, but nothing of the kind happened under Napoleon. The Concordat did not extend to the army. Napoleon ended the Revolutionary dream of creating citizen-soldiers, erecting the army into a caste apart, but he did not want his men to carry any more of their past selves into the ranks than was necessary, and that included, if possible, their religion. In place of a sense of duty to an abstract Nation, he allowed them real comradeship and a new set of values that turned on loyalty to each other, to the commanders, and to himself, personally. It was the Emperor to whom oaths were now sworn; Napoleon, not an abstract entity, gave them their eagles. Instead of a Christian heaven, Napoleon held out the earthly paradise of the Imperial Guard, which could only be reached by valour in war, and when war came it was seized on as an opportunity, not recoiled from in dread. Put another way, the men were highly motivated when they broke camp after almost two years in barracks, a singular triumph of leadership.

There were ironic but very real parallels between the new army forged in the camps and the Church of the old monarchy Napoleon sought to make it forget. The French Church had been made the First Estate for a reason: it was a sealed world, the most privileged body in a society built on privilege. It tried its own members in its own courts; it paid no taxes, but extracted great wealth from the rest of France while offering it great services in return; its members were distinguished from the rest of society by their dress and their way of life; the Church offered men of relatively low standing the best chance of advancement in the world. All this was now the prerogative of the Grande Armée. There was more still: the internal divisions of the old First Estate had more than a faint echo of those of the new military caste. The wealthy, powerful bishops were now the marshals; the mass of grumbling, underpaid and overworked parish clergy – intent on rising if they could – were the regiments of the line; the Imperial Guard were the new equivalent of the wealthiest, most privileged regular orders of monks, who never dirtied their hands with parochial tasks but performed specialised, elite roles within the First Estate. Both the old First Estate and the new army were laws unto themselves, with their own codes of conduct, their own family feuds and, above all, their own sense of difference and superiority. The marshals now took precedence at all official ceremonies, as once the clergy had done; the army was always the most visible and numerous presence at any state event. It never ran the state, it never controlled the levers of power – nor, indeed, had the Church under the Bourbons – but the state was run for its benefit. The age of the citizen-soldier died in the Channel camps. Instead, Napoleon created a new elite caste in French society, which was meant to set society a new ethos. He offered the uprooted conscripts an alternative universe, and it was probably as close to paradise as he felt he came himself.

The obvious happiness Napoleon felt in the camps, and when he was about this work, slips from his pen most poignantly in unguarded moments. 'But for this wretched trial, I would already be in the middle of the camps,' he wrote to Soult from Paris in June 1804.[59] The 'wretched trial' was that of Cadoudal and Moreau, who had conspired to kill him. Napoleon was irritated, more than intimidated, when he was busy, a powerful example of his own psychological training at work. A few weeks before he broke camp, and in the midst of his rages at the navy and all its workings, as the time of the camps came to an end, he told Cambacérès – who didn't know one end of a musket from the other and cared less – 'I have just reached Boulogne. In an hour, I shall review 100,000 infantry . . . The troops are very fine, and I am extremely satisfied with all I see here.'[60] He forgot to whom he wrote in his joy, for that is what it was. Napoleon's pride simply glows in these words, and well it might.

It is not improbable that his feelings had spread throughout the ranks by 1805. There is one piece of hard evidence that might support this: when camp was broken, and the long, hard march to southern Germany began, the order was given so quickly, after such intense secrecy, that there was predictable confusion everywhere. Most of the officers and men had no clear idea where they were going, and even the Guard thought it was heading back to Paris; many assumed they were moving north to Holland, as a prelude to invading England. It was a near ideal chance to desert, but on that entire march of several weeks only a handful did so. In Davout's corps of 30,000 the number did not reach double figures; in Soult's it was somewhere between thirty and forty.[61] When the scale of the problem of getting these men from their homes to the camps is recalled, Napoleon's achievement is brought home in no uncertain terms.

Napoleon had created the finest army in the world, and he had done so according to his own lights. He had thought his plans out in the years between the victory of Marengo and the creation of the Channel camps. As he recounted on St Helena, he had laid out his blueprint in Italy:

When the Austrians held Italy, they tried without success to make soldiers of the Italians. They deserted as fast as they could be assembled, or if they were forced to march towards the enemy, they ran at the first shot. It was impossible to constitute a single regiment. When I conquered Italy and began to raise levies, the Austrians made fun of me, and said I would never succeed . . . that fighting was not in the Italian character . . . Despite all that, I enrolled thousands of Italians who fought bravely with the French, and who never abandoned me in my adversity. Why? I abolished the lash and the cane used by the Austrians. I promoted soldiers with talent; several generals emerged among them. I put honour and emulation in the place of terror and the lash.[62]

The Italian troops fought well on the Italian front in 1805, in Spain and in Russia. They were also the first army Napoleon had created from raw, unwilling recruits and trained according to his own methods.

There were those who mocked the work of the Channel camps then, and some still do. On 15 August 1804 – Napoleon's birthday, and the date that would later become an imperial holiday, 'St Napoleon's Day' – he held a mass review of 60,000 troops, less than a third of the whole, on a hill near Boulogne. He distributed the crosses of the Legion of Honour to the troops, surrounded by relics of France's military past, and also medals for the coming 'English campaign'. British observers found it ridiculous. Historians since have agreed; Nicholas Rodger sees it as Napoleon dreaming at other people's expense.[63] At the time this was dangerous complacency. The army might have been impotent when it faced the sea, but if and when it turned inland, the rest of Europe had nothing to match it. Nor was Napoleon dreaming while he sat on his dais, seeming to gaze out towards Dover. This review was followed by a thorough inspection of the army, a purge of several divisional headquarters,[64] and, later, the transfer of the Guard to Boulogne. Napoleon fretted often about British espionage along the coast, but he need not have worried; they did not understand what they saw, or they would not have gone with such alacrity into war. Once again, he won a major victory because his rivals – here the British – failed to take him seriously, and their continental allies, Vienna and St Petersburg, who would soon have to do the real fighting, would not have followed London so readily. Predictably, Madame Junot waxed as lyrical about the day as the British sneered sarcastically. She called it simply 'the greatest sight the world had yet seen'.[65] Even she did not know the half of it – or the third – for the Grande Armée was still to reach its peak. As in the assemblies of Milan, in the murk of the Po Valley or the committee rooms of the Luxembourg Palace in the dark days of his first winter in office, after the coup of Brumaire, the 'month of fogs', Napoleon worked well in the shadows, this time in the mists of the Flemish fens which shrouded the birth of his greatest personal creation, a genuine weapon of mass destruction, but a thing of wonder nonetheless. He had truly created a mass from a thousand scraps, and his enemies had not the faintest idea.

14

EMERGENCE OF THE THIRD COALITION

Towards the Real War, 1803–1805

Napoleon and his enemies had been busy in the field of diplomacy in these months, but in very different ways. Napoleon set about consolidating his grip on western Europe, an activity which, in turn, heightened the unease of the other powers. His actions were small-scale, however, for he had no possibility of forging grand alliances. Save for the Batavians, the Swiss, Spain and the small German states, the new French Empire was alone. In contrast, the British set to work reforging their alliance with the other great powers, all of which – ominously – still referred to the newly crowned Emperor as merely 'the Head of the French State', showing as much a lack of faith in his potential for longevity in power as a snub to the pretensions of the imperial coronation.

Napoleon had yet to antagonise any of the continental powers in a war of his own regime's making, but he was developing an approach to international relations that was new and unsettling. Napoleon's disquieting behaviour was of quite another order than crude military threats; he had his 'mass' of the Grande Armée to assemble before he could dare to act in such a manner. Thierry Lentz has pinpointed two distinct, antagonistic approaches to the international reordering of Europe that all statesmen saw was required after the wars of the 1790s. On the one hand was the traditional eighteenth-century concept of a balance of powers – and equilibrium – and on the other hand that of a 'system', or several systems, which drove Napoleon's thinking, in which great powers organised the continent into hegemonic blocks or spheres of influence around themselves.[1] Napoleon's approach was as much of a break with the past as the radical democracy of the Jacobins, in the minds of an older generation of diplomats, his own foreign minister, Talleyrand, increasingly included.

There was only one real hegemonic arrangement practicable in the circumstances of Europe after the Peace of Amiens: a partition of the continent between France and Russia, and Russia was the only other great power with whom Napoleon could conceivably hope to form a working relationship. He saw this quickly, and worked for it from as early as the Franco-Russian Treaty of Paris of October 1801. In the first article of the secret convention that went with the formal treaty, the new First Consul and the new Tsar, Alexander I, who had ascended the throne following the assassination of his father, Paul I, only the preceding March, arrogated to themselves 'the invariable intention of a just equilibrium between the Houses of Hohenzollern [Prussia] and Austria', while Article XI went further still, as Napoleon and Alexander accorded themselves the right 'to re-establish a just equilibrium in the different parts of the world'.[2] Here, couched in the language of the old diplomacy, was the first clear manifestation of the new. Alexander vacillated about this approach, for the practical reason that it proved hard for traditional Russian interests to accommodate themselves to clear lines of demarcation. Agreeing to help Napoleon 'manage' the two major German states in their mutual interest did not prove too difficult for Alexander. France and Russia both disliked the Habsburgs, if for different reasons, and they both despised Prussian weakness, but it was harder for him to shed commitments to protect some of the small German states linked to the Romanovs by marriage, or less tangible allegiances to the House of Savoy, whose ruler, Charles-Emmanuel IV, had been deposed by the French. He was confined to his only remaining territory, the island of Sardinia, whereas the Knights of Malta, whom Napoleon had personally overthrown on his way to Egypt, were a much more practical preoccupation for Alexander.

At the heart of Russian policy for more than a century had been the search for secure access to an all-year, warm-weather port. By the late eighteenth century, with Russian control of the Black Sea consolidated, first Tsar Paul and then Alexander strove to create something like a corridor along the Mediterranean, which had to run the gauntlet of the Ottomans in the Dardanelles, but then depended on being able to count on safe passage in the central Mediterranean, which in turn relied upon Malta and good relations with the Neapolitan Bourbons. Napoleon found it difficult, if not initially impossible, to accommodate this aspect of Russian ambition, but before 1805 he did not return to the Directory's policy of trying to extend French domination in Italy to the southern kingdom of Naples, although he unsettled Alexander and infuriated the British by maintaining a French military presence there, as the British did in Malta. At another level, he never fully appreciated why Alexander felt so compelled to interfere in matters so far removed from his borders.

Nevertheless, Napoleon worked very hard to make a friend of the new Tsar and, if he failed to do so by 1805, when Russia was the first power to join Britain in the Third Coalition, he was able to convince him of the potency of 'the system' two years later. Alexander had to be persuaded in that most time-honoured manner of monarchs, on the field of battle. In the meantime, he clung to the advisers whose concern was for a traditional 'balance', which the new French hegemony in the west had upset, and who were also concerned about Russia's lucrative trade with Britain.

The trade treaty concluded between France and Russia was highly valued by Napoleon, if mainly as a sign of goodwill. In contrast, Russian raw materials fed the needs of the Royal Navy, just as its grain poured into the incomparably large market of urban Britain. Moreover, these exports were almost entirely in the hands of the great court nobility who surrounded Alexander, and who had connived in his father's violent death.[3] In the competition for Russian support between Britain and France in the winter of 1803–4, Britain held the distinct advantage for those around the throne.

Whatever his own inclinations – and they were still unformed and fluctuating – Alexander was far from ready to adopt the new diplomacy of pan-continental systems in the years before the war. It all came to a head when Alexander proposed a peace plan in 1803, which, although it offered to recognise all the satellite republics of France – those of Italy, Batavia and Helvetica – insisted on French military withdrawal from all of them, and called for territorial compensation for the House of Savoy elsewhere in Italy. Napoleon rejected the proposal, something that even his most trenchant critic, Paul Schroeder, admits he had good reason to do – 'Bonaparte's claim that Russia's terms were worse than Britain's . . . was correct.'[4] For his part, Napoleon was taken aback by the Tsar's genuine anger at the execution of the duc d'Enghien, partly in a spirit of aristocratic solidarity, but even more because he felt an obligation to the ruler of Baden, whose territory had been violated. It was an exercise in mutual incomprehension, which was eventually overcome, if not in time to stop a war.

Britain was an irreducible enemy and, once hostilities began in 1803, it began her traditional search for continental allies to engage the French on land. Even when Napoleon had been all but driven from the Caribbean, he still clung to his control of the Channel coast, and extended his grip across northern Germany after 1803, from his own fear of attack, when he occupied the Electorate of Hannover, whose ruler was George III, and the Hansa ports along the North Sea coast. Moreover, once the Peace of Amiens had dissolved, the British returned to their previous policy of insisting that peace was only possible if the Bourbons were restored.

Austria was very reluctant to fight in these years, and her interests in the Balkans meant that potentially she could be isolated from Russia. Despite the compensation of the former Republic of Venice, Napoleon saw Austria as a continued threat in northern Italy, and the feeling was reciprocal; the River Adige alone separated the two powers from the lands of the new Kingdom of Italy, a region that had once been the richest province of the Habsburg Monarchy and was now the jewel in Napoleon's crown, his own original power base. More serious still had been the careful French cultivation of the south German princes to the point that, by 1804, it was clear to Francis himself that Germany had become a dangerous place for Austria, rather than a stronghold.

Austrian interests had much to gain from a restoration of the European 'balance', which would reduce the French presence in Italy, and circumscribe their influence in Germany, a set of objectives that might be achieved by negotiation but could only be feasible in war if supported by a coalition financed by Britain and supported in the field by Russia. Francis did not want war save on these terms. Those who knew most about the state of the army led by his brother, the Archduke Charles, did not want war at all, warning in 1804 that the army could muster only 40,000 effective troops, for it had never really recovered from the campaigns of 1796–1800. Moreover, Charles had sent a mission to Russia that revealed how unprepared Alexander was for war as well. In the meantime, however, Francis had signed a preliminary treaty with Russia in November 1804, which envisaged the two powers fielding armies of 235,000 Austrians and 115,000 Russians, with the prospect of British subsidies. Charles had been kept in the dark about this, and he was able to counter with his own information.[5] As Gunther Rothenberg, the major historian of Archduke Charles, has put it, 'Charles had told the unburnished truth, but at this point, the Emperor and his ministers preferred to live in wilful ignorance.'[6]

Even Charles had no real idea of what awaited; his reports dwelt almost entirely on the weakness of his own forces and those of the Russians. He had no idea of the new military power Napoleon was amassing, nor did he, or anyone else in Vienna, fully realise the cynical plans already concocted between the British and Russians, which entailed Austria doing most of the actual fighting in any new war with France. On the one hand, Britain and Russia agreed that neither of them wanted, or would take, any direct benefits from victory. This was quite genuinely a war to restore the balance of power in Europe, although the end result, as outlined in their agreement, the joint leadership of a league of secondary states,[7] bore more than a passing resemblance to the Napoleonic concept of 'systems', without France: 'They never disagreed on this hegemonic goal, the central aspect of their alliance . . . Both felt that Europe needed them much more than they needed Europe.' This represented a level of detachment Napoleon could never aspire to, had he so wished, and a degree of cynicism that at least rivalled his own. For all their high-mindedness, their plan was for an Austrian war effort – Prussian participation was welcome, but acknowledged to be unlikely – and this was deliberately concealed from Vienna.[8]

These were the shark-infested waters in which Napoleon's diplomacy could not penetrate the major courts of Europe for long, but where Austria's proved wholly wanting. Aristotle asserted that some men were born to be slaves; the servants of the Habsburgs, Charles excepted, must have appeared so to Napoleon, Pitt and Alexander. By 1804, Austria had become belligerent, but in the worst possible circumstances, deluded by its allies and oblivious of its own weakness. In the first phases of negotiations for a new coalition, the Austrians had been cautious in their commitments to Alexander, but there was a determined 'war party' in Vienna, led by Cobenzl and Colloredo, the former 'an accomplished courtier, if little else', and the latter the Emperor's old tutor. They set out to discredit Charles' damning report on the state of the army, and succeeded. Gradually, they persuaded Francis to listen to General Mack, who had a disastrous record as a field commander in the 1790s, but who asserted that the army could be reformed, enlarged and turned around almost immediately. He was believed. For their parts, Cobenzl and Colloredo found the prospect of a Russian alliance and £400,000 of British subsidy too good an opportunity to ignore, despite the fact that the Russians would not arrive for months, and that there was not enough time to spend the British money properly on the army.[9]

When Francis began to mobilise troops, in anticipation of war, he did so in ways that played directly into Napoleon's hands, and revealed expansionist ambitions – however traditional and predictable – which could only strengthen France where it was most essential for her interests. The Habsburgs had long sought to obliterate Bavaria as a state and annex it directly to their German possessions. In the 1780s, Joseph II had proposed that the Bavarian Elector simply swap his state, over which the Wittelsbach dynasty had ruled from the early Middle Ages, for the Austrian Netherlands, a scheme which resurfaced in modified form at Amiens, when Vienna floated the idea of receiving Bavaria as compensation for the loss of the Austrian Netherlands to France.

In 1804–5, Francis simply seemed set on naked aggression, massing what troops he had on the Bavarian border, when Charles had advised him they would be better deployed elsewhere. The result was to drive Max Joseph, the Elector, even further into Napoleon's camp. Having already gained greatly from the reorganisation of Germany, Max Joseph had still hesitated to commit wholly to any alliance for fear of war, but in autumn 1805 it was Cetto, his own ambassador in Paris, not Talleyrand, who raised the point that the Habsburgs had threatened Bavaria with extinction no fewer than five times since Max Joseph had become Elector in 1798.[10] Austrian illusions transformed cautious Wittelsbach ambition into fear, from which only Napoleon could profit, and in just the manner he needed most in the circumstances of 1805, with war imminent. The other, smaller German princes had fewer qualms than Bavaria, for whom coming into the Napoleonic camp meant losing her status as the third most important state of the old Reich, for all she would gain from a French alliance. Francis himself had guaranteed this was no longer any issue, however.

The contingents of Napoleon's German allies were not large, nor were these troops of frontline quality; the largest contingent was the Bavarians, at 25,000,[11] and they quickly showed their limited worth in the field when the whole army withdrew north, towards the French advance, in September 1805, when the Austrians entered Bavaria, exposing Munich and forcing Max Joseph to leave his capital.[12] The military capacity of the south German states would improve vastly in the years to come, under French tutelage. Nevertheless, and far more importantly, Napoleon's troops now had free passage through the Rhineland states of Baden, Nassau and Württemberg, and the operational base he most wanted in Bavaria, and got at Max Joseph's request. No one but Napoleon among the leaders of the great powers, save the marginalised Archduke Charles, was thinking in practical military terms during the months prior to the outbreak of war.

Napoleon had been hard at work trying to consolidate his lines and his rear as war approached, but in this crucial case Vienna did his work for him.

In truth, Napoleon had little alternative but to develop his concept of hegemonic blocks. France had no substantial allies, nor, realistically, was it going to find them. This was his salient weakness, and the one on which the British pinned their hopes. Paul Schroeder has seen Napoleon's sphere of influence as 'a great coalition of satellites and allies' deliberately assembled against the British.[13] It was, in fact, nothing of the kind. There is no doubt that Napoleon's consolidation of his grip on most of western Europe was seen as a challenge to the balance of power. For Napoleon, however, all these steps – with the important exceptions of his occupation of the Batavian Republic and Hannover – were not a direct threat to Britain or Russia. Napoleon saw them as essential buffers against Austria. Taken together, the cluster of territories now bound to France one way or another did indeed amount to a considerable pool of material and human resources, but they did not constitute the potential power of a grand coalition of the great powers. The only major military asset Napoleon acquired 'ready-made' was the Spanish navy, which was crippled at Trafalgar. Napoleon knew how weak he actually was, and it drove his creation of the new army, and spurred on his wider reform of France. The only conscripts in the Grande Armée who were not from what was now called 'old France' or 'the Interior', were Rhinelanders, Piedmontese and Belgians, for the great annexations came after, not before, the war of 1805. Their numbers were not negligible, but neither did they match the grandiose numbers of Russian and Austrian troops the leaders of the Coalition believed they could put in the field against him.

There were not enough men under Napoleon's control to match those of the Coalition. Rather he had profited from the weakness and fear of the states in the power vacuum between his enlarged France and the Habsburgs. Bavaria was the prime case in point, but all the other German princes who had gained from his protection also dreaded a reordering of Germany led by Austria. This reversal of the standing of the Habsburgs was probably Napoleon's greatest diplomatic achievement, and in 1804–5 it reaped its reward. The first stage in this process came with the great territorial redistributions agreed in 1802, through the secularisation of all the ecclesiastical states which disappeared along with forty-five of the fifty-one imperial free cities. The result was to forge closer bonds between Napoleon and the princes who had benefited from this, nor was the only result of this process the strengthening of the *Mittelstaaten* at the expense of the smallest states. The price was paid not just by the states that disappeared, but by the Habsburgs, in two ways.

The first of these was purely practical; the small German states – the prince-bishoprics, the imperial free cities and tiny fiefs of the Imperial Knights, who were the next in line for extinction, although their turn would only come in 1806, after Napoleon had defeated the Coalition in the field – were important sources of support for the Habsburgs. They provided significant numbers of officers and men for the Austrian army; in theory, they were serving the Holy Roman Emperor, but in effect they were Austrian soldiers – many of Vienna's leading statesmen, the most famous of whom was Metternich, were not Austrians, but came from these small states. The impact of this loss on the Austrian military establishment at a time of mounting tensions was particularly serious, as Francis steadfastly refused to allow conscription in his realms, seeing it as a destabilising French revolutionary invention. Added to this, in May 1802 the Hungarian Diet, the noble parliament over which Francis had very little control, refused to agree to his requests for military aid on the scale he sought.

The second price the Habsburgs paid was less tangible at first, but was soon seen to be even more serious. In his role as Holy Roman Emperor, but to the distinct advantage of the Austrian state, Francis, like his predecessors, had been the protector not just of the smaller states from the *Mittelstaaten*, but of all German states from each other. Not only had the disappearance of the small states deprived Austria of its loyalest supporters, it destroyed the confidence of all members of the Reich in its leadership. They felt confirmed in this view, when

Francis – in an act as illegal and unilateral as any Napoleonic fiat – proclaimed himself 'Emperor of Austria' on 10 August 1804. This was a wholly new, unprecedented title, which showed his intention to abandon his interests in the old Reich, and this was not lost on contemporaries. Legally, it was in complete defiance of the rule that no German prince could assume a royal title within the boundaries of the Reich, except the Holy Roman Emperor himself, which is why the Hohenzollerns styled themselves kings of Prussia, rather than Brandenburg, their heartland. There were attempts by Dalberg, the Chancellor of the Holy Roman Empire, to rally the Imperial Knights and the other German princes around the concept of an empire based on a 'third Germany' without Prussia or Austria, but all knew the immediate future lay in alliances with Napoleon, and Napoleon had little interest in Dalberg's appeal to him to help. When war broke out in 1805, most of the German princes knew where they stood, and it was no longer with Austria.

All this had been achieved because Napoleon had been allowed to step into the vacuum alone. Alexander had co-operated with him in the crucial initial stages, seeking aggrandisement for the German houses traditionally linked to the Romanovs, and withdrew his blessing when it was too late. The Habsburgs were momentarily too preoccupied with trying to regain the advantage in Italy while, in a very short-sighted, narrow analysis of the nature of Napoleonic power, as Paul Schroeder has pointed out, the British 'paid little attention to [Germany] and cared less'. Napoleon's veritable revolution in German affairs played no part in British motivations to return to war.[14]

After Austria, the most important German state, based on its military reputation, was Prussia. Christopher Clark has put Prussian policy in a nutshell when he says that the policy of neutrality adopted by Frederick-William II in 1795 hardened into a system under his successor, the passive Frederick-William III.[15] On the whole, it had served Prussia well; she had profited from the territorial reorganisation of Germany in two useful ways, the straightforward acquisition of territory and, as the leading Protestant state in the Reich, by the disappearance of so many Catholic states from the Imperial Diet. All this had come without the commitment to France the southern states had had to make. Prussia would be the most junior partner in any alliance, with either France or Russia, and the Queen, a more forceful figure than her husband, was still of the view that a Russian alliance would make Prussia wholly dependent on her gigantic neighbour. If there were to be a French alliance, the King said it should be one which 'would let France do whatever it wanted to Austria, so long as it left Prussia alone'.[16] Moreover, Frederick-William fully realised he could not afford war,[17] in contrast to Francis in Vienna.

However, when war between Britain and France resumed in 1803, and Napoleon took a direct strategic interest in the North Sea coast, as he had to, it was very hard for him to leave Prussia alone. There had been signs of this during the pan-European blockade of Britain of 1800–1, when joint Franco-Russian pressure had forced Frederick-William to occupy Hannover to help everyone else seal the coasts, and did so only because Napoleon said he would if Prussia did not. Frederick-William withdrew as quickly as he could, disturbed by the souring of relations with London, but two years later, when Napoleon needed to secure the same coastline, he showed Frederick-William that he made promises, not threats. A French army corps under Bernadotte rapidly ensconced itself in the ancestral home of George III, right on the Prussian border. It has been seen as a 'complete disregard for Prussian sensibilities'[18] but, in the light of recent experience, Frederick-William saw it coming, and, in the circumstances of 1803, Napoleon would have left himself open to attack had he done otherwise. In Napoleon's mind, Prussia had benefited substantially from the reordering of Germany, and she could at least tolerate this predictable step, which, if it made life difficult for Berlin with London, posed nothing like the problems it might create for him if he left the coast open for the British. He was right: Prussia kept out of the war in 1805, swallowing even Napoleon's violation of neutrality – his clearest act of open aggression – when he marched French troops across the small Prussian enclaves of Ansbach and Bayreuth.

It went further. At the very moment Napoleon abandoned the projected invasion of Britain and broke camp at Boulogne, he offered Hannover to Prussia in an effort to ensure its neutrality by undermining its relations with Britain. His exasperation with Prussia is apparent in his letter to Talleyrand from Pont-de-Briques, written the day he broke camp:

In giving Hannover to Prussia, I am doing them a favour which, without exaggeration, increases their force of 40,000 men and improves the position of their state, in the same way Genoa would do for Piedmont [that is, giving Prussia better outlets to the sea and more ports], and just as I guarantee the integrity of its territory, so Prussia guarantees that of my present states . . . I am making this offer to Prussia, but they must listen to me: I will not be able to offer it again in a fortnight. If the present of Hannover to Prussia, leading to this power to declare itself for me, frightens Austria and Russia . . . and frees me from the worry of a war at sea, I will consider myself recompensed for this great increase in Prussian power. But once I have broken camp . . . I cannot halt again; my project for a maritime war has failed; and so I shall gain nothing from giving Hannover to Prussia. She must decide immediately.[19]

Prussia did indeed accept, but, true to past behaviour, remained neutral, and Napoleon was in no position to take reprisals, nor did he do so until Prussia entered the war on the side of the Coalition a year later. His priority was to secure internal lines, of which Hannover was a part. In truth, he did not care if Prussia fought with him, for his main concern was, as he said, to protect his northern flank from a maritime attack, thus freeing Bernadotte's corps for action. Neutrality would do, and was handsomely rewarded, but in a way, he hoped, that would prevent an alliance with Britain, which it merely postponed. If Napoleon's offer of Hannover to Prussia was couched in terms of aggression, it was bluff and everyone knew it.

The whole point of drawing Frederick-William into his plans stemmed from weakness, for the whole business was an acknowledgement that, for all the might of the Grande Armée, Napoleon could not defend the North Sea coast properly while waging war elsewhere. Once on campaign, he would have no army with which to threaten Prussia, for the Channel defences of France itself had been stripped down to a bare minimum of the poorest quality troops, even as Napoleon wrote to Talleyrand in these terms. As for Britain and Russia, they realised that Prussia was determined to stay neutral. After the 'war party' was perceived to be gaining the upper hand with Francis, they concentrated their efforts on Vienna, well aware of how unreliable Prussia could be as an ally, and that she was as unwilling to risk working with Austria as she was with France.

Elsewhere, the pro-French elites who now controlled the satellite states of Italy and Batavia knew they had little to hope for from the restorations promised by the Third Coalition. With fresh memories of their fates after the French reversals of 1798–9, they stood by France, however reluctantly in some cases. The only power of any size in Napoleon's orbit was Spain, whose decline was well known. Napoleon commanded a wide degree of loyal, but ineffectual, support, the price of moving into power vacuums rather than achieving crushing victories in war over rival powers. Napoleon took this very much to heart in his march up the Rhine in the autumn of 1805.

All this left Austria alone against Napoleon, in any future war, until Russia could mobilise. Only the Neapolitan Bourbons went into the field with them, and, in contrast to Austria, they received direct military support from both the Russians and the British, who had immediate strategic interests in their territory. Effectively abandoned by the other powers, for all Russia and Britain wanted him to fight the French at their bidding, Francis had feared Napoleon would seek election for the imperial crown in these years, for he would have had a majority among the princes by 1804. This is the real source of Francis' consternation at the form of Napoleon's coronation as King of Italy in Milan on 26 May 1805. Napoleon had himself crowned with the Iron Crown of the Lombards, a relic closely associated with Charlemagne, who wore it as King of the Lombards, a title held in conjunction with that of Holy Roman Emperor. This gesture was less to do with Franco-Austrian tensions in Italy, significant as these were in the origins of the war, than with a perceived threat to the House of Habsburg's hold on the imperial throne.[20] The days of the Holy Roman Empire had been numbered, if not from the secularisations of 1802, then certainly from Francis' proclamation of himself as Emperor of Austria in 1804. He formally dissolved it on 6 August 1806, in the wake of his crushing military defeat by France, when it would have been impossible to prevent Napoleon doing as he pleased about the future of the Reich. In the autumn of 1805, that particular nightmare still lay in the future.

Napoleon nevertheless felt that what he held had to be consolidated with great urgency in these years, and his actions provoked fear in quarters like London and Vienna, where anything he did was suspect in all circumstances, but also in St Petersburg, as has been seen. Napoleon was, in fact, at his most pragmatic at this time, reordering the territories he already controlled, with two overriding aims only, to secure his rear and flanks, on a wide European front, and to garner as much financial and material support from his hegemony as he could. Napoleon's approach to the internal affairs of his satellites in 1805 can be gauged quite simply on how effectively they responded to his demands for support, financial more than military. The Swiss produced the substantial sums of money and the moderate contingent of troops asked of them and were left alone; Napoleon made no attempt to interfere in the workings of the Act of Mediation.

It was more complicated in the Batavian Republic and his own Kingdom of Italy, however. The Dutch proved, initially if not in the following years, less problematic, for in their case Napoleon's dissatisfaction with their state's lack of direction matched that of many segments of the Dutch political elites; even if they had very different ideas from Napoleon's about what to do, they were just as concerned by the sense of drift in their republic, at a time of crisis. For radicals, the fear of defeat and an Orange restoration concentrated many minds, and gave Napoleon a fragile point of agreement with them that he sought to exploit.

Napoleon had intervened quickly and ruthlessly in the internal affairs of the Dutch in 1801 when, in September, French troops forcibly closed the Batavian parliament, worried by the growing tensions between the radical republican and more moderate factions. The new constitution Napoleon imposed – 'the Regency of State' – sought to placate not only moderate republicans, but Orangeist supporters of the pre-revolutionary order, by re-establishing, at least in theory, a degree of local autonomy based on the traditional provinces, and creating a collegiate executive, felt to be more in keeping with Dutch political culture. In this spirit, the Batavian Republic was briefly rechristened 'the Batavian Commonwealth'. In fact, the process of centralisation and the professionalisation of the government went on; the real change came through Napoleon's attempt to introduce the spirit of *ralliement* and *amalgame* to the Dutch political classes, as the Orangeist elites returned to positions of power and influence. This was a very influential policy, in the long term, for 'the Regency of State was the first attempt to find a middle way between the old regime and the revolution.'[21]

In the short term, however, the Dutch republicans, both moderate and radical alike, saw only the failure of this policy to achieve real reconciliation and, as a result, a climate of 'political and conceptual confusion' developed in the years 1801–5. For the Dutch, this stemmed from the alien nature of the Napoleonic political culture imposed on them, rather than the new institutions of government as such. They found Napoleon's blending of the old monarchy and the French Revolution increasingly coloured by militarism 'enigmatic', as one Dutch scholar has put it, and so 'the reconciliation of all the parties proclaimed so insistently since 1801 was still awaited; political energy seemed to have deserted the nation'.[22] Napoleon had his own, very concrete reasons for being unhappy with his attempt to transport his own political vision to the Dutch, but the failure of the Regency of State as a viable regime only impinged on him with the resumption of the war with Britain, after 1803. While he was in Brussels in July 1803, in the first months of the war, he remarked to Cambacérès, of the Dutch delegation in London, 'I have spent a long time with . . . the Batavian commission [to London]. They have promised much; we shall see if they keep their promises.'[23] Over the next two years, he complained of administrative confusion which held back his invasion plans and the seeming flood of British contraband into Dutch warehouses and hiding places. One of the first things he demanded of the Dutch in the late spring of 1805 was to do something about 'the Dutch granges and stables ... full of English merchandise', and he threatened to send in French patrols to deal with it; 'this is a violation of territory, but also the only way to oppose such scandalous smuggling'.[24]

Napoleon attributed this sort of problem to the weak, collegial executive he had given the Dutch, in a concession to their political traditions, worries that began to surface among some of the Dutch themselves.[25] However, in a very emphatic letter to Talleyrand in April 1804, he voiced clearly his belief that his attempt to export *ralliement* and *amalgame* to the Dutch had failed, that the Orangeists were now in the pocket of the British, and undermining both his own grip on the country and the safety of the republicans, radical and moderate alike, who had served the French. He listed four specific points to Talleyrand that caused the most alarm: there were no Dutch Catholics in the government or the assemblies, or the administration at any level, despite amounting to one-third of the population, 'and without contradiction, that part most attached to France' like religious minorities everywhere, and where Napoleon saw discrimination against them, he saw the creeping return of the old order; that the composition of the 'Asiatic Council' – the committee responsible for running the Dutch overseas empire – had been surreptitiously purged of all those members loyal to France and replaced by 'men known for their attachment to the English cause, [and] who have all their assets in England'; that, by an ordinance of 6 March, the local government of Amsterdam had reassigned all the special pews in churches, transferring them from the government officials they were meant for – from families who had served the French and the Batavian Republic – 'to men who had embraced the English cause and been amnestied almost the same day, [while] those who have always supported the cause of France were dishonoured and driven off'; that over the past three months, local government had undergone a quiet purge 'wholly in favour of the English, [which has united local government] as one voice, complaining about the French alliance'.

Napoleon may have become paranoid as the war with Britain unfolded, but it was paranoia that reflected the fears of his foreign collaborators and affirmed his commitment to them. If French troops were evacuated from Batavia, not only would he have the British on his borders, but what would become of 'the finest part of the Dutch nation'? This is why, he told Talleyrand, he was now ready to intervene in Dutch internal affairs, 'to assure the Dutch friends of France of their influence and consideration'. Before he did, he needed to know two things, however: if the Dutch could not live with their present constitution, what sort of amendments or changes should be made? Who were the men who should occupy the leading posts? Napoleon meant it.

The future relationship of the Dutch to the French Empire brought economic misery and military and political oppression, but in 1804–5 Napoleon was determined to protect not only his northern flank, but his friends, and this meant restoring to power 'those sane men who have held posts since the entry of the French [in 1795] and who are, today, without employment'.[26] On the last day of 1804, Napoleon told Talleyrand to tell the Batavian ambassador to Paris, the lawyer and leading 'gadfly' of Dutch republicanism, Rutger Jan Schimmelpenninck, to draw up a new constitution for his country,[27] which he did. It created a one-man executive, entitled 'the Grand Pensionary', an archaic title from the old Republic Napoleon and Talleyrand had plucked out, and Schimmelpenninck, a moderate reformer who had served both the French and the old regime, was given the post. The new constitution curbed civil rights considerably and tightened central control, while – for all it created a stronger executive – still acknowledging the traditions of Dutch republican political culture, around which even pro-French radicals had been rallying during the uncertain times of the Regency of State.[28]

Schimmelpenninck's tenure of power lasted but a year; when the dust had momentarily settled on the military campaigns, Napoleon replaced him – he was not ruthlessly deposed and thrust aside, but 'reassigned to other duties', which really meant running his extensive estates[29] – with a satellite kingdom under his brother, Louis. Nevertheless, this particular exercise in regime-change was about men, as well as institutions. In his short time in power, Schimmelpenninck brought back many moderate republicans, the most prominent among them the financial expert Issac Gogel, the educational reformer Adriaan van den Ene, and the veteran French loyalist Johannes Goldberg, if no real radicals. Most of them survived into Louis' service, as did the new institution of a strong executive power and its inevitable corollary, a more unitary, centralised state, at odds with Dutch history, but henceforth its central pillar. Schimmelpenninck had kept some avowed Orangeists in important posts – some even in the police[30] – but the overt opposition of the supporters of the old order to the regime-change of 1805[31] had ensured that men like Gogel now tied themselves firmly to the new order, when, until that point, they had been essentially suspicious of Napoleon.

When Louis took his new, illegal and unprecedented – in the pure sense of the term – throne in 1806, 'the constitution Napoleon gave him had simply scratched monarchy onto the pre-existing republican traditions'.[32] Napoleon was momentarily happy with his work, but as Louis began to prove himself a more unreliable, incompetent ally than anything the locals had produced in the preceding decade, he soon lamented that he had created so powerful an executive. He had been warned by one of his loyalest, most trusted Dutch supporters, Karel Veurhuell, an admiral made Minister of the Navy – a key post for Napoleon – who had been a staunch Orangeist, like most of the navy, but whose direct service under Napoleon had converted him to unswerving loyalty.[33] He had told all and sundry that the new constitution 'gives the head of the government much more power than any number of kings have had'.[34] When Louis mishandled his power, Napoleon stripped him of it with a ruthlessness bordering on cruelty, and his solution was to annex the country directly to France. That lay four years hence, however.

In the meantime, he had no cause to repent of his hasty action. The Dutch had no military support to offer Napoleon. Indeed, he had to promise Schimmelpenninck that the country would still be protected by the weak forces he had left in Boulogne and the northern Rhineland after the campaign began[35] – but his worries were less about getting the Dutch to contribute financially to the war effort than of sedition. He had responded to the growing crisis in the Batavian Republic – as it was now called once again – in a way which secured it for him, and for the friends of the French; it had reaffirmed his loyalty to the same kind of collaborators he told Eugène – in 1806, as his new Viceroy in his Kingdom of Italy – to 'treat well ... The patriot party is the one that has always been the most energetic for France.'[36] The dangers of war, and the need to secure his hegemony, had brought Napoleon back, in some manner, to his roots, the trappings of monarchy notwithstanding. However, by December 1805, Napoleon was warning the Dutch they had to pay for the French troops on their soil, and that 'in the midst of the enormous expenses I am obliged to bear, Holland must help me'.[37] These words were written from the Habsburg palace of Schönbrunn, after the triumphs of the 1805 campaign. The price of victory was high, and, one way or another, it would shatter more than one long-standing working relationship.

There remained the Kingdom of Italy to consolidate. Napoleon had made himself its king, a step which had unsettled not just the other powers, but many of his loyalest supporters in Milan. It signified a tighter control – and so a more deep-running subordination to France – than some of his most prominent collaborators wanted, Melzi d'Eril chief among them. Napoleon was his own master in the Kingdom of Italy, much more so than elsewhere in his hegemony, perhaps even more than in France itself. Unlike the former Dutch Republic, or France for that matter, the Kingdom of Italy was a new, composite entity, most of whose component parts had either been under foreign rule, or, like the former Papal Legations around Bologna, had seen themselves as subject provinces to a leech-like metropole, Rome, to which they felt no loyalty. Only the ex-Duchy of Modena had any claim to a political identity of its own, or a coherent political culture that reached beyond a city wall, what Italians then as now termed *campanilismo*, the loyalty of the parish church spire.

As the needs of defence and the costs of a major war bore down on him for the first time as supreme leader, Napoleon now had cause to feel qualms about the modest sense of national unity he had actually fostered among the elites of the Kingdom. There was a pro-Austrian faction in the Lombard core of the Kingdom, and it was numerous, but its adherents had neither the institutional heritage nor quite the financial resources of the Dutch Orangeists. In Milan, Napoleon's problems came from within the confines of his own creation, but they were limited to the more conservative reforming elements of the political class, centred on Melzi, whose prime concern was to increase the autonomy of the Kingdom of Italy, a concern which heightened when the union of the crowns became a reality as Joseph and then Louis refused the Iron Crown. The underlying fear was – correctly gauged – that Napoleon would increasingly subordinate Italian to French interests.

Melzi's timing could not have been worse. In the course of the Amiens negotiations, as has been seen, Napoleon was indeed risking virtually everything to secure international recognition for the Italian Republic, as it still was, and continued to make this a condition of his dealings with everyone. The terms he laid down to Prussia in August 1805, as the real war finally began, included an unambiguous demand that the Italian state be fully recognised by Berlin. The diplomatic costs had been as high as imaginable, a continuing battle that did not render Napoleon amenable to compromising his hold on what he had regarded as his real power base from the outset. Talleyrand sided with Melzi, believing that at least the outward trappings of independence would make international recognition easier to achieve. Napoleon began in this mode, but his brothers scotched these efforts for him.

The real point of no return, however, came with the mounting costs incurred by the onset of war, which brought long-standing problems between Melzi and Napoleon to a head, and Melzi's defiance could not have been more ill judged. These problems ranged from the particular to those of a more fundamental nature. Following the reconquest of the territories of the Cisalpine Republic in 1800, Napoleon had continued the practice he had been encouraged into under the Directory of stationing a French army there, and he continued to do so, throughout the years of peace in which the Italian Republic existed, that is, during Melzi's entire tenure as its Vice-President. These troops amounted to about 40,000 men, not in itself a large contingent, but they were paid for by Milan, and their commander, Murat, saw himself as above and beyond Melzi's authority. It was the principle of the thing for Melzi, although he recognised he needed them there to protect the Republic from Austria.[38]

Melzi, predictably, had a very fraught relationship with Murat and hoped the creation of the country's own army, which was well under way by 1804–5 and numbered almost 70,000 men by 1805, would be met by a reciprocal reduction of French troops on its soil.[39] The onset of war put paid to this: Napoleon could not realistically have reduced his presence on his only direct frontier with Austria. In the summer of 1805, there were 125,000 Austrian troops in Venice and the Tyrol, all menacing the Kingdom, as opposed to only 80,000 on the border with Bavaria,[40] making it clear where Francis intended to concentrate his efforts.

Melzi's hopes of seeing French financial demands and its military presence in the Republic of Italy reduced rose after the Peace of Amiens, but when he reformulated his wider requests for reform in 1805, at the creation of the Kingdom, these demands, which had featured so prominently for so long, disappeared as war loomed. Melzi continued to seek a range of constitutional changes during the conversion of the Republic into the Kingdom, but, in complete contrast to his approach to Dutch affairs, Napoleon did almost nothing to alter the institutional framework of the Kingdom of Italy in 1805. There was no reason for him to do so, for it was here, more than in France, that he had been able to realise his political ideas, and he was not about to dismantle his own work. Melzi hit upon the very aspects of the constitution Napoleon prized most. He wanted to create more electoral colleges, expanding them by 50 per cent,[41] which ran directly counter to Napoleon's belief that fewer colleges, covering wide areas, increased their role. The net result was a strong continuity in the institutions from the Republic to the Kingdom.

Melzi, however, had a longer historical perspective than Napoleon. Lombardy had been the milch cow of the Habsburg Monarchy; it produced more in revenues than any other province, and more than all the lands of the Hungarian side of the monarchy put together. Freedom from Habsburg rule had raised hopes among its major taxpayers – patricians with extensive, productive rural estates – that the new regime would bring prosperity. The Napoleonic reforms brought many potential benefits, but they remained just that, potential, because Napoleon stationed a large army there, even in time of peace, and continued to make huge demands on the treasury as war approached. This exploded in July 1805 when, in his efforts to squeeze more revenue out of Italy on a more regular basis, Napoleon raised tariff duties to worryingly high levels and, in a shocking step for many in the Milan government, created duties and fees for the registration of legal transactions of kinds hitherto unknown there. Napoleon accepted the rejection of his project by the legislature in Milan on 13 July; a modified, more temporised project was passed four days later by the narrow margin of thirty-three to twenty-five.[42] These measures led one high-ranking member of the government to explode in terms Melzi may have nurtured, but never dared voice: 'We will show these French dogs that we are Italians.'[43] Melzi interpreted this as the result of the absence of real political independence, and this is why he regarded the union of the crowns in Napoleon's person as so dispiriting. Napoleon's insistence that an Italian division be sent to Boulogne to serve with the French at Milan's expense appeared, in this light, not just as an extra burden, but as a slight to the sovereignty of the Republic.

In 1804, Melzi attempted to get a promise from Napoleon that the crowns would become separate after his death, that, whoever his French successor was, he would not wear the Iron Crown as well, a view shared by Talleyrand. This was coupled to a demand that all public posts be reserved for citizens of the Kingdom; that is, Melzi did not want Frenchmen taking over the higher echelons of government. Napoleon sensed the subtext of this quickly enough: Melzi wanted him to withdraw from direct involvement in Italian affairs. There had been other tensions. Despite Melzi's insistence that Roman Catholicism be made the official religion of the state, with others only tolerated, in contrast to France, he had still clashed with Napoleon over the terms of the Concordat between the Republic and the Vatican, which Melzi found far too accommodating to Rome. This had almost led to his resignation as Vice-President in June 1804, a sign of Melzi's preoccupation with sovereignty and independence as much as an indication of his anti-clericalism.[44] Nevertheless, Napoleon and Melzi had more in common than not. Melzi welcomed the institution of monarchy, because it would strengthen the state internally and, hopefully, it would make Italy appear as a permanent fixture in Europe. He agreed with Napoleon that the new kingdom should emerge as the most powerful and influential power south of the Alps, as the touchstone of a new, reformed peninsula; both men saw the Kingdom of Italy as a regional power in the making. Napoleon would not let go of his first stronghold, however.

On the same day as they made their peace over the Italian Concordat – an argument Melzi largely won – he wrote to his foreign minister, Marescalchi, that this was the one issue on which Napoleon would not listen to reason,[45] as he did not agree to reserve the bureaucracy for Italian nationals. Melzi wanted Napoleon to call himself 'the constitutional king of the Italian Republic'. Moreover, he wanted the head of state to reside in Milan, or to appoint a Viceroy for Life, who had to be an Italian.[46] Melzi's days were numbered, and Napoleon used the creation of the Kingdom to remove him, and install Eugène as his Viceroy – a non-Italian, but resident in Milan – and Melzi's bitter rival, Antonio Aldini, as his prime minister.

There was another factor at work among the political elites of the

Kingdom of Italy which isolated Melzi and had made Napoleon's life easier, at least within the narrow confines of elite politics. Italy had been rocked by violent, widespread popular revolts both in the late 1790s and even after the French reconquest; resentment still festered in its countryside and, as has been seen, even some of the larger provincial cities like Padua were not immune to revolt if French power seemed endangered, as it could well have been again, in 1805, with a considerable Austrian force massed on its eastern border. An intrinsic distrust of the masses, largely absent in the Netherlands, made it much easier for Napoleon to convert many radical Italian reformers to authoritarianism. It was about survival in a hostile world, in the short term and, probably more importantly, the only means by which to reform a recalcitrant people along revolutionary, enlightened lines. Put another way, many Italian radicals saw Napoleon as a protector from internal as well as international threat, and regarded a strong, authoritarian state as the only way to reform their new country. They had abandoned consensus from 'the bottom up', as it were, and could work with Napoleon more easily as a result.

In common with only a segment of pro-French Dutch patriots, most Italian radicals, who were far more embattled, came to see the strengthening of the state as 'the only way to educate and discipline the popular masses and to overcome the conditions of social and cultural backwardness that had condemned the democratic experiments of 1796–99 to failure', as Carlo Capra has put it with an incisive, unadorned clarity, which matched the mixture of hard-eyed realism and determined reformism they shared with Napoleon.[47] When Napoleon took direct control, in the first moments in the life of the new kingdom between the dismissal of Melzi and the institution of Eugène, he kept his word and was good to the radical patriots, bringing them into high office and low, in contrast to the relative moderation of Schimmelpennick in the Batavian Republic, the other major satellite state.

Melzi's ready replacement as Eugène's new prime minister was a man with a very radical past, Aldini. The partnership Aldini formed with Eugène over the next nine years was emblematic of the new Napoleonic vision: a revolutionary radical, still bent on reform, but now convinced of the need for a strong, authoritarian state, in harness with a younger man, a Napoleonic bureaucratic born and bred.

The pragmatism of 1804–5 was driven by ruthless expediency, although, for the moment, Napoleon recognised certain limits, which were increasingly seeming to be hindrances to him in a crisis. He modified his new taxes for the Kingdom of Italy; he tried to acknowledge Dutch political traditions in his constitutional intervention of 1805; he bullied the Spanish mercilessly, but he left the Swiss in peace when they gave him what he wanted. Intervene and demand he did, however, driven by the financial needs of an unprecedentedly large war effort. Money and military needs exposed the fissures in his relationship with Melzi; they forced him not only to dictate a political settlement to the Dutch, but one which overturned his own previous policies. Napoleon reserved his most overt aggression for the states within his own hegemony in the build-up to war.

His enemies possessed far more potential resources than those of the territories under Napoleon's control, but he marshalled what was at his disposal much better, through superior organisation. Men were delivered through conscription, and they had to be, for France had no worthwhile allies. Money was another matter. As has been seen, France was in the throes of a financial crisis in 1803–5, and the Dutch had been caught up in it as well, as their trade with Britain ceased and the rest of their international commerce retracted severely, as the blockade tightened. It was all the more important that the Kingdom of Italy, relatively untouched by the crisis, contribute yet more. Memories among most of the reformers in these states of the harsh, if short, restorations of 1798–9 were fresh enough in 1804–5 for Napoleon to retain their support, if only just.

His desperation as well as his concern to consolidate, not expand, are clear in his letter to Talleyrand of 22 August, already cited. As he broke camp and began 'the great pirouette' of turning his back on the Channel, towards the Rhine, he outlined limited goals but revealed an aggressive determination to act as he felt necessary. He insisted that Prussia

guarantee to me, the integrity of my present states . . . If I am asked what my actual frontiers are, I will say: the Rhine to the German [North Sea] coast; in Italy, they are the borders of my own kingdom and Tuscany. The King of Prussia will guarantee to me and my descendants my kingdom of Italy . . .

As for Prussia, so for the other powers. When he fought, it would be in the first instance to protect Bavaria from Austrian expansionism, 'to defend a House I love, and that it is in my interests to protect, you will explain this [to the Prussian ambassador] and make him understand the meaning of this question', just as he was to tell the Bavarian ambassador that the French army was on its way to help Max Joseph. It was all Austria's fault, on every front: the Habsburgs had brought war to Germany by entering the field, and 'the ills of war will rebound on those on those who provoke it'.

Napoleon made an interesting comment in his castigation of the Austrians, asking them to end their troop movements, hostile acts against 'a France engaged in a maritime war which is in the cause of all nations'. There is a substantial body of evidence that Napoleon meant this, which is why his actions that very day are called a 'pirouette'; he had given all his attention to the 'descent on England', and now had to perform a volte-face of gargantuan proportions. War with Austria was not what he wanted, at least for the time being. The vicious circle of it all emerges best in the particular, not in the grand diplomatic strategies of Russia or Britain: France and Austria were the two regional powers engaged in the bitter local war. Napoleon had broken the terms of all the preceding treaties when he intervened in Switzerland, yet that intervention had given the Swiss stability. Subsequently, he had been called upon to withdraw his troops, with which he had effected the Act of Mediation, and he went through the motions; by 1805 he could say with reason, as he did, '[for Austria] to fill the Tyrol with troops when I evacuate Switzerland, is to declare war on me'. Above all, he made it clear that in future he would not even pretend to be bound by any arrangements but his own:

As for Holland, I don't want to give any kind of guarantee. If the war with England goes on for long, and this people, without colonies, without firm land, no longer wishes to live separately, I want nothing to bind me on this particular point. It is the same for Switzerland. I will respect the Act of Mediation, as long as the Swiss keep it; should they ever violate it, I will no longer recognise their independence.[48]

These are among the most significant, prophetic words Napoleon ever committed to paper, and they remained in a private American library, the Pierpont Morgan, until republished by the diligence of the Fondation Napoléon in 2008. This was the moment when Napoleon threw down more than a military gauntlet to the Austrians. He was ready to go beyond annexing Batavia if he felt the need; he was prepared to do the same to Switzerland, if it seemed necessary. It amounted to an assertion that he would disregard all his promises in future. He had 'played to the whistle', as the saying goes, up to now, if not 'to the spirit of the game'. Even his most determined detractor, Paul Schroeder, admits grudgingly that the war of 1805 'did not exactly result from these acts of [Napoleon's] aggression; instead, it represented their purpose'.[49] Napoleon had gone beyond the terms of treaties in annexing Piedmont and Liguria, and by intervening in Switzerland. His actions were not illegal in the Netherlands, and not at all in Germany, where Austria was the lawless expansionist, if the international relations of the period are subject to scrutiny of this kind. Napoleon had played more than his part in the destabilisation of western Europe between 1803 and 1805, but he had not been alone. Britain and Russia lured Austria into the field, and there is no doubt that Napoleon was reacting to this in 1805, not provoking.

There is another important element in his words to Talleyrand. In 1805, as aggressive as those words were, they did not spell out a policy of expansion – that would only emerge after the military triumphs of 1805–7 – but, rather, a ruthless determination to hold on to what he had gained, fairly or not, up to that point. The first phase of the War of the Third Coalition was a defensive war on Napoleon's part. As Philip Dwyer – like Schroeder, far from an admirer of Napoleon – has pointed out, it would have been difficult for him to do otherwise, for 'Napoleon's foreign-political decisions conformed to the material and political interests of the new elite.'[50] That elite still thought in defensive terms; its cynicism emerged in the ruthless exploitation of the resources under its control, but not in a policy of expansion. Dwyer has characterised this as an 'ideological consensus', while many diplomatic historians have dismissed ideology as a real motive in the genesis of the War of the Third Coalition, the first of the entirely 'Napoleonic wars'. In truth, Napoleon did rally the elites of his own empire around him for reasons that had their roots in the ideology of revolutionary, enlightened reform, which had caused the small groups of collaborators now in power around him in the 'foreign departments' of France and the satellite states to side against their old rulers, just as the majority of French Revolutionaries had now 'rallied'.

Yet, in 1805, these ideological origins of his support were overlain by the realpolitik of survival. If he failed to maintain the status quo – a hegemony which was not as territorially large as that achieved by the Directory by 1798 – his fate would be grim, just as it would be for those who had first brought him to power. He was defending not so much the gains made at Campo Formio, Lunéville or Amiens, but the great advances of the late 1790s. The costs of the new army, based almost entirely in France, were compounded by the financial crisis of 1804, and cast minds back to the relative ease with which such expense had been borne before 1799, when the war had paid for itself or, rather, when foreigners had paid for the war: in this context the satellite states were now seen to be indispensable to France. When Napoleon roused the legislators of the Kingdom of Italy to reject his new taxes in 1805, he was actually reviving the economic imperialism begun – during his absence in Egypt – by the commercial treaties of February and July 1798, which completely subjugated the Cisalpine Republic to Directorial France.[51]

Napoleon inherited far more than the Directory's foreign policy. As the needs of war grew, he could not turn his back on the mass of French taxpayers he had done so much to win around. Napoleon had hard reasons to refuse to cede the territory he held, and they were to do with the internal dynamics of French revolutionary politics, not a lust for conquest. It would have been political suicide to do anything else. Napoleon was only just achieving stability within France; there had been serious plots against him; not all – especially within the army – had accepted the creation of the Empire; he had no obvious heir. What may have been provocation to the other powers was inviolable obligation within the French elites, financial and political alike. The loss of Saint-Domingue made the retention of the new captive markets of western Europe all the more imperative.

There is no doubt that, by 1805, Napoleon was in full personal control of French foreign policy, and that of his allies and satellite states as well. Thierry Lentz has seen the victories of 1805 as the first turning point in Napoleon's worsening relationship with Talleyrand, which culminated in the latter's resignation in 1807.[52] In fact, Talleyrand was increasingly pushed aside over anything to do with the Kingdom of Italy, and the 'peace party' centred on Joseph and himself was marginalised in 1803, over the renewal of war with Britain. Napoleon could not realistically have followed their advice and maintained the support of the French elites. This is epitomised by British insistence on a new commercial treaty at the time of Amiens, which would have awakened the fears of an influx of British goods, the shadow of the collapse of the fragile French textile industry and, politically, the memories of the perceived 'treason' of Louis XVI in allowing a comparable arrangement in the 1780s. In its place, renewed French control of northern Italy allowed the cynical dismantling of the silk industries of Lombardy and Piedmont, which began in 1802, and the supply of cheaply imported raw silk to feed the once rebellious city of Lyon. These were interests Napoleon had to listen to for his own well-being, just as Alexander had to heed the commercial connections of his great court nobles in the same years. It was as well for many in France that Napoleon, not the 'peace party', had such a tight grip on foreign policy. It was also a salutary lesson that empires are not built by one man, but by collaborative effort.

For all his personal control, what Napoleon could do was still limited, or so he thought, until he saw how powerful the Grande Armée actually was and, 'being Napoleon', he did wait to see before he thought in more than defensive terms. Napoleon was not yet in a position to be an aggressive expansionist; he had only just gathered a new army to replace the exhausted shambles he had had to take into the field in 1800. This was still about survival. If the war was brought about by 'Napoleon simply being Napoleon', that Napoleon was not yet the insatiable conqueror he may later have become. He was, however, the unscrupulous leader of an equally unscrupulous 'rogue state', and his political and personal survival depended on being and doing this very well. In that sense, he was 'simply being Napoleon', surviving and prospering at the expense of other aggressors.

Others, the Austrians above all in 1805, played into Napoleon's hands, under-estimating him and over-confident in themselves, just like Sieyès after Brumaire. The British had the best vantage point to observe the work of the Channel camps, and Napoleon was always looking over his shoulder for them, but, while Nelson was wilfully blind to danger when he raised his telescope to his blind eye to 'see no ships', his masters remained culpably oblivious to the great beast of prey only a few miles off their shores. The German states would not have come as easily into the orbit had it not been for a justified fear of Austria; Spain was drawn into an alliance – and just about held to it – by British expansionism; 'Jacobin' reformers in Italy, the Rhineland and the Low Countries clung to him, often in sour temper, because he was their only bastion against the horrors of reactionary reprisals, and a return to a past from which they had excluded themselves. Their position never changed over the years of Napoleonic rule, and is perfectly encapsulated in the words of the mayor of Alessandria in Piedmont, the former Jacobin Barrocchio, who wrote to Fouché in the midst of another war with Austria, in 1809, that: 'My political existence depends on the fate of the government, its enemies are my enemies, and it was not long ago that, in their joy at the Austrian advance, they showed their true opinions.'[53]

Louis XVIII, from exile, still breathed fire and brimstone on the men who had killed his brother, and his promises to confiscate all the national lands, kill the regicides and abolish the revolutionary reforms – in which he came to include Napoleon's – were continually reasserted. This was all fresh in the memory in 1805. Napoleon had been raised to office to prevent the return of the old order in 1799. Now, in power, his surest support came from all those for whom defeat meant annihilation, rather than from a thirst for victory, and he included himself among them. Great horizons awaited, but they had not arrived quite yet.

The relationship between the Russians and the British was not straightforward in shaping the Third Coalition, and Paul Schroeder has pointed, astutely, to the fact that they were the only true global powers of the time as an important part of this. Georges Lefebvre argued that the crux of the War of the Third Coalition was a clash of two imperialisms, French and British, which Schroeder has challenged, redefining it as one among three imperialisms, incorporating Russia.[54] Perhaps this refinement is not quite the measure of the times either, however, in that it overestimates Napoleon's reach. With the end of French naval power and the loss of Saint-Domingue, France was now more of a regional European power, as opposed to a colonial, Atlantic force, than at any other time since European expansion began. France had become the dominant power in western Europe and, as such, her interests and approaches to international relations now bore more resemblance to those of the Habsburgs than to the truly global concerns and visions of either Russia or Britain. Napoleon may have nurtured hopes of regaining foreign colonies, but these were not his realistic goals. Austria was the regional power on its way down, whereas France was in the ascendancy and usurping its place, but it was a competition between comparable powers for the same ground. Their enmity should not disguise this fact, any more than the crushing

military superiority Napoleon was bringing to life, as yet still unknown
to the rest of world in these years. Napoleon was winning a bloodless
war against the Habsburgs in Germany, thereby creating a 'mass' of
yet another kind out of the small parcels of the German states. Gillray
produced a sneering engraving of Napoleon 'baking' German thrones
'to order' but the joke was on Britain. Nevertheless, Napoleon still had
to be watchful and nervous about his grip on northern Italy, given the
porous frontier there. Just as the Habsburgs had no idea of the shock
that awaited them in the form of the Grande Armée, Napoleon did
not yet fully realise Austrian military weakness, although he had sent
several observers into southern Germany to assess just that in 1804,
and in all his plans for war in 1805 he bore in mind the good account
the Austrian army had always given of itself in the 1790s.

Compared to Britain and Russia, Napoleon and the Habsburgs still
shared common limitations, for all Napoleon's burgeoning strength.
Like Austria, and in stark contrast to Russia and Britain, Napoleon
had no safe heartland to retreat to, a fact which enabled Alexander and
Pitt to calculate the odds as they did.[55] They interpreted Napoleon's
consolidation as aggression to be contained, whereas Austria, once
deluded into thinking she could challenge Napoleon, saw the prospect
of a successful war as a means to redress her previous losses. To seize
Bavaria was a step towards consolidation for Francis, just as annexing
Piedmont and Liguria were Napoleon's means to preserve his gains
in northern Italy. Both powers were looking for gains, but gains that
had as much to do with consolidating themselves as expanding, for
it was still about the struggle for control of western Europe, without
reference to wider horizons.

These limited horizons were often reflected in Napoleon's mis-
calculations when dealing with both Britain and Russia, for he
adapted more readily than he would have liked to recognise to the
role of 'Emperor of the West', and of the west alone. His insistence
on continuing to garrison several coastal fortresses in the Kingdom
of Naples, and in Tuscany, created unease in the Russians, just as it
pushed the British to war; they were prepared to go to war to keep their

own hold on Malta, in the same region. The British and the Russians took fright at the very presence of the French in the Mediterranean, which posed no direct threat, but made them uneasy about the safety of their longer lines of communication to India and through the Black Sea, respectively. When war broke out, Napoleon considered the campaign in southern Italy a secondary front, but the Russians and British poured considerable resources into it. This was not a conflict about immediate threats to their territory, as far as Britain and Russia were concerned, save in the Kingdom of Naples, but about wider issues of security which, if he were allowed to continue unchecked, Napoleon might eventually be able to interfere in. What underlay the British attitude was the conviction that he would continue to expand and menace, although it was not necessarily the Russian view.

What finally convinced Alexander to form an offensive alliance with the British, provided they could lure Austria into the war, was Napoleon's annexation of the satellite republic of Liguria – the old Republic of Genoa – to France. Liguria was about 1,500 miles from St Petersburg. Moreover, Napoleon annexed it to secure his internal line of communication between France and the Kingdom of Italy, something he had been pondering since 1799, simply because Liguria was too weak to protect itself from British attack, and the pro-French government of the satellite republic – a weak, small minority drawn from the Genoese elites with little popular support – needed France. Indeed, when the prospect of annexation by the Kingdom of Italy was raised, the Ligurians themselves sought annexation to France as the lesser of the two evils. Faced as they were with an internal economic crisis they could not surmount, and growing financial demands from Napoleon, the actual spur to annexation came from the Ligurian government itself. Napoleonic rule proved catastrophic for the Genoese, but that lay in the future.[56] The Ligurian delegates at Napoleon's coronation in Milan took the opportunity to tell him that 'where there is no freedom of the seas for a commercial people, the need arises to unite with a more powerful flag'.[57] In 1805, that it was their decision, hardly made gladly but still their own, went unremarked by the members of the nebulous anti-French coalition. To the British and Russians, Genoa was a good potential naval base, and another sign to Russia and Britain that Napoleon's grip on the region was too firm for comfort, and his proclivity to do away with even satellite republics was worrying.

The unilateral – aggressive – nature of the annexation was infuriating, but it was hardly on a scale with the partitions of Poland or Austrian designs on Bavaria. Rather, French piecemeal expansion in the region seemed cumulative. Conversely, Britain took no interest in Napoleon's growing power in southern and central Germany, which was Austria's main concern and one of Alexander's worries. Whereas Russia and Britain were drawn together by fear of what Napoleon might do, Austria was the member of the coalition who feared what he had actually done. Yet the Austrians also knew when Napoleon was more of an impediment to their own expansionist ambitions than an active threat, something that escaped Alexander and which the British were not interested in discerning.

Vienna was on her guard, and had considered war when Napoleon stepped beyond the terms of Lunéville in annexing Piedmont, but was hardly shocked. Napoleon needed it to secure Lombardy, which was as vital to his interests as it had been for the Habsburgs. When Charles-Emmanuel of Piedmont threatened France's hold on Lombardy – now the Cisalpine Republic – in 1798, by negotiating with Austria when he had signed an agreement with France to allow free passage through Piedmont to the Cisalpine Republic, the Directory knew he had to go. Napoleon made attempts to restore him, fully realising the powerful loyalty he commanded from his subjects, but when Charles-Emmanuel showed himself undependable again, after much hesitation Napoleon annexed the region to France for strategic reasons. When Charles-Emmanuel allied quickly with the British, and let them use Sardinia, where he took refuge, as a base, Napoleon felt confirmed in his distrust of him. Austria had long coveted Piedmont, yet Vienna did not have any sympathy for Charles-Emmanuel, whose dynasty had long sought to set the French and Austrians against each other for its own advantage. Francis knew how treacherous an ally the Savoyards could be, and he understood Napoleon's logic there; he was an aggressor – no other power knew it so well – but the Austrians knew this was not a direct threat to them. Franco-Austrian rivalry was bitter and all the more determined because it was so localised, but it was calculable on both sides. Alexander, however, could not grasp why Napoleon so adamantly refused to countenance any territorial compensation for Charles-Emmanuel. The depths of Napoleon's feelings on the matter are clear in the letter to Talleyrand, already quoted above, written just as he broke camp in Boulogne on 22 August 1805:

I will hear no talk about the King of Sardinia. That is it, just as with the Bourbons: it is having been weak enough even to discuss the issue that has cost me all the present quarrels. I will never consent to let him have Corfu [an idea of Alexander's] ... his alliance with England cost him his throne; his conduct in Sardinia will not let me be drawn into giving comfort to an enemy.[58]

There were other things that antagonised Napoleon that the other powers did not understand either, and this became an important issue in turning Alexander personally against Napoleon. Alexander neglected to weigh Napoleon's intransigence over the House of Savoy in 1804–5 not just against his conciliatory attitude to them in 1800, when he entertained a restoration, but beside his usually generous treatment of deposed royals. When the Stadholder of the Netherlands formally renounced his claims to the title for a financial settlement, Napoleon awarded his son the small German states of Fulda and Corvey. Vienna at least grasped the importance of Piedmont to French interests, however much it opposed them, because northern Italy was just as important to Austria. Austria and France were about to defend themselves, and to seize what they could, largely from each other and, in the case of Napoleon, for his useful but essentially harmless allies. Britain and Russia had other interests, less tangible, but urgent in their own minds.

The origins of few wars have attracted so much sharp disagreement as that of the Third Coalition. This was the first 'war' Napoleon could call his own, as it were. He had not inherited the hostilities of 1805 from the Directory; foreign policy had been in his hands, and his almost alone, from the outset of the Consulate. There is no doubt that he was at the helm or that he steered France into war. It follows that for most historians he was its cause, and some go further to claim that he caused it, which is not quite the same thing. The positions over this are as fiercely held as those surrounding the start of the First World War, and not dissimilar. In 1961, the German historian Fritz Fischer asserted in his famous book *Griff nach Weltmacht* that Germany had, indeed, caused the First World War, that it had done so deliberately, and had been planning a war of aggression since at least 1912. Fischer went further, and tried to establish a continuity between German policy in 1912–14 and Hitler's war plans. Similarly, Paul Schroeder and Desmond Seward[59] have not shrunk from comparing Napoleon with Hitler, the former on the specific grounds that he believes Napoleon never had precise aims in his wars. It should be added that Fischer's thesis was based on hard evidence, not extrapolations about what Napoleon 'was like'. This is an extreme position, but its arguments tend to revolve around the war of 1805 more than the subsequent campaigns.

Such an approach fails to take much into account, and those who see in 1805 only Napoleonic aggression forget Austrian ambitions in Bavaria, which were of an expansionist character that Napoleon himself had yet to adopt in Europe. He had an inheritance to defend, and if his war aims bear comparison to those of either the Second or Third Reichs, it was that Napoleon had to frame them with regard to his domestic situation, in a way that only the British had to consider at the time. Francis of Austria wanted Bavaria because the Habsburgs had for a century thought it logical to expand; Napoleon wanted northern Italy, the Rhineland and the Low Countries because they had become essential to the French economy, and because he was expected to retain them by the revolutionary political classes, not because Louis XIV a century earlier had marched his armies to the Rhine against the same House of Austria Napoleon now faced. In 1805, he was not a free agent. Defending these regions had to take priority over his own vision in 1805; when he was attacked – and he did not strike the first blow – he had to abandon his own dream, the conquest of Britain, to deal with French interests.

The first phase of the War of the Third Coalition is also too readily subsumed by almost all historians into a 'second hundred years war' between Britain and France, but this is not the most useful way to see it. A geo-political struggle between the two powers does indeed explain much about the renewed war of 1803, even if it is hardly the whole story. By 1805, with the loss of Saint-Domingue and the withdrawal from Egypt, France had changed – possibly regressed – as a power. Following these losses, it was now far more important for Napoleon to defend northern Italy, the Rhine and his German allies than to invade Britain, for French interests were no longer those of a colonial, Atlantic empire, but those of a rising regional power.

Ideology in its purest form played little part in the origins of the war of 1805, as most scholars agree. The great – and small – houses of Europe may have despised Napoleon, but they did business with him when it suited them. His most loyal allies, the Wittelsbachs, recoiled from the marriage of one of their daughters, Augusta, to Eugène de Beauharnais – forgetting he was a scion of an old, distinguished noble house – but they agreed, noses held firmly.[60] It would be wrong to discount ideology in British dealings with Napoleon, so popular, in its nature and its audience, was the propaganda of the period; nor can the aversion of Francis to the institution of conscription be read in any light other than that of an abiding fear of the influence of the French Revolution, when all common sense – of which Archduke Charles had become the sole Austrian repository by 1805 – called for its adoption.

The resurgence of French military power – engendered first by the ideologically driven domestic reforms of the Revolutionaries – had upset decades of given assumptions among the other powers, whose calculations rested on French weakness. The renaissance of effective French militarism enabled the new regime to assert itself successfully in the traditional contested spaces with the Habsburgs, northern Italy, southern and western Germany and the Low Countries. Outwardly, this resembled an older struggle with geo-political origins, because it took place in the same regions, and its practical result would be the acquisition of this power vacuum by either France or the Habsburgs.

It was not quite this simple, however. The eruption of the French Revolution, and the emerging character of the Napoleonic new order, had altered the character of international relations in Europe. Whether or not it was still a redoubt of Jacobin, democratic king-killers, France was still a rogue state in the eyes of the old dynasties, under ever-shifting regimes, of which Napoleon's was but one more, perhaps actually more sane than the rest to the eyes of the other powers, but just as aggressive. The other powers could not be sure if they were dealing with a regime that would conform to pre-1789 Bourbon behaviour and ambitions. Perhaps, but perhaps not.

The war was made possible by traditional Habsburg ambitions and the now inviolate determination of the new French political elites to hold on to the gains of the 1790s. It was driven by something else, however, which was not ideological in itself, but was derived from ideology. No one was more aware of this rogue status, or the sound reasons for it, than Napoleon. A certainty for all their enemies was that the French revolutionaries had begun the war out of naked ideological aggression coupled with avaricious expansionism. Henceforth, the problem for the other powers became less the complexion of whatever regime ruled France at a given time than its lack of stability and, therefore, its unpredictability. Napoleon could not dispel this impression, and where scholars like Paul Schroeder show their strongest arguments is in claiming that Napoleon did nothing to try to dispel it, and that his actions conformed to that of a rogue leader of a rogue state. This is the context in which Schroeder's famous remark belongs, that French foreign policy – and so the outbreak of war – was the result of 'Napoleon doing what Napoleon did'. He did what the French did when they were strong enough: he fought Austria for the narrow ground between them. However, in 1805, the only war he wanted was with Britain, the relic of a now irrelevant colonial struggle that neither he nor the British felt they could abandon, because the new power of France had upset a European configuration predicated on French weakness .

Napoleon's 'pirouette' of August 1805 was not his wish. These were not times of wild optimism or extravagant ambition for Napoleon. His cast of mind slipped out in a letter he wrote to the 23-year-old Eugène, in June 1805, which gave him general advice about his new role in Milan, but he concluded thus: 'visit the fortresses and all the famous battlefields. It is probable that, before you are thirty, you will have to fight, and it is a great advantage to know the terrain.'[61] As it turned out, Napoleon's prediction was one year out; Eugène did not have to fight on his own ground until 1813. The real point, however, is that if Napoleon was ever in thrall to an image of himself as the invincible, insatiable conqueror, he did not feel that way as the storm clouds gathered in 1805.

Whatever the tortuous calculations of the new allies, they were all wrong. Their hopes and ambitions soon foundered on the power of the Grande Armée. Napoleon was more than ready for war, more than anyone knew, himself included. No one else was. He had called his enemies' bluff and for once in the history of conflict it really was all over by Christmas.

THE LEAP IN THE DARK: AUTUMN 1805

Napoleon had no choice but to turn and face the Allies in September 1805. They, not he, had chosen the time to strike, for they knew that almost his entire army was on the Channel coast. The Austrians were marching on France, trampling over Napoleon's German allies as they went: on 14 September, 72,000 Austrian troops occupied Munich unopposed, only nine days after Napoleon left Boulogne for Paris; the smaller German states could only be next in line. The Russians were behind them, and Tsar Alexander had promised his Habsburg allies that 75,000 troops would reach Bavaria by 20 October.[1] More could follow, the Allies concluded, before Napoleon had got his army to the Rhine to check them. If this happened, they would be able to choose where to fight, as well as when. It would take a manoeuvre of unprecedented speed by Napoleon to reverse this situation and reach the Austrians before they reached France. Time seemed to be on the side of the new, Third, anti-French Coalition.

The new alliance had come into being through the belief shared by the Habsburgs, Russia and Britain that they were stronger than Napoleon and, by any rational calculation, they had good reason to think their chance to extinguish the new regime in France had come. The Allied commanders were immune to the image of invincibility Napoleon had spun around himself for the French public, just as they were indifferent to his genuine successes in the two Italian campaigns which had made him appear a new Alexander the Great to supporters of the Revolution, inside and outside France. Their troops in the field outnumbered Napoleon's by over two to one: their total mobilised forces came to over 400,000 compared to the 210,000 of the Grande Armée, and they had already neutralised the 25,000-strong Bavarians, his largest ally. The Allied soldiers were almost all professionals, most of them veterans. The Coalition knew little about Napoleon's new army, but they were aware that, by 1805, much of the Grande Armée was composed of untried and originally recalcitrant conscripts. The Russians could summon reserves of over 100,000, even if they were still far away. Compared to this, Napoleon had stripped the defences of his empire bare for the offensive of 1805. Eugène held northern Italy with only 30,000 men in the front line and 25,000 in the fortresses behind the lines; hastily trained National Guards were all that stood between the Channel coast and the British. Even worse, Napoleon had bled France dry to create the Grande Armée, and was now compromising his fragile, hard-won restoration of civil order to raise a reserve of replacements in anticipation of the casualties to come. Whereas the Austrians and Russians went to war with the promise of mountains of British gold to pay the costs of conquest, Napoleon had put at risk the financial stability Gaudin had worked so hard to achieve, before a shot had even been fired. The Allies went to war certain they had ample reserves of men and money, so much that they felt no risk of domestic disorder behind them. Napoleon was straining every sinew of his new regime to meet the challenge.

Alongside this were Napoleon's own shortcomings as a commander. Even the most sympathetic examination of the Italian and Egyptian campaigns exposes his weaknesses, more than his talents. Objective scrutiny yields much to fear for his fate against the massed forces of the Allies. However successful the First Italian Campaign, the Second had hinged on victory at Marengo, a near-run thing, which was not won by Napoleon's own tactics, and owed much to luck. His victory over the Mamelukes at the Battle of the Pyramids, however spectacular, bore no relationship to the realities of European warfare; rather, it foreshadowed the colonial wars of the coming century, where technologically superior European troops overwhelmed the less advanced armies of African and Asian societies. If the logistical preparations for the Second Italian Campaign had marked a distinct improvement from those for Egypt and Syria, this was hardly to set a high standard, for the failures of Egypt and even more, of the advance into Syria, were undeniable and catastrophic. Napoleon had moved too fast, and so too unprepared, up the Nile from Alexandria to Cairo, through difficult country; he set off in truly slapdash fashion up the coast of Palestine, a few months later. In 1805, he had to move even larger forces across Alpine country with winter approaching; the crossing of the Alps to Italy in 1796 and 1800 had been brief, if difficult, affairs, hardly on the scale demanded now.

Above all, Napoleon was as untried as his peasant conscripts, when it came to commanding so big an army over so vast a theatre of operations. Only the First Italian Campaign really ranked as a shining success in his career to date, but Napoleon's whirlwind conquest of the Po Valley in 1796 was not won against the main Austrian army. Nor had he faced the Russians, who swept the French out of Italy and Switzerland while he was in Egypt, triggering the crisis that led to Brumaire. The Italian and Egyptian campaigns had all been 'side-shows', and Napoleon had admitted his lack of experience in leading the main army when he handed command of the German front to Moreau in 1800.

Moreau was gone now, skulking in American exile and offering his sword to the Allies. Napoleon was on his own, in charge of a far bigger army than he had ever led before, fighting on a front that was utterly unknown to him. His plan was to seek a major engagement with the Austrians as soon as he could, before the Russians could arrive. If Marengo, his largest battle to date, was the benchmark, there was a strong possibility he might lose the great encounter he now sought. To bring about this quick battle, Napoleon would have to move the Grande Armée a huge distance, at great speed, into barren, rugged mountain country at the very time of year the weather became worst. If the Nile and Syrian campaigns are taken as a guide to his abilities to march armies a long way over hard country, there was every prospect he would lose his Grande Armée before he had a chance to lose a battle. This was the unadorned truth.

Everything rational and tangible was against Napoleon, from the resources of his empire to his own record as a soldier. Yet, his troops, officers and men alike, were young, trained and armed to a degree of excellence to which no other army of the period could aspire. His state machinery, from the pen-pushers in the prefectures and the ministries to the ruthless 'enforcers' of the Gendarmerie, had been reinvigorated; the reforms of the Revolution and the Consulate had welded France into a more efficient state than any of its continental rivals. Above all, Napoleon was possessed of an energy, guile and ready intelligence absent from those who now opposed him. Few clashes in history have pitted the old against the new, youth against age, so emphatically as when the French pushed across the Rhine and then up its course in October and November.

As the murk of a cold, gloomy Alpine autumn descended on the Grande Armée, its soldiers bore the fate of their leader and his whole creation with them. Nor was it merely the survival of the new imperial regime that hung in the balance. The whole new world brought into being by the French Revolution in 1789 would be swept away along with Napoleon, should they fail. The snow-clad peaks and looming pine trees made of the march the stuff of Wagnerian opera, as the war-of-the end-of the-world drew closer, save that the hero was now Figaro, bent on victory over the old gods by intelligence and craft, as well as courage. Napoleon, like Figaro, was not just bent on overthrowing the old gods, but upstaging them. In the shadow of the mountains, through the darkness of the forest, destiny beckoned.

ACKNOWLEDGEMENTS

There are many debts, of many kinds, bound up with this book. It was conceived with the help of my agent, Robert Dudley, and nurtured by Neil Belton, at Faber & Faber. Richard Collins gave it much needed shape and Donald Sommerville saved me from many errors. It also grew into a wider project, which began after it was first drafted, but which proved a crucial influence in its final form. The Leverhulme Trust's generous award of the Major Research Fellowship for the project *Napoleonic Civilisation* drew this book into its web, and enabled me to rethink its wider parameters. This was a fortunate conjuncture, as well as the fruits of a timely award.

A work of this kind inevitably builds on foundations laid by others, and even the most passing glance at its references will show the debt owed to so many scholars who continue to fire the 'Napoleonic Renaissance'. The historiography of a period so long seen as barren and sterile has been invigorated inestimably in the last two decades by a myriad of contributions from many quarters, and there would have been no point in yet another life of Napoleon without the work of my friends and colleagues far across the globe. In this sense, every footnote is a tribute to each of them. A new generation of scholars cluster around Napoleon like his brilliant marshals and ministers, yet even among such company, several must stand out, and these debts have become as personal as they always were professional. Steven Englund, Luigi Mascilli Migliorini, Philip Dwyer, Geoffrey Ellis and Alan Forrest have already produced fine lives of Napoleon; Jacques-Olivier Boudon has done more than any single scholar to enthuse and inspire a new generation of French researchers to enter the field, both through his writings and his teaching. Annie Jourdan has given us all much to think about and be thankful for. This book would not so much be the lesser without them, as pointless. Above all, however, the herculean labours of Thierry Lentz and Peter Hicks of the Fondation Napoléon in Paris have given Napoleonic studies the new, seminal impetus they deserve, and this book would have had no reason for being without the new edition of Napoleon's correspondence they are producing. Lentz's own new history of the First Empire is formidable enough in itself, but the new *Correspondance* will now become the starting point for all future work on Napoleon I, and this book is but the first attempt to make use of its riches, which have been acquired with so much patience, hard labour and impeccable scholarly standards. If the present work has any intrinsic merit, it stems from having put this unparalleled resource to quick use.

For reasons of space I have not included a bibliography in this volume but I intend to include a bibliographical essay in my second volume.

The support of everyone mentioned above is deeply appreciated, as the magnitude of the task grew on me each day. They, at least, were fortunate enough to remain at arm's length from the fray. Others were less fortunate: Sue, my wife, Munro Price, whose leave corresponded with mine in Paris, my colleagues at Lady Margaret Hall – Geraint Thomas, Grant Tapsell and, above all, Ambrogio Caiani – bore the brunt like stolid *grognards*. Even my cat, the well-dubbed Louis, stood guard on the manuscript in the manner of the marmalade Mameluke he has become. Quiet words kept me afloat. My late friend of many years, Philippe Béchu, with his belief that it was 'in me'; Claire Béchu, who told me it was time for 'my' Napoleon; and my former student, Jo Godfrey, now a history editor of the finest calibre, who simply told me 'it will be good'. I hope 'destiny' proves them right.

Many years ago, when we were both young lecturers and sharing a house in York, the late Jim McMillan was busy writing a life of Napoleon III, while I finished my thesis. He hoped to return to it one day, and even then, so many years ago, told me it was my destiny to write 'the life' of the 'wee big man' for our times. He never came back to Napoleon III, nor will he see this book, but it is for him. Jim would have seen the irony of the subtitle, and I can see his smirk. A biography seems the best way to thank him for his own life.

Charbury-Oxford
St Patrick's Day, 2013

NOTES

INTRODUCTION THE FORCE OF DESTINY

1 Alexandre de Beaumarchais, *Le Mariage de Figaro*, Act V, Scene III. Translated from *Beaumarchais. Théâtre* (Paris, 1980), ed. Jean-Pierre de Beauharnais, p. 535.

2 Jean-Jacques Rousseau, *The Confessions* (1781; English trans. J. M. Cohen, London, 1971 edn), pp. 282–3, 287, 291.

3 For a study of this phenomenon across the life of the French old regime, from Molière to Beaumarchais: Yves Morand, *La conquête de la liberté de Scapin à Figaro* (Paris, 1989).

4 Steven Englund, *Napoleon: A Political Life* (New York, 2004), p. xiv.

5 Robert S. Alexander, *Napoleon* (London, 2001), p. 236.

6 Cited in Annie Jourdan, *Napoléon. Héros, imperator, mécène* (Paris, 1998), p. 106.

7 Beaumarchais, *Le Mariage de Figaro*, Act V, Scene XIX, p. 574.

8 Jourdan, *Napoléon*, p. 104.

9 Jourdan, *Napoléon*, p. 101, notes this in the case of Parisian intellectual circles.

10 Joseph Conrad, *Nostromo* (Oxford, 2009 edn), p. 414.

11 Pieter Geyl, *Napoleon: For and Against* (1949; London, 1965 edn), p. 21.

12 In *London Review of Books*, vol. 34, no. 13, 5 July 2012: David Runciman on Robert Caro, *The Years of LBJ*: vol. iv, *The Passage of Power* (New York, 2012).

13 Conrad, *Nostromo*, p. xv. Conrad cited from: 'Preface', *The Nigger of the Narcissus* (Oxford, 1984), p. i.

14 *Napoléon Bonaparte, Correspondance générale*, vols I–VII, ed. Thierry Lentz (Paris, 2004–10).

15 Jesús Pabón, *Las ideas y el sistema Napoleonicos* (Madrid, 1944), p. 14.

1 LIFE ON THE EDGE

1 For a clever juxtaposition of all the fact and fiction, see the first two chapters of Dorothy Carrington, *Napoleon and his Parents: On the threshold of history* (London, 1988).

2 Cited in Luigi Mascilli Migliorini, *Napoléon* (French trans., Paris, 2006), p. 23.

3 Antoine-Marie Graziani, *La Corse Génoise. Économie, société, culture. Période moderne, 1453–1768* (Ajaccio, 1997), pp. 36–41.

4 Graziani, *La Corse Génoise*, pp. 104–5.

5   Michel Vergé-Franceschi, *Napoléon, une enfance corse* (Paris, 2009), p. 152.

6   Carrington, *Napoleon and his Parents*, p. 61.

7   Vergé-Franceschi, *Napoléon*, pp. 201–2.

8   Vergé-Franceschi, *Napoléon*, p. 210.

9   Carrington, *Napoleon and his Parents*, pp. 88–9, sees the urban elite as imbued with 'vendetta culture' pursued at law.

10   Graziani, *La Corse Génoise*, pp. 142–3.

11   Vergé-Franceschi, *Napoléon*, p. 185.

12   Ibid.

13   Vergé-Franceschi, *Napoléon*, pp. 260–4.

14   Michel Vergé-Franceschi, *Paoli, un Corse des Lumières* (Paris, 2005), p. 103.

15   Carrington, *Napoleon and his Parents*, p. 33.

16   Carrington, *Napoleon and his Parents*, p. 37.

17   To Paoli, 12 June 1789, *Napoléon Bonaparte. Correspondance générale*, vol. I, *Les Apprentissages, 1784–1797* (Paris, 2004), no. 29, pp. 76–7. See note 7, p. 78, for the meticulous research by Thierry Lentz, showing how dubious is the provenance of this famous letter.

18   Vergé-Franceschi, *Paoli*, pp. 353–4.

19   Vergé-Franceschi, *Paoli*, pp. 366–7.

20   Carrington, *Napoleon and his Parents*, brilliantly juxtaposes the myth and reality of the 'flight' in the first two chapters of her book.

21   Carrington, *Napoleon and his Parents*, pp. 53–61, 90–2.

22   Carrington, *Napoleon and his Parents*, p. 102.

23   Carrington, *Napoleon and his Parents*, p. 99.

2   FRANCE

1   Luigi Mascilli Migliorini, 'Napoleon and Classicism: His contemporaries' judgement', in *L'Europa Scopre Napoleone, 1793–1804*, 2 vols, ed. Vittorio Scotti-Douglas (Alessandria, 1999), vol. i, pp. 233–40, at p. 238.

2   David Bien, 'The Army in the French Enlightenment: Reform, Reaction and Revolution', *Past & Present*, 85 (1979), pp. 68–98.

3   Philip Dwyer, *Napoleon: The Path to Power, 1769–1799* (London, 2007), p. 26.

4   Cited in Migliorini, *Napoléon*, pp. 30–1.

5   Dwyer, *Napoleon*, pp. 31–2.

6   Dwyer, *Napoleon*, pp. 26–32.

7   Andy Martin, *Napoleon the Novelist* (Cambridge, 2000), p. 44.

8   Cited in Martin, *Napoleon the Novelist*, p. 40.

9   Robert Darnton, *The Literary Underground of the Old Regime* (Cambridge, Mass. and London, 1982), pp. 226–32.

10   Martin, *Napoleon the Novelist*, pp. 12–13.

11   For a lively, humorous account of this, Martin, *Napoleon the Novelist*, pp. 7–33.

12   To Labitte, 'marchand de drap', from Paris, c. 23 Sept. 1785, *Correspondance générale*, vol. I, no. 6, p. 48; to Amielh, Directeur du Petit Séminaire, Aix-en-Provence, from Valence, c. 25 Nov. 1785, ibid., no. 7, p. 49.

13   To La Guillaume, Intendant de Corse, from Ajaccio, c. 19 Nov. 1786, *Correspondance*

générale, vol. I, no. 9, pp. 51–2.

14 To La Guillaume, Intendant de Corse, undated nos 15, 16, 17, 18, 19, *Correspondance générale*, vol. I, pp. 58–64; to Brienne, undated, *c*. Nov. 1787, no. 13, ibid., p. 56; and idem, 24 Nov. 1787, no. 14, ibid., pp. 57–8.

15 To Don Luciano, 28 March 1789, *Correspondance générale*, vol. I, no. 23, pp. 68–70.

16 To Matteo Buttafoco, 23 Jan. 1793, *Correspondance générale*, vol. I, no. 44, pp. 91–6.

17 To Giubega, June 1789, *Correspondance générale*, vol. I, no. 28, pp. 74–5.

18 Jean Defranceschi, *La Jeunesse de Napoléon* (Paris, 2001), pp. 155–6.

19 To Joseph, from Auxonne, 8/9 August 1789, *Correspondance générale*, vol. I, no. 34, p. 81.

20 Cited in Miglioroni, *Napoléon*, p. 36.

21 To Letizia, 15 April 1789, *Correspondance générale*, vol. I, no. 25, p. 72.

22 Vergé-Franceschi, *Paoli*, pp. 444, 450.

23 Defranceschi, *La Jeunesse*, p. 170.

24 Vergé-Franceschi, *Paoli*, pp. 454–5.

25 Vergé-Franceschi, *Paoli*, pp. 451–2, 456–7.

26 Defranceschi, *La Jeunesse*, pp. 168–9.

27 Defranceschi, *La Jeunesse*, pp. 175–6.

28 Dwyer, *Napoleon*, pp. 109–10.

29 Migliorini, *Napoléon*, pp. 61–2.

30 Defranceschi, *La Jeunesse*, pp. 210–12.

31 Cited in Defranceschi, *La Jeunesse*, p. 220.

32 Vergé-Franceschi, *Paoli*, pp. 469–80.

33 Dwyer, *Napoleon*, p. 135.

34 Cited in David Chandler, *Campaigns of Napoleon* (London, 1967 edn), pp. 23–4.

35 Chandler, *Campaigns*, pp. 21–2.

36 Chandler, *Campaigns*, pp. 27–8.

37 Chandler, *Campaigns*, pp. 26–7; Dwyer, *Napoleon*, p. 140.

38 For the full plan: to Bouchotte, Minister of War, 24 Brumaire, Year 2 (14 Nov. 1793), *Correspondance générale*, vol. I, no. 111, pp. 142–8.

39 Dwyer, *Napoleon*, p. 141.

40 Chandler, *Campaigns*, pp. 27–8. Dwyer, *Napoleon*, p. 141, who attributes this, possibly, to Smith's bad conscience for having attacked ships full of civilians.

41 To the Municipal Officers of Beausset, 12 Oct. 1793, *Correspondance générale*, vol. I, no. 90, p. 130.

42 To Capt. Perrier, 22 Vendémiaire, Year 2 (13 Oct. 1793), *Correspondance générale*, vol. I, no. 91, p. 130.

43 To Berlier, Chef de Bataillon, 14 Messidor, Year 2 (12 July 1793), *Correspondance générale*, vol. I, no. 204, p. 186.

44 To Chauvet, Commissaire Ordonnateur, *c*. mid-Oct. 1793, *Correspondance générale*, vol. I, no. 95, pp. 132–3.

45 To Brigadier Gassendi, 27 Vendémiaire, Year 2 (18 Oct. 1793), *Correspondance générale*, vol. I, no. 101, p. 136.

46 To Dupin, Adjoint to the Minister of War, 4 Nivôse, Year 2 (24 Dec. 1793), *Correspondance générale*, vol. I, no. 127, p. 54.

47 Dwyer, *Napoleon*, p. 141.

48 For the latter supposition: Gabriel Girod de l'Ain, *Désirée Clary* (Paris, 1959), pp. 21–7.

49 Girod de l'Ain, *Désirée*, pp. 33–4.
50 Girod de l'Ain, *Désirée*, p. 17.
51 Girod de l'Ain, *Désirée*, pp. 12–20, for a well-researched portrait of the family and their world.
52 Dwyer, *Napoleon*, p. 154.
53 Dwyer, *Napoleon*, p. 155, after considerable study, is of this opinion.
54 Dwyer, *Napoleon*, p. 176.
55 Cited in Dwyer, *Napoleon*, p. 179.
56 Andrea Stuart, *Joséphine: The Rose of Martinique* (Basingstoke and Oxford, 2004 edn), pp. 170–1.
57 Stuart, *Joséphine*, p. 177.
58 The traditional date is 15 October 1795.
59 Cited and translated in Stuart, *Joséphine*, p. 173.

3 THE CONQUEST OF ITALY

1 To the Executive Directory, Nice, 7 Germinal, Year 4 (27 Mar. 1796), *Correspondance générale*, vol. I, no. 422, p. 302; to the Executive Directory, Nice, 8 Germinal, Year 4 (28 Mar. 1796), ibid., no. 424, p. 303.
2 Cited in Chandler, *Campaigns*, p. 56.
3 Expressed directly in Jonathon Riley, *Napoleon as a General. Command from the Battlefield to Grand Strategy* (London, 2007), p. 152.
4 Bouches-du-Rhône, Var, Vaucluse and Basses-Alpes (today Alpes-Maritimes): the core of the Provence region.
5 To the Executive Directory, Nice, 8 Germinal, Year 4 (28 Mar. 1796), *Correspondance générale*, vol. I, no. 426, p. 304.
6 Napoleon to Faipoult, French Minister to Genoa, Nice, 8 Germinal, Year 4 (28 Mar. 1796), *Correspondance générale*, vol. I, no. 422, p. 302.
7 Migliorini, *Napoléon*, pp. 465–6, 469.
8 To Masséna, Nice, 8 Germinal, Year 4 (28 Mar. 1796), *Correspondance générale*, vol. I, no. 427, p. 305.
9 To Executive Directory, Nice, 8 Germinal, Year 4 (28 Mar. 1796), *Correspondance générale*, vol. I, no. 426, p. 304.
10 To Berthier, Nice, 9 Germinal, Year 4 (29 Mar. 1796), *Correspondance générale*, vol. I, no. 429, p. 306.
11 Riley, *Napoleon as a General*, p. 140.
12 To Carnot, Lodi, 25 Floréal, Year 4 (14 May 1796), *Correspondance générale*, vol. I, no. 597, p. 398.
13 To the Executive Directory, Lodi, 25 Floréal, Year 4 (14 May 1796), *Correspondance générale*, vol. I, no. 599, p. 399.
14 To the Executive Directory, Lodi, 27 Floréal, Year 4 (16 May 1796), *Correspondance générale*, vol. I, no. 602, p. 401.
15 Alain Pillepich, *Milan, capitale napoléonienne, 1800–1814* (Paris, 2001), pp. 23–4.
16 Stendhal, *Rome, Naples et Florence* (1826; Paris, 1987 edn), p. 28.
17 The figures are drawn from Chandler, *Campaigns*, p. 95.
18 Chandler, *Campaigns*, p. 95.

19 To Berthier, Milan, 2 a.m., 6 Prairial, Year 4 (25 May 1796), *Correspondance générale*, vol. I, no. 629, p. 416.

20 To General Despinoy, 7 Prairial, Year 4 (26 May 1796), *Correspondance générale*, vol. I, no. 653, p. 418.

21 T. C. W. Blanning, *The French Revolutionary Wars, 1787–1802* (London, 1996), p. 167.

22 To the Executive Directory, 22 Pluviôse, Year 5 (10 Feb. 1797), *Correspondance générale*, vol. I, no. 1367, p. 833.

23 Simon Schwarzfuchs, *Napoleon, the Jews and the Sanhedrin* (London, 1979), pp. 22–3.

24 To the Executive Directory, 27 Pluviôse, Year 5 (15 Feb. 1797), *Correspondance générale*, vol. I, no. 1379, p. 839.

25 Englund, *Napoleon*, p. 115.

26 Cited in Englund, *Napoleon*, p. 116.

27 Dwyer, *Napoleon*, p. 298.

28 Dwyer, *Napoleon*, pp. 299–300.

29 Migliorini, *Napoléon*, pp. 463–72.

30 *Les vies des hommes illustres de Plutarque*, vol. 7 (Paris, 1818), p. 295. A reprint of an eighteenth-century translation with which Napoleon's generation was familiar.

31 Jacques-Olivier Boudon, *La France et l'Empire de Napoléon* (Paris, 2006), pp. 43–52.

32 To Joséphine, Mamirolo, 2 p.m., 29 Messidor, Year 5 (17 July 1796), *Correspondance générale*, vol. I, no. 783, p. 505.

33 Dwyer, *Napoleon*, pp. 301–2.

4 THE CISALPINE REPUBLIC

1 Englund, *Napoleon*, p. 111.

2 To the Executive Directory, Milan, 25 Floréal, Year 4 (14 May 1797), *Correspondance générale*, vol. I, 1549, pp. 941–2.

3 Dwyer, *Napoleon*, pp. 248–72.

4 Dwyer, *Napoleon*, p. 268.

5 To the Executive Directory, Nice, 8 Germinal, Year 4 (28 Mar. 1796), *Correspondance générale*, vol. I, no. 426, p. 304.

6 To the Piedmontese Patriots, Nice, 11 Germinal, Year 4 (31 Mar. 1797), *Correspondance générale*, vol. I, no. 447, p. 315.

7 Carlo Zaghi, *Il Direttorio Francese e La Repubblica Cisalpina*, 2 vols, I: *La Nascita di Uno Stato Moderno* (Rome, 1992), p. 137.

8 Dwyer, *Napoleon*, pp. 305–6.

9 To the Executive Directory, Milan, 8 Nivôse, Year 5 (28 Dec. 1796), *Correspondance générale*, vol. I, no. 1549, pp. 941–2.

10 To the Executive Directory, Milan, 25 Floréal, Year 4 (14 May 1797), *Correspondance générale*, vol. I, no. 1549, pp. 941–2.

11 To Carnot, Member of the Executive Directory, Milan, 22 Prairial, Year 4 (10 June 1796), *Correspondance générale*, vol. I, no. 666, p. 437.

12 To Carnot, Member of the Executive Directory, Milan, 11 Fructidor, Year 4 (28 Aug. 1796), *Correspondance générale*, vol. I, no. 882, p. 561.

13   Zaghi, *Il Direttorio*, vol. I, p. 178.
14   Ibid.
15   Zaghi, *Il Direttorio*, vol. I, pp. 184–5.
16   Carlo Zaghi, *L'Italia di Napoleone. Dalla Cisalpina al Regno. Storia d'Italia*, vol. 18
     (ed. Galante Galassa) (Turin, 1986), p. 177.
17   To the Executive Directory of the Cisalpine Republic, Passarino, 22 Vendémiaire,
     Year 6 (15 Oct. 1797), *Correspondance générale*, vol. I, no. 2156, p. 1250.
18   To the Executive Directory of the Cisalpine Republic, Mombello, 15 Messidor,
     Year 5 (5 July 1797), *Correspondance générale*, vol. I, no. 1751, p. 1041.

5 WIDER LESSONS

1   As cited in Dwyer, *Napoleon*, p. 299.
2   See especially, Dwyer, *Napoleon*, p. 229.
3   *Le Congrès de Rastatt (le 11 juin, 1798 au 28 avril, 1799), Correspondance et
    documents* (2 vols, Paris, 1912–13), ed. P. Montalerot and L. Pingaud, p. 84.
4   To Talleyrand, Paris, 25 Nivôse, Year 6 (14 Jan. 1798), *Napoléon Bonaparte,
    Correspondance générale*, vol. II, *La Campagne d'Egypte et d'Avènement, 1798–1799*
    (Paris, 2005), no. 2300, pp. 29–31.
5   To the Executive Directory, Paris, 5 Ventôse, Year 6 (25 Feb. 1798), *Correspondance
    générale*, vol. II, no. 2315, pp. 36–9.
6   To General Brune, Paris, 22 Nivôse, Year 6 (11 Jan. 1798), *Correspondance générale*,
    vol. II, no. 2296, pp. 27–8.
7   To Berthier, Commander-in-Chief, Army of Italy, Paris, 18 Pluviôse, Year 6 (6 Feb.
    1798), *Correspondance générale*, vol. II, no. 2309, p. 34.
8   To the Central Administration, dept Var, Toulon, 24 Floréal, Year 6 (15 May 1798),
    Correspondance générale, vol. II, no. 2478, p. 122.
9   To the Executive Directory, Toulon, 28 Floréal, Year 6 (17 May 1798),
    Correspondance générale, vol. II, no. 2489, p. 126.
10 To the Military Commission of the 9th Military Division, Toulon, 27 Floréal, Year 6
    (16 May 1798), *Correspondance générale*, vol. II, no. 2483, p. 124.
11 Dwyer, *Napoleon*, p. 445.
12 To Joseph, aboard the *Orient*, 4 Prairial, Year 6 (25 May 1798), *Correspondance
    générale*, vol. II, no. 2500, p. 132.
13 To Letizia, aboard the *Orient*, 9 Prairial, Year 6 (28 May 1798), *Correspondance
    générale*, vol. II, no. 2510, p. 138.
14 Henry Laurens, *L'expédition d'Égypte, 1798–1801* (Paris, 1997), pp. 29–30.
15 To the Executive Directory, Milan, 29 Thermidor, Year 5 (16 Aug. 1797),
    Correspondance générale, vol. I, no. 1908, p. 1118.
16 Dwyer, *Napoleon*, p. 354.
17 To Berthier, on board at port in Malta, 21 Prairial, Year 6 (9 June 1798),
    Correspondance générale, vol. II, no. 2514, p. 140.
18 To the Administration of dept Aegean Sea, HQ, Malta, 26 Prairial, Year 6 (14 June
    1798), *Correspondance générale*, vol. II, no. 2528, p. 147.
19 To Garat, Minister of the French Republic in Naples, Malta, 25 Prairial, Year 6
    (13 June 1798), *Correspondance générale*, vol. II, no. 2524, p. 145.

20 To the Consuls of the French in Tunis, Tripoli and Algiers, Malta, 27 Prairial, Year 6 (15 June 1798), *Correspondance générale*, vol. II, no. 2552, p. 149.
21 *Al-Jabarti's Chronicle of the French Occupation, 1798. Napoleon in Egypt* (English trans., Princeton and New York, 1993).
22 Paul Strathern, *Napoleon in Egypt: 'The Greatest Glory'* (London, 2007) pp. 85–6.
23 Strathern, *Napoleon in Egypt*, pp. 86–9.
24 Strathern, *Napoleon in Egypt*, pp. 90–1.
25 Strathern, *Napoleon in Egypt*, p. 96.
26 Strathern, *Napoleon in Egypt*, p. 107.
27 Strathern, *Napoleon in Egypt*, p. 118.
28 Strathern, *Napoleon in Egypt*, p. 132.
29 Laurens, *L'expédition*, p. 129.
30 Strathern, *Napoleon in Egypt*, pp. 132–3.
31 Laurens, *L'expédition*, p. 151.
32 Dwyer, *Napoleon*, p. 397.
33 Laurens, *L'expédition*, p. 155.
34 Laurens, *L'expédition*, pp. 134–6.
35 Cited in Strathern, *Napoleon in Egypt*, p. 138.
36 Laurens, *L'expédition*, p. 210.
37 Laurens, *L'expédition*, pp. 130–9, 168–71.
38 Dwyer, *Napoleon*, pp. 377–8.
39 Dwyer, *Napoleon*, p. 388.
40 Dwyer, *Napoleon*, pp. 389–90.
41 Laurens, *L'expédition*, pp. 238–9.
42 As translated and cited in Dwyer, *Napoleon*, p. 407.
43 Cited in Laurens, *L'expédition*, pp. 268–9.
44 Laurens, *L'expédition*, p. 469.
45 As translated and cited in Englund, *Napoleon*, pp. 137–8.

6 IN A SINISTER FOG

1 Dwyer, *Napoleon*, p. 255–62.
2 Patrice Gueniffey, *Le Dix-huit Brumaire. L'épilogue de la Révolution française* (Paris, 2008), p. 229.
3 Jacques Norvins de Montbreton, *Histoire de Napoléon*, 4 vols (Paris, 1833), ii, p. 4. As rightly questioned by Gueniffey, *Le Dix-huit Brumaire*, pp. 229–30.
4 Cited in Gueniffey, *Le Dix-huit Brumaire*, pp. 233–4.
5 Cited in Stuart Semmel, *Napoleon and the British* (New Haven and London, 2004), p. 21.
6 Gueniffey, *Le Dix-huit Brumaire*, p. 203.
7 Gueniffey, *Le Dix-huit Brumaire*, p. 212.
8 Pierre Serna, *La République des Girouettes* (Paris, 2005), p. 433.
9 Serna, *La République*, pp. 445–6.
10 Isser Woloch, *Napoleon and his Collaborators: The making of a dictatorship* (New York, 2001), pp. 16–17.
11 Jean-Denis Bredin, *Sieyès. La clé de la Révolution française* (Paris, 1988), pp. 436–9.

12 Dwyer, *Napoleon*, pp. 483–4.
13 As translated and cited in Englund, *Napoleon*, p. 164.
14 Englund, *Napoleon*, p. 165.
15 Dwyer, *Napoleon*, pp. 501–2.

7 THE PERILS OF OFFICE

1 Bredin, *Sieyès*, p. 463.
2 Bredin, *Sieyès*, p. 466.
3 Bredin, *Sieyès*, pp. 483–4.
4 Bredin, *Sieyès*, pp. 470–2.
5 Bredin, *Sieyès*, p. 484.
6 Chandler, *Campaigns*, pp. 264–5.
7 Chandler, *Campaigns*, p. 265.
8 Chandler, *Campaigns*, pp. 278–81.
9 Chandler, *Campaigns*, p. 301.
10 Cited in Rory Muir, *Tactics and the Experience of Battle in the Age of Napoleon* (New Haven, 2000), p. 78.
11 Muir, *Tactics*, p. 207.
12 Cited in Muir, *Tactics*, p. 164.
13 Cited in Chandler, *Campaigns*, p. 296.
14 To Gen. Moreau, Milan, 28 Prairial, Year 8 (17 June 1800), *Napoléon Bonaparte. Correspondance générale*, vol. III, *Pacifications, 1800–1802* (Paris, 2006), no. 5444, p. 306.
15 Muir, *Tactics*, p. 135.
16 To Francis II, Holy Roman Emperor, Marengo, 27 Prairial, Year 8 (16 June 1800), *Correspondance générale*, vol. III, no. 5440, pp. 303–4.
17 To Christian VII, King of Denmark, Lyon, 11 Messidor, Year 8 (30 June 1800), *Correspondance générale*, vol. III, no 5477, pp. 319–20.
18 To Carnot, Min. of War, Milan, 28 Prairial, Year 8 (17 June 1800), *Correspondance générale*, vol. III, no. 5443, p. 306.
19 To Gen. Brune, Commander-in-Chief of the Army of the Reserve, 25 Thermidor, Year 8 (13 Aug. 1800), *Correspondance générale*, vol. III, no 5600, pp. 369–70.
20 To Carnot, Paris, 18 Fructidor, Year 8 (5 Sept. 1800), *Correspondance générale*, vol. III, no. 5632, p. 384.
21 To Francis II, Holy Roman Emperor, Mortefontaine (Calvados), 10 Thermidor, Year 8 (29 July 1800), *Correspondance générale*, vol. III, no. 5578, p. 361.
22 To Talleyrand, Paris, 16 Thermidor, Year 8 (4 Aug. 1800), *Correspondance générale*, vol. III, no. 5595, p. 367.
23 To Carnot, Paris, 26 Fructidor, Year 8 (15 Sept. 1800), *Correspondance générale*, vol. III, no. 5643, p. 388.
24 To the Landgrave of Hesse-Kassel, Paris, 4 Vendémiaire, Year 9 (26 Sept. 1800), *Correspondance générale*, vol. III, no. 5662, p. 396; to the Landgrave of Hesse-Darmstadt, Paris, 4 Vendémiaire, Year 9 (26 Sept. 1800), *Correspondance générale*, vol. III, no. 5663, p. 396.
25 To Joseph, Paris, 28 Vendémiaire, Year 9 (20 Oct. 1800), *Correspondance générale*, vol. III, no. 5700, pp. 411–12.

26 To Carnot, Paris, 26 Fructidor, Year 8 (13 Sept. 1800), *Correspondance générale*, vol. III, no. 5643, p. 388.

27 'La comparison d'Alexandre le Grand avec Jules César', *Les vies des hommes illustres de Plutarque*, vol. vii, ed. and trans by Amyot (Paris, 1818 edn of 1769 original), pp. 295, 300.

28 Migliorini, *Napoléon*, pp. 235–6.

29 Cited in Woloch, *Napoleon and his Collaborators*, p. 92.

30 Valérie Huet, 'Napoleon I: a new Augustus?', *Roman Presences: Receptions of Rome in European Culture, 1789–1945*, ed. Catherine Edwards (Cambridge, 1999), pp. 53–69, 54.

31 Darrin M. McMahon, *Enemies of the Enlightenment: The French Counter-Enlightenment and the Making of Modernity* (Oxford, 2001), pp. 128, 132, 134–5.

32 Woloch, *Napoloen and his Collaborators*, pp. 206–7.

33 Cited in McMahon, *Enemies of the Enlightenment*, pp. 150–1.

34 McMahon, *Enemies of the Enlightenment*, p. 151.

35 To Fouché, Milan, 30 Floréal, Year 13 (20 May 1805), *Correspondance générale*, vol. V, *Boulogne, Trafalgar, Austerlitz, 1805* (Paris, 2008), no 10092, p. 325.

36 To Fouché, 30 Aug. 1806, *Napoléon Bonaparte. Correspondance générale*, vol. VI, *Vers le Grand Empire, 1806* (Paris, 2009), no. 12819, p. 766.

37 To Joseph, 31 May 1806, *Correspondance générale*, vol. VI, no. 12206, p. 475.

38 A. F. Lebrun, *Opinions, rapports et choix d'écrits politiques de Charles-François Lebrun, Duc de Plaisance* (Paris, 1829), pp. 77–8.

39 Cited in Isser Woloch, *The New Regime: Transformations of the French Civic Order, 1789–1820*, (New York, 1994), p. 68.

40 Woloch, *New Regime*, p. 68.

41 To Fouché, 13 Nivôse, Year 9 (3 Jan. 1801), *Correspondance générale*, vol. III, no. 5878, p. 497.

42 To Talleyrand, 30 Fructidor, Year 9 (17 Sept. 1801), *Correspondance générale*, vol. III, no. 6494, pp. 781–2.

43 Napoleon to Joseph, 17 Ventôse, Year 10 (8 March 1802), *Napoléon et Joseph. Correspondance intégrale, 1784–1818*, ed. Vincent Haegele (Paris, 2007), no. 95, p. 73.

44 To Talleyrand, 22 Brumaire, Year 10 (13 Nov. 1801), *Correspondance générale*, vol. III, no, 6642, pp. 850–1.

45 To Talleyrand, 30 Pluviôse, Year 10 (19 Feb. 1802), *Correspondance générale*, vol. III, no. 6779, p. 915.

46 Napoleon to Joseph, 21 Ventôse, Year 10 (12 Mar. 1802), *Napoléon et Joseph*, no. 101, p. 76.

47 To Talleyrand, 30 Pluviôse, Year 10 (19 Feb. 1802), *Correspondance générale*, vol. III, no. 6780, p. 916.

48 Joseph to Napoleon, 17 March 1802, *Napoléon et Joseph*, no. 108, p. 79.

49 Emmanuel de Waresquiel, *Talleyrand. Dernières nouvelles du Diable* (Paris, 2011), p. 103.

50 de Waresquiel, *Talleyrand*, pp. 104–5.

51 To Alexander I, Emperor of Russia, 18 Vendémiaire, Year 10 (10 Oct. 1801), *Correspondance générale*, vol. III, no. 6549, pp. 805-6.

52 To Alexander I, Emperor of Russia, 27 Pluviôse, Year 10 (16 Feb. 1802), *Correspondance générale*, vol. III, no 6770, p. 909.

53 *Les Grands Traités du Consulat. Documents diplomatiques du Consulat et de l'Empire*, ed. Michel Kerautret (Paris, 2002), vol. I, p. 197.
54 *Les Grands Traités*, vol. I, p. 244.
55 Cited in Migliorini, *Napoléon*, p. 223.

8 TAKING POWER

1   Marie-Blanched'Arneville, *Parcs et Jardins sous la Premier Empire. Reflets d'une société* (Paris, 1981), p. 31.
2   See Frédéric Bluche, *Le Bonapartisme. Aux origines de la droite autoritaire, 1800–1850* (Paris, 1980), for the classic definition of this policy.
3   Germaine de Staël, *Ten Years' Exile* (English trans., Fontwell, 1968), pp. 15–16.
4   Englund, *Napoleon*, p. 224.
5   To Berthier, 19 Ventôse, Year 12 (10 Mar. 1804), *Napoléon Bonaparte. Correspondance générale*, Vol. IV, *Ruptures et Fondation*, (Paris, 2007), no. 8726, pp. 633–4.
6   To Real, Conseiller d'État, 24 Ventôse, Year 12 (15 Mar. 1804), *Correspondance générale*, vol. IV, no. 8736, p. 640–1.
7   François-René de Chateaubriand, *Napoléon* (Paris, 1969 edn), p. 141.
8   Chateaubriand, *Napoléon*, pp. 141–2, 176.
9   Migliorini, *Napoléon*, p. 237.
10 To Talleyrand, 27 Ventôse, Year 12 (18 Mar. 1804), *Correspondance générale*, vol. IV, no. 8746, p. 645.
11 To Murat, 28 Ventôse, Year 12 (19 Mar. 1804), *Correspondance générale*, vol. IV, no. 8747, p. 646.
12 Woloch, *Napoleon and his Collaborators*, p. 106.
13 To Cambacérès and Lebrun, 4 Pluviôse, Year 10 (24 Jan. 1802), *Correspondance générale*, vol. III, no. 6738, p. 894.
14 To Champagny, Min. of Int., 9 Frimaire, Year 13 (30 Nov. 1804), *Correspondance générale*, vol. IV, no. 9431, p. 965.
15 To Daunou, 9 Frimaire, Year 13 (30 Nov. 1804), *Correspondance générale*, vol. IV, no. 9432, p. 966.
16 Yves Bénot, 'Il gruppo della "Décade Philosophique": Un tentative di resistenza intelletuale (1799–1803)', in *Napoleone e gli intelletuali. Dotti e 'hommes de lettres' nell'Europa napoleonica*, ed. Daniela Gallingani, pp. 83–114, at p. 98.
17 Henry Lachouque and Anne S. K. Brown, *The Anatomy of Glory: Napoleon and his Guard* (English trans., London, 1997), pp. 28–9.
18 Philip Mansel, *The Eagle in Splendour. Napoleon and his Court* (London, 1987) pp. 14–15.
19 Mansel, *The Eagle in Splendour*, pp. 14–15.
20 Lachouque and Brown, *Anatomy of Glory*, p. 29.
21 Woloch, *Napoleon and his Collaborators*, pp. 90–9, at p. 92.
22 Woloch, *Napoleon and his Collaborators*, p. 94.
23 Englund, *Napoleon*, p. 222.
24 Jacques Godechot, *Les Institutions de la France sous la Révolution et l'Empire* (Paris, 1968), pp. 575–6.
25 Bredin, *Sieyès*, pp. 471–2.

26 Godechot, *Les Institutions*, p. 575.
27 Woloch, *Napoleon and his Collaborators*, p. 157.
28 Ambrogio A. Caiani, *Louis XVI and the French Revolution, 1789–1792* (Cambridge, 2012), *passim*.
29 Timothy Wilson-Smith, *Napoleon and his Artists* (London, 1996), pp. 102–5.
30 To Talleyrand, 16 Fructidor, Year 9 (3 Sept. 1801), *Correspondance générale*, vol. III, no. 6458, p. 767.
31 For a recent, incisive analysis of the constitution: Emanuele Pagano, *Enti locali e Stato in Italia sotto Napoleone. Repubblica e Regno d'Italia (1802–1814)* (Rome, 2007), pp. 21–6.
32 Georges Lefebvre, *Napoléon* (Paris, 1941), pp. 134–6.

9 THE GREAT REFORMS

1 Englund, *Napoleon*, p. 188.
2 Marie-Cécile Thoral, 'Small state, Big society: the Involvement of Citizens in Local Government in Nineteenth-Century France', in *The Napoleonic Empire and the New European Political Culture*, ed. M. Broers, P. Hicks and A. Guimera (Basingstoke, 2012), pp. 59–69.
3 Alison Patrick, 'French Revolutionary Local Government, 1789–1792', in *The French Revolution and the Creation of Modern Political Culture*, vol. II, *The Political Culture of the French Revolution*, ed. Colin Lucas (Oxford, 1988), pp. 399–420.
4 Geoffrey Ellis, *The Napoleonic Empire* (2nd edn, Basingstoke, 2003), pp. 28–30.
5 Cited in Jacques-Olivier Boudon, *Histoire du Consulat et de l'Empire* (Paris, 2003 edn), p. 75.
6 Howard G. Brown, *Ending the French Revolution: Violence, Justice and Repression from the Terror to Napoleon* (Charlottesville and London, 2008), p. 301.
7 To General Hédouville, 11 Pluviôse, Year 8 (31 Jan. 1800), *Correspondance générale*, vol. III, no. 4914, p. 60.
8 Clive Emsley, *Gendarmes and the State in Nineteenth-Century Europe* (Oxford, 2000), pp. 60–1.
9 To Fouché, 5 Frimaire, Year 9 (26 Nov. 1800), *Correspondance générale*, vol. III, no. 5804, pp. 460–1.
10 To Berthier, 1 Thermidor, Year 10 (20 July 1802), *Correspondance générale*, vol. III, no. 7030, pp. 1036–7.
11 To Moncey, 10 Frimaire, Year 11 (1 Dec. 1802), *Correspondance générale*, vol. III, no. 7330, p. 1175.
12 Emsley, *Gendarmes*, pp. 61–2.
13 To Lagrange, 7 Floréal, Year 11 (27 April 1803), *Correspondance générale*, vol. IV, no. 7612, pp. 118–19.
14 Emsley, *Gendarmes and the State*, pp. 59–60.
15 Emsley, *Gendarmes, passim*.
16 Brown, *Ending the French Revolution*, p. 327.
17 Emsley, *Gendarmes*, p. 71.
18 Alan Forrest, 'The Ubiquitous Brigand: The Politics and Language of Repression', in *Popular Resistance in the French Wars. Patriots, Politics and Land Pirates*, ed. C. J. Esdaile, (Basingstoke, 2005), pp. 25–44.

19 To General Hédouville, 2 Pluviôse, Year 8 (22 Jan. 1800), *Correspondance générale*, vol. III, no. 4897, p. 51.

20 Alan Forrest, *Déserteurs et Insoumis sous la Révolution et l'Empire* (Paris, 1988), pp. 33–4.

21 Forrest, *Déserteurs et Insoumis*, pp. 53–4.

22 For a concise, clear analysis of the reforms: Ellis, *The Napoleonic Empire*, pp. 35–40.

23 To Gaudin, 25 Germinal, Year 8 (13 April 1800), *Correspondance générale*, vol. III, no. 5179, p. 178.

24 Rip Kain and E. Baignet, *The Cadastral Map in the Service of the State: A History of Property Mapping* (Chicago and London, 1984,), pp. 228–31.

25 To Gaudin, 7 Germinal, Year 8 (28 Mar. 1800), *Correspondance générale*, vol. III, no. 5151, p. 166.

26 To Gaudin, 1 Frimaire, Year 9 (22 Nov. 1800), *Correspondance générale*, vol. III, no. 5796, p. 457; *idem*, 8 Frimaire, Year 9 (29 Nov. 1800), no. 5808, p. 462.

27 To Gaudin, 18 Fructidor, Year 9 (5 Sept. 1801), *Correspondance générale*, vol. III, no. 6469, p. 772.

28 To Gaudin, 8 Fructidor, Year 9 (26 Aug. 1801), *Correspondance générale*, vol. III, no. 6458, p. 759.

29 To Gaudin, 22 Fructidor, Year 9 (9 Sept. 1800), *Correspondance générale*, vol. III, no. 6486, pp. 778–9.

30 To Fouché, 5 Vendémiaire, Year 13 (27 Sept. 1804), *Correspondance générale*, vol. III, no. 9253, p. 891.

31 Geoffrey Ellis, *Napoleon* (Harlow, 1997), p. 172.

32 To Cambacérès, 15 Vendémiaire, Year 13 (7 Oct. 1804), no. 9320, p. 920.

33 To Haüy, 19 Pluviôse, Year 11 (8 Feb. 1803), *Correspondance générale*, vol. IV, no. 7464, p. 46.

34 Lefebvre, *Napoléon*, p. 79.

35 Boudon, *Histoire*, pp. 80–4.

36 Jacques-Olivier Boudon, *Ordre et Désordre dans la France Napoléonienne* (Paris, 2008), p. 173.

37 Joseph Fouché, *Mémoires*, 2 vols (second edn, Brussels, 1825), i, p. 157.

38 Napoleon to Joseph, 1 Thermidor, Year 9 (20 July 1801), *Napoléon et Joseph*, no. 87, p. 69.

39 To Portalis, 25 Vendémiaire, Year 10 (15 Oct. 1801), *Correspondance générale*, vol. III, no. 6589, p. 820.

40 Napoleon to Joseph, 1 Thermidor, Year 9 (20 July 1801), *Napoléon et Joseph*, no. 88. pp. 69–70.

41 Bernard Plongeron, *Conscience religieuse et Révolution. Regards sur l'historiographie religieuse de la Révolution française* (Paris, 1969), p. 226.

42 Boudon, *Histoire*, p. 83.

43 Ibid.

44 Boudon, *Ordre et Désordre*, p. 173.

45 To Cambacérès, 9 Brumaire, Year 11 (31 Oct. 1802), *Correspondance générale*, vol. III, no. 7254, p. 1142.

46 To Fesch, 11 Brumaire, Year 11 (2 Nov. 1802), *Correspondance générale*, vol. III, no. 7260, pp. 1145–6.

47 To Régnier, 1 Prairial, Year 12 (21 May 1804), *Correspondance générale*, vol. IV, no. 8887, pp. 711–12.

48 Boudon, *Ordre et Désordre*, p. 190.

49 Boudon, *Ordre et Désordre*, p. 184.

50 Boudon, *Ordre et Désordre*, p. 190.

51 To Bernadotte, 11 Floréal, Year 8 (1 May 1800), *Correspondance générale*, vol. III, no. 5219, p. 201.

52 To General Hédouville, 2 Pluviôse, Year 8 (22 Jan. 1800), *Correspondance générale*, vol. III, no. 4897, p. 51.

53 To General Brune, 9 Pluviôse, Year 8 (29 Jan. 1800), *Correspondance générale*, vol. III, no. 4909, pp. 57–8.

54 To Bernier, Bishop of Orléans, 24 Frimaire, Year 12 (16 Dec. 1803), *Correspondance générale*, vol. IV, no. 8433, pp. 514–15.

55 To Régnier, 27 Frimaire, Year 12 (19 Dec. 1803), *Correspondance générale*, vol. IV, no. 8476, p. 531.

56 Staël, *Ten Years' Exile*, p. 14.

57 Boudon, *Ordre et Désordre*, pp. 184–5.

58 To Régnier, 20 Messidor, Year 12 (9 July 1804), *Correspondance générale*, vol. IV, no. 8999, p. 768.

59 To Fesch, 11 Brumaire, Year 11 (2 Nov. 1802), *Correspondance générale*, vol. IV, no. 7260, pp. 1145–6.

60 To Fouché, 15 Vendémiaire, Year 13 (7 Oct. 1804), *Correspondance générale*, vol. IV, no. 9328, pp. 924–5.

61 The former is a Catholic symbol created by the Jesuits, and almost synonymous with them in this period. The latter was a lay organisation, also their creation.

62 To Fesch, 11 Brumaire, Year 11 (2 Nov. 1802), *Correspondance générale*, vol. IV, no. 7260, pp. 1145–6.

63 To Talleyrand, 15 Vendémiaire, Year 13 (7 Oct. 1804), *Correspondance générale*, vol. IV, no. 9334, p. 927.

64 *Napoleon: His Court and Family: Memoirs of Madame Junot, Duchesse d'Abrantès*, 3 vols (English trans., London, 1883), ii, pp. 274–6.

65 To Champagny, 18 Thermidor, Year 13 (6 Aug. 1805), *Correspondance générale*, vol. V, no. 10516, pp. 541–2.

66 *Napoleon: His Court and Family*, ii, pp. 304–9.

67 Jean-Clement Martin, *La Vendée et la France* (Paris, 1987), pp. 108, 272–3, 281–2, 331.

68 To General Hédouville, 2 Pluviôse, Year 8 (22 Jan. 1800), *Correspondance générale*, vol. III, no. 4897, p. 51.

69 To Bernadotte, 11 Floréal, Year 8 (1 May 1800), *Correspondance générale*, vol. III, no. 5219, p. 201.

70 All quotations from Portalis' *Premier Discours* are taken from *Naissance du Code Civil*, ed. P. A. Fevet (Paris, 1989).

71 Pierre Vialles, *L'Archchancelier Cambacérès, 1753–1824* (1908; Paris, 2006 edn), p. 218.

72 Vialles, *L'Archchancelier*, pp. 213–14.

73 Jean-Louis Halpérin, 'Le regard de l'historien', in *Le Code Civil, 1802–1804. Livre de Bicenteniare* (Paris, 2004), pp. 43–58, at p. 50–1.

74 Halpérin, 'Le regard', p. 53.

75 David Bell, 'Culture and Religion', in *Old Regime France*, ed. W. Doyle, (Oxford, 2002), pp. 78–104. For the classic study, Robert R. Palmer, *Catholics and Unbelievers in Eighteenth-Century France* (Princeton, 1939).

76 Jean-Louis Halpérin, *L'Impossible Code Civil* (Paris, 1992), pp. 271–2.
77 Halpérin, *Impossible Code*, pp. 276–7.
78 Fevet, *Naissance du Code Civil*, p. 265.
79 Halpérin, *Impossible Code*, pp. 282–3.
80 Halpérin, *Impossible Code*, p. 273.
81 Staël, *Ten Years' Exile*, p. 18.

10 INTO THE BRIGHT SUN

1   Englund, *Napoleon*, pp. 196–200.
2   Jourdan, *Napoléon*, p. 211.
3   To Cambacérès, 23 Nivôse, Year 10 (13 Jan. 1802), *Correspondance générale*, vol. III, no. 6716, p. 883.
4   To Cambacérès, 8 Brumaire, Year 11 (30 Oct. 1802), *Correspondance générale*, vol. III, no. 7251, p. 1140. Lebrun was a native of Normandy.
5   To Barbé-Marbois, 9 Brumaire, Year 11 (31 Oct. 1802), *Correspondance générale*, vol. III, no. 7252, p. 1140.
6   Gavin Daly, *Inside Napoleonic France: State and Society in Rouen, 1800–1815* (Aldershot, 2001).
7   Daly, *Inside Napoleonic France*, p. 268.
8   Alexander Grab, *Napoleon and the Transformation of Europe* (Basingstoke, 2003), p. 116.
9   To d'Affray, 22 Germinal, Year 11 (12 April 1803), *Correspondance générale*, vol. IV, no. 7564, pp. 96–7.
10 Grab, *Transformation*, p. 119.
11 To the Members of the Small and Great Councils of the Canton of Berne, 8 Messidor, Year 11 (27 June 1803), *Correspondance générale*, vol. IV, no. 7765, p. 187.
12 To Murat, 20 Ventôse, Year 11 (11 Mar. 1803), *Correspondance générale*, vol. IV, no. 7519, pp. 72–3.
13 To Gen. Morand, 19 Germinal, Year 11 (9 April 1803), *Correspondance générale*, vol. IV, no. 7560, pp. 93–4.
14 Semmel, *Napoleon and the British*, p. 30.
15 Graciela Iglesias Rogers, *British Liberators in the Age of Napoleon: Volunteers under the Spanish Flag in the Peninsular War* (London, 2013), pp. 15–17.
16 To Decrès, 25 Nivôse, Year 11 (15 Jan. 1803), *Correspondance générale*, vol. IV, no. 7425, pp. 30–2.
17 Cited in *Napoléon à Sainte-Hélène*, 'L'Evangile selon Gourgaud', ed. Jean Tulard (Paris, 1981), p. 460.
18 Laurent Dubois, *Avengers of the New World: The story of the Haitian Revolution* (Cambridge, Mass., 2004). pp. 231–3.
19 Dubois, *Avengers*, p. 233.
20 Dubois, *Avengers*, p. 239.
21 Cited in Pierre-Louis Roederer, *Oeuvres*, 6 vols (Paris, 1856), iii, p. 334.
22 Instructions pour Lequoy-Mongiraud, 24 Nivôse, Year 9 (14 Jan. 1801), *Correspondance générale*, vol. III, no. 5923, p. 519.
23 Dubois, *Avengers*, p. 247.

24 Jacques Norvins de Monbreton, *Souvenirs d'un historien de Napoléon*, 3 vols (Paris, 1896–7), ii, pp. 405–6.

25 Cited in Tulard, *Napoléon à Sainte-Hélène*, p. 240.

26 Dubois, *Avengers*, pp. 253–5.

27 Cited in Tim Matthewson, *A Proslavery Foreign Policy: Haitian-American Relations during the Early Republic* (Westport, 2003), p. 101.

28 Cited in Paul Finkelman, *Slavery and the Founders. Race and Liberty in the Age of Jefferson* (New York, 1996), p. 134.

29 Matthewson, *Proslavery Foreign Policy*, p. 107.

30 Michael Zuckerman, 'The Power of Blackness: Thomas Jefferson and the Revolution in Saint Domingue', in Zuckerman, *Almost Chosen People: Oblique biographies in the American Grain* (Berkeley, 1993), n. 76, pp. 203–4.

31 Matthewson, *Proslavery Foreign Policy*, p. 99.

32 Matthewson, *Proslavery Foreign Policy*, p. 107.

33 Matthewson, *Proslavery Foreign Policy*, p. 106.

34 Norvins, *Souvenirs*, ii, p. 34.

35 Norvins, *Souvenirs*, ii, pp. 366–7.

36 To Berthier, 18 Messidor, Year 11 (7 July 1803), *Correspondance générale*, vol. IV, no. 7791, p. 199.

37 Cited in Matthewson, *Proslavery Foreign Policy*, p. 101.

38 Cited in Tulard, *Napoléon à Sainte-Hélène*, p. 240.

39 Matthewson, *Proslavery Foreign Policy*, pp. 108–10.

40 Cited in Tulard, *Napoléon à Sainte-Hélène*, p. 476. The Noailles and the La Rochefoucauld were among the oldest and proudest noble families in France, with extensive links to the Vendean region, as well as colonial commercial interests.

41 Norvins, *Souvenirs*, ii, pp. 37, 39.

42 Joachim Kühn, *Pauline Bonaparte: Napoleon's attendant star* (English trans., London, 1937), p. 64.

43 Kühn, *Pauline*, pp. 70–2.

44 To Pauline (in Port-Républicain, Saint-Domingue), 25 Ventôse, Year 10 (16 Mar. 1802), *Correspondance générale*, vol. III, no. 6814, p. 934.

45 There had been rumours that Pauline had been having an affair with a young officer: Kühn, *Pauline*, p. 73.

46 To Pauline, 12 Messidor, Year 10 (1 July 1802), *Correspondance générale*, vol. III, no. 6979, p. 1012.

47 *Napoleon: His Court and Family*, ii, p. 245.

48 Kühn, *Pauline*, pp. 76–8.

49 *Memoirs of Count Miot de Melito*, ed. Gen. Fleischmann (English trans., London, 1881), 2 vols, i, p. 512.

50 Dubois, *Avengers*, p. 292.

51 E. Wilson Lyon, *Louisiana in French Diplomacy* (Norman, 1934), pp. 142–3.

52 Frank W. Brecker, *Negotiating the Louisiana Purchase: Robert Livingston's Mission to France, 1801–1804* (London, 2006), pp. 106–7.

53 Brecker, *Negotiating the Louisiana Purchase*, pp. 54–6.

54 Lyon, *Louisiana*, p. 136, n. 31.

55 Lyon, *Louisiana*, pp. 136, 140.

56 Cited in Lyon, *Louisiana*, p. 124.

57 To Talleyrand, 3 Germinal, Year 11 (24 Mar. 1803), *Correspondance générale*, vol. IV, no. 7535, p. 79.

58 To Talleyrand, 11 Nivôse, Year 11 (1 Jan. 1803), *Correspondance générale*, vol. IV, no. 7406, pp. 20–1.

59 To Tsar Alexander I, 20 Ventôse, Year 11 (11 Mar. 1803), *Correspondance générale*, vol. IV, no. 7513, p. 66.

60 To Frederick-William II of Prussia, 20 Ventôse, Year 11 (11 Mar. 1803), *Correspondance générale*, vol. IV, no. 7517, p. 70.

61 To Régnier, 11 Nivôse, Year 11 (1 Jan. 1803), *Correspondance générale*, vol. IV, no. 7405, p. 20.

62 To Chaptal, Min. of the Interior, 20 Pluviôse, Year 11 (9 Feb. 1803), *Correspondance générale*, vol. IV, no. 7466, p. 47.

63 The British had used the term earlier, when demanding Napoleon evacuate the Batavian Republic and recognise British sovereignty over Malta.

64 The hated Eden Commercial Treaty of 1786.

65 The 1713 Treaty of Utrecht had been a humiliation for the French; it obliged them to demolish the fortifications of Dunkirk under British supervision.

66 To Talleyrand, 4.30 a.m., 20 Floréal, Year 11 (10 May 1803), *Correspondance générale*, vol. IV, no. 7629, p. 127.

67 To Talleyrand, 23 Floréal, Year 11 (13 May 1803), *Correspondance générale*, vol. IV, no. 7638, pp. 131–2.

11 TOWARDS EMPIRE

1   Cited in Bernard Chevalier, 'Deux femmes pour un Empereur: Joséphine et Marie-Louise', in *Napoleone, Le Donne. Protagoniste, Alleate, Nemiche*, ed. Massimo Colesanti (Rome, 2009,) pp. 15–26, at p. 21.

2   To Joséphine, Pont-de-Briques, 25 Thermidor, Year 13 (13 Aug. 1805), *Correspondance générale*, vol. V, no. 10560, pp. 564–5.

3   Gueniffey, *Le Dix-huit Brumaire*, pp. 256–7.

4   Gueniffey, *Le Dix-huit Brumaire*, pp. 294–5.

5   Chevalier, 'Deux femmes', p. 20.

6   To Joséphine, Calais, 18 Thermidor, Year 12 (6 Aug. 1804), *Correspondance générale*, vol. IV, no. 9062, p. 798.

7   To Hortense, Pont-de-Briques, 27 Thermidor, Year 12 (15 Aug. 1804), *Correspondance générale*, vol. IV, no. 9103, p. 819.

8   *Napoleon: His Court and Family*, ii, p. 296.

9   *Memoirs of Count Miot de Melito*, i, p. 502.

10 *Napoleon: His Court and Family*, ii, p. 233.

11 Fauvelet de Bourrienne, *Memoirs of Napoleon Bonaparte* (English trans., London, 1903), pp. 211–12. The specific incident Bourrienne relates takes the questionable form of a reconstructed conversation, but its content is certainly consistent with Lucien's dislike of Joséphine, which was well known.

12 To Jérôme, Milan, 20 Prairial, Year 13 (9 June 1805), *Correspondance générale*, vol. V, no. 10224, p. 401.

13 To Jérôme, 16 Floréal, Year 13 (6 May 1805), *Correspondance générale*, vol. V, no. 9986, p. 274.

14 To Letizia, 2 Floréal, Year 13 (22 April 1805), *Correspondance générale*, vol. V, no. 9877, p. 224.

15 To Cambacérès, 25 Floréal, Year 13 (13 May 1805), *Correspondance générale*, vol. V, no. 10037, p. 300.

16 To Pius VII, 4 Prairial, Year 13 (24 May 1805), *Correspondance générale*, vol. V, no. 10121, pp. 339–40.

17 To Pius VII, 1 Fructidor, Year 13 (19 Aug. 1805), *Correspondance générale*, vol. V, no. 10604, pp. 587–8.

18 Jacques-Olivier Boudon, *Le Roi Jérôme, frère prodigue de Napoléon (1784–1860)* (Paris, 2008), p.85.

19 To Jérôme, 20 Prairial, Year 13 (9 June 1805), *Correspondance générale*, vol. V, no. 40244, p. 401.

20 To Murat, 30 Floréal, Year 13 (20 May 1805), *Correspondance générale*, vol. V, no. 10094, p. 326.

21 Charlene M. Boyer Lewis, *Elizabeth Patterson Bonaparte: An American Aristocrat in the Early Republic* (Philadelphia, 2012).

22 Boudon, *Jérôme*, pp. 95–8.

23 His two illegitimate sons were by his Polish mistress, Maria Walewska, born in 1809, and by Elénore Denuelle de la Plaigne, a young lady-in-waiting to his sister Caroline, in 1806.

24 To Hortense, La Tour d'Ordre, 24 Thermidor, Year 13 (12 Aug. 1805), *Correspondance générale*, vol. V, no. 10552, pp. 558–60.

25 *Napoleon: His Court and Family*, ii, p. 295.

26 Fouché, *Mémoires*, i, p. 190.

27 Cited in Migliorini, *Napoléon*, p. 239.

28 Figures from Boudon, *Histoire du Consulat et de l'Empire*, p. 150.

29 Boudon, *Histoire du Consulat et de l'Empire, passim*.

30 Englund, *Napoleon*, 147.

29 Boudon, *Histoire du Consulat et de l'Empire, passim*.

31 Cited in Thierry Lentz, *Nouvelle Histoire du Premier Empire*, vol. i, *Napoléon et la Conquête de l'Europe, 1804–1810* (Paris, 2002), p. 23.

32 Cited in Boudon, *Histoire du Consulat et de l'Empire*, p. 147.

33 Lentz, *Nouvelle Histoire*, i, p. 42.

34 Cited in Lentz, *Nouvelle Histoire*, i, p. 74.

35 Lentz, *Nouvelle Histoire*, i, pp. 75–7.

36 Cited in Lentz, *Nouvelle Histoire*, i, p. 77.

37 Cited in Gilbert Martineau, *Madame Mère: Napoleon's Mother* (English trans., London, 1978), p. 60.

38 Lentz, *Nouvelle Histoire*, i, p. 86.

39 Lentz, *Nouvelle Histoire*, i, p. 79.

40 Lentz, *Nouvelle Histoire*, i, p. 90.

41 Lentz, *Nouvelle Histoire*, i, pp. 109–10, n. 1, p. 110.

12 WAR WITH BRITAIN

1 *Napoleon: His Court and Family*, ii, pp. 257–8.

2 *Napoleon: His Court and Family*, ii, p. 311.

3 Frédéric Rousseau, *Service militaire au xix siècle: de la résistance à l'obeisance. Un siècle d'apprentissage de la patrie dans le département de l'Herault* (Montpellier, 1998), p. 79.

4 This is traced with admirable precision in Aurélien Lignereus, *La France rébellionaire. Les resistances à la gendarmerie (1800–1859)*, pp. 24–31.

5 Forrest, *Déserteurs et Insoumis*, p. 53.

6 To Fouché, 18 Thermidor, Year 13 (6 Aug. 1805), *Correspondance générale*, vol. V, no. 10520, p. 545.

7 To Gen. Lacuée, Director of War Administration, 17 Thermidor, Year 13 (5 Aug. 1805), *Correspondance générale*, vol. V, no. 10513, pp. 539–40.

8 To Berthier, 20 Thermidor, Year 12 (18 Aug. 1804), *Correspondance générale*, vol. IV, no. 9069, p. 803.

9 To Berthier, Cologne, 28 Fructidor, Year 12 (15 Sept. 1804), *Correspondance générale*, vol. IV, no. 9215, pp. 871–2.

10 To Lacuée, 28 Vendémiaire, Year 13 (20 Oct. 1804), *Correspondance générale*, vol. IV, no. 9356, p. 935.

11 To Champagny, Min. of Interior, 19 Thermidor, Year 13 (7 Aug. 1805), *Correspondance générale*, vol. V, no. 10524, p. 546.

12 To Gen. Lacuée, Director of War Administration, 19 Thermidor, Year 13 (7 Aug. 1805), *Correspondance générale*, vol. V, no. 10529, p. 548.

13 This entire section is based on Lentz, *Nouvelle Histoire*, i, pp. 134–9.

14 Remi Monaque, 'Trafalgar: A French point of view', in *A Great and Glorious Victory: New Perspectives on the Battle of Trafalgar*, ed. Richard Harding (Barnsley, 2008), pp. 70–9, at p. 72.

15 To Decrès, 21 Floréal, Year 12 (1 May 1804), *Correspondance générale*, vol. IV, no. 8866, pp. 700–1.

16 Cited in N. A. M. Rodger, *The Command of the Ocean: A Naval History of Britain, 1649–1815* (London, 2004), p. 531.

17 Rodger, *Command*, p. 530.

18 To Decrès, 27 Thermidor, Year 13 (15 Aug. 1805), *Correspondance générale*, vol. V, no. 10574, p. 574.

19 To Decrès, 4 Fructidor, Year 13 (22 Aug. 1805), *Correspondance générale*, vol. V, no. 10623, p. 596.

20 Monaque, 'Trafalgar: A French point of view', p. 74.

21 To Decrès,29 Messidor, Year 13 (18 July 1805), *Correspondance générale*, vol. V, no. 10419, p. 492.

22 To Allemand, Comdt Rochefort, 7 Thermidor, Year 13 (26 July 1805), *Correspondance générale*, vol. V, no. 10459, pp. 510–11.

23 To Decrès, 25 Thermidor, Year 13 (13 Aug. 1805), *Correspondance générale*, vol. V, no. 10555, pp. 561–2.

24 Rodger, *Command*, pp. 532–3.

25 Rodger, *Command*, pp. 533–4.

26 To Decrès, 25 Thermidor, Year 13 (13 Aug. 1805), *Correspondance générale*, vol. V, no. 10556, p. 562.

27 Rodger, *Command*, p. 2.

28 Rodger, *Command*, pp. 2–44 on this period in the Royal Navy.

29 Rodger, *Command*, pp. 17, 22.

30 Rodger, *Command*, p. 26.

31 Rodger, *Command*, p. 529.
32 Lentz, *Nouvelle Histoire*, i, pp. 148–9.
33 Rodger, *Command*, pp. 530, 536.
34 Rodger, *Command*, p. 530.
35 Cited in Jacques Garnier, *Austerlitz, 2 décembre 1805* (Paris, 2005), p. 38.
36 To Villeneuve, 27 Messidor, Year 13 (16 July 1805), *Correspondance générale*, vol. V, no. 10412, pp. 489–90.
37 To Gen. Marmont, Comdt Camp of Utrecht, 26 Messidor, Year 13 (15 July 1805), *Correspondance générale*, vol. V, no. 10405, p. 487.
38 To Berthier, 1 Thermidor, Year 13 (20 July 1805), *Correspondance générale*, vol. V, no. 10427, pp. 495–6.
39 To Fouché, 3 Thermidor, Year 13 (22 July 1805), *Correspondance générale*, vol. V, no. 10433, pp. 498–9.
40 To Decrès, 8 Thermidor, Year 13 (27 July 1805), *Correspondance générale*, vol. V, no. 10469, pp. 516–17; to Rear Admiral Gourdon, Comdt Ferrol squadron, 8 Thermidor, Year 13 (27 July 1805), ibid., no. 10472, p. 519.
41 To Fouché, 21 Thermidor, Year 13 (9 Aug. 1805), *Correspondance générale*, vol. V, no. 10538, p. 551.
42 To Fouché, 21 Thermidor, Year 13 (9 Aug. 1805), *Correspondance générale*, vol. V, no. 10539, p. 552.
43 To Decrès, 22 Thermidor, Year 13 (10 Aug. 1805), *Correspondance générale*, vol. V, no. 10542, p. 553.
44 To Decrès, 27 Thermidor, Year 13 (15 Aug. 1805), *Correspondance générale*, vol. V, no. 10574, p. 574.
45 To Decrès, 4 Fructidor, Year 13 (22 Aug. 1805), *Correspondance générale*, vol. V, no. 10618, p. 594; to Vice-Admiral Ganteaume, 4 Fructidor, Year 13 (22 Aug. 1805), ibid., no. 10626, pp. 597–8; to Villeneuve, 4 Fructidor, Year 13 (22 Aug. 1805), ibid., no. 10631, p. 601.
46 Garnier, *Austerlitz*, p. 30.
47 To Berthier, 5 Fructidor, Year 13 (23 Aug. 1805), *Correspondance générale*, vol. V, no. 10633, pp. 601–2; to Dejean, Director of War Admin., 5 Fructidor, Year 13 (23 Aug. 1805), ibid., no. 10640, p. 605.
48 To Decrès, 4 Fructidor, Year 13 (22 Aug. 1805), *Correspondance générale*, vol. V, no. 10623, p. 596.
49 To Talleyrand, 28 Thermidor, Year 13 (16 Aug. 1805), *Correspondance générale*, vol. V, no. 10586, p. 579; to Talleyrand, 30 Thermidor, Year 13 (18 Aug. 1805), ibid., no. 10594, p. 583.
50 Cited in Garnier, *Austerlitz*, p. 39.
51 On the estimable performance of the French and Spanish fleets: Agustín Guimera, 'Trafalgar. Myth and History', in *A Great and Glorious Victory*, pp. 41–57.
52 Rodger, *Command*, pp. 537–42.
53 Rodger, *Command*, p. 542.
54 Rodger, *Command*, pp. 543–4.
55 Guimera, 'Trafalgar. Myth and History', pp. 53–4; Monaque, 'Trafalgar: A French point of view', pp. 76–7.
56 Monaque, 'Trafalgar: A French point of view', p. 76.
57 Guimera, 'Trafalgar. Myth and History', p. 64.

58 Richard Glover, *Britain at Bay: Defence Against Bonaparte, 1803–1814* (London, 1973), pp. 12–15.

59 Rory Muir, *Britain and the Defeat of Napoleon, 1807–1815* (New Haven, 1996), p. 17.

13 THE CREATION OF A MASTERPIECE

1   John Elting, *Swords Around a Throne: Napoleon's Grande Armée* (New York, 1988), p. 58.

2   Muir, *Tactics*, p. 35.

3   Muir, *Tactics*, p. 158.

4   Chandler, *Campaigns*, p. 371.

5   Cited in Garnier, *Austerlitz*, pp. 167–70. Berthezène's memory may have been at fault as Morland's command, part of the Guard cavalry, would not have had the strengths described either at the start or during the campaign.

6   Garnier, *Austerlitz*, p. 167.

7   To Berthier, from Cologne, 28 Fructidor, Year 12 (15 Sept. 1804), *Correspondance générale*, vol. IV, no. 9215, pp. 871–2.

8   To Berthier, 8 Floréal, Year 12 (28 April 1804), *Correspondance générale*, vol. IV, no. 8847, p. 694.

9   To Marmont, 21 Ventôse, Year 12 (12 Mar. 1804), *Correspondance générale*, vol. IV, no. 8731, pp. 637–8.

10 Elting, *Swords Around a Throne*, p. 60.

11 Jacques Morvan, *Le soldat impérial, 1800–1814*, 2 vols (Paris, 1904), i, pp. 280–3.

12 *Nelson: The New Letters,* ed. Colin White (Woodbridge, 2005), p. 53.

13 Cited in Bruno Colson, *Napoléon. De la Guerre* (Paris, 2011), p. 261.

14 To Davout, 14 Messidor, Year 12 (3 July 1804), *Correspondance générale*, vol. IV, no. 8984, pp. 762–3.

15 *Napoleon: His Court and Family*, ii, p. 323.

16 White, *Nelson: The New Letters*, p. 54.

17 Riley, *Napoleon as a General*, p. 12.

18 Muir, *Tactics*, pp. 75–6.

19 Morvan, *Le soldat impérial*, i, p. 291.

20 Morvan, *Le soldat impérial*, i, pp. 283, 296.

21 Muir, *Tactics*, pp. 76, 77.

22 Riley, *Napoleon as a General*, p. 83.

23 From Napoleon's writings collated in Colson, *Napoléon*. pp. 259–60.

24 Cited in Colson, *Napoléon*, p. 260.

25 Michael Broers, 'The Revolutionary and Napoleonic Wars', in *The Changing Character of War*, ed. Hew Strachan and Sibylle Scheipers (Oxford, 2011), pp. 64–78, at p. 66–7.

26 Cited in Colson, *Napoléon*, p. 259.

27 Muir, *Tactics*, p. 91.

28 Riley, *Napoleon as a General*, p. 83.

29 Cited in Colson, *Napoléon*, pp. 255–7.

30 Colson, *Napoléon*, p. 107.

31 Morvan, *Le soldat impérial*, i, p. 290.

32 Muir, *Tactics*, p. 107.
33 Morvan, *Le soldat impérial*, i, p. 295.
34 Morvan, *Le soldat impérial*, i, p. 289.
35 Lachouque and Brown, *Anatomy of Glory*, p. 51, n. 7.
36 Lachouque and Brown, *Anatomy of Glory*, p. 37.
37 Cited in Colson, *Napoléon*, p. 258.
38 Cited in Colson, *Napoléon*, p. 259.
39 Cited in Colson, *Napoléon*, p. 163.
40 Lachouque and Brown, *Anatomy of Glory*, p. 38.
41 Lachouque and Brown, *Anatomy of Glory*, p. 51.
42 *Napoleon: His Court and Family*, ii, p. 320–1.
43 Morvan, *Le soldat impérial*, i, p. 301.
44 Alan Forrest, *Napoleon's Men: The Soldiers of the Revolution and Empire* (London, 2002), p. 136.
45 Forrest, *Napoleon's Men*, pp. 134–5.
46 John A. Lynn, 'Towards an Army of Honor: The Moral Evolution of the French Army, 1789–1815', *French Historical Studies*, 16, no. 1 (1989), pp. 152–73.
47 Morvan, *Le soldat impérial*, ii, pp. 5–9.
48 Lynn, 'Army of Honor', p. 167.
49 Cited in Colson, *Napoléon*, p. 160.
50 Cited in Colson, *Napoléon*, p. 159.
51 Cited in Colson, *Napoléon*, p. 163.
52 To Berthier, Ostend, 26 Thermidor, Year 12 (14 Aug. 1804), *Correspondance générale*, vol. IV, no. 9098, p. 816.
53 All cited in Colson, *Napoléon*, p. 162.
54 Cited in Colson, *Napoléon*, p. 260.
55 Morvan, *Le soldat impérial*, i, pp. 295–7.
56 Forrest, *Napoleon's Men*, pp. 155–6, for examples.
57 David Bell, *The First Total War: Napoleon's Europe and the birth of warfare as we know it* (New York, 2007), pp. 152, 245.
58 Elting, *Swords Around a Throne*, p. 99.
59 To Soult, 14 Prairial, Year 12 (3 June 1804), *Correspondance générale*, vol. IV, no. 8929, p. 733.
60 To Cambacérès, Pont-de-Briques, 16 Thermidor, Year 13 (4 Aug. 1805), *Correspondance générale*, vol. V, no. 10496, p. 532.
61 Morvan, *Le soldat impérial*, ii, pp. 15–16.
62 Cited in Colson, *Napoléon*, p. 160.
63 Rodger, *Command*, pp. 529–30.
64 Morvan, *Le soldat impérial*, i, pp. 293–4.
65 *Napoleon: His Court and Family*, ii, p. 326.

14 EMERGENCE OF THE THIRD COALITION

1 Thierry Lentz, *Nouvelle Histoire du Premier Empire*, vol. iii, *La France et l'Europe de Napoléon, 1804–1814* (Paris, 2007), pp. 679–80.
2 'Traité de Paix de Paris avec la Russie, 7, 8 et 10 octobre, 1801', Kerautret, *Grands Traités*, pp. 214, 217.

3   Marie-Pierre Rey, *Alexander I: The Tsar Who Defeated Napoleon* (English trans., DeKalb, 2012), pp. 3–9.

4   Paul W. Schroeder, *The Transformation of European Politics, 1763–1848* (Oxford, 1994), pp. 247–8.

5   Gunther E. Rothenberg, *Napoleon's Great Adversary: Archduke Charles and the Austrian Army, 1792–1814* (Stroud, 2007 edn), pp. 100–1.

6   Rothenberg, *Napoleon's Great Adversary*, p. 102.

7   Schroeder, *Transformation*, pp. 260, 261.

8   Schroeder, *Transformation*, p. 261.

9   Rothenberg, *Napoleon's Great Adversary*, pp. 98–102.

10   Michael Kaiser, 'A Matter of Survival: Bavaria becomes a Kingdom', in *The Bee and the Eagle: Napoleonic France and the End of the Holy Roman Empire, 1806*, ed. Alan Forrest and Peter H. Wilson (Basingstoke, 2009), pp. 94–111, at p. 98.

11   Chandler, *Campaigns*, p. 384

12   Rothenberg, *Napoleon's Great Adversary*, p. 115.

13   Schroeder, *Transformation*, p. 245.

14   Schroeder, *Transformation*, p. 238.

15   Christopher Clark, *The Iron Kingdom: The Rise and Downfall of Prussia, 1600–1947* (London, 2007 edn), pp. 298–9.

16   Schroeder, *Transformation*, pp. 254–5.

17   Clark, *Iron Kingdom*, p. 299.

18   Clark, *Iron Kingdom*, p. 300.

19   To Talleyrand, Pont-de-Briques, 4 Fructidor, Year 13 (22 Aug. 1805), *Correspondance générale*, vol. IV, no. 10629, pp. 598–600.

20   For a perceptive, succinct account of this process: Michael Rowe, 'Napoleon and State Formation in Central Europe', in *Napoleon and Europe*, ed. Philip G. Dwyer (London, 2001), pp. 204–24.

21   Matthijs Lok and Martijn van der Burg, 'The Dutch Case: The Kingdom of Holland and the Imperial Departments', in *Napoleonic Empire*, ed. Broers, Hicks and Guimera, pp. 100–11.

22   Wyger Velema, 'Louis Napoléon et la Mort de la République', in *Louis Bonaparte. Roi de Hollande*, ed. Annie Jourdan (Paris, 2010), pp. 31–44, at p. 33–4.

23   To Cambacérès, Brussels, 7 Thermidor, Year 11 (26 July 1803), *Correspondance générale*, vol. IV, no. 7863, pp. 230–1.

24   To Talleyrand, 30 Floréal, Year 13 (20 May 1805), *Correspondance générale*, vol. V, no. 10095, p. 326.

25   Lok and Burg, 'The Dutch Case', *passim*.

26   To Talleyrand, 7 Floréal, Year 12 (27 April 1804), *Correspondance générale*, vol. IV, no. 8845, pp. 692–3.

27   To Talleyrand, 10 Nivôse, Year 13 (31 Dec. 1804), *Correspondance générale*, vol. IV, no. 9479, p. 991.

28   Velema, 'Louis Napoléon', pp. 34–6.

29   Simon Schama, *Patriots and Liberators: Revolution in the Netherlands, 1780–1813* (New York, 1977), p. 500.

30   Schama, *Patriots and Liberators*, pp. 469–73.

31   Velema, 'Louis Napoléon', pp 35–6.

32   Velema, 'Louis Napoléon', p. 39.

33   Schama, *Patriots and Liberators*, p. 469.

34 Cited in Velema, 'Louis Napoléon', p. 37.

35 To Schimmelpenninck, 7 Vendémiaire, Year 14 (20 Sept. 1805), *Correspondance générale*, vol. V, no. 10899, p. 748.

36 Cited in Michael Broers, *Europe under Napoleon, 1796–1814* (London, 1996), p. 126.

37 To General Dejean, Min. of War Admin., 6 Nivôse, Year 14 (27 Dec. 1805), *Correspondance générale*, vol. V, no. 11229, pp. 915–16.

38 Pillepich, *Milan*, p. 567.

39 Pillepich, *Milan*, p. 569.

40 Lentz, *Nouvelle Histoire*, i, p. 153.

41 Carlo Capra, 'La Fine della Repubblica Italiana', in *La formazione del primo Stato italiano e Milano capitale, 1802–1814*, ed. Adele Robbiati Bianchi (Milan, 2006), pp. 719–32, at p. 725.

42 Alain Pillepich, 'La politique italienne de Napoléon en 1805', in *Napoléon Bonaparte. Correspondance générale*, Vol. V, 1805 (Paris, 2008), pp. 928–41, at p. 935–6.

43 Cited in Pillepich, 'La politique italienne', p. 935.

44 Michael Broers, *The Politics of Religion in Napoleonic Italy: The War against God, 1801–1814* (London, 2002), pp. 146–7.

45 Cited in Capra, 'La Fine', p. 725.

46 Capra, 'La Fine', pp. 725–6.

47 Capra, 'La Fine', p. 721.

48 To Talleyrand, Pont-de-Briques, 4 Fructidor, Year 13 (22 Aug. 1805), *Correspondance générale*, vol. V, no. 10629, pp. 598–600.

49 Schroeder, *Transformation*, p. 240.

50 Philip G. Dwyer, 'Napoleon and the Drive for Glory', *Napoleon and Europe* (London, 2001), ed. Philip G. Dwyer, pp. 118–35, at p. 125.

51 Pillepich, *Milan*, p. 590.

52 Lentz, *Nouvelle Histoire*, iii, p. 687.

53 Cited in Michael Broers, *Napoleonic Imperialism and the Savoyard Monarchy, 1773–1821: State Building in Piedmont* (Lampeter, 1997), p. 273.

54 Schroeder, *Transformation*, pp. 264–5.

55 Schroeder, *Transformation*, pp. 263–5.

56 Antonia De Francesco, *L'Italia di Bonaparte. Politica, statualità e nazione nella peninsula tra due rivoluzioni, 1796–1821* (Milan, 2011), pp. 101–5.

57 Cited in De Francesco, *L'Italia di Bonaparte*, p. 72.

58 To Talleyrand, Pont-de-Briques, 4 Fructidor, Year 13 (22 Aug. 1805), *Correspondance générale*, vol. IV, no. 10629, pp. 598–600.

59 Desmond Seward, *Napoleon and Hitler: A Comparative Biography* (London, 1988).

60 Kaiser, 'A Matter of Survival', pp. 102–4.

61 To Eugène, Milan, 18 Prairial, Year 13 (7 June 1805), *Correspondance générale*, vol. V, no. 10224, pp. 386–8, at p. 388.

THE LEAP IN THE DARK: AUTUMN 1805

1 Chandler, *Campaigns*, pp. 382–3.

INDEX